EXAM PREP™

Network+

Melissa Craft

Mark A. Poplar

David V. Watts

Will Willis

CORIOLIS

Network+ Exam Prep

The Coriolis Group, LLC
14455 N. Hayden Road, Suite 220
Scottsdale, Arizona 85260

480/483-0192
FAX 480/483-0193
http://www.coriolis.com

Library of Congress Cataloging-in-Publication Data
 Network+ exam prep /by Melissa Craft ... [et al.].
    p.   cm.
 Includes index.
 ISBN 1-57610-412-5
  1. Electronic data processing personnel--Certification.   2. Computer technicians--Certification Study guides. 3. Computer networks--Examinations Study guides.   I. Craft, Melissa.
 QA76.3.N48   1999
 004.6--dc21   99-31053
                                                CIP

Printed in the United States of America
10   9   8   7   6   5   4   3

Publisher
Keith Weiskamp

Acquisitions Editor
Shari Jo Hehr

Marketing Specialist
Cynthia Caldwell

Project Editor
Meredith Brittain

Technical Reviewer
David Stabenaw

Production Coordinator
Kim Eoff

Cover Design
Jesse Dunn

Layout Design
April Nielsen

CD-ROM Developer
Michelle McConnell

CORIOLIS

14455 North Hayden Road, Suite 220 • Scottsdale, Arizona 85260

Coriolis: The Training And Certification Destination™

Thank you for purchasing one of our innovative certification study guides, just one of the many members of the Coriolis family of certification products.

Certification Insider Press™ has long believed that achieving your IT certification is more of a road trip than anything else. This is why most of our readers consider us their *Training And Certification Destination*. By providing a one-stop shop for the most innovative and unique training materials, our readers know we are the first place to look when it comes to achieving their certification. As one reader put it, "I plan on using your books for all of the exams I take."

To help you reach your goals, we've listened to others like you, and we've designed our entire product line around you and the way you like to study, learn, and master challenging subjects. Our approach is *The Smartest Way To Get Certified*™.

In addition to our highly popular *Exam Cram* and *Exam Prep* guides, we have a number of new products. We recently launched Exam Cram Live!, two-day seminars based on *Exam Cram* material. We've also developed a new series of books and study aides—*Practice Tests Exam Crams* and *Exam Cram Flash Cards*—designed to make your studying fun as well as productive.

Our commitment to being the Training And Certification Destination does not stop there. We just introduced *Exam Cram Insider*, a biweekly newsletter containing the latest in certification news, study tips, and announcements from Certification Insider Press. (To subscribe, send an email to **eci@coriolis.com** and type "subscribe insider" in the body of the email.) We also recently announced the launch of the Certified Crammer Society and the Coriolis Help Center—two new additions to the Certification Insider Press family.

We'd like to hear from you. Help us continue to provide the very best certification study materials possible. Write us or email us at **cipq@coriolis.com** and let us know how our books have helped you study, or tell us about new features that you'd like us to add. If you send us a story about how we've helped you, and we use it in one of our books, we'll send you an official Coriolis shirt for your efforts.

Good luck with your certification exam and your career. Thank you for allowing us to help you achieve your goals.

Keith Weiskamp
Publisher, Certification Insider Press

ABOUT THE AUTHORS

Melissa Craft (Glendale, AZ) is a Senior Consulting Engineer for MicroAge, a global systems integrator headquartered in Tempe, Arizona. MicroAge provides IT design, project management, and support for distributed computing systems. Melissa develops enterprise-wide technology solutions and methodologies for client organizations. These technology solutions touch every part of a system's life cycle—from network design, testing, and implementation, to operational management and strategic planning.

Aside from earning a bachelor's degree from the University of Michigan, Melissa has several technical certifications, including CompTIA's Network+, Microsoft's MCSE, Cisco's CCNA, Novell's Master CNE, and Citrix's CCP. Melissa is a member of the IEEE, the Society of Women Engineers, and American MENSA, Ltd. Melissa currently resides in Glendale, Arizona with her family, Dan, Justine, and Taylor, and her two dogs, Marmaduke and Pooka. She can be contacted at **mmcraft@compuserve.com**.

Mark A. Poplar (Riverside, CA) is the Senior Technology Engineer for Business Computing Solutions. His certifications include MCSE, CCNA, CCDA, and CNA, as well as the new Network+ certification. He has worked on designing, installing, and troubleshooting LAN and WAN networks for small to medium sized businesses throughout Southern California. He provides knowledge and insight that shows experience in the field, and he shares it in a manner that shows experience in the classroom. Mark can be reached at **mpoplar@earthlink.net**.

David V. Watts (Houston, TX) was born in Basildon, Essex, England. He has lived and worked in the United States since 1988. He has spent most of that time in northern Virginia and Maryland, working for companies ranging in size from 250 to 150,000 users. David is a Novell CNE, a Microsoft MCSE+I and MCSD, and a Network+ Certified Technician.

David is a great believer in self-study. In his professional life, he keeps Sir Arthur Conan Doyle's maxim in mind: "When you have eliminated the impossible, whatever remains, however improbable, must be the truth." You can contact him at **dwatts@wt.net**.

Will Willis (Lewisville, TX)—MCSE, A+ Certified Technician, Network+ Certified Technician, B.A.—is a Network Systems Manager responsible for a switched/routed 10/100MB Ethernet and Frame Relay TCP/IP LAN/WAN that connects multiple sites in Texas and California. His duties include vendor relations (negotiating and securing goods and services as needed), administering/ managing the entire network, and resolving desktop support/user issues. Administration includes responsibility for documentation, establishing corporate standard operating procedures, maintaining tape backup schedules, antivirus strategies, server maintenance and upgrades, and ensuring the reliability and availability of network resources to the company.

Will started out as a help desk tech, providing technical support over the phone for PC hardware and software, and later moved up to a desktop/LAN support specialist position at another company, working on an 8-person team that supported a 3,000+ user multiple-site network. Currently, Will administers NT 4 servers running BackOffice applications Exchange Server 5.5, IIS 3 and 4, SQL Server 6.5, and SMS 1.2. When not busy being a techie, he enjoys spending time with his family and writing and recording original music. Will can usually be reached at **wwillis@inside-corner.com**.

ACKNOWLEDGMENTS

I would like to thank the following people.

➤ Justine, Taylor, and Dan, for patiently supporting me in my writing and being a wonderful family.

➤ Christine Herfurth, for teaching me how to write, and for being my mom.

➤ Pete Rourke and Frank Tanner, for providing me with all the technical resources and contacts that I asked for.

➤ My boss, John Hetrick, for encouraging me in this pursuit.

➤ Meredith Brittain and Shari Jo Hehr from Coriolis, for their diligence in getting this book published. Also, thanks to the other members of the Coriolis team: Kim, Robert, Cynthia, Jesse, and April.

➤ My co-authors, Mark, Will and David, for all their excellent work, and for keeping up with such an aggressive schedule.

—Melissa Craft

I'm surprised by how many people are needed to make a project like this culminate in a quality finished product I can be proud of. To all those who have helped take this from an idea to a book, I give my thanks. Thanks also to my co-authors, Will Willis, Melissa Craft, and David Watts, three of the highest quality professionals in the technology field. They have been dedicated from the start to providing readers with knowledge they can apply every day as they strive for excellence. My thanks too, for the professionals at Coriolis who worked to help us reach our goal, and to my personal assistants, Justin Mihn and Steven Dunney, for their fine editing and photography skills.

Finally though, my ultimate thanks go to my wife, Annette, and my daughters, Melissa and Kimberly. They taught me that life is beautiful and truly worth living.

—Mark A. Poplar

Acknowledgments

I would like to thank my parents. I have had the pleasure of getting to know them better over the past few years, and I cherish that time. I love you. For anyone who knows me, it goes without saying that half the credit for this book belongs to my wife, Siobhan Chamberlin. Without her I would not have been capable of pulling this off. I am glad you are in my life. I also want to mention my sister, Catherine, and her husband Jeff. I miss talking to you! It is always inspiring to see others developing new skills and moving their lives in new directions. So it is with utter sincerity that I thank my brother, John Watts. I am proud of you! And thank you, Barbara, for being there. I also want to congratulate Peter Chamberlin, who has taught us all valuable lessons in determination. Moira, Siobhan's mother, I am so happy things worked out for you. There are others whom I hope to inspire to reach greater heights–Zevi Mehlman (Zevster), Sam Singh, Sam Rao, and Marco Alvarado. You guys have a lot of potential; I hope you use it to the greatest advantage. I want to thank Will Willis, for whom I have gained great respect. The regulars at the MCPmag forums are too numerous to mention, but Smokey and Chris come to mind. I also want to thank Melissa and Mark, who worked hard on this book. Shari Jo, Meredith Brittain—thank you for the help, you're both great. Thanks to all my colleagues at Shell, including Graham, Mark, Marcus, Erik and Susan. Finally— to my lifelong buddy Michael Cook. It's worth going back to England just to have a beer with you. And, of course, Puppy and Ratty—two of the weirdest dogs you'll ever know!

—David V. Watts

I would like to first and foremost thank my wonderful wife, Melissa, and son, Duncan, whose support was critical to my success in writing this book. I also thank Mom, Dad, and Alexandra Willis, Donna, Melba, and Bill Duncan. I thank Ken, Charles, Ian, Nick, and Matt for making me realize we weren't going to be the next great rock band and that college was where I needed to be! Florence Estes, Chet and Loretta Dillon. My 4th grade teacher Mr. Donovan for helping me realize I had a lot more potential than I was showing. High school teacher Beverly Johnson for impacting my life. Mark Herrmann for helping keep me motivated during my certification studies. Mark Malott for getting me out of Stream. Ace and Peter. Shiner Bock. The U.S. Air Force for NOT accepting me into officer school. Kim for all the years of friendship. The financial services gang at Imprimis. David for keeping me sane during those "up all night/gotta meet the deadline" sessions. ForumGuys William/"Smokey" and Chris. The MCPmag forum regulars. Shari Jo and Meredith for their guidance. Special thanks to my co-authors for their outstanding work in bringing this book to fruition. To anyone I didn't get to mention, it's Coriolis's fault for not giving me enough space! :-)

—Will Willis

CONTENTS AT A GLANCE

TABLE OF CONTENTS

CHAPTER 6
THE DATA LINK LAYER 197

PART II NETWORKING PRACTICES

INTRODUCTION

Welcome to *Network+ Exam Prep*! This new book from Certification Insider Press offers you interactive activities and numerous hands-on projects that reinforce key concepts and help you prepare for the exam. This book also features troubleshooting tips for solutions to common problems that you will encounter.

The companion interactive CD-ROM features a unique test simulation environment with two complete practice exams that allow you to test your skills and knowledge, making this the perfect study guide for the Network+ certification exam. The exam questions have been specially written based on the content of the book to reinforce what you have learned. These materials have been specifically designed to help individuals prepare for CompTIA's Network+ exam. Answers to end-of-chapter review questions are also found on the CD-ROM.

The big technology question for the '90s and beyond is, "Are you certified?" Certification is rapidly becoming the key to professional career enhancement for network engineers, technicians, software developers, Web designers, and even professional office workers.

If you're ready to dig right in, skip to the "About The Book" section later in this Introduction.

WHY GET CERTIFIED?

The benefits to certification reach farther than just adding some letters behind your name. Those letters stand for a significant body of knowledge that you have obtained and a certain level of professional achievement and competence. These are all highly valued by the IT industry.

Employers and recruiters also value these certifications. Employers grant advancement opportunities based on certifications, and recruiters prefer applicants who are certified. In addition, customers show more confidence in technicians who are certified. Some customers require that the technicians assigned to their accounts maintain certain levels of certification. It's obviously to the technician's advantage to be certified.

About CompTIA

CompTIA, short for Computing Technology Industry Association, was formed in 1982. Currently, 7,500 members make up the CompTIA trade association. CompTIA works with Value Added Resellers and integrators of all sizes.

CompTIA established the A+ certification to provide entry-level technicians with vendor-independent, recognized qualifications. CompTIA also offers the CDIA (Certified Document Imaging Architech) for document imaging and the new Network+ certification for network technology skills. These certifications identify skills and knowledge required for competent job performance.

How It Started—The A+ Certification

The A+ certification is a precursor to the Network+ certification program offered by CompTIA. This certification is able to confirm the competency of entry-level computer technicians. The level of competency is deemed to be at least six months of experience.

Sylvan Prometric, a testing administration company, first offered the A+ certification exam in 1993. In 1998, CompTIA revised the A+ exam. Today, there are over 65,000 A+ certified technicians around the world.

The Network+ Certification

CompTIA created the Network+ certification-testing program to ascertain the networking knowledge of technicians with one one-half to two years of experience in the Information Systems industry. This test focuses on vendor-independent networking technologies, with a focus on understanding TCP/IP.

Network+ certification is a logical next step for an A+ certified technician. It offers a path to entering the networking industry. Network+ can help a technician gain greater recognition for knowledge, which may translate into a strategic career move, whether that is with an existing employer or a new position. The test provides a measurable skill set that can verify that the candidate has a baseline of networking skills. Not only does a technician benefit, but a company hiring for positions requiring network skills now has a standard on which it can base recruits.

CERTIFY ME!

So you are ready to become a CompTIA Certified Network Technician. The examinations are administered through Sylvan Prometric (formerly Drake Prometric).

Registering for an exam is easy. To register to take an exam with Sylvan Prometric, call 1-800-77-MICRO. This is the same number to use when taking the A+ certification exam. The Sylvan Prometric associates will assist you in selecting the closest exam location. If you need directions, they will be able to give those to you as well.

When you call to register, have the following information ready:

➤ Your name, organization (if any), mailing address, and phone number.

➤ A unique ID number (e.g., your Social Security number).

➤ The name of the exam you wish to take.

➤ A method of payment (e.g., credit card number or prepaid voucher). If you pay by check, payment is due before the examination can be scheduled. The fee to take each exam varies; check CompTIA's Web site (**www.comptia.org**) for specific fees.

ADDITIONAL RESOURCES

One of the best sources of information about CompTIA certification tests comes from CompTIA itself. Because technologies change frequently, the best place to go for exam-related information is online.

If you haven't already visited the Network+ certification pages, do so right now. As of this writing, the Comptia certification page resides at **www.comptia. org/ct_certs/index.htm** and the Network+ certification page is at **www.comptia.org/networkplus/index.htm**. Note that it may not be there by the time you read this, or it may have been replaced by something new, because Web sites change regularly. If this happens, please read the next section, "Coping With Change On The Web."

The options in the page's left-hand column point to important sources of information for CompTIA certifications, including:

➤ **Certifications News** Pulls up the page that discusses the latest news about CompTIA and its certifications.

➤ **Contacts** Links directly to a page that contains email addresses for CompTIA departments, in case you have any questions.

The links in the center of the page link directly to the various certifications that CompTIA offers. Use the Network+ icon to jump to summaries of all historical data about Network+, benefits of certification, frequently asked questions (FAQs), and other information. The Network+ page has a link to training resources, including organizations offering training and links to materials.

Of course, these are just the high points of what's available in the CompTIA certification pages. As you browse through them—and we strongly recommend that you do—you'll probably find other information we didn't mention here that is every bit as interesting and compelling.

Other than the CompTIA pages, there are a few other sites that are worth visiting on your journey to Network+ certification. The first is **ExamCram.com** at **www.examcram.com**. This site is a place to get information on all sorts of certification exams, including those from Microsoft, Novell, and CompTIA. The Network+ certification exam has a lot of objectives in common with Microsoft's Networking Essentials certification exam and with Novell's Networking Technologies certification exam. The information for those two tests can be a real help for the Network+ exam.

Another site to visit is Braindump Heaven. This site is a collaborative dump of information from people who have taken certification exams and are willing to tell others what to expect from them. The site is located at **http:// 209.207.167.177/**. A link to the Network+ braindump is located at the bottom of the left-hand column.

A truly helpful site is What IS. What IS offers a quick summary about any networking or computer technology term. Not only does the site offer the ability to search for terms and find their meanings, but the site has white papers explaining networking concepts. The address for this site is **www.whatis.com**.

Finally, do not be afraid to explore the vendors' support, education, and training Web pages. A great deal of networking information can be found on Novell's support Web site at **http://support.novell.com** and **http://developer. novell.com/research/appnotes.htm**. Cisco maintains a tremendous knowledgebase at **www.cisco.com**. Microsoft has its own support knowledgebase at **http://search.microsoft.com**.

COPING WITH CHANGE ON THE WEB

Sooner or later, all the specifics we've shared with you about the CompTIA certification pages, and all the other Web-based resources we mention throughout the rest of this book, will go stale or be replaced by newer information. In some cases, the URLs you find here may lead you to their replacements; in other cases, the URLs will go nowhere, leaving you with the dreaded 404 error message, "File not found."

When that happens, please don't give up! There's always a way to find what you want on the Web, if you're willing to invest some time and energy. To begin with, most large or complex Web sites—and CompTIA's qualifies on both counts—offer a search engine. As long as you can get to the site itself, you can use this tool to help you find what you need.

The more particular or focused you can make a search request, the more likely it is that the results will include information you can use. For instance, you can search for "Training and Certification" to produce a lot of data about the subject in general, but if you're specifically looking for, for example, the Preparation Guide for the Network+ Exam, you'll be more likely to get there quickly if you use a search string such as: "CompTIA Network Exam" AND "Preparation Guide".

Finally, don't be afraid to use general search tools like **www.search.com**, **www.northernlight.com**, **www.altavista.com**, or **www.excite.com** to find related information. Although CompTIA offers the best information about its certification exams online, there are plenty of third-party sources of information, training, and assistance in this area that do not have to follow a party line like CompTIA does. The bottom line is: If you can't find something where the book says it lives, start looking around.

ABOUT THE BOOK

Networking is the hottest topic in the information systems industry. If you want to move to the top of the IT field, you have to know and understand networking at a detailed level. This book will get you started and serve as a reference along the way.

This book is filled with hands-on projects that cover every aspect of understanding, installing and managing a PC network. The projects are designed to make what you learn come alive through actually performing the tasks. Also, every chapter includes a range of practice questions to help prepare you for the Network+ certification exam. These features are offered to reinforce your learning, so you'll feel confident in the knowledge you have gained from each chapter.

The book is divided into two parts, according to the two broad categories of Network+ exam objectives. Part I, Networking Technology, consists of Chapters 1 through 11, and Part II, Networking Practices, is made up of Chapters 12 through 16.

Chapter 1 begins with a review of the OSI Reference Model and network topologies. Then, Chapter 2 takes you through basic network operating systems. Chapter 3 reviews networking protocols. Chapter 4 covers the internal and external systems that are used in networking. Next, Chapters 5 through 7 delve deeper into the functions of the lower OSI protocol layers. Chapters 8 and 9 focus on the TCP/IP protocol stack. Chapters 10 and 11 discuss remote access and network security. Chapters 12 through 14 discuss installation, system components and change control practices. Chapter 15 explains best practices for network administration, and the last chapter—16—discusses troubleshooting methods.

Finally, there is one appendix, which provides a list of all the Network+ exam objectives and tells you where these objectives are covered in the book. A glossary that defines all of the acronyms and technical terms used in this book follows the appendix.

Features

To aid you in fully understanding Network+ concepts, there are many features in this book designed to improve its value:

➤ **Chapter objectives** Each chapter in this book begins with a detailed list of the concepts to be mastered within that chapter. This list provides you with a quick reference to the contents of that chapter, as well as a useful study aid.

➤ **Illustrations and tables** Numerous illustrations of screenshots and components aid you in the visualization of common setup steps, theories, and concepts. In addition, many tables provide details and comparisons of both practical and theoretical information.

➤ **Hands-on projects** Although it is important to understand the theory behind networking, nothing can improve upon real-world experience. To this end, along with theoretical explanations, each chapter provides numerous hands-on projects aimed at providing you with real-world implementation experience.

➤ **Chapter summaries** Each chapter's text is followed by a summary of the concepts it has introduced. These summaries provide a helpful way to recap and revisit the ideas covered in each chapter.

➤ **Review questions** End-of-chapter assessment begins with a set of review questions that reinforce the ideas introduced in each chapter. These questions not only ensure that you have mastered the concepts, but are written to help prepare you for the Network+ certification exam.

Text And Graphic Conventions

Wherever appropriate, additional information and exercises have been added to this book to help you better understand what is being discussed in the chapter. Icons throughout the text alert you to additional materials. The icons used in this book are as follows:

The Note icon is used to present additional helpful material related to the subject being described.

Each hands-on activity in this book is preceded by the Hands-On Project icon and a description of the exercise that follows.

Tips are included from the author's experience that provide extra information about how to attack a problem, how to approach network installation and configuration, or what to do in certain real-world situations.

The cautions are included to help you anticipate potential mistakes or problems so you can prevent them from happening.

WHERE SHOULD YOU START?

This book is intended to be read in sequence, from beginning to end. Each chapter builds upon those that precede it, to provide a solid understanding of Network+. After completing the chapters, you may find it useful to go back through the book and use the review questions and projects to prepare for the Network+ certification test.

SYSTEM REQUIREMENTS

To complete the projects in the book, you will need access to a file server and a workstation. You should also have access to network operating system software, including Novell NetWare and Microsoft Windows NT Server. These projects are not mandatory; however, the projects will give you experience using this resource as a prospective server administrator.

The recommended software and hardware configurations are described in the following sections.

Workstation Clients

➤ Windows 95, Windows 98, Windows 2000, or Windows NT

➤ Pentium with 16MB of RAM minimum

➤ VGA monitor

➤ Mouse or pointing device

➤ Network interface card connected to a network

➤ Hard disk with at least 110MB free

➤ CD-ROM drive

➤ Internet access and a browser

File Server

➤ Listed in Microsoft's Hardware Compatibility List and compatible with Novell NetWare

➤ 32-bit bus computer with a Pentium 90MHz or faster processor

➤ VGA or better resolution monitor

➤ Mouse or pointing device

➤ High-density 3.5-inch floppy disk drive

➤ CD-ROM drive

➤ 48MB or more memory

➤ One or more hard disks with at least 250MB of disk storage free

➤ Network interface card for network communications

➤ Tape backup system (recommended but not required)

➤ Modem (recommended but not required)

➤ Printer (recommended but not required)

System Requirements For Exam Prep Software

➤ 8MB RAM (16MB recommended)

➤ VGA/256 color display or better

➤ 6X CD-ROM Drive

➤ Windows NT 4, Windows 95, Windows 98, or Windows 2000

ABOUT THE CD-ROM

To become a CompTIA Certified Network Technician, you must pass a rigorous certification exam that provides a valid and reliable measure of technical proficiency and expertise. The CD-ROM that comes with this book can be used in conjunction with the book to help you assess your progress in the event you choose to pursue Network+ certification. The CD-ROM contains specially designed test simulation software that features two 75-question practice exams. These content-based questions were expertly prepared to test your readiness for the official Network+ certification examination.

Practice Exam Features

➤ 75 questions

➤ 90-minute timed test to ensure exam readiness

➤ Questions that can be marked and answered later

Software

The Network+ Exam Prep's companion CD-ROM contains elements specifically selected to enhance the usefulness of this book, including the following utilities:

➤ *PPPShare Pro*—An evaluation version of a proxy server that enables multiple networked computers to share a single Internet connection that can be dial-up TCP/IP, ISDN, ADSL, cable modem, or Ethernet.

➤ *EventReader(tm) for Windows NT(tm)*—A configurable utility that can read the event log from multiple Windows NT workstations and servers. This tool enables an administrator to collect event information and store it in ODBC-compliant databases for later evaluation and baseline tracking.

➤ *OstroSoft Internet Tools*—OstroSoft has developed a complete suite of Internet utilities. This suite includes domain scanner, port scanner, ping, traceroute, netstat, Whois client, Finger utility, FTP client, mailbox watcher, and HTML document watcher, among others.

➤ *Alot MoniCA*—This utility is for those who are curious to know what happens when they are not using their computers. Alot MoniCA lets you know who was using your standalone or networked computers, and when and what they were doing.

➤ *Find for NetWare*—Wiredred software created this little utility to find open files and locked files by user. It looks just like the Windows 95 File Find utility and is very easy to use.

- ➤ *LMHosts Generator*—Netadmintools developed this snappy utility for Windows networks with more than 10 computers. It generates an LMHOSTS file automatically, plus the batch file to use in distributing it to other computers.

- ➤ *MacView*—Another Wiredred utility, this tool displays and searches for MAC-layer addresses on your NetWare servers. Automatically cross-references MAC address to over 1,600+ vendors.

- ➤ *Quiktakes for NetWare*—Wiredred utility that displays realtime NCP traffic loads of the file server.

- ➤ *Salvage 98 for NetWare*—Wiredred utility that can salvage deleted files in NetWare. Uses a Windows Explorer style interface.

- ➤ *SNMP Trap Watcher*—This tool is designed to receive SNMP traps from network equipment, including routers, switches, and workstations. Traps are sent when errors occur on the network.

Solutions To End-Of-Chapter Questions

For further help in making sure you are prepared for the Network+ certification exam, we have included solutions for the end-of-chapter review questions on the CD-ROM.

PART I

NETWORKING TECHNOLOGY

## CHAPTER ONE

BASIC NETWORKING KNOWLEDGE

After Reading This Chapter And Completing The Exercises, You Will Be Able To:

➤ Define the layers of the OSI Reference Model and identify the protocols, services, and functions that pertain to each layer

➤ Demonstrate understanding of basic network structure, including the characteristics of star, bus, mesh, and ring topologies, their advantages and disadvantages, and the characteristics of segments and backbones

Network basics are the entry point to an exciting world of connectivity. Computers, servers, and mainframes all connect to the network. Network segments connect to hubs, routers, switches, and other infrastructure equipment that connects many segments together into an internetwork. The internetwork connects to the Internet. People connect their home PCs to the network by dialing in. It's all connectivity—and it is all based on the concepts introduced in this chapter.

The Comptia Web site lists the many fundamental concepts that you must understand before you take the Network+ certification exam. Two fundamental concepts covered in this chapter are the OSI Reference Model and the basics of network structure.

Beware how small these two concepts seem! They are actually essential to understanding later chapters of this book that address how everything works together.

This chapter will be chock full of acronyms. TLAs (three-letter acronyms) are confusing and nearly limitless nowadays, but many test-takers fail to realize their importance until they take an exam on networking concepts. It helps to write acronyms down along with the words that they stand for so that you can commit them to memory.

OVERVIEW OF BASIC NETWORK STRUCTURE

Originally, computers were standalone devices with proprietary operating systems. Networks grew from the need to share data among different types of systems. The following sections will review the way that networks evolved and the various methods of connecting computers together into a network.

History Of Computers And Networks

Unlike most trends in life, computers started big and became smaller. The first computers were huge—the size of rooms or buildings. They were difficult to use, requiring punch cards, punch card readers, and punch card printers in order to put some data in or get some data out.

Computers became smaller over time. Eventually, multiple consoles, or terminals, were added so that people could access data simultaneously. The computer's main processor was limited as to how many terminals it could support, so a *front-end processor (FEP)* was added to increase the numbers of terminals. The need to increase the distance from the computer prompted the use of telephone wires multiplexed between multiple terminals. *Multiplexing* means that several data transmissions can transfer across the telephone wire at seemingly the same time. Even though the use of computers grew, they were still very large and so expensive that only large enterprises would purchase them and develop programs for them.

Soon, companies wanted their large computers to connect together and share data. To satisfy this need, manufacturers created their own networking architectures. IBM created SNA (Systems Network Architecture), and Digital Equipment Corporation created DECNet. Although today SNA and DECNet can be used on non-IBM and non-Digital computers, back then IBM computers could connect only to other IBM computers, and Digital computers could connect only to other Digital computers. These groups of connected computers were the first homogeneous networks.

A radical change in computer circuitry—the integrated circuit chip—started the microcomputer age. Now, microcomputers are typically called PCs (which stands for personal computers). PCs made computer technology affordable for the general population. Because of the availability of computing power, small businesses, noncritical business units within large businesses, schools, and homeowners bought PCs and used them to handle their computing needs. This started a "sneakernet" in the workplace. Literally, people transferred data by walking around "in sneakers" with disks of data.

The government was the first entity to create a true network; it was called ARPANET. ARPANET was created by the Advanced Research Projects Agency (ARPA) in the 1970s for the purpose of sharing radar data. Since then,

ARPANET has grown into what is now the Internet. The ARPANET designers set out to fulfill two requirements:

➤ Interconnectivity

➤ Interoperability

Interconnectivity is the ability to connect to a network and transfer data. Mainframes already had this ability when the ARPANET designers started. Mainframes could connect to a wire and transfer data to another mainframe by the same manufacturer. The problem with simply providing interconnectivity was that it did not provide for different types of computers being able to communicate with each other.

Interoperability is the ability of different types of operating systems to transfer data between them, such as in file transfers or printer output. Because the different operating systems had such different technologies, the ARPANET designers had their work cut out for them. They eventually designed the basis of the Transmission Control Protocol/Internet Protocol (TCP/IP) protocol suite. It is called a *suite* because it has four layers of protocols that interoperate with each other, with the operating system, and with the network. Based on these concepts, ARPANET was the first heterogeneous network, where many different types of computers were able to share data. The same layered approach to protocols is also used by the OSI (Open Systems Interconnection) Reference Model, as will be discussed later in this chapter.

Network Components

Network structure can be confusing. People will walk right into a wiring closet (a central termination point for cables and hubs), then close their eyes, cross their fingers, and back out quickly before someone asks them to describe what's in there. Wiring closets look horrifyingly complex, what with wires coming from every direction and all those lights on the hubs and routers. When people are back at their desks, the network seems much neater—one wire comes out of the PC and disappears into the wall.

What Are The Basic Components Of A Network?

The answer is simply:

■ **A client** The computer requesting the use of a service

■ **A server** The computer responding to the client with the service

■ **A physical medium** The network interface card and the wire data travels on, or air for wireless networks

■ **A common language** The network protocol used for communication and transmitting data across the physical medium

That explains where the wires come from. Cablers take great pains to create a wiring scheme that is convenient for an enterprise to use. Cables are usually hidden between walls, like telephone wires are, and fed back to a central point, which is the wiring closet. Wiring closets are a matter of convenience. If all the wires come to the same termination point, they can be connected with whatever hubs or switches or other networking equipment is being used to provide a connection. If the type of hub, switch, or other network equipment changes, the wires do not need to be recabled to accommodate the change, unless the equipment requires a different type of wire.

The wires themselves provide the path for the data to travel over or transmit across. Wires are considered a physical medium. The wires are usually connected to a computer via a *network interface card (NIC)*. Wireless networks are an exception to the rule that networks require a cable of some sort. Instead, the physical medium is the air that carries microwaves, radio waves, or light waves.

Another important component of a network is the server. *Servers* are computers that provide a service or, more commonly, multiple services to the network. The use of a common storage area is a key advantage of networks. This common storage area is provided by file services. Some of the other services that network servers provide are print services for sharing printers, messaging services for sending email, and Web services for accessing HTML pages.

The computers that connect to the wire are servers, clients, or both. Generically, any computer connected to the network is called a PC, computer, station, host, node, or network node. The term *node* is also applicable to any router, gateway, or device that is assigned a logical address and connected to the network. On TCP/IP networks, the term *host* is commonly used for any device that has been assigned a logical network address. A *client* is the term for any computer that requests the use of a service on the network. A computer can both share its services and use the services of another server or client/server in the network. This arrangement is called *peer to peer* computing. Each computer is an equal, or peer, of the others in what it can share and attempt to access.

Host is a term used on TCP/IP networks for any device that is assigned a logical address.

The final component that enables the wires, the servers, and the clients to work together is the protocol, or set of protocols, that is used to transfer data across the wire. At a network computer that is sending data, protocols are used to break down the data being transmitted into a bitstream format that the network will understand. At a network computer that is receiving data, protocols are used to rebuild the data into the format that the receiving computer will understand. Figure 1.1 depicts various network components.

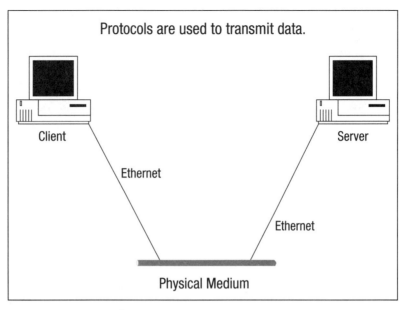

Figure 1.1   Network components.

THE OSI REFERENCE MODEL

In 1977, the International Organization for Standardization (which uses the acronym ISO because of its French translation) established a subcommittee to develop a data communication standard to promote interoperability, so that operating systems from multiple vendors would be capable of networking with each other. The Open Systems Interconnection (OSI) Reference Model was the result of this effort.

General Purpose Of The OSI Reference Model

The purpose of the OSI Reference Model was to raise networking standards so that they were universally accessible. ISO also wanted multiple vendors to be able to develop their hardware and software so that they could be used with other vendors' products.

The OSI Reference Model serves the networking industry as a guideline for network data-transmission tasks. It does not specify a specific standard that can be used for data transmission itself, but it provides the ideal framework for a standard.

There are many types of computers today—more than when ISO started its project. Every piece of hardware or software in a computer can be different from the corresponding components in another computer. Sending a piece of information from one computer to another is a complex problem. The ISO subcommittee members responded to this issue by dividing and conquering.

They began with the required network functions and separated them into logical areas, or *layers*. Each layer included the function of how to interact with the other layers above and below, in order for data to transmit between layers. This approach yielded two benefits:

➤ The problem of networking was much easier to understand because the functions were divided. Vendors could concentrate on specific functions that they wished to provide in networking. For example, a Layer 2 switch need only concentrate on the functions and protocols at the Physical and Data Link layers. On the other hand, a file-transfer application should understand the Application layer and the Presentation layer. As long as the remaining protocol layers are in use on the computer, a file-transfer application does not need to include those functions in its programming.

➤ With the functions separated, they could be optimized within their protocol. The modularity of protocols enables easy replacement of older, nonoptimal protocols when newer ones are developed. Network optimization through protocol modularity has been demonstrated particularly with the Ethernet protocol. Ethernet was originally a 10Mbps Physical and Data Link layer specification. Since then, there has been Fast Ethernet at 100Mbps, and Gigabit Ethernet at 1Gbps. If the network is running the TCP/IP protocol stack over Ethernet, the Ethernet portion can be upgraded to a newer version without replacing much more than the protocol itself, hubs, switches, network interfaces, and cables. All the network applications running on the computers do not need to be upgraded at the same time because they exist at a different protocol layer.

After the OSI Reference Model was released, some network protocols already existed, such as the TCP/IP protocol suite. These protocols did not match perfectly with the OSI Reference Model, but there is enough correspondence to be able to use the Reference Model layers to describe the functions provided by the various protocols within the suites. It is not uncommon to see a protocol that belongs to one of those suites described as equivalent to an OSI Reference Model protocol layer.

Layers Of The OSI Reference Model

The OSI Reference Model consists of seven layers: Physical, Data Link, Network, Transport, Session, Presentation, and Application. Each of these layers handles specific functions, as described in Table 1.1. When a source computer (the one sending data) communicates with a destination computer (the one receiving data), the source computer sends data through the protocol layers in its own computer first. The peer layers in the destination computer receive this data.

Table 1.1 The functions of the seven OSI layers.

Layer Number	Layer Name	Functions
1	Physical	Network media, connection specifications, electrical and electromagnetic signaling
2	Data Link	Organizes data into frames, assigns physical addresses, handles error and flow control
3	Network	Assigns network segment addresses and logical node addresses, packages data into datagrams, routes data between segments
4	Transport	Responsible for connection-oriented, reliable data transmission, flow control, error control, and message multiplexing
5	Session	Handles dialog control, including establishing, maintaining, and synchronizing the dialog
6	Presentation	Data transfer syntax, format of data, encryption, decryption, compression, and expansion
7	Application	User interface to the network, network applications

A good way to remember the layers of the OSI Reference Model, from Layer 7 to Layer 1, is using the mnemonic device: All People Seem To Need Data Processing; see Table 1.2.

Figure 1.2 demonstrates the way that a source computer communicates with a destination computer. If a service at the Transport layer needs to send data to the destination computer, the service will eventually communicate with the Transport layer on that destination computer. This communication between corresponding layers on different computers is called *peer-layer communication*.

Table 1.2 Mnemonic device for the order of the layers of the OSI Reference Model.

Mnemonic	Layer Name	Layer Number
All	Application	Layer 7
People	Presentation	Layer 6
Seem	Session	Layer 5
To	Transport	Layer 4
Need	Network	Layer 3
Data	Data Link	Layer 2
Processing	Physical	Layer 1

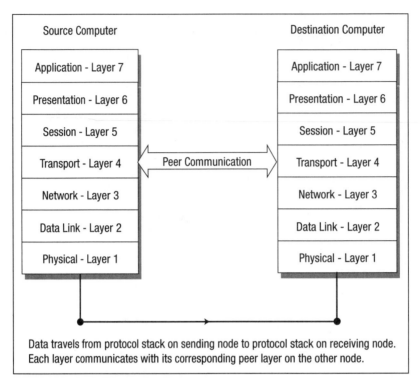

Figure 1.2 shows:

Source Computer		Destination Computer
Application - Layer 7		Application - Layer 7
Presentation - Layer 6		Presentation - Layer 6
Session - Layer 5		Session - Layer 5
Transport - Layer 4	Peer Communication	Transport - Layer 4
Network - Layer 3		Network - Layer 3
Data Link - Layer 2		Data Link - Layer 2
Physical - Layer 1		Physical - Layer 1

Data travels from protocol stack on sending node to protocol stack on receiving node. Each layer communicates with its corresponding peer layer on the other node.

Figure 1.2 OSI Reference Model layers and peer-layer communication.

The source Transport layer does not, however, communicate directly with the destination Transport layer. Instead, the source Transport layer requests a service of the Network layer on the source computer. The Network layer then requests a service of the Data Link layer, which subsequently requests the service of the Physical layer such that the data can be sent along the network medium in a bitstream format. The destination computer receives the data at the Physical layer. It reassembles the bitstream and forwards it to the Data Link layer. The transmission is further sent up the protocol stack until it reaches the receiving Transport layer. At this point, the transmission is processed by the destination computer.

Most of the layers of the OSI Reference Model use headers to encapsulate data received from higher protocol layers. In fact, a transmission contains two parts—the header and the data.

The header contains control information about how to handle the message at that protocol layer. The type of control information varies from layer to layer, to reflect the functions that occur at the different layers. As each message is passed from an upper layer to a lower layer on the sending computer, the next layer adds a header to the data. Each subsequent layer considers the previous headers to be simply a part of the data it encapsulates.

1

The second process that happens as a message passes from an upper-layer protocol to a lower layer is fragmentation. *Fragmentation* is the process in which data from an upper layer is broken into smaller packets of data. A header is added to each fragment. At the Physical layer, the data is broken into raw bits and there is no header.

When data is received by the Physical layer at the destination computer, the data is reassembled into the Data Link layer's packets. At the Data Link layer, the header is stripped off the packets, and they are reassembled into the Network-layer packets. This process is repeated for each layer until the data reaches the destination layer service and is acted upon.

Table 1.3 shows the name applied to the type of data that can be expected at each layer. These names generally reflect the fragmentation of the data because bits are the smallest fragment of data, frames are the next largest, and so on through the protocol stack.

 It is important to note that the OSI Reference Model is not actually used for sending data from one computer to another. It is simply a concept to apply to other protocols.

When a protocol stack is used, it can contain some or all of the protocol layers. The functions of more than one OSI protocol layer might be incorporated into a single protocol created by a vendor. There will not always be a one-to-one correspondence between actual protocols in use and the OSI Reference Model. The following sections describe each of the OSI layers in detail.

Layer 1: Physical

The Physical layer defines the mechanical and electrical requirements of the network medium and of the interface to that medium. This layer includes the following specifications:

➤ **Hardware** The type of medium—whether cable or wireless, type of cable, type of interface, including specification of the connector pins

Table 1.3 Data packet names used at each OSI protocol layer.

OSI Protocol Layer	Data Packet Type
Physical	Bits
Data Link	Frames
Network	Datagrams
Transport	Segments
Application	Messages
All layers	Packets

> ➤ **Physical connection and topology**   How the medium is interconnected with the network nodes

> ➤ **Data transmission**   Electrical or electromagnetic signaling; how the one and zero bits are translated to voltages, light, or other signals

> ➤ **Data receipt**   Signaling receipt, including translation of the electrical signals into one and zero bits

Layer 2: Data Link

In general, the Data Link layer organizes frames of data from the zeros and ones received from the Physical layer and encapsulates into frames the data received from the Network layer. Functions include error detection, error correction, flow control, and hardware addressing. The Data Link layer is typically considered to have two sub-layers:

> ➤ Media Access Control (MAC) layer

> ➤ Logical Link Control (LLC) layer

The MAC layer is the lower of the two sub-layers and is directly above the Physical layer. The MAC layer is of particular interest because it specifies the physical, or hardware, address. The MAC address is commonly *burned in*, or encoded as part of the network interface card. Each MAC address must be unique on an internetwork. When the MAC address is applied by the vendor, it does not need to be managed. Some specifications require vendors to use certain ranges of MAC addresses in order to ensure that the MAC address of each interface is unique.

 MAC addresses are preset on Ethernet network interface cards at the factory.

The LLC layer is the upper of the two sub-layers and is directly below the Network layer. The LLC sub-layer is the portion of the Data Link layer that specifies error control and flow control.

Layer 3: Network

The primary objective of the Network layer is *routing*: moving data from one network segment to another network segment. When there are multiple, connected segments, the network is called an *internetwork*.

The Network layer routes data by providing a network address and a node address. The network address is applied to the network segment. Each segment must have a network address that is unique on an internetwork. The node address is a logical address and is usually different from the MAC address. The node address must also be unique on the internetwork.

The Network layer's header provides routing. This header includes the source network and node address, as well as the destination network and node address. The Network layer inspects the destination Network-layer address. Using a routing table or a realtime calculation of the best route, the Network layer sends the packet to the next transit point, which is called a *router*.

Data at the Network layer is organized into datagrams. A *datagram* is a logical unit of information transmitted at the Network layer. The services at the Network layer are considered both connectionless and unreliable. *Connectionless service* means that there is no established communication between the source and destination nodes. *Unreliable service* implies that data delivery is neither confirmed nor denied.

Layer 4: Transport

The Transport layer provides a connection-oriented, reliable delivery service. This layer compensates for the fact that the Network layer and lower layers are connectionless and unreliable.

A Transport-layer data transmission may be termed reliable, but that does not mean that data is always delivered. Instead, the data is *confirmed* as delivered. This is an important distinction because a break in an internetwork can deny the data transmission without other layers being aware of it. Even though the Transport layer won't know about the break in the internetwork, the Transport layer can determine whether or not the data was transmitted.

When data is not delivered to the destination computer, or when it is received incorrectly, the Transport layer recognizes the error and notifies upper-layer protocols. The application either takes corrective action or informs the end user that the data was not delivered appropriately.

One Transport-layer function is *data multiplexing*. This means that the data is divided up to be sent over multiple channels to optimize performance.

The Transport layer uses mechanisms to determine when data has been delivered correctly. These mechanisms include:

➤ Acknowledgment responses

➤ Sequencing

➤ Flow control

Acknowledgment responses are commonly known as ACKs. The sending, or source, computer expects an ACK response to the sent data within a certain amount of time. After the timeout value has expired, the data is considered not to have been received by the destination computer.

Sequencing is the assignment of sequence numbers to the data segments. When a message is sent, it is fragmented into smaller pieces, called *segments*, at the Transport layer. Because data can travel over different paths through an internetwork, it is possible that the data will arrive out of order. Sequence numbers enable the Transport layer to reassemble the segments in the correct order.

Flow control enables one side of the data transmission to tell the other side when the rate of data transmission must be slowed or could be sped up. One type of flow control is known as *windowing* because the rate of flow is considered a window. The window can increase or decrease in size, and it is sometimes called a *sliding window*. Either side can notify the other of the need to decrease the rate of flow or of an opportunity to increase the rate of flow.

Layer 5: Session

The Session layer handles the dialog between two computers. It establishes, maintains, synchronizes, and manages the dialog between the source and destination computers.

Additionally, the Session layer communicates to upper layers about problems with file transfers (such as lack of disk space) and with printing (such as when the printer is offline or out of paper).

At the Session layer, two protocols are widely used:

➤ NetBIOS

➤ Remote Procedure Calls

NetBIOS (Network Basic Input/Output System) is often confused with NetBEUI (NetBIOS Extended User Interface) and is therefore thought to be a protocol stack in and of itself. However, NetBIOS is really a Session layer API (Application Programming Interface) that can run over many different protocol stacks, including NetBEUI, TCP/IP (Transmission Control Protocol/Internet Protocol), and Novell's IPX (Internetwork Packet Exchange) protocol stack.

Remote Procedure Calls are commonly known as RPCs. Like NetBIOS, RPCs can run over many different protocol stacks. RPCs are a popular method for accessing messaging systems and databases. One of the most popular RPCs involves the way Microsoft Outlook uses RPC communication to access Microsoft Exchange Server mailboxes. RPCs make remote commands in an application appear as though they are local. End users cannot tell whether those commands are local or remote.

Layer 6: Presentation

The Presentation layer is responsible for the way that data is formatted. In some Presentation-layer protocol specifications, both the source and destination computers agree on the format of the data before the data is sent. Different operating systems use different methods of text formats and graphics formats. For example, an IBM mainframe uses EBCDIC text formatting, whereas a PC uses ASCII. There are many graphics formats available. A Unix computer may format the graphic in JPEG format, whereas a PC may use JPG—a slightly different graphic format of the same specification. Translating the text format or the graphic format occurs at the Presentation layer.

Data format is the syntax of the information being transferred. Both the sending and the receiving computers must understand the syntax. Syntax issues include:

➤ **Compression and expansion**   *Compression* is a technique for using fewer data signals to represent the same amount of information. There are many ways of compressing data; most will replace a repetitive series of bits with a shorter series. This process is somewhat equivalent to replacing all the "and" words in a paragraph with an "&" (ampersand) symbol. *Expansion* is the technique of taking compressed data and translating it back to the full data format. This process is equivalent to replacing the "&" with "and" again.

➤ **Encryption and decryption**   *Encryption* is a method of protecting data so that it cannot be deciphered without knowing the code. Encryption coding is a complex system, regardless of the method used. Encryption is like creating a puzzle and mixing up the pieces. *Decryption* is the method of decoding an encrypted message. Decryption is like solving a puzzle to make a full picture.

Layer 7: Application

The primary objective for the Application layer is to provide the interface for the end user into the network. Another function of the Application layer is to manage the communication between source and destination applications.

The services of the Application layer are the most familiar to the end user. There are file transfer services, virtual terminal applications, directory services, network management services, and electronic messaging services.

TOPOLOGIES

Topologies are the various possible layouts or shapes of a network. A topology can be either the logical layout or the physical layout.

The *physical topology* is the actual appearance of the network. This includes the network nodes, the media, and any hardware devices used with the media. The shape of the connected devices and their wires makes up this physical topology.

The *logical topology* is the way that data flows throughout the network. A shape comes from following the data from a sending device through the media and passing whichever nodes are in the path. This path through the network is the logical topology.

Media Types

One of the characteristics of every physical topology is the type of medium that is being used. So before we delve into the actual physical topologies, we will briefly discuss the media that those topologies use. Chapter 4 discusses more comprehensive details of these media. Media can be of several types:

➤ Copper twisted–pair cable

➤ Coaxial cable

➤ Fiber optic cable

➤ Unbounded media, such as microwaves, infrared, laser, and radio

Copper Twisted-Pair

Copper twisted–pair cable comes in two basic types: unshielded twisted-pair (UTP) and shielded twisted-pair (STP). Each type contains two or more pairs of copper wires that are twisted around each other. UTP is more common than STP. The main advantage of twisted-pair wiring is that it is commonly used in telephone networks. It is a mature technology that can be used with telephone technology. The disadvantage of twisted-pair is that it is sensitive to electromagnetic interference (EMI), which is also called *crosstalk*.

Coax

Coaxial cabling comes in many different types, but all of them are referred to as "coax." A coaxial cable is made up of a central conducting wire, surrounding insulation, an outer conductor, and the exterior plastic coating. The advantage of using coax is that it is a fairly mature and stable technology. Coax has a higher tolerance to EMI than twisted-pair does. A disadvantage is that the cabling is somewhat bulky and difficult to manipulate. Even though it is less susceptible to EMI, it can still be affected by EMI. Table 1.4 lists the various coax types.

Table 1.4 Types of coaxial cable.

Coax Name	Ohms	Usage
RG-8	50 ohm	Ethernet, called thicknet
RG-11	50 ohm	Ethernet, called thicknet
RG-58	50 ohm	Ethernet, called thinnet
RG-59	75 ohm	Cable TV
RG-62	93 ohm	ARCNET

Fiber Optic

Fiber-optic cabling is made of light-conducting plastic or glass fibers that are encased within a protective cladding, which is then surrounded by a protective sheath. Fiber optics are lightweight and can carry more conductors than copper twisted-pair or coaxial cabling can. Fiber optics have several advantages. Fiber optics are not susceptible to EMI; they do not leak signals; and they have a slower rate of signal attenuation so that they can carry signals for longer distances.

Unbounded Media

Unbounded media are those types of transmission media that can transmit and receive data without an electrical or optical conductor. These media include microwave, radio, laser, and infrared techniques.

Microwaves are very short radio waves that are more than 890MHz (megahertz) per second. Microwaves can be set up on satellites or between two points on the planet. One of the main requirements of microwaves is that the two end points are within the line of sight of each other. When microwave units are installed with interfering objects between them, or are so far apart on land that the curvature of the Earth prevents the two end points from reaching each other in a direct line, they will not perform. The main advantage to microwave technology is the potential high bandwidth. Microwave technology also has the same benefit as all unbounded media in that no cabling or trench digging is needed to install it.

Radio waves have the main advantage of being able to broadcast in all directions. There is no need for the end points to be in direct line of sight. Shortwave radio is used for global systems. Local systems use VHF or UHF. Radio is subject to various regulations by national and international agencies, so it is not often the first choice. Radio is extremely vulnerable to EMI and to eavesdropping.

Laser is based on a narrow light beam that is modulated into pulses that represent the data signals. The bandwidth possibilities for laser are much higher than for microwaves. Lasers fall prey to bad weather, but are otherwise resistant to EMI, jamming, and eavesdropping. Lasers do require specific alignment and have a short transmission distance.

Infrared communication is becoming more common as many printers and laptops come readily equipped with infrared photodiodes. This type of communication can reach high bandwidth rates. However, infrared has a limited distance of about 150 feet or less.

Media-Access Methods

Each topology has a media-access method. A *media-access method* is the set of rules governing how a source computer can gain entry to the network, how transmission occurs, and how to release the use of the network. The three methods are as follows:

➤ Polling

➤ Contention

➤ Token passing

Polling

Polling, shown in Figure 1.3, is a way for data to access the media, also called a *channel*, that designates a controller device as the channel-access administrator. The *channel-access administrator* polls each of the other devices to ascertain whether the devices have data to communicate. When the channel-access administrator sends a request for data to another device, it is starting the polling

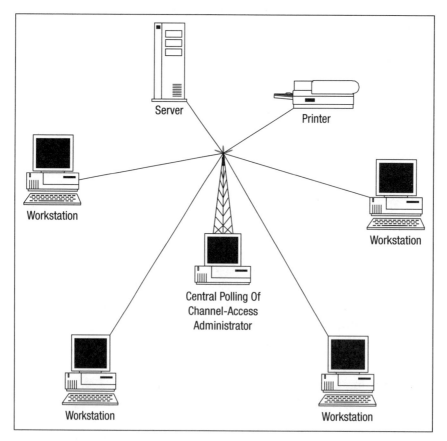

Figure 1.3 Polling as a media-access method.

1

process. After receiving the request, a device that needs to transmit data sends it through the channel-access administrator. The channel-access administrator then polls the next network node in a predetermined order. Protocol specifications have rules to limit how long each network node is permitted to send data through the channel-access administrator.

Advantages to polling are:

➤ Data throughput can increase to the channel administrator's threshold. After reaching the threshold, the data throughput will not be decreased, but it cannot increase either. *Throughput* is a measure of the data that can be sent through the media at a point in time.

➤ Access to the media is centrally located, and the traffic throughput is predictable, because the network has a single threshold in the channel-access administrator. In some polling systems, the channel-access administrator can grant priority to a network node.

The disadvantages to polling are the main reasons that polling is seldom used. These disadvantages are:

➤ The channel-access administrator is a single point of failure. If the channel-access administrator fails to poll for data, then the network cannot function.

➤ The polling process creates a significant amount of overhead. This overhead takes several forms: requests for data, acknowledgments that data was received, and time spent listening for data.

Contention

When the media-access method is *contention*, all the network nodes can begin transmitting data whenever they have data ready to transmit. Unlike the polling method, the contention method has no central channel administrator that manages when data is transmitted. In this method, nodes simply send data whenever they need to, regardless of any other network node's activity.

The result of this strategy—in which multiple network nodes can access the media as needed (as depicted in Figure 1.4—each network device can transmit data to the network at the same time)—is the potential for collisions. A collision occurs when two network nodes transmit data at the same time, and the transmissions literally collide on the wire. At the Physical layer, the signals get all mixed up and are unusable for both transmissions.

One version of contention access attempts to avoid collisions by having the stations "listen" for network traffic and transmit only if the medium is free of traffic. This method is called CSMA, which stands for Carrier Sense, Multiple Access.

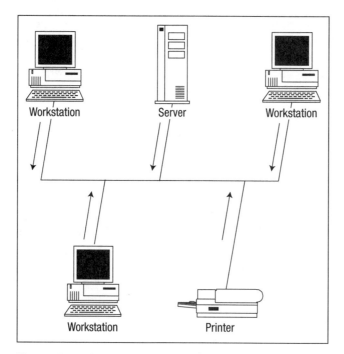

Figure 1.4 Contention as a media-access method.

Some CSMA protocols also provide for collision detection. They are called CSMA/CD, which stands for Carrier Sense, Multiple Access with Collision Detection. When the protocol detects a collision, it initiates a retransmission of the data, usually after waiting for a short, random-length period of time. CSMA/CD provides for a backoff algorithm to determine this random-length period of time. Ethernet and the IEEE 802.3 protocol are two examples of CSMA/CD protocols. The IEEE is the Institute of Electrical and Electronics Engineers. The IEEE has created many protocols and networking standards. Of these standards, the 802.x series is the most recognized because it addresses various protocol specifications that are used today.

Other CSMA protocols employ methods to avoid collisions. These protocols are called CSMA/CA, which stands for Carrier Sense, Multiple Access with Collision Avoidance. This type of protocol uses systems such as time-sliced media access or transmission requests to gain access to the media. LocalTalk, which was developed by Apple for networking Macintosh and Apple computers, is an example of a CSMA/CA protocol.

The advantages of contention media-access methods are:

➤ Contention protocols are simple with little overhead.

➤ With light traffic, data throughput is high and can nearly meet the bandwidth capacity of the media.

The disadvantages of contention media-access methods are:

➤ Because network stations can transmit whenever they need to, there is very little predictability.

➤ No priorities can be given to certain network stations. If a server or a critical network node requires better or faster access to the network media, or needs access for longer periods of time, contention will not provide it.

➤ At higher traffic levels, data throughput rates can become far less than the capacity of the media because so many collisions and retransmissions occur.

Token Passing

The key to the token passing media-access method is the token. A *token*, in this context, is a specially formatted frame of data. The format of the frame tells the network nodes that the frame is a token and not a data frame. The token is passed from node to node. When a node receives the token, the node can transmit data. If there is no data to transmit, the node transmits the token, passing it on to the next node in line. See Figure 1.5 for an example.

The token-passing method grants each network node equal opportunity to access the network. Each network node knows the station to which it must send the token next and the station from which the token will be received.

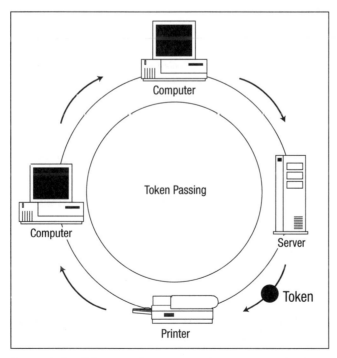

Figure 1.5 Token passing as a media-access method.

There are rules to limit the time that a station can control the token, although some token-passing protocols enable priority setting for certain network nodes to lengthen their limit. Because the token is sent to each node in an orderly fashion, network access is predictably available.

Two types of token-passing protocols are the IEEE 802.4 Token Bus and the IBM Token Ring protocols. IBM Token Ring is nearly identical to the IEEE 802.5 protocol and is compatible with it.

The advantages of a token-passing media-access method are:

➤ Token passing is suitable for automated equipment devices because it is easy to determine when a station will be able to transmit and for how long.

➤ The ability to have a flexible priority system in token passing makes it preferable for mission-critical network stations.

➤ Traffic management is the main benefit of token passing. The use of the token to control which node may transmit provides an equal-opportunity network. This, in turn, keeps data moving on the wire. When there is a high-traffic situation, token passing usually offers the highest data throughput of any media-access method.

Disadvantages of token passing include:

➤ The token-passing protocol is complex and has a fair amount of overhead involved in the creation and passing of the token throughout the network. Light traffic has less data throughput because of the overhead.

➤ Token passing requires management of the network. When a computer is turned off, the neighboring nodes must be adjusted so they know where to send the token to or where it will be received from. Other network-management functions are needed to handle fault detection in the network, recovery, and monitoring.

Now that we have reviewed media types and media-access methods, we will discuss the types of shapes, or topologies, in which they are used. These shapes consist of a combination of point-to-point and multipoint connections.

A *point-to-point* connection is the link that exists between only two devices. A point-to-point link—shown in Figure 1.6—implies that the bandwidth is dedicated between the two devices. It is common to use a point-to-point connection when a computer dials in to a network because it connects to a remote-access server and does not share the link.

A *multipoint connection* is a link that exists between three or more computers, arranged so that they can all access the link. In a multipoint connection—shown in Figure 1.7—the bandwidth on the link is shared among all the nodes. This is a typical connection type for local area networks (LANs). LANs typically interconnect many nodes on a single cable.

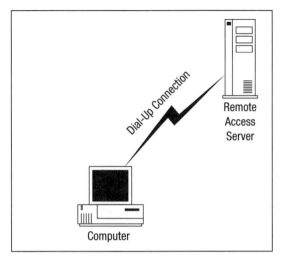

Figure 1.6   Point-to-point link.

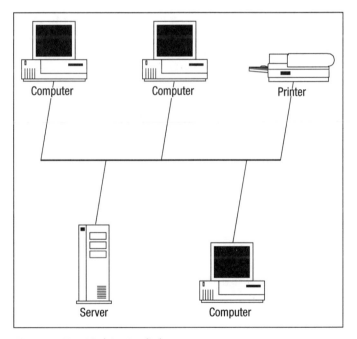

Figure 1.7   Multipoint link.

Topology Types

The star, bus, mesh, and ring topology types are discussed in the following sections.

Star Topologies

Star topologies consist of multiple point-to-point links connected to a central device. In a logical star topology, the center of the star controls the data throughput. In a physical star topology, the center of the star connects the arms of the star to enable data exchange between the end nodes.

In a physical star topology, as shown in Figure 1.8, the center device is usually called a hub, a concentrator, a multistation access unit, or a multiport repeater. There is a difference between an active hub and a passive hub. An active hub regenerates the signal it receives from an end node before sending it on. A passive hub is not a repeater and does not participate in signal regeneration; instead, it just enables the connection of the nodes.

The logical star topology is used in polling media-access methods. The data must always flow through the central polling device, which is the channel-access administrator, before it can go to the destination on the network. Data flows in a star shape, always flowing from the end node to the central polling device to another node.

The star topology can be used physically just to connect the end nodes, but a different topology can be used logically for the same network. For example, data can travel in and out of each wire to a node, from a node to the center to a node, until it makes a complete ring. In this way, the data flow is a logical ring topology, but the physical shape of the network is a star topology.

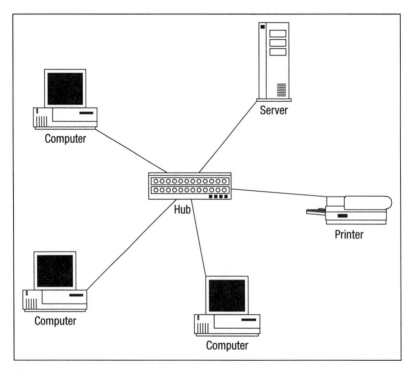

Figure 1.8   A physical star topology.

Physical star topologies tend to use twisted-pair wiring, both shielded and unshielded. This is evident in both Ethernet 10BaseT and IBM token ring topologies because they both can be set up in a physical star topology using UTP (unshielded twisted-pair).

The advantages of star topologies include:

➤ Stars are easy to troubleshoot because they have a central point to isolate the failure.

➤ Stars can be organized in a hierarchy, or a type of pecking order. This organization lends star topologies a measure of flexibility where traffic flow can be isolated on peripheral stars, whose centers are placed where an end node would be, but an upper-level star still contains the main traffic.

The disadvantages of star topologies are:

➤ On a physical star topology, the cabling for each node must be brought to a central point where the hub is located (usually the wiring closet). This requires more cabling than a network that connects nodes in a serial formation.

➤ The center in both the physical and the logical star topologies gives it a single point of failure. If the center device or hub fails in the star topology, this failure can disable the entire star network.

An example of a physical star topology is Ethernet 10BaseT. This topology uses a central device called an Ethernet hub with unshielded twisted-pair connected to each node.

Bus Topologies

Bus topologies are a true multipoint connection. A bus topology, as seen in Figure 1.9, has a linear shape to it. When used in a logical bus topology, a node transmits data to all nodes on the network, where the data stops at each node on its travels through the network. In a physical bus topology, each network node is attached to the same cable in a serial fashion.

A physical bus topology requires that the ends of the network are terminated. *Termination* means that a device is connected to each end of the cable to mark its beginning and end. The terminating device ensures that data signals do not reflect back through the network in the direction from which they came.

Bus topologies are often set up with coaxial cabling, both thicknet and thinnet. The most popular logical bus topology is Ethernet, which uses a contention media-access method (CSMA/CD). Ethernet 10Base5 is an example of a physical bus topology using coax.

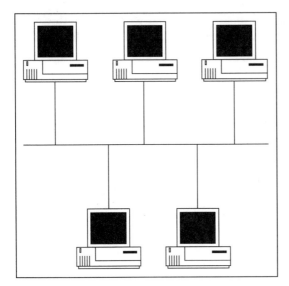

Figure 1.9 A bus topology.

One advantage of bus topologies is:

➤ The physical bus topology uses the least amount of cable for any topology requiring cabling.

A disadvantage of bus topologies is:

➤ Physical bus topologies are difficult to troubleshoot. Because nodes are all attached to the same cable, if there is a fault in the cable, it is difficult to pinpoint where to look for the fault. A fault in the cable will cause the entire segment to fail.

Mesh Topologies

There are so many connections in a mesh topology that it is difficult to think about it in terms of point-to-point. However, a mesh topology is simply that— a series of point-to-point connections between each node on the network.

Mesh topologies exist in only a physical sense. They are typically depicted in diagrams as a "cloud," as is shown in Figure 1.10. The connections within the cloud are usually not depicted because the mesh topology can have many more connections inside the cloud. Mesh topologies are often public networks that a private enterprise connects to on either side. The private enterprise knows of the end points where it connects, but does not know about the inner connections of the public network.

Pure mesh topologies—in which each and every node has a connection to each and every other node—are rare. More commonly, a partial mesh topology is created. In a partial mesh topology, many of the nodes are connected to many

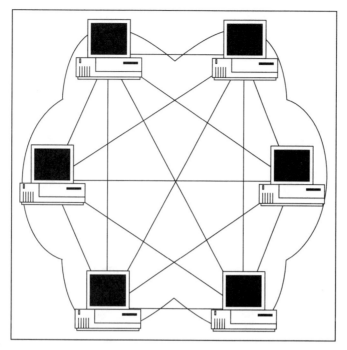

Figure 1.10   A mesh topology.

of the others, and most of them have at least two or more point–to–point connections with other nodes in the mesh.

An example of a mesh topology is Frame Relay, a wide area network (WAN) protocol that uses multiple redundant, meshed connections to maximize data throughput.

The main advantages of mesh topologies are:

➤ With so many connections available, a message made of three frames can have each frame travel a different route from the sending node to the destination node. This flexibility maximizes the data throughput.

➤ Meshed connections are redundant. If there is a break in the point–to–point link between any two nodes in the mesh, the network itself does not fail. Instead, data is sent over different routes in order to transmit through the network.

The disadvantages of mesh topologies include:

➤ Pure mesh topologies are simply impractical. After a certain number of nodes have been added to the network, adding more interfaces to any particular node may be impossible.

➤ Mesh topologies require a lot of cable. Because of the multiple connections, this topology uses more than does any other physical topology.

➤ There is a certain amount of overhead involved in mesh topologies in order to manage how data is transmitted from one node to another node, regardless of which path the data takes.

Ring Topologies

The ring topology can exist in both a logical and a physical sense. The logical ring topology transmits data in a circular fashion, starting with the sending node and continuing throughout the network until reaching the initial node again. Whereas the logical ring topology can be used with a different physical topology, the physical ring topology always uses a logical ring topology. See Figure 1.11 for an example of ring topology.

The physical ring topology is best described as a closed loop of point-to-point connections. In the physical ring topology, a node has two connecting points on its network interface card. One of the connecting points is the *ring-in* point, which is where the data is expected to be received from. The other connecting point is the *ring-out* point, which is where the station transmits data out to the network. Neighboring nodes will have one node's ring-in port connected to the next node's ring-out port. This means that data will have a logical path from a ring-out port of one node to the ring-in port of the next node, then out its ring-out port and on to the next node's ring-in port, and so on throughout the ring.

Ring topologies usually use token passing for the media-access method. One example of a ring topology is Fiber Distributed Data Interface (FDDI). FDDI

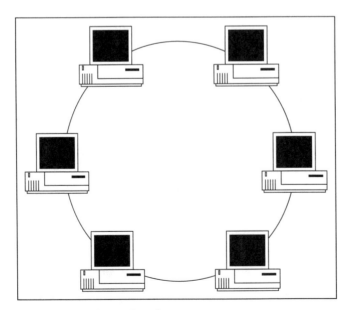

Figure 1.11   A ring topology.

uses a dual ring of fiber-optic cables. The second ring is a redundancy factor used to maintain the network's connectivity even when there is a break in one of the rings.

IBM's token ring is another example of a ring topology that uses a token-passing media-access method on a single ring. Although token ring may be set up in a physical and logical ring, it can also be set up in a logical ring topology, but using a physical star topology. When a token ring network is set up with a physical star topology, it uses a central device called a MSAU (Multistation Access Unit) or MAU (Media Access Unit, or Media Attachment Unit). Token ring MAUs can be connected together to increase the size of the single ring. This is done by connecting the ring-in port on the first MAU to the ring-out port on the other MAU, and then connecting the ring-out port on the first MAU to the ring-in port on the second. In this way, the ring is completed throughout the MAUs. Figure 1.12 shows how the data flows through this scheme in a logical ring.

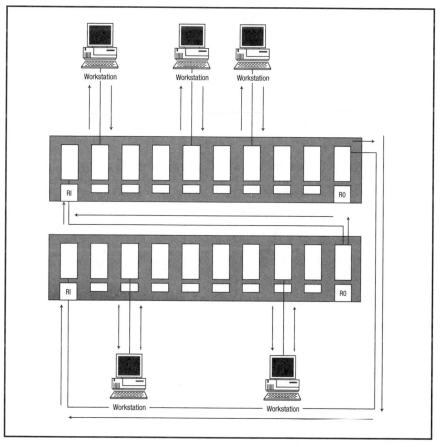

Figure 1.12   A physical star topology with logical ring data flow.

The advantage of a ring topology is:

➤ Physical ring topologies use very little cabling because they need to be wired only in a point-to-point manner between nodes.

The disadvantages of a ring topology are:

➤ Physical ring topologies are difficult to troubleshoot because it is hard to pinpoint where a network failure has occurred.

➤ If there is a fault with any of a physical ring's connections, the entire ring fails. A ring topology therefore has a low tolerance for network faults. FDDI uses a redundant ring to become more fault tolerant. In token ring, a MAU in a physical star topology using the logical ring is able to *wrap* ports when a fault occurs so that the ring can be maintained intact even when there are multiple faults on the network.

INTERNETWORK CHARACTERISTICS

Throughout this chapter, we have used the terms *network, segment,* and *LAN (local area network)* almost interchangeably. These terms are, however, somewhat different from each other and from an *internetwork. Backbone* is a new term describing a type of network characteristic. Because these terms are important for understanding networking, we will define them here:

➤ **Backbone** A backbone is a segment that provides the primary path through the network, connecting multiple network segments.

➤ **Internetwork** An internetwork is any group of computers that are connected in a way that allows users to exchange data and share services. There are no geographic boundaries set on an internetwork.

➤ **LAN** LAN stands for "local area network." A LAN is a group of computers that are linked in a way that enables their users to share data and services, and that are located in close proximity geographically (usually within the boundaries of a building or campus).

➤ **Network** A network is a group of computers that are able to communicate with each other. "Network" can refer either to a LAN or to a segment that exists within a LAN. Sometimes, "network" refers to a WAN (wide area network) or to an internetwork.

➤ **Segment** A segment is a portion of a network that is bounded by bridges, switches, or routers.

Characteristics Of Segments And Backbones

What the definitions in the previous section state is that *network* is a generic term. A network describes any segment within a LAN. It can describe the LAN itself. It is sometimes even used to describe an internetwork, which is the whole enchilada—segments, LANs, and wide area network links, no matter what they may link to.

The smallest section of a network is the segment. A segment can be discussed on a physical or a logical level. At the physical level, it is a portion of any network that is bounded by bridges, switches, or routers. A segment can be any type of topology, either a point-to-point or a multipoint link.

Using the definition that a segment is bounded by bridges, switches, and routers, let's examine what happens when bridges and switches and routers are added to a network. A bridge operates at the Data Link layer of the OSI Reference Model. The bridge receives frames of data from one physical segment and forwards them onto another physical segment. Bridges usually require similar topologies on both sides of the interface. There are a few exceptions to this rule, such as translational bridges, but normally an Ethernet segment can be bridged only with another Ethernet segment. A Layer 2 switch operates at the same layers as a bridge does.

When data moves from a source network through a bridge or a Layer 2 switch, it does not go through all the OSI layers. Instead, the bridge only looks at the Data Link layer, determines from the MAC address where the data should be sent, and forwards it through that interface. Bridges learn the MAC addresses of the nodes connected to the bridge's directly connected segments. Figure 1.13 depicts the bridging principle.

Routing is the function of moving data between dissimilar network segments. Routers operate at the Network layer of the OSI Reference Model. When a router examines data it receives, it looks at the logical network address and forwards it out the interface that leads to that particular network. This process requires that the router know which interfaces lead to which networks. The router performs routing by creating a routing table, making forwarding decisions, and learning new routes. (A detailed discussion of routing appears in Chapter 5.) When a router is included in a network, the network is considered an internetwork.

Figure 1.14 depicts routing. Note how similar routing is to bridging. A type of networking hardware called a *brouter* combines a bridging functionality with a routing functionality. A brouter will bridge when it can (working at the Data Link layer), and route when it cannot bridge (working at the Network layer).

Segments can be connected into internetworks in all sorts of ways. Many internetworks grow haphazardly, with segments being connected into an

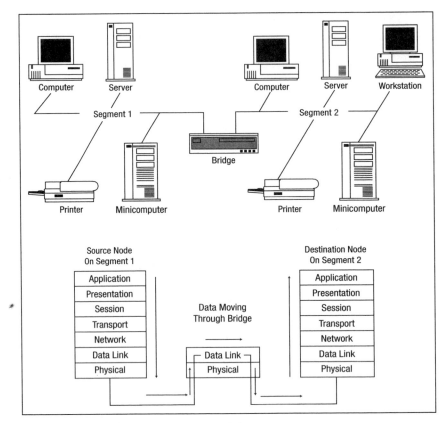

Figure 1.13 Bridging at the Data Link layer.

existing internetwork on an as-needed basis. When not planned, an internetwork can become very difficult to manage. Here's why:

➤ Data throughput can become increasingly degraded.

➤ Segments can be unreachable because they are out of the range of a routing protocol being used.

➤ There can be multiple broadcasts of the same data because redundant paths are created when new segments are added.

These are a few problems that can arise when no planning goes into the network infrastructure. Using a backbone can mitigate some planning problems. A backbone is a special segment that provides the primary path for data flow throughout a network. An internetwork may have several campus-area backbones, or it may use a single wide-area backbone.

How a backbone is set up depends on several factors: which segments have the highest data transmission rates, the type and size of data sent, and the quality of the transmission service required.

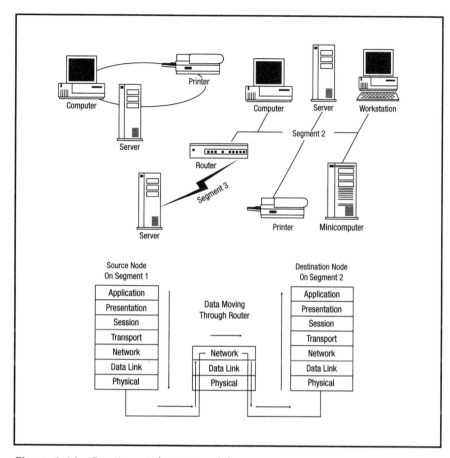

Figure 1.14   Routing at the Network layer.

The segments that have the most data to exchange would best be routed directly to the backbone. These segments include those with mainframes and servers, because end users from different locations in the internetwork might need to access their services. In a campus network that has a consolidated printing room, the printers segment can also be routed directly to the backbone.

The type and size of the data transmitted on the internetwork can determine whether a segment should be routed directly into the backbone. For example, if a workgroup of end users were located on two separate segments in the same building, and those users exchanged large graphics files between their segments, it would be better to isolate the traffic between those two segments, rather than stress the backbone with excessively large file transfers.

Quality of service is a way of ensuring that certain data types receive higher priorities or more bandwidth. For example, when video data is sent, it needs to have a higher quality of service than a file transfer does. Very few users complain if a file transfer has momentary pauses. Users might complain, however, if a video being viewed stopped in the middle or if, during a video conference, the president's speech did not match the movements of his mouth.

Some backbones are installed to ensure simplicity in a network. Still others are made to provide redundant paths. In any case, the backbone of an internetwork must be reliable because it is the primary path for data exchange. Quite often, the backbone network will be a high-capacity specification, such as a FDDI (Fiber Distributed Data Interchange) ring or an ATM (Asynchronous Transfer Mode) network. Figure 1.15 illustrates a backbone in an internetwork.

Backbones are used to interconnect multiple segments together. It is considered bad form to link up a single device to a backbone. It is better to connect that single device to a segment and then to connect the segment to the backbone.

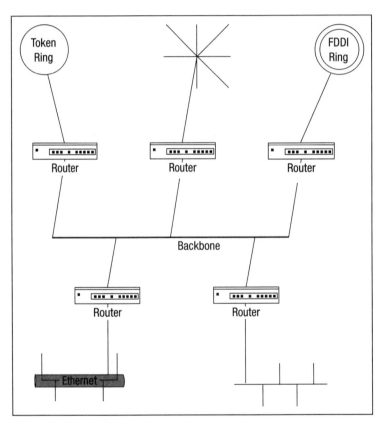

Figure 1.15   Backbone in an internetwork.

CHAPTER SUMMARY

The two networking fundamentals you need to understand are:

➤ The layers of the OSI Reference Model, and the protocols, services, and functions that pertain to each layer

➤ Basic network structure, including the characteristics of star, bus, mesh, and ring topologies, their advantages and disadvantages, and the characteristics of segments and backbones

There are four basic components in a network: a client computer that is requesting a service, a server computer that is fulfilling service requests, the media that connects them, and the protocol, which is a set of rules governing how the data is transmitted.

The ISO created the OSI Reference Model. The OSI Reference Model is used as a method for understanding networks. The ISO took a layered approach to the OSI model, which enables vendors to concentrate on the networking function that they need to provide, rather than creating proprietary monolithic networking hardware and software.

The OSI Reference Model consists of these seven layers:

➤ **Physical** The Physical layer is where data is placed onto the wire in the bitstream format. The Physical layer handles the electric or electronic signaling of the data. The Physical layer also specifies the media–access method and the physical topology to be used.

➤ **Data Link** The Data Link layer consists of two sub-layers—the Media Access Control (MAC) sub-layer and the Logical Link Control (LLC) sublayer. The Data Link layer organizes data into frames. A physical address (also known as a MAC address) is assigned to the node at this layer.

➤ **Network** The Network layer handles the movement of data between segments, a process called *routing*. A logical network address is assigned to the network segment, and a logical node address is assigned to the station at this layer.

➤ **Transport** The Transport layer provides a reliable, connection-oriented service. The Transport layer ensures that data is sent through acknowledgment messages (ACKs), that sequencing is used to assemble data in the correct order, and that flow control is used to maximize throughput.

➤ **Session** The Session layer is directly applicable to dialogs that are created between two network nodes. The Session layer establishes, manages, and terminates the dialog.

➤ **Presentation** The Presentation layer handles the formatting of data. Two nodes will agree on the data format at the Presentation layer. Also, encryption, decryption, compression, and expansion are all handled at the Presentation layer.

➤ **Application** The Application layer is where services such as electronic messaging and file transfers take place. This is the layer where the end user will interact with the network.

Media-access methods are the ways that data can be placed on the media. The three types are polling, contention, and token passing. Polling uses a channel-access administrator to poll each node to determine whether it has data to transmit. Contention allows any node to transmit data whenever necessary. CSMA/CD (Carrier Sense, Multiple Access with Collision Detection) and CSMA/CA (Carrier Sense, Multiple Access with Collision Avoidance) are two types of contention methods. Token passing uses a special frame called a token, which is passed from node to node in order to grant the nodes permission to transmit data.

Physical topologies describe the shape or layout of the network. A logical topology describes the shape of the data flow through the network. The following are four basic topologies used:

➤ **Ring** A ring topology is in the shape of a ring, where each node is connected in point-to-point links to two neighboring nodes until the last node is connected to the first, completing the ring. The ring topology has a lot of overhead and is difficult to troubleshoot when a cable fault occurs.

➤ **Star** A star topology is in the shape of a star. It has a central device, which is connected to every other node on the segment in a point-to-point link. The star topology is easy to troubleshoot.

➤ **Mesh** The mesh topology consists of multiple, redundant, point-to-point links. Mesh topologies require a lot of cable to connect all the nodes.

➤ **Bus** The bus topology is a multipoint link where all the nodes are connected to the same cable. Bus topologies are hard to troubleshoot when there is a cable fault because it's difficult to pinpoint the fault.

Topologies are applicable to individual segments. A segment is a portion of a network that is bounded by bridges, switches, and routers. A special type of segment is a backbone. Backbones are the primary path for data transmission throughout a network.

Review Questions

1. Which layer of the OSI Reference Model provides a reliable, connection-oriented datastream?

   a. Presentation

   b. Transport

   c. Session

   d. Data Link

2. Which layer of the OSI Reference Model manages the dialog between two network nodes?

   a. Physical

   b. Transport

   c. Data Link

   d. Session

3. Which layer of the OSI Reference Model contains both the Logical Link Control sub-layer and the Media Access Control sub-layer?

   a. Physical

   b. Network

   c. Data Link

   d. Presentation

4. Which layer of the OSI Reference Model provides routing functionality?

   a. Network

   b. Application

   c. Transport

   d. Data Link

5. Which layer of the OSI Reference Model is responsible for services such as electronic messaging?

   a. Physical

   b. Presentation

   c. Application

   d. Network

6. Which layer of the OSI Reference Model handles data-format issues such as encryption and compression?

    a. Physical

    b. Data Link

    c. Transport

    d. Presentation

7. Which layer of the OSI Reference Model places data on the wire and manages signaling?

    a. Physical

    b. Data Link

    c. Presentation

    d. Transport

8. Which of the following network devices will operate at the Network layer? [Choose the two best answers]

    a. Router

    b. Hub

    c. Bridge

    d. Brouter

9. Which of the following topologies consists of a central device with end nodes connected in point-to-point links to it?

    a. Mesh

    b. Star

    c. Ring

    d. Bus

10. Which topology consists of multiple, redundant, point-to-point links?

    a. Mesh

    b. Star

    c. Ring

    d. Bus

11. Which topology is a multipoint connection where all computers access the same single cable?

    a. Mesh

    b. Star

    c. Ring

    d. Bus

1

12. Which of the following is a disadvantage of using a mesh topology?
   a. A cable fault is difficult to locate and disables the entire segment.
   b. It uses a tremendous amount of cabling.
   c. It requires knowledge of the neighboring nodes.
   d. It needs a controlling device to grant access to the media.

13. Which of the following is a disadvantage of using a bus topology?
   a. A cable fault is difficult to locate and disables the entire segment.
   b. It uses a tremendous amount of cabling.
   c. It requires knowledge of the neighboring nodes.
   d. It needs a controlling device to grant access to the media.

14. Which of the following requires ring-in ports to be connected to ring-out ports for two to be connected?
   a. Hub
   b. Repeater
   c. MAU
   d. Router

15. Which of the following is the best option to connect to a backbone?
   a. Client
   b. Server
   c. Printer
   d. Segment

HANDS-ON PROJECTS

End users access the network through the Application layer. Workstations access an internetwork through the Network and Data Link layers. We will be examining the setup of Network layer and Data Link layer addresses on various operating systems, and the Telnet application that accesses network services.

Project 1.1

The first portion of this hands-on project shows you how to set up the HyperTerminal application on a Windows 95/98/NT workstation so that you can Telnet to a router. Telnet is an Application-layer service that provides terminal emulation.

The second half of this hands-on project will let you examine the Network-layer address that is assigned to a Cisco router. All Cisco routers use the Cisco IOS (Internetwork Operating System). This exercise applies to IOS v11.x (a current version). To complete this hands-on project, you must first complete the

first part of this hands-on project, using a Cisco router's IP address, and you
must be connected to a network with a Cisco router.

To set up the HyperTerminal application:

1. On the Windows desktop, click on Start.

2. Select Programs.

3. Select Accessories.

4. If HyperTerminal is an option, select it; otherwise, select Communications
and then select HyperTerminal. (Note: Some PCs must have
HyperTerminal installed with the Add/Remove Programs icon in the
Control Panel. A newer version of HyperTerminal may be available from
www.hilgraeve.com.)

5. The HyperTerminal folder will open. Double-click on the Hypertrm icon.

6. In the first dialog box, type a name such as TEST, select an icon, and click
on OK.

7. In the Connect To dialog box, select TCP/IP (Winsock) from the Connect
Using drop-down list. As shown in Figure 1.16, the dialog box will change
to allow an IP address and port number.

8. If you have a Cisco router available, enter its IP address. The standard Telnet
port number is 23, but some network devices may be configured with
custom ports. If so, change the port number. If you do not know, leave 23.

9. Click on OK. HyperTerminal is configured. To connect, click on the Call
menu and select Call.

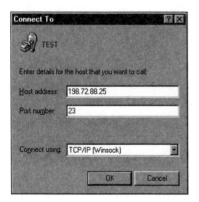

Figure 1.16 HyperTerminal configuration of IP address for Telnet access.

To examine the Network-layer address that is assigned to a Cisco router:

1. From the HyperTerminal window, click on the Call menu and select Call. The window will begin a Telnet session with the target router.

2. Press the Enter key.

3. The Cisco router may request a password to connect. If so, enter the password. If not, you should be in User EXEC mode at a prompt that is similar to ROUTER>. This prompt is the router name followed by the > symbol.

4. Type "enable" and press Enter.

5. Type the password and press Enter. The router will be in Privileged EXEC mode, and the prompt will be similar to ROUTER#.

6. Type "show interface ethernet0". (If the router does not have an Ethernet interface, you may try "show interface serial0" or "show interface tokenring0".)

7. The router will display output that shows how the interface is configured, including the Network-layer addresses that have been assigned to it. These are the first few lines of a typical output of this command, including the Data Link layer's MAC address of the interface (0000.203b.b3cd) and the IP address, which is the logical Network-layer address (199.72.88.25):

```
Router#show interface tokenring0
Tokenring0 is up. Line protocol is up.
  Hardware is TMS380, address is 0000.203b.b3cd (bia 0000.203b.b3cd)
  Description: Testing router
  Internet address is 199.72.88.25/24
  .......
```

Project 1.2

This hands-on project contains three parts, each pertaining to Network-layer addresses. The first part will show you how to view the MAC and IP addresses of an interface installed in a Windows 95 or Windows 98 workstation. The second part of this project will show you how to view the Network-layer address configured on a NetWare 5 server. The third part will show you how to view the Network-layer IP address configured on a Windows 98 or Windows NT 4 workstation.

To view the addresses on a Windows 95 or Windows 98 workstation:

1. On the Windows desktop, click on Start.

2. Select Run.

3. In the dialog box, type "winipcfg".

4. Click on OK.

5. If there are multiple network interface cards or modems on the workstation, you can click on the drop-down box and select the interface whose address you want to view.

6. Click on the More Info button to expand the amount of information available about that interface. The Adapter Address shows the Data Link layer's MAC address of the interface. The IP address displays the Network-layer IP address assigned to the interface. See Figure 1.17 for an example of WINIPCFG output.

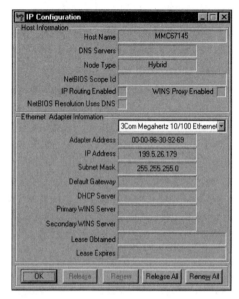

Figure 1.17   WINIPCFG output.

To view a NetWare server address:

1. At the NetWare 5 server, go to the console prompt. The console prompt on a NetWare 5 server looks like "SERVER:" (the server name followed by a colon). If the console is not at the console prompt, press Alt+Esc until the console prompt appears. The Alt+Esc key combination pages through all the console screens on a NetWare server.

2. Clear the screen by typing "cls" and pressing Enter.

3. Type "config" and press Enter. This step will show all the interfaces on the computer and their configurations. There may be several screens' worth of information. Press Enter until you have viewed all of them. See Figure 1.18 for the NetWare configuration screen.

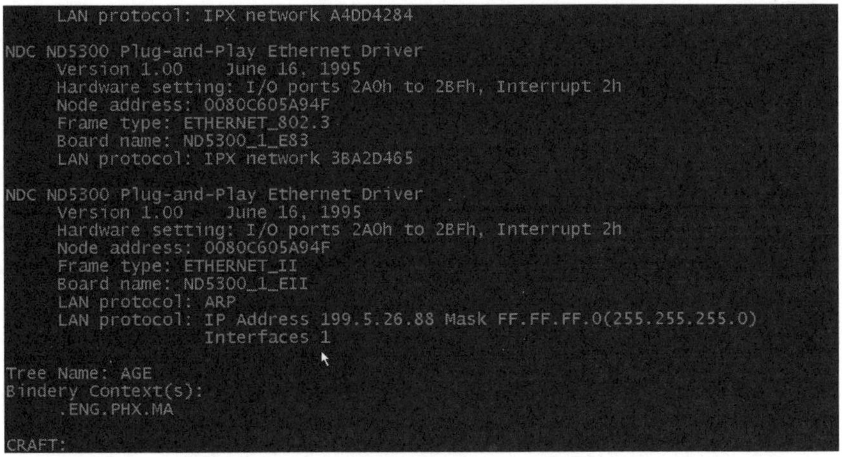

```
      LAN protocol: IPX network A4DD4284

NDC ND5300 Plug-and-Play Ethernet Driver
    Version 1.00     June 16, 1995
    Hardware setting: I/O ports 2A0h to 2BFh, Interrupt 2h
    Node address: 0080C605A94F
    Frame type: ETHERNET_802.3
    Board name: ND5300_1_E83
    LAN protocol: IPX network 3BA2D465

NDC ND5300 Plug-and-Play Ethernet Driver
    Version 1.00     June 16, 1995
    Hardware setting: I/O ports 2A0h to 2BFh, Interrupt 2h
    Node address: 0080C605A94F
    Frame type: ETHERNET_II
    Board name: ND5300_1_EII
    LAN protocol: ARP
    LAN protocol: IP Address 199.5.26.88 Mask FF.FF.FF.0(255.255.255.0)
                  Interfaces 1

Tree Name: AGE
Bindery Context(s):
    .ENG.PHX.MA

CRAFT:
```

Figure 1.18 NetWare configuration screen.

To view the address on a Windows 98 or Windows NT Workstation:

1. Click on Start.

2. Click on Programs.

3. Select the DOS Prompt or Console Prompt option.

4. At the prompt, type "ipconfig" or, if you want more information, "ipconfig /all", and press Enter. This command will display the IP addresses applied to the various interfaces on the workstation. The output is similar to the following:

```
Windows 98 IP Configuration

        Host Name . . . . . . . . . : MMC67145
        DNS Servers . . . . . . . . :
        Node Type . . . . . . . . . : Hybrid
        NetBIOS Scope ID. . . . . . :
        IP Routing Enabled. . . . . : No
        WINS Proxy Enabled. . . . . : No
        NetBIOS Resolution Uses DNS : No

0 Ethernet adapter :

        Description . . . . . . . . : PPP Adapter.
        Physical Address. . . . . . : 44-45-53-54-00-00
        DHCP Enabled. . . . . . . . : Yes
        IP Address. . . . . . . . . : 0.0.0.0
        Subnet Mask . . . . . . . . : 0.0.0.0
        Default Gateway . . . . . . :
```

```
            DHCP Server . . . . . . . . : 255.255.255.255
            Primary WINS Server . . . . :
            Secondary WINS Server . . . :
            Lease Obtained. . . . . . . :
            Lease Expires . . . . . . . :

    1 Ethernet adapter :

            Description . . . . . . . . : Xircom Performance Series XPS
                                          Ethernet Adapter Dr
            Physical Address. . . . . . : 00-80-C7-FE-C6-8D
            DHCP Enabled. . . . . . . . : Yes
            IP Address. . . . . . . . . : 169.254.134.70
            Subnet Mask . . . . . . . . : 255.255.0.0
            Default Gateway . . . . . . :
            DHCP Server . . . . . . . . : 255.255.255.255
            Primary WINS Server . . . . :
            Secondary WINS Server . . . :
            Lease Obtained. . . . . . . : 02 21 99 10:26:17 AM
            Lease Expires . . . . . . . :

    2 Ethernet adapter :

            Description . . . . . . . . : 3Com Megahertz 10/100 Ethernet +
                                          56K PC Card
            Physical Address. . . . . . : 00-00-86-30-92-69
            DHCP Enabled. . . . . . . . : No
            IP Address. . . . . . . . . : 199.5.26.179
            Subnet Mask . . . . . . . . : 255.255.255.0
            Default Gateway . . . . . . :
            Primary WINS Server . . . . :
            Secondary WINS Server . . . :
            Lease Obtained. . . . . . . :
            Lease Expires . . . . . . . :
```

NETWORK OPERATING SYSTEMS

After Reading This Chapter And Completing The Exercises, You Will Be Able To:

➤ Explain the purpose of the operating system and its role in networking

➤ Describe the features of major network operating systems, including Microsoft Windows NT, Novell NetWare, and Unix

➤ Identify network clients and their interoperability as clients and peers

➤ Describe the directory services of the major network operating systems

Network operating systems are the providers for the network. They provide services to other computers. Services, in the form of file and printer sharing, are the reason for connecting computers in the first place.

PURPOSE OF THE OPERATING SYSTEM

The primary purpose for any network operating system (NOS) is to provide services to the internetwork. *Servers* are the computers that run the network operating system and provide various services to clients. *Clients* are workstations that access services through the use of client software, typically referred to as a requester. The client software and the NOS both use a network protocol stack to transmit data.

That network protocol stack must be the same for both a client and a server. *Protocols* are the sets of rules that govern the way that data is transmitted. A protocol is like a language that both computers need to understand and speak in order to communicate.

A network operating system may provide any or all of the following types of services to users:

➤ File services

➤ Printer sharing

➤ Electronic messaging or email services

➤ Database services

➤ Web services

➤ Dynamic addressing services

These are only a few examples of the services that network operating systems can provide. Older network operating systems focused almost solely on sharing files and printers. Back when a 5MB hard drive cost $5,000 or more, the ability to share hard-drive space was a precious commodity. Printers were also exceptionally expensive. Because it was rare that any one user would send a constant data stream of prints to a printer, sharing printers could reduce the cost of printer hardware and maximize its utilization.

What grew from the sharing of files and printers was the need to secure those files and printers from unauthorized users. *Share-level security*—the process of setting a general password for a file or a printer and giving that password to authorized users—was easily defeated. The password would be given by an authorized user to an unauthorized user for temporary use, or the password would be taped to a monitor on a desk, and all sorts of security leaks would occur.

NOSs soon required the administration of user accounts that were granted access to files and printers. This level is considered "user-level" security. In this system, a user is given an authenticating identifier, usually called a *login ID*, and an associated password. The network administrator grants individual users access to the appropriate resources, as shown in Figure 2.1.

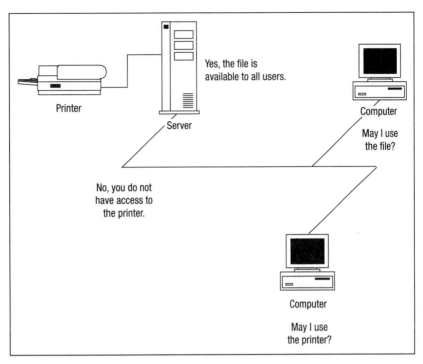

Figure 2.1   Sharing files and printers with user-level security.

Groups were created to simplify the security management of a NOS. It is easier to grant file access to a group, and then add or remove user accounts from that group, than it is to keep track of individual security access. Some NOSs include a group called EVERYONE, or WORLD, which includes all the user accounts within that NOS's directory, so that any resource can be granted universal access.

A NOS includes utilities for the following:

➤ Managing the directory of users

➤ Managing files and shared disk space

➤ Monitoring the server's performance

➤ Managing printing resources

➤ Archiving data to a backup tape or other archival system

➤ Managing client access

The NOS is usually intended to work with a specific protocol, which is considered its native protocol. With the movement toward more and more interoperability, most NOSs now will support many different protocols in addition to their native protocols. The protocols do not necessarily come "out of the box"; some must be installed onto the NOS as part of an add-on package. Almost all NOSs support the Transmission Control Protocol/Internet Protocol (TCP/IP) protocol.

MAJOR NETWORK OPERATING SYSTEMS

Many operating systems can share files and printers with other systems on an internetwork. For example, Windows 95 and Windows 98 can both share files and printers with any other Windows PC using the same protocol. *Peer-to-peer networking* is an arrangement in which a Windows PC shares files and printers while also being used as a workstation by an end user.

However, a major network operating system is typically dedicated to serving files, printers, and other services to the internetwork. Some NOSs do not even have access to the server's files and printers from the server console. Instead, the network administrator must connect from a workstation and receive proper network authentication to be able to manipulate and administer those items. The use of dedicated servers on a network is called *server-based networking* or *client/server computing.* Figure 2.2 shows a peer-to-peer network and a server-based network.

The following sections review some of the major network operating systems and a few that are less trendy.

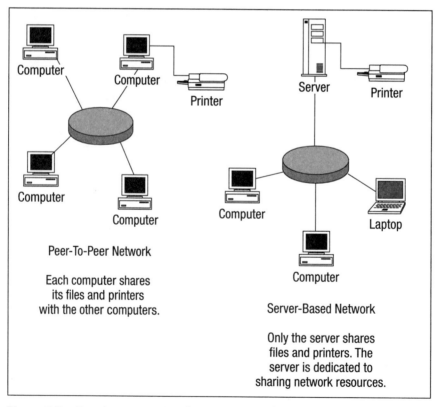

Figure 2.2   Peer-to-peer network versus server-based network.

The following sections consist of a crash course in network operating systems. The most popular NOSs are reviewed in detail, including core concepts and administration requirements. The rest of the book will refer to these NOSs and will describe how to use them.

2

Microsoft Windows NT 4

Microsoft created Windows NT as a 32-bit operating system with advanced multitasking capabilities. It came with two versions: Workstation and Server. The first versions (3.1, 3.5, and 3.51) of NT, which stands for New Technology, had the same GUI (graphical user interface) as Microsoft Windows 3.1. The new technology that NT came with was behind the scenes and was evident in NT's multitasking capabilities. Windows NT 4 uses the same GUI as Windows 95.

Domains

Windows NT uses a logical organizational scheme called *domains* for its computers and users. This scheme is similar to a workgroup organization. Each computer is designated as a member of a domain. Each user is created as a member account of the domain. The domain requires a special computer, called a *primary domain controller (PDC),* to maintain the database of users and computers that are members of the domain. There can be only one PDC per domain.

Additional domain controllers, called *backup domain controllers (BDCs),* can be installed into the domain to provide a measure of redundancy. When the primary domain controller is down, the backup domain controller authenticates users so that they can access network resources such as files and printers. The backup domain controller cannot be used to create new users in the domain. If the primary domain controller fails or is removed from the domain for another reason, a backup domain controller can be promoted to primary domain controller so that it can be used to create new users.

The primary domain controller maintains security information for the users and computers. This information is located in the SAM (Security Account Manager) database, which is located on the PDC and replicated on the BDCs, if there are any.

Because the domain structure is a logical organization, the physical location of a workstation does not matter. A workstation can be a member of any domain on the internetwork. (However, placing many workstations with a small amount of bandwidth between themselves and a domain controller is not an optimal network design.)

Example Of A Trust Relationship

Trust relationships are complex. Imagine that the domain in the internetwork is a country on a planet. Each computer is like a city in the country. Several countries (domains) are on the planet (internetwork). Each country has its own security policies. If a visitor from England wants to visit a city in Iraq, then Iraq must trust England and allow visas. However, if England does not trust Iraq, then Iraq's visitors cannot visit any of the English cities. Trust relationships are nonreciprocal, or one-way.

Trusts are nontransitive as well as nonreciprocal. If France trusts Iraq, and Iraq trusts England, that does not automatically mean that France trusts England. In fact, domain trust relationships do not flow through from one domain to another, so network security is maintained.

An internetwork can have multiple domains, but multiple domains make security more complex. Each primary domain controller has its own security database (the SAM). If the users of one domain need to access resources available on computers that are members of another domain, the standard separate domain configuration will not work. Therefore, Microsoft uses a *trust relationship* to overcome this issue. The trust relationship can enable a single authenticated logon for a user to access any resource in any domain if that user has been granted access to it.

A single trust relationship creates one-way access. Therefore, for two domains to have access to each other, two trust relationships must be set up. Domain A must trust Domain B, and Domain B must trust Domain A. A trust relationship is created so that users can access network resources in another domain. This access includes being able to log on to computers in the other domain. Without the right trust relationship, the users' domain will not even appear in the logon screen.

The main drawback to domains is the precise planning required. Domains tend to be difficult to rename or redefine. A change at that level is typically done only through reinstalling software and manually changing each member server's and workstation's domain membership. Because changes are so problematic, you should create a domain plan before implementing Windows NT. This plan should also take into account the growth of the enterprise and potential changes, such as mergers or migrations.

Several standard multidomain models can assist in domain planning. The domain models are depicted in Figure 2.3. These models are:

➤ **Single Domain Model** A single domain consists of a PDC and workstations. There may or may not be BDCs. There are no trust relationships with any other domains.

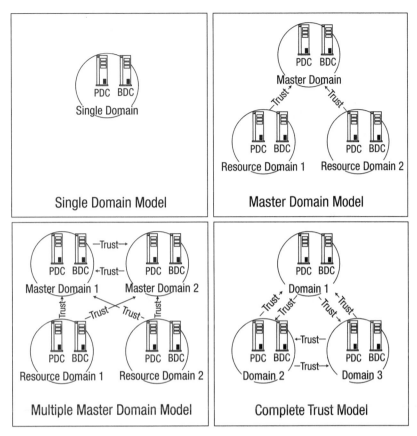

Figure 2.3   Domain models.

➤ **Master Domain Model** This model consists of a master domain and one
or more resource domains. The master domain contains the user accounts.
The resource domains contain the resources available on the internetwork.
Each resource domain trusts the master domain, and that trust relationship
enables the user accounts to access the resources.

➤ **Multiple Master Domain Model** The multiple master domain consists
of two or more master domains and one or more resource domains. Each
resource domain contains resources on the internetwork. Each master
domain contains user accounts. Each master domain trusts the other master
domain(s). Each resource domain trusts all of the master domains.

➤ **Complete Trust Model** The complete trust model is somewhat like a
mesh network. All domains trust all other domains. This particular model gets
unwieldy when there are more than a few domains on the internetwork, so it
is rarely implemented in a network with a large number of domains.

In Windows NT, security is applied using user accounts and two types of
groups: global groups and local groups. A user account is actually a "global user

account" when it is created in a domain. Local user accounts also reside on every workstation and server. The default administrative account in Windows NT is the global *administrator* account. The same factors that apply to local groups apply to local users, and the same factors that apply to global groups apply to global users.

A local group is created in a separate security database on the server. (So is a local user account, for that matter.) The local group is "local" to the server, so the security contained within it does not get applied to any other server or workstation in that or any other domain. Local user accounts and groups can be granted access only to local server resources.

A global group is created in the domain security database on the primary domain controller. (So is a global domain user account.) The global group and the global user can be made members of a local group on any server in the domain or can be made members of local groups in any domain that trusts their own. Being in the domain security database gives them access to the other computers through security membership and through trust relationships.

Always remember that a local group or account cannot travel outside its server; it stays put. The global groups and users can travel through the domain and trusting domains, so they can be made members of local groups on servers within their domain or trusting domains.

 The NT groups are confusing to manage. It is easy to just give up and grant rights to any group or any user that will accept them. Unfortunately, the result is that some people can access what they need to, others have more rights, and yet others have fewer. The easiest way to manage security under Windows NT is to follow the Microsoft-recommended strategy, which is to:

1. Create a global user account.

2. Create a global group and make the user account a member of a global group.

3. Create local groups and make the global group a member of appropriate local groups.

4. Grant the local groups appropriate access to files, printers, and other network resources.

Utilities

To create any type of user or group, use the Windows NT utility called the *User Manager For Domains*. Security is applied to user accounts, group accounts, and general policies in this utility. Password-protection policies are set here specifically. User Manager For Domains is automatically included on NT Server, but an administrator can install the client version and manage the domain from a connected client computer.

2

Windows NT has a utility similar to User Manager called Server Manager. Server Manager manages member computers of NT domains and their shared resources. Members can be Windows NT workstations, Windows NT servers, or Windows For Workgroups PCs. Windows 95 and Windows 98 PCs access a domain as though it were a workgroup, so they do not appear in this utility. An administrator can manage a domain by executing the process to synchronize domain controllers so that backup domain controllers' security databases are equivalent to the PDC's, adding members to and removing members from the domain, and promoting a BDC to a PDC. The administrator can manage other member computers by viewing the list of connected users, viewing shared resources, managing the services running on those computers, and sending messages to connected users.

To set up protocols for NT, use the Network icon in Control Panel. This icon sets up adapters, as well as services such as DHCP (Dynamic Host Configuration Protocol) and RAS (Remote Access Service). In the Control Panel, adapters, protocols, and services are added as components. For example, a token-ring adapter could be used with TCP/IP and RAS. Or an Ethernet adapter could replace the token ring, or NWLink (Microsoft's version of IPX [Internetwork Packet Exchange]) could replace TCP/IP, and so on. The combinations show how the modularity of the OSI (Open Systems Interconnection) Reference Model really works.

Performance Monitor and Event Viewer are both used for fault and performance management. Performance Monitor is best known for its realtime graphs of server performance based on the *counters*, or items of service, being monitored. Performance Monitor can also create written reports, and it supports alerts for the counters, making Performance Monitor a powerful tool.

The SNMP (Simple Network Management Protocol) service must be installed in order for some TCP/IP counters to appear in the Performance Monitor list.

The Event Viewer is an essential troubleshooting tool. Any error that occurs on an NT Server appears in the Event Viewer. The Event Viewer window uses different icons, depending on the messages being sent to it. Red alert icons represent critical warnings. They indicate a serious problem that may cause denial of service. If any network service has a startup error, the error and its cause appear as a series of events in the Event Viewer. For example, a common problem is that a network adapter card fails if it uses the same interrupt as a modem. Errors can include:

➤ Network services that failed because they did not find the required protocol

➤ Protocols that failed because they did not find the adapter card to bind to

➤ Adapter cards that failed due to an interrupt being used by another card

RAS, the Remote Access Service, provides the ability to attach remote nodes via a point-to-point protocol connection. A remote node can act as though it is attached to the server, or to the domain, even though it's connected via a modem or ISDN (Integrated Services Digital Network) line. The node can use the Network Neighborhood, connect network drives, use email, and otherwise function as part of the network.

 One of the key things to remember is that TCP/IP is a universal protocol. Each operating system on the network can use TCP/IP.

In Microsoft Windows NT, TCP/IP utilities include the following:

➤ Diagnostic commands, including **arp**, **hostname**, **ipconfig**, **lpq**, **nbtstat**, **netstat**, **ping**, **route**, and **tracert**

➤ Connection utilities, including finger, ftp, lpr, Telnet, and tftp

➤ Management and services, including DHCP Manager, DNS Manager, Internet Information Server, and SNMP Service

Table 2.1 lists the major utilities that are part of Windows NT.

Table 2.1   Utilities included in Microsoft Windows NT.

Utility	Can Be Used To:
User Manager	Create, change, and delete user accounts; grant and revoke network resource rights; create password-protection policies; establish security policies.
Server Manager	Manage the domain; synchronize domain controllers; promote a BDC; manage member computers in the domain; change file and resource shares; send messages to connected users.
Network icon in Control Panel	Add, change, or remove adapters, services, and protocols.
Performance Monitor	Monitor counters for services; create performance graphs and reports; set alerts to monitor.
Event Viewer	Review the errors and information messages that occur on the server and domain.
Remote Access Service	Attach remote nodes via PPP (Point-To-Point Protocol) connections.
ARP (Address Resolution Protocol)	Resolve IP addresses to MAC (Media Access Control) addresses.
Hostname	Specify the IP hostname.
Ipconfig	Display the IP configuration for the server.
Lpq	Obtain the status of an IP-based print queue.
Nbtstat	View NetBIOS over TCP/IP protocol statistics and current connections.

(continued)

Table 2.1   Utilities included in Microsoft Windows NT *(continued).*

Utility	Can Be Used To:
Netstat	Provide TCP/IP protocol statistics and current connections.
Ping	Determine whether a remote host can be reached via TCP/IP.
Route	Manipulate the routing table on a server that is acting as a router connected to two separate segments.
Tracert	Trace the route from the server to an IP destination address.
Finger	Display information about a user who is logged in to a host that is running the Finger service.
FTP (File Transfer Protocol)	Transfer files via TCP/IP.
Lpr	Print a file to an IP-based printer.
Telnet	Access a Telnet host as a remote terminal.
tftp (trivial file transfer protocol)	Transfer files via UDP (User Data Protocol), a connectionless Transport layer protocol in the IP stack.
DHCP Manager	Serve a group of IP addresses to network-connected computers so that an address can be reused when a computer has become inactive.
DNS Manager	Maintain a mapping between hostnames and IP addresses.
Internet Information Server	Provide Web services to the internetwork.
SNMP Service (Simple Network Management Protocol)	Send messages on the internetwork when an IP-based host encounters errors.

Microsoft Windows 2000

The next version of Windows NT Server will be called Windows 2000 Server. It will support file, print, application, Web, and remote access services. Application services are provided by a terminal service that enables client computers to run Windows graphical terminal emulation of the server at their desktops. The planned releases of the Windows 2000 Server series will include SMP (symmetrical multiprocessing) support. Higher-level releases will also support clustering (using multiple redundant servers) and load balancing (being able to distribute connections and application loads across multiple servers). The most important feature of this network operating system is the addition of an Active Directory Service.

The Active Directory Service is a distributed directory service of users, groups, computers, and other network resources. It offers a single point from which to administer the network. It removes the separate domain structure with connecting trust relationships. The Active Directory Service is a secured hierarchical tree of organizational units that can be organized in many ways, such as the example in Figure 2.4.

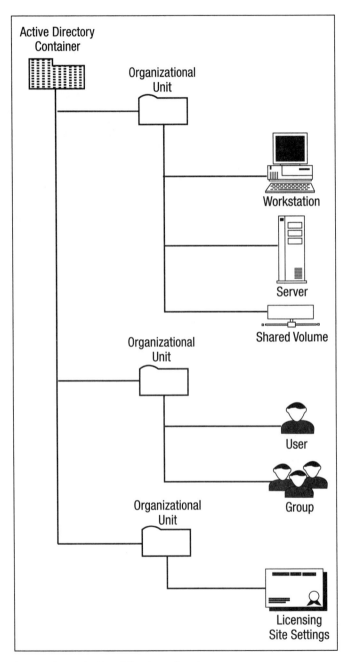

Figure 2.4   Active Directory Service.

The Active Directory Service simplifies network resource access for users, and it enhances administration capabilities for network administrators. The Active Directory Service is similar to Novell Directory Services (NDS) and is based on the X.500 standard specification for directory services. It enables the following:

➤ **Resource Management** The Active Directory Service provides a scalable, hierarchical tree repository for users, groups, and resources. Administrators may have variable access rights and levels at different levels of the tree.

➤ **Single Access Points** The Active Directory Service can consolidate directories, integrating an electronic messaging directory or other directories of resources. It also facilitates users' access to resources.

➤ **Single Authentication** Using a single directory can enable a single login to access all network resources, eliminating the requirement of multiple logins.

Novell NetWare

Novell NetWare, one of the first network operating systems, is one of the most popular. It was originally created for the simple purpose of sharing hard-drive space. The oldest versions are rare and are no longer supported. Three versions of NetWare, which are 32-bit network operating systems, can be purchased today. These versions are:

➤ NetWare 3.x

➤ NetWare 4.x

➤ NetWare 5.x

Each version of NetWare has core features and services that are identical. What Novell NetWare does best is to provide file and print services to client computers. Additional services are run as NLMs on NetWare servers. NLMs (NetWare Loadable Modules) are executables in the NetWare operating system. NLMs are similar to daemons that run under Unix.

NetWare offers extended file attributes and extensive rights access capabilities to files and directories. File attributes are applied to individual files. Access rights can flow from a directory down through the directory structure and are applied to all the files within that structure. The file attributes and access rights are the same across the various NetWare versions. The main difference between versions is that the utilities used to apply file attributes and access rights in NetWare 3.x are command-line or DOS-menu based, and the utility used in NetWare 4.x and 5.x is the NetWare Administrator.

File attributes are extended beyond standard DOS file attributes. To change a file attribute, the administrator can use either the FLAG command-line utility or the NetWare Administrator program in NetWare 4.x and 5.x. The file attributes available in NetWare are listed in Table 2.2.

Table 2.2 File attributes available in NetWare.

Attribute	Abbreviation	Description
Archive Needed	A	Set automatically when a file is changed to flag it for backup.
Copy Inhibit	Ci	Prevents users from copying Macintosh files.
Can't Compress	Cc	Sets automatically when no significant amount of space is saved by compressing a file.
Don't Compress	Dc	Prevents NetWare from compressing a file or directory.
Delete Inhibit	Di	Prevents a file or directory from being deleted.
Don't Migrate	Dm	Prevents a file or directory from being migrated to a high-capacity storage unit.
Don't Suballocate	Ds	Ensures that the file takes up only whole blocks, rather than suballocated blocks, on the server's hard drive.
Immediate Compress	Ic	Compresses files immediately.
Migrated	M	Sets automatically when a file has been migrated.
Hidden	H	Prevents users from seeing the file when listing directory contents.
Indexed	I	Activates turbo FAT indexing on the file.
Purge	P	Causes files to be deleted immediately, without being able to be salvaged.
Rename Inhibit	Ri	Prevents users from renaming a file or directory.
Read Only	Ro	Prevents a file from being modified, renamed, or deleted.
Read Write	Rw	Enables a file to be modified, renamed, or deleted.
Shareable	S	Enables multiple users to access the same file simultaneously.
System	Sy	Indicates a system file and is a combination of Read Only and Hidden.
Transactional	T	Indicates a NetWare Transaction Tracking System file.
Execute Only	X	Prevents users from modifying, renaming, erasing, or copying a file. This attribute cannot be removed once it is set.

Security access is different from a file attribute. Security access is set on a file or directory for a specific user or group. In NetWare 3.x, access rights are set in SYSCON. In NetWare 4.x and 5.x, access rights are set in the NetWare

Administrator. Access rights can also be granted or revoked through the **rights** command, which is executed at the DOS command line. NetWare access rights are listed in Table 2.3.

All versions of NetWare support multiple client types. These client types include DOS, Windows 3.1, Windows For Workgroups 3.11, Windows 95, Windows 98, Windows NT, OS/2, Macintosh OS, and Unix. A special file-system support enables the different operating systems to store and access files on the server. This file-system support is in the form of a *namespace*. Namespaces are loaded onto a NetWare volume, which is a portion of the server hard disk or hardware RAID array and shared out to end users.

Novell developed the IPX (Internetwork Packet Exchange) protocol stack based on the XNS (Xerox Network System) protocols. All versions of NetWare run on this proprietary protocol stack. All versions of NetWare support the TCP/IP protocol stack, but NetWare 5.x runs TCP/IP as a native protocol. When older versions of NetWare run TCP/IP, they must also run IPX in order to function. NetWare 5.x is unique in that it can run on TCP/IP alone.

NetWare 3.x

The main characteristic of NetWare 3.x is the *Bindery*. The Bindery is the database that contains user, group, and security information and that resides on each NetWare server. The Bindery forces an administrator to manage the user database on a per-server basis. The default administrative account on the NetWare 3.x server is *supervisor*.

For example, in a network with 12 servers and 100 users, each user would need 12 user accounts to be able to log in to each server. The result would be 1,200 user accounts to be managed by an administrator. Synchronizing passwords between the multiple servers would become cumbersome, and overall administration would be difficult.

Table 2.3 Access rights available in NetWare.

Access Right	Abbreviation	Description
Access Control	[A]	Grant, revoke, or change the rights of other users to the file.
Create	[C]	Create a new file or a directory.
Erase	[E]	Erase or delete an existing file or directory.
File Scan	[F]	View the contents of a directory.
Modify	[M]	Change the attributes of a file or rename it.
Read	[R]	Read or open an existing file.
Supervisor	[S]	All available rights.
Write	[W]	Write data to an existing file.

To handle most of the NetWare administration, the administrator runs utilities on a client workstation. NetWare 3.x uses a significant number of DOS-based utilities. The main utility for managing users, groups, and security access is SYSCON, a DOS-based, menu-driven utility. For files and directories, the FILER utility—along with several command-line utilities, such as FLAG, NDIR, NCOPY, and RIGHTS—isused to manipulate files on the NetWare server.

NetWare 3.x also includes server-based utilities. These are NLMs that load on the server and provide basic menu-driven or command-line control over server functions. These utilities are limited to the server's protocols, performance parameters, and services running on the server. Two of these utilities are MONITOR and SET. The MONITOR utility displays performance statistics—including CPU utilization and memory statistics—for the server. The **SET** command is used to change server parameters to improve the server's performance in a variety of ways, from disk management to memory buffers.

NetWare 4.x

The main advance from NetWare 3.x to NetWare 4.x is *Novell Directory Services (NDS)*. NDS is a database of network resources that is distributed across multiple servers. NDS replaces the Bindery. Servers can contain copies of database sections, or *replicas*, so that the database is available to users attempting to access network resources. The default administrative account in NetWare 4.x and 5.x is ADMIN, which is usually located in the Organization container.

The database enables a single user account for each user, regardless of the number of NetWare 4.x and 5.x servers on the network that participate in their NDS tree. This structure, shown in Figure 2.5, greatly simplifies the administration needs of the network.

In addition to the single-login feature, NetWare 4.x introduced the concept of a *single seat of administration*. This is the capability to administer the network from a single management station, using the fewest number of tools. The concept was accompanied by the NetWare Administrator program (see Figure 2.6).

NetWare Administrator is a graphical administrative program that has access to each NDS network resource and utility on the network. The NetWare Administrator enables the administrator to view each network resource in its position in the tree. The NetWare Administrator consists of a window with a single pane. The top of the NetWare Administrator window starts with the tree [root] object. Below the [root], the pane lists the container units, which act like folders or directories on a hard drive because they hold either other container units or leaf objects, plus the contents of any expanded container units. *Leaf objects* are network resources or services that appear as icons in the NDS tree. A leaf object does not contain any other objects.

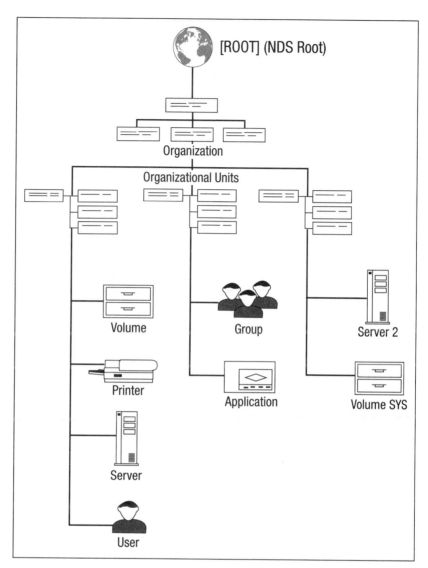

[ROOT] (NDS Root)

Organization

Organizational Units

Volume

Group

Server 2

Printer

Application

Volume SYS

Server

User

Figure 2.5   Novell Directory Services.

To manage a network resource or container object, the administrator can double-click on a leaf object, or right-click on a container object and select Details. The administrator can create new user objects, which are the users' login accounts, as well as a variety of other objects that represent network resources. The NetWare Administrator program offers a single seat of administration because it can access and manage any resource in the tree as long as the logged-in user has been granted the rights to manage them.

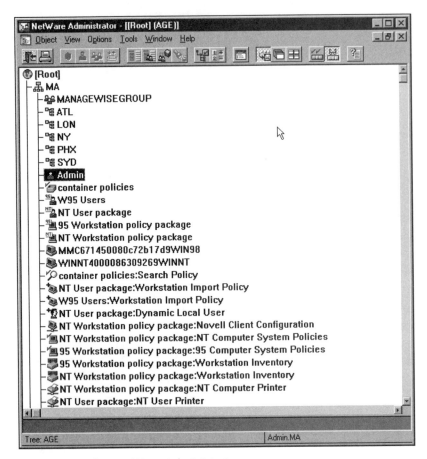

Figure 2.6 The NetWare Administrator program.

Additionally, NetWare 4.x consolidated the SET command-line server-based utility into SERVMAN, a server-based, menu-driven utility. The SERVMAN utility, displayed in Figure 2.7, was incorporated into the MONITOR utility for NetWare 5.x. SERVMAN includes help facilities to assist the administrator with the usage of various SET parameters.

NetWare 5.x

NetWare 5.x is the latest version of NetWare, offered in late 1998. This version is very similar to NetWare 4.x and can coexist in the same NDS tree. The major differences in NetWare 5.x are as follows:

➤ Pure IP integration

➤ Java-based GUI console on the server

➤ Integration with Internet services (Netscape's FastWeb Server, DNS, and DHCP management integrated with NDS)

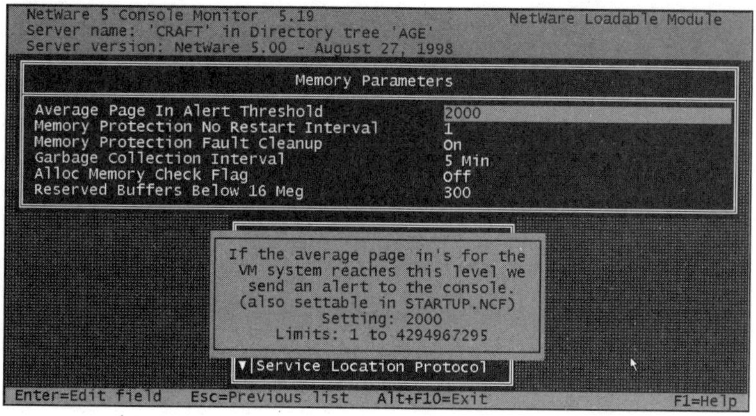

2

```
NetWare 5 Console Monitor  5.19              NetWare Loadable Module
Server name: 'CRAFT' in Directory tree 'AGE'
Server version: NetWare 5.00 - August 27, 1998

                          Memory Parameters
  Average Page In Alert Threshold          2000
  Memory Protection No Restart Interval    1
  Memory Protection Fault Cleanup          On
  Garbage Collection Interval              5 Min
  Alloc Memory Check Flag                  Off
  Reserved Buffers Below 16 Meg            300

            If the average page in's for the
            VM system reaches this level we
            send an alert to the console.
            (also settable in STARTUP.NCF)
                  Setting: 2000
             Limits: 1 to 4294967295

             ▼ Service Location Protocol
  Enter=Edit field   Esc=Previous list   Alt+F10=Exit         F1=Help
```

Figure 2.7 The server-based SERVMAN utility.

➤ Z.E.N.works (Zero Effort Networks)

➤ NAL (NetWare Application Launcher)

➤ NDPS (Novell Distributed Printing Services)

A critical difference for NetWare 5.x is that it can run the TCP/IP protocol on both clients and servers without any other protocol stack. Previous versions required a combination of TCP/IP and IPX tunneling to use NetWare on a TCP/IP internetwork.

Another difference for NetWare is a new Java-based GUI console, called ConsoleOne, that runs on the server console. Previous versions of NetWare did not have a graphical interface on the server. Instead, the console was purely command-line and text-menu based, as shown in Figure 2.8. The new Java console requires an administrator to log in and provides a view of the NDS trees

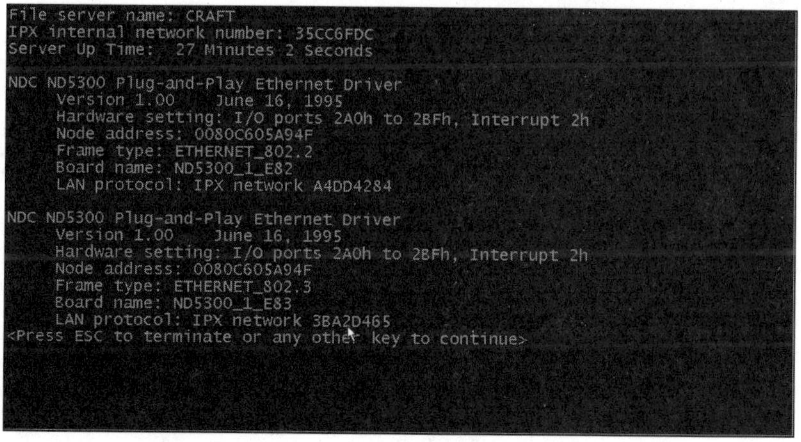

```
File server name: CRAFT
IPX internal network number: 35CC6FDC
Server Up Time:   27 Minutes 2 Seconds

NDC ND5300 Plug-and-Play Ethernet Driver
     Version 1.00    June 16, 1995
     Hardware setting: I/O ports 2A0h to 2BFh, Interrupt 2h
     Node address: 0080C605A94F
     Frame type: ETHERNET_802.2
     Board name: ND5300_1_E82
     LAN protocol: IPX network A4DD4284

NDC ND5300 Plug-and-Play Ethernet Driver
     Version 1.00    June 16, 1995
     Hardware setting: I/O ports 2A0h to 2BFh, Interrupt 2h
     Node address: 0080C605A94F
     Frame type: ETHERNET_802.3
     Board name: ND5300_1_E83
     LAN protocol: IPX network 3BA2D465
<Press ESC to terminate or any other key to continue>
```

Figure 2.8 Traditional NetWare server console.

on the internetwork. However, the graphical console is simply an additional screen that sits on the console. The administrator can press Alt and Esc to move to other screens, which almost all consist of text-based menus and a command-line console. The reason for this is that most NetWare applications did not have graphical screens, and the new version needed to be backward compatible.

The Internet functionality of NetWare 5.x is greater than any in earlier versions. Novell developers took some TCP/IP tasks and integrated them into Novell Directory Services. These tasks specifically included the distribution of dynamic IP addresses through the DHCP protocol and domain-name resolution through DNS. NetWare 5.x also includes a Web service—Netscape's FastWeb server, which can be integrated into NDS by requiring login authentication to a specific NDS tree for security.

Novell created a group of network management tools called Z.E.N.works (Zero Effort Networks). A reduced set of Z.E.N.works tools ships with NetWare 5.x. Z.E.N.works is completely integrated into the NDS tree and extends the capabilities of the NetWare Administrator program. New objects, such as workstation objects, appear in the tree so that the administrator can manage a network inventory.

Additionally, the NetWare Application Launcher, called NAL, ships with NetWare 5.x. This utility enables the administrator to create application objects for programs that are installed on the network. The application object may even be created to install applications to the workstation. In NDS, application objects are secured, so a user must be granted rights to an application before that application's icon will appear in the user's NAL window on his or her workstation.

Finally, Novell developed a new printing system in partnership with Xerox and Hewlett-Packard. This printing system takes advantage of 32-bit Windows printing architecture and extended printer capabilities. This system is called *Novell Distributed Printing Services,* or NDPS. NDPS enables end users to browse through their Network Neighborhood icons for printers. After finding one, users can simply click on the icon to print to that printer. The NDPS printers are objects within the NDS tree, and security can be applied to prevent users from printing to inaccessible printers.

NetWare Utilities
The essential utility for managing NetWare is the one that provides access to user accounts. In NetWare 3.x, this was SYSCON, a DOS-based menu-driven utility. In NetWare 4.x and NetWare 5.x, this is NetWare Administrator.

NetWare utilities come in three types. Tables 2.4, 2.5, and 2.6 discuss some of the essential utilities to be aware of on the server and on a workstation. Please note that other NetWare utilities are available as well.

Table 2.4 Server-console utilities and applicable NetWare version.

Utility Name	NetWare Version	Function
MONITOR	All NetWare versions	Displays performance statistics in a text menu.
ConsoleOne	NetWare 5.x	Displays limited NDS tree information in a graphical Java-based screen.
SET	All NetWare versions	A command-line utility used to set configuration parameters.
SERVMAN	NetWare 4.x	A text-menu utility assisting in SET parameters. SERVMAN functions were merged into MONITOR for NetWare 5.x.
CONFIG	All NetWare versions	A command-line utility used to display current adapters and their configurations.
INETCFG	NetWare 4.x and 5.x	A text-menu utility used to display protocols, adapters, and configurations.
INSTALL or NWCONFIG	All NetWare versions	A text-menu utility used during and after installation to configure the hard drive, volumes, startup configuration files, and NLM applications.
PCONSOLE	All NetWare versions	A text-menu utility used to display printer functionality and statistics.
NDPS Manager	NetWare 5.x	A text-menu utility used to display NDPS printer functionality and statistics.

Table 2.5 Client menu-driven utilities and applicable NetWare version.

Utility Name	NetWare Version	Function
SYSCON	NetWare 3.x	A text-menu utility for managing users, groups, and security.
FILER	All NetWare versions	A text-menu utility for managing files on a NetWare server.
SALVAGE	NetWare 3.x	A text-menu utility for undeleting files on a NetWare server volume. This functionality was incorporated into FILER for NetWare 4.x and 5.x.
NetWare Administrator	NetWare 4.x and 5.x	A Windows graphical application that enables management of the entire NDS tree and its network resources, including users, groups, and security.
NDS Manager	NetWare 4.x and 5.x	A Windows graphical application that enables management of the NDS database replication throughout the internetwork.

(continued)

Table 2.5   Client menu-driven utilities and applicable NetWare version *(continued)*.

Utility Name	NetWare Version	Function
DNS/DHCP Manager	NetWare 5.x	A Windows graphical application that enables management of DNS and DHCP functions.
RCONSOLE	All NetWare versions	A text-menu utility that runs a terminal emulation of a selected server console. This utility requires that REMOTE.NLM and RSPX.NLM are loaded on the target server in order for that server to appear as an option for terminal emulation.

Table 2.6   Client command-line utilities used in all NetWare versions.

Utility Name	Function
FLAG	Changes the NetWare extended attributes for files that reside on a NetWare server.
NDIR	Lists the contents of a directory that resides on a NetWare server and enables sorting based on the NetWare extended attributes.
NCOPY	Copies files residing on a NetWare server and enables the retention of extended attributes and rights to the file after the copy has been completed.
RIGHTS	Displays, grants, and revokes rights to a file on a NetWare server.

In NetWare 4.x and later, most NetWare functions can be managed from the NetWare Administrator window. For example, each of the command-line utilities is redundant because the NetWare Administrator will allow you to change file attributes, list a directory's contents, copy files with retention of security and attributes, and display rights. Also, the NetWare Administrator window includes a menu called Tools, which displays additional tools that can be launched from this single utility.

Unix

Unix is a peer-to-peer network operating system originally developed by Bell Laboratories for use on minicomputers. It is unique because the original operating system was not proprietary. There are many versions of Unix available today. Each version is slightly different, but they all share the same core features and benefits.

The common element of Unix is the use of TCP/IP as the core protocol stack. The Unix environment allows both a peer-to-peer networking model and a server-based networking model. Traditional Unix systems are hosts that provide user access through dumb terminals.

Unix has both a graphical interface and a text command-line interface. Even when the graphical interface is used, a command-line window can be opened to enter Unix commands. Unix commands tend to be cryptic and awkward. For example, the command *lp* is used to print a file. The commands also vary among different versions of Unix because they can have one of three different shells. A *shell* is the command interface. The three types are Bourne, Korn, and C.

Several graphical user interfaces are available. The most popular are X-Windows and Motif, which function similarly to Microsoft Windows.

The administration for a Unix server starts with the *superuser* or *root* account. This account is named "root" and has the capability to override file permissions. Each version of Unix has different types of administrative utilities, but the core of Unix administration lies in the configuration files located in the /etc directory.

The /etc/passwd file contains user information. To add a user account, the administrator can simply edit this file. The basic format of the file is that each row represents a user account. Each row contains fields that are separated by colons (:). The fields are:

➤ **login-id** The user login account.

➤ **password** The user's password.

➤ **user account number (uid)** A numerical identifier for the account. The root account has the user account number 0.

➤ **group account number (gid)** Identifies the group that the user is assigned to.

➤ **user information** The user's real name.

➤ **home directory** The path to the user's login directory.

➤ **shell** Used for the user's initial shell program. This field can be empty if the default shell will be used. The default shell is /usr/bin/sh.

Groups are contained in the /etc/group file. Each row in this file represents a different group, and each row consists of four fields separated by colons (:). The fields are group-name, password, group account number (gid), and comma-delimited list of users. Note that the gid is created in this file and cross-linked to the /etc/passwd file. The user's login ID, which is created in the /etc/passwd file, is applied in the comma-delimited list of users in the /etc/group file.

Another configuration file that Unix servers contain is the /etc/hosts file. The hosts file contains a table of hostnames mapped to their IP addresses. The format of this file is:

```
#IP-Address hostname alias
127.0.0.1 localhost loghost
218.5.88.24 myserver
```

Services that Unix servers provide to the network are listed in the /etc/services file. The file maps the services with their port numbers and protocol. The format of the services file is:

```
#services port/protocol
ftp 21/tcp #File Transfer Protocol
telnet 23/tcp #Telnet
smtp 25/tcp #Simple Mail Transfer Protocol
tftp 69/udp #Trivial File Transfer Protocol
www 80/tcp #Hypertext transfer or World Wide Web
```

The **ifconfig** command is essential for managing an interface on a Unix server. This command assigns addresses, enables and disables the interface, and assigns the protocols to the interface. The **ifconfig** command is executed in the startup scripts for the server so that the server is initialized with networking interfaces enabled appropriately.

The **netstat** command is used to display the network status for the Unix server. The **netstat** command can show the status of sockets and server processes, management statistics, and routing tables.

SCO Unix

SCO developed an Intel-processor-based Unix operating system: SCO Unix. This platform is a network operating system that provides file services, printer services, and Web services.

SCO Unix supports both virtual disks and RAID (Redundant Arrays of Inexpensive Disks). Virtual disks organize data in multidisk systems such that the multiple disks appear to the end user as a single hard drive. RAID versions supported are:

➤ **RAID 0** Striped array of multiple nonredundant disks.

➤ **RAID 1** Mirroring, or parallel data duplication onto two disks.

➤ **RAID 4** Disk striping with a reserved disk for parity. Block-interleaved undistributed parity array.

➤ **RAID 5** Disk striping with parity striped across all disks. Block-interleaved distributed parity array.

SCO Unix supports SMP (symmetric multiprocessing) of systems with more than one processor. It also supports NFS (Network File System), which was developed by Sun Microsystems. NFS allows long file names of up to 256 characters and enables the sharing of files with remote file systems. SCO Unix print services are standard LPD (Line Printer Daemon) systems that support printer sharing.

The SCO Unix directory is the NIS (Network Information Services), which enables a single server to manage a group of systems. NIS extends the database of system information—such as hostnames, addresses, and usernames—across multiple servers over the TCP/IP protocol.

SCO Unix provides for multiple client types, including Unix, DOS, Windows 3.1, Windows For Workgroups 3.11, Windows 95, Windows 98, Windows NT, and OS/2. SCO also provides for a NetWare gateway so that it can connect to NetWare servers and use their services.

SCO Unix provides full support for the Internet. This support includes an SMTP (Simple Mail Transport Protocol) based electronic messaging application. The server portion is a mail transfer subsystem, and clients can be either SCOmail or Netscape Navigator SCOmail. Other Internet applications are Netscape FastTrack Server, http daemon (Hypertext Transfer Protocol service), and nntp (Network News Transfer Protocol) support for electronic newsgroups.

Linux

Linux is unique because it is free. Linus Torvalds created this Unix-based operating system, with the assistance of other developers, as freely distributed operating source code. Linux is a multitasking, multiuser, and multiplatform NOS (network operating system), which means that it can run several applications for several different users and can be installed onto systems using different types of CPUs.

All of the source code for Linux is available and may be freely distributed. There are commercial applications for Linux that can be installed on a Linux server. Linux supports several Unix file systems on local disks, including its own, which provides for up to 4 terabytes of files and for file names of up to 255 characters.

Like all Unix operating systems, Linux includes complete TCP/IP protocol support. Standard utilities are ftp, Telnet, and SNMP.

Sun Microsystems' Solaris

Sun Microsystems created the Solaris version of Unix. Solaris is multiplatform; it can run on a system with an Intel CPU as well as on a SPARC station. The processing can be either 32-bit or 64-bit. The 64-bit processing capacity improves performance by up to 10 times. The Solaris operating system is fully integrated with TCP/IP and other open standards, ensuring interoperability on a heterogeneous internetwork. Solaris adheres to the POSIX, Unix 98, and X/Open standards for application portability. Solaris also adheres to Internet Engineering Task Force (IETF) and WWW Consortium standards for Internet services interoperability.

Solaris is extensible using device drivers, STREAMS, and file systems. Device drivers enable the Solaris kernel to access I/O devices, such as network interface cards, CD-ROMS, and tape drives. Solaris drivers can be installed and removed on a station without rebooting. STREAMS is an application programming interface (API) that can be used by new service modules to provide greater functionality. File systems are used by Solaris to configure the disk volumes and file compatibility. When a new file system is installed, Solaris has a new way to configure disks and their files.

In short, all network operating systems have a lot in common. They have a way to share files, share printers, manage the network, and interoperate with various protocols. Table 2.7 shows the summary of major network operating systems.

Table 2.7 Summary of major network operating systems.

NOS	Protocols	Features
Windows NT 3.x	TCP/IP, NetBEUI, IPX, DLC	Domain structure, file and printer sharing, Windows 3.1 GUI, SMP capable, software RAID, RAS, Services for Macintosh, runs SMB (Server Message Block) over TCP/IP.
Windows NT 4.x	TCP/IP, NetBEUI, IPX, DLC	Domain structure, file and printer sharing, Windows 95 GUI, SMP capable, software RAID, RAS, greater Internet awareness, Services for Macintosh, runs SMB over TCP/IP.
Windows 2000	TCP/IP, NetBEUI, IPX, DLC	Active Directory Service, file and printer sharing, Windows 95 GUI, SMP capable, software RAID, RAS, Internet aware and browser integration, Services for Macintosh, supports TCP/IP natively.
NetWare 3.1x	TCP/IP, IPX, AppleTalk	Bindery structure, file and printer sharing, Novell's text interface, supports mirroring and duplexing, uses NLMs to add other software features, highly intelligent login script features, DOS-based tools, supports multiple clients, including OS/2, Macintosh OS, Unix, and Windows. TCP/IP is added protocol, not native support.
NetWare 4.x	TCP/IP, IPX, AppleTalk	Novell Directory Services, file and printer sharing, Novell's text interface, supports mirroring and duplexing, uses NLMs to add other software features, login script features with enhanced capabilities for NDS structure, DOS-based and Windows-base tools, supports multiple clients, including OS/2, Apple, Unix, and Windows. TCP/IP is added protocol, not native support.

(continued)

Table 2.7   Summary of major network operating systems *(continued)*.

NOS	Protocols	Features
NetWare 5.x	TCP/IP, IPX, AppleTalk	Novell Directory Services, file and printer sharing, Java graphical interface, supports mirroring and duplexing, uses NLMs to add other software features, hierarchical login scripts with enhanced NDS features, tools are mainly Windows based, supports multiple clients, including OS/2, Apple, Unix, and Windows. Has remote connectivity and Internet Web services built in, supports TCP/IP natively.
Unix	TCP/IP	Network Information Services, file and printer sharing, full Internet applications and utilities, supports RAID, uses daemons to add services, has a cumbersome command-line interface, best clients are other Unix machines but supports DOS, Windows, and OS/2.

Other Network Operating Systems

Although Windows NT/2000, NetWare, and Unix are widely used, there are, and have been, other network operating systems. Some enterprise internetworks are built almost entirely on some of these network operating systems. Others have a single server located here or there. Either way, it is not unlikely for a network technician to run into one of these NOSs.

Windows For Workgroups

Microsoft Windows For Workgroups is a version of Windows 3.1 that includes peer-to-peer networking. This networking includes some rudimentary tools for file and printer sharing, as well as a scheduler and electronic mail. Windows For Workgroups was one of the first peer-to-peer networking products that was easily accepted by enterprises. This acceptance was due mainly to the fact that the enterprises' existing 16-bit applications would still operate under Windows For Workgroups, but would not always operate under Windows NT. Later, Microsoft introduced Windows 95 and Windows 98, with peer-to-peer networking capabilities incorporated into the operating system. The main limitation to this type of network is that only other Microsoft Windows systems can participate as peers on the network. Windows For Workgroups, Windows 95, and Windows 98 all have the capability of using the Microsoft TCP/IP protocol stack for accessing network resources.

Banyan Vines

Vines (Virtual Network System) is a NOS that Banyan Systems developed. Vines is based on a Unix kernel, uses TCP/IP natively, and runs on Intel-based systems. Vines offers file and printer sharing and electronic communications services.

Banyan created StreetTalk, a global naming service, for Vines. StreetTalk offers an enterprisewide three-level hierarchical context for naming users, printers, servers, and other network resources. The standard naming convention is item@group@organization. The item portion can be a user, nickname, list, or service.

Vines can support multiple clients: DOS, Windows, OS/2, Unix, and Macintosh. The file system is Unix based and utilizes name-space support for non-Unix file-naming conventions.

OS/2 Warp Server

IBM offers OS/2 Warp Server as its own network operating system. OS/2 is a 32-bit operating system that was codeveloped by IBM and Microsoft. OS/2 is similar to Windows NT in that it uses the domain concept. A domain controller server manages the domain's security information. This server contains the domain control database and user and group information files. These can be replicated on backup domain controllers.

OS/2 Warp Server provides file services and manages access to files with access rights. Print services are provided with network print queues and printer pools. Warp Server enables the sharing of serial devices—not only serial printers, but also modems.

OS/2 Warp Server's native protocol is NetBEUI, but it also supports the TCP/IP protocol stack. It supports DOS, Windows, OS/2, and Macintosh clients. Warp Server includes Internet service capabilities, including an HTTP (Hypertext Transfer Protocol) service, LDAP (Lightweight Directory Access Protocol) client, and dynamic IP clients for Windows 95, NT, and OS/2.

Apple Macintosh Networks

Apple developed networking as part of the native operating system so that connecting to the network is transparent to end users. When a server is dedicated to providing files and printers to Apple computers, it is called an AppleShare Server. The Chooser application displays the network resources that are available to the user within the local zone. Zones are a form of workgroup computing. Computers belong to various zones. Through the *zone information protocol (ZIP)* and the *name binding protocol (NBP)*, the zone resources are available to the internetwork, regardless of the physical location of the computer. For example, if a computer in Paris is assigned to the Executive zone, and a computer in London is assigned to the Executive zone, then the resources of both computers will be displayed in the Executive zone in the Chooser application.

2

In AppleTalk, each node and network is assigned a Network layer address. There are node addresses from 1 to 254 available for each network address. If the number of addresses needs to be increased, multiple network addresses can be assigned to a single network. This system is called a *cable range*. A seed router dynamically assigns the node addresses. This system works behind the scenes through the AppleTalk protocol so that users are completely unaware of the networking transactions taking place.

AppleTalk is the native protocol used by Apple Macintosh computers and printers in a peer-to-peer network. The AppleTalk protocol is available on many network operating systems, including Windows NT's Services for Macintosh, Novell NetWare, and various Unix versions. AppleTalk has its own versions of Ethernet (EtherTalk), token ring (TokenTalk), and Fiber Distributed Data Interchange (FDDITalk). AppleTalk also has a proprietary protocol called LocalTalk, which runs 230Kbps over unshielded twisted-pair.

SELECTING A NETWORK CLIENT

Which clients work best with which operating systems? That is a good question, especially when you're trying to decide what to install or which clients to implement in a new network.

The first item to determine is what type of connectivity is required across the internetwork. Using a single protocol, if possible, is the best choice, because it reduces the complexity and overhead of the internetwork. The only protocol that is supported by every network operating system is TCP/IP. If TCP/IP is the main, or sole, protocol stack implemented, then the best client is one that supports TCP/IP.

Consider the following when developing a client access program:

➤ What resources will the client application use on the workstation? If two client applications provide the same types of network access, but one client uses far less of the workstation's processing power, then it is the better choice.

➤ What types of access will the client provide? If two clients can access the same system, but one client has more capabilities, then that one is the better choice.

➤ Will you need the ability to implement a standard across an enterprise network? When there are multiple client access programs running, it is far more difficult to manage workstations. The best option is to maintain a standard type of client access program and then to control versions so that all workstations operate at the same version level.

Server-Based Vs. Peer-To-Peer Clients

Large enterprise networks tend to be server based. The size of the corporation increases the distance between members of the same business unit, forcing the centralization of their common network resources.

Time zones also play a part in the movement toward server-based computing. For example, if two people in the same business unit are in two separate time zones, there may be several hours separating when they are logged in to the network. Using a peer-to-peer networking scheme would prevent access to resources for several hours. A server-based environment enables the resources to be available, regardless of time zone, because servers are typically online 24 hours per day, 7 days per week.

Peer-to-peer networking is more difficult for administrators to manage. New peers can start sharing files without the administrator's knowledge. This can sometimes cause network bandwidth problems, especially if files are shared over wide area network (WAN) links. Many large internetworks have implemented rules that restrict peer-to-peer networking in order to avoid these types of problems.

Networks that are located in a single site or that are much smaller are more likely to be peer-to-peer networks. A peer-to-peer network initially provides a reduction in costs because it can be implemented on users' existing workstations with the time and productivity savings of networking. Besides, a peer-to-peer network does not require a large investment in a complex server. The network is managed by end users, so it does not always require a dedicated administrator.

Many client operating systems include a client access program to enable the OS to access servers. Vendors usually provide the client access program that will access their own servers. For example, all Apple Macintosh computers can access AppleShare servers because the client access program is built into the operating system. OS/2 Warp workstations can access OS/2 Warp servers. Unix workstations can access Unix servers. Most of these workstations also run the TCP/IP protocol and can access TCP/IP services.

Windows 3.1 Clients

Microsoft Windows 3.1 and DOS are legacy client workstations on internetworks all over the world. These clients dominated the network several years ago. Many organizations developed proprietary applications that worked only on DOS or Windows 3.1 clients. Besides the issues with licensing and concerns over process change, proprietary applications are a major reason for Windows 3.1 clients to remain on an internetwork.

Plain DOS and Windows 3.1 clients do not have built-in networking capabilities. Therefore, peer-to-peer networking clients cannot be used to access

2

servers. For these clients to access servers, a client access program must be installed. Novell NetWare ships an IPX and IP client to access their servers. Likewise, Windows NT Server ships a client to access Windows NT Servers, and Unix servers ship with clients as well.

The problem is that none of these clients work on all network operating systems at once. The clients act as TSRs (terminate-and-stay-resident programs) and tend to stay at the lower memory area (the first 640K). Windows 3.1/DOS clients do not handle lower memory usage well. When more memory is used, less is available to applications. Sometimes adding a client access program can degrade performance of a workstation beyond acceptable limits. Whenever you're adding client access programs, the client should be tested and compared to any alternatives before implementation to ensure that performance will be acceptable.

Windows 95 And 98

Microsoft Windows 95 and Windows 98 are closely linked in their architecture. It's a good bet that if a network client works on Windows 95, it will also work on Windows 98. Both of these operating systems ship with network clients. Figure 2.9 displays some of the options available in Windows 98.

Clients that ship with Microsoft Windows 95 and 98 are the Microsoft clients. As shown in the screen, additional vendors' clients are available in the operating system. These are typically not the latest clients that can be installed, and they might not provide the greatest functionality.

Windows 95 and 98 are backward compatible with many Windows 3.1 clients. Using these clients is not recommended because they can cause the same memory issues under Windows 95/98 as they did under Windows 3.1. Additionally, these legacy clients can be difficult to install under Windows 95/98.

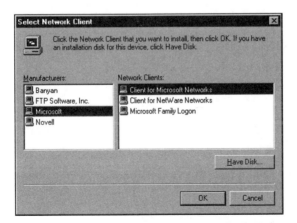

Figure 2.9   A list of some of the Windows 98 network clients, accessed from the Network icon in the Control Panel.

The best choices for network clients are the 32-bit client access programs offered by vendors. These 32-bit clients use memory in a much more effective way than legacy clients do. The vendors' network clients are programmed to have the optimal access to the network, with extended options available to them. The vendors' network clients may offer a greater variety of protocol support as well. The native Microsoft Windows 98 clients are modular and support various protocols. Some of these protocols are shown in Figure 2.10.

There are several choices for accessing a Novell NetWare network from Windows 95/98. The Microsoft Client for NetWare Networks will access a NetWare network in Bindery mode. An additional service for NDS enables the Microsoft client to access a Novell Directory Services tree. Novell offers a 32-bit client for NetWare networks that functions in both Bindery mode and NDS mode. The Novell client is recommended because many NDS-integrated capabilities require it, such as Z.E.N.works' workstation management capabilities.

For peer-to-peer networking, the Microsoft client for Microsoft networks is the correct choice. The Microsoft client will access any other Microsoft network server, whether it is a peer server or a Microsoft Windows NT Server. The main consideration when selecting the protocol is that it is the same one used on the peers and servers that need to be accessed.

Windows NT Workstation

Windows NT Workstation is nearly identical to Windows NT Server. Windows NT Workstation ships with Microsoft clients for NetWare and for Windows NT servers. Like Windows 95/98, the Microsoft client for Microsoft networks is used for peer-to-peer networking, as well as for accessing NT domains.

Novell offers a NetWare 32-bit client for Windows NT that, like the client for Windows 95/98, is required for using many NDS-integrated capabilities. Other vendors offer Windows NT clients for their servers as well.

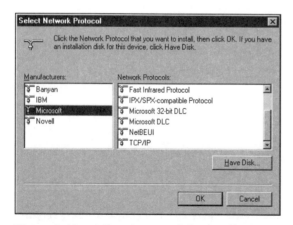

Figure 2.10 A list of some of the Windows 98 network protocols, accessed from the Network icon in the Control Panel.

Unlike Windows 95/98, legacy Windows 3.1 and DOS clients do not work. Windows NT does not work with TSRs or with programs that directly access hardware components. Many of the legacy clients are both TSRs and access the network interface card directly. This is why they do not work.

Dumb Terminals

Dumb terminals are not much more than keyboards and monitors that access a host computer and run programs on it remotely. Mainframe computers, minicomputers, and many Unix servers provide terminal services to dumb terminals. They also provide services to terminal emulation programs.

A *terminal emulation program* is a software application that runs on a PC. It mimics the functionality of standard dumb terminal hardware, enabling it to run host applications on the PC. Many enterprise networks require end users to use both host applications and PC applications. Terminal emulation programs enable users to have both host applications and PC applications without investing in two sets of hardware. This system also saves on desktop real estate.

Telnet

Telnet is a protocol that enables terminal emulation over TCP/IP. It is also the name of the application that uses the Telnet protocol. Using Telnet is similar to using any terminal emulation program. Telnet uses the Internet name or the IP address of the Telnet host, along with the host's port number, which is usually the default port 23. Typically, all operating systems have a Telnet application, and its command executable is nearly always *telnet.* The Telnet application window is shown in Figure 2.11.

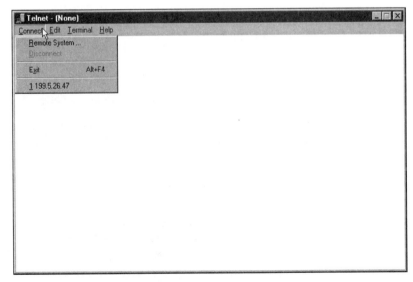

Figure 2.11   Telnet application window.

DIRECTORY SERVICES

Directory services are becoming more essential as enterprise internetworks grow in size and complexity. The directory service provides a means of cataloging network resources and login accounts in a single repository. The directory service catalog enables the use of a single login, sometimes even for networks with different types of network servers. An added benefit is the capability of managing from a single management station.

Novell Directory Services

Novell Directory Services are integral to the newer versions of the NetWare operating system. Novell has developed a product called *NDS for NT*, which enables management of NT domains through a single Novell Directory Service tree.

The main consideration for NDS is how to design the tree. The tree design is based on the objects that are within it, so a clear understanding of these objects will assist in the design and ongoing maintenance of the NDS tree.

An NDS object represents a physical or logical resource within the internetwork. Common objects represent users, groups, servers, printers, applications, and workstations. The options available for the objects are called the *NDS schema*. This is the definition of the objects and properties that can be installed in the NDS tree. Applications can extend the schema of the tree. For example, a backup program might add a backup object to the NDS tree so that the administrator can check the status of a backup. This object is not part of the current standard NDS schema. If the schema is extended on one NDS replica, but not another, then the NDS directory must be synchronized.

The three types of objects are:

➤ **[root]** There is a single [root] object in every tree. This object holds all other objects.

➤ **container** Container objects can contain other objects.

➤ **leaf** A leaf object represents a resource and cannot contain any other objects.

Each object type has properties. A specific object will have values for each property. For example, a leaf object for a user will have the property of First Name, and the value of that First Name property might be John. A sample NDS tree design is shown in Figure 2.12.

When the tree is created, it should mirror the physical location of network resources and users. No container object should span a WAN link. That means that each physical location should have its own container object to hold its resources. Below those container objects, further container objects can be placed to hold a logical organization or grouping of resources. Here are some standard rules to follow.

2

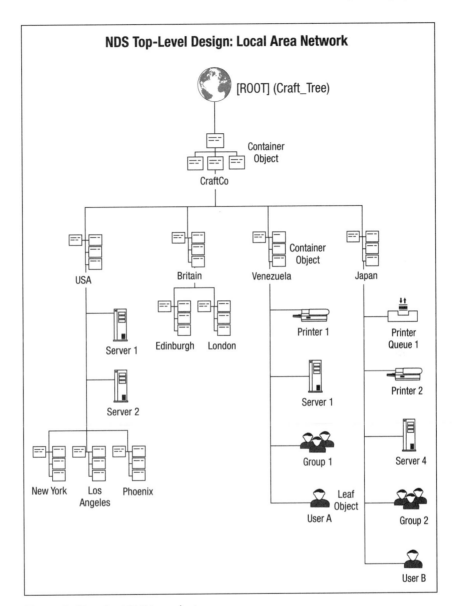

Figure 2.12   An NDS tree design.

➤ Design the top of the NDS tree to reflect the physical locations of the enterprise.

➤ Do not allow a container unit to span a WAN link.

➤ Keep the bottom of the tree wider than the top of the tree; expand wider as the tree gets deeper.

➤ Use container units at the bottom of the tree as logical groups.

➤ Design the bottom of the tree to mirror sites, divisions, and business units, and make sure the login scripts and rights are designed before implementation.

Active Directory Service

The Microsoft Windows 2000 Active Directory Service is a directory view over a single or multiple domain structure. Like Windows NT 4 domains, the Active Directory depends on trust relationships to ensure that security is enabled throughout the directory. Unlike older NT domains, the Active Directory automatically creates trust relationships. The Active Directory also makes the trust relationships *transitive*, unlike older NT domains. Transitive trust relationships are such that if Domain A trusts Domain B, and Domain B trusts Domain C, then Domain A implicitly trusts Domain C. This relationship is depicted in Figure 2.13.

The basic container unit of the Active Directory is the domain, which serves as both a security and an administrative boundary. The combination of domains and transitive trust relationships builds an Active Directory domain tree. The only requirement is that the domains use a contiguous Domain Name Service (DNS) namespace; that is, the domains are all part of the same TCP/IP–based company.com domain name. When there are domains that do not have the same DNS namespace, the Active Directory trees are combined to create a *forest*.

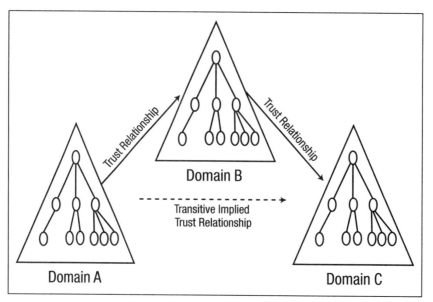

Figure 2.13 Transitive trust relationship in Active Directory.

Within the domain structure of an Active Directory tree are organizational unit containers that enable the hierarchical view of objects. The organizational units also allow administrative rights to be granted to different portions of the domain unit—an improvement over the "all or nothing" strategy of older NT domain administrative rights.

X.500

Both Novell Directory Services and Active Directory Service are based somewhat on the X.500 directory standard. The X.500 standard has been around since it was offered by the CCITT (International Telegraph and Telephone Consultative Committee) in 1988. X.500 is a protocol standard that specifies a model for linking multiple local directory services to form a single, global distributed directory. A server that contains a partition of the global directory and the index of directory information is called a *Directory System Agent (DSA)*. Through the DSA, users perceive the entire directory to be available from the local server.

Administrators are able to maintain the database from the local DSA by manipulating the entries that describe the network resources and users. Each entry has a unique identifier called a *Distinguished Name*. The Distinguished Name contains information about the location of the network resource within the hierarchical tree.

Lightweight Directory Access Protocol

Lightweight Directory Access Protocol (LDAP) is an Internet standard for locating and managing network resources across diverse directories. LDAP is like an index of directories. It can access directories such as DNS, which is a globally accessible table of domain names and their corresponding IP addresses in the TCP/IP protocol stack. DNS works well as a mapping system, but requires end users to know which domain name to search for. With LDAP, users do not need to know the domain name or the IP address, but can search the DNS directory and look at what is available.

Another type of directory would be a messaging system or the directory services of network operating systems such as NDS or Active Directory. Both NDS and Active Directory are LDAP compliant, which means that an LDAP client can access and browse the NDS and Active Directory hierarchical trees. The LDAP protocol is capable of browsing X.500-compliant directories. The LDAP client is not the same as the proprietary NDS or Active Directory client. Instead, the LDAP client can access multiple directories.

LDAP directories are organized into a hierarchical tree with the following aspects that are very similar to NDS:

> ➤ The root of the tree

> ➤ Country information containers

> ➤ Company, state, or national organization containers

> ➤ Organizational unit containers

> ➤ Individuals and shared network resources

File Services

File services are the core functions of most servers. File services enable the storage and sharing of data and applications.

NFS

NFS is the Unix Network File System. It uses Remote Procedure Calls (RPCs) to provide transparent file access to users on remote hosts.

When a user accesses a file via NFS, an RPC call is placed to the NFS server. This call uses the file name, the user's user ID, and the group ID to determine the access rights to the specified file. To ensure proper file access, user and group IDs must be the same on both the client and the host machine.

NTFS

NT File System (NTFS) was created to overcome some of the shortcomings of the 16-bit File Allocation Table (FAT) system used by DOS. NTFS has the following capabilities:

> ➤ Support for long file names

> ➤ File and/or directory access control

> ➤ File and/or directory compression

> ➤ Large partition support

> ➤ Volume space addition capabilities

The NTFS file system supports long file names that are both case sensitive, for Unix programs, and case insensitive, for DOS, OS/2, and Windows programs. NTFS maintains an 8.3 file name for files, along with their longer file names, so that a DOS program can open it.

NTFS provides the capability of assigning user access to files and to directories. Whereas User Manager For Domains is where user accounts are created and added to groups, Windows NT Explorer is where users are assigned permission to files and directories. Another capability of NTFS is compression. File compression is available as the property of individual files under the Windows NT Explorer utility.

2

Large partitions are an indispensable facility of file servers. NTFS supports large partitions through the use of volumes. A volume associates a single drive letter with a collection of free-space areas that can be spread across several hard drives. The volume can be expanded by adding free space from another hard drive on the server. The Disk Administrator utility manages volumes.

NetWare File System

Novell NetWare has a file system that is transparent to users. NetWare is a network operating system that is designed to serve files to client workstations. The NetWare file system has features that are specially designed to support a variety of clients.

When you're installing or configuring a NetWare server through the INSTALL or NWCONFIG NetWare Loadable Module, the basic division of a hard disk is a NetWare partition. A volume is the logical division of hard disk space. Like NTFS, the NetWare file system can concatenate multiple free-space areas into a volume that can be shared by users. When a volume is shared, users perceive it as a single drive letter. NetWare can support volumes up to 32 terabytes.

In the NetWare file system, the namespace specifies the way that a client will be able to save files. For example, the DOS namespace will save files with an 8.3 file-name format. The LONG namespace is used to enable long file names for OS/2 and Windows 95/98/NT clients. Namespaces are provided as a special NetWare Loadable Module with the .NAM extension. Namespaces are available to support multiple client file systems.

The NetWare file system provides for security, in the form of *trustee assignments,* that applies to files and directories. A trustee assignment is an explicit granting of a security right to a user or group. When security is applied to a directory, its files and subdirectories inherit the same security unless it is explicitly denied through an *inherited rights filter.* An inherited rights filter stops certain rights from being inherited down the directory tree.

The NetWare file system supports file compression and data migration. Both file compression and data migration must be enabled on the NetWare volume before files can be compressed. The FLAG utility or the NetWare Administrator program can be used to change the way that files are individually compressed or migrated.

CHAPTER SUMMARY

Network operating systems are special-purpose operating systems designed to share files and printers and other services on an internetwork. All servers run a network operating system. There are two basic types of network operating systems:

➤ Peer to peer

➤ Server based

Peer-to-peer network operating systems run on computers that can act as servers and as client workstations at the same time. Server-based network operating systems are dedicated to providing services to the internetwork.

Many network operating systems are available. These include Microsoft Windows NT/Windows 2000 servers, Novell NetWare, various types of Unix, Microsoft Windows For Workgroups, Microsoft Windows 95/98, Banyan Vines, IBM OS/2 Warp Server, and AppleShare servers. All of these network operating systems can run over the TCP/IP protocol.

Microsoft Windows NT is a 32-bit network operating system that provides file and print services to the internetwork. It can provide services to many different types of client operating systems. Microsoft Windows NT servers depend on a domain structure to provide a single login to the Windows NT network. Servers can have one of three roles: primary domain controller (PDC), backup domain controller (BDC), or Member Server.

➤ A PDC is the owner of the domain's user and security information database, called the Security Account Manager (SAM).

➤ A BDC maintains a copy of the PDC's SAM so that security information is available for clients even if the PDC becomes unavailable.

➤ A member server belongs to the domain, and domain users can access its services if granted the rights. When there are two or more domains, a trust relationship can enable domain users from one domain to access the other domain's resources.

The planned release of Microsoft Windows 2000 is the upgraded version of Windows NT. It maintains the same types of services available in Windows NT. The addition of Active Directory Services is the principal improvement over Windows NT.

Novell NetWare is a dedicated 32-bit network operating system. NetWare is based on a proprietary protocol, IPX (Internetwork Packet Exchange). Three versions are commercially available today:

➤ NetWare 3.x is based on a Bindery system. The Bindery is the database on each server that contains the user and security information for that server. NetWare 3.x servers do not share security information with each other. For each server, a user must have a separate account. This becomes cumbersome as the number of servers increases.

➤ NetWare 4.x servers participate in the Novell Directory Services (NDS) tree for user and security information. NDS is a hierarchical structure of users and security information that enables a single login for each user. The tree is a database that is distributed across multiple servers. Users can browse the network resources in the NDS tree as though the NDS database were available locally, although the database is replicated throughout the internetwork. Both NetWare 3.x and 4.x require IPX in order for the server to operate.

➤ NetWare 5.x participates in the same NDS tree structure. NetWare 5.x no longer requires IPX. The NetWare 5.x kernel can run over pure TCP/IP. NetWare 5.x includes new capabilities, including Web server and workstation management.

Unix is a nonproprietary network operating system that can work in host mode and in peer-to-peer mode. Unix uses the TCP/IP protocol stack as its native protocol. All types of Unix have both a text command-line interface and a graphical interface that is similar to Windows. The command-line interface uses cryptic commands to operate the server. There are different types of Unix— some developed by vendors and others developed within the public domain. The following are various types of Unix:

➤ SCO Unix

➤ Linux

➤ Sun Microsystems' Solaris

Network clients are the computers that use the services provided by servers. The computers require some form of client program that will enable them to access the network services. Many client operating systems include client programs to access various servers; some clients do not. Server vendors offer client access programs along with the server network operating system. The vendor's client programs are the best choice for accessing a single, proprietary network operating system. The most popular clients are Microsoft Windows computers.

DOS and Windows 3.1 servers require a client access program for all networks because these operating systems do not include networking components. Windows 95/98 and Windows NT Workstation all include the client access programs for Microsoft Windows networks and for Novell NetWare networks.

Dumb terminals are the minimal hardware required to send input to a host computer and to receive output from it. A dumb terminal generally consists of a keyboard, a monitor, and a network connection of some type. Dumb terminals are used with mainframe computers, minicomputers, and Unix hosts. Terminal emulation software is used on a client computer to enable the client to run as though it were a dumb terminal. Telnet is a type of terminal emulation software that is specific to the TCP/IP protocol. Directory services are becoming increasingly essential to networking. The following directory services enable universal access to network resources.

➤ NDS organizes network resources in a hierarchical tree. NDS is a database that is distributed across network servers so that the directory appears as though it is available locally.

➤ Active Directory Service is the Microsoft Windows 2000 directory service. Based upon the older Windows NT domain system, it assists in creating the correct trust relationships to establish network resource access.

➤ X.500 is the CCITT directory services standard established in 1988. It is most similar to NDS (which is based on X.500) in its organization of a tree. The X.500 tree has a root, which represents the world. The root contains country information. Country information containers hold organization containers. Organization containers hold organizational unit containers. Organizational units contain the network resources and user accounts.

➤ Lightweight Directory Access Protocol (LDAP) was created to enable universal directory access.

File services are available on all types of network operating systems. The file system that provides the file services varies greatly among the various NOSs. File systems determine the size and configuration of server hard drives, as well as the file-name formats that can be supported. Network File System (NFS) is a Unix file service. NT File System (NTFS) is the Microsoft Windows NT file system that supports volumes and long file names. The NetWare file system uses namespaces to provide file services to multiple types of clients.

REVIEW QUESTIONS

1. Which of the following devices runs a network operating system?

   a. Printer

   b. File server

   c. Dumb terminal

   d. DOS-based computer

2. What services can a server provide to the internetwork? [Choose the three best answers]

   a. File services

   b. Printer sharing services

   c. Electromagnetic interference

   d. Web services

2

3. Which of the following network operating systems uses domains to group servers and security information?

   a. Sun Microsystems' Solaris

   b. Novell NetWare 4.x

   c. Banyan Vines

   d. Microsoft Windows NT 4

4. What type of computer is the holder of the Security Account Manager (SAM) for the domain?

   a. Member server

   b. DHCP server

   c. Primary Domain Controller

   d. Workstation manager

5. What network operating system uses a Bindery?

   a. Linux

   b. Novell NetWare 3.x

   c. Microsoft Windows 2000

   d. Novell NetWare 5.x

6. How do NetWare 4.x and NetWare 5.x organize user and security information?

   a. In a hierarchical tree structure

   b. In a separate, server-based flat database

   c. In a replicated domainwide database

   d. In the passwd file in the /etc directory

7. Where are groups specified in a Unix server?

   a. As objects in the NDS tree

   b. As objects in the Active Directory

   c. As entries in the /etc/groups file

   d. In the Bindery on the Unix server

8. Which of the following are server-based network operating systems?

   a. Linux

   b. Microsoft Windows For Workgroups

   c. Microsoft Windows 98

   d. Novell NetWare

9. Select the network operating system that uses StreetTalk.

   a. Banyan Vines

   b. Novell NetWare

   c. Microsoft Windows NT

   d. Microsoft Windows 2000

10. Select the two network operating systems that organize computers, users, and security information into domains.

    a. SCO Unix

    b. Novell NetWare 3.x

    c. IBM OS/2 Warp Server

    d. Microsoft Windows NT Server 3.51

11. Which protocol was developed by Novell for NetWare network operating systems?

    a. TCP/IP

    b. AppleTalk

    c. IPX

    d. DECNet

12. Acme Garages recently acquired Widget, Inc., and is merging the two internetworks. Tracy is hired to determine the best plan to merge them. There are OS/2 Warp Servers, Apple Macintosh clients, Windows 98 clients, Novell NetWare servers, and SCO Unix servers on either or both of the internetworks with multiple protocols. One of Acme's network design goals is to reduce the number of protocols to one. Which one of the following protocols should Tracy select for use in the merged internetwork?

    a. AppleTalk

    b. TCP/IP

    c. DECNet

    d. IPX

13. Organs Co. has a Novell NetWare 3.x network that runs IPX over Ethernet. The accounting department must access a Telnet application from the State Department as a new requirement. What must the administrator add to the clients for this to work?

    a. A client access program for AppleShare servers

    b. The AppleTalk protocol stack

    c. The TCP/IP protocol stack

    d. The NetBEUI protocol stack

2

14. Grant's Pharmacies currently runs Unix servers with Wyse terminals to access host programs. A new requirement is to use Microsoft Office 2000 applications but still run the Unix host programs for the Research department. The Research department is very short of space on the desktop. Which of the following will the administrator have to install? [Choose the two best answers]

a. PCs

b. Dumb terminals

c. Terminal emulation software

d. Client access programs for NFS

15. Which of the following is the directory services standard that was offered by the CCITT?

a. TCP/IP

b. Active Directory

c. X.500

d. NDS

16. Select the file system that is used on Unix servers.

a. NTFS

b. Network File System

c. FAT

d. FAT32

17. Which of the following file systems will support volume sets and long file names on Windows NT servers?

a. NFS

b. FAT

c. HPFS

d. NTFS

18. What is the system used by NetWare servers to be able to serve files to multiple client operating systems?

a. Namespaces

b. NetWare Loadable Modules

c. NTFS volumes

d. NFS

HANDS-ON PROJECTS

Project 2.1

This hands-on project will show you how to set up a peer-to-peer network with two Windows 98 computers. For this project, you will need two Windows 98 computers with network interface cards, a hub, and/or the appropriate cables to connect them. We will designate one of the computers as PC1 and the other as PC2. They will belong to a workgroup called "PCGroup." We will install the client for Microsoft Networks on both computers, using the TCP/IP protocol. If the network you are using already has a TCP/IP address scheme, then use that. If not, we will use the addresses for the two PCs from Table 2.8.

To set up a peer-to-peer network:

1. The first item is to install the network interface card (adapter) driver. Note that this driver may already be installed if the adapter is recognized by the operating system, so this step may simply be verification of the driver installation. Start by clicking on the Start button.

2. Click on Settings.

3. Select Control Panel.

4. Double-click on the Network icon. You are now in the Network dialog box.

The actions up to this point will have the same result as right-clicking on the Network Neighborhood icon and selecting Properties.

5. Click on the Add button.

6. Select Adapter and click on Add.

7. In the Manufacturers pane, select the manufacturer of the adapter card. In the Network Adapters pane, select the card. Then, click on OK. You should be returned to the Network dialog box.

If there is a driver from the manufacturer, select the Have Disk button instead of the manufacturer and adapter card, and point to the location of the driver. For example, if the driver is on a disk and in the Win98 directory, select A:\Win98 for the location of the driver.

Table 2.8 Practice TCP/IP Addresses.

PC Name	IP Address Subnet Mask
PC1	199.99.9.1 255.255.255.0
PC2	199.99.9.2 255.255.255.0

2

8. If there was no networking functionality on the workstation, then Windows 98 may prompt for adding a client and a protocol. This exercise will add the client for Microsoft Networks and TCP/IP protocol separately. To add the TCP/IP protocol, click on the Add button.

9. Select Protocol and click on Add.

10. In the Manufacturers pane, select Microsoft. In the Network Protocols pane, select TCP/IP. Then, click on OK. Input the TCP/IP addresses from Table 2.8. You should be returned to the Network dialog box.

11. The final element to installing networking functionality is the client. To install this, click on the Add button.

12. Select Client and click on Add.

13. In the Manufacturers pane, select Microsoft. In the Network Clients pane, select the Client For Microsoft Networks. Then, click on OK.

14. To change the name of the PC, select the Identification tab and change the name under Computer Name.

15. To make the PC part of the workgroup, on the Identification tab change the workgroup name to PCGroup.

16. To share files in a peer-to-peer arrangement, the Windows 98 PC has to do more than participate in a workgroup. It must also have the service enabled for file and printer sharing. To add this service, click on the Add button.

17. Select Service and click on Add.

18. In the Manufacturers pane, select Microsoft. In the Network Services pane, select File and Printer Sharing for Microsoft Networks. Click on OK.

19. After each of the networking elements has been added, click on the OK button at the bottom of the Network dialog box. You will be prompted to reboot the PC; go ahead and reboot it.

The previous set of exercises should be repeated for the second PC, using the other TCP/IP address and PC name as stated in Table 2.8.

20. Once the PC has rebooted and you have logged in, right-click on the Network Neighborhood icon and select Properties.

21. In the Network dialog box, click on the File And Printer Sharing button.

22. Make sure that the I Want To Be Able To Give Others Access To My Files checkbox is not checked Click on OK.

23. Click on OK for the Network dialog box.

24. Double-click on the My Computer icon.

25. Right-click on the C: drive and select Sharing. The File Sharing dialog box will appear.

26. On the Sharing tab, select the radio button for Shared As.

27. Change the Share name to "Cdrive".

28. Note that the access type is Read Only. If you want users to be able to edit or delete files on your PC, you should change the access type to Full. Assign a password if you wish; then, click on the OK button.

Project 2.2

This hands-on project will review the way that an administrator can manage users and security on a NetWare 5.x network. In this exercise, you will create a user account, create a group, assign the user to the group, grant the group rights to a file, and change the extended properties of that file. You will use the NetWare Administrator program to complete all these tasks.

To start NetWare Administrator:

1. Using a Windows 95, Windows 98, or Windows NT workstation, browse the Network Neighborhood and select the NetWare server. Double-click on it to display its volumes.

2. Double-click on the SYS volume to expand its contents.

3. Double-click on the Public folder.

4. Double-click on the Win32 folder, and then double-click on NWADMN32.EXE to execute the NetWare Administrator program.

To create a user account:

1. In the NetWare Administrator window, browse to the organizational unit where you want to place the user account and press the Insert key.

2. Select User from the list and click on OK.

3. Type in the user account's login name and the last name of the user. Check the Define Additional Properties checkbox and click on the Create button.

4. The User Properties dialog box will appear. This is the dialog box used to manage the user's information and capabilities on the network. Feel free to click on each of the buttons and look at the available options.

5. Click on OK or Cancel when you're finished. (OK will save any changes that you made while looking at the Properties box. Cancel will keep the user account, but not save any changes.)

To create a group:

1. While the NetWare Administrator window displays, select the organizational unit where you want to place the group account. Click on the Object menu and select Create.

2. Select Group from the list and click on OK.

3. Type the name of the Group. Check the Define Additional Properties checkbox; then, click on the Create button. The Group Object Properties dialog box will appear.

2

To assign the user to the group:

1. While still viewing the Properties dialog box for the group you created, click on the Members button on the right side of the box.

2. Click on the Add button.

3. If the user account does not appear in the left pane of the dialog box, browse through the NDS tree until you find the user account in the left pane. Select the user account and then click on OK. The user account, with its full NDS context, will appear in the Group Members window.

To grant the group rights to a file:

1. While still viewing the Properties dialog box for the group you created, click on the Rights To Files And Directories button.

2. Click on the Add button.

3. Within the Browse pane in the right-hand side of the dialog box, browse through the NDS tree and double-click on the SYS volume of a server to expand it. (The SYS volume is named SERVERNAME_SYS, where Servername is the name of the server containing the volume.) Double-click on the Public directory to expand it.

4. In the Available Objects pane, on the left-hand side of the dialog box, select the Rights.exe file and click on OK.

5. The file will appear in the Files And Directories window; below it, the Read and File Scan checkboxes will be checked. Check the Write and Modify checkboxes.

6. Click on OK to save the changes to the group.

To change the extended file properties:

1. In the NetWare Administrator window, locate the organizational unit that contains a server SYS volume.

2. Double-click on the SYS volume to expand the directories within it.

3. Double-click on the Public directory to expand the files and directories within it.

4. Double-click on the Rights.exe file to display its properties.

5. Click on the Attributes button.

6. Check the Shareable and Immediate Compress checkboxes.

7. Click on OK to save the changes to the file.

## CHAPTER THREE

MAJOR NETWORKING PROTOCOLS

After Reading This Chapter And Completing The Exercises, You Will Be Able To:

➤ Understand what protocols are and why they are so important

➤ Explain the historical development of the three major protocols: IPX/SPX, TCP/IP, and NetBEUI

➤ Explain the addressing schemes for IPX/SPX, TCP/IP, and NetBEUI

➤ Detail the advantages and disadvantages of each protocol

➤ Know when each protocol is used most often

This chapter discusses three of the major networking protocols in use today. Because we are concerned primarily with personal computers (PCs), we will concentrate on protocols applicable to that platform. As you will see, the three protocols we'll discuss were designed for a specific need. For example, vendor need drove the design of IPX/SPX. In contrast, the need for a protocol that met a projected worldwide requirement, independent of vendor specifications, drove the design of TCP/IP.

Protocols make the networking world go 'round. Without them, we would have no networks, no Internet, and no jobs for all the network engineers out there. Over time, protocols have come and gone as the scale of networks has increased.

The protocols used on a network can affect the network's scope and performance significantly. We will cover these effects as we examine each of the three protocols. We'll also discuss addressing and how each protocol enables you to uniquely identify hosts on a network.

Before we launch into a discussion of the three major particular protocols, we'll explain why we need protocols in the first place. When you know what they are used for, you will understand more readily the subtle nuances of each major protocol used on PCs today.

WHAT ARE PROTOCOLS USED FOR?

When PCs first emerged, the mere fact of having one was enough of a wonder. You could prepare documents, make lists and databases, and calculate spreadsheets faster than ever before. Although these early PCs fulfilled their functions with great efficiency, they were not quite ready for prime time. First, they operated relatively slowly, and second, they didn't make it easy to exchange data with other PC users.

People quickly identified these failings and compared PCs with mainframe computers. With the mainframe, a central processor processed all data and stored all files. When coupled with terminals, the mainframe also allowed users to share both the processor and the data. It was not long before the light bulb went on and people realized that this model could work very well for PCs, too.

Terminals coupled with the mainframe were known as *dumb* terminals. All the terminal did was open a window into the mainframe's space. It didn't really process anything at all, but was merely a screen that allowed you to interact with the mainframe. In this respect, PCs—which shifted processing power to the user—offered a great advantage. Although the PC at that time was expensive for a home user, when compared to the price of a mainframe, it was a bargain.

People logically wanted to follow the mainframe model while taking advantage of the PC's local processing power. That combination led to the birth of the local area network (LAN) that we know today. To make the combination work, however, you need a couple of things. First, you need a big brain in the network's center to process data, to figure out who is who, and to share printers and anything else attached to the network. Next, you need a road leading to and from every host on the network. Finally, you need a common language.

The big brain in the network's center is the network operating system—a super operating system for controlling the network's activities, managing security, and sharing devices. The road connecting each host is the network's cabling—a path between one host and every other host. And the common language is the subject of this chapter—the protocol.

Never confuse protocols with operating systems. Protocols are portable. Once defined, you can adapt them to run on different cabling in networks with different network operating systems. Operating systems are often less forgiving to adaptation.

Why do so many different protocols exist? Well, the answer in general terms is scale. In the PC's early days, the machines were not cheap enough for everyone to use one at home, or even at businesses. And PCs still were relatively rare.

Therefore, when vendors sat down to design a protocol allowing these rare and expensive PCs to communicate with each other, the problem's scale was small. Therefore, the solution that vendors developed was also small in scale.

By the late 1960s, however, people had concluded that the limits on a network's size were too arbitrary. Think about the military, for example. The military needs a way for computers to talk to each other across multiple networks and over great distances. This is not a small-scale problem suitable for a small-scale solution. In response to such increasingly sophisticated needs, vendors began to develop new protocols with new capabilities.

We will address these new protocols as we go through this chapter. The three protocols discussed, although very different, represent, in effect, an evolution. Each was designed to solve a specific problem at a given time, and each was superseded as our networking needs grew.

Before we move on, we should note one final point. Protocols allow hosts to send and receive data. To facilitate this, the protocol's job is partly to allow you to uniquely identify hosts on a network. For example, if you have 200 hosts on a LAN, and two of those hosts are called Bob, how can your computer know which Bob you mean when you send something?

Well, each protocol uses an addressing scheme. The addressing scheme, however—and this is very important—lies atop another addressing scheme. That underlying addressing scheme uniquely identifies each host by the Media Access Control (MAC) address burned into the host's network interface card (NIC). Unfortunately, MAC addresses (which are discussed in more detail in Chapter 6) are completely arbitrary and difficult to remember. Moreover, on most network cards you cannot change MAC addresses, and you cannot easily group hosts together by their MAC addresses because the addresses can vary widely.

So each protocol uses its own addressing scheme, which allows you to change addresses and to group hosts logically. Each protocol also uses its own method for translating between its addressing scheme and the MAC addresses. In all cases, though, the protocol's addressing scheme is *always* translated into the MAC addressing scheme in order for computers to talk to each other.

Now, we're ready to discuss the three major protocols used on LANs today:

➤ IPX/SPX

➤ NetBEUI

➤ TCP/IP

Internetwork Packet Exchange/Sequenced Packet Exchange (IPX/SPX)

Vendors have fought several battles for dominance in the network operating systems market. In the 1980s, Novell emerged as the big winner with its NetWare product. Moreover, as NetWare became increasingly popular, so did the protocol suite that Novell designed for the network operating system (NOS)—IPX/SPX.

To say that Novell designed the IPX/SPX protocol is somewhat misleading, however, because Novell had a helping hand from Xerox. During the early development of Ethernet, Xerox had designed a protocol called Xerox's Network Systems (XNS). Novell later based its development of IPX on Xerox's XNS protocol. Similarly, Novell based its development of SPX on Xerox's earlier design for the Sequenced Packet Protocol (SPP).

Because Novell included IPX/SPX in every box of NetWare sold, IPX/SPX soon became a standard of sorts. At that time, no one really worried about other issues, such as the Internet, because the idea of major networks with hundreds of PCs was still new. For its time, IPX/SPX did a good job on LANs, and Novell still supports it today. Over time (a very long time), however, IPX/SPX will likely disappear. Until then, we all should know what it is, what it does, and how it does it.

Overview

As you will see, two of the major protocols in use today— IPX/SPX and TCP/IP—have two distinct parts. The first part is *connectionless*; the second part is *connection based*. The distinction between the two parts pivots on your need (or lack of need) to guarantee that sent data will arrive at the destination host. If you don't need a guarantee, then a connectionless protocol is adequate. If you do need a guarantee, then a connection-based protocol is needed.

You might wonder why we don't use connection-based protocols all the time. After all, if you can guarantee delivery, why not do it? The answer lies in the overhead required for connection-based protocols. More data has to go down the road to establish and maintain a connection between two or more hosts. Moreover, the more data you send, the more overhead is required. So, if you do not absolutely need a dedicated connection, why waste bandwidth?

In this discussion, *bandwidth* refers to how efficiently you are using the road's width. For example, a connectionless protocol might need to send three pieces of data from one host to another. In that situation, the protocol doesn't care how the data gets there. So the data can drive as it wants, changing lanes, accelerating a bit, or slowing down without problems. This method is efficient because the protocol does not manage the data's driving from the back seat. In contrast, a connection-based protocol controls the driving process and might even use a whole lane of highway to complete the communication. Without such control, the protocol could not guarantee that the data would reach its destination and not take a detour to the beach.

Within the IPX/SPX protocol suite, IPX is connectionless and SPX is connection based. If you need to guarantee the delivery of data, use SPX. If you don't need to guarantee the delivery of data, use IPX.

Protocols In The IPX/SPX Suite

Remember that IPX/SPX is a *suite,* or collection, of protocols that work together. No one protocol in a suite can perform all the tasks required of a fully functional NOS enterprise protocol. Because of this, the suite includes several protocols that collectively can do the job. These protocols are:

➤ Internetwork Packet Exchange (IPX)

➤ Sequenced Packet Exchange (SPX)

➤ Routing Information Protocol (RIP)

➤ Service Advertising Protocol (SAP)

➤ NetWare Link Services (NLSP)

➤ NetWare Core Protocol (NCP)

Let's look at each protocol to see what function it performs in the suite. Although we will not discuss these protocols at length, familiarity with their capabilities will help you understand what IPX/SPX, as a suite, does and does not do.

As you will see, all protocols have several functions in common. Chief among these is getting data from point A to point B, sometimes with a guarantee and sometimes without. Protocols also must provide a way for hosts and servers to find available network resources and services. In addition, other components of the network must communicate using one or more protocols in the suite.

Internetwork Packet Exchange (IPX)

IPX provides connectionless communication. Because other protocols in the IPX/SPX suite use it for their functionality, IPX is a centerpiece of the suite. Although the protocol cannot guarantee delivery of data, its lack of overhead gives it the advantage of speed.

IPX performs internetworking routing and logical network addressing (which is different from the physical or MAC-level addressing discussed in the "Addressing Schemes" section later in this chapter).

Sequenced Packet Exchange (SPX)

SPX provides connection-based communication and is used when guaranteed delivery is required. Guaranteed delivery inherently means the protocol will operate more slowly than protocols that do not guarantee delivery. SPX's slowness is attributable to its ability to maintain the connection between hosts and to check the integrity of data as it is received.

SPX complements IPX. It allows the protocol suite to fragment, sequence, and reassemble packets. These functions are requirements of guaranteeing delivery of data. First, you need to break up into fragments any data too big to fit into a single packet. Next, you need to add a sequence bit to those fragments so the receiver knows in which order they go. Finally, you need to know how to reassemble the fragments. SPX answers these needs.

Routing Information Protocol (RIP)

To understand the role of RIP, we first need to know a little about a network component called a router. (Routers are discussed in detail in Chapter 7.) A *router* is a network component that decides where to send packets of data. By storing in its memory both a table of addresses and routes to those addresses, a router knows how to get data from point A to point B. Such knowledge becomes extremely important as networks get larger and you can no longer have the luxury of having all hosts on one long piece of cable.

RIP uses IPX to pass routing-table information from one router to another. Thus, a key component of the router's intelligence (its routing table) is disseminated throughout the network and improves the network's efficiency.

Service Advertising Protocol (SAP)

It is all well and good to network a bunch of computers together, but how does each host on the network know which services are available to it? The answer mimics real life: The services advertise—and advertising is the function of SAP.

Each router on an IPX network has an agent on it called, not surprisingly, a SAP agent. Much as the router maintains its routing table, the SAP agent maintains a server information table, which lists each service that has advertised. When a host wants a service, it contacts the SAP agent to find out where the service is.

NetWare Link Services Protocol (NLSP)

Because RIP and SAP are older protocols, they perform inefficiently. For example, RIP periodically broadcasts an entire routing table. Depending on how many routers you have on your network, such broadcasting can generate a lot of extra traffic.

To redress the inefficiencies of RIP and SAP, Novell designed a more sophisticated protocol called *NetWare Link Services Protocol (NLSP)*. NLSP elects one router as the designated router (DR) to collect and collate all data into a central database of routing information. This central database is then passed to each router.

NLSP is more efficient than the RIP/SAP combination and therefore is more popular.

NetWare Core Protocol (NCP)

The protocols mentioned so far provide underlying functionality for the hosts and the network. In other words, these protocols not only distribute information about where each host or network service is located, but also provide a service whereby a piece of data can travel from one point on the network to another. NetWare Core Protocol (NCP), in comparison, provides services to client applications. With NCP, hosts have a method for making calls to a NetWare server for services, such as printing.

Novell originally developed NCP to operate over IPX. However, in the latest version of NetWare, which allows TCP/IP to be the default protocol, Novell adapted NCP for use in that protocol suite also.

 If you read Microsoft documentation, you might have some difficulty finding information on IPX/SPX. That's because you're looking under the wrong name. Microsoft's implementation of IPX/SPX is known as NWLINK and was designed to offer functionality across network operating systems. The typical protocol in use on Microsoft networks is TCP/IP.

IPX/SPX And The OSI Model

In Chapter 1 of this book, we talked about the Open Systems Interconnection (OSI) model. This model describes the many functions occurring in networked computers. Protocols with their checkered developmental pasts, rarely wholly adhere to the OSI model.

Precisely mapping OSI functionality to IPX/SPX functionality is impossible. Nevertheless, you can devise an approximate mapping. Refer to Chapter 1 for a discussion of the significance of each layer of the OSI model.

As you can see in Figure 3.1, most of the core IPX/SPX functionality maps to the Network and Transport layers of the OSI model. SPX fits in at the Transport layer.

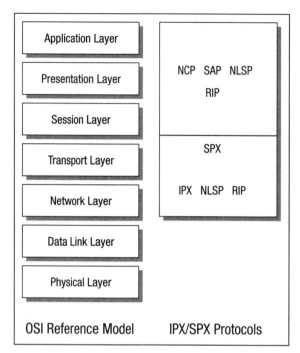

Figure 3.1   IPX/SPX and the OSI model.

You should note that the NLSP and RIP protocols in the IPX/SPX protocol operate at more than one layer of the OSI model. Don't worry too much about these protocols (unless you plan to become a NetWare engineer). For the Network+ certification, all you need is a general knowledge of what each protocol does.

Addressing Schemes

Now you know quite a bit about IPX/SPX—some of the major protocols in the suite and how they interact with network components such as routers. Let's move on to discuss how IPX/SPX identifies hosts on the network.

One caution worth repeating: There are two types of addressing schemes. The first is sometimes called a *logical addressing* scheme, and the other is sometimes called a *physical addressing* scheme. The difference between them is that you can manipulate the logical addressing scheme, but you cannot manipulate the physical addressing scheme. The physical addressing scheme refers to the MAC address built into every network card. This address cannot be changed and is the only true way to ensure that there are no duplicate addresses on your network.

When we talk about a protocol addressing scheme, we really are talking about an addressing scheme—other than the physical addressing scheme—that the protocol can use. A protocol address is usually configurable and is easier to remember than the MAC address. A protocol address either uses a scheme that completely differs from the physical addressing scheme (as with TCP/IP, as you will see later in this chapter) or adds information to the MAC address for additional functionality. Whichever method is used, however, all protocol addressing schemes will be translated to MAC addresses.

Now we'll look at IPX/SPX and explain how it addresses hosts and other network components. The IPX/SPX protocol suite uses several kinds of addresses:

➤ IPX network address

➤ Internal IPX address

➤ Station IPX address

➤ Socket identifier

The addressing scheme for IPX/SPX is straightforward once you understand why the protocol needs four address types. Let's discuss each one in turn.

IPX Network Address
Networks are complex beasts—lots of different cables attached to lots of components allow lots of data to flow. Servers and hosts on an IPX/SPX network need a way to know where they are in the grand, tangled cable scheme of things. If a server or host doesn't know where it is, then it will not understand how to get data from one point of the network to the next point.

 IPX/SPX is intrinsically linked to NetWare, so much so that the two terms are sometimes used interchangeably. The practice, although inaccurate, is not uncommon, so you should be aware of it. Novell designed the IPX/SPX protocol suite for its NetWare NOS. Therefore, because IPX/SPX was the default protocol for the NetWare NOS, their identities virtually fused. Thus, networking examples involving IPX/SPX commonly use NetWare as the NOS. In conversation, people often confuse the two terms.

On an IPX/SPX network, each network segment needs an address that uniquely identifies it. In NetWare, this address is assigned to the server. Basically, assigning an address means that the cable attached to the server's network card is christened—for example, "B4E578A1." But how did "B4E578A1" gets its name? Does that number follow some format? (We hope so, because as names go, it's not very catchy.)

The IPX network address, in fact, is an eight-digit hexadecimal number. Although this eight-digit number might make you scratch your head a bit, it holds no significance. It does follow some simple rules, though. These rules for the IPX network address are:

➤ The address must be eight digits long.

➤ Two segments on the network cannot have the same IPX network address; the segments must have unique addresses.

➤ You cannot use 00000000, FFFFFFFF, or FFFFFFFE for an address because they have been reserved.

As you can see, these rules necessitate documenting your network because if you end up with two network segments with the same IPX network address, you will experience routing difficulties.

 You can ensure that an eight-digit IPX network address is globally unique by applying for a registered IPX network number in the Novell Network Registry. You can reach the Registry by phone at 1-408-577-7506 or by email at **registry@novell.com**.

Internal IPX Address

Every *server* on an IPX/SPX network also has a unique address. The *internal IPX address* is a unique eight-digit number used to identify a server. To make sure this address is unique, it is usually generated randomly when the server is installed.

If the address is not unique, then both servers with the address will fail to connect to the network—not a desirable result. Consequently, although you can change the address, we suggest that you just leave it alone.

Station IPX Address

The *station IPX address* is a unique 12-digit number used to identify each device on an IPX network. We use the term *device* rather than *host* because routers, as well as hosts, need unique addresses.

The station IPX address is a 12-digit number, whereas other addresses are 8-digit numbers, because Novell designed IPX/SPX to use the MAC address—also a 12-digit number—as the unique identifier. This was not a bad idea because MAC addresses ensure that we have no duplicates on a network. The downside, however, is that the IPX address, like the MAC address, is not easily remembered.

When communicating on the network, the host uses an address combining the IPX network address and the station IPX address, with colons separating the values.

Socket Identifier

The final piece of the IPX/SPX addressing puzzle is the socket identifier. The *socket identifier* is unique for each *process* running on an IPX/SPX server. Service and protocol developers and designers usually assign socket identifiers. Do not change them.

IPX uses the socket identifier when it needs to address a packet to a particular process running on a server. For example, a packet addressed to RIP on a server would have the RIP socket identifier added to it so the server would know for which process the packet was intended.

Now that you know what each of these addressing components is designed to do, IPX/SPX addressing might seem more logical. Table 3.1 lists four network components and the address types they use.

When To Use IPX/SPX

Now that you are on your way to becoming an IPX/SPX expert, you should begin thinking about the circumstances under which you might use IPX/SPX rather than other protocols. When will you most likely come across it now? What about in the future?

IPX/SPX has been a mixed blessing for Novell's NetWare. During the 1980s, the protocol suite, because it was both routable and fast, gave NetWare an edge over its competitors. Over the years, however, TCP/IP has emerged as the de facto standard for protocols, leaving older NetWare systems with a problem—lack of native support for the most popular protocol on the planet. Why did this occur?

First, IPX/SPX is a proprietary protocol, designed and controlled by Novell. When you start talking about adopting a protocol globally, however, an independent, standards-based protocol clearly wins out over a proprietary protocol.

Second, when you think about the Internet, its millions of hosts, and its broad definition of a segment, you can see that IPX/SPX wouldn't work very well with this scenario. Imagine trying to figure out the IPX network address for each segment!

Table 3.1 Address types of common network components.

Component	Address Type
Server	Internal IPX address
File sharing	Socket identifier
Network cable	IPX network address
Host	Station IPX address

So, is IPX/SPX still used? Yes. In fact, you will encounter IPX/SPX on just about every Novell network with which you work. Don't be fooled by sales figures and market share analyses indicating the protocol's imminent demise. The product still sells in very respectable numbers, and you will use it time and again.

Novell nevertheless is moving away from IPX/SPX. In its latest release, NetWare 5, you can (for the first time) choose between TCP/IP and IPX/SPX as the default protocol. This development probably marks the beginning of the protocol's end. Although IPX/SPX will endure for quite some time in order to provide backward compatibility (new NetWare 5 servers will need to talk to older NetWare 3.x and 4.x servers), the writing is on the wall.

 When you're configuring a NetWare or Microsoft Windows NT server to use IPX/SPX, be careful about the frame type you select. Frames and frame types are discussed in detail in Chapter 6.

Microsoft did not adopt IPX/SPX as its default protocol, but chose TCP/IP instead. Microsoft, however, did develop an IPX/SPX-compatible protocol called NWLINK. Why? Because NetWare servers rather than Microsoft servers dominated the market at that time. To win customers, Microsoft included NWLINK to allow its servers to communicate with NetWare servers.

NetBIOS Extended User Interface (NetBEUI)

Of the three protocols discussed in this chapter, NetBEUI was designed with the smallest scope in mind. When designing IPX/SPX and TCP/IP, developers considered large networks with 200 or more hosts, but NetBEUI remains firmly in the territory of smaller networks.

You will encounter NetBEUI often because Microsoft uses it extensively in its operating systems. Built-in limitations, however, mean that on the modern network, the protocol cannot match the power and flexibility of IPX/SPX or TCP/IP. Consequently, we will not discuss NetBEUI at length, but we will cover all the key points.

Overview

To understand why anyone would design a protocol with NetBEUI's limitations, you should be aware of the evolution of LANs. One of the first networked PC configurations was the workgroup. A *workgroup* is generally a collection of between 20 and 200 PCs that share data and resources but do not require a central server. Thus, a workgroup does not need a sophisticated protocol. Another network device, using different protocols, handles any connections made outside of the workgroup (to other workgroups or to mainframe computers).

To move beyond the workgroup's limited functionality and limited host capabilities, IBM contracted with Sytek in the early 1980s to design a small and fast protocol: NetBEUI. The first NetBEUI protocol was released commercially in 1985. IBM's strategic alliances at that time ensured NetBEUI's continuing survival, and today, the protocol is available in every Microsoft Windows operating system.

 Note that a similar-sounding protocol, NetBIOS—Network Basic Input/Output System—is NetBEUI's parent. NetBEUI represents NetBIOS after Microsoft enhanced the parent protocol for its operating systems. Hence the "Extended User Interface" portion of the NetBEUI name.

During the creation of NetBEUI, IBM maintained a strategic alliance with Microsoft to develop LAN Manager, a network operating system intended for sale under the IBM banner. When the alliance dissolved, Microsoft went on to create its Windows NT product. You'll still find bits and pieces of LAN Manager within Windows NT, however, and one of those bits is NetBEUI.

Microsoft's inclusion of NetBEUI in its operating system marked the protocol's big break. Windows 3.1 was the first useful, Microsoft-developed graphical user interface (GUI) for DOS. But Windows 3.1 had one failing: It could not be networked. To fix this shortcoming, Microsoft released a product, Windows For Workgroups (WFW), which used the NetBEUI protocol. Suddenly, many people had NetBEUI on their desktops.

 In Windows For Workgroups, protocols do not load as part of the Microsoft Windows operating system, but are invoked by the Disk Operating System (DOS) instead.

NetBEUI And The OSI Model

In contrast to the IPX/SPX and TCP/IP protocols discussed in this chapter, you can think of NetBEUI as simplistic, and that's a fair assessment. Because of its simplicity, NetBEUI does not involve many layers of the OSI model. (Refer to Chapter 1 for a discussion of each layer in the OSI model.)

As shown in Figure 3.2, NetBEUI operates only at the Transport and Network layers of the OSI model. Moreover, as a less-than-sophisticated product, it does not employ a suite of protocols with many definitions. You won't have to memorize multiple protocols with different functions for NetBEUI, as you

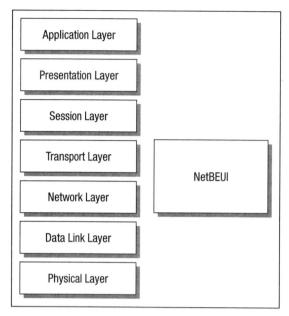

Figure 3.2 NetBEUI and the OSI model.

must for IPX/SPX and TCP/IP. Such simplicity makes NetBEUI easier to understand, but limits its usefulness.

Addressing Schemes

As mentioned earlier, NetBIOS was the original name of the protocol that IBM released. To create NetBEUI, Microsoft extended NetBIOS. Consequently, one potential area of confusion involves each protocol's naming scheme, so let's clear this up right away. NetBEUI's naming conventions adhere to NetBIOS's naming conventions. That is, when creating NetBEUI from NetBIOS, Microsoft did not extend the naming-convention component. As a result, most discussions of NetBEUI's naming schemes often refer to "NetBIOS names" instead. Following suit, we will alternate between referring to NetBEUI and to NetBIOS in this section. So, don't get confused—you're just absorbing one quirk of the true networking insider.

Now we'll introduce the NetBEUI addressing scheme. What you'll find will probably surprise you. You've probably used NetBEUI (or at least, the NetBIOS naming scheme) for a long time without ever knowing it.

If you have ever installed a Microsoft Windows 9x operating system with networking, you probably remember being asked to enter a computer name. That computer's name is used commonly seen when you open Network Neighborhood (see Figure 3.3).

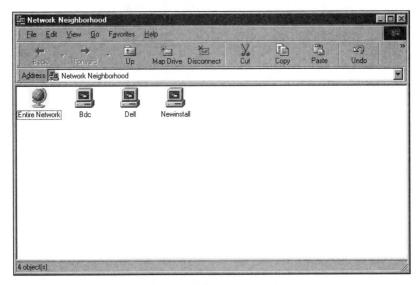

Figure 3.3 A typical Network Neighborhood screen.

But what communicates that computer's name? NetBEUI! Despite what you might have thought about this older, more limited protocol, NetBEUI currently is an integral part of all Microsoft operating systems. If you turn NetBEUI off, your computer's name will disappear from Network Neighborhood.

Unlike the addressing scheme of other protocols, NetBIOS's addressing scheme is simple to understand and easy to use. Here it is: The NetBIOS address is 16 characters long and must be unique. Microsoft reserved the address's last character as a suffix that differentiates between different functions or services offered by a particular server or host. Therefore, you are left with 15 characters. For those characters, you can type whatever you want, as long as the address is unique and does not include any spaces.

Let's examine the reserved sixteenth character. Networked computers need both to take things from the network and other hosts and to give other things back. For example, a host might need to print a document on a printer attached to a remote server. That is, the host needs to take the server's functionality and use it. The same workstation also might have a folder that is shared for everyone's use. That is, the host needs to give something back.

With Microsoft Windows NT, such giving and taking raises some good questions. For instance, how does a machine know what services are out there? The computer's ability to contact another computer by name does not explain how the computer knows that a folder is shared. That sixteenth bit offers the solution.

Something called *Windows Internet Name Service (WINS)* clearly illustrates how this sixteenth bit works. A WINS server runs on a Microsoft Windows NT network and maintains a database of all computer names and available services. With this database, WINS helps your hosts find each other. (Chapter 9 covers this topic in detail.)

We've touched upon WINS here because a quick look at its database reveals the sixteenth character's use, as shown in Figure 3.4.

As you can see, some computers on this network are registered multiple times. Why? Because each service that a host offers is registered individually. If you look at the highlighted text, you will see the computer's name followed by "[20h]". The "20" indicates that this computer runs the file-server service. Any host that can share files will have an entry like this, whether it's a Microsoft Windows NT host or a Windows 9x host. The "h" after the number indicates that the number is a hexadecimal number.

What are the most common sixteenth-character numbers and their meanings? Table 3.2 lists this information.

A list including other, less common sixteenth characters and their meanings would be quite extensive. You can learn much about what is taking place on your network by looking at the WINS database. For this chapter, however, the database simply illustrates the use to which Microsoft has put that sixteenth bit.

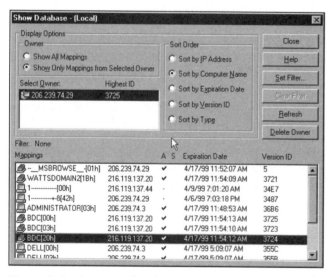

Figure 3.4 An example of a WINS database.

Table 3.2 Sixteenth characters in NetBIOS addresses.

Name	Number	Meaning
<computername>	00	Workstation service
<computername>	06	RAS Server service
<computername>	20	File Server service
<domain>	00	Domain name
<domain>	1B	Domain Master Browser
<Inet~Services>	1C	Internet information server
<computername>	2B	Lotus Notes Server service
<IRISMULTICAST>	2F	Lotus Notes
<username>	03	The name of the currently logged on user

When To Use NetBEUI

Our discussion of NetBEUI has almost exclusively detailed its limitations. Consequently, you might conclude—mistakenly—that it has no use. Paradoxically, the fundamental problem with NetBEUI is that its strengths generally turn into its weaknesses.

The best place to use NetBEUI is exactly the place for which it was designed: a workgroup. For example, suppose that a doctor needs you to install in her office 10 computers that can share some folders and printers. This scenario is perfect for using NetBEUI for two reasons.

First, NetBEUI requires almost no setup. Once installed, it is ready to go. You won't confront any weird parameters (beyond assigning unique computer names) or any glitches with getting computers to find each other. How will they find each other without your expert help? Broadcasting. When Host 1 wants to find Host 2, it will send a message to all the networked machines, announcing, "Hey, Host 2! Here's something for you!" All the machines will look at the packet to see if it is intended for them, but only the intended recipient will process the data.

Second, for small networks, in which bandwidth rarely raises concerns, NetBEUI offers a great solution. You can probably see how NetBEUI's bandwidth use could cause problems for larger networks, however. Such potential problems explain why Microsoft developed WINS servers to handle this function.

The NetBEUI protocol achieved its intended purpose: It's a small protocol with a resultant limited memory footprint that can self-tune to adjust the rate at which data is sent to fit a given situation. NetBEUI also offers excellent recovery of transmission errors.

So what great flaw has prevented this protocol from wider deployment on modern networks? NetBEUI is not routable. Because Microsoft never intended the protocol to provide a way to transmit data from one network to another, it incorporated only limited addressing capabilities. Large networks, however, just can't handle widespread broadcasting comfortably. The entire organism just gets bogged down and lethargic.

Because NetBEUI lacks the ability to route packets between networks, its usefulness is limited. Although developers have written interfaces allowing NetBEUI to use TCP/IP or even IPX/SPX for routing, the interfaces are inefficient and unnecessary. If you need TCP/IP or IPX/SPX to use NetBEUI, why not just use either exclusively?

Over the next five years, NetBEUI will probably be used less and less, but you should not overlook it. If you plan to install a network that fits NetBEUI's scope, this protocol might be your best option.

TRANSMISSION CONTROL PROTOCOL/INTERNET PROTOCOL (TCP/IP)

Since the introduction of computers and computer networks, their importance has grown exponentially. As you have surely noticed while reading this chapter, the history of computers is littered with protocols that seemed good at the time but soon proved inadequate, either because of fundamental restrictions on the protocol's use (NetBEUI) or because of concerns regarding its addressing scheme (IPX/SPX).

From the consumer's perspective, the Internet materialized overnight. One day it didn't exist. The next day, television and radio commercials began urging people to "get connected." The Internet, however, required some standards to ensure reliability, dependability, and long-term staying power. In essence, such standards would foster a controlled environment in which an impartial but expert group could propose, test, and accept innovations. Only then would the standards group introduce its successful innovations to both vendors and users.

Fortunately, the Internet's historical development largely embraced this ideal. Many governing bodies now define standards for Internet operations, register organizations' names for use on their Web sites, and assign IP addresses for use on corporate LANs. Sometimes the Internet can seem like a pretty wild place, but in truth, much of what goes on behind the scenes adheres to strict rules.

You might not realize this, but protocols, just like your favorite applications, come in versions, too. A new version of a protocol, as is the case with TCP/IP, can take a long time to develop and rarely gets released with the great fanfare heralding other software releases. A new version of a protocol is developed incrementally and typically interests only those behind-the-scenes people (maybe you?) who keep their networks running day and night.

The current version of TCP/IP is version 4, more commonly known as IPv4. A new version currently in development will be called IPv6 (version 5 was never developed). Later, we'll look at this developing version and discuss its importance for the years ahead. But first, we'll discuss TCP/IP's importance to the computing world in general and to the Network+ certification process in particular.

This chapter's discussion of TCP/IP attempts to minimize duplication of information covered elsewhere in this book, but if information provided here reappears in Chapter 8 or 9 as well, that information is critical. TCP/IP arguably represents the most important protocol suite around today. A solid knowledge of its inner workings is essential not only for achieving certification but also for succeeding with the real-world computer tasks you will undertake.

Overview

Without TCP/IP, the Internet would not exist. TCP/IP forms the fundamental building blocks of the Internet. An independent committee—the Internet Engineering Task Force (IETF)—controls its development by evaluating and testing proposals for change. This rigorous process ensures that nothing drastic and disastrous strikes overnight, leaving us unable to function on the Internet.

The IETF's official Web site at **www.ietf.org** allows you to join the IETF listserv if you want to receive notices and join discussions. The IETF home page contains a link to all current RFCs (Requests For Comments) and links to other important Internet sites that can give you information on protocol developments and name registration. If you click on the Internet Assigned Numbers Authority (IANA) link, the Web page that appears provides information on how IP addresses are assigned and provides links to RFCs that are relevant to the process. It also contains an excellent glossary of Internet terms.

Some organizations have only recently introduced TCP/IP into their networking environments. Before moving to TCP/IP, many of these organizations used a network operating system (NOS) that employed a proprietary protocol, such as IPX/SPX. Their move to TCP/IP, however, has strained the TCP/IP resource pool. We will discuss the source of this strain, as well as possible strategies to relieve it.

TCP/IP represents a global acceptance of a networking language. Using the protocols in this suite is the price of admission to the Internet. If you don't use TCP/IP, then you can't get on. Of course, its easy implementation, strong management tools, and well-understood operations have not hurt.

You cannot overstate TCP/IP's power and prevalence. Even vendors who have expended considerable time and resources developing their own protocols have accepted that TCP/IP is here to stay.

Protocols In The TCP/IP Suite

Just as IPX/SPX is a protocol suite, TCP/IP is also a protocol suite—a group of protocols interacting to provide all the necessary features. Although it would technically be possible for one protocol to provide all of these needed services, it would be unable to do so efficiently. Also, it is important to remember that in the protocol world, small is beautiful. A small protocol is generally an efficient protocol. And in the world of networks, efficiency is even more valued than small size because the network's topology limits the amount of information that can pass through a cable.

The TCP/IP suite provides the following services:

➤ The delivery of frames from one host to another (TCP and IP)

➤ The ability to download files from one host to another (FTP)

➤ The ability to connect to mainframe systems and to access programs (Telnet)

➤ The ability to use IPCONFIG and WINIPCFG to get basic diagnostic information from a host

➤ The ability to determine the route that a frame took when it traveled from source to destination (TRACERT)

FTP stands for File Transfer Protocol. TRACERT stands for Trace Route. Chapters 8 and 9 cover TCP/IP, including the services listed above, in greater detail.

Like IPX/SPX, TCP/IP actually represents two protocols, each with a different feature set. Together, these two protocols constitute the suite's core functionality. The TCP component provides connection-based functionality; the IP component provides connectionless functionality. The rules for connection-based and connectionless functionality that apply to IPX/SPX also apply to TCP/IP. A connection-based protocol can guarantee delivery, but at the expense of higher overhead and its resultant slowness. A connectionless protocol performs more quickly, but cannot guarantee delivery.

TCP/IP's wealth of diagnostic tools and compatible applications has contributed significantly to its popularity. These are discussed in great detail in Chapters 8 and 9. Don't confuse the roles of each of its components, however. For example, FTP downloads and uploads files. Because many applications on the market bill themselves as FTP or variations of FTP, you might mistake them for the protocol itself. These applications, however, only use the underlying FTP protocol; they are not the protocol itself.

TCP/IP And The OSI Model

Not surprisingly, TCP/IP does not match the OSI model perfectly. Moreover, TCP/IP developers modeled the protocol on the ARPA model (named after the organization that developed the protocol) instead.

As shown in Figure 3.5, the ARPA model's four layers roughly map to the OSI model, from the Physical layer to the Application layer, and thus provide a wide range of functionality. Chapter 8 discusses each layer of the ARPA model in detail. For now, just remember that the TCP/IP protocol suite includes functionality for virtually everything you might want to do on a network.

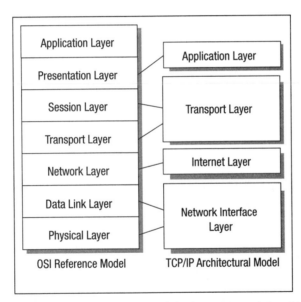

Figure 3.5   The ARPA model of TCP/IP and the OSI model.

Addressing Schemes

TCP/IP uses a highly structured addressing scheme, designed for easy use while allowing for billions of possible networked hosts. Moreover, with TCP/IP, the developers always envisioned the network as one that crossed great distances. Consequently, the addressing scheme they developed had to accommodate many hosts in different locations. In addition, the scheme needed to assign addresses in such a way that the host's location could be determined and a route to it could be discovered. The scale of this addressing scheme represented an enormous step, given that the networks in use at the time of TCP/IP development counted hosts in tens.

The addressing scheme of TCP/IP, nevertheless, has served the network community well, though it has recently begun to show its age. As the Internet changes, and more hosts join every day, TCP/IP clearly demands further development in order to provide enough unique addresses for all the hosts and devices needing connectivity to the Internet.

What do we have right now? The current version of TCP/IP can accommodate more than four billion unique IP addresses. That is, with TCP/IP, four billion individual hosts theoretically can be on the Internet at one time! How does the protocol do this?

Remember that an IP address has two unique parts. The first part, known as the network ID, designates the network on which that host resides. The second part, known as the host ID, designates the unique host. Hosts on the same network will share a network ID, but will never share a host ID.

Thus, this scheme allows organizations to have their own unique network IDs and allows the hosts on their networks to have unique host IDs. Moreover, because the addresses are regulated, the protocol guarantees that each host ID is unique worldwide. Ranges of IP addresses are categorized into classes (A, B, C, D, and E). Only Class A through Class C addresses, however, name networks. Class A, B, and C addresses differ according to the number of unique networks and hosts that their addresses will support. (Don't worry about Class D and Class E addresses; they are reserved for special purposes.)

When we refer to a Class A, B, or C address, we are referring to a network address. Each class can support a limited number of unique network IDs. For example, a Class A address can support a maximum of 126 unique network IDs. In comparison, a Class B address supports 16,384 unique network IDs, and a Class C address supports a whopping 2,097,152 unique network IDs.

Each class, along with supporting a fixed number of unique network IDs, also supports a fixed number of unique host IDs. Class A supports the greatest number of unique host addresses: 16,777,214. Class B supports 65,534 unique host addresses, which is more than adequate for most corporations today. Class

Table 3.3 Network and host IDs supported by Class A, Class B, and Class C
addresses.

Class	Number Of Networks	Number Of Hosts
A	126	16,777,214
B	16,384	65,534
C	2,097,152	254

3

C supports 254 unique host addresses. The address classes, along with their
network and host ID limits, are shown in Table 3.3.

Why does the number of supported network IDs for each class increase when
the number of host IDs for that class decreases? To understand this structure,
you must understand IP addresses. An IP address consists of four numbers.
Because each number is one byte long, that number, in decimal terms, is limited
to being between 0 and 255.

> IP addresses are actually binary numbers converted to decimal
> numbers. We convert the numbers because we can remember and
> understand decimal numbers more easily than binary numbers.
> Chapter 8 explains how to convert decimal addresses to binary
> addresses and vice versa.

As we noted earlier, an IP address includes two parts—a network ID and a host
ID. Because we have a limited number of digits with which to create an IP
address (four numbers between 0 and 255), we also have a finite total of digits.
The numbers in the left part of an IP address represent the network ID, and the
numbers in the right part of an IP address represent the host ID. The fewer
digits used for the network ID leave more remaining digits for the host ID. The
opposite is also true; a very large network ID leaves fewer numbers with which
to create unique host IDs.

In a Class A network, the first number of the IP address's four numbers
represents the network ID. The three remaining numbers represent the host ID.
With so many numbers available for host IDs, a Class A network is considered
larger than networks of other classes.

In a Class B network, the first two numbers of the IP address's four numbers
represent the network ID. The two remaining numbers represent the host ID.
With fewer numbers available for host IDs, a Class B network supports fewer
unique hosts, but more networks.

Finally, in a Class C network, the first three numbers of the IP address's four
numbers represent the network ID. The single remaining number represents the
host ID.

You might wonder how the servers and routers on a network know which part of the IP address's four-digit number represents the network ID and which part represents the host ID. The answer involves something called the *subnet mask*, which blocks out the network ID.

For example, we learned that in a four-digit Class A address, the first number represents the network ID and the last three numbers represent the host ID. We also learned that these numbers are limited to a value between 0 and 255. If we have a Class A address of 1.0.0.0, the first number—1—represents the network ID, and the three other numbers—0.0.0—represent the host ID. (The three zeros can also indicate that the IP address has not yet been assigned to a host.)

To create a subnet mask for this Class A address, we would increase the first number representing the network ID to the greatest value possible—255—but leave the three numbers representing the host ID set to 0. Thus, the subnet mask becomes 255.0.0.0.

With an IP address and a subnet mask, you can discover whether you and the host share the same network. If you and the host share the same network ID and subnet mask (in this case, 255), then you both are located on the same network. Conversely, if you and the host do not share the same network ID and subnet mask, then you and the host are located on different networks. Similar calculations occur all the time on your networked computers. Chapter 8 explains the process in detail.

A final point: Our discussion of basic TCP/IP addressing has assumed an ideal world in which all hosts in a corporation are located on the same network. Of course, such convenience rarely occurs in the real world. You can better serve your organization's real-world networking needs by further subdividing your network and host IDs with custom subnet masks. The process for creating such custom masks involves taking bits from your host ID and assigning them to your network ID. Such shifting gives you more unique network IDs, but fewer unique host IDs. You cannot achieve the reverse, however—that is, you can never create more host IDs. Just remember that as you create more network IDs, you reduce the possible number of host IDs.

When To Use TCP/IP

Determining which networking scenarios call for TCP/IP used to be more challenging. Early versions of Novell NetWare used IPX/SPX as the default protocol and therefore did not need TCP/IP. NetWare 5, however, allows you to choose between IPX/SPX and TCP/IP. Another popular network operating system, Microsoft Windows NT, uses TCP/IP as its default protocol.

So when would you use TCP/IP today? How about whenever you want to connect to the Internet? The Internet's use of TCP/IP has scored an enormous point in the protocol's favor. Wouldn't you want to use the same protocol as the largest network in the world?

Communicating with hosts and devices that speak the same language as your network is easier. If your computer runs TCP/IP, then it can communicate better with other hosts running TCP/IP. Even without running TCP/IP, your computer can still communicate with other hosts running TCP/IP, but you will need additional devices for translation purposes.

When deciding on a protocol, you should also weigh TCP/IP's many other advantages over other protocols. As a well-understood and well-supported protocol, TCP/IP offers a wealth of tools for capitalizing on its feature set. Moreover, many current and developing applications now take advantage of those features. There really isn't any good reason not to use TCP/IP.

TCP/IP Version 6 (IPv6 Or IPng)

As a de facto industry standard, TCP/IP will probably remain the preferred protocol for many years. Our discussion of TCP/IP, however, would be incomplete if we did not discuss the protocol's future. TCP/IP, as the protocol of the Internet, was developed specifically to allow hosts around the world to communicate. As a result, the protocol is used more widely than all the protocols that came before it.

TCP/IP, however, has also become a victim of its own success. The Internet as we know it today is not the one that TCP/IP's developers originally envisioned. Those original architects foresaw much smaller networks using TCP/IP to connect to the Internet, and did not anticipate the millions of eager users who go online now. Not surprisingly, as the Internet's size and uses have grown and diversified, TCP/IP's original design has begun to groan and strain under the weight.

TCP/IP's addressing scheme, for example, has not weathered the Internet's growth without revealing significant weaknesses. As we discussed earlier, the protocol's current addressing scheme will support more than four billion unique hosts. Although that capacity might sound staggering, current Internet growth rates indicate that it will be exceeded within a decade!

With a four-billion-host capacity, couldn't TCP/IP support just about everyone? Think about it. Try to imagine all of the uses we could discover for the Internet (not merely our current uses projected on a larger scale). For example, every car could become a host on the Internet, downloading traffic and accident reports, signaling its location, and performing other tasks. Toasters and ovens could become hosts, allowing you to check on your roasting dinner from work, change the cooking temperature if necessary, and ensure that a hot meal awaits your return home. Televisions across the country could download movies and software and transmit family photographs to relatives living on the other side of the world.

Now, how many televisions are in the world today? How about all those cars, toasters, and ovens? When you imagine the future in these terms, four billion doesn't sound like very much at all.

Because of this projected growth and diversification, the IETF has embarked on developing the next generation of TCP/IP, known by two abbreviations—IPng (IP next generation) and IPv6 (IP version 6). Documentation frequently uses the abbreviations interchangeably because they represent the same thing.

Note The IPv6 area directors of the IETF recommended IPv6 at the Toronto IETF meeting on July 25, 1994, as documented in RFC 1752, "The Recommendation for the IP Next Generation Protocol." The Internet Engineering Steering Group approved the IETF's recommendation on November 17, 1994, making the recommendation a proposed standard.

To summarize, we need a new version of TCP/IP to accommodate the skyrocketing number of hosts on the Internet. A new version, however, must respond to other, even more complex issues as well. TCP/IP needs additional features to support the Internet's increasingly diverse uses. For example, pushing video across the Internet demands a process that's completely different from the process of transmitting secure documents. During the current TCP/IP suite's development, however, its architects did not anticipate these and other, equally challenging, demands.

After learning about these weaknesses of the current version of TCP/IP, you may wonder why we devoted so much discussion to that outdated version rather than to the new and improved version. Protocol development differs from application, spreadsheet, or database development. Changes occur infrequently, and those changes that do occur are slow and migratory. You probably won't confront IPv6 in the working world for several years. Even then, you will discover that it's designed to run alongside the current version of TCP/IP. Moreover, given the current version's widespread use, IPv6 will not become predominant for a long time.

What changes can you expect with the protocol's new version? Consider the following major improvements:

➤ An increased address space size, from 4 numbers (32 bits) to 16 numbers (128 bits)

➤ New extensions allowing for data integrity checks and encryption

➤ A new type of address, called an *anycast address*, which allows a frame to be sent to specific host groups rather than to be broadcast to all of your network's computers

➤ More efficient routing of frames from source to destination host

These changes will alleviate the four most common problems on the Internet today. The first change addresses our need to increase the availability of unique network and host IDs. The second change responds to our rapidly growing use of the Internet to purchase goods and services by guaranteeing our privacy and security during such transactions. Without this guarantee, millions of people not yet using the Internet for commerce will never begin. The third change answers our need to minimize traffic on the Internet. Why broadcast a frame to all of your network's computers when you intend it for only 200 hosts? The final change will increase transmittal speeds by fine-tuning routing information.

If you want to get an idea of what IPv6's increase of the IP address from 4 to 16 digits means, consider this: On a pure IPv6 network, 340,282,366,920,938,463,374,607,431,768,211,456 unique IP addresses can be created. Is that enough for you?

As we have observed, these changes represent an evolutionary, rather than a revolutionary, transformation. In other words, IPv6 builds on existing structure and features rather than reinventing the wheel. This approach offers good news because it will enable developers to provide backward compatibility.

A more extensive discussion of IPv6 is beyond the scope of this book. When you become a proficient user of the current version, however, you should at least daydream about the future—a little knowledge never hurts.

CHAPTER SUMMARY

Protocols are the agreed-upon languages that computers speak. Without such agreement, you need special network devices to translate languages. This chapter discussed three major suites: IPX/SPX, NetBEUI, and TCP/IP.

IPX/SPX is a suite of protocols designed by Novell. IPX/SPX became popular because it was the default protocol for the most popular network operating system of the 1980s: Novell's NetWare. In NetWare 5, IPX/SPX is now an optional protocol.

➤ Protocols in the IPX/SPX suite include IPX, SPX, RIP, SAP, NLSP, and NCP.

➤ IPX is a connectionless protocol. SPX is a connection-based protocol.

➤ The IPX/SPX protocol suite maps to the following layers of the OSI model: Application, Presentation, Session, Transport, and Network.

➤ IPX/SPX uses four types of addresses: the IPX network address, the internal IPX address, the station IPX address, and the socket identifier.

NetBEUI is NetBIOS with some Microsoft-added enhancements.

➤ NetBEUI was designed for workgroups with between 20 and 200 hosts.

➤ NetBEUI maps to the Transport and Network layers of the OSI model.

➤ NetBEUI retained the NetBIOS naming scheme. This name is limited to 16 characters. Because the sixteenth bit is reserved, the name's effective limit is 15 characters. The sixteenth bit of a NetBIOS name identifies services running on a host or server.

➤ NetBEUI's main failing is its inability to route. Thus, you cannot use it to join different network segments.

➤ Although NetBEUI lacks some of the features other protocols offer, it still suits small networks. It is small and fast with good error control.

TCP/IP is the reigning protocol champion. Most networks use it, including the biggest network in the world—the Internet.

➤ TCP/IP is defined by consensus. The IETF has defined processes for channeling enhancements to the protocol suite. This governing structure ensures industry agreement on new features and prevents new features from "breaking" old ones.

➤ Protocols and services in the TCP/IP suite include, but are not limited to, TCP, IP, FTP, Telnet, IPCONFIG, and TRACERT.

➤ IP is a connectionless protocol. TCP is a connection-based protocol.

➤ TCP/IP maps to the following six layers of the OSI model: Application, Presentation, Session, Transport, Network, and Data Link.

➤ TCP/IP addressing supports three classes of IP addresses, known as Classes A, B, and C. Class A addresses support the greatest number of hosts but the least number of networks. Class C addresses support the least number of hosts but the greatest number of networks.

➤ For a network to use a TCP/IP address, it also must know the host's subnet mask.

➤ The current version of TCP/IP, known as IPv4, allows for more than 4 billion hosts.

➤ The Internet's growth and diversification has prompted the IETF to evaluate proposals for the next generation of TCP/IP. This version is known as IPng (IP next generation) or IPv6 (IP version 6). IPv6 will allow many more hosts and offer better addressing capabilities, enhanced security, and more efficient routing of frames.

REVIEW QUESTIONS

3

1. If hosts on a network do not use the same protocol, what problem will this most likely cause?
   a. The network will be slow because the hosts will have to translate each frame they receive.
   b. The hosts will be unable to communicate with each other.
   c. The hosts will not start.
   d. You will receive messages and files, but they will appear in a different language.

2. Why do so many protocols exist?
   a. To address different needs.
   b. Because most protocols are designed to run on specific cable types.
   c. Because different NICs use different protocols.
   d. Because different operating systems support different protocol stacks.

3. IPX/SPX was originally designed for use with which network operating system?
   a. Unix
   b. Microsoft Windows NT
   c. Linux
   d. Novell NetWare

4. Which one of the following statements is correct?
   a. IPX is a connection-based protocol.
   b. IPX is a connectionless protocol.
   c. IPX is part of the TCP/IP protocol suite.
   d. IPX is based on NetBEUI.

5. Which one of the following statements is correct?
   a. SPX is an application, not a protocol.
   b. SPX cannot be routed.
   c. SPX is not used in networks today.
   d. SPX is a connection-based protocol.

6. Which one of the following IPX/SPX protocols moves routing table information between routers?

   a. NCP

   b. NLSP

   c. RIP

   d. FTP

7. Which one of the following IPX/SPX protocols participates in advertising available services?

   a. RIP

   b. SAP

   c. NCP

   d. NLSP

8. Which one of the following protocols was designed for efficiency and therefore is beginning to replace RIP and SAP?

   a. IPX

   b. SPX

   c. TCP/IP

   d. NLSP

9. Which statement best describes the difference between a logical addressing scheme and a physical addressing scheme?

   a. A logical addressing scheme is used internally on the network, and you never know what the address is. A physical addressing scheme can be changed.

   b. A physical addressing scheme is stamped onto all components in a host. With a logical addressing scheme, you must visit each PC to note each component's address.

   c. A logical addressing scheme can be changed. A physical addressing scheme cannot be changed.

   d. A physical addressing scheme is specific to a network. A logical addressing scheme is not.

10. Which address types are used in an IPX/SPX network?

    a. IP address

    b. Socket identifier

    c. Home address

    d. Station SPX address

11. What is the address type given to each segment of an IPX/SPX network called?
    a. Internal IPX address
    b. A segment address
    c. IPX network number
    d. Socket identifier

12. To directly access the Internet, you can use either TCP/IP or IPX/SPX. Is this statement true or false?
    a. True
    b. False

13. NetBEUI was originally designed for which type of network?
    a. Local area network
    b. Wide area network
    c. Standalone PCs
    d. Workgroups

14. NetBEUI is an enhanced version of which protocol?
    a. SAP
    b. NetBIOS
    c. TCP/IP
    d. IPX/SPX

15. What is the maximum number of characters you can use in a NetBIOS address?
    a. Up to 16 characters with no spaces
    b. Up to 16 characters with spaces
    c. Up to 15 characters with no spaces
    d. Up to 15 characters with spaces

16. To which two layers of the OSI model does NetBEUI map?
    a. Application layer
    b. Transport layer
    c. Data Link layer
    d. Network layer

17. What is NetBEUI's most significant limitation?

    a. NetBEUI is too fast for some network cables.

    b. NetBEUI cannot be routed.

    c. NetBEUI works only in Windows For Workgroups network operating systems.

    d. NetBEUI does not allow you to share printers.

18. TCP/IP is the default protocol for Novell NetWare 5. Do you agree or disagree with this statement?

    a. Disagree. The default protocol for NetWare 5.0 is IPX/SPX.

    b. Agree. TCP/IP is the only choice.

    c. Disagree. You can use either IPX/SPX or NetBEUI.

    d. Disagree. TCP/IP is now optional. You can choose between it and IPX/SPX.

19. TCP/IP is a vendor-specific protocol. Is this statement true or false?

    a. True

    b. False

20. Which two of the following protocols are parts of the TCP/IP suite?

    a. IPX

    b. FTP

    c. SAP

    d. Telnet

21. TCP/IP addresses fall into different classes. Which two of the following represent a valid class address for identifying hosts on your network?

    a. Class A

    b. Class D

    c. Class E

    d. Class B

22. Which class of addresses supports the largest number of hosts but the smallest number of networks?

    a. Class C

    b. Class A

    c. Class D

    d. Class B

23. What two things do you need for a properly configured TCP/IP address?

    a. A unique IP address

    b. A default gateway

    c. A unique network ID and a shared host ID

    d. A subnet mask

24. TCP/IP version 6 is currently the most common protocol used on the Internet. Is this statement true or false?

    a. True

    b. False

HANDS-ON PROJECTS

Project 3.1

In the first hands-on project, we will look at the properties that are available for each of the three protocols discussed in this chapter. For this exercise, we will use a Microsoft Windows 9x machine.

As you will see, the more features a protocol provides, the more options there are to be configured. This is both a blessing and a curse. If there are lot of options, there is more room to make a mistake. The fewer the options, the easier the protocol is to use. This session assumes that you have all three of the protocols installed (if you don't, you need to install Microsoft Networking to be able to complete this exercise).

To view protocol properties:

1. Open the Network dialog box. Do either of the following:

    ➤ Right-click on the Network Neighborhood icon on your desktop and choose Properties.

    ➤ Click on Start | Settings | Control Panel and double-click on the Network icon.

    If you do not see the Network Neighborhood icon on your desktop, you probably do not have any network functions installed. (As stated earlier, you will have to install Microsoft Networking before you can perform the steps in this exercise.)

2. A fairly typical Network dialog box is shown in Figure 3.6. In this case, the network card is called a "Realtek RTL8029 Ethernet Adapter."

3. Notice which protocols have been installed. In Figure 3.6, you can see that IPX/SPX is loaded. The arrow next to the name is followed by the device to

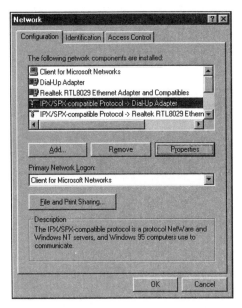

Figure 3.6   A Network dialog box.

which that protocol is bound. In this case, IPX/SPX is mentioned twice, which indicates that either the dial-up adapter or the NIC can use it. Click on the scrollbar to the right of the list of protocols. How many protocols are installed?

4. Click on the entry for IPX/SPX (if you have two entries, you can click on either one). Next, click on Properties. You will see the dialog box shown in Figure 3.7.

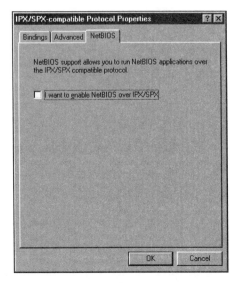

Figure 3.7   The IPX/SPX Properties dialog box.

5. As you can see in Figure 3.7, there are three tabs in this dialog box. Let's look at each tab in turn. Click on each tab as we discuss it, but don't change any of the default settings. On the NetBIOS tab, if you check the I Want To Enable NetBIOS Over IPX/SPX checkbox, you will allow NetBIOS to be encapsulated and passed around the network by IPX/SPX. This is one way to route NetBIOS frames.

6. Click on the Advanced tab. There are several options on this tab. Some of these—such as the Network Address—should be familiar to you after reading this chapter. Others—such as the Frame Type—might still be a bit of a mystery. This option is discussed in Chapter 6. Do not change this option because doing so could prevent you from communicating on the network.

7. Click on the Bindings tab. This tab lists all the networking services on the system that can use this protocol. Checking and unchecking boxes in this tab enables or disables protocols. Once again, exercise caution when making changes in this area, because some changes can prevent you from connecting to the network.

With three tabs, the IPX/SPX protocol is a fairly complex protocol. However, it offers a lot of functionality. Next, we are going to take a look at NetBEUI. You'll find that it is a far easier protocol to work with.

8. Click on Cancel to return to the Network dialog box. Scroll down the list until you find an entry for NetBEUI. If you have two entries, you can select either one. Click on the protocol name and then click on Properties. You should see the dialog box shown in Figure 3.8.

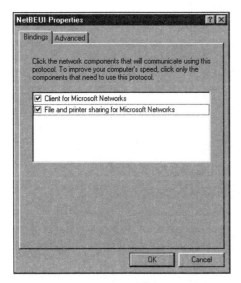

Figure 3.8 The NetBEUI Properties dialog box.

9. The NetBEUI Properties dialog box has only two tabs. The first is the Bindings tab, which lists all the networking services on the system that can use this protocol. Click on the Advanced tab.

   In the Advanced tab, there are only two options, and you rarely have to change the defaults that have been entered.

   Because NetBEUI has few options to configure, it is easy to get working. However, remember the inherent limitations that it poses on your clients.

10. Finally, we will look at the options that are available in the TCP/IP Properties dialog box. Click on Cancel to return to the Network dialog box.

11. If you have two listings for TCP/IP, you can select either one and then click on the Properties button. However, if you select TCP/IP | Dial-Up Adapter, you will first see a warning dialog box, which informs you that TCP/IP settings can vary between different dial-up connections. In this case, it is better to set the TCP/IP properties in the Dial-Up Networking Wizard. For the purposes of this exercise, you can click on OK. You should see a dialog box like that shown in Figure 3.9.

    As you can see, TCP/IP has seven tabs of information that you can configure—by far the most of any of the protocols we have looked at. The first tab displayed is the IP Address tab. This is where you enter the unique IP address and the subnet mask for your host. In the example shown in Figure 3.9, the Obtain An IP Address Automatically option has been

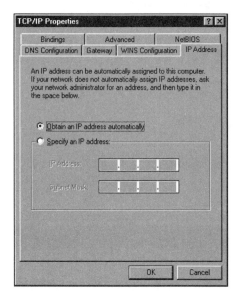

Figure 3.9 The TCP/IP Properties dialog box.

selected. This means that, when the host boots up, it contacts a service on the network to get most, if not all, of its necessary settings. This option is discussed in more detail in Chapter 9.

12. Click on each of the tabs to see the options that are available. Do not change options because doing so could prevent you from accessing the network. If you do not remember if you have changed an option or not, then click on the Cancel button to exit the dialog box.

13. When you have finished looking at the properties in this dialog box, click on Cancel. This returns you to the Network dialog box. Click on Cancel here to close the dialog box without saving any changes you have made.

Project 3.2

One of the most important topics discussed in this chapter is name resolution. Although there are several methods of name resolution in use today, one of the most common methods that you will find on a Microsoft network is the Windows Internet Name Service (WINS).

In this project, we will use WINS to assign names to computers, and then, using a Windows 9x host, we will use WINS to help us confirm that the new hostname and IP address have been accepted correctly. To perform the steps of this exercise, you must have a Microsoft Windows NT computer running the WINS service (almost all Microsoft networks have such a machine) and a host computer. (We used a Microsoft Windows 98 machine, but you could just as easily use Microsoft Windows 95 or another Microsoft Windows NT machine to perform the same steps.)

We will be using three TCP/IP utilities during this exercise. These utilities will be discussed in detail in Chapters 8 and 9 of this book. We will only be using their most basic functionality at this time.

To use WINS to assign names to computers:

1. Select a computer name that you think is unique on your network. For the purposes of this exercise, I will use the name NETWORKCERT.

2. On the Windows 98 client, click on Start|Run. This opens the Run dialog box. In the Open box, type "command" and press Enter. This will open an MS-DOS prompt on the desktop.

3. Now we will use a TCP/IP utility: PING. At the MS-DOS prompt, type "ping networkcert" and press Enter.

4. If this computer name has not been used on your network, you should receive a message that says "unknown host networkcert". This indicates that the host is unknown to all name resolution services on your network (and WINS in particular). If this is the case, you can proceed with the following steps.

If you did not see this message, then the computer name probably exists on your network. Pick a name that you know does not exist and use the **ping** command as shown in Step 3 to test for the computer name's existence. You cannot proceed until you have a computer name that is not used on your network. (Computer names can be a maximum of 15 characters long with no spaces.)

5. Once you have a unique computer name, we need to find an IP address we can assign to it. For the purposes of this exercise, we are going to use the TCP/IP address of the Microsoft Windows 98 machine (our host). At the command prompt on the host, type "ipconfig" and press Enter.

6. This will display basic TCP/IP information for your host computer. One of the parameters is called "IP Address." Write this address down on a piece of paper.

With these two pieces of information (a unique computer name and an IP address), we are now ready to go to the management tool for WINS. This is called the "WINS Manager". This tool resides on a Microsoft Windows NT Server.

Log on to the Microsoft Windows NT Server using an administrative account. If you do not log on as an administrator, you will not be able to complete the final steps of this exercise.

7. Once you are logged on to the Microsoft Windows NT Server, you will need to locate and start WINS Manager by selecting Start | Programs | Administrative Tools (Common) | WINS Manager. A typical WINS Manager display is shown in figure 3.10.

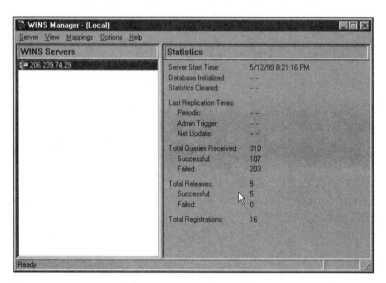

Figure 3.10   A typical WINS Manager screen.

Two types of entries (known as registrations) are recorded by WINS. Entries of the first type, which are collected by hosts as they broadcast their names when they are turned on, are dynamic in nature. The second type, which can be entered manually and will remain in the database at all times, are known as *static mappings*. We will be using the latter type for this exercise.

8. To bring up the Static Mappings dialog box, select Mappings | Static Mappings on the drop-down menu. The Static Mappings dialog box is shown in Figure 3.11.

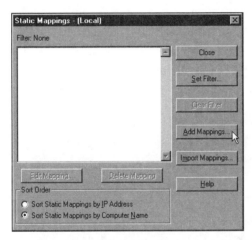

Figure 3.11   The Static Mappings dialog box.

Although the Static Mappings dialog box shown in Figure 3.11 does not have any entries, the dialog box on your system might have some. Be careful not to delete any of these entries, because it could lead to problems with hosts contacting these systems on your network.

9. Click on the Add Mappings button to bring up the Add Mappings dialog box. This is where you will enter the name and IP address of the system we want to add, which we determined in Steps 1 through 6. In the Name field, enter the unique computer name. Press Tab to move the cursor to the IP Address field.

10. In the IP Address field, enter the IP address that you wrote down earlier. Finally, on the right-hand side of the dialog box, make sure the Unique option (which is the default option) in the Type field is selected. Do not change this option.

11. Click on the Add button. You will be returned to a blank Add Mappings dialog box. Click on Close to be returned to the Static Mappings dialog box.

12. You will see several entries in the Static Mappings dialog box for the computer name you just entered. Click on Close and the exit WINS Manager by clicking on Server | Exit.

The tasks at the server are complete. Next, we will return to the Microsoft Windows 98 host to see if we can now find the new computer name on your network.

13. If you closed the MS-DOS prompt on the Microsoft Windows 98 host, you will need to open a new one. To do this, click on Start | Run, type "command", and then press Enter.

14. At the MS-DOS prompt, type "ping networkcert". (If you used a unique computer name other than networkcert, substitute that instead.)

15. You should see a result similar to that shown in Figure 3.12. You will receive the "Destination host unreachable" message because, despite the computer name being resolved to an IP address (as shown in brackets on the first line), the computer did not reply. This is because it does not really exist on the network.

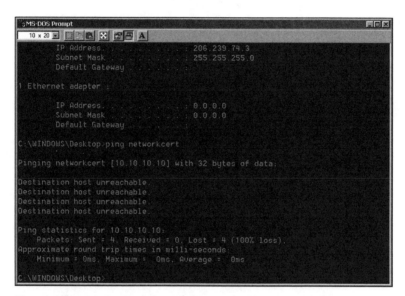

Figure 3.12   A PING with a WINS resolved computer name.

16. Because this exercise has introduced a computer name that does not really exist, you should go back and remove the entries you added in Steps 7 through 10. Once you have arrived at the Static Mappings dialog box, highlight the entries you added (hold down the Ctrl key on the keyboard and click on each one), and then click on the Delete Mappings button. This will remove the entries from the WINS database.

## CHAPTER FOUR

ESSENTIAL ELEMENTS OF NETWORKING

After Reading This Chapter And Completing The Exercises, You Will Be Able To:

➤ Design and install a fault-tolerant network

➤ Understand all six major RAID levels

➤ Create a volume set

➤ Design a network installation utilizing the most efficient network media

➤ Understand the roles of the various elements that make up a network

---

When a network is planned, much consideration is given to the basic hardware elements that make up the workstations and the servers. Management often pays particular attention to such things as CPU speeds, hard drive space, and RAM. Network professionals know that in addition to these highly visible areas of concern are elements that provide the network with the ability to function as a unit rather than just as a number of independent computers. In fact, these elements are often more important than the individual workstations and servers that make up the network. These elements include networking media, fault-tolerant disk configurations, and tape backups. Network professionals are relied upon to explain these areas to management in a manner that will allow the proper options to be considered before the network is installed. Ignorance in these areas can result in a network that functions as less than the sum of its components; ignorance in some areas can often result in the loss of critical data.

In this chapter, we will cover some of the elements that turn a collection of computers into a functional data-processing network. This chapter will provide you, the networking professional, with the information you need to decide how your network will be connected and how your data will be secured. We will be covering some common hard-disk configurations, such as:

➤ Disk mirroring

➤ Disk duplexing

➤ Disk striping

➤ Disk volume sets

135

We will cover Physical-layer media topics, including:

➤ Cabling uses and lengths

➤ Ethernet types and speeds

➤ Bandwidth types

➤ Gateway types and roles

REDUNDANT ARRAYS OF INEXPENSIVE DISKS (RAID)

The technology of RAID was first presented in 1987 in a paper titled "A Case for Redundant Arrays of Inexpensive Disks (RAID)," written by Patterson, Gibson, and Katz and published at the University of Berkeley. RAID's original attractive feature was the ability to improve a system's I/O capability. Multiple disks containing the same data allowed the system to read and write information in different physical locations. If one disk was busy responding to an I/O request, another disk could respond to a different request. This arrangement eliminated the bottleneck of I/O requests, common at the time, which resulted in I/O requests being held up in queues awaiting processing. Thus, the concept of disk striping was developed. *Disk striping* is a technique used to bind multiple disks together as a single volume, referred to as a *stripe set*. In disk striping, data is broken down into data chunks and distributed across the multiple disks in the array. *Disk striping with parity* provides for a compressed duplication of data that can be used to reconstruct the data in the event of a disk failure.

Fault Tolerance

The main reason for the implementation of RAID in business today is to provide a degree of fault tolerance. *Fault tolerance* can be defined as a resistance to failure. It is not absolute and exists only in degrees. With disk storage, the question is not if your disk will fail, but when. This measure of each disk drive's durability is known as the Mean Time Between Failures (MTBF) and is measured in hours.

RAID Levels 0 Through 5

The Berkeley RAID paper introduced five methods or levels of RAID, referred to as RAID 1 through RAID 5. Level 1 is disk mirroring. Levels 2 through 5 are forms of disk striping with parity. Disk striping with parity is the method of fault tolerance that provides the fastest read/write performance. Many additions and changes have been made since RAID's conception. Some companies have tried promoting levels like 10 and 53, but the only one not defined in the Berkeley paper (but included here) is RAID level 0.

RAID 0: Disk Striping Without Parity

RAID 0 is simple disk striping. Data is distributed across two or more disks for faster read/write access. No redundancy is involved and, hence, there is no ability to retrieve data from the set in the event of a single disk failure. Performance here is very high, and no storage space is lost to redundancy. This method, however, is rarely used; when it is used, it is in systems where data is simply passing through, such as in print servers. RAID 0 should not even be included with the fault-tolerance grouping because this level of RAID provides no fault tolerance at all. Figure 4.1 shows disk striping without parity.

RAID 1: Disk Mirroring Or Duplexing

RAID 1 is also a simple form of RAID, but it is a very effective method. Most widely used with small businesses, it can provide data redundancy and recovery while maintaining the additional benefit of tolerance in the event of a single disk failure.

RAID 1 uses disk mirroring to duplicate the information stored on a disk. Disk mirroring provides the same type of I/O read/write advantages as disk striping does. Two disks attached to the same controller duplicate each other, as shown in Figure 4.2. In addition, this method introduces a basic form of fault tolerance.

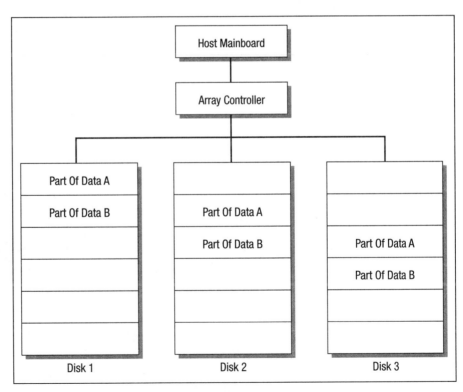

Figure 4.1   RAID 0: disk striping without parity.

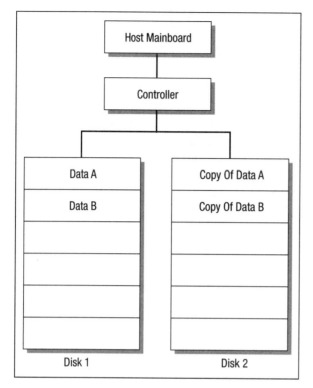

Figure 4.2 RAID 1: disk mirroring.

In the event of a single disk failure, the controller automatically uses the remaining disk to continue, uninterrupted, with processing data. This fault-tolerant capability can be further extended by providing duplicate controllers. This arrangement, known as *disk duplexing,* is shown in Figure 4.3. In fact, all components can be duplicated, up to and including duplicate servers on duplicate power supplies. This, of course, brings up the only real disadvantage to RAID 1: cost. Twice as much disk storage must be purchased as will actually be used.

RAID 2: Disk Striping With Error Correction

RAID 2 stripes bits of data across multiple disks. For parity, it uses a Hamming error correction code (ECC), which can be used to reconstruct data in the event of a single disk failure. This technique was developed in the 1950s for large arrays of disks and is extremely inefficient when compared with RAID 5. This method is rarely, if ever, still used.

RAID 3: Disk Striping With Single-Disk Parity

RAID 3 also uses the disk-striping technique. RAID 3 replaces the ECC technique with a single disk used for parity. This parity data is contained on a single, dedicated disk (Figure 4.4), allowing the data to be reconstructed in the

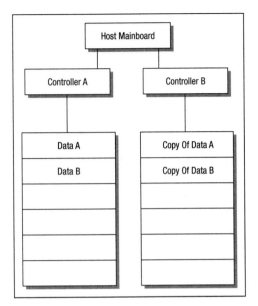

Figure 4.3   RAID 1: disk duplexing.

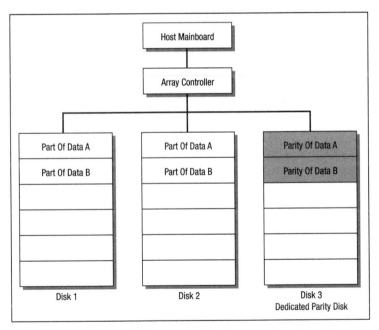

Figure 4.4   RAID 3: disk striping with dedicated parity drive.

event of a single disk failure. The amount of storage space available is the total number of drives less one. Three drives are the minimum required, but efficiency is greatly increased as more drives are added. RAID 3 is also less desirable when compared with RAID 5. With a dedicated parity drive, the I/O performance is greatly reduced because the system can respond to only one I/O request at a time.

RAID 4: Disk Striping With Single-Disk Parity In Blocks

RAID 4 uses the same disk-striping technique as RAID 3. The main difference is the storing of data in large chunks. RAID 3 distributes data at the block level, as opposed to distributing data in bits. When data is changed, the parity drive must process a change for larger parity chunks, causing much slower performance in write operations. RAID 4 is rarely implemented.

RAID 5: Disk Striping With Distributed Parity In Blocks

RAID 5 is the most widely implemented method of RAID. Data is striped across all disks in the array at the block level. The parity data is also distributed across the multiple disks at the block level, allowing the data to be reconstructed in the event of a single disk failure. The data and its parity are always written on different disks, as shown in Figure 4.5. RAID 5 supports a

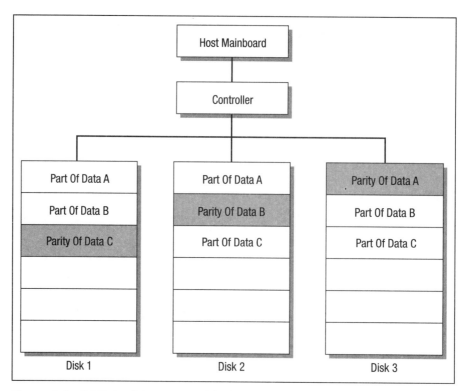

Figure 4.5 RAID 5: disk striping with distributed parity.

minimum of 3 and a maximum of 32 disks. Efficiency is greatly increased because the equivalent of only one drive is lost to parity. Write performance suffers, however, as more disks are added, due to data having to be written across each disk in the array.

Table 4.1 provides a comparison of these RAID methods. Levels 2 and 4 have no practical use and can basically be ignored.

Hardware RAID Vs. Software RAID

One important consideration in the implementation of RAID is the method of design. Although RAID is available as a software implementation in operating systems such as Windows NT, the primary implementation of RAID has been hardware based. The major server makers, such as Compaq and Hewlett-Packard, have specially designed controllers, such as the Smart Array Controller, which handle the array configuration. Adaptec has SCSI controllers, such as the AA130 series controller card, which are designed to handle this.

The main difference to consider lies in the nature of the configuration. Software RAID configurations, such as those provided in Windows NT, are provided by the operating system. The RAID configuration does not exist until the operating system is booted. In a stripe set, the data is spread across the disk volume, which doesn't exist until the system is booted. Simply put, in a software RAID configuration, you cannot boot from a stripe set. What is required to implement software RAID is a separate boot drive on a separate boot partition. In contrast, with a hardware RAID configuration, the disk array is configured and operational before the booting of the operating system and therefore does not require a separate partition. In addition, the system can boot even with a drive missing from the array. The hardware RAID can be a little more costly, because it requires a special controller, but it does provide additional fault-tolerance benefits.

Table 4.1   Standard RAID levels.

RAID Level	Minimum Number Of Drives	Brief Description
RAID 0	2	Disk striping without parity
RAID 1	2	Disk mirroring, disk duplexing
RAID 2	3	Disk striping; dedicated drive using error correction code (ECC)
RAID 3	3	Disk striping at byte level with dedicated parity drive
RAID 4	3	Disk striping at block level with dedicated parity drive
RAID 5	3	Disk striping at block level with distributed parity

Volume Sets

Volume sets are multiple disks or partitions of disks that have been configured to read as one drive. Each member of the volume set is called a *volume*. The maximum number of segments allowed in an NT or NetWare volume set is 32. Hardware-implemented volume sets can hold up to 255 segments. Volume sets have no parity and provide no fault tolerance. Volume disks are often made of leftover partitions on numerous disks that need to be combined to provide enough space to be usable. Volume sets allow you to create the largest continuous space from your hard drives. Refer to Figure 4.6.

Newer RAID Classifications

The RAID Advisory Board, considered the authority on fault tolerance, has issued new classifications that have extended the principles originally expounded in the Berkeley Paper. These newer classifications are listed as follows:

➤ Failure Resistant Disk System (FRDS)

➤ Failure Resistant Disk System Plus (FRDS+)

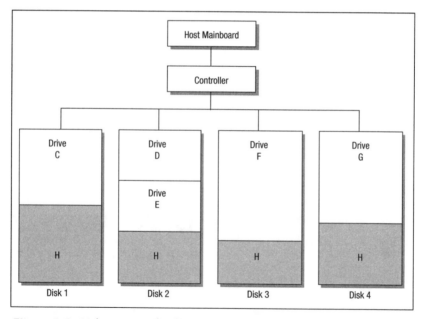

Figure 4.6 Volume set. The free space left on each drive is combined as drive letter H.

➤ Failure Tolerant Disk System (FTDS)

➤ Failure Tolerant Disk System Plus (FTDS+)

➤ Disaster Tolerant Disk System (DTDS)

➤ Disaster Tolerant Disk System Plus (DTDS+)

4

No longer confined to disk failures, these guidelines involve all components of the disk system. Criteria are established for protection against data loss due to such reasons as:

➤ External power failures

➤ Cache component failure

➤ Host I/O bus failure

➤ Device channel failure

➤ Controller failure

Although these criteria are very well designed, the industry has been slow to adopt them. Most industry personnel still refer to RAID levels 0 through 5 when discussing the implementation of fault tolerance.

PRIMARY CABLE TYPES

Several types of cable can be used in networks:

➤ Coaxial cable

➤ Twisted-pair cable (shielded or unshielded)

➤ Fiber-optic cable

Coaxial Cable

Coaxial cable, commonly referred to as "coax," is usually made of a solid copper core, insulated and surrounded by braided metal, and covered with a thick plastic or rubber covering (Figure 4.7). Coax is most widely used for data transmissions. Sometimes it contains an additional foil covering; this kind of coax is known as "dual shielded." Coax can also be found in a quad-shielded

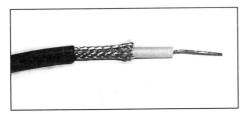

Figure 4.7   Coaxial cable ("coax").

form for areas that might experience high interference. The single-shielded form is light, easy to use, and fairly inexpensive. At one time, it was the most common form of cabling used in new data-network installations. It is also widely used for cable TV transmissions and at telephone-company switching offices.

The core of the cable carries the electronic data signal. The wire mesh provides the grounding. It is important that the two elements be separated by the insulation layer. Should these elements touch, a "short" would result, causing loss of data and ending the transmission of data on your network.

If two wires should get too close, they may produce electronic interference with each other. This interference, known as *crosstalk*, can cause many problems on a network.

One major advantage of coaxial cable is its resistance to crosstalk and other interference. Coax also is more resistant to attenuation than is twisted-pair cable. *Attenuation* is the loss of signal that occurs as data is transmitted across a network. Attenuation is the reason to pay careful attention to distances and to cable-length maximums when planning your installation. Most attenuation is very difficult to detect without a network analyzer, but can result in data being transmitted over and over until the packets are received intact.

Thinnet

Thinnet coaxial is the most commonly used coaxial cable. It is usually about .25 inches or less in diameter and is most often used in Ethernet (10Base2) or ARCnet environments. Each segment branches off from the main line with a T-shaped connector known as a BNC (British Naval Connector) (see Figure 4.8). This connector then branches off to another segment or plugs directly into the network adapter on the back of the CPU (central processing unit). There can be no open links in this architecture. All open ends must be capped with a terminator rated with no less than 50 ohms impedance.

Thinnet has a maximum distance of approximately 185 meters or about 600 feet. After this distance, the signal will start to experience attenuation.

Thinnet cable falls into the RG-58 coaxial family as described in Table 4.2.

Figure 4.8   BNC (British Naval Connector), connecting segments of thinnet coaxial cable.

Table 4.2   Common thinnet coaxial cables.

Cable	Description
RG-58 /U	Solid copper core
RG-58 A/U	Stranded wire core
RG-58 C/U	Military specification of RG-58 A/U
RG-59	Broadband transmission such as cable television
RG-62	ARCnet network specific

4

Thicknet

Thicknet coaxial, most commonly used as the "backbone" of a coaxial network, is usually about .375 inches in diameter. Thicknet is common today in TV networks, and it is not usually installed in newer computer networks due to its difficulty to install as well as its relatively high expense. In Ethernet networks, it's known as 10Base5.

Thicknet can be installed a maximum distance of approximately 500 meters or about 1,640 feet before attenuation begins.

Thinnet Vs. Thicknet

Thinnet is more flexible, less expensive, and easier to install. Thicknet has a thicker core that provides for a longer distance. Often, a network is designed with a thicknet backbone and thinnet branches. Twisted-pair cable is quickly replacing the entire use of coaxial cable in networks.

Twinaxial

Twinaxial cable is another type of coaxial cable. It contains two insulated carrier wires twisted around each other. This type of cable is commonly found in IBM mainframe environments or used with AppleTalk networks.

Twisted-Pair Cable

Twisted-pair cable comes in two modes:

➤ Unshielded twisted-pair (UTP)

➤ Shielded twisted-pair (STP)

The Electronics Industries Association/Telecommunications Industries Association (EIA/TIA) has categorized UTP into five groups known throughout the industry as CAT1 through CAT5 cabling (category numbers are plainly marked, as shown in Figure 4.9):

➤ **Category 1** Voice-grade UTP cable, commonly used in normal telephone transmission. This cable is not suitable for data transmissions, but works well for short-distance voice transmissions.

Figure 4.9 Category numbers are clearly marked on twisted-pair cable.

➤ **Category 2** Data-grade UTP cable or data-grade transmission cable capable of supporting data transmissions up to 4Mbps. Not commonly used anymore.

➤ **Category 3** Data-grade UTP or STP cable or data-grade transmission cable capable of supporting data transmissions up to 10Mbps. This was the most widely used cable a few years back. It was perfect for the standard 10Mbps transmissions on a 10BaseT network.

➤ **Category 4** Data-grade UTP or STP cable or data-grade transmission cable capable of supporting data transmissions up to 16Mbps. This cable was most commonly used in the IBM token ring environment.

➤ **Category 5** Data-grade UTP or STP cable, data-grade transmission cable capable of supporting data transmissions up to 100Mbps (or more). This high-bandwidth transmission is required for Fast Ethernet, the transmission medium of choice today. This cable is the most flexible, inexpensive, and easy to install, and it is the most commonly used cable in new installations.

Standards are currently being discussed for Category 6 cable. At this time, there has not been agreement as to the requirements, and therefore Category 6 cable is not yet available.

Unshielded twisted-pair (UTP) cable, regardless of category, has a maximum distance of 100 meters (approximately 328 feet). Shielded twisted-pair (STP) cable can support longer distances, depending on the type of shielding used. STP is less flexible and therefore a little more difficult to use, but its resistance to crosstalk and electromagnetic interference make it a requirement in certain locations. Also, due to the shielding, extra steps must be taken to ensure that the shielding is properly grounded. Both shielded and unshielded twisted-pair can be used with all 10BaseT or 100BaseT networks. The most common difference is that UTP is used primarily in Ethernet, and STP is used almost exclusively in ARCnet or IBM networks.

Twisted-pair cable consists of four pairs of two wires, as shown in Figure 4.10. The common Ethernet usage requires only two pairs. Twisted-pair connects to an Ethernet port using an RJ-45 connector, which is a little larger than a phone jack plug (see Figure 4.11). Be sure that you know how to identify RJ-45 and BNC connectors; they are used extensively throughout networking.

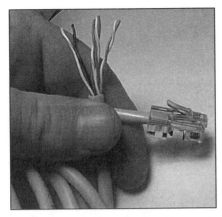

Figure 4.10   Standard twisted-pair cable consists of four pairs of twisted wire.

Figure 4.11   RJ-45 connector used in Ethernet.

Fiber-Optic Cable

Fiber-optic cabling, also known as "fiber optics" or "optical fiber," is finding increasing usage in the computer industry. Fiber-optic cable uses light rather than electricity as its transmission medium. Because there is no interference or crosstalk, fiber optics are available in single and multifiber mode. This means that multiple networks can transmit at the same time through the same cable segment. Fiber-optic cable is also capable of transmission speeds up to 10Gbps and distances as long as 2 kilometers. Fiber-optic cable is also the most secure cable because it is immune to electromagnetic interference (EMI) and eavesdropping. There are, however, limitations imposed when fiber-optic cable is used in an Ethernet network. These limitations are related to the nature of Ethernet and not to the capability of fiber-optic cable.

The core of the fiber-optic cable is made up of one or more plastic or glass fibers. The light signal passes through this core. A plastic "cladding" surrounds the core and is covered with another layer of plastic called "buffer." Usually two of these (one for each direction) are encased in a hard plastic or plenum "jacket" (see Figure 4.12).

With all its advantages, fiber-optic cable should be the cable of choice, except for its biggest drawback: cost. Everything associated with fiber optics—cable,

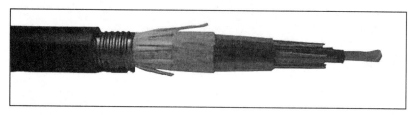

Figure 4.12 Fiber-optic cable.

adapters, hubs, network card, and so on—is much more expensive than for its twisted-pair counterpart.

Figure 4.13 gives you an easy comparison of the main cable types and their maximums, and Table 4.3 provides a comparision of network cables.

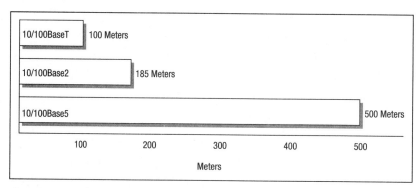

Figure 4.13 Comparison of common cable lengths.

Table 4.3 Comparison of network cables.

Cable Type	Cable Grade	Maximum Length	Maximum Bandwidth	Relative Cost
Thinnet coax (10Base2)	Data-grade	185 meters	10Mbps	Medium
Thicknet coax (10Base5)	Data-grade	500 meters	10Mbps	Medium
Twisted-pair, Category 1	Voice-grade	100 meters	Not networkable	
Twisted-pair, Category 2	Data-grade	100 meters	4Mbps	Very low
Twisted-pair, Category 3 (10BaseT)	Data-grade	100 meters	10Mbps	Very low

(continued)

Table 4.3   Comparison of network cables *(continued)*.

Cable Type	Cable Grade	Maximum Length	Maximum Bandwidth	Relative Cost
Twisted-pair, Category 4 (10BaseT)	Data-grade	100 meters	16Mbps	Very low
Twisted-pair, Category 5 (10BaseT)	Data-grade	100 meters	100Mbps	Very low
Fiber optic (100BaseFX/ 1000BaseFX)	Data-grade	2,000 meters	10,000Mbps	Very high

Cabling And Fire Code Considerations

Polyvinyl chloride (PVC) is the common component in most types of coaxial cable. PVC coaxial is very flexible and easy to install. The problem with this cable lies in the gas it produces when it burns. This poisonous gas is the reason many fire codes now require the use of Plenum cable. This cable is required in building areas where fires would most likely spread gas throughout the structure.

Plenum cable contains special fire-resistant materials that produce a minimum amount of smoke if burned. This smoke is not poisonous as with PVC cable. The drawback to using this cable is that it is more expensive and a lot less flexible, making installation a tougher and costlier process. When planning a major cabling installation, be sure to refer to your local fire and building codes, or consult a licensed contractor.

Fiber Distributed Data Interface (FDDI)

Fiber Distributed Data Interface (FDDI, pronounced fiddy) was first introduced in the mid-1980s. FDDI is a high-speed data-transfer technology designed to extend the capabilities of existing local area networks. Its specifications are similar to token ring, using both the dual-ring topology as well as the token-passing media-access method. FDDI uses monomode (single strand) or multimode (multiple strand) fiber-optic cable, over which passes 100Mbps data transmissions. FDDI provides all the capability of token ring, the speed of Fast Ethernet, and the security, reliability, and speed of fiber-optic cable. It truly is a very beneficial technology that is used primarily for high-speed backbones. Its only drawback is that, like all fiber-optic solutions, it is very expensive to implement.

Copper Distributed Data Interface (CDDI)

Copper Distributed Data Interface (CDDI) is the implementation of the FDDI standard using electrical cable rather than fiber-optic cable. The use of UTP or STP cable brings the distance limitations, security concerns, and other drawbacks of these cabling methods, essentially removing the main benefits of the FDDI technology. Fast Ethernet provides the same data-transmission speeds using Ethernet technology; therefore, CDDI is not widely implemented.

Fiber Channel

Fiber channel is a full gigabit-per-second data-transfer technology. It was designed in 1992 as a joint effort of IBM, Hewlett-Packard, and Sun Microsystems. This technology implements IP and SCSI protocols over copper or fiber-optic cabling for distances up to 10 kilometers. Fiber channel (sometimes spelled fibre to differentiate from fiber optic) is still evolving and may find more implementations as peripherals for gigabit technologies become more affordable.

IEEE STANDARDS FOR ETHERNET TOPOLOGIES

The IEEE (Institute of Electrical and Electronic Engineers) is a professional organization that has defined many standards used in cabling as well as in many other areas of networking. This book, as well as any book on electronics or computer networks, will refer often to these standards. These standards have been accepted throughout the computer industry, so you'll need to be familiar with them.

10BaseT

10BaseT is the IEEE 802.3 specification for running Ethernet at 10Mbps over shielded or unshielded twisted-pair wiring. The maximum length for a 10BaseT segment is 100 meters (328 feet).

10Base2

10Base2 is the IEEE 802.3 specification for running Ethernet at 10Mbps over thinnet coaxial cable. The maximum length for a 10Base2 segment is 185 meters (607 feet).

10Base5

10Base5 is the IEEE 802.3 specification for running Ethernet at 10Mbps over thicknet coaxial cable. The maximum length for a 10Base5 segment is 500 meters (1,640 feet).

100BaseTX

100BaseTX, known as Fast Ethernet, is the IEEE 802.3u specification for running Ethernet at 100Mbps over shielded or unshielded twisted-pair wiring. 100BaseTX uses only two pairs of twisted-pair wires and is still subject to the distance limitation of twisted-pair cabling, 100 meters (328 feet). Category 5 cable is the minimum class of UTP cable that can support 100BaseTX technology. Specifications for Fast Ethernet do not support the use of coaxial cable. With the lower cost today of 100Mbps components, 100BaseTX has begun to replace 10BaseT as the choice for new installations.

100BaseT4

100BaseT4 technology allows the use of Fast Ethernet technology over existing Category 3 and Category 4 wiring. Utilizing all four pairs of wiring and transferring the collision-detection function onto a separate pair makes this possible. This does, however, eliminate the possibility of installing a full duplex transmission mode. This is not the preferred method of a 100BaseT and is used only where Category 3 cable is already in place.

100BaseFX

100BaseFX is the specification for running Fast Ethernet over fiber-optic cable. This technology combines speed with distance and security. In consideration of the expense of fiber-optic architecture, 100BaseFX is currently limited as an infrastructure backbone. The continual decline in the cost of fiber-optic components may someday change that.

100BaseVG-AnyLAN

100BaseVG (Voice Grade)-AnyLAN is the IEEE 802.12 specification that allows data transmissions of 100Mbps over Category 3 (data-grade) cable. This was designed as a joint effort of IBM and Hewlett Packard to allow organizations to utilize their existing network and cabling infrastructure. This specification supports both Ethernet and token ring topologies. Although it is a good choice for utilizing current Category 3 infrastructures, its architecture is strictly proprietary and is provides no benefits over 100BaseTX for new installations.

1000BaseX

1000BaseX, known as gigabit Ethernet, is the IEEE 802.3z specification for data transmissions of 1,000Mbps. Gigabit Ethernet is currently used as a laser-based data-transmission technology and uses fiber-optic cabling to provide major bandwidth between switches and hubs. Specifications are currently under design to utilize gigabit Ethernet technology over currently installed Fast Ethernet infrastructures. Gigabit Ethernet is the newest technology, and, with the insatiable demand for higher bandwidth, it will continue to evolve as a major player.

ADDITIONAL NETWORKING CONSIDERATIONS

Although networks may appear to be just a collection of hardware and cable, there are many more things to consider when planning a network. In Chapter 5, we'll cover more advanced design concepts and additional hardware components that are used in networks. Let's finish this chapter with a look at a few more of the options you will need to think about when designing your basic network.

Full And Half Duplexing

Data traverses the networking wire so fast that it appears to the average user that all computers are sending and receiving data at the same time. Nothing could be further from the truth. Not only can only one computer at a time transmit, but it cannot receive and transmit across the same wire at the same time. If two computers attempt to transmit at the same time on the same wire, the packets will collide and all data will need to be resent. Here is where the concepts of full and half duplexing become important. Assume that you have a computer connected directly to its server. When the computer sends a request to the server, the server responds and data is sent back across that wire. Packets are being sent in both directions but in only one direction at a time. This situation is called *half duplexing*. A good correlation to this is the CB radio. One person calls out and then waits while the second person responds. The second person then waits while the first person responds. Both parties are in communication but only one can transmit at a time. Half duplexing has been the standard for 10Mbps networks for a long time.

Now let's examine full-duplex transmission. This is like the current analog telephone, in that both parties can listen and speak at the same time. With the replacement of coax cable with twisted-pair cable comes the opportunity for more than one data path within a cable and, with it, the technology of full duplexing. Twisted-pair cable has eight wires inside, allowing for multiple data paths, as opposed to coax, which is limited to one core transmission path. Data can now travel in one direction on one pair of wires while data travels in the opposite direction on another pair. Both pairs are inside the same plastic jacket and are connected to the same RJ-45 connectors. Full Duplex Ethernet transforms 10Mbps transmissions into 20Mbps transmissions. At 200Mbps, Full Duplex Fast Ethernet has quickly become a top choice for networks requiring the maximum bandwidth possible between switches and servers.

WANs And LANs

Most of the time, the first grouping of computers you will work with will be located on the physical premises and connected using the same cable infrastructure. This setup is known as a *local area network* (LAN). It might be on different floors or even in different buildings, but it's all in the same local area.

Now let's assume that you have a LAN in Chicago and another LAN in Los Angeles. Your CEO decides to share data between the two. A dedicated phone line is installed, and a router is put on each end. Now, when the people in Los Angeles need a file from a server in Chicago, they pull it down just like it was in the next room. This combination of LANs, or single computers over a wide area using various methods of remote access, is known as a *wide area network* (WAN). WANs can span cities or states and can even cross international borders.

Servers And Clients

Before the evolution of the modern PC (personal computer) network, the data-processing environment was basically split into two groups. In one group, the larger networks provided a central computer, such as an IBM System 38 or an HP Unix. These networks are known as mainframes. All data was centrally stored and processed on this system. The users accessed this system through a number of remote terminals with attached keyboards. The other group consisted of small, standalone PCs, which usually provided a single function, such as word processing. As PC networks began to evolve, many of these standalone PCs were connected together in order to share files and documents. This arrangement eventually evolved into the networking systems that are most common today. This system combines the centralized data storage found in the mainframe systems with the localized processing of the PC.

Centralized functions in a LAN or WAN are processed through a server. This server can be a file server or database server for data storage and retrieval or a special-function server, such as an access server or a print server. The function of the server is to provide services to the workstations known as clients. The actual processing of data is done by the clients. This setup is known as *client/ server processing.*

Smaller networks may still function well as peer-to-peer networks—those in which data is not centrally located. Even those networks will often have the main data located on one or more specific computers. The biggest drawback to a peer-to-peer network is the inability to properly secure the data. It is often scattered all over the network.

Network Adapters

We have already covered the types of cabling and topologies used in a network. Just as important as correct usage of cabling is the interface that connects the cable to the network nodes. *Nodes* are any processing elements that are connected to the network to which data flows. Nodes include computers, servers, printers, hubs, and routers. These interfaces are known as *network adapters* or network interface cards (NICs), because most of them are cards that insert into a slot on the mainboard. Part of the adapter is on the exterior for connection to a cable, whereas the major part is inserted into the computer case and connected to the mainboard of the processing unit.

Baseband And Broadband Signal Transmissions

There are two types of connections used to transmit signals across transmission media: baseband and broadband. A comparison of the two can be seen in Figure 4.14.

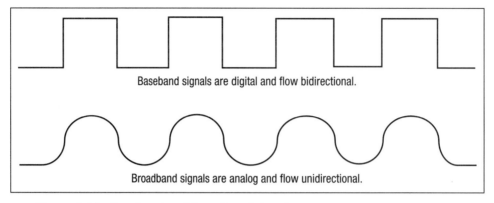

Figure 4.14   Baseband and broadband signals.

Baseband Transmission

A baseband transmission uses digital signaling. Digital transmissions are sent over a single wire in binary code and over a single transmission frequency. This signal uses the entire bandwidth of the cable as a single channel to transmit the signal in the form of electrical pulses or beams of light. The most common example of baseband transmission is the standard Ethernet network.

Broadband Transmission

A broadband transmission uses analog signaling. Analog transmissions are sent in the form of optical or electromagnetic waves over multiple transmission frequencies. Broadband transmission allows for multiple signals to be carried at the same time, as is done with TV signal transmissions, the most common form of broadband transmission. Broadband transmission is unidirectional. In order for it to be used to transmit data back and forth between nodes, it must be split into two channels. Sometimes two cables are used—one to send and one to receive.

Often, it is necessary to translate between analog and digital signals. This requirement is most common when data is sent across public telephone lines. In this instance, a modulator/demodulator (a modem) is used to modulate and demodulate the signal between digital and analog.

Multiplexing

Often a single broadband cable is used to transmit multiple signals using a method of sharing known as *multiplexing*. The unit attached to each end of the cable, which is used to combine and then seperate the different signals, is called a *multiplexer* (or *demultiplexer*). The two main methods of multiplexing are Time Division Multiplexing (TDM) and Frequency Division Multiplexing (FDM), sometimes known as Wavelength Division Multiplexing (WDM). As the names imply, TDM uses time slices to divide the transmission, and FDM divides the channel into separate frequencies. Both methods are very effective and quite widely used.

Gateways

There are many types of hardware and software gateways that are usually identified by their purpose. Although gateways can function at all seven layers of the Open Systems Interconnection (OSI) Reference Model, in this chapter we are more interested with those gateways that relate to the lower layers. Gateways of these types can be used to connect any form of transmission media or method to another, such as a LAN to a WAN, or either one of those to a mainframe. Routers, bridges, switches, and access servers are common pieces of hardware that are sometimes used as gateways. When used as gateways, these devices change the methods of data transmission, but they do not change the nature of the data in any way. These hardware devices and their usage will be discussed in more detail in Chapters 5 and 13.

Software gateways operate at the upper layers of the OSI Reference Model. The majority of them are application-oriented gateways, which are used to make data from one application usable in another. Although a separate computer may be used to translate anything from protocols to application data, this function is still performed as a software-related function and should not be mistaken for a hardware gateway.

Gateways are often necessary when dissimilar applications or network environments are connected. A multihomed computer is used to convert protocols between the IBM Systems Network Architecture (SNA) network and the Windows-based Ethernet network. Protocol conversion needs to be done before these two networks can share common data. Usually a software program, such as Microsoft's SNA server or Novell's Systems Application Architecture (SAA) server, is used.

Another popular protocol gateway is the Simple Mail Transfer Protocol (SMTP) gateway. This gateway uses the services of the TCP/IP protocol at the transport layer for sending and receiving messages. With the integrated nature of the Internet, often mail messages cross multiple dissimilar platforms before reaching their final destinations. Implementation of the SMTP gateway allows for the data conversions that make this possible.

Network administrators must ensure that they are using the correct gateway for the task required. This is where knowledge of the OSI Reference Model becomes important. Simply attaching an IBM AS400 onto an Ethernet hub will not allow you to pull OS/400 data into a Windows spreadsheet. Another major concern with gateways is to be sure that they can handle the amount of data you want to transmit. Bottlenecks often occur at gateways when data transmissions cannot pass through at network speed. Figure 4.15 shows a protocol gateway.

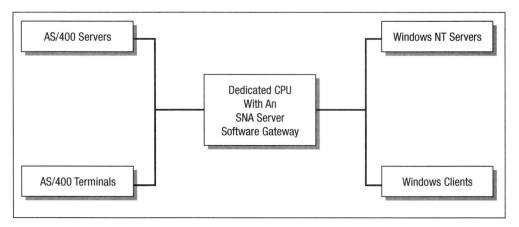

Figure 4.15 An SNA server protocol gateway.

Chapter Summary

The chapter began with an overview of the different types of RAID. Fault tolerance using RAID (Redundant Arrays of Inexpensive Disks) is designed to prepare for disk failure. RAID 0 does not provide parity and will not prevent data loss upon disk failure. RAID 1 is disk mirroring, which maintains an exact duplicate of data on a separate hard drive that can continue operating if the primary disk fails. RAID 5, the most common fault-tolerant solution implemented, is disk striping with parity distributed across all disks. Software RAID is configured by the operating system and therefore cannot contain the operating system. Hardware RAID is independent of the operating system and will boot to an operating system loaded on its volume. The chapter also discussed the different types and characteristics of cabling. Twisted-pair cable (10BaseT) has a maximum distance of 100 meters or about 328 feet. Thinnet coax (10Base2) has a maximum distance of 185 meters or about 600 feet. Thicknet coax (10Base5) has a maximum distance of 500 meters or about 1,640 feet. Category 5 twisted-pair cable is most commonly used to support 100Mbps transmissions. Fiber-optic cable is capable of transmission speeds up to 10Gbps and distances as long as 2 kilometers. Plenum cable is fire resistant and is used when called for in fire and building codes.

Finally, the chapter covered data-transmission methods. Half duplexing sends packets in only one direction at a time, whereas full duplexing can send packets in both directions at the same time. Baseband transmission uses digital signaling and is bidirectional. Broadband transmission is analog and is unidirectional.

REVIEW QUESTIONS

1. What is the minimum number of disks needed to create RAID level 1?
   a. One
   b. Two
   c. Three
   d. Four

2. What is the minimum number of disks needed to create disk striping?
   a. One
   b. Two
   c. Three
   d. Four

3. How is parity maintained in RAID level 5?
   a. On a dedicated disk
   b. There is no parity in RAID 5
   c. In blocks across the array
   d. In bits across the array

4. Which RAID level provides no fault tolerance at all?
   a. RAID 0
   b. RAID 1
   c. RAID 3
   d. RAID 5

5. What is the maximum number of disks allowed in a disk array?
   a. 2
   b. 3
   c. 32
   d. There is no limit

6. What percentage of disk space can be used for data with RAID 1?
   a. 33
   b. 50
   c. 100
   d. It depends on the number of drives used

7. Which method of fault tolerance provides the fastest read/write performance?

   a. Disk duplexing

   b. Disk mirroring

   c. Disk striping with parity

   d. A volume set

8. In a coax cable, how is the data signal carried?

   a. Using pulses of light through the core

   b. Coax is used only for voice-grade signal transmissions

   c. Electronically through the wire mesh

   d. Electronically through the core

9. Which type of network can span cities and even international boundaries?

   a. LAN

   b. WAN

   c. MAN

   d. CAN

10. Attenuation is defined as:

    a. Transmissions from two cables interfering with each other

    b. Loss of data due to a short

    c. Loss of signal strength over distance

    d. Loss of transmission capability due to lack of termination

11. A BNC connector is used with:

    a. Fiber-optic cable

    b. Thinnet coaxial cable

    c. Twisted-pair cable

    d. All of the above

12. Disk mirroring is what RAID level?

    a. RAID 0

    b. RAID 1

    c. RAID 3

    d. RAID 5

4

13. The maximum distance for thinnet is:
    a. 100 meters
    b. 185 meters
    c. 500 meters
    d. 2 kilometers

14. The maximum distance for thicknet is:
    a. 100 meters
    b. 185 meters
    c. 500 meters
    d. 2 kilometers

15. What is the longest cable segment allowed when installing 100BaseTX?
    a. 100 meters
    b. 185 meters
    c. 500 meters
    d. 200 meters

16. The maximum distance for UTP cabling is:
    a. 100 meters
    b. 185 meters
    c. 500 meters
    d. 2 kilometers

17. You have one disk with 600MB, one with 1.1GB, and one with 320MB. What method would allow for the largest continuous space?
    a. Disk striping
    b. Disk mirroring
    c. Disk duplexing
    d. A volume set

18. Which cable standard uses only two pairs of twisted-wire cable in UTP?
    a. 10BaseT
    b. 100BaseTX
    c. 100Base T$
    d. All of the above

19. Which category of network cable is rated for use with 100BaseTX?

    a. Category 5

    b. Category 4

    c. Category 3

    d. Category 2

20. Gigabit Ethernet specifies data transfers at:

    a. 10Mbps

    b. 100Mbps

    c. 1,000Mbps

    d. Gigabit Ethernet can be any speed as long as it's on fiber-optic cable

21. 100BaseVG-AnyLAN was designed to provide for:

    a. Data transmissions of 100Mbps over Category 3 cable

    b. Voice transmissions of 100Mbps over Category 5 cable

    c. Voice transmissions of 100Mbps over fiber-optic cable

    d. Voice transmissions of 100Mbps over any LAN cable

22. 100BaseTX, known as Fast Ethernet, is the IEEE 802.3u specification for running:

    a. Ethernet at 100Mbps over twisted-pair cable only

    b. Ethernet at 100Mbps over coaxial or twisted-pair cable

    c. Ethernet at 100Mbps over twisted-pair cable on segments over 100 meters

    d. 100BaseTX is still experimental and no specifications have been fully defined

23. 10BaseT is the IEEE 802.3 specification for:

    a. 10Mbps Ethernet over twisted-pair cable

    b. 10Mbps Ethernet over thinnet coaxial

    c. 10Mbps Ethernet over thicknet coaxial

    d. 10Mbps Ethernet over any type of cable

24. 10Base2 is the IEEE 802.3 specification for:

    a. 10Mbps Ethernet over twisted-pair cable

    b. 10Mbps Ethernet over thinnet coaxial

    c. 10Mbps Ethernet over thicknet coaxial

    d. 10Mbps Ethernet over any type of cable

25. 10Base5 is the IEEE 802.3 specification for:
    a. 10Mbps Ethernet over twisted-pair cable
    b. 10Mbps Ethernet over thinnet coaxial
    c. 10Mbps Ethernet over thicknet coaxial
    d. 10Mbps Ethernet over any type of cable

26. Which type of cable provides protection from EMI and eavesdropping?
    a. Thicknet coaxial
    b. Fiber optic
    c. Insulated copper core
    d. Shielded twisted-pair

27. Multiplexing is a method used to:
    a. Carry multiple signals across a baseband network
    b. Carry multiple signals across a broadband network
    c. Allow both baseband and broadband transmissions to transmit across the same cable at the same time
    d. Transmit across multiple cables from a hub or concentrator

HANDS-ON PROJECTS

Project 4.1

In this project, you will mirror two hard disks you have installed on Windows NT Server version 4.0. This is a software RAID level 1 configuration. Then, we will break the mirror set we set up.

To begin, you must have installed a hard drive equal or greater in size to the one you wish to mirror with proper SCSI ID settings (if applicable). The drive may also need to be low-level formatted if that was not already done at the factory.

To view the disk configuration information:

1. Make sure you have logged on with an account that has administrator rights.
2. Click on Start | Programs | Administrative Tools | Disk Administrator.
3. Click on the partition containing your C: drive and look at the bottom of the screen to tell which is the primary partition (see Figure 4.16).
4. Click on each partition to find the same information about each one.

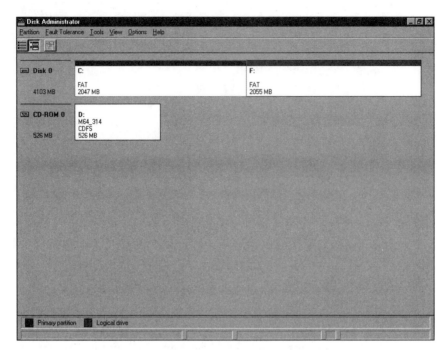

Figure 4.16   Disk Administrator window in Windows NT 4.

To create a mirror set on a Windows NT 4 operating system:

1. In order to create a mirror, Windows NT 4 you should have only one drive currently partitioned and containing data. The second drive should be identified but showing as free space. These will be identified as Disk 0 and Disk 1.

2. Click on the partition of the drive you wish to mirror.

3. Hold down the Ctrl key; then, click on the free space of the second drive so that both the partition and the drive are highlighted.

4. Go to the Fault Tolerance menu and click on Establish Mirror. Now you have established the mirror. The second drive will create an exact duplicate of the first. From this point on, all data written to the drive will be written on both drives.

5. Go to File | Commit Changes and click on Commit Changes Now.

6. You will be prompted to reboot, after which your second drive will begin to copy the data from the initial drive. Click on the second hard drive with your mouse, and the message at the bottom of the screen will read "Mirror Set (INITIALIZING)." Let the computer run until it reads "Mirror Set (HEALTHY)." You will need to refresh if you keep this window open in order to see the change from "INITIALIZING" to "HEALTHY" when the synchronization is complete.

7. Only partitions are mirrored, not drives. If you have more than one partition on your drive, you will need to repeat this procedure for each partition you wish to mirror.

8. Now you should have two mirrored drives with identical sized partitions. The primary drive will have a small asterisk at the top designating it as the primary partition.

9. We must now prepare for potential disk failure by having a boot disk available that points to the bootable partition on the mirrored drive. This information is in the BOOT.INI file that is read upon startup. It usually looks something like this:

```
[boot loader]
timeout=30
default= multi(0)disk(0)rdisk(0)partition(1)\WINNT="Windows NT
Server Ver 4.00"
[Operating Systems]
multi(0)disk(0)rdisk(0)partition(1)\WINNT="Windows NT Server Version
4.00"
multi(0)disk(0)rdisk(0)partition(1)\WINNT="Windows NT Server Version
4.00 [VGA mode]" /basevideo /sos
```

10. To create a fault-tolerant disk, start with a blank (NT) formatted floppy.

11. Enter Windows Explorer and copy from your C: drive the files BOOT.INI, NTLDR, NTDETECT.COM, and NTLDR. (This is for SCSI disks only.)

12. Open the BOOT. INI file on the floppy using Notepad and alter the file as shown:

```
[boot loader]
timeout=30
default= multi(0)disk(0)rdisk(1)partition(1)\WINNT="Windows NT
Server Ver 4.00"
[Operating Systems]
multi(0)disk(0)rdisk(1)partition(1)\WINNT="Windows NT Server Version
4.00"
multi(0)disk(0)rdisk(1)partition(1)\WINNT="Windows NT Server Version
4.00 [VGA mode]" /basevideo /sos
```

This will allow you to boot to the second drive in the set in case this first drive is not bootable. Keep in mind that in the event that either drive fails the remaining drive will continue to operate until the system is powered down.

To break the mirror set:

1. Following the steps outlined above, open the Disk Administrator.

2. Highlight the mirror set that you wish to break.

3. From the Fault Tolerance menu, select Break Mirror.

4. You will be prompted to confirm that you wish to break the selected mirror.

5. Click on Yes.

Although this will not affect the data contained on either partition, it is always advisable to have a good backup before taking any action like this affecting your configuration.

Project 4.2

In this project, you'll learn how to properly install a network adapter in a Windows 95 workstation. You'll learn how to determine what network adapter is installed in your computer, running Windows 95, and how to determine if the adapter is properly installed.

To install a network adapter, you must first physically insert it into a card slot on the motherboard and be sure it is securely fastened. Then, you need to install the software drivers.

To install the software drivers:

1. Click on Start | Settings | Control Panel.

2. Double-click on the Add New Hardware icon and click on Next to start the wizard.

3. Click on Yes to let Windows detect the adapter for you. Windows will locate the new adapter for you. You will be prompted to insert the Windows 95 CD-ROM, and the drivers will be loaded. If Windows cannot find the adapter or the drivers, you may need to click on Have Disk and insert the driver diskette into drive A:.

4. Click on OK to reboot, and then refer to the next part of this project to be sure your adapter is installed and configured properly.

To locate the Network Adapter setup information:

1. Click on Start | Settings | Control Panel.

2. Double-click on the System icon.

3. Click on the Device Manager tab and locate the Network Adapter icon.

4. Double-click on the Network Adapter icon, and then double-click on the network adapter. Read the Device Status box located in the center. It should read, "This device is working properly."

5. Click on the Resources tab, and locate the Interrupt Request (IRQ) setting and the Input/Output (I/O) Range.

6. Look in the Conflicting Device List area and check that it reads "No conflicts".

PHYSICAL LAYER CONNECTIVITY

After Reading This Chapter And Completing The Exercises, You Will Be Able To:

➤ Define and explain the Physical layer of the OSI Reference Model

➤ Identify the various types of network interface cards

➤ Install and configure a network interface card

➤ Troubleshoot common problems with network interface cards

➤ Identify and resolve hardware resource conflicts

➤ Identify the purpose of hubs, MAUs, patch panels, and transceivers

➤ Describe the difference between intelligent and unintelligent hubs

➤ Design a simple network using the Hierarchical Model

The Open Systems Interconnection (OSI) Reference Model, which we explained in Chapter 1, maps the convergence of two separate nodes as they share information from Application layer to Application layer (see Figure 5.1). The nodes might differ in presentation methods or transport protocols, but they eventually funnel down to the one layer where they must converge. Even though the Network layers may communicate to find the correct address, and the Application layers may communicate to transfer the data from the server to the client, their only physical connection occurs at the lowest layer, the Physical layer. This is the layer where the two nodes meet and connect to transfer signals in their most basic form, the bit.

Let's look again at our definition of the Physical layer. The Physical layer defines the mechanical and electrical requirements of the network medium and the interface to that medium. This layer includes:

➤ Hardware

➤ Physical connection and topology

➤ Data transmission

➤ Data receipt

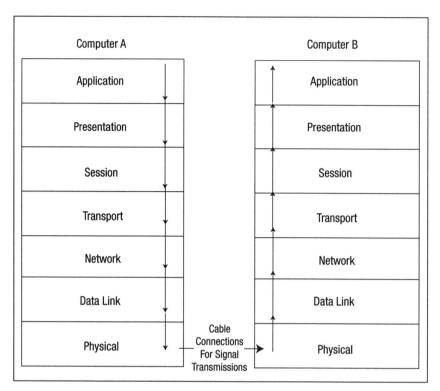

Figure 5.1   Connectivity in the Physical layer of the OSI model.

The Physical layer also defines all the mechanical, electrical, procedural, and functional specifications for the activation, maintenance, and deactivation of the physical link between communicating network systems. The specifications defined in this layer include such characteristics as physical connectors, maximum distances for transmissions, voltage levels and timings, and physical data rates.

In Chapter 4, we looked at the advantages and limitations of different types of cabling connecting the various network devices. We explained the IEEE (Institute of Electrical and Electronics Engineers) standards for Ethernet topologies and some of the basic differences between local area networks (LANs) and wide area networks (WANs). In this chapter, we will look at the physical connectivity of this layer, where the various devices of the network attach to the cables. We will also cover hubs, both managed and unmanaged.

The first item we need to discuss is the network adapter. This device attaches your personal computer to the Physical layer of the network. Network adapters work at the core of the Physical layer. Network adapters also account for a large percentage of the connectivity problems associated with the Physical layer. When network nodes fail to communicate, network administrators will concentrate their efforts on the network adapters. This is the area where the majority of communication problems will need to be resolved.

NETWORK INTERFACE CARDS

Network adapters, also known as *network interface cards (NICs)*, are very important devices in network connectivity. NICs can vary greatly in quality, performance, and cost. It's common for network planners or managers to take great care in understanding all the processing and storage components they choose to include in a computer and then to attach it to the network with the least expensive NIC they can find. A common misconception is that all NICs are pretty much the same. This misconception is a result of the lack of understanding of the NIC's function and of how the quality of the NIC can greatly affect the performance of your network. Let's take a look at the infamous NIC and see how it really works.

The Media Access Control (MAC) Address

The MAC address is unique to each NIC and is known by many names, including the *physical address*, the *node address*, and the *PROM (programmable read-only memory) address*. The MAC address, however, is the only identifier that the node responds to. All other references to this node—IP/IPX addresses, NetBIOS names, etc.—must be resolved to the MAC address to be recognized by the node.

The MAC address is composed of six sets of two-digit numbers. The first three sets identify the manufacturer, and the second three sets are unique to the NIC. Later chapters will discuss this address more; for now, just remember that this is the address that identifies this NIC and the node to which it's attached on the network. The MAC address is also inserted into the header frames and used to identify which packets need to be processed by the attached processing unit. Packets have no way to identify which computer or application they are looking for. Only the MAC address allows the node to process the frame it receives. Now, let's look at the procedure it uses to do this.

The Role Of The NIC In Networking

The Physical layer transmits and receives the raw bitstream over a physical medium, usually cabling. The NIC is the nodes' connection or interface to that physical medium. The NIC converts the parallel data chunk received from the CPU into the serial stream of bits carried across the cabling. In order to do this, the NIC needs to modify the digital signal pattern (1s and 0s) used by the PC to fit the type of cabling to which the NIC is attached. It helps determine which signals will be used to represent the binary 1 and 0, and then divides the bitstream into packets. The NIC then converts the bit values of these packets into electrical signals and transmits the sender's information across the cabling in the appropriate packets. The forms and methods used to do this differ greatly depending on the network architecture being used. For example, an Ethernet interface card uses a much different method than a token-ring adapter uses.

On the receiving end, the NIC constantly monitors all packets transmitted across the network to determine if a particular packet is destined for the node to which the NIC is attached (see Figure 5.2). If the destination address on the incoming packet does not match the node, then the packet is immediately discarded. The packet is chosen for processing only if one of the following conditions is true:

➤ The MAC address listed as the destination in the packet header matches the address of the node to which the NIC is attached.

➤ The header of the packet indicates that this packet is being *broadcast*—that is, it's being sent to all the nodes on the network.

➤ The header of the packet indicates that this packet is being multicast—that is, it's being sent to a select group of nodes on the network, of which this node is a member.

Upon capturing the packet destined for the node, the NIC strips off any overhead or addressing bits from the serial bitstream and converts the remaining

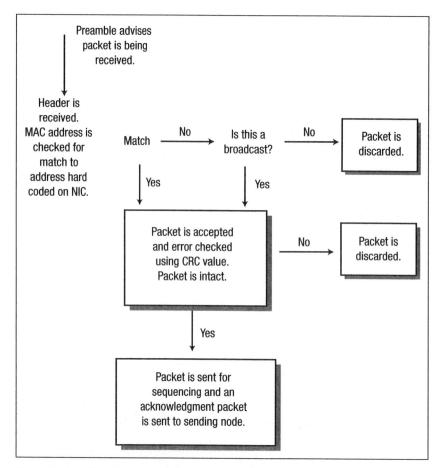

Figure 5.2   Flow of data packet through a receiving NIC.

Preamble (64 bits)	Ethernet Address Of Destination (48 bits)	Ethernet Address Of Sender (48 bits)	Packet Length (16 bits)	'Message Data (368 12K bits)	Error Checking Information (32 bits)

Figure 5.3   Format of a standard Ethernet packet.

bits into a parallel data chunk. This data chunk is then passed on for use in the application. (Figure 5.3 shows the makeup of a sample packet.)

The most common network architecture being installed today is Ethernet. We will concentrate on the Ethernet NIC because it is the one that most network administrators will need to understand. Ethernet NICs can be purchased as 10Mbps (traditional), 100Mbps (for use with Fast Ethernet) or 10/100Mbps (versatile because it can be used on networks where different nodes are transmitting/receiving at different transfer rates). They have traditionally been manufactured using the Industry Standards Architecture (ISA), which supports both the 8- and 16-bit architectures. Currently, there is a major change underway to the PC 98 specification, which requires networking to be done utilizing the Peripheral Component Interconnect (PCI) standard. PCI offers many major advantages over the previous ISA cards and will eventually replace them in PC networking.

Because of its versatility, the most common card is the 10/100Mbps Ethernet card. In networks with 10Mbps hubs in use and a plan to eventually upgrade to 100Mbps architecture, this card can save a lot of time and expense by eliminating the need to change all the NICs in the network.

Industry Standards Architecture (ISA) Network Cards

ISA network cards have served network computing well for many years. They were designed for the earlier generations of microprocessors. The ISA bus standards were developed in the 1980s and evolved with the EISA (Extended Industry Standard Architecture) standard designed at the time for the arrival of the 386 processor. They provided data paths as wide as 16 bits and maximum transfer rates up to 16MB per second. For the DOS applications in use at the time, this rate was adequate. Faster, more demanding applications required more demanding processors, and the ISA standard has now proven to be inadequate to serve today's demanding networking needs. The replacement that has come of age is the Peripheral Component Interconnect (PCI) standard.

Peripheral Component Interconnect (PCI) Network Cards

The PCI standard is an open local-bus specification standard. In 1992, PCI Special Interest Group (PCI SIG) was formed by major industry leaders to maintain the specification as an easy-to-implement, stable technology and to contribute to its establishment as an industrywide standard. PCI cards have quickly begun to replace the older ISA/EISA cards. PCI cards have a different type of mainboard connectivity than ISAs. Let's compare the two cards and see why PCI is clearly the better of the two.

Comparison Of Data Transfer Speeds

Current Pentium processors accept 32-bit data paths and process up to 500MB per second. This amount is far more than the traditional ISA bus could transfer. The new PCI bus is designed to provide throughput rates up to 528MB per second, thereby providing the transfer speed adequate to prevent the bottlenecks that occur when the processor is transmitting data faster than the NIC can handle. In addition, the clockspeeds provided by the PCI card go as high as 66MHz, whereas the ISA/EISA cards are limited to 8.25MHz. It is easy to see why networks using older, less capable ISA/EISA network cards can severely hinder the networking capabilities of their faster Pentium computers. Table 5.1 compares the different architectures.

These numbers show the superior performance of PCI adapters. This alone would be a compelling reason to choose them over the ISA/EISA standard. The development of bus mastering technologies has made the newer network adapters an even better choice.

Bus Mastering

Bus mastering is a bus accessing method in which the NIC takes control of the bus in order to send data in the bus directly to the system memory. This is achieved without help from the CPU, thereby lowering the CPU utilization needed by the card and freeing it for usage by the demanding applications being run. This arrangement improves system performance during large data transfers. Most ISA devices do not support bus mastering and require intervention of the CPU in order to transfer data. In multitasking operating environments, this situation can cause a significant performance loss as the CPU processing power is continually diverted from the number of application tasks being performed in parallel. Bus mastering was originally introduced with the advent of the EISA standard, but the PCI architecture has combined it with the significantly faster transfer rates to greatly improve data transfer performance.

Table 5.1 Comparison of network adapter architectures.

Bus Type	Maximum Width	Maximum Speed	Capacity
ISA	16 bits	8.25MHz	16.5MB/second
EISA	32 bits	8.25MHz	33MB/second
PCI	64 bits	66MHz	528MB/second

Installation And Configuration

In addition to network interface cards, there are many other components that can increase the functionality of a computer system. Modems for remote communication, tape devices for external storage, and sound cards for sound are just a few. These devices have to be physically connected to a signal transfer path by cable attachments or by direct insertion into the mainboard. In addition, the system must be told how and through which transfer paths the signals will be moving. This is done by assigning the resources that the device will use, such as its IRQ (interrupt request) and its I/O and by installing the appropriate driver, which is a small software program that helps the operating system understand the communication needs of the device. Until Plug and Play was developed, it seemed that this would continue to be the most difficult part of any component installation.

Plug And Play

Plug and Play is an independent set of computer-architecture specifications that manufacturers can use to create devices that are capable of being installed without user intervention. Plug and Play requires that both the device and the operating system support this architecture. Most devices sold today—such as NICs, modems, and sound cards—utilize the Plug and Play architecture.

Installing a NIC with Plug and Play enabled is simple. (Refer to the "Hands-On Projects" section at the end of the chapter for a step-by-step guide.) Installing a NIC without Plug and Play enabled is more difficult and can entail utilization of oncard jumpers, manufacturer's configuration software, or both. In any event, drivers for the card must be loaded for the device to function properly.

If your operating system incorrectly identifies your NIC, or if it configures it to conflict with another device, you might have to disable the Plug and Play support feature that comes with your card.

Windows 95 and 98 allow you to disable Plug and Play support for your network interface card using the following steps:

1. Run the setup software that comes with your card and set the card to non-Plug and Play mode.

2. Click on Start | Settings | Control Panel and double-click on the System icon.

3. Click on Device Manager, double-click on Network Adapters, and select your network adapter. Click on Remove.

4. In the Control Panel, double-click on Add New Hardware and manually reinstall the network adapter. If your network card is not on the list, click on Have Disk and insert the manufacturer's disk when prompted.

5. If you continue to have problems, there might be conflicting hardware resources. We will cover some methods of resolving hardware conflicts later in this section, as well as in more detail in Chapter 16.

Jumpered Cards

Many of the older network cards have miniature pins, which require the card to be "jumpered" or connected in order to route the current flow on the card for the resources you are going to use. A tiny connector is placed over two pins to connect the flow.

This method has since been replaced by software configurations (you use a setup program to configure the card) and by assigning the configuration through Plug and Play.

Network Interface Card Drivers

The network interface card needs driver software to tell it how to communicate with the other hardware in the system as well as with the operating system. This software is provided by an interface standard. Available standards include Transport Driver Interface (TDI) standards and Network Driver Interface Specification (NDIS), both of which are used in Windows environments, and the Open Data–Link Interface (ODI), which is heavily used in Novell and AppleTalk networks. These drivers make it possible to bind multiple protocols to the same NIC, so that the card can be used by multiple operating systems. You install the appropriate driver for the operating system under which the NIC will function, and you use the Bindings tab to be sure that the protocol is properly bound to the adapter. Figure 5.4 shows where your Bindings can be verified in a Windows NT environment.

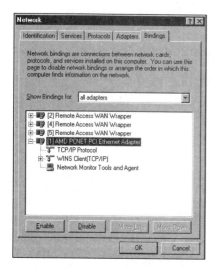

Figure 5.4   Bindings tab in the Windows NT Network Properties window.

Interrupt Requests

The two most important items to configure on your NIC are the interrupt request (IRQ) line and the memory address settings. The IRQ is the direction that the device uses to channel its communications to the CPU. The memory address, or range of addresses, is the location where the device stores its information. It is important to remember that two devices cannot use the same IRQ or the same memory address at the same time. This conflict is the most common cause of network interface card failure. Table 5.2 shows the standard assignments of IRQs in the X86 and Pentium class systems.

There is more to the IRQ than a simple numbering structure. The priority that is assigned to the request for the CPU is based on the IRQ number. The lower the IRQ, the higher the priority of the device assigned to it. This is why certain numbers have already been assigned by the operating system. Efficient operations require that some devices have a higher priority than others.

Newer Pentium computers have two chips with eight IRQs each. The first chip controls the second. The second chip must receive its interrupt signal through IRQ 2 on the first chip. This is channeled through IRQ 9 on the second chip. Never change the association of IRQ 2.

Table 5.2 Standard IRQ settings.

IRQ	Bus Slot Type	Standard Function
0	None	System timer
1	None	Keyboard controller
2	None	Second IRQ controller
3	8-bit	Serial port 2 or 4
4	8-bit	Serial port 1 or 3
5	8-bit	LPT 2, parallel port 2
6	8-bit	Floppy-disk controller
7	8-bit	LPT 1, parallel port 1
8	None	Realtime clock
9	8-bit	Redirected from IRQ 2
10	16-bit	Available
11	16-bit	Available
12	16-bit	PS/2 mouse
13	None	Math coprocessor
14	16-bit	Hard-disk controller
15	16-bit	Available

When adding devices, you should determine which IRQs are available and then assign the next lowest IRQ to the device you are installing. In most systems, the network interface is assigned the IRQs 5, 7, or 10, depending on which ones have already been taken. IRQs are often shared by devices, too. It is important to remember that these devices must not use the same interrupt at the same time. Network adapters are almost always in use, so never assign a network adapter to a shared IRQ.

Memory Addresses

Another resource that often causes hardware conflicts is the memory address. The problem is the same: Two devices cannot share the same memory address. There are two types of configurable memory: the I/O address and the direct memory access (DMA). Both of these are expressed in hexadecimals, and both can be found in Device Manager, as shown in Figure 5.5. (Locating and reconfiguring these is discussed in this chapter's "Hands-On Projects" section. Troubleshooting these conflicts is discussed in Chapter 16.)

Network Card Diagnostics

With the advanced features now available in network interface cards and operating systems comes an additional set of potential problems. Fortunately, the diagnostic tools now available are up to the task. Many NICs now have built-in troubleshooting and diagnostic programs that allow the user to determine the cause of a problem, whether it's related to the configuration of the card or to the malfunctioning of the hardware itself. These programs check communications to the Ethernet controller by sending packets to and receiving packets from the adapter using the DMA channel. These programs can also test the board's interrupt level and transmit and receive packets of various sizes

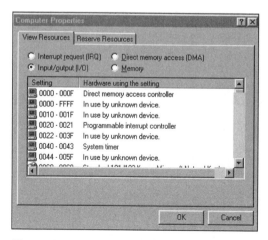

Figure 5.5 IRQ, I/O, and DMA settings in Windows 95 Device Manager.

when loopback testing is in progress. This testing state is called the *loopback mode*.

Loopback testing is a method in which the output and input wires are crossed or shorted in a manner that allows all outgoing data to be routed back into the network interface card. This will determine whether the transceiver on the card is functioning properly. A loopback plug is a device used for loopback testing. Many cards now have internal loopback capabilities that allow the diagnostic testing to be done without the loopback plug.

If you discover that your network card has resource conflicts, you can change the interrupt request (IRQ), the I/O base address, or the memory range. Here is the method used to change these items using Windows 95:

1. Double-click on the System icon in Control Panel.

2. In the System Properties window, click on Device Manager.

3. Double-click on Network Adapters.

4. Double-click on the network card you have installed.

5. Click on the Resources tab. Figure 5.6 shows the Resources tab of a card's Properties window.

6. Highlight the IRQ, I/O range, or memory range that you want to change.

7. Uncheck the Use Automatic Settings checkbox.

8. Click on the Change Settings button.

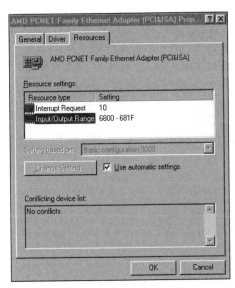

Figure 5.6   Resources tab of the Properties window for a network card in Windows 95.

9. Change the value to a resource not being used; then, click on OK.

10. If no conflicts are listed, you can restart the computer to change the values.

Token Ring Adapters

IBM's token ring adapters have traditionally been ISA or Microchannel devices with a 4 or 16Mbps transfer capability. IBM has since produced a new line of token ring adapters using the PCI bus architecture. These new adapters allow token ring to support the same 32-bit bus mastering capabilities as their Ethernet counterparts. These adapters also include wiring compatibility with standard twisted-pair (STP) and unshielded twisted-pair (UTP) cabling and can support such advanced features as full duplexing, 100Mbps data transfer, and automatic ring speed detection, while maintaining the ring-passing architecture that has made them popular. These adapters also incorporate standard Plug and Play features, such as automatic configuration of I/O, memory, and IRQ.

So far, we have discussed the network interface card, the types of cards available, and factors to look for in choosing the right card. We have discussed installing and configuring a network card, and we have learned how to troubleshoot some of the common configuration conflicts that can occur with these devices. Now, let's take a closer look at the network that these adapters connect us to.

IMPLEMENTATIONS OF THE PHYSICAL LAYER

The previous chapters have defined a number of specifications regarding implementation of the Physical layer. These specifications can be categorized as either LAN or WAN specifications.

LAN Specifications

LAN Physical-layer implementations include, but are not limited to:

➤ **Ethernet** A baseband LAN specification for operating at 10Mbps over coaxial or twisted-pair cable.

➤ **Fast Ethernet** A LAN technology specification for 100Mbps data transfer.

➤ **Token ring** A token-passing LAN topology that transfers data at up to 16Mbps using a star topology.

➤ **Fiber Distributed Data Interface (FDDI)** A dual-ring, token-passing 100Mbps LAN topology using fiber-optic cable.

Ethernet

Ethernet is the most widely implemented LAN specification. Started as a project by the University of Hawaii in the 1960s and further developed through a joint venture of Digital, Intel, and Xerox in the 1970s, Ethernet was defined by the IEEE 802.2 work group. In the early 1980s, the IEEE 802.3 specification was developed with slight variances of this original Ethernet specification and still holds the name. This more common implementation of Ethernet operates at 10Mbps over coaxial cable and uses a method called Carrier Sense Multiple Access/Collision Detection (CSMA/CD) to ensure that only one packet is on the network at any given moment. Although the 802.2 and 802.3 specifications are very similar, they are not identical and special measures must be implemented if you wish to allow both types to coexist on the same network. It is best however, to choose one of the two and standardize it throughout your network.

Fast Ethernet

Fast Ethernet is becoming more popular as its implementation costs continue to decrease. Disagreements as to the exact specifications and the method of network access have allowed this technology to become fragmented into categories, most of which were defined in Chapter 4.

Token Ring

IBM developed token ring in the 1980s, when IBM dominated the computing industry. Token ring is a token-passing LAN defined by IEEE standard 802.5. It operates at either 4 or 16Mbps in a star topology. Token ring is still used extensively, although not as much as in the past. New token-ring technologies capable of 100Mbps data transfers may bring a resurgence in the popularity of token–ring architecture.

Fiber Distributed Data Interface (FDDI)

FDDI is a 100Mbps token-passing, dual-ring LAN using fiber-optic cable. FDDI uses two rings traveling in opposite directions. For more information on FDDI, refer to Chapter 4.

WAN Specifications

WAN Physical-layer implementations include, but are not limited to:

➤ **High Speed Serial Interface (HSSI)** The standard for high-speed serial communications over WAN links.

➤ **X.21bis** The Physical-layer standard used in older X.25 networks.

➤ **Switched Multimegabit Data Service (SMDS)** A high-speed broadband packet-switching service that sends data at up to 44Mbps over public lines, much faster than the X.25 networks.

High Speed Serial Interface (HSSI)

High Speed Serial Interface (HSSI) is considered the network standard for high-speed serial communications over WAN links. HSSI includes frame relay,

T1, T3, E1, and ISDN lines. It has been continuously reviewed for standardization and acceptance, but because no standards have been developed or agreed upon, the term "HSSI" generally applies to all high-speed serial links. The use of high-speed serial data transfer is becoming more common as the methods and costs continue to become more favorable. Branch offices that formerly communicated by fax, phone, or mail are finding that direct links of computer sites is much more efficient and less time consuming than previous methods. Video conferencing to remote locations—previously unavailable due to high bandwidth requirements—is being implemented in greater degrees. The HSSI technology will continue to evolve as the need for more immediate and more global communication methods are required by the demanding needs of business. This area will also provide computer professionals with great opportunities for job growth and advancement because technicians who can understand and implement these high-speed connectivity solutions will be in demand.

X.21bis

X.21bis supports synchronous, full-duplex, point-to-point transmissions with speeds up to 19.2Kbps. At one time, X.21bis was considered a high-speed data-transmission method. The Physical-layer implementation used in X.25 has since proven to be extremely slow and outdated. Most companies that have used X.21bis for X.25 data transmissions have since upgraded to faster technologies.

Switched Multimegabit Data Service (SMDS)

Switched Multimegabit Data Service (SMDS) is the Physical-layer implementation for data transmission over public lines at speeds between 1.544Mbps (T1) and 44.736Mbps. Defined by IEEE 802.6, this is an extremely fast and efficient method of data transfer. Its implementation provides large bandwidth over digital service lines using time division multiplexing for signal transmission. Digital service lines or channels are classified in ranges from DS0 to DS4. Digital service lines are still very expensive, so SMDS isn't used in a large segment of the general networking community. As computer technology continues to decrease in price, so will the cost of digital services. Then, the use of this technology and these DS channels will become more attractive to the bandwidth-hungry IT community.

NETWORK CONNECTIVITY COMPONENTS

If a network consists of just two computers, a single crossover cable can be used to connect the two. Most networks, however, consist of multiple computers, printers and servers, all of which need to be connected to each other or to a central device through which all their signals can pass. The most common and least expensive device for this purpose is known as a hub.

Hubs And Their Role In The LAN

A *hub*, also known as a *concentrator* or a *multiport repeater*, is the central intersection of two or more cable connections. Hubs physically connect all the wires of the network in order to connect the components. Hubs can be very simplistic devices for simple concentration functionality, or they can become a center point for the management and troubleshooting of your network traffic.

Unintellegent Hubs

Most hubs are considered *unintelligent* or *passive* hubs due to their inability to learn, process, or utilize any of the information that passes through them. Their sole function is to distribute the signals received through a connected port to the other ports on the hub. These hubs are strictly Physical-layer devices that do not consider the address of the node or segment where the signal originated from or the address of the node for which it is intended. Some multiport devices provide the same concentrator functions as hubs, but also route or filter packets to ports and segments based on the addresses of the sending or destination nodes. These are known as switches and routers. Because these processes are handled at the Data Link and Network layers, they will be covered in detail in Chapters 6 and 7. Other types of hubs—called *active hubs*—can boost the strength of the signal before they pass it on through the other ports.

Often, these hubs are stackable, which means that they can be added to each other to increase the size of the network. They normally come with an even number of ports (4, 8, 12, 16, or 24). You can use stackable hubs in larger networks by attaching other hubs at the end of the cable to boost the signal and send it on through all their ports. Because they provide no filtering, all hubs linked to the central hub are part of the same collision domain, which we have already learned can accommodate only one packet at a time.

If a network node is past the allowable distance for the length of the cable being used, an active hub can be used to provide additional signal strength and to prevent attenuation or lost packets. Hubs that are used solely for boosting the signal to extend the maximum cabling distance are known as *repeaters*. For example, if you had a computer 150 meters from your closest hub, you could not extend CAT5 cable from the hub to the computer. This distance would exceed the 100-meter maximum allowed for CAT5 cable. You would then have attenuation, resulting in CRC (Cyclical Redundancy Check) errors, and many packets would need to be retransmitted. The easy solution would be to insert a repeater at the midpoint; this repeater would boost the signal strength and allow the signal to go another 100 meters from the location of the repeater.

Hubs most often come in 10Mbps or 100Mbps combinations. Many now also come with autosensing features that allow 10Mbps or 100Mbps transfers to take place, depending on the capability of the network interface in use by the node.

If the hub doesn't have this autosensing feature, a workstation will not be able to communicate with another using a different transfer mode. For example, connecting a computer with a 10Mbps card to a hub that is strictly 100Mbps will result in an inability to transfer packets of any kind. This also applies to other network components, such as routers or bridges, with 10Mbps ports. These devices will be unable to function on a 100Mbps network. A lot of time is often lost running NIC diagnostics, checking cable connections, and performing other troubleshooting techniques, only to find that all the hardware works correctly, but just can't work on the same network. Unless your network cards and components have autosensing features, 10Mbps and 100Mbps components cannot operate on the same network.

Hubs can also be very useful for interchanging media types, such as fiber or coax. With the appropriate adapters, it is not uncommon to have a fiber-optic cable attached to a hub with 24 or more ports. Attached to these ports will be 24 workstations connected with CAT5 cable running 10Mbps. The fiber-optic cable is connected hundreds of yards away to another hub or to switches operating at the core of the network.

Intelligent Hubs

Intelligent hubs, also known as *managed hubs*, take advantage of their location in the network to provide the administrator with a variety of tools that can be used to monitor the performance of the network. These tools can range from simple to those that are designed to implement high-end monitoring technologies. Different vendors implement a variety of monitoring techniques. Many have evolved into well-defined standards. The most efficient and most widely recognized of these techniques used on managed hubs is known as RMON.

RMON is the *remote monitoring* standard that provides network administrators with comprehensive network-fault diagnosis and performance information. RMON was established in 1992 by RFC 1271 for use in Ethernet networks. This standard defines nine groups of monitoring elements, each providing specific sets of data to meet common network-monitoring requirements. Most implementations of RMON do not use all nine groups, but some go as far as supporting detailed packet analysis and network accounting functions. They cause the minimum amount of network disruption possible and can be a very valuable tool to administrators trained sufficiently to implement and understand them.

Some managed hubs have a more limited monitoring role, yet they provide administrators with some idea of network performance. These hubs use SNMP (Simple Network Management Protocol) to collect and analyze data about the network. SNMP uses this data to establish a baseline for normal network operation. Network traffic is continuously compared to this baseline to determine if any abnormalities occur. The administrator sets the level of deviation considered allowable, and then special detectors known as *agents* monitor the network and report any aberrations that occur. When such an event occurs, an alarm known as an *SNMP trap* is sent out, notifying the administrator that something in network activity differs from the established norm.

Hubs have always provided the center for the concentration of network connections. The continuously changing needs of the network have evolved to make this position as "network central" usable for a variety of other network functions. The hub has also evolved from its role as the point where computers are connected and bandwidth is shared. Devices that no longer share the same bandwidth in the same collision domain, but provide dedicated bandwidth to each port, are quickly replacing the hub. The use of switches that can provide full bandwidth on each port have begun to make the network wiring closets sophisticated centers of network monitoring and management. We will learn more about these devices when we learn about the Data Link and Network layers in Chapters 6 and 7.

Multistation Access Unit

A Multistation Access Unit (MAU, or sometimes MSAU) is a hub that is used in an IBM token-ring network. Although MAUs are very similar in appearance to hubs, they have a different topology. The MAU organizes the connected nodes into an internal ring and uses the RI (ring in) and RO (ring out) connector to expand to other MAUs on the network. In addition to passing the packets around the ring, the MAU serves as a repeater to boost the signal as it passes it on. When shielded IBM cables are used, up to 30 MAUs can be connected, supporting up to 260 nodes.

MAUs, like their Ethernet counterparts, are now being made with intelligent network-monitoring capabilities. They even have the capability to manage and route between multiple architectures.

Transceivers

A *transceiver* is a coined word that combines "transmitter" and "receiver." In networking, a transceiver is a device that can both transmit and receive a signal. The term "transceiver" also refers to fiber-optic networks and is similar in nature to a repeater. The IEEE 802.3 specification standards refer to a transceiver as a MAU or Media Access Unit (not to be confused with the IBM MAU). In Ethernet networks, the transceiver is a chip built onto the network interface card. It is the chip that both sends and receives the signal. In wireless networks, the transceiver is the access point where the signal is broadcast or received and forwarded into the network. Whatever the architecture, the main definition of a transceiver remains the same: It transmits and receives a signal.

Patch Panels

A *patch panel* is a place where the wiring used in twisted-pair networks converges. The internal wiring in these cables connects to the back of this panel. An additional cable, called a *patch cable*, connects the link to the workstation outlet to the hub, switch, or other connectivity device it needs to link to. The main benefit of a patch panel is that it provides a central location for control of the links to the network. A patch panel also requires a minimum amount of effort to change the destinations of the links. If the cable coming out of the wall were wired directly into a hub or concentrator, imagine the trouble you would encounter should you decide to move workstations to another hub or to troubleshoot a specific link. With a patch panel, you have only to change the connection of the patch cable to move the connection of the corresponding workstation.

Patch panels have no intelligent or processing capabilities. Patch panels require no power and have no functions of their own except to gather and hold the connected wires. Sometimes patch panels are mounted in rows on racks, or they may be mounted or embedded in a wall. It is best to always maintain access to the rear of a patch panel in order to provide standard troubleshooting and maintenance. A smart administrator will also have the outlets numbered and a chart showing where each link connects.

THE HIERARCHICAL MODEL OF NETWORK DESIGN

The functions of hubs, routers, and bridges can easily get clouded as networks begin to grow. Without structure, networks become a stream of continuous bottlenecks and openings, much like a four-lane highway that turns into a single-lane residential street and then back into a highway. It is important to design a network in which the appropriate uses of the network devices provide for the maximum data flow. The Hierarchical Model describes a network as logical components where the functions can be defined. This model helps the administrator know where to place the network components for the most efficiency.

The Hierarchical Model has three basic layers—the Core layer, the Distribution layer, and the Access layer—each of which has a function. Figure 5.7 shows the layers of the hierarchical model and their relationships. The functions described in this model are designed to provide the maximum bandwidth while filtering data to the end user in the most efficient manner. Access lists and filters are placed at the levels that will provide the least amount of disruption to the data flow. Routers, with access lists and filters, require that packets be examined and processed before passing them to the next node. The fewer the packets subjected to this examination, the faster the flow of data will be.

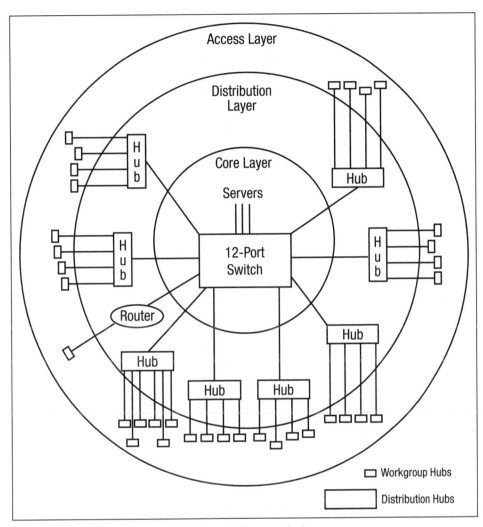

Figure 5.7   The Hierarchical Model of network design.

For example: Suppose that you need to provide a filter for a group of five salespeople on one hub so that they cannot access the accounting department servers. These servers are currently being accessed by 600 users across the entire domain. It would be much more efficient for a router to examine each packet going from the hub upon which the five users are located than it would be to examine every packet going into the router to the accounting department, where packets from hundreds of users are passing. The number of packets needing to be examined would be much smaller and therefore would have much less effect on the response times of the network.

Let's look at the three layers, their functions, and their most appropriate uses.

The Core Layer

The Core layer is the backbone of the network. It should be designed for high-speed packet switching. This layer should provide fault tolerance and redundancy because any disruption at this level would affect a large number of users. There should be no manipulation of packets at this level (as is done by access lists or filtering). Access lists are implemented on a router to control whether traffic is blocked or forwarded from the router's interface. If large numbers of packets must be compared against the access lists before they are allowed to continue on the network, slowdowns or bottlenecks will result. The main purpose of the Core layer is to get the data to the Distribution layer at the fastest possible speed. High-end, high-speed switches and routers are used at this level to increase the speed and bandwidth of the network.

In a centralized processing environment, the servers would be attached at this level. The higher the bandwidth the better, so use of Fast Ethernet technology and full duplexing is recommended. In larger networks, even Gigabit Ethernet with fiber-optic cable might be used. Dual-network interface adapters in each server—connected to two different hubs or switches for redundancy—would provide additional fault tolerance. No devices that would restrict flow should be between the servers and these hubs or switches. Out of these ports would flow data to other network distribution devices. No end users should be connected at this level. This level is designed strictly to provide high-bandwidth data flow between the data servers and the Distribution layer.

The Distribution Layer

The Distribution layer functions as the separation point between the Core layer and the Access layer of the network. The Distribution layer devices implement security access policies for the distribution of packets to groups within the network. These policies can be in the form of access lists on routers, or they can be done through the use of domain or workgroup rights and permissions maintained by the logon servers. Virtual LANs (VLANs) become defined at this level, and static or dynamic routing protocols become separated. This level takes the high-speed data transfer from the Core layer and begins to define its access from the network. Router, switches, and bridges are often used at this level to provide access to hubs and switches where multiple workstations connect.

The Access Layer

The Access layer is where the workstation connects to the network. It is at the Access layer where the hubs reside and where the workgroups access the network through microsegmentation. *Microsegmentation* is the process of using switches to divide the network into numerous collision domains, thereby providing higher bandwidth to the member workgroups. The Access layer provides the access for remote sites using wide area technologies, such as ISDN, leased lines, or Frame Relay.

Routers, bridges, switches, and hubs are all used extensively at this level to segment the network and to further implement security and access policies.

Network Redundancy For Fault Tolerance

Networks using the Hierarchical Model need only one path from any workstation to the data source. This path may be routed through a number of networking devices that direct the flow of data traffic. As with all network components, these devices are subject to failure. Failure of devices at the Access layer will often affect a small group of users. Failure of the same devices at the Core layer can affect a large part of the network, or even the entire network.

Network redundancy policies call for the duplication of paths, particularly at the Core layer. With duplicate data paths in place, the network can continue to function should a device fail. This is like having two freeways that lead from work to home. If one is blocked due to an accident, then you can take the other freeway to get home. When the network is properly designed, this redundancy can also decrease the utilization on each path by distributing the packets among both paths, much like traffic is reduced when half the autos use one freeway while the rest use the other. Figure 5.8 shows the Hierarchical Model with redundancy implemented.

In switched networks, switches often have redundant links to each other. This redundancy can cause circular data movements, or loops, in which data can

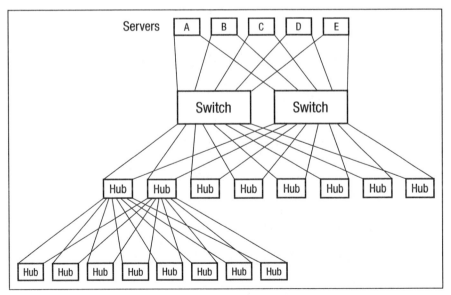

Figure 5.8 The Hierarchical Model with redundant links for fault tolerance.

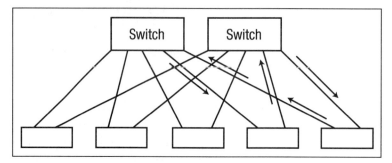

Figure 5.9   Physical Data Link loop.

continue along in a circular path between two or more devices until its assigned "time to live" expires (see Figure 5.9) and the packet ceases to exist. To prevent this situation, the IEEE designed specification 802.1d, the spanning tree protocol.

Virtual Local Area Networks (VLANs)

With the advances made in switching technologies came newer ideas for how to use them. One of the best and most implemented ideas for the use of switches is the virtual local area network, or VLAN for short. VLANs can become complex in their implementation and a real nightmare in their administration. They have found their way into the more advanced network designs and will probably continue to evolve as a major instrument in network design technology.

A VLAN, in its simplest form, is a logical grouping of network nodes, usually defined by the ports on a common switch. The member nodes can be grouped in any manner the designer wishes, although the purpose is usually to define them by their common purpose. Although the nodes may be members of the same network and share a common infrastructure, they are virtually in different groups. You may have four people in a room of an office with all four on different virtual networks, unable to access each other's data. What would be the benefit of this setup?

Let's suppose that your company occupies a 20-story building. Your company's management has decided that each floor should handle the company's operations in a different country. Each floor should have its own sales staff, personnel manager, and accounting department. On the main floor is the server farm, where all the data is kept on file servers. (This data includes accounting, management information, sales information, and so on.) The VLAN would be implemented at the core switch—a 240-port Catalyst, for example. Here, all the accounting people would be on one LAN, personnel managers on a different LAN, and the sales staff on another. All employees would go through the same switch to access the others within their LAN and to access their respective

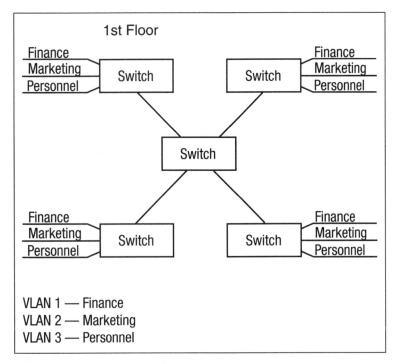

Figure 5.10   A VLAN configuration.

servers. They would not be able to access the VLAN or servers of the other departments. Figure 5.10 illustrates a VLAN configuration.

The security benefits of this arrangement are obvious. Users could not access areas not on their VLAN, even with the passwords of others. Broadcasts would also be unable to pass over the VLAN boundaries, so this would cut down on network congestion. In general, there would be separate networks with their own collision domains and their own security zones. This sounds good. How can this create a problem?

Let's suppose that the department on the sixth floor purchases a color laser printer. Not everyone will be able to use it. You might see how this could become a problem. So, although there are benefits in setting up VLANs, they must be done in a well-designed manner.

CHAPTER SUMMARY

The *network interface card (NIC)* is a device that attaches the computer to the network cable. The NIC converts the parallel data chunk into a serial stream of bits to carry across the wire. The MAC address of the destination computer is in the header of the packets (also called *frames*) sent across the wire. A packet sent to all computers on the network is called a *broadcast*. A packet sent to a group of computers on the network is called a *multicast*.

Network interface cards available for use in PCs can be ISA (16 bit), EISA (32 bit), or PCI (64 bit). Bus mastering support available in EISA or PCI cards can provide significant improvement in speed and performance.

Plug and Play architecture is designed to provide automatic configuration of computer components. Sometimes, however, Plug and Play might need to be disabled to prevent conflicts. The NDIS and ODI are standards for a single NIC to be used by multiple operating systems.

The three configurations that must be made when installing a NIC are the IRQ, the I/O address, and the DMA. IRQ numbers represent the priority of the link to the CPU. The lower the number, the higher the priority of the interrupt. Two devices cannot transmit on the same IRQ at the same time.

Hubs share their bandwidth between ports; switches provide full bandwidth on each port. Active hubs boost the strength of the signal as it passes through the hub, but passive hubs do not. Intelligent or managed hubs have network monitoring and diagnostic capabilities. In token-ring environments, Multistation Access Units are hubs where workstation cables converge.

The Hierarchical Model for designing networks identifies three layers: the Core layer, the Distribution layer, and the Access layer. Fault Tolerance in network design means duplicating the routes that packets use to traverse the network.

REVIEW QUESTIONS

1. Which of the following would not be considered a LAN specification?
    a. Ethernet
    b. Fast Ethernet
    c. Fiber Distributed Data Interface
    d. High Speed Serial Interface

2. PCI network interface adapters are designed to accommodate what architecture?
    a. 8 bit
    b. 16 bit
    c. 32 bit
    d. 64 bit

3. The NDIS and ODI standards are designed to provide what benefit to network adapters?

    a. They can be configured without user intervention.

    b. A single card can be used by multiple protocols.

    c. They can send parallel chunks of data across the wire.

    d. They can automatically detect and reconfigure IRQ conflicts.

4. What is the relevance of the IRQ number?

    a. The higher the number, the more priority the request gets.

    b. The lower the number, the more priority the request gets.

    c. There is no relevance; it's just the number of the path to the CPU.

    d. It determines which slots the cards are placed in.

5. Which is *not* a layer of the Hierarchical Model for designing networks?

    a. Access layer

    b. Core layer

    c. Physical layer

    d. Distribution layer

6. Which of the following would not be considered a WAN specification?

    a. X.21bis

    b. Switched Multimegabit Data Service

    c. Token ring

    d. High Speed Serial Interface

7. An active hub provides what function that a passive hub does not?

    a. It boosts the signal before sending it out.

    b. It can monitor all traffic on the network.

    c. It routes packets based on IP addresses.

    d. It has special functions that alert administrators when problems arise.

8. Which parameters need to be configured when you install a network interface card? [Choose the three best answers]

    a. IRQ

    b. I/O address

    c. DMA

    d. Com Port

5

9. Which of the following is designed to assist in monitoring network activities?

    a. A passive hub

    b. An intelligent hub

    c. A stackable hub

    d. A passive hub

10. The cable used between the patch panel and the hub is called a:

    a. SCSI cable

    b. A bidirectional cable

    c. A patch cable

    d. A hub cable

11. Which network device can be used to connect multiple devices providing full bandwidth on each port?

    a. Hub

    b. MAU

    c. Switch

    d. Transceiver

12. When an SNMP agent determines that a baseline has been exceeded, what does it do?

    a. It illuminates an LED on the hub.

    b. It sends out an SNMP trap.

    c. It begins a shutdown of the active hub.

    d. It records the situation in the SNMP log.

13. You intend to create an Ethernet 10BaseT network of three computers. In addition to network cards and network cable, what other item do you need?

    a. Router

    b. MAU

    c. Hub

    d. Bridge

14. The digital bitstream consists of a series of 1 and 0 values known as:

    a. Primary

    b. Secondary

    c. Binary

    d. MACs

15. The ISA NIC on a Windows 95 workstation is not functioning. Where would you look to determine whether there are any resource conflicts?

    a. Network diagnostics

    b. Control Panel | System | Device Manager

    c. Control Panel | Ports | Settings

    d. Control Panel | Network | Adapters

16. Upon capturing the packet destined for the node, the serial bitstream is converted into what form?

    a. Serial data chunks

    b. Parallel data chunks

    c. Parallel bitstreams

    d. None of the above

17. What is the most common network architecture being installed today?

    a. Token ring

    b. Ethernet

    c. ARCnet

    d. None of the above

18. Which device works at the Physical layer of the OSI model?

    a. Router

    b. Switch

    c. Hub

    d. Bridge

19. Network redundancy policies for fault tolerance require which of the following?

    a. Using all switches or all hubs but never mixing the two.

    b. Creating duplicate paths for data transfers.

    c. Duplicating all routed paths with bridges in case of router failure.

    d. Using switches to create loops for circular data movements in large networks.

20. RFC 1271 established a remote monitoring standard for networks. This standard is known as:

    a. HSSI

    b. RayMond

    c. X.25

    d. RMON

21. IRQ 2 on the first chip in a Pentium set is channeled to which IRQ on the second chip?

    a. 7

    b. 9

    c. 11

    d. 15

22. A repeater should be used when a CAT5 cable length exceeds how many meters?

    a. 10 meters

    b. 100 meters

    c. 1,000 meters

    d. None of the above

23. The Physical layer includes which of the following?

    a. Data transmission

    b. Hardware

    c. Physical connection and topology

    d. All of the above

24. A High Speed Serial Interface includes which of the following:

    a. T1 lines

    b. Frame Relay

    c. ISDN

    d. All of the above

25. At which layer of the Hierarchical Model should a router with access list filters not be placed?

    a. Core layer

    b. Distribution layer

    c. Access layer

    d. Physical layer

HANDS-ON PROJECTS

Project 5.1

In this project, we will redesign a network of about 400 users. We'll use the Hierarchical Model to maximize the amount of bandwidth we can provide to end users and to increase the speed of data transfers.

Suppose that Apex Fabrics has hired you as administrator for a Windows NT 4 network. The company is using TCP/IP as its main protocol. For the past two years, this network has been in a state of continuous expansion. Your predecessor continued to add components as the workstations were added to the network. There are currently about 400 workstations connected to the network. You have taken time to diagram the network, and the configuration you have is shown in Figure 5.11. The network has extremely poor performance in a majority of areas. During peak times of the day, many workgroups come to a virtual halt.

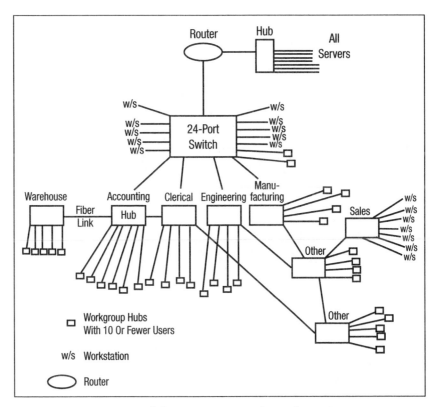

Figure 5.11 Diagram of the current network configuration.

Your manager has provided this additional information:

➤ All workstations are within the 100-meter limit, except for the warehouse, which has a fiber-optic link installed to it.

➤ The CEO is concerned that the sales staff may want information from the engineering or accounting servers. Access lists have been configured on the router to restrict them from accessing these two servers.

➤ All the unused ports in the switch were filled with miscellaneous workstations that were added later.

➤ The switch has 100Mbps capability on all ports as well as a fiber-optic link available.

➤ Management does not wish to spend any more money at this time.

To redesign this network, we start at the Core layer:

1. The Core layer is designed for speed. This layer is where the servers are connected directly to the switch. Servers should never have between them any routers using access lists to restrict flow. All links from this layer should be connected to hubs, to other switches, or to routers to WANs or stub networks. Any backbone links to remote areas, such as the fiber-optic link, should be off this layer. Begin your redesign of the network by drawing the Core layer. Your drawing should look similar to Figure 5.12.

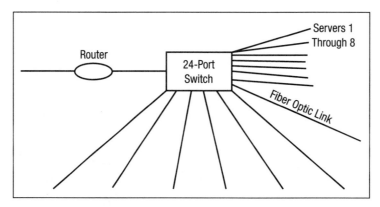

Figure 5.12   The Core layer of the Apex Fabrics network.

2. To extend the Core layer, add links to the Distribution layer to your drawing. This layer consists of hubs, switches, or routers that are connected directly to the ports on the hub. All hub links to workgroup hubs should be as evenly distributed as possible. Routers with access lists can be added at this level to implement security policies. Your drawing should resemble Figure 5.13.

3. Next, add links to the Access layer. The Access layer consists of workgroup hubs and is the layer where all workstations are connected to the network. There should be no crosslinks of hubs connected to other Distribution-layer hubs. Additional hubs branching off access layer hubs in a daisy-chain fashion can become a problem and should be avoided if possible. Instead, with additional ports still available on the distribution hubs, any additional workgroup hubs should be connected to these ports and not off a port on the workgroup hub. Your final drawing should look similar to Figure 5.14.

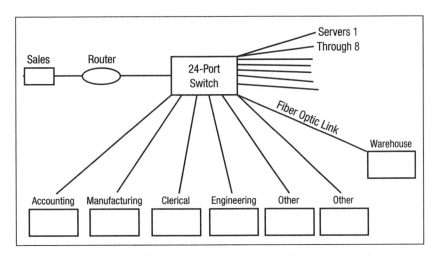

Figure 5.13 The Distribution layer of the Apex Fabrics network.

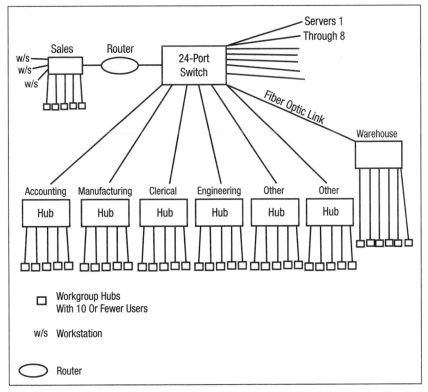

Figure 5.14 The Access layer of the Apex Fabrics network.

Project 5.2

In this project, we will install a 3Com network interface adapter using Plug and Play in Windows 95. We will then change the setting for the IRQ and the I/O address to resolve a conflict.

To install a network adapter:

1. With the power off, insert the card into the slot on the mainboard, taking proper care to ensure proper grounding.

2. Replace the cover and reattach the power cable.

3. Turn the computer on.

4. When Windows starts, it will notify you that new hardware has been found and will prompt you to insert the driver disk into drive A:.

5. Insert your 3Com driver disk into drive A: and press Enter.

6. Your computer will load the driver and will advise you to reboot.

7. After you reboot, go to Settings | Control Panel | System | Device Manager and double-click on Network Adapter.

8. Double-click on the 3Com adapter to open the Properties window.

9. Click on the Resources tab.

10. Assume that, under Conflicting Device List, the Resources tab says:
    Interrupt Request 05 used by:
    Creative AWE64 16-bit Audio (SB16 compatible)

To change the IRQ setting:

1. Uncheck the Use Automatic Settings checkbox.

2. Double-click on Interrupt Request to open the Edit Interrupt Request window.

3. Click on the down arrow next to "value" to find the lowest value that reads No Devices Are Conflicting".

4. Click on OK to return to the Resources tab. Verify that No Conflicts is displayed under the Conflicting Devices list.

5. Click on OK until all Properties windows are closed; then, restart your computer.

The procedure is the same to change the I/O address settings.

THE DATA LINK LAYER

This chapter discusses the Data Link layer of the Open Systems Interconnection (OSI) model and the major events that occur—and don't occur—at this layer. In addition, as you read this chapter, you will see that the Data Link layer and other layers of the OSI model have different, but complementary, purposes. Moreover, you will gain a better understanding of hosts and how they interact on the network, including the method by which each host—among the millions in existence today—uniquely identifies itself.

We will also discuss the major network component that operates at the Data Link layer: the bridge. You will find out what the bridge does, when you would use one, what its advantages and disadvantages are, and where its functionality might be lacking.

We will also explain why the standards of the Institute of Electrical and Electronics Engineers (IEEE) are so important in networking. Although the IEEE has established many standards, we will focus on three: those that apply to Ethernet, token ring, and Logical Link Control (LLC).

Next, we will examine data frames. As an example of how frames can differ, we will look closely at Ethernet frames and at how the various IEEE standards alter their structures.

Finally, we will discuss two important functions that occur at the Data Link layer: transmission synchronization and flow control. This discussion will help you understand some of the fundamental ways that hosts on your network communicate.

OVERVIEW OF THE DATA LINK LAYER

By now you should be familiar with the OSI model. The Data Link layer is part of the OSI reference model; its role involves passing frames from the Physical layer to the Network layer and vice versa.

There is more to the Data Link layer than passing frames, however. As you can see in Figure 6.1, the Data Link layer sits right above the Physical layer, and the data that comes off the cable, through the Physical layer into the Data Link layer, is just a set of bits. The Network layer does not understand these bits. It needs a translator, something to package those bits in a way it can use. Enter the Data Link layer.

When data moves up through the layers of the OSI model, the Data Link layer plays a central role in transferring information between the Physical and Network layers. After the Physical layer passes the bits to the Data Link layer, the Data Link layer packages the bits and then gives them to the Network layer to process.

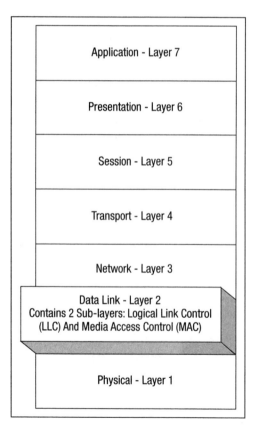

Figure 6.1 The Data Link layer's position in the OSI model.

Similarly, when data moves down through the layers of the OSI model, the Data Link layer plays comparable role in reverse. After it receives information from the Network layer, the Data Link layer packages the bits for the Physical layer's subsequent processing. These packages of bits are also called *data frames.*

The format of a data frame depends upon the network's topology. For example, an Ethernet data frame does not use the same structure as a token-ring data frame. These formats are discussed in more detail later in this chapter.

As data is passed from the top layer of the OSI model (the Application layer) down to the bottom layer (the Physical layer), each layer adds information to the data frame. If the Presentation layer adds information to the data frame of the sending host, that information is delivered to the Presentation layer on the receiving end.

No intelligence is involved in this process. For example, if the Network layer adds information to the data frame and then passes the frame to the Data Link layer, the Data Link layer does not examine that particular information, and is not aware of its existence. Furthermore, although data flows through the OSI model vertically, each layer in the model "thinks" the data flow is a horizontal communication. In other words, when the Session layer at the origin passes data to the Session layer at the destination, neither layer considers itself to be in a vertical hierarchy.

Like most of the layers of the OSI model, the Data Link layer also adds information, called a *header* and a *trailer*, to the data. Headers and trailers aid in the synchronization of frames. Without them, the network software would not know where a frame belonged in a sequence.

The Data Link Layer And Error Control

The Data Link layer plays an important role in something we all take for granted—the error-free transfer of packets. Because the Data Link layer can read the headers and trailers of frames, it can provide error-free transmission between hosts. Note that we are not talking about the integrity of the data itself, but about the delivery of the data frames from one place to another. The Data Link layer achieves error-free transmission through several methods.

First, the Data Link layer provides frame acknowledgments. When the Data Link layer receives a frame, it replies to the sender, saying, in effect, "Yep, got that one!" In addition, the Data Link layer not only sends these acknowledgment notices, but also waits for them. And if it does receive an acknowledgment, it re-sends the data frame.

Also, when the Data Link layer receives a frame, it performs error checking to make sure that the frame did not get corrupted on its journey and that the layer does not pass bad frames up the OSI model. If the Data Link layer discovers an error, it discards the frame without sending a frame acknowledgment. Because the sender does not receive the frame acknowledgment, it retransmits the data frame. This process is discussed in more detail later in this chapter, when we discuss frames and transmission synchronization.

It is the Data Link layer that accesses the network cable. When a data frame is passed to the Physical layer on its way to the cable, the Physical layer might reject it because the network is busy. The Data Link layer manages this process and retransmits frames as necessary.

Finally, the Data Link layer inspects every frame a host receives to see if the frame belongs to that host. The layer inspects the destination address of each frame. If the address matches the host's address, the Data Link layer sends the frame to the next layer in the OSI model. If the addresses do not match, the layer discards the frame.

As you can see, the Data Link layer is a busy place. It provides some essential services that make the job of working with computers easier. With your knowledge of the Data Link layer in hand, let's now talk about a network component that operates at this layer.

THE MEDIA ACCESS CONTROL (MAC) ADDRESS

Throughout this book, and particularly in this chapter's discussion of bridges, you will encounter the term *Media Access Control (MAC) address* or *MAC address* of a host. Because the term appears throughout subsequent chapters on TCP/IP (Transmission Control Protocol/Internet Protocol and routers, you need to understand what the MAC address is, how it came to be, and why it is important.

A MAC address is a six-octet number that uniquely identifies a host on a network. Because it is unique, it is very useful. All hosts on a network, including network devices such as printers and routers, must be uniquely identified. In other words, when data is sent from one host to another, something within that data frame must say, "Hey, you're meant for host XYZ!" Similarly, when host XYZ looks at a data frame, it must be able to recognize itself as the frame's intended recipient.

Myriad addressing schemes are available. Sometimes, as with token ring, the scheme depends entirely on the network's underlying topology. Other times, the addressing scheme depends on the protocols being used. (You learned more about these schemes in Chapter 3.) None of the addressing schemes, however, works at the right layer in the OSI model. Worse, none of them uses a standard way of uniquely addressing hosts.

Although the addressing schemes mentioned above are effective, they are not guaranteed to generate unique addressing. For instance, with TCP/IP, it is not uncommon for duplicate IP addresses to be assigned. Hosts on a network, however, require guaranteed unique addressing, and such addressing must be employed universally. Moreover, because hosts recognize only the MAC address and will not process information without a MAC address, such a universally employed, guaranteed-unique addressing scheme must utilize a MAC address.

The heart of addressing takes place at the Data Link layer, and the Data link layer is concerned with MAC addresses. Where did they come from?

 Several terms are used to describe the MAC address, including *network address, NIC address,* or *physical address.* They all mean the same thing.

The IEEE answered the need for such a scheme when it issued a proposal that network card manufacturers assign a unique number to every network card when it is manufactured. According to the proposal, such a unique number would contain a series of six octets. The first three octets in the series would identify the card's manufacturer. The last three octets in the series would be unique to that card and be assigned by the manufacturer. Network card manufacturers throughout the world accepted the proposal.

Because manufacturers now burn a series of six unchangeable octets into each network card's ROM, the method provides a unique addressing scheme. The Data Link layer can identify hosts by this ID and be assured that the correct host is contacted.

The IEEE assigns the first three octets of the series to each manufacturer. This identifier is known as the Organizationally Unique Identifier (OUI). A complete MAC address—that is, an address with both an OUI and the last three octets the manufacturer assigned to the card—is called the *Universal LAN MAC address.* An example of a MAC address is shown in Figure 6.2. The utility used to display the address is WINIPCFG. (This utility is covered in more detail in Chapter 9.) In this utility, the MAC address is called *the adapter address.*

Next, we will discuss bridges and the good use they make of the MAC address.

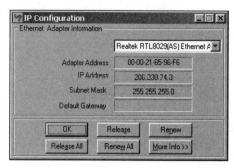

Figure 6.2   An example of a MAC address. In this case, it's called *adapter address*.

BRIDGES AND BRIDGING

As you are introduced to network components, you might start to get glassy eyed. Remembering what each component does and how the components vary can sometimes be difficult. But understanding the OSI model can help. If you understand the OSI model and the functions of each of its layers, then knowing which layer a network component works in will help you understand that component's capabilities.

In Chapter 5, you read about hubs and repeaters. One limitation of those devices is their lack of any real intelligence. They operate at the OSI model's Physical layer, and not much analysis goes on at the Physical layer to allow hubs and repeaters to make decisions.

This limitation does not apply to the bridge, however. The bridge operates at the OSI model's Data Link layer and benefits from the information to which it has access. A *bridge* is a network device that can join two local area networks (LANs) together. After a bridge is installed, the two joined LANs operate as one, with each individual LAN operating as one segment of the same network.

A bridge connects to the two LANs at the same time and has a network connection for every physical connection the bridge makes. There is more to bridges than that, though. A bridge can read the destination host's MAC address from the packets it receives, compare the MAC address to an internal table, and then determine whether to pass the frame from one segment to the other.

In Figure 6.3, you see an example of two LANs joined by a bridge. Each LAN is now considered to be a segment. Let's say that Host A on Segment 1 sends a packet on its segment, destined for Host C. The bridge receives this packet, reads the MAC address, compares it to the internal table, realizes that Host C is on the same segment, and discards the frame. The bridge does this because it assumes that the destination host is on the same segment, so the host must have

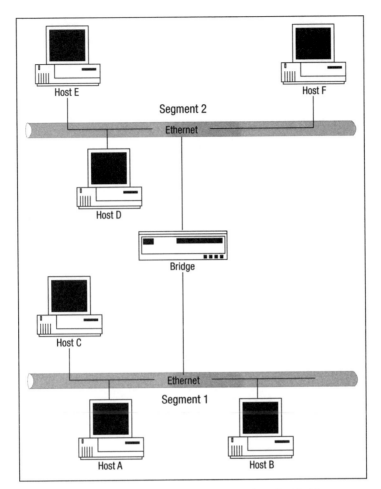

6

Figure 6.3   Two network segments joined with a bridge.

received the frame. Because the receiving host is on the same segment as the sending host, there is no need for the bridge to perform any action.

Okay, now let's imagine that Host A sends a packet destined for Host D. Without a bridge or some other network component, this could not be done. But in the situation shown in Figure 6.3, the bridge receives the packet, reads the MAC address, realizes that the destination host is not on the same segment, and passes the data to Segment 2. Everyone is happy, and the data got through.

The bridge's processes are called *filtering* and *forwarding*. The bridge filters frames on the network and then forwards those frames that need forwarding to the destination segment.

You can see that a bridge can relieve congested networks. Let's assume you have a busy network with lots of packets going across the cable. One solution to the traffic problem is to set up two segments joined by a bridge. With a bridge, not all packets are traversing the cable, so hosts do not have to look at packets not meant for them.

Another neat function a bridge can perform is the joining of segments using different cabling types. Let's say you have one segment that uses 10BaseT and another that uses 10Base2. You could join these two cabling schemes together with a bridge, thus allowing the clients to share data.

A bridge also can connect more than two segments together. When a bridge connected to three segments receives a frame with a MAC address not in the bridge's internal table, the bridge takes the easy route and forwards the frame to all other segments.

What you cannot do with a standard bridge is join two segments that employ different media-access schemes. For example, a standard bridge cannot join an Ethernet segment and a token-ring segment.

You should know that several types of bridges are available. You also should know, however, that making hard-and-fast rules about what a bridge does is difficult. The information on bridges in the preceding paragraphs, although correct, does not tell the whole story. We will go into more detail later in this chapter.

Bridges sound like a great deal. But despite their advantages, they have a downside. Here are their disadvantages:

➤ Because they do more work, bridges are slower than repeaters. Bridges must get a packet, examine the MAC address, and determine whether the packet should be discarded or forwarded. All that computation takes time.

➤ Bridges always forward broadcast packets. If a host on a segment broadcasts a packet, the packet will propagate throughout every segment connected by bridges. Consequently, although bridges can help with traffic congestion on your network, you first should determine what kind of traffic causes the congestion. Bridges will not help with broadcast traffic.

➤ Because a bridge operates at the Data Link layer, it shares that layer's limitations. The Data Link layer allows the dropping and forwarding of packets, but nothing else. Thus, a bridge cannot communicate with other network devices. If a bridge gets flooded with packets, it has no means to ask everyone to hold off for a moment. Instead, the bridge just gets overwhelmed and starts to drop or discard packets.

➤ Bridges are more complex than repeaters and cost more to purchase. So you will spend more time administering them, and they will leave you with less change in your pocket.

The Bridging Address Table

We still have not answered the question: How does the bridge know whether a MAC address is on Segment 1 or Segment 2? The answer is the bridging address table.

The *bridging address table*, held in the bridge's memory, is a list of MAC addresses and the segment that each host is on. When a frame arrives, the destination's MAC address is read, compared to the bridging address table in memory, and then sent on its way.

That sequence raises another question: How do MAC addresses and information get into the table? The question has two answers. First, with the first generation of bridges, someone had to enter the information manually. (And yes, it was as bad as it sounds.) This type of bridge is still available and can be effective for small networks. But wouldn't it be nice if the bridge did the hard work for you? That's what learning bridges do.

Learning Bridges

A *learning bridge*—also called a *smart bridge*—builds its bridging address table on its own, rather than requiring you to enter information manually. Figure 6.4 illustrates a learning bridge.

When you turn on a learning bridge for the first time, its bridging address table is empty. If a learning bridge reads a packet's MAC address and finds no matching entry in its address table, the bridge does two things. First, it adds an entry for the packet's MAC address to its bridging address table so it can route the packet more intelligently next time. Next, the bridge sends the packet to all segments to which the bridge is attached.

Although this routine may not sound very impressive, remember that we are talking about computer technology, where everything happens in seconds. Even on a complex network, a learning bridge will broadcast packets for less than a minute—all the time it needs to read those MAC addresses and build its bridging address table.

Of course, if you turn the learning bridge off, you are back to square one. When you turn the learning bridge back on, it will have to go through the same process again until it has entries for the MAC addresses on each segment.

If a MAC address changes from one segment to another, the learning bridge updates its address table with the new information. Such automatic updating allows you to move printers and computers around without fear that the bridge will make errors in routing.

Learning bridges also include an aging parameter, which you can set. The aging parameter allows you to instruct the learning bridge to delete from its address table entries it has not heard from in a certain period of time.

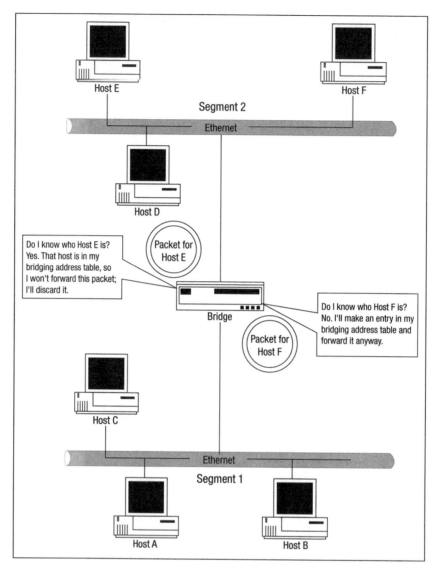

Figure 6.4 A learning bridge.

Deciding When To Use A Bridge

We have covered almost all the information you should know about bridges and how they work. Before we move on to other topics, however, it would be useful to look at a bridging scenario. In this scenario, we will use bridges to join three LANs into a single LAN with three segments; by doing so, we will demonstrate one of the most important concerns you will have when using bridges on your network—looping.

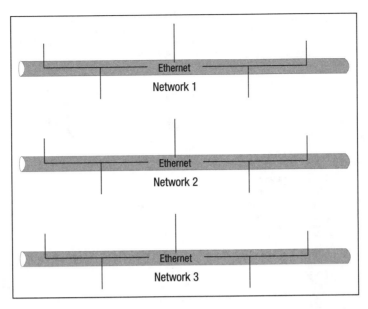

Figure 6.5   Three separate LANs.

Figure 6.5 illustrates what our hypothetical network looks like before we install bridges. As you can see, we have three LANs not connected in any way. We want to join these LANs so that users can share information.

When we install our bridges, we will build in redundancy in case one of our bridges goes bad. Because we do not want to overwork any of our bridges, we will not connect any bridge to more than two segments. The three LANs connected with bridges is shown in Figure 6.6.

It looks like these three LANs have been joined into a single LAN with three segments. Users should be sending documents back and forth and sharing folders. But wait!

You first realize that something is wrong when you try to open a document stored on the server, and the hourglass freezes on your screen. Next, you try to retrieve your email, but it takes forever to come up. What's wrong?

You have been introduced to the problem of looping when using bridges. The trouble stems from the multiple routes available between a sender and a destination. Let's say that Host C sends a packet to Host F. In this situation, two bridges—Bridge 1 and Bridge 2—will see the packet, and both will forward the frame. Bridge 1 will pass it to Segment 1, and Bridge 2 will pass it to Segment 2.

Bridge 3 will receive the packet sent to Segment 1 and then will forward it to Segment 2. About this time, Host F will receive two packets of the same

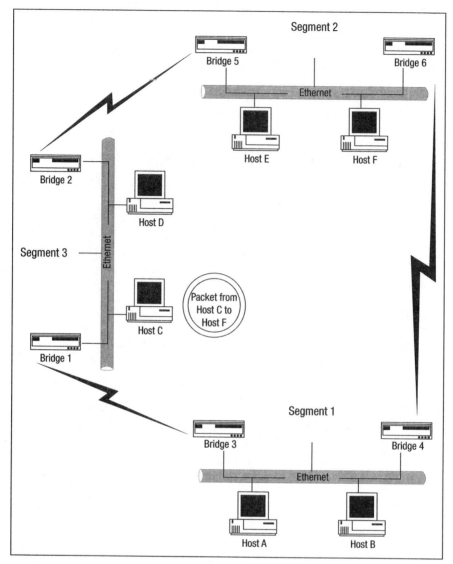

Figure 6.6 Three separate LANs connected with bridges.

information. This is a problem because it will cause network congestion as duplicate packets are moved around the network.

Now, imagine that the forwarded packet was a broadcast packet. Remember that bridges always forward broadcast packets. Do you see what will happen next? Because there are multiple routes between the sender and a destination, we have a loop! That broadcast packet will bounce around forever. Soon, your network will exhibit some very poor performance.

Looping arises primarily when frames at the Data Link layer have not been assigned a *time to live (TTL)*. When a network gets flooded with these types of packets, the situation is called a *broadcast storm*.

Transparent Bridging

To prevent looping, you need more intelligence in your bridges. Fortunately, more intelligent bridges are available, and they use a process known as *transparent bridging* to alleviate looping. With transparent bridging, the bridges on your network tell each other which ports on the bridge should be opened and closed, and which ports should be forwarding packets and which should be blocking them.

Bridging is called *transparent* when the bridges take care of the technicalities of the process themselves, without any other devices being aware of the bridging process.

Not all bridges have the transparent bridging capability. If your network's bridges lack this capability, be careful when designing your network infrastructure. Placing bridges in the wrong places can seriously damage your network's health!

THE INSTITUTE OF ELECTRICAL AND ELECTRONICS ENGINEERS (IEEE)

You didn't think you were out of the woods yet as far as standards go, did you? Because we still must consider another important set. When the OSI model for networking emerged, so did a set of specifications defined by the Institute of Electrical and Electronics Engineers (IEEE).

These specifications deal with a very specific area of networking—network interface cards (NICs) and network media, more commonly known as cables. Thus, the IEEE specifications apply to the OSI model's Physical and Data Link layers. Many of the most important committees working in technology today—such as the American National Standards Institute (ANSI) and International Organization for Standardization (ISO) —have adopted the IEEE's standards.

When the IEEE evaluated the OSI model, it decided that the Data Link layer did not include enough granularity. Consequently, the Institute divided the layer into two parts: the Logical Link Control (LLC) sub-layer and the

Media Access Control (MAC) sub-layer. The 802.2 specification defines functionality at the LLC layer, and the 802.3 and 802.5 specifications define standards at the Physical layer.

The 802 Series Of Specifications

The IEEE assigns two distinct sets of functions to each of these two sub-layers. Specification 802.2 defines the functions of the LLC sub-layer. At the LLC sub-layer, the following functions occur:

➤ Frame sequencing

➤ Frame acknowledgment

➤ Frame traffic control

➤ Link establishment and termination

At the MAC sub-layer, the following functions occur:

➤ Frame delimiting

➤ Frame error checking

➤ Media access management

The MAC sub-layer communicates directly with the NIC. The LLC sub-layer operates above the NIC.

Table 6.1 outlines the 802 specifications and their respective numbers. We will not cover all of them in detail, but you should understand what each

Table 6.1   IEEE 802 categories.

Specification Name	Description
802.1	Overview of project 802, including internetworking
802.2	Logical Link Control (LLC)
802.3	For bus networks that use Carrier Sense Multiple Access With Collision Detection (CSMA/CD), such as Ethernet
802.4	Token bus
802.5	Token ring
802.6	Metropolitan area network
802.7	Broadband Technology Advisory Group
802.8	Fiber Optic Technology Advisory Group
802.9	Voice/data integration on LANs
802.10	Standard for interoperable LAN security
802.11	Wireless networks
802.12	Demand priority access LAN (100BaseVG–AnyLAN)

specification defines. Don't worry if some of the terms are unfamiliar. Later in this chapter, we will cover in detail the significant terms you should memorize, including 802.2, 802.3, and 802.5—the three most common specifications you will encounter in your work on networks.

You might be wondering why all these standards begin with "802." The specifications were named after the year and month of their inception: 1980 (80), February (2) Although you need not remember this, it is an interesting bit of trivia.

802.1

The 802.1 standard defines specifications for the OSI model's Physical and Data Link layers. The standard allows two IEEE LAN stations to communicate over a LAN or wide area network (WAN) and often is referred to as the "internetworking standard."

802.2

The 802.2 standard defines the LLC sub-layer for the entire series of protocols covered by the 802.x standards. This standard specifies the adding of header fields, which tell the receiving host which upper layer sent the information. You will most commonly see this standard used with IEEE 802.3, 802.4, 802.5, and 802.6. We will discuss it in detail a little later in this chapter.

802.3

Because of its association with Ethernet, the 802.3 standard is probably the most widely used. It specifies Physical-layer attributes, such as signaling types, data rates, and topologies. It also specifies the media access method used: Carrier Sense Multiple Access With Collision Detection (CSMA/CD.) This method will be discussed in greater detail later in this chapter.

802.4

The 802.4 standard is commonly used in factories to define how production machines should communicate with each other. The standard establishes a common protocol for use in connecting these machines. It is unlikely that you will see this standard used in corporate LANs.

802.5

The 802.5 standard is often associated with the token-ring topology. The two differ, however. For example, 802.5 does not specify a particular topology or transmission medium. We will discuss these differences in more detail later in this chapter.

802.6

The 802.6 standard uses the Distributed Queue Dual Bus (DQDB) technology to transfer high-speed data between nodes. A metropolitan LAN is a LAN covering a metropolitan area. It is larger than a LAN and more commonly referred to as a wide area network (WAN).

802.7

The 802.7 standard defines the design, installation, and testing of broadband-based communications.

802.8

Rather than a standard in itself, the 802.8 standard actually describes a group of people who advise the other 802-standard committees on various fiber-optic technologies and standards. This group is called the Fiber Optic Technical Advisory Group.

802.9

The 802.9 standard focuses on the integration of voice and data transmissions and uses isochronous Ethernet (IsoEnet.)

802.10

The 802.10 standard focuses on security issues by defining a standard method for protocols and services to exchange data securely by using encryption mechanisms. Because it does not depend on any particular transmission media or encryption method, this standard can apply to any of the other 802 standards.

802.11

The 802.11 standard defines implementations for wireless technologies, such as infrared and spread-spectrum radio.

802.12

The 802.12 standard is based on 100VG-AnyLAN, which uses a 100Mbps signaling rate and a special media-access method allowing for 100Mbps data traffic over voice-grade cable.

Three Important 802 Specifications

Now we will discuss three of the IEEE standards in more detail. We have chosen 802.2, 802.3, and 802.5 because they are the most common specifications you will be expected to know about when you venture into the world of networking (and when you take the Network+ certification exam).

You can find out more about the IEEE's work by visiting its Web site at **www.ieee.org**. To find more information on the specifications covered in this chapter (as well as those not covered), visit the Web site at **standards.ieee.org**.

Because the specifications for each of the 802 standards exceed 250 pages, we won't attempt to discuss them comprehensively. Instead, we will briefly describe what each specification addresses.

802.2: Logical Link Control

With the Logical Link Control sub-layer, the IEEE created a single framework that embraces multiple LAN implementations. Thus, even if the implementations of different network topologies varied, the 802.2 specification could still be used.

The Logical Link Control specification details how the Data Link layer is divided into two sub-layers: the Logical Link Control sub-layer and the Media Access Control sub-layer. The Logical Link Control sub-layer maintains a link between two hosts and sends data across the network.

The division of the Data Link layer allows some of its functions to be shared among LAN implementations, and other functions to be adapted to the network's topology. The result is more flexibility.

Token ring and Ethernet provide examples of this division. In these two implementations, the LLC sub-layer structure is identical, but the MAC sub-layer is different. Specification 802.2 defines the LLC sub-layer. The MAC sub-layer specifications vary and have their own 802 specifications. (We will discuss two of the major specifications in the next two sections.)

802.3: Carrier Sense Multiple Access With Collision Detection (CSMA/CD) Access Method And Physical Layer Specifications (Ethernet)

The 802.3 specification covers a lot of ground. Rather than try to sum up the specification in a few sentences, we will benefit more from looking at each of the terms in this long title.

➤ **Carrier Sense** With all the different packets being thrown onto the network cable, you might wonder how a computer knows that it is okay to add another one. What if another packet comes flying by at the very second a host wants to send data? Well, that's the heart of carrier sense. The term *carrier sense* means that the host will check the cable for a carrier signal. If a signal is present, then the cable is considered busy and the host waits before sending out its packets. If no carrier signal is present, then the host puts its packets on the cable.

➤ **Multiple Access** This term means that any host on the network can send data whenever it wants. It does not have to wait for others to finish or wait for a turn in a queue. Multiple access explains why 802.3 often is associated with Ethernet and why token ring topology is defined in other specifications (802.4 and 802.5). (Topologies were covered in Chapter 1.)

➤ **Collision Detection** Of course, nothing is perfect. Carrier sense sounds good, but what if something still goes wrong? With the speed packets travel on a cable, a collision might still occur when a host sends data onto the cable. A collision can occur when a host tries to send data when the packets from another host are monopolizing the cable. So the Collision Detection component of 802.3 defines a standard for remedying this problem. When a collision occurs, a host should wait for a short, random period of time before trying to re-send data. This is called the *backoff algorithm*. The backoff algorithm ensures that two computers do not get denied at the same time, wait for the same period of time, and then try again at precisely the same moment.

 Collisions, although inevitable, are not good for your network. A small number is okay, but if you get a lot of collisions, then you may assume that your network is flooded. You can alleviate flooding by segmenting your network with bridges and routers. Bridges were covered earlier in this chapter. Routers are covered in the next chapter and offer significant benefits over a bridge.

Before we get too carried away with the 802.3 standard, let's clarify. The 802.3 standard does not define Ethernet, although the two terms are often used interchangeably. The differences between the two are largely historical. Xerox invented Ethernet in 1972. Its first commercial implementation, made available in 1980, represented a joint venture between Xerox, Digital Equipment Corporation (DEC), and Intel and was called, appropriately enough, Version 1.

The IEEE standards for networking improved upon the Version 1 specification for Ethernet. The improved specification offered some benefits, but also meant that Ethernet and a network that used 802.3 could not coexist on the same network. Not to worry. Xerox, DEC, and Intel got back together and came up with Version 2 of Ethernet, which is compatible with the 802.3 standard and closely associated with it. (You will find the details of these changes discussed later in this chapter in the "Frames And Their Relationship To The IEEE Standards" section.)

So remember, these two specifications are different. Moreover, the 802.3 standard encompasses many different implementations. The most common one that you will encounter is 10BaseT, discussed in detail in Chapter 4.

To summarize, 802.3 is a set of rules that determines how network devices attempt to share network cable. This standard is still commonly known as Ethernet.

802.5: Token-Ring Access Method And Physical Layer Specifications

Token-ring topology was covered in Chapter 1. Let's review some basics here so you can see how they fit in with what we have already discussed. Unlike a bus topology, such as Ethernet, token ring controls who does what and when by using a token.

This token—a small data frame—is passed around the ring from host to host, and a host can transmit data only if it holds the token. If it holds the token, the host transmits data and then the token continues along the ring to the next host downstream.

The first host that is turned on monitors the ring for any problems by sending a data frame to the next host in the ring. This data frame is passed around until it returns to the originating host. If the data frame completes the circle, all is well. If it does not, built-in logic enables the host to detect where the break is and logically fix the ring.

 Try not to get trapped into thinking that token ring networks are actually shaped like a ring. Remember, there are logical as well as physical rings. There is also such a beast as a token bus, as defined in 802.4. Refer to Chapter 1 if you have questions about this.

As with Ethernet, the token-ring design emerged several years ago. But it took a long time from its conception in 1969 to its commercial implementation in the 1980s. The driving force behind token ring was, and still is, IBM. Even the IEEE used IBM's presentation of the token-ring topology as the basis of its specification.

Much like we saw with 802.3, the IEEE has tweaked the token-ring standard since it was defined. Furthermore, the IBM token-ring standard no longer complies 100 percent with the IEEE standard. However, the differences between the two standards are not significant.

Because token ring is a fairly common implementation, you will likely encounter it as you go to work on networks.

FRAMES AND THEIR RELATIONSHIP TO THE IEEE STANDARDS

Throughout this book, you'll see the terms *frames* and *packets* used often. In this section, we will define frames and packets and explain how some of the IEEE standards affect them.

We'll look at what actually goes across the cable when a packet of data is sent from Host A to Host B. What is a packet and what does it contain? And what does the IEEE have to do with all this? We'll look at one of the most common network topologies: Ethernet. Ethernet offers a great example because it has seen many changes over the years.

Let's start at the beginning. Data is picked up from a hard disk, is sent across a piece of cable, and arrives at a destination host. The sending host packaged the data, and the receiving end knew what the data was and how to process it. How does this happen? The two hosts abide by a set of rules detailing where in a packet of data certain bits of information can be found.

When you send a piece of data across a wire, a lot more information beyond the piece of data is being transmitted. In addition to the data packet itself, you also need the packet's destination, the packet's sender, and information about the type of packet being sent. The identifying information getting passed across the cable can exceed the size of the actual data. But this information is important, and not just to the hosts. Every network component, from bridges to routers, needs to know the format of a packet before the component can know what to do with the packet.

Chapter 3 provided information on three major protocols. One of those protocols was IPX/SPX (Internetwork Packet Exchange/Sequenced Packet Exchange), which is most often used in Novell NetWare LANs. If you have ever configured a NetWare LAN (or a Microsoft Windows NT Server using NWLINK, Microsoft's version of IPX/SPX), you know that you must choose a frame type. If you choose the wrong one, the server will be unable to communicate with all its mates on the network.

You must choose a frame type because Ethernet, a widely used network specification, has undergone some changes over time. With each change, the format for frames has been altered, and if your packets don't let everyone know which Ethernet variation your network uses, they won't be able to communicate.

Ethernet uses four basic frame types:

➤ Ethernet II

➤ IEEE 802.3 raw

➤ IEEE 802.3 with 802.2

➤ IEEE 802.3 with 802.2 SNAP

(We'll discuss terms like *raw* and *SNAP* as we proceed, as well as detail the differences among the frame types.)

Ethernet II

The Ethernet II frame type is a direct descendent of the original Ethernet specification established by Xerox, DEC, and Intel and of the revised version that is compatible with the IEEE's 802.3 standard. Figure 6.7 illustrates what an Ethernet II frame includes.

The Ethernet II frame type is basically the parent for all other Ethernet frame types. Because the fields in its frame appear in the other three frame types, we should examine them closely:

➤ **Destination Address** The destination address provides the address of the host that should receive a frame.

➤ **Source Address** The source address tells the receiving host who sent the frame.

6

Figure 6.7 The structure of an Ethernet II frame.

➤ **Frame Type** The Frame Type field names the protocol that sent the frame. The receiving host needs the information to determine to which protocol it should pass the frame. The two most widely used protocols today are IPX/SPX and TCP/IP.

➤ **Data** This is the packet's data. The data field can contain any kind of data, but it must be 64 bytes in length. If the data being sent is not 64 bytes in length, the data gets padded to 64 bytes.

➤ **Frame Check Sequence** The Frame Check Sequence field ensures that all of a frame's data frame arrives. The field does this by performing a Cyclical Redundancy Check (CRC), which is a type of mathematical calculation. The calculation generates a value, which is then added to the end of the frame. When the receiving station gets the frame, that station performs the same CRC. After calculating the value, the receiving station compares it to the value at the end of the frame. If the values match, the data arrived intact; if the values do not match, the data is considered corrupted and is discarded.

Once you have the fields of the Ethernet II frame defined, its operation is pretty straightforward. Wouldn't it be nice if that were all we had to worry about?

802.3 Raw

The situation changed when the IEEE defined its 802.3 standard. The original Ethernet specification is not completely compatible with the 802.3 standard, as pictured in Figure 6.8. The IEEE changed the name and function of one field in the frame, and that change triggered other developments for the Ethernet frame.

By the way, the term *raw* in the 802.3 standard is not, for once, an acronym. It actually means "raw," indicating a bare-bones 802.3 frame without embellishment. Now, let's define the field that the IEEE changed in the Ethernet specifications.

The Frame Length field specifies the length of a frame—that is, how long the entire frame is. The maximum length for an 802.3 frame is 1,518 bytes. The Frame Length field replaced the Frame Type field of Ethernet II. Without the Frame Type field, however, the host cannot determine to which protocol a sent frame belongs. Thus, an 802.3 frame can be misrouted. The IEEE soon addressed the unfortunate loss of the Frame Type field.

802.3 With 802.2

The 802.3 with 802.2 frame corrected some of the previous 802.3 frame type's limitations. The 802.3 with 802.2 frame was not initially adopted, however,

Figure 6.8   The structure of an IEEE 802.3 frame.

because it did not exist until after the IEEE had defined and adopted the 802.3 frame. After it became available, however, it was used. Let's look at what the 802.2 standard brought to the frame party, as illustrated in Figure 6.9.

As you can see, the 802.3 with 802.2 frame added three fields to the Ethernet II frame: DSAP, SSAP, and Control. These three fields restored the frame-type information lost with the 802.3 frame and created fields for future expansion. The Frame Type field addressed the basic problem of routing. Let's define these extra fields:

➤ **Destination Service Access Point (DSAP) and Source Service Access Point (SSAP)**   The meanings of the terms *destination* and *source* in Destination Service Access Point (DSAP) and Source Service Access Point (SSAP) should be obvious—they pertain to the sending and receiving hosts. But what does the term *Service Access Point (SAP)* coupled with these terms mean? The SAP restores the functionality of the Frame Type field used with Ethernet II frames. The SAP informs the receiving host which protocol the frame is

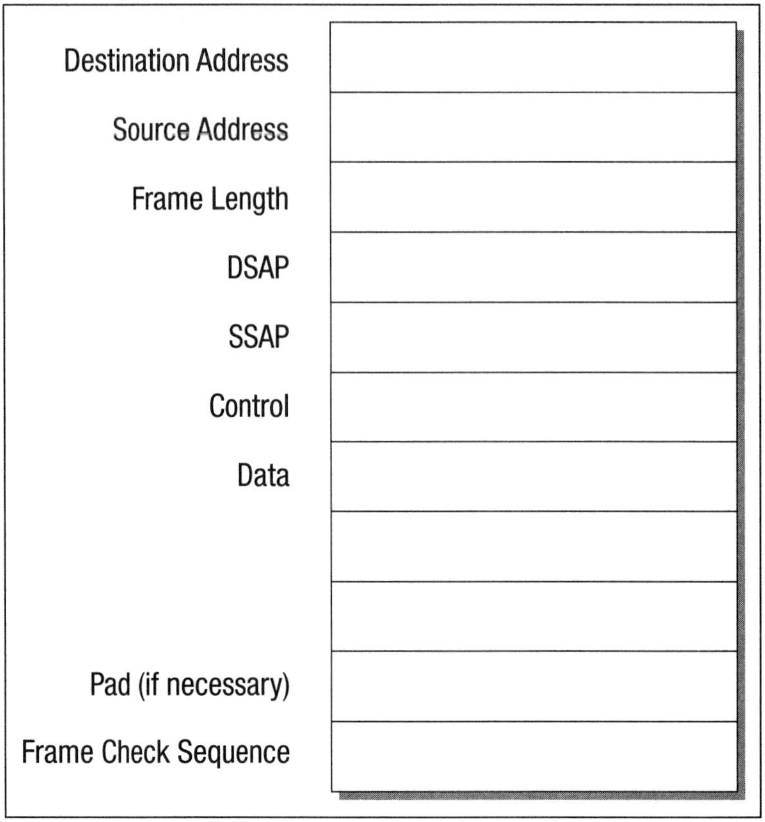

Destination Address	
Source Address	
Frame Length	
DSAP	
SSAP	
Control	
Data	
Pad (if necessary)	
Frame Check Sequence	

Figure 6.9 The structure of an 802.3 with 802.2 frame.

intended for. Because the DSAP and SSAP fields are each only one byte long, however, there was some concern about the 802.3 with 802.2 frame.

➤ **Control** The Control field is used for protocol administrative services and is not directly related to our discussion.

Before we proceed, you should know one final nugget of information about the 802.3 with 802.2 frame. This frame's name may seem baffling. How can a frame be both 802.3 and 802.2? The 802.2 frame encapsulates the actual data. The 802.3 frame then encapsulates the 802.2 frame. So the data, in effect, wears two pairs of gloves. First you put the 802.2 glove over the raw data. Then, you put another glove, an 802.3 glove, over the first 802.2 glove.

IEEE 802.2 Subnetwork Access Protocol (SNAP)

Networks have changed rapidly. Just when something new that is designed to address a networking problem hits the market, a new problem arises and the development cycle begins again.

This cycle characterizes the development of the 802.2 SNAP frame, which was created in response to concerns about the extra fields added to the 802.2 frame component of the 802.3 with 802.2. Because advances in networking technology occur rapidly, the one-byte length of the DSAP and SSAP fields seemed minuscule. These fields' small lengths limited to 256 the number of different protocols that could be identified. And many of those numbers were already reserved when the IEEE introduced the 802.3 with 802.2 frame. Before long, network professionals began calling for change.

Pressure, primarily from Apple and the TCP/IP community, was brought to bear to persuade the IEEE to revisit the situation. From these discussions, another frame type for Ethernet and token-ring networks emerged: 802.2 with SNAP. Figure 6.10 illustrates the new frame type.

You will notice that the 802.2 SNAP frame has yet another field: Protocol Identification. This new field opens the window for acceptance of many different protocols.

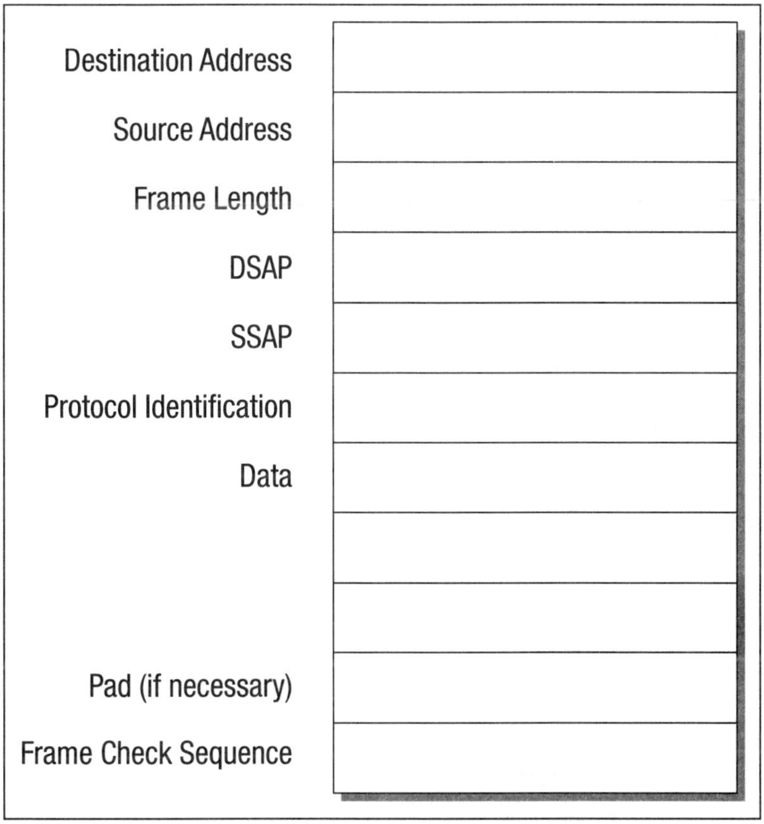

Figure 6.10   The structure of an IEEE 802.2 SNAP frame.

The Protocol Identification field serves the same purpose as the DSAP and SSAP fields in a 802.3 with 802.2 frame, with one exception. The field is five bytes long, leaving more room for new protocols.

How does a router know whether to use the protocol information provided in the DSAP or SSAP fields or the information provided in the Protocol Identification field? When the protocol information appears in the Protocol Identification field, the DSAP and SSAP fields have values of "AA." If the router finds this information in the DSAP and SSAP fields during a simple check, the router then reads the information in the Protocol Identification field.

That wraps up our discussion of frames, the types of information they contain, and the different frame types you will routinely see used on your IPX/SPX network. As you have learned, choosing an incorrect frame type will cause communication problems, so you should set things up correctly.

Finally, you should consider how to select frame types on a Microsoft Windows NT Server. Although Microsoft Windows NT Server offers an automatic selection process for frame types, it also allows you to select them manually. To do so, go to the General tab of the NWLink IPX/SPX Properties dialog box. Fill in the Internal Network Number and Adapter fields, select the Manual Frame Type Detection radio button, and click on the Add button. In the Manual Frame Detection dialog box that appears (see Figure 6.11), select the frame type you want and click on Add.

TRANSMISSION SYNCHRONIZATION

In addition to packaging data into frames and transferring information between the Physical and Network layers, the Data Link layer performs another important function: transmission synchronization. *Transmision synchronization* is a means whereby systems can agree on when data will be transmitted between them.

How does a network device know which signals are significant? Much of this work actually occurs at the Physical layer, but at this layer, the focus is on the individual bit. The Data Link layer focuses on entire frames.

The receiving device needs to know when to measure the signal on a cable because it has no other way of knowing when to start interpreting all the signals

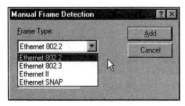

Figure 6.11   Manually selecting frame type in Microsoft Windows NT 4.

passed back and forth. Once a communication starts, the hosts must agree on a starting point and an ending point. With those points agreed upon, the receiving host knows when the flow of frames is finished and can move on to other things. Moreover, the receiving host must ensure that the data it received is free of errors. We discussed this process briefly in the section on the Frame Check Sequence field of frames. Now, we will look at that field in more detail.

Three methods are available for transmission synchronization:

➤ Asynchronous transmission

➤ Synchronous transmission

➤ Isochronous transmission

To achieve transmission synchronization, even more bits are added to frames. However, the added bits are based not on the frame type, but on the synchronization type.

Asynchronous Transmission

Synchronization of bits—known as *bit synchronization*—occurs at the Physical layer. Synchronization of entire frames of data occurs at the Data Link layer. The two types of synchronization, however, share some features.

In bit synchronization, a start bit and a stop bit are added to a transmission so that the receiving station can know when a particular bit has been transferred. Asynchronous transmission at the Data Link layer uses the same idea. A start bit is added to the start of a frame to tell the receiver that a part of the transmission has begun. Similarly, a stop bit is added to the end of the frame to tell the receiver that a part of the transmission has concluded.

An extra bit, called the *parity bit*, is also added to the end of each frame. This is shown in Figure 6.12. When communication between two devices is about to begin, the devices agree on whether they are going to use even or odd parity.

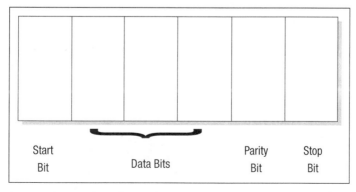

Figure 6.12 Asynchronous transmission.

With even parity, the addition of all the parity bits in a frame will add up to an even number. In this situation, if a receiving station agrees on even parity and then gets a frame where the parity bits add up to an odd number, the station knows that the frame has been corrupted. Odd parity works similarly.

This method has one failing, however. If multiple bytes are corrupted, the parity bit addition can still work out correctly. In this situation, the receiving host would not detect the corruption.

In asynchronous transmissions, the two hosts maintain their own internal clocks and do not sync with each other. The start bit tells the receiving station to begin checking for data.

This synchronization method is very effective, is well established, and is well understood. However, the method also introduces a lot of overhead. Because a parity bit is added to every byte of data, the frame's size quickly balloons by 20 to 30 percent. Such size increases also slow this method. Also, errors in multiple bits with this method can fool the receiving host into thinking that no error has occurred when something actually has gone wrong.

Synchronous Transmission

Synchronous transmission uses the Cyclical Redundancy Check (CRC) to check for errors. But the method adds more than the CRC to a frame.

In synchronous transmission, the sending and receiving hosts use the same clock. To achieve this, the timing information is included in the frame itself. Bits are added if a frame is not the correct size, and some strings of control characters are also added for synchronization. Because this information is read from the frame, you can be sure that both the sender and the receiver have the same data.

Synchronous transmission uses a CRC to protect against transmission errors. This method offers better protection than the parity bits used with asynchronous transmissions because the receiver cannot be fooled by errors in multiple bytes.

Along with the accuracy advantages of CRC over parity bits, you also will see a performance boost with synchronous transmission because the overhead is far less, and not as many extra bits must be added. The only downside to this method involves its greater complexity.

Isochronous Transmission

When we get to isochronous transmission, we have come full circle. We saw earlier that in asynchronous transmission, the sender and the receiver each figured out their own timing. In the case of synchronous transmission, the sender and the receiver agreed upon the timing. With isochronous transmission, one host relinquishes this responsibility to a third party.

Isochronous transmission requires a separate device on the network, which generates a clock signal that creates time slots. When hosts and other devices wish to communicate, they fill an available time slot with data. Beyond this, the hosts themselves do not do the processing; the central device takes care of everything.

Although isochronous transmission requires little overhead, the method also creates a single point of failure on your network. If the clock signal device fails, you'll experience big trouble. Consequently, you must make sure that any device you choose is fault tolerant.

FLOW CONTROL AT THE LOGICAL LINK CONTROL (LLC) SUB-LAYER

6

Another function of the Data Link layer is flow control. Flow control ensures that your network continues to work and that the amount of data moving around does not overwhelm certain components.

On a typical network, you will find several hundred devices all working together. These devices include hosts, servers, bridges, routers, printers, and many others. If they all operated similarly and had the same capabilities with fully distributed and equitable access, then you wouldn't need flow control. You do need flow control, however, because these network components are trying to answer requests from hundreds and possibly thousands of different devices all at the same time. When a channel of communication opens, a negotiation has to take place to make sure that each device knows what signals are being sent (as with transmission synchronization) and how many can be accepted at one time. Flow control deals with the latter requirement.

Let's look at an example. Say you're working at a grocery store. It is your job to put all the groceries into bags after their bar codes are scanned. A family with a lot of groceries has started to be served. The cashier is working as fast as he can. Groceries are coming toward you, and you are trying to bag them as fast as you can. But it is easier to swipe the bar codes than it is to bag the items, so a backlog starts to form. No matter how hard you work, the groceries continue to back up. Before long, the checkout clerk has finished, and you are left with a huge pile of groceries and a long line of people waiting to be served.

The same thing can happen on your network if one host has a super network card and can put data onto the cable at incredible speeds, but the host that receives the data is much slower. With this problem left uncorrected, you will probably lose data because the receiver just cannot keep up.

Flow control can alleviate this problem. An example of flow control is shown in Figure 6.13. With flow control, two devices talk to each other. The sending

Figure 6.13   Flow control demands agreement.

device can ask, "How much data can I send at a time?" The receiving host can reply, "Send me eight frames and then wait. When I am ready for some more, I'll tell you." Flow control even allows a network device to ask a sending host to stop for moment while it does something else.

Let's discuss how flow control works. First, you should know that the Data Link layer uses two types of flow control. These two methods are called:

➤ Guaranteed flow control

➤ Window flow control

With guaranteed flow control, a dialog takes place before any data is sent, so the sending and receiving hosts can agree on a rate of transmission. Once they agree on a rate, the communication will take place at the guaranteed rate until the sender is finished. The guaranteed rate for the duration of the communication will not vary. (That is why it is considered guaranteed.)

With window flow control, a more complicated process occurs. The receiving host buffers the data it receives to allow the sending host to get a little ahead of itself. A buffer is a small piece of memory. The receiving device stores incoming data until it can process it. After processing the data, the receiving host sends to the sending host an acknowledgment that the processing has taken place.

The amount of data that the receiving host can buffer will vary. The sending host needs to know how much data can be buffered before it can expect to get an acknowledgment. This amount is referred to as the *window*.

Networking being what it is, there are two types of windows:

➤ Static window

➤ Dynamic window

A static window is a fixed size. The receiving host dictates the size of this window. For example, if the window on the receiving host is 10, then the sender will not send any more data if there are 10 frames outstanding without an acknowledgment. This window type is illustrated in Figure 6.14.

With a dynamic window, the receiving host dynamically alters the size of the window when the network device or host is very busy (it reduces the size of the window) or when it is idle (it increases the size of the window). This method offers greater flexibility and, if you're given a choice, is the preferred method. Unfortunately, for the most part, you cannot choose.

 A dynamic window is also sometimes called a *sliding window* or a *floating window*.

You can sometimes can alter the way buffers and windows work with servers. On a NetWare server, for example, you can create additional buffers, thereby allowing the server to service more requests.

One of the most common methods by which a device with a dynamic window tells the sending host that its buffer is nearly full is by sending a *choke packet*. When the sending host receives a choke packet, it knows to stop sending. The sending host then gradually sends more data until it receives another choke packet from the receiving host, causing it to throttle back.

The flow-control concept is basically common sense. Devices cannot process information beyond their capabilities. Given that networks are made up of many components and devices with differing capabilities, flow control allows them all to work together.

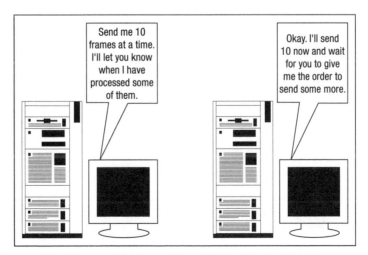

Figure 6.14   A static window.

CHAPTER SUMMARY

In this chapter, we discussed the role of the Data Link layer of the OSI model and its functions. Primary among its functions is the processing of bits as they are passed up from the Physical layer. The Data Link layer also plays a significant role in error control and can add a header and a trailer to a frame for packet sequencing. Sequencing helps the receiving host determine the order in which it should reassemble packets.

The Data Link layer also sends an acknowledgment when it receives a packet. If a sending host does not receive an acknowledgment, the sender re-sends the message. The Data Link layer also performs error checks on the packet and does not send a receipt acknowledgment if it discovers an error. Failure to receive an acknowledgment forces the sender to re-send the message.

We also discussed the Media Access Control (MAC) number, known by many names, including *adapter address* and *network address*. The MAC number, a unique number branded into every network interface card manufactured today, is used to route packets. The Data Link layer examines the MAC address to determine whether the host is the intended host for a packet. The MAC address is a six-octet number. The first three octets represent the organizationally unique identifier, which the IEEE assigns to each card manufacturer. The last three octets represent a unique address for the specific card. The MAC address is also known as the *universal LAN MAC address*.

The most significant network component operating at the OSI model's Data Link layer is the bridge. The bridge connects two LANs together. When connected, the two LANs operate as two segments of the same LAN. The bridge keeps an addressing table listing MAC addresses and segment numbers. The addressing table tells the bridge which segment of the network a host is on. When a bridge looks at a packet, it determines whether the host is on the same segment as the bridge interface or on a different segment. If the packet is on a different segment, then the bridge passes the packet to the correct segment. If the host is on the same segment, then the bridge discards the packet.

A bridge can alleviate traffic congestion on a segment. However, a bridge always forwards broadcast packets and, consequently, is not a foolproof solution for network congestion. In addition, a bridge is fairly dumb. It does not analyze the packets it receives; it merely forwards or discards them. Its limited intelligence stems from its operation at the OSI model's Data Link layer.

A bridge can be used to join two segments using different topologies, such as joining a 10BaseT network with a 10Base2 network. You cannot join dissimilar media-access methods with a bridge, however. Thus, you cannot use a bridge to join a token-ring network and an Ethernet network.

The bridging address tables of older bridges required manual configuration. Newer (and smarter) bridges, known as learning bridges, can build these tables dynamically. When designing a network with bridges, you must be careful not to include loops in your design. Such loops could allow packets to circle your network endlessly, generating congestion.

The Institute of Electrical and Electronics Engineers (IEEE) has developed specifications designed to standardize network communication. These specifications, known collectively as the 802 specifications, have evolved over time. Three of the most important 802 specifications are:

➤ 802.2, which defines the Logical Link Control sub-layer

➤ 802.3, which defines Collision Sense Multiple Access With Collision Detection (CSMA/CD) and is more commonly known as Ethernet

➤ 802.5, which defines a standard for the token-ring topology

The IEEE divided the OSI model's Data Link layer into two parts: the Logical Link Control (LLC) sub-layer and the Media Access Control (MAC) sub-layer. The LLC sub-layer remains consistent from one topology to another (i.e., from Ethernet to token ring), but the MAC sub-layer can vary.

We also discussed *frames*, the logical blocks that are sent across a cable. A frame contains both the data itself and many kinds of control information. The frame's format and content depend on the frame type used. Frame types provide a standard way for packaging data. For two hosts to communicate using IPX/SPX, both must agree on the frame type. IPX/SPX uses four frame types: Ethernet II, Ethernet 802.3 raw, 802.3 with 802.2, and 802.3 with 802.2 SNAP. Microsoft Windows NT Server allows you to choose an automatic selection for frame type, but because some network interface cards do not support this option, you usually should set the frame type manually.

In our discussion of transmission synchronization, we discussed the methods a host uses to recognize the signals on the cable. Transmission synchronization resembles the bit synchronization that takes place at the OSI model's Physical layer, except that it concerns an entire frame rather than a single bit. The three kinds of transmission synchronization are asynchronous, synchronous, and isochronous.

Finally, we discussed flow control. Flow control ensures that the amount of information transmitted does not overwhelm any single network device, be it a host, a bridge, or a router. The two types of flow control are guaranteed flow control and window flow control. Guaranteed flow control is negotiated before a transmission begins and does not change until the transmission is complete. With window flow control, the receiving station buffers the incoming data and sends acknowledgments as it processes frames.

The two kinds of windows in flow control are static and dynamic. A static window uses a fixed number of frames. A dynamic window varies in size, depending on how busy the device is.

REVIEW QUESTIONS

1. The Data Link layer sits between which two levels of the OSI model?
   a. Application layer
   b. Network layer
   c. Physical layer
   d. Session layer

2. One of the key functions that occurs at the Data Link layer is:
   a. Putting bits onto the cable
   b. Error control
   c. Making sure the user is logged on
   d. Learning routes to other hosts

3. Before frames can be passed from one host to another, the receiving host must be uniquely identified. What is the unique identifier that eventually must be resolved?
   a. The IP address
   b. The IPX address
   c. The computer name
   d. The MAC address

4. Which one of these is a good example of a MAC address?
   a. 00-00-86-16-4E-CB
   b. 10-00-86-16-4E
   c. 10-00-86-16-4E-CB-01
   d. 00-00-86-16-4E

5. What is the best way to find out the MAC address on a Windows 9x client?
   a. Control Panel | Network | Network Card | Properties.
   b. Double-click on Network Neighborhood and select NIC from the File menu.
   c. Use the **WINIPCFG** command.
   d. PING 127.0.0.1.

6. Which of the following network devices operates at the Data Link layer?

    a. Router

    b. Gateway

    c. Bridge

    d. All of the above

7. Which of the following best describes a bridge?

    a. A bridge is used to filter traffic on a network segment.

    b. A bridge is used to join two segments so they behave like a single segment.

    c. A bridge works as an interface to the Internet.

    d. A bridge allows dissimilar topologies to talk to each other.

6

8. A bridge keeps a list in memory that allows it to determine which segment a host resides on. What is this table called?

    a. Bridge router

    b. Bridging table

    c. Bridging address lookup table

    d. Bridging address table

9. Which of the following could be considered a failing of bridges?

    a. They are expensive.

    b. They can make communications on your network slower.

    c. They always forward broadcasts.

    d. They do not work with token-ring networks.

10. Which IEEE standard applies to Ethernet?

    a. 802.5

    b. 802.3

    c. 802.2

    d. 802.1

11. Which IEEE standard applies to token ring?

    a. 802.3

    b. 802.6

    c. 802.5

    d. 802.7

12. What is the collision sensing process used by Ethernet called?

    a. CSMA/CD

    b. CSMD/CA

    c. CSMC/DA

    d. CDCA/MA

13. Which two of the following are valid Ethernet frame types?

    a. 802.2 with SNAP

    b. 802.3 raw

    c. 802.2 raw

    d. Ethernet II

14. Which type of transmission synchronization uses an agreed-upon third-party timing mechanism?

    a. Asynchronous

    b. Duplex

    c. Synchronous

    d. Isochronous

15. What are the two types of flow control that occur at the Logical Link Control sub-layer?

    a. Continuous

    b. Guaranteed flow control

    c. Window flow control

    d. Maximum flow control

16. A receiving host can have two types of windows. What are they?

    a. Static window

    b. Dynamic window

    c. 10-byte window

    d. 8-byte window

17. What is a common term used to describe a window that varies in size?

    a. Variable window

    b. Window of opportunity

    c. Sliding window

    d. Open window

18. You install two identical Microsoft Windows NT Servers on your network. You are using the IPX/SPX protocol. One of the servers is working fine, but the other cannot talk to other servers or clients. What is a likely cause?

    a. IPX/SPX is not routable.

    b. Microsoft Windows NT works only with TCP/IP.

    c. You need to wait for the servers to sync up.

    d. The servers have different frame types set.

19. Which IEEE standard defines Logical Link Control?

    a. 802.2

    b. 802.3

    c. 802.7

    d. 802.10

HANDS-ON PROJECTS

The following hands-on projects will review details about the subjects covered in this chapter. Because we have discussed network components to which you might not have access, we have tried to keep these exercise requirements to a minimum configuration. However, by the very nature of the topic, we have assumed that you have either NWLINK (IPX/SPX) already installed on your computer or the ability to install it.

Project 6.1

In this chapter, we discussed MAC addresses and how they are unique on a network. The following steps walk you through two methods of finding out what the MAC address is for the computer you are currently working on. It is a good idea to remember both ways because you will often find yourself sitting at a host that supports only one method.

We then will look at a command-line utility that allows you to find out the MAC address of a remote computer on your network. This exercise assumes that you are using the Windows 9x operating system.

Portions of this exercise will work as detailed only if you have either a network interface card or a dial-up adapter installed on your system.

To find out the MAC address of a computer via a command prompt:

1. Go to a command prompt. To do this, do one of the following:

    ➤ Go to Start | Programs | MS-DOS Prompt.

    ➤ Go to Start | Run. Type "command" and press Enter.

2. You should now be looking at a window called the MS-DOS Prompt. At the command prompt, type "ipconfig /all | more" and press Enter.

If the results of this command scroll off the screen before you can read them, then you most likely forgot to type the "| more" command. This command will prevent the information from scrolling off the screen before you have had time to read it.

3. You should see an entry that looks like Figure 6.15.

Notice that this utility displays the MAC address under the title "Physical Address." This is another name for the MAC address. This command provides you with additional information, such as the IP address and subnet mask of the host.

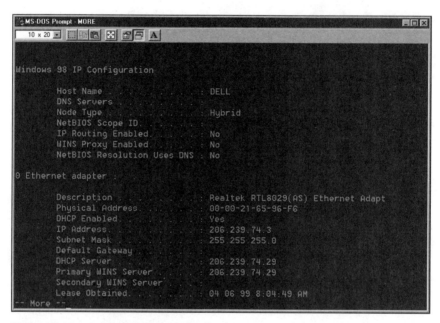

Figure 6.15 An IPCONFIG example.

4. If the command prompt is displaying "--more--", then press Enter until it returns you to the "C:>" prompt (or the drive letter of the drive that the command prompt defaulted to).

5. When the command prompt is displayed correctly, type "exit" to return to the desktop.

To view the same information from the WINIPCFG utility (a good utility that doesn't ship with Microsoft Windows NT):

1. Click on Start | Run. Type "winipcfg" and press Enter.

Notice that the MAC address is displayed on the first screen and that Microsoft used the name "Adapter Address."

If you compare the numbers shown with both utilities, they should be the same.

Next, we will look at a utility that allows you to quickly find out the MAC address of another computer on your network. First, we will have to find out a computer name.

2. Double-click on the Network Neighborhood icon on the Windows 9x desktop. If you cannot see the Network Neighborhood icon, it is most likely because you have an application open. Minimize the application by clicking on the Minimize button in the upper-right corner of the screen.

3. You should see a window that contains the names of all the other hosts available on your network. Write down the names of one or two of them for use in the following exercise.

4. Go to a command prompt.

5. Type "nbtstat –a <computername>" where the <computername> parameter should be replaced with one of the names you wrote down while looking at the Network Neighborhood window.

If you did this correctly, you should see a result that looks something like Figure 6.16.

Figure 6.16 An example of NBTSTAT with -a.

The result set of this command displays the MAC address of the host as the final entry. The other results refer to the NetBIOS names that the computer has registered. (This was discussed in detail in Chapter 3. The NBTSTAT command will be discussed in more detail in Chapter 9.)

Project 6.2

In the following exercise, we are going to look at the frame types that a Microsoft Windows NT 4 Server uses by default when NWLINK has been installed. Then, we'll look at how you can change the frame type.

Be careful when performing the steps in this exercise. Follow each step exactly as detailed. That especially includes clicking on Cancel when directed to (rather than on OK). If you do not follow the precise steps as outlined, it is possible that your server will no longer be able to participate on your network. If this occurs, you will have to reset the server to the state it was in before you did this exercise. No permanent damage can occur on the server if you follow the steps and document each change you make.

Our first step is to find out which protocols are currently installed on the server.

To check the protocol type and prepare to change frame type:

1. Click on Start | Settings | Control Panel to open the Control Panel.

2. Double-click on the Network applet.

3. Click on the Protocols tab. You will see a display like the one in Figure 6.17.

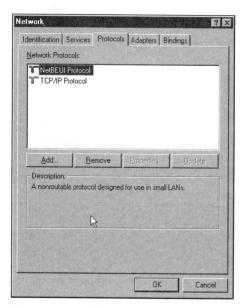

Figure 6.17   The Protocols tab in the Network applet.

Four protocols have been installed. One of these protocols is NWLINK IPX/ SPX Compatible Transport. This is the name Microsoft gives to the IPX/SPX protocol. If you do not see this listed in the Protocols tab, then the server you are currently sitting at does not have NWLINK installed. It is easy to install NWLINK, but it will require a reboot to complete the installation. If you are unsure whether you are have sufficient security rights to reboot the server, don't worry. We have included figures illustrating what you would see if you perform the following steps.

To install IPX/SPX:

Follow these steps only if you do not have IPX/SPX installed and wish to install it now.

1. Click on the Add button in the Network applet. This opens the Select Protocol dialog box. This dialog box shows all of the available protocols that ship with Microsoft Windows NT Server.

2. Select NWLINK IPX/SPX Compatible Transport from the list and click on OK.

3. You will now be prompted for the Microsoft Windows NT Server CD so the necessary files can be loaded onto your system. If the path specified for your CD-ROM is incorrect, type the correct path before proceeding.

4. If you have Remote Access Server installed on your system, you will be asked if you want to bind IPX/SPX with your RAS connections. If you are unsure whether you want to do this, click on Cancel.

5. You will then be returned to the Protocols tab of the Network applet. Now you will see NWLINK IPX/SPX Compatible Transport listed. The installation was successful.

6. Before you can look at the properties for this protocol, you must close the Network applet. Click on OK.

7. You will then see the Network Settings Change dialog box. This dialog box is telling you that the protocol is not fully functional until the server has been rebooted. For the purposes of this exercise, it is not important for the server to be rebooted. Click on No when you see this dialog box.

To view the default properties that have been assigned to the NWLINK IPX/SPX Compatible Transport:

1. Open the Network dialog box. This time we will use a shortcut: Right-click on Network Neighborhood and select Properties. The Network applet opens.

2. Click on the Protocols tab to see the names of the protocols that have been installed.

3. Click on NWLINK IPX/SPX Compatible Transport, and then click on Properties.

You will now find yourself at the NWLINK IPX/SPX Properties dialog box. This is the dialog box in which you can select frame types. The default setting is Auto Frame Type Detection. This setting enables Microsoft Windows NT Server to automatically determine the frame type to use. However, because some network interface cards are not compatible with this feature, we will look at how you can add a specific frame type.

4. Click on Add. This will take you to the Manual Frame Detection dialog box.

5. Click on the arrow next to the Frame Type drop-down box to list all of the available frame types.

All of the frame types discussed in this chapter are listed. You can choose any of them. If NWLINK IPX/SPX Compatible Transport was already installed on your server, then it is *not* advised that you make any permanent changes in this dialog box, because doing so could cause the server to stop communicating on your network.

To remove the protocol from the server:

If the protocol was already installed, you should *not* follow the remaining steps in this exercise. In the remaining steps, we will be removing the protocol for the server. (It is advisable to not have unnecessary protocols installed on a system because they can affect performance.)

1. Click on Cancel to close the Manual Frame Detection dialog box.

2. Click on Cancel to close the NWLINK IPX/SPX Compatible Transport dialog box.

Make sure that the NWLINK IPX/SPX Compatible Transport protocol is highlighted. This is very important. It is essential that you do not remove any protocols other than those that you added yourself during this exercise.

3. Click on Remove. The dialog box shown in Figure 6.18 will appear on your screen.

4. Click on Yes. The protocol will now be removed from the server.

5. You will be returned to the Network dialog box. Click on OK to close this dialog box.

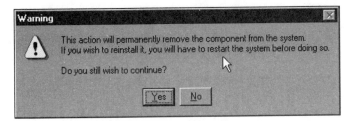

Figure 6.18   The warning dialog box.

6. You will now see the Network Settings Change dialog box. This dialog box asks if you want to restart your server. In this case (because we have just installed some software and then removed it), it is suggested that you click on Yes. If this server cannot be rebooted at this time, don't worry; it will still operate on your network. Just make sure that you schedule a reboot in the near future.

6

## CHAPTER SEVEN

THE NETWORK AND TRANSPORT LAYERS

After Reading This Chapter And Completing The Exercises, You Will Be Able To:

➤ Explain the purpose of routing and the Network layer

➤ Discern between a router and a brouter

➤ Distinguish between routable and nonroutable protocols

➤ Explain what default gateways and subnetworks are and why unique network IDs are needed

➤ Distinguish between static and dynamic routing

➤ Explain the purpose of the Transport layer

➤ Distinguish between connectionless and connection-oriented data transmission.

➤ Explain name resolution

Moving data from segment to segment on a network occurs at the Network layer of the OSI (Open Systems Interconnection) Reference Model. Moving data *reliably* occurs at the Transport layer of the OSI Reference Model. Because these layers handle data movement between different segments, they are fundamental to networking.

THE NETWORK LAYER

Figure 7.1 displays the location of the Network layer within the OSI Reference Model protocol stack. Note that the Network layer is also commonly referred to as Layer 3.

The primary functions of the Network layer are:

➤ Logical node addressing

➤ Logical network segment addressing

➤ Routing

➤ Routing protocols

➤ Routing hardware

Unique Network Addresses

Within any internetwork, each network segment is identified by its own unique logical network address. Pay attention to the word *unique*. No network segment can have the same logical address as any other network segment. The same rule applies to node addresses. No workstation on the internetwork can have the same network/node-address ID as any other node.

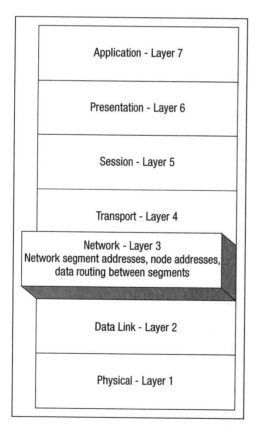

Figure 7.1   The Network layer within the OSI Reference Model.

Routing—the process of moving data from one segment to another—is similar to sending a letter. A network address is like a street, and the node address is like the house number. When you send a letter to a house, the letter's address must have both the street name and the house number for the letter to get to the right place.

The data-packet header includes the source-node address, which is similar to a letter's return address. The source-node address tells the destination node where to send responses. The data-packet header also includes the destination-node address, which is where the data packet will be sent. Unique network addresses ensure that data packets reach the correct destinations and that responses reach the correct source nodes. The way that a network address and a node address combine creates a unique address, as shown in Figure 7.2.

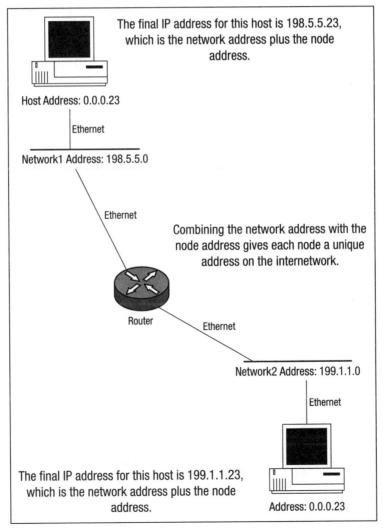

Figure 7.2   Network and node addresses combine to create unique addresses.

IPX And IP Network Addresses

Two of the most common protocol stacks are IPX (Internetwork Packet Exchange) and TCP/IP (Transmission Control Protocol/Internet Protocol). Each of these protocol stacks uses Network-layer addresses, but in different ways.

The IP address is 32 bits long and defines both the address for the network segment and the address for the network node. An IP address uses a subnet mask and classes of IP addresses to determine which portion of the 32-bit IP address is the network address and which portion is the node address. For example, an IP address of 199.5.128.3 with a mask of 255.255.255.0 has a network address of 199.5.128.0 and a node address of 0.0.0.3. (IP addresses are discussed in more detail in Chapter 3.)

In contrast, the IPX protocol stack uses a 32-bit network address and a 48-bit node address. The 48-bit node address is normally copied directly from the MAC (Media Access Control) address of the network interface. IPX addresses are usually specified in a hexadecimal format. The IPX network address for a segment might be a100bef6, whereas the IPX node address might be a0900000123b. MAC addresses are burned into the network interface card by the manufacturer. Each manufacturer is given a separate series of addresses to use on their cards so that all MAC addresses are unique.

Routing

Routing is the process of moving data from one segment to another. Routing typically occurs between dissimilar network types, but can also be established between similar network types. After routing is established between them, separate network segments are assembled into an internetwork.

It is a good idea to route data in many instances, including:

➤ If you need more nodes on the network than the physical cable can provide.

➤ If you need to connect to wide-area-network links, which are dissimilar enough to require routers. This reason is basically the need to connect networks that are geographically distant from each other.

➤ If you want to concentrate network traffic between nodes that communicate the most with each other. A good network routing design provides the ability to divide traffic so that bandwidth utilization is reduced. Such a design places the computers that communicate most with each other on a common segment so that the largest amount of network traffic remains on that segment.

Routing occurs at the Network layer. The Network-layer addresses are used to locate the network segment to which data should be forwarded. The OSI Network layer's data-packet header includes both the source and destination addresses to be used for routing. For efficiency and effectiveness, a networked computer does not need to know how to send data all the way through an internetwork to its final destination. Instead, the only thing that the computer needs to know is which router on the local network segment is responsible for sending that data toward that destination.

A router needs to know the following:

➤ The networks that the router is directly connected to

➤ The routers that are attached to those networks

➤ The routing table of networks that each of those routers knows about

From this information, each router can determine where to send data. It doesn't matter whether the data will be sent to a computer on a directly connected network or whether the data will be sent to the next router in the path to the destination network.

The table of networks maintained by the router is known as a *routing table*. The routing table consists of records that link four basic types of information. Each record represents a single route. The information includes:

➤ Router addresses on locally connected networks

➤ The networks to which those routers can forward data

➤ The locally connected networks that the neighboring routers are connected to

➤ How much it costs (in distance, time, or other metrics) to use that route to the network

In protocol terms within the router, the Network layer receives the packet from the Data Link layer. Then, the router checks for errors or data corruption. If there are problems with the packet, the router discards it. If there are no errors, the router checks for the destination address. The router then checks the destination address against its routing table. The router determines which neighboring router can send the packet on to the destination, and which locally connected network that router is on. Finally, the router forwards the packet to the next router in the path.

Routing itself is somewhat different for various protocols. The basic functionality is the same, but each protocol stack has its own processes at the Network layer. One function that most protocols perform is the fragmentation of packets into smaller units between the Network layer and the Data Link layer. The router must be able to assemble the Data Link layer's fragments into Network-layer packets before examining the Network layer's packet header. Other functions are not the same. For example, TCP/IP uses a subnet mask to expand the number of network segments within an address class. An IP router must know the subnet mask to determine which addresses are local and which are not.

Internetworking Equipment

Getting data from one segment to another requires some form of equipment to move the data. The equipment must decide which data should be sent on to which network segment.

Routers

A *router* is the computer equipment that performs routing between segments on the internetwork. Routers work at the Network layer because their main function is to route data from one network segment to another.

Routers are usually special computers that have multiple interfaces to various network types. These types of routers, which are dedicated to routing data between network segments, tend to be compact boxes—stackable or rack-mountable—that do not have monitors or keyboards.

Another type of router is one that is not dedicated to routing. Many servers can act as routers. Microsoft Windows NT Server can forward data between two network segments if it has multiple network interface cards. This function is, by default, disabled. For example, both Novell NetWare and Unix can route data, too. Depending on the version of the operating system, or on the desired routing functionality, an additional routing package may need to be installed. However, basic routing capabilities are becoming more common as part of a network operating system.

Routers operate with three core processes. The fewer processes that a router must run, the more efficient the router is at providing the core function of routing. The three processes are:

➤ Route lookup

➤ Network layer forwarding

➤ Routing-table maintenance, if dynamic routing is used

Route lookup is the process of examining each incoming data packet to discover its Network-layer destination address and looking at the routing table to determine where to forward it. A router uses the destination address in the packet to look up the next router in the routing table.

The routing table can quickly become large and complex. Nodes that are local to a router—attached to a network segment to which the router is also directly attached—must have an entry in the routing table. This entry must include both the network address and the node address. Efficiency in routing is reached when the nodes are not local. In these cases, the router needs to know only which network number a data packet will be sent to and requires only a single entry for that network in its routing table. Further economies can be used when a logical network design enables the router to add network numbers into groups for forwarding onto the same route. This process is called *route summarization*.

After the router has looked up the route, it performs the Network-layer forwarding. *Network-layer forwarding* is the process of modifying a data packet's Network-layer header appropriately to forward it to the next router or destination. This process is a set of packet manipulations where the router changes the MAC address to reflect the next router's address, increments any hop-count fields to prevent looping, decrements any time-to-live fields to prevent looping, and recomputes the header checksum to ensure accuracy.

Routing-table maintenance is a process used by dynamic routing protocols for ensuring that the routing table is always up to date with changes made on the internetwork. Router responsibilities are summed up in Table 7.1.

7

Brouters

Some situations require the same two segments to be routed with one protocol but bridged with another. A *brouter* is used to perform this function. It acts as a router for routed protocols and acts as a bridge for nonroutable protocols.

 Bridges are covered in detail in Chapter 6.

Bridges are similar to routers in their connectivity functions. Bridges connect network segments together so that they can function like a single network segment. Usually a bridge will connect segments that use the same physical topology so that the number of nodes that participate in that network segment can be increased. Some bridges enable two different physical topologies to be connected.

Bridges filter data packets between network segments by deciding whether to forward each data packet received from the connected networks. The decision is based on the destination MAC address of the packet. The bridge maintains a table of the MAC addresses on each connected network to make the decision.

Table 7.1   Router responsibilities.

Router Responsibility	Result
Optimize routing paths	Select the "best" route, using a routing algorithm to determine which route is nearest or fastest.
Operate efficiently	Utilize as little processing and memory overhead as possible so that moving data is the primary function.
Maintain stability	Provide network uptime even during stressful traffic conditions.
Routing	Transport packets over networks to reach the destination.

The difference between bridges and routers is that bridges work at the Data Link layer and routers work at the Network layer. A router becomes more efficient at connecting dissimilar topologies because it doesn't matter which physical topologies are connected to a router. A router can segment more traffic from traversing between the two segments because it looks at a data packet's network address and discerns which segment that packet should be forwarded to. Reducing the number of users on a network segment increases performance through the associated reduction of bandwidth utilization.

 Whether you use a router or a bridge, a good guideline to follow is to have 80 percent or greater of the packets transmitted on a segment destined for other nodes on that segment.

Imagine a network that uses both SNA (Systems Network Architecture) traffic, which cannot be routed, and IP traffic, which is optimally routed. In this network, a brouter is one option for providing connectivity between network segments. The brouter would route IP traffic and bridge SNA traffic. A brouter is complex because of its capability to determine which protocols to bridge and which to route. That complexity makes it difficult to optimize the network. Instead of using a bridged protocol, other options—such as a gateway solution or encapsulation—can be used to enable connectivity for the nonroutable protocol.

The Routing Process

A router, such as the one shown in Figure 7.3, follows a set process when moving data from Node A to Server 1. This figure uses TCP/IP addressing with standard Class C subnet masks on each segment of 255.255.255.0.

1. Node A prepares the data packet and sends it with the local router's physical address (MAC address) and the destination address (the Network layer's network address and node address of the destination computer).

2. Router 1 receives the packet and accepts it because of the MAC address.

3. Router 1 checks its routing table for the destination network 193.123.48.0.

4. The routing table shows that this network is connected to Router 1's Interface 3, which has the address 193.123.4.2. The routing table also shows that the neighboring router that can lead to the destination network has an IP address of 193.123.4.1.

5. Router 1 strips off its own MAC address from the packet and replaces it with the MAC address of Router 2's Interface 1.

6. Router 1 then forwards the packet through its Interface 3 to Router 2.

7. Router 2 receives the packet and accepts it because of the MAC address.

8. Router 2 knows that the network 193.123.48.0 is locally connected to its Interface 2.

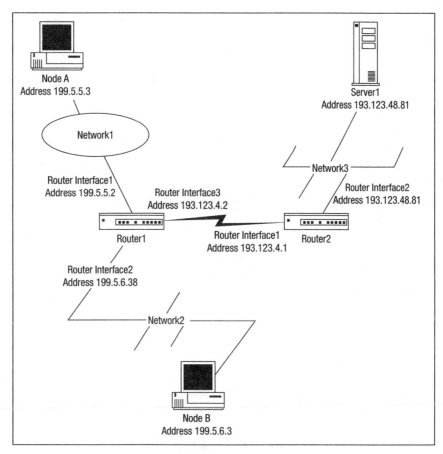

Figure 7.3   The routing process.

9. Router 2 strips off its own MAC address from the packet and replaces it with the MAC address of Server 1.

10. Router 2 forwards the packet to Server 1.

Routable And Nonroutable Protocols

Not all protocols can be routed. A *routable protocol* is one that provides a Network-layer address for network segments and nodes. Network-layer addresses are required for data to be transmitted from one network segment to another without a forwarding bridge capability or encapsulation technique.

Examples of routable protocols are the TCP/IP and IPX protocol stacks. TCP/IP specifies IP, the Internet Protocol, as its Network-layer protocol. IP specifies network and node addressing. IP addresses are assigned for both the network address and the node address. IPX, the NetWare Internet Packet Exchange protocol, also specifies network and node addressing. However, unlike IP, IPX network addresses are assigned and IPX node addresses are copied from the MAC-layer address that is burned into the network interface card.

Examples of nonroutable protocols are DLC (Data Link Control), NetBEUI (NetBIOS Extended User Interface) and SNA (Systems Network Architecture). Neither DLC nor IBM's SNA provide for a Network-layer addressing scheme.

Encapsulating Nonroutable Protocols

One option for enabling nonroutable protocols to travel throughout the internetwork is to *encapsulate*, or tunnel, the nonroutable protocol within a routable protocol. This type of encapsulation is the process of carrying one protocol's frames as the data portion inside another protocol's frames. Tunneling is used for one of two reasons:

➤ A nonroutable protocol is being used on the network, and the other protocol is used to route it through an internetwork.

➤ The number of protocols will be reduced on the internetwork to simplify the network overhead and management.

Many enterprise networks have been built around legacy mainframes and minicomputers that contain mission-critical databases and applications. IBM mainframes and minicomputers use SNA, a nonroutable protocol. Other mainframes use LAT (Local Area Transport) which is also nonroutable. The methods that enterprise networks use to provide access to their legacy equipment usually include bridging, brouting, or tunneling.

Default Gateways And Subnetworks

The *default gateway* is the designated address of a router that can forward all traffic to the internetwork. For network nodes, the default gateway is the IP address of a router on the segment where the node resides. Network nodes do not need a default gateway to communicate with nodes on their segment. They need to know where to send data when they need to communicate with nodes on other segments. The default gateway's IP address is used for this type of traffic.

IP routing is based entirely on the network portion of the destination address. Traditionally, each Unix IP host maintained a list, or table, of network numbers. For each network number, a gateway was listed. To reduce the need to maintain multiple lists, especially for hosts on segments with a single router, default gateways were introduced. Default gateways are used when a network number does not exist in the network number table. Today, the default gateway is usually the only gateway address used on end nodes. Networked computers depend on the routers to know how to move the data packets throughout the internetwork.

The following is the process that a network node follows when sending data and using the default gateway's IP address:

1. Data is received by the IP stack, specifying the destination IP address.
2. The IP stack checks to see if the destination IP address is on the same network as the source node is—a local IP address.
3. If the destination IP address is determined to be a remote address, the source node forwards the packet to the default gateway address.

Routers can be configured with default gateways, too. Some networks designate certain routers as *smart routers*. These smart routers have full routing tables with intelligent paths to all network segments on the internetwork. A smart router is best placed in a central location and on the backbone of an internetwork. Routers that are configured with a reduced set of routing instructions can forward data quickly and with low router overhead. Using a default gateway address on a router is a good choice for routers on *stub networks*, where the router is the single path of internetwork access for all nodes on the network. Figure 7.4 displays a router that uses a default gateway.

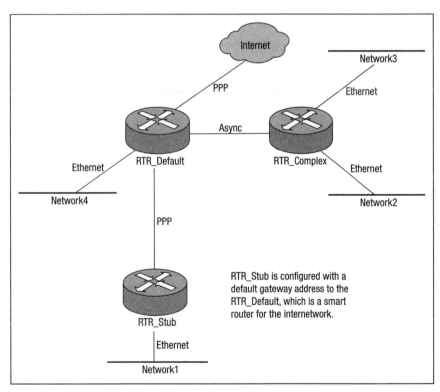

Figure 7.4   Using a default gateway.

A *subnetwork* is a subset of addresses within an IP network address. The use of a subnet dates back to the original IP networks, which used Class A addresses. A Class A address can contain 16,777,213 hosts. That many hosts would cause a huge traffic and administration problem if all the hosts had to be connected to the same network segment. In fact, the network would become saturated with traffic and fail.

Subnetworking allows an IP network address to be distributed across multiple separate network segments. (For more about IP subnetworks, see Chapter 8.)

Static And Dynamic Routing

When a packet is received by a router, the router looks at the header. The header of the Network-layer packet contains the IP address of the source computer and the network and node address of the destination computer. The router looks at the network address of the destination. If the packet is not destined for a directly connected network segment, then the router needs to find out where to send the packet. Because the host is not locally accessible, the router checks the routing table for the next host to forward the packet to.

The routing table can be created in two ways. An administrator can manually create the routing table, or a routing protocol can dynamically create the routing table and maintain it with updates whenever a route changes on the internetwork.

There are two general types of dynamic routing protocols:

➤ Distance-vector routing protocols

➤ Link–state routing protocols

Static Routing

A routing table can be created when a network administrator enters a route to another network into a router's routing table. This manual entry of routes into the routing table is called *static routing*.

A static routing table is best used in a small network that isn't changed often. When an internetwork becomes large or is changed often, static routing becomes difficult to manage. In large internetworks, or those that have multiple, varied changes to the internetwork configuration, the use of dynamic routing through routing protocols is the best choice for implementation.

Dynamic Routing: Distance-Vector Routing Protocols

Distance-vector routing protocols are an older type of routing protocol. They use the *distance* to the destination network and the *vector*, or direction, of the destination network.

To define the distance to a network, a distance-vector routing protocol typically uses a hops metric or a ticks metric. *Hops* are the number of routers that must be crossed before reaching the network. *Ticks* are measurements of time, about 1/18th of a second, that show how long it will take for data to reach the other network.

To prevent packets from traveling endlessly throughout an internetwork, a limit is usually placed on the number of hops. In both IP RIP (Routing Information Protocol) and IPX RIP (also called Routing Information Protocol), which are both distance-vector protocols, the limit to the number of hops is 15. The 16th hop or beyond is considered an unreachable network.

A routing table itself contains basic information about the various network paths. This table can differ somewhat for various individual routing protocols, but contains the same basic information for all of them. Each routing record, or line in the routing table, contains the information needed to forward data. A routing record typically contains the following information:

➤ The network number to which data will be forwarded

➤ The address of the next router in the path to the destination network, or identification of the local interface to transmit that data through

➤ The time, hops, or other metrics used to evaluate the distance or cost of that route

➤ An aging statistic for the record

When a distance-vector router first comes online on the internetwork, it advertises its presence to its neighboring routers on the internetwork. Neighboring routers are those that are connected to segments that are directly connected to a router, as shown in Figure 7.5.

Each router periodically broadcasts its entire routing table to its neighbors. The periodicity can be different depending on the routing table. For example, AppleTalk's RTMP (Route Table Maintenance Protocol, a distance-vector protocol) broadcasts every 10 seconds, IP RIP broadcasts every 30 seconds, and IPX RIP broadcasts every 60 seconds. These broadcasts are used to build the routing table initially and to update it thereafter.

Not only does a routing protocol create and update the routing table, it also performs a *route selection*. Route selection occurs when the router determines which routes are the best to use when there are multiple routes to the same network. A redundant route is not unusual because it provides connectivity if a path fails. However, the redundant routes show up in a router as it's receiving updates from its neighbors. The routing protocol typically looks at the time factor (ticks) first and selects the route with the smallest number of ticks. This

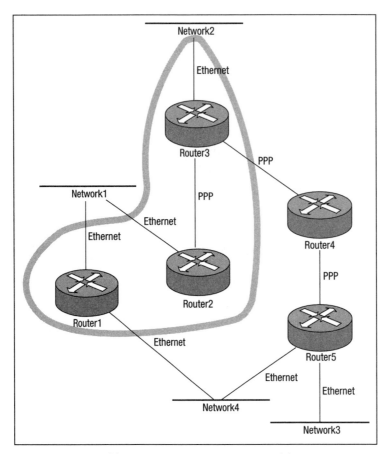

Figure 7.5 Neighboring routers. Router2's neighbors are Router1 and Router3.

process ensures that optimal routes are selected. When the ticks are identical, the router then selects the route with the fewest number of hops. When both the hops and the ticks are identical, the router keeps both routes in its table and sends data through either one.

When a router is taken off the network, or the network address is removed from use, the routing table does not automatically delete the invalid routes. So how do routers know when the network is no longer there? Each routing record in the routing table has an aging number with it. Every time the router receives an update, the routing protocol looks at the aging number. The router keeps the record in the routing table for a short duration, a threshold number of update periods. When the router receives updates without the record, it looks at the aging number of the route in the table already. If the aging number is less than the threshold number, the routing protocol keeps the record in the table and increments the aging number. If the aging number is at or above the threshold number, the routing protocol discards the route.

The time that it takes for all routers on the internetwork to propagate a change is called *convergence*. The shorter a convergence time is for the internetwork, the more efficient and effective the internetwork is at routing data.

One problem with routing protocols is making sure that a routing loop does not occur. Take, for example, the network depicted in Figure 7.6. In this network, assume that Router1 goes down. Currently, Router2 says that Network1 is 1 hop away, and Router3 says that Network1 is 2 hops away. When Router1 goes down, Router2 hears from Router3 that Network1 is 2 hops away, so Router2 drops the old route and adopts the new one. Router2 sends the update out that Network1 is now 3 hops away. Router3 drops its old route and adds it back in so that Network1 is 4 hops away. This bouncing of routes back and forth will continue until the route to Network1 is more than 15 hops away from one of the routers. Then, the routers will drop the route.

7

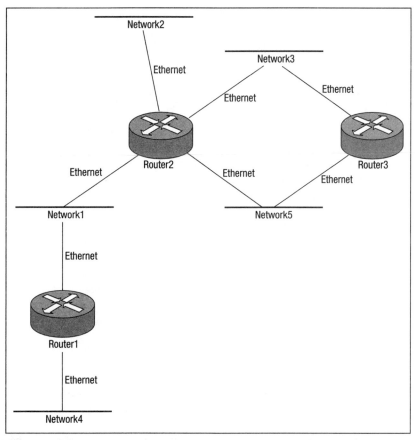

Figure 7.6   A routing loop.

Split horizon was developed to minimize routing loops, although it does not completely eliminate them. With a *split horizon*, the router does not send any routing updates back to where it learned those routes. In our example, because Router3 learned of Network1 from Router2, Router3 would not advertise to Router2 that it had a path to Network1.

Another twist to split horizon is called *poison reverse*. Instead of not sending routing updates at all, poison reverse sends routing updates back to the router they were learned from with a destination marked at 16 hops, which makes that route unreachable.

Besides developing mechanisms to decrease problems like routing loops, distance-vector protocols have other strengths. A distance-vector protocol is an older, proven routing protocol. It works well on small internetworks, especially those with high-speed links.

Distance-vector protocols have a few weaknesses, too, however. Distance-vector protocols create a tremendous amount of utilization overhead. Each router broadcasts its entire routing table to its neighbors periodically. As routing tables grow more complex, the overhead grows as well.

The fact that routers broadcast their entire routing tables only to neighbors causes a problem in two areas. The first is that convergence takes a long time because the routing updates are stored, then forwarded, throughout the internetwork. The second is that the information that is sent through the internetwork is mainly secondhand information. The router learned about a path from its neighbor, which learned about the path from its neighbor, and so on, in grapevine fashion. This usage of secondhand information causes routing loops.

The weaknesses of distance-vector protocols contributed to the development of link-state protocols, which developers hoped would circumvent these problems in the future.

Dynamic Routing: Link-State Routing Protocols

Link-state routing protocols were designed specifically to address the limitations of distance-vector routing protocols. Link-state protocols are more complex than distance-vector protocols and create overhead on the router's CPU. However, link-state protocols do not create unnecessary overhead on the network bandwidth, they do not use secondhand information, and they have a fast convergence time. Examples of link-state protocols include those in Table 7.2.

Table 7.2 Link-state protocols.

Link-State Protocol	Abbreviation	Protocol Stack
Open Shortest Path First	OSPF	TCP/IP
NetWare Link Services Protocol	NLSP	IPX
Intermediate System to Intermediate System	IS-IS	OSI

Link-state routers use a *hello* packet to announce their presence on the internetwork, as well as to ascertain whether a router can be reached.

To update other routers, a failure on the internetwork triggers a flood of link-state advertisements (LSAs) throughout the internetwork. A *flood* is the broadcast of the LSA to every router in the internetwork's area. The LSA causes each router to recalculate the routing table with the inclusion of the failure data. The LSA contains the information about only the network that has changed. The inclusion of only updated information limits the size of LSA packets.

The flood mechanism is the main reason that a link-state-routed network has a fast convergence. The LSA is broadcast to each router. This means that each router receives firsthand information about network changes. This reduces the time for the network to converge. LSAs ensure that each router knows the topology of the internetwork and can compute the optimal route for each destination network.

To determine which paths are the best, link-state routing protocols assign a cost metric, or *link state*, to each path. An administrator can assign the cost metric for a given path to override the protocol-assigned metric. The link-state cost metric takes into account more than the number of routers that are crossed (hops) or the amount of time that it takes to reach a distant network (ticks). The link-state cost metric includes information about the type of network connection over which the data will be transmitted.

OSPF is a link-state routing protocol in the TCP/IP protocol stack. OSPF stands for Open Shortest Path First. OSPF was built for large, autonomous systems by the Internet Engineering Task Force (IETF) as an Interior Gateway Protocol. An *autonomous system* is a group of routers and network segments that share routing information freely with each other. An enterprise internetwork can be designed to contain one or more autonomous systems. The number of autonomous systems depends on the size, complexity, and organization of the network infrastructure.

NLSP is a link-state routing protocol in the IPX protocol stack. NLSP stands for NetWare Link Services Protocol. NLSP was developed to exchange routing information with IPX RIP in a hierarchical manner. The NLSP routers were designed to exchange NLSP routing information with each other and NLSP servers. NLSP servers and routers work with RIP, which communicates with end stations. A hierarchical routing environment can create routing areas of RIP and NLSP that link together into routing domains, which are autonomous systems. The routing domains can be linked to create a global enterprise internetwork.

7

Route Summarization

Routers can use a process call *route summarization* to reduce the size and overhead of the routing table. When routes are not summarized, the router must maintain a route to every network segment in the internetwork. Summarization is the capability of grouping network segments together by their addresses' leading bits, as long as the direction for sending data to those segments is the same.

Taking Figure 7.7 as an example, if all the network addresses began with the same leading bits, such as 198.5.192.0, then router R4 could send all data with those leading bits to router R2. The actual addresses could be 198.5.212.0,

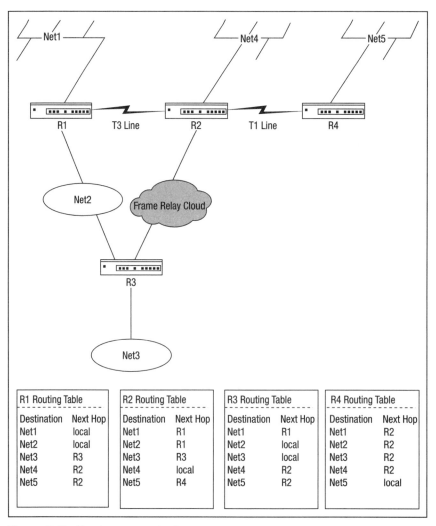

Figure 7.7 Route summarization.

198.5.193.0, 198.5.229.0, and 198.5.243.0, which appear to be vastly different but actually have the same 198.5.192.0 bits in common. The result is that router R4 reduces its routing table to a single entry.

For route summarization to be effective, network addresses should be assigned in a logical grouping.

THE TRANSPORT LAYER

Figure 7.8 shows the Transport layer in relation to the OSI Reference Model. The Transport layer is also referred to as Layer 4.

Protocols at the OSI Transport layer perform several functions:

➤ Multiplexing of transport connections onto network connections

➤ Error detection and recovery

➤ Flow control

➤ Sequence control

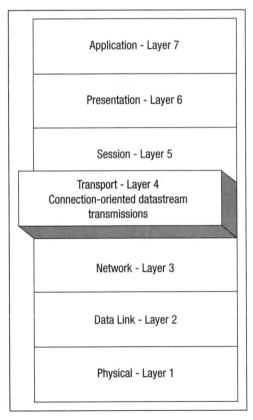

Figure 7.8   The Transport layer in the OSI Reference Model.

Transport-layer services are end-to-end services. Intermediate systems do not process the Transport layer. Instead, Transport-layer protocol segments are delivered to the destination computer in the same structure that they were transmitted in.

Multiplexing

Transport-layer services enable multiple applications to use the same Transport-layer datastream. The data from upper-protocol layers, and ultimately from the applications themselves, is multiplexed through segmentation and reassembly of each application's packets. The multiplexing function itself occurs when the data is received from the Session layer.

One of the most well-known multiplexing protocols is Winsock, which is based on the Berkeley Sockets API (Application Program Interface). Winsock is a Session-layer protocol that works with the multiplexing facility of Transport-layer protocols so that many Windows applications can use the same TCP/IP connection without even being "network-aware." Figure 7.9 shows how multiplexing works.

After data from upper layers has been multiplexed at the Transport layer, the only way that one application can be discerned from another is by looking at the port number of the data packet. When the data is received at the destination node, the Transport layer separates the data by port number and reassembles it so that the correct applications receive the correct data.

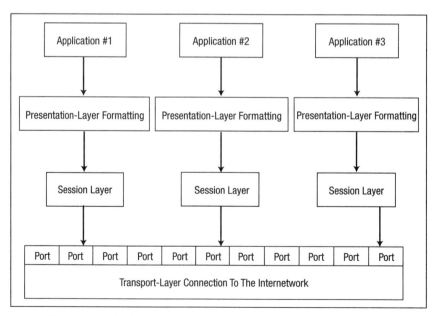

Figure 7.9 Multiplexing.

The Connection Orientation

The Transport layer is best known for *connection-oriented* services. Connection-oriented services are considered reliable because their mechanisms can verify whether or not data was received at the destination node.

The following is an overview of the connection–oriented transmission:

1. An application on the source computer sends a request to send a message to the destination computer. This message verifies that the destination computer can accept data.

2. The source node sends the data to the destination.

3. The Transport layer expects ACK (acknowledgment) packets from the destination node within a specified period of time. Acknowledgment packets ensure that no data is lost, damaged, or duplicated.

4. When ACK packets are received, the connection continues until all data transmission is complete, at which time the connection is closed.

5. When ACK packets are not received at the source computer, the source computer re-sends the data. After a certain number of retries, the connection is closed and the upper-layer protocols are notified of the problem.

6. The application receives the notification that data cannot be sent and notifies the user.

When the transmission is not reliable, it is called *connectionless*. Sometimes it is simply unnecessary to know whether data was sent. And if that information is not needed, why use all the extra overhead? That is where a connectionless Transport-layer service comes into the picture.

Connectionless transport does not use ACK packets. The application does not need to know whether the data was transferred. DHCP (Dynamic Host Configuration Protocol) is an upper-layer protocol that uses a connectionless Transport-layer protocol. The sending computer and the destination computer do not create the session. In fact, the sending DHCP Server simply doles out a dynamic address with the expectation that it will be received by the destination computer. If a dynamic address is not received, the server is not obligated to dole out the address again, because the computer could have been disconnected from the network for several reasons.

Flow Control

Flow control is a service—performed at the Transport layer—that manages how data is sent on a network that is experiencing various levels of congestion. Data flow must be managed for a couple of reasons:

➤ A high-speed computer can generate traffic faster than some network components can receive it.

➤ Multiple computers transmit data simultaneously.

The Transport layer manages flow control with a mechanism called *windowing* or a *sliding window*. Windowing is a conversation between the sending computer and the destination computer in which the destination computer tells the sending computer how much data it can receive between acknowledgments. This amount of data is the window, and it slides to a larger amount when there is less congestion on the network, then slides to a smaller size when there is more congestion on the network. The sending computer does not wait for an acknowledgment before sending the next segment of data. Instead, it sends a group of data segments before receiving acknowledgments. Otherwise, the network would be too slow, and the purpose of using windowing (which is to optimize data transmission with the network traffic conditions) would be defeated.

Sequence Control

The way that data is transmitted at the Transport layer, with the multiplexed datastream and the sliding window mechanism, data can be received out of order. Transport-layer services manage the sequence of data by reassembling segments in the correct order. A sequence number is assigned to each data segment at the Transport layer. As the data is received by the destination computer, it is reordered, as shown in Figure 7.10.

The Transport layer provides its services above the Network layer. The services at the Network layer are best-effort, nonguaranteed services. They manage locating and sending data to another computer, and they must rely on upper-layer services to provide reliability.

Conversely, the Transport layer depends on the Network layer to determine which hostnames are mapped to network addresses and which path to take to a given destination.

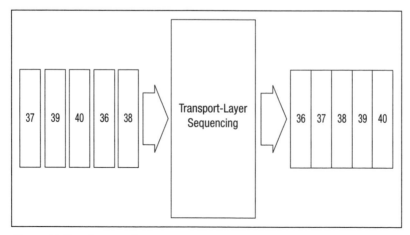

Figure 7.10 Sequencing.

Examples of Transport-layer protocols include:

➤ Transmission Control Protocol (TCP)

➤ User Datagram Protocol (UDP)

➤ Sequenced Packet Exchange (SPX)

Transmission Control Protocol

Transmission Control Protocol (TCP) is one of the Transport-layer protocols of the TCP/IP protocol suite. TCP tracks the individual data segments that the data is divided into.

On the Internet, for example, when an HTML file downloads into a computer from a Web server, the server's TCP layer does the following:

1. Divides the file into multiple packets.

2. Assigns a sequence number to each packet.

3. Forwards each packet to the IP Network layer.

IP receives the packets individually. It uses the same destination address, but might forward each packet to the destination on a different route. The receiving computer might receive the packets out of order. The receiving computer's TCP layer reassembles them in order and sends the file to the upper layers until it is displayed in the Web browser.

TCP is a connection-oriented protocol, and is therefore reliable. TCP ensures that the data is received by the end node. If one or more of the packets from the HTML file cannot be downloaded, TCP lets upper-layer protocols know. They, in turn, pass that message to the Web browser, which then displays an appropriate error message to the end user.

Table 7.3 shows the TCP header fields.

Table 7.3 TCP header fields.

Field	Length	Function
Source Port	16 bits	The source port number of the application that is initiating the data transfer. For example, the port number for Telnet is 23.
Destination Port	16 bits	The destination port number of the application that data is being transferred to.
Sequence Number	32 bits	The sequence number of the first data octet in this segment of data.

(continued)

Table 7.3 TCP header fields *(continued)*.

Field	Length	Function
Acknowledgment Number	32 bits	This control bit states the number of the sequence of data expected to be received next. The ACK number is sent for error correction. If no error in data receipt has occurred, then this field's value will be at or above the sequence number of the correctly received segment incremented by one. When TCP receives this type of ACK, it can assume that all of the segments with a value less than this number have been received.
Data Offset	4 bits	This number shows the point in the TCP packet where data starts.
Reserved	6 bits	Always set to zero. This area is reserved for future use.
Control Bits	6 bits	Each bit has a different significance. The first bit is the Urgent Pointer, the second bit is the ACK, the third bit is the Push function, the fourth bit is the connection reset, the fifth bit is synchronization of sequence numbers, and the last bit is the finish indicator of no more data from the sender.
Window	16 bits	This field indicates the number of data segments that the sender is willing to accept next. It works with the acknowledgment field to show which sequence number to start counting the window from.
Checksum	16 bits	Checksums are used for error detection. If the segment contains an odd number of header and text bit values to be checksummed, the last octet is padded with zeroes to form a 16-bit checksum. The pad is not transmitted as part of the segment. The checksum is calculated at the destination computer. If the checksum is not the same as the number in the header, the data is considered to be corrupt. TCP does not send an acknowledgment for a segment with a bad checksum.
Urgent Pointer	16 bits	If the urgent control bit is set in the Control Bits field, then this field will contain the sequence number of the octet following the urgent data.
Options	Variable # of bits	This field includes optional data and is a multiple of 8 bits.
Padding	Variable # of bits	This field contains the padded bits for the checksum field.

User Datagram Protocol

The User Datagram Protocol (UDP) is a Transport-layer protocol in the TCP/IP protocol stack. UDP and TCP are never used together. A network application will use either the TCP protocol or the UDP protocol.

UDP is a connectionless protocol. Connectionless protocols use less overhead than connection-oriented protocols do. UDP does not ensure that a packet arrives at its destination.

UDP is best used for short bursts of traffic. Some Application-layer protocols can use either UDP or TCP. FTP is an example of an Application-layer protocol that can use either UDP or TCP. These applications use the same port number when using UDP as they do when using TCP. TCP programs take advantage of the control data and reliability that TCP provides. UDP programs take advantage of the speed that UDP provides. Streaming or realtime applications are more likely to use UDP because of the faster network response.

Some of the applications that take advantage of the faster transmission that UDP provides are:

➤ DNS—Domain Name Service

➤ NTP—Network Time Protocol

➤ BOOTP—Boot Protocol

➤ DHCP—Dynamic Host Configuration Protocol

➤ TFTP—Trivial File Transfer Protocol

➤ NFS—Network File System

In each of these applications, the UDP protocol can provide a fast data transmission on the internetwork. When compared to the TCP header fields in Table 7.3, the UDP header fields, described in Table 7.4, show how much less overhead is consumed by UDP.

Sequenced Packet Exchange

SPX, or the Sequenced Packet Exchange protocol, is the Transport-layer protocol of NetWare's IPX protocol stack. SPX is a reliable, connection-oriented protocol.

SPX takes advantage of all the services that a Transport-layer protocol can have. It provides multiplexing, flow control, acknowledgments, and sequence control. SPX provides reliability over the IPX protocol, which is a connectionless Network-layer protocol.

SPX Printing

Specific services take advantage of the SPX protocol for its reliability. One service that uses SPX is NetWare's queue-based print services. The SPX

Table 7.4   UDP header fields.

Field	Length	Function
Source Port	16 bits	The source port number of the application that is initiating the data transfer. For example, the port number for Telnet is 23.
Destination Port	16 bits	The destination port number of the application that is receiving the data transfer.
UDP Length	16 bits	The number of bytes of data being sent.
UDP Checksum	16 bits	This field contains the result of an algorithm performed on the length of the header and data. The receiving node will perform the same algorithm and compare the result to the number oin this field to determine if there is an error. If error detection is unnecessary, UDP provides for this field being equivalent to zero.

protocol is used to ensure that the data packets placed in the NetWare queue are in the correct order and all accounted for. Printing data packets must be in the correct order and accounted for so that a printer does not spew out pages of indecipherable codes. When printing data packets are not all there and in order, the printer misses an escape character code and does not know that a formatting code is a formatting code, so it prints that formatting code. The print job never recovers from this type of error.

If printing problems occur on a NetWare queue-based network, it's helpful to check the SPX values of the client software. An administrator can adjust the protocol settings for SPX to increase the connections that SPX creates. This adjustment can stabilize printing in a volatile environment. Figure 7.11 shows

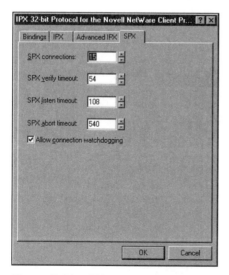

Figure 7.11   SPX protocol properties on a Windows 98 NetWare client.

the NetWare client 32, 32-bit IPX/SPX protocol properties of a Windows 98 PC. The default values are depicted here. The SPX connections value is the one that should be increased first. Using 60 SPX connections will typically cure an SPX-based printing problem. Timeouts can also be increased to stabilize the printing environment.

Name Resolution

Name resolution provides the ability for a network user to access an internetwork service without having to know the Network-layer address. Many protocol stacks use name resolution to simplify network access.

Domain Name Service

Domain Name Service (DNS) is a mapping mechanism and service in the TCP/IP protocol stack. It maps IP addresses to hostnames. People use names to help them remember how to access internetwork services. It is much easier to remember **myftpserver.mycompany.com** than it is to remember 199.5.25.81.

DNS servers receive requests from clients asking for an address to match the name that the client knows. If the DNS server has the address matching the name on file, it responds to the client. If the DNS server does not have the address matching the name on file, it passes the request to a higher-level DNS server. This process continues until the DNS request is passed to a root DNS server. If the root server cannot resolve the name to an IP address, the DNS servers pass an error message back through to the client. Many DNS servers maintain a cache of addresses so that frequently accessed services can be quickly responded to.

DNS is a hierarchical system. The highest level of the naming hierarchy is the suffix of the hostname. The common codes for this suffix are listed in Table 7.5.

Table 7.5 Hostname suffixes.

Naming Suffix	Meaning
gov	Government
com	Commercial
edu	Educational
int	International organization
mil	Military
net	Network related
org	Miscellaneous organization
arpa	Special facility used for reverse translation
two-letter codes	Abbreviations indicating the country of origin

The next level of the naming hierarchy is sometimes called a *zone,* or a local domain. The domain is the part of the name that represents an enterprise, organization, or other group. Further division of the name is allowed so that there can be subdomains. A sample domain name is **mycompany.com**. This name represents a group of IP addresses. Each service in the network, and each computer in the network, is given a *fully qualified domain name*. The fully qualified domain name is **host.mycompany.com** or **service. mycompany.com**.

DNS servers are actually software-based applications that run on a network server. Versions of DNS are available for all types of network operating systems, including Unix, Windows NT, and NetWare. Each DNS server application uses its own method for storing, retrieving, and dispensing the mapped addresses to requesting clients. The similarity between them all is the fact that each DNS application uses DNS to communicate with the clients and follows the formatting rules so that any DNS client can receive a mapped address from any DNS server.

DNS Clients

The DNS client is usually implemented as part of the TCP/IP protocol client. The client software has the following two functions:

➤ Sending a name-to-address resolution request to a DNS server

➤ When a failed resolution error is received, appending a domain-name suffix to the name and retrying the name-to-address resolution request

The DNS server is always configurable in the client software. The client software usually allows more than one DNS server to be defined. Multiple DNS servers are useful in the case of a server failure or numerous internetwork changes.

Windows Internet Name Service

Windows Internet Name Service (WINS) is used to map a NetBIOS name to an IP address. WINS is used on Windows PCs with the TCP/IP protocol stack. WINS differs from DNS in two significant ways:

➤ WINS is a dynamic service. WINS tables for name resolution are built without human intervention, whereas DNS files must be configured and managed by an administrator.

➤ WINS resolves NetBIOS names to IP addresses, whereas DNS resolves domain/hostnames to IP addresses. These are two different types of names, so they cannot be substituted for each other.

The dynamic nature of WINS works this way:

1. A WINS client boots up.
2. The WINS client contacts the configured WINS server address.

3. The WINS server registers the client's NetBIOS name and IP address.

4. If the NetBIOS name is already in use, the WINS server rejects the registration and sends an error message to the client, instructing it to change its name.

Service Advertising Protocol

Service Advertising Protocol (SAP) is the mechanism used by NetWare to provide to clients the names and addresses of services available on the network. SAP is a Transport-layer protocol that works in concert with IPX RIP, the Routing Information Protocol, to dynamically build tables of network services on every NetWare server and router.

SAP periodically broadcasts its SAP table to neighboring NetWare routers and servers. The SAP table contains the name of a service and its associated Network-layer address. Each server builds a table based on the information received. Basically, SAP tells the network what is available and where it is, whereas RIP tells the network how to get to it.

NetWare servers and routers maintain the SAP table, and clients gain access to services through transparent RIP requests to the NetWare server. These requests are transparent because the end user does not see these requests; they happen automatically.

CHAPTER SUMMARY

The Network layer and the Transport layer form the core logic for a protocol stack. Most protocol stacks can work over multiple Physical layer and Data Link layer protocol specifications, and do not specify any particular ones. The method of accessing internetwork services is left to the logic in the Network and Transport layers. Upper layers provide the end-user interface and supporting mechanisms, but are unaware of how data is transmitted throughout the internetwork.

The Network layer provides two basic functions:

➤ Specifying logical network addresses and logical node addresses

➤ Routing data throughout the internetwork

Logical addressing is an essential foundation to routing data throughout the internetwork. The Network layer provides for both a network address, which is applied to a segment on the internetwork, and a node address, which is applied to a computer or network device on the internetwork. The network address is similar to a street name, and the node address is similar to a house number. The combination of house number and street name is unique so that messages are delivered to the correct house.

Each network address on the internetwork is required to be unique throughout the internetwork. Each node address is required to be unique on an individual segment. The combination of the two creates a unique Network-layer address.

Routing is the movement of data throughout an internetwork, from one segment to the next, until the data reaches its correct destination. Routing requires special routing equipment, either a router or a brouter, to move the data. Servers can act as routers when they have multiple network interface cards and are configured to forward data from one segment to another. A router works at the Network layer. The router does the following:

➤ Receives data packets

➤ Determines the destination of each packet

➤ Selects a route to send the packet on

➤ Strips the Network-layer header off the packet and creates a new one to indicate the next passage through the internetwork

➤ Forwards the data to the next router in the path toward the destination

Brouters perform the same function as routers do, but brouters add a level of complexity. A brouter is a combination of a bridge and a router. A brouter determines whether a packet is supposed to be bridged. A bridge decides whether to forward a packet, depending on the destination address.

The need for bridging packets is usually determined by the type of protocols used on the internetwork. Routable protocols are best transmitted via routers. However, nonroutable protocols—like IBM's SNA (Systems Network Architecture)—must be either bridged or encapsulated within a routable protocol to traverse the internetwork.

Routers maintain a table of routing information, which they use to determine how to send data. The table can either be manually configured by an administrator (this type of routing is static) or be dynamically built and maintained by a routing protocol (this type of routing is dynamic).

The two basic types of routing protocols are:

➤ Distance vector

➤ Link state

A distance-vector routing protocol uses the distance to the destination network—typically measured in hops (the number of routers to cross)—and the direction, or vector, in which data is sent. Distance-vector routers send their entire routing tables to the neighboring routers to update them, have a slow convergence time, and are susceptible to routing loops. Split horizon and poison reverse are two mechanisms that attempt to prevent routing loops. IP

RIP (Routing Information Protocol), IPX RIP, and RTMP (Route Table Maintenance Protocol) are all distance-vector protocols.

A link-state routing protocol uses a cost metric and link-state advertisements to create and update routing tables. The link-state router announces its presence on the internetwork by sending a hello packet to its neighbors. The neighbors add the new route to their tables and send a link-state advertisement (LSA) to the rest of the internetwork. Each router copies the information from the LSA into its routing table and then forwards it. Link-state protocols are more complex to run on a router, but have a fast convergence time and have very low network-bandwidth overhead. IP OSPF (Open Shortest Path First) and IPX NLSP (NetWare Link State Protocol) are both link-state protocols.

The Transport layer offers several services in its protocol specifications:

➤ **Multiplexing** Taking data received from multiple upper-layer protocols and interweaving them to create a single datastream for transmission across the internetwork. This is accomplished by using specific port numbers to represent the sending upper-layer protocol. For example, SMTP (Simple Mail Transport Protocol) uses port 25.

➤ **Connection-oriented transport** Using acknowledgment packets to ensure that data arrives at the destination computer.

➤ **Connectionless transport** Not using acknowledgments in order to reduce overhead and increase transmission speed.

➤ **Flow control** Windowing, or a sliding window, of the number of data segments that a destination computer is capable of receiving. Flow control optimizes the data transmission so that it matches the congestion on the internetwork—reducing transmission size when the network is congested, and increasing it when the network has more bandwidth available.

➤ **Sequence control** Ensuring that the data received by the destination computer can be reassembled in the correct order. The sending computer's Transport layer assigns sequence numbers to each data segment and forwards them to the Network layer. The Network layer can route the data through multiple paths on the internetwork. The data segments can be sent along different paths and arrive out of order. The destination computer's Transport layer reorders the segments according to the sequence numbers.

The TCP/IP protocol suite has two types of Transport-layer protocols. TCP (Transmission Control Protocol) is a reliable, connection-oriented transport. UDP (User Datagram Protocol) is an unreliable, connectionless transport.

The IPX protocol suite uses a single Transport-layer protocol. SPX (Sequenced Packet Exchange) is a reliable, connection-oriented transport. SPX is utilized by services that require reliability.

Name resolution is the method that various protocol stacks use to make services more accessible to end users. It is easier to remember a name than a complex number. The TCP/IP protocol stack uses DNS (Domain Name Service) to resolve IP addresses to IP service names. Windows PCs use WINS (Windows Internet Name Service) with the TCP/IP protocol stack. NetWare servers use SAP (Service Advertising Protocol) to ensure that clients can access NetWare services.

REVIEW QUESTIONS

1. How many computers connected to the same hub can use the same node address?

    a. 1

    b. 8

    c. 16

    d. 10

2. George has a network of a single segment and uses a network Class C IP address of 191.5.16.0 with the default mask of 255.255.255.0. George adds a new hub and router to the network and connects both the hub and the single segment to different interfaces on the router. George attempts to use the same network address, but different node addresses, on both router interfaces, but receives an error. Why did George receive an error?

    a. Because there were no computers connected to the hub.

    b. Because the router should use the same node address for each of its interfaces.

    c. Because the network address should be unique for each interface.

    d. Because the router was not IP-compatible.

3. Grant is the network administrator on an internetwork that has an IBM mainframe using SNA, and NetWare servers using IPX. Grant knows that SNA is not encapsulated. He has a single piece of equipment connecting his network segment to the backbone that is attached to the mainframe and servers. What type of equipment is connecting the segment to the backbone?

    a. Router

    b. Brouter

    c. MAU

    d. Repeater

4. Which of the following is required to route data through an internetwork?

   a. Repeater

   b. MAC address

   c. Subnet mask

   d. Network address

5. Which OSI protocol-layer header does a router change before forwarding data to a different segment?

   a. Data Link

   b. Network

   c. Transport

   d. Session

7

6. What is the difference between a routable and a nonroutable protocol?

   a. A routable protocol lacks a Network-layer addressing scheme.

   b. A nonroutable protocol lacks a Network-layer addressing scheme.

   c. A routable protocol needs to multiplex a datastream.

   d. A nonroutable protocol needs to multiplex a datastream.

7. Which of the following is a nonroutable protocol?

   a. IP

   b. IPX

   c. DLC

   d. NetBEUI

8. Ken is adding a branch office of seven users on a single hub to the internetwork by connecting them via routers and a fractional T1 connection. The router at the home office is a smart router with knowledge of all the network segments contained in its routing table. Which of the following should Ken configure on the branch router?

   a. Systems Network Architecture

   b. User Datagram Protocol

   c. Sequence control

   d. Default gateway

9. Which type of routing is demonstrated when a network administrator manually configures each route on the internetwork routers?

   a. Default routing

   b. Subnet routing

   c. Static routing

   d. Dynamic routing

10. Which of the following are the types of dynamic routing protocols?
    [Choose the two best answers]
    a. Distance vector
    b. Default gateway
    c. Link state
    d. Subnetworking

11. Which routing protocol uses a hello packet to announce a router's presence
    on the internetwork?
    a. RTMP
    b. IP RIP
    c. IPX RIP
    d. NLSP

12. What mechanism is used by distance-vector routing protocols as a
    prevention measure against routing loops?
    a. Open Shortest Path First
    b. Poison reverse
    c. Flow control
    d. Multiplexing

13. What Transport-layer function enables multiple applications to use the same
    Internet connection?
    a. Multiplexing
    b. Connectionless transport
    c. Flow control
    d. Sequence control

14. When a Transport-layer protocol uses ACKs to verify that data is received
    by a destination computer, which function is it using?
    a. Name resolution
    b. Connectionless transport
    c. Connection-oriented transport
    d. Congestion control

15. Which of the following mechanisms is used to manage data transmission to
    minimize network congestion at the Transport layer?
    a. Split horizon
    b. Name resolution
    c. Connection-oriented transport
    d. Windowing

16. What method ensures that data packets are assembled in the correct order?
    a. Split horizon
    b. Connectionless transport
    c. Sequence control
    d. Sliding window

17. Which of the following is the connection-oriented Transport-layer protocol used with IP?
    a. TCP
    b. UDP
    c. RIP
    d. OSPF

7

18. What is the Transport-layer protocol used with IPX?
    a. TCP
    b. UDP
    c. SPX
    d. DNS

19. Which of the following protocols is used in concert with RIP to enable service access to network clients?
    a. DNS
    b. WINS
    c. NetBIOS
    d. SAP

20. Which protocol resolves NetBIOS names to IP addresses?
    a. Domain Name Service
    b. Windows Internet Name Service
    c. Service Advertising Protocol
    d. NetBIOS Extended User Interface

21. Which protocol resolves IP hostnames to IP addresses?
    a. DNS
    b. WINS
    c. SAP
    d. NetBEUI

HANDS-ON PROJECTS

These projects examine routing and name resolution. The routing example requires a Windows NT 4 Server with two network interface cards and full administrative access to the computer or domain. The name-resolution example requires a NetWare 5 server, a client, and administrative access to the Novell Directory Services Tree.

These exercises are intended to be run on a test or lab network. They are not intended to be used on a production internetwork because changing some properties on the production internetwork could cause performance problems. The IP addressing scheme for the test network should be available for these exercises.

Project 7.1

This project sets up routing on a Microsoft Windows NT 4 Server and then executes a diagnostic program to determine the route to a destination network. Windows NT 4 Server includes a Multiprotocol Router that can route IP RIP, forward BOOTP packets, and route IPX RIP. This exercise shows you how to enable static routing on the server without the MPR component. The Windows NT 4 Server should have at least two network interface cards, and both the cards and TCP/IP should be configured on the server.

To set up routing on a Microsoft Windows NT 4 Server and then execute a diagnostic program to determine the route to a destination network:

1. Boot the Windows NT 4 Server.
2. Log on as Administrator of the computer or domain, or equivalent.
3. Click on Start|Settings|Control Panel.
4. Double-click on the Network icon. The Network properties window for the NT Server will open.

Steps 3 and 4 can be replaced by right-clicking on the Network Neighborhood icon on the desktop and selecting Properties.

5. Select Protocols.
6. Select Microsoft TCP/IP.
7. Click on Properties. The Microsoft TCP/IP Properties dialog box will open.
8. Click on the Routing tab.

9. Check the Enable IP Forwarding option. At this point, the server is capable of routing between the two network interface cards and their connected segments.

10. Click on OK to save the changes; then, reboot the server.

11. Log on to the NT Server.

12. Open a Command Prompt window.

13. Type "route print" and press Enter. This command will display the routes configured in the Windows NT routing table.

14. Type "route add *ip-address* mask *subnet-mask gateway-ip-address* metric *hops*" where *ip-address* is the IP address of the destination subnet, *subnet-mask* is its subnet mask, *gateway-ip-address* is the address of the router that will lead to the destination subnet, and *hops* is the number of routers that must be passed to get to the destination. Press Enter.

15. Type "route print" and press Enter. The new static route should appear in the Windows NT routing table.

16. Type "tracert *ip-address*" to display the route taken to the destination network.

Project 7.2

This project will configure DNS on a NetWare 5 server. This process uses the Novell Directory Services tree as a repository for DNS information.

To configure DNS on a NetWare server and Novell Directory Services tree:

1. If DNS is not installed into the Novell Directory Services tree, then the first step is to install it. To do so, boot up the client workstation.

2. Open the Network Neighborhood by double-clicking on it.

3. Open the NetWare 5 server by double-clicking on it.

4. Open the SYS volume by double-clicking on it.

5. Open the DNSDHCP folder by double-clicking on it.

6. Double-click on the SETUP.EXE application to begin the installation.

7. Click on Next at the welcome screen.

8. Accept the default path for the file installation and click on Next.

9. Click on Next to copy the snap-in files.

10. Type the path as "SYS:PUBLIC\WIN32" and click on OK.

11. Click on Yes to read the readme file.

12. Close the file and click on OK to finish. DNSDHCP is now installed on the NetWare server, and the DNSDHCP extensions are available on the NetWare Administrator in the Win32 directory (NWADMN32.EXE).

13. Start the NetWare Administrator by executing "SYS:PUBLIC\WIN32\NWADMN32.EXE".

14. Click on the Tools menu and select the DNSDHCP Management console.

15. The DNSDHCP Console starts. There are two tabs—one for DNS and another for DHCP. Select the DNS Services tab.

16. Click on Create Object and select DNS Server.

17. Click on OK and select the NetWare server that will carry the DNS Service.

18. Name the DNS Server and provide its domain name.

19. Click on the All Zones object on the DNS Service tab; then, click on the Create button on the toolbar.

20. Choose a zone and click on OK.

21. Click on Create to establish the domain as a zone.

22. To designate resources that can be resolved from IP addresses to names, the next step is to create a resource record. The resource record contains the IP address and the name to resolve for any resource in the zone. After resource records are created, DNS will be installed and will now resolve those resource records.

CHAPTER EIGHT

TCP/IP FUNDAMENTALS

After Reading This Chapter And Completing The Exercises, You Will Be Able To:

➤ Name the governing bodies of the Internet and TCP/IP suite

➤ Understand the architectural model of TCP/IP

➤ Understand TCP/IP addressing

➤ Name and define the major protocol of the TCP/IP suite

➤ Understand the role of TCP/IP sockets and ports

➤ Define Domain Name Service (DNS) and describe how it works

The Transmission Control Protocol/Internet Protocol (TCP/IP) is an industry de facto standard suite of protocols developed in 1969 by the U.S. Department of Defense Advanced Research Projects Agency (DARPA). The term TCP/IP is a catchall to mean anything related to TCP/IP internetworking technologies, which includes both protocols and defined practices.

The original design goal of TCP/IP was to develop a high-speed communication mechanism for use over packet-switched networks. The protocols being defined were required to be independent of the underlying operating systems and network architecture (cable type) so that dissimilar networks would be able to communicate with each other. The original experiment was on ARPANET. This network has since grown into the Internet that we know today.

Although TCP/IP has a set of published standards, it does not follow that all TCP/IP stacks are the same. Although all of them adhere to the standards, they also add their own customizations to better fit the specific operating systems and other requirements they have. An example of this is the Microsoft TCP/IP stack, which has other mechanisms built in to allow different types of name translation. This customization can sometimes lead to incompatibilities.

This chapter addresses TCP/IP in a general way, covering the TCP/IP protocol suite and how it is governed, along with its architectural model as it relates to the Open Systems Interconnection (OSI) Reference Model. This chapter also explains TCP/IP addressing and discusses protocols that aid in troubleshooting TCP/IP and those that help it operate efficiently.

IP GOVERNING BODIES

Volunteer organizations have emerged to manage the development of the TCP/IP suite of protocols. These organizations attempt to ensure that TCP/IP is developed in a coherent way, and they promote the use of the Internet. These governing bodies do not dictate TCP/IP specifications, however. Opinions on proposed changes are considered and decisions are arrived at by consensus. Because IP addresses are a finite resource, these governing bodies control how and when they are assigned.

A complete process has been defined that allows for proposals of new features or for altering the way the suite works. The standards by which the suite works are published as Requests For Comments (RFC.) These RFCs cover network services, protocols and their implementations, and policy matters relating to the suite.

Internet Activities Board (IAB)

This board was established in 1983 to help coordinate the design, management, and engineering of the Internet. This group operates in a technical advisory capacity to the Internet Society. Beneath the IAB are two task forces: the Internet Engineering Task Force and the Internet Research Task Force.

Internet Engineering Task Force (IETF)

The IETF is responsible for specifying the protocols used on the Internet and for defining the architecture of the Internet. Membership in the IETF is completely voluntary. Also, anyone may attend their meetings and participate.

Internet Research Task Force (IRTF)

The IRTF is the research arm of the IAB. The scope of the research it performs includes Internet protocols, applications, architecture, and technology.

Internet Assigned Numbers Authority (IANA)

The IANA organization has responsibilities in three interrelated areas: Internet protocol addresses, domain names, and protocol parameters. These include the root server system. The IANA's goal is to "preserve the central coordinating functions of the global Internet for the public good."

THE ARCHITECTURE OF TCP/IP

You were introduced to the Open Systems Interconnection (OSI) Reference Model in Chapter 1. The TCP/IP suite of protocols follows a similar four-layer conceptual model, which I'll discuss to help you visualize how data is passed through the TCP/IP stack from an application to the network cable.

The TCP/IP model is called the ARPA model, after the U.S. government agency that initially developed TCP/IP. This model maps functionality against the OSI Reference Model.

 Because the TCP/IP standards are voluntary, you might find that different implementations vary slightly from what is presented here. However, this discussion will outline the model that has been used by Microsoft and most other TCP/IP implementations.

The TCP/IP architectural model has four layers, which are listed here in order from bottom to top:

➤ Network Interface layer

➤ Internet layer

➤ Transport layer

➤ Application layer

The order of these layers, starting at the bottom, illustrates the flow of data from the network cable through to the application on the desktop. Data comes in at the Network Interface layer, and your applications gain access to resources from the Application layer.

Applications and protocols that are considered part of the TCP/IP suite map to at least level one of this four-layer model. As you can see in Figure 8.1,

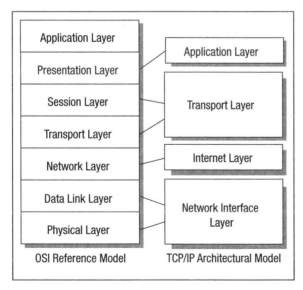

Figure 8.1   The relationship between the TCP/IP architectural model and the OSI Reference Model.

some layers of the TCP/IP architectural model actually map to more than one layer of the OSI Reference Model.

The Network Interface Layer

At the bottom of the TCP/IP architectural model is the Network Interface layer. The purpose of this layer is to send and receive frames. *Frames* are single packets of information. This layer pulls frames from the network and puts them on the network. This layer maps to the Physical and Data Link layers of the OSI model.

One of TCP/IP's strengths is that it was designed to be independent of the underlying network access method, so it works regardless of whether the physical network is token ring or Ethernet. This independence also allows TCP/IP to be more easily adapted for new technologies as they become available.

The Internet Layer

This layer is responsible for addressing, packaging, and routing functions. Protocols operating at this layer of the model encapsulate packets into Internet datagrams. All necessary routing algorithms are run here also.

The core protocols of the TCP/IP suite that run at the Internet layer include IP, ARP, ICMP, and IGMP; each offers a specific service at this layer:

➤ IP (Internet Protocol) is responsible for IP addressing and for the fragmentation and reassembly of packets. It is a routable protocol.

➤ ARP (Address Resolution Protocol) resolves Internet-layer addresses (TCP/IP addresses) to Network-layer addresses (Media Access Control [MAC] addresses) of hosts on the same physical network.

➤ ICMP (Internet Control Message Protocol) is responsible for diagnostic functions and for reporting on errors regarding the delivery of IP packets.

➤ IGMP (Internet Group Management Protocol) manages IP multicast groups.

The Internet layer of the TCP/IP model maps to the Network layer of the OSI Reference Model.

The Transport Layer

Protocols at the Transport layer provide for communication sessions between computers. This layer provides the Application layer with session and datagram services. The two protocols that operate at this layer are TCP (Transmission Control Protocol) and UDP (User Datagram Protocol).

TCP provides a connection-oriented, reliable communication service. TCP establishes the connection and the sequencing, and acknowledges packets as they are sent through the "three-way handshake," which is covered later in this chapter. TCP can also recover from errors by resending packets. This protocol is used for one-to-one communications. It is commonly used when a large amount of data is being sent.

UDP is a connectionless, unreliable communication service. This protocol is used when the amount of data being transferred is small or when the application itself provides reliability. The amount of data sent over UDP is generally very small, meaning that all the data to be sent can fit into a single packet. UDP provides one-to-one and one-to-many communications.

The Transport layer maps to the Transport layer and to part of the Session layer of the OSI Reference Model.

The Application Layer

The Application layer provides applications with the ability to access the services of the other layers of the TCP/IP architectural model. The Application layer also defines the protocols that the applications can use to do this. Many protocols currently operate at this level, and new ones are being developed all the time.

Common protocols that operate at this level include HTTP, FTP, and SMTP; management protocols that operate at this level include DNS (discussed later in this chapter) and SNMP:

➤ HTTP (Hypertext Transfer Protocol) is used by Web browsers to transfer pages and files. You use this protocol for browsing the World Wide Web (WWW).

➤ FTP (File Transfer Protocol) is used for file transfer between two hosts.

➤ SMTP (Simple Mail Transfer Protocol) is used for the transfer of messages and attachments.

➤ DNS (Domain Name Service) is used to resolve hostnames to IP addresses.

➤ SNMP (Simple Network Management Protocol) is used to provide network devices with a method to report network management information to a management console. These network devices include routers, bridges, and intelligent hubs.

The Application layer of the TCP/IP model maps to the Presentation layer of the OSI Reference Model.

FUNDAMENTAL CONCEPTS OF TCP/IP ADDRESSING

When you send a letter to someone in the mail, you need to know the person's address, and this address needs to be unique. The address might look something like this:

Donald Somebody
113 Somewhere Road
Whatever, TX 77479-6255

This address uniquely identifies where Mr. Somebody lives so the post office can route the letter to him. The address is divided into distinct parts: The street name, city, and ZIP code tell the post office where the person lives. The name of the person tells the post office which individual this letter is intended for. All this information is needed to make sure that the letter is delivered to the correct person.

The same principle applies to computer networks. In order to ensure that a packet arrives at its intended destination, the destination needs to have a unique address. The address must identify both the network where the packet should go and the unique individual computer that the packet is intended for.

In computer terms, this unique identifier is the MAC address of the network card. A MAC address looks something like this: 09-00-90-97-12-08. Because MAC addresses are branded into network cards as they are manufactured, it is pretty safe to assume that each one is unique. The problem is that MAC addresses are difficult to remember. Because TCP/IP reduces the 6-byte MAC address to a 4-byte address, the address is easier to remember.

From the outset, the TCP/IP suite of protocols was designed with wide area networks (WANs) in mind. It was recognized that a protocol would need to be routable to many different networks and would need to uniquely identify individuals with ease. In this case, *routable* means that communication should be possible between two hosts on entirely different networks if they are connected via a router or other device. Communication also needs to be independent of the underlying systems that process the packets, whether they are mainframe systems, corporate PC networks, or individuals with dial-up connections to the Internet.

The original specification allowed a TCP/IP address to be a 32-bit number. For ease of use, it has become customary to break this number into four 8-bit fields called *octets*. This number is a binary number, which most people find difficult to remember. So, for the sanity of those using it every day, it is common practice to express these octets as decimal numbers. When this is done, the address is considered to be in *dotted decimal notation*. Here is an example of a binary notation translated into a dotted decimal notation:

```
Binary notation:   11000000   00010111   11100110   01101110
Decimal notation:  192.23.230.110
```

The first part of the IP address denotes the network the computer is on. This portion of the address is called the *network ID*. The second portion identifies the individual computer. This portion of the IP address is called the *host ID*. (This will be explained in more detail later in this chapter.) Each host that participates on a network must have a unique combination of a network ID and host ID. This is collectively known as a host's IP address.

Binary numbers and their implications are explained in the "Binary And Decimal Number Systems" section later in this chapter.

The Five Classes Of IP Addresses

When the TCP/IP suite was developed, the designers decided that there must to be way to define both an individual network and the computers that were a part of that network (known as *hosts*.) This addressing scheme would need to identify networks of different sizes. To this end, the Internet community defined five classes of networks, to be known as Classes A, B, C, D, and E. Of these, only three (A, B, and C) were used to define specific networks and hosts. The other two were set aside for specialized tasks (IP multicasting, for example).

The three classes vary by the number of hosts they can support. Remember, an IP address is a 32-bit number. Each IP address has two parts: a network ID and a host ID. By setting aside parts of the number to identify the network and parts to identify the host, you can allow for both large and small networks.

You can easily tell which class a network ID belongs to by looking at the first octet of the address. Each class has a value that falls within a particular range.

Class A Networks

Class A networks are very large. In a Class A network, the first octet specifies the network ID, and the following three octets identify the host ID. As shown in Table 8.1, this scheme allows for a potential of 16,777,214 hosts on a single Class A network. The first octet of a Class A address has a value of between 1 and 126. The remaining 24 bits of the address identify the host ID. The high-order bit is always zero.

Class B Networks

Class B networks are assigned to midrange to large networks. In a Class B network, the first two octets specify the network ID, and the following two

Table 8.1 Default network IDs.

Class	Network ID Range	Network ID Portion	Host	Number Of Hosts
A	1–126	w	x.y.z	16,777,214
B	128–191	w.x	y.z	65,534
C	192–223	w.x.y	z	254

octets identify the host. As shown in Table 8.1, this scheme allows for a potential of 65,534 hosts on a single Class B network. The first octet of a Class B address has a value of between 128 and 191. The remaining 16 bits of the address identify the host ID. The two high-order bits are always 1 0.

Class C Networks

Class C networks are assigned to small networks. In a Class C network, the first three octets specify the network ID, and the following one octet identifies the host. As shown in Table 8.1, this scheme allows for a potential of 254 hosts on a single Class C network. The first octet of a Class C address has a value of between 192 and 223. The remaining 8 bits of the address identify the host ID. The three high-order bits are always 1 1 0.

Class D And Class E Networks

Class D networks are used for broadcasting messages to many hosts, a process called *multicasting*. Class E is reserved for experimental purposes and is not currently used. Neither of these classes is used to identify individual networks and hosts and therefore are not discussed further in this chapter.

You may have noticed that there is a missing number in this list, 127. That's because 127.x.y.z has been reserved for use as a loopback for testing and interprocess communication on the local computer. Also, 255 has been reserved for broadcasting. Therefore, these numbers should never be used on your network.

If you want to use the public Internet, then your network ID must be unique. Therefore, you do not get to choose your TCP/IP address. However, you can subnet your address. This will be discussed later in this chapter.

Network IDs

As mentioned earlier, the network ID specifies the network portion of the IP address. Expressed on its own, the network ID is not an IP address. A complete IP address requires a network ID and a host ID. All hosts sharing the same network ID are considered to be on the same network and can communicate with each other. All hosts on the same physical network that need to communicate with each other should share the same network ID.

The network ID must be unique within your network. Networks with different network IDs cannot communicate without the help of other equipment, such as a router. If your network is going to be connected directly to the Internet, then the network ID must be unique on the Internet also. This is why network IDs are regulated by the Internet Information Center (InterNIC).

As noted earlier, the addresses 127 and 255 have been reserved, so these should not be used on your network. You also cannot have a network ID that contains only zeros. Figure 8.2 shows a Class C address with its network ID and host ID portions highlighted.

Host IDs

Host IDs are used to uniquely identify a client or resource on your network. This means that no two systems on the same network can share a host ID. If this happens, you have what is called an *IP conflict*. Also, each byte in the host ID will be between 1 and 254. The host ID cannot be all ones because this scheme is used for broadcasts.

In simple terms, then, the network ID is the portion of the IP address showing which subnet a computer is on. The host ID is the portion that uniquely identifies the host on a given subnet.

Binary And Decimal Number Systems

Before going any further, we need to understand how the binary number system works. We are all familiar with the decimal system because we use it every day. Unfortunately, computers "speak" only binary. One of the many amazing things that goes on in your computer all the time is the conversion of everything you do into binary.

A decimal number is Base10. Each placeholder is a multiple of 10 larger than the one preceding it. This means that the decimal system has placeholders that

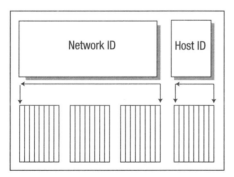

Figure 8.2   A Class C address showing the network ID and host ID portions.

can each contain one of 10 values, 0 through 9. Each digit in a decimal number is a multiple of a placeholder. Some decimal placeholders are:

100000   10000   1000   100   10   1

Let's say you want to express the number 192. We know what this looks like on paper, but if you place the number under the placeholders you get a clearer view of what it means.

100000	10000	1000	100	10	1
			1	9	2

As you can see, you have one 100, nine 10s, and two 1s, which equals a total of 192.

Binary, on the other hand, is Base2. Each placeholder is a multiple of two larger than the one preceding it. This means that the binary system has placeholders that can each contain one of two values: 0 or 1. Each digit in a binary number is a multiple of a placeholder. Some binary placeholders are:

128   64   32   16   8   4   2   1

To express 192 decimal in binary format, you would write 11000000. In binary, it looks like this:

128	64	32	16	8	4	2	1
1	1	0	0	0	0	0	0

That is one 128 and one 64.

As you can see, binary numbers can become very long, making them more difficult to remember or recognize at a glance. That is why IP addresses are converted to decimal. Binary-to-decimal conversions are used when calculating custom subnet masks. A *subnet mask* is a 32-bit address that is used to mask or "screen" a portion of the IP address. When applied, this mask tells you which part of the IP address is the network ID and which part is the host ID.

Subnet Masks And Subnetting

Now that you know about IP addresses and the basic network classes, it's time to consider how the computer systems "know" which part of the address is the network ID and which is the host ID. In a simple world, this would be easy because the InterNIC assigns TCP/IP addresses and they all have a defined number of possible hosts and standard or default subnet masks. But this is the real world, and sometimes the needs of organizations force them to adapt their IP address range to suit themselves.

About the only thing you can tell at a glance is what class the address range is from. It is impossible to tell, simply by looking at an IP address, which part is the network ID and which part is the host ID. So how do the systems and routers of your network know?

What you need is a simple method to take an IP address and break it into its two parts accurately. Fortunately, this is just what the subnet mask was designed to do. Each class comes with a default subnet mask, but due to network constraints (and just plain common sense), most organizations—especially those large enough to have a Class A or Class B address—create their own custom subnet masks to better fit their needs.

Consider a large organization that has a Class A address. The total number of client IDs available is almost 17 million. Now, for IP to work, all of these computers would have to exist on the same physical network!

Clearly, this is not practical and exceeds the specifications for all cabling systems. Also, many organizations are dispersed in multiple offices or even across continents. Even in the case of a Class B network, having this many computers would saturate your network with packets and prevent hosts from being able to communicate with each other. Therefore, networks are divided into manageable sizes and are connected by routers or some other network device.

This is done by breaking down the single network ID you are assigned into many unique network IDs and then connect them together. This is done through assigning a custom subnet mask. Each section of the physical network needs to have a unique subnet mask (and therefore a unique network ID). How this is done, and how you can work out the network ID based on custom subnet masks, will be discussed later in this chapter.

Subnet Masks

The three network classes already mentioned have a default subnet mask, as shown in Table 8.2.

As you can see, each number that corresponds to a value in the network ID is filled with a 1 in the subnet mask. Each bit that corresponds to a part of the host ID is filled with a zero.

If you need to break your network ID into smaller networks, you can create a "custom" subnet mask. This will be discussed later, but in simple terms, you can

Table 8.2 Default subnet masks.

Class	Default Subnet Mask (Decimal)	Default Subnet Mask (Binary)
A	255.0.0.0	11111111.00000000.00000000.00000000
B	255.255.0.0	11111111.11111111.00000000.00000000
C	255.255.255.0	11111111.11111111.11111111.00000000

"borrow" bits from the host ID to further define the network ID. This mask can then be used in the same way as a default subnet mask to define those computers on the same network.

It is necessary to have the IP address and the subnet mask in order to ascertain the IP address of a host. Even though there are default subnet masks given to each class, many organizations have created custom subnet masks.

It is important to note that the network ID remains the same for all users, but the portion the network recognizes as the network ID is changed by using a subnet mask.

So how does IP use this information to figure out whether a packet was intended for a client on the local network? The answer is something called *ANDing*. ANDing is a process where the IP address of the sending machine is matched against its subnet mask. Matching bits are assigned a value of 1. The same process is performed on the destination host's IP address. Comparing the results tells us whether the two hosts are on the same network (a perfect match means they are.) Every time a packet is sent from one IP client to another, IP internally performs the ANDing to work out where the host is. If the host is on the same network, the packet is forwarded. If not, the packet is sent to an IP router or to a default gateway, as explained later in this chapter.

This is how ANDing works. The sending host's IP address is ANDed with its subnet mask to generate a value. Then the destination IP address is also ANDed. If the two results match, then the two hosts are on the same network and the packet is forwarded directly to the host. If they are different, then the hosts are not on the same network and the packet is sent to the default gateway.

So let's look at an example of how ANDing works. Let's say that the host—with an IP address of 192.124.19.10 with a default subnet mask—is trying to send a packet to 192.124.19.142 with a default subnet mask.

The initial ANDing at the host is as follows:

```
IP Address (Decimal):  192.124.19.10
Subnet Mask:           255.255.255.0
IP Address (Binary):   11000000  01111100  00010011  00001010
Subnet Mask:           11111111  11111111  11111111  00000000
ANDing Result:         11000000  01111100  00010011  00000000
```

Then, the destination IP address is ANDed in the same way:

```
IP Address (Decimal):  192.124.19.142
Subnet Mask:           255.255.255.0
IP Address (Binary):   11000000  01111100  00010011  10001110
```

```
Subnet Mask:        11111111  11111111  11111111
ANDing Result:      11000000  01111100  0001001
```

When you compare the ANDing results, you will see
therefore, both hosts reside on the same subnet and t⌐
forwarded directly. Because this whole process runs
have to perform this task manually. However, it is us⌐⟍
where a packet should be sent.

Subnetting

Subnetting is the process of breaking your assigned IP address range into smaller
clusters of hosts that better fit your business need. You might want to do this for
several reasons:

➤ Your users and resources are dispersed at different physical locations.

➤ Your users are physically dispersed in the same location.

➤ You have specific security requirements.

➤ You want to mix different cabling types.

➤ You want to reduce traffic congestion on a particular segment of your
   network.

You can never gain additional host IDs from subnetting; in fact, you lose host
IDs when you subnet. However, you can create additional network IDs to make
your network more manageable.

Remember, a network ID is determined through a combination of the assigned
network ID and the subnet mask. By manipulating the subnet mask (making it
larger by borrowing bits from the host ID), you can create multiple network
IDs from the single one assigned to your organization.

Whatever the reason for your need to subnet, you need certain information
before you can proceed. Once you have this information, you will know how
many different network IDs you will have to create. The information you will
need to gather includes the following:

➤ The number of physical segments your network has

➤ The number of hosts you'll need on each segment

Every client requires a unique host ID, and each physical network segment
requires its own network ID.

As mentioned earlier, network IDs are assigned by InterNIC. IP addresses are
getting scarce, so it is imperative that you make good use of the one you have
been given. Each IP address assigned has an associated default subnet mask. The
combination of the subnet mask and the IP address allows you to determine
which part of the address is the network ID and which part is the host ID.

To create additional network IDs, you alter the subnet mask by taking bits from the host-ID portion of the address and adding them to the network ID. When you create additional network IDs, you have fewer bits for the host ID, so you can have fewer hosts. This is the price you pay for added flexibility.

It is highly recommended (and mandatory when using some routers) that the new bits be contiguous with the subnet mask, meaning that the bits must be high-order bits (bits starting on the left-hand side of the octet).

The number of bits that you move from the host ID to the network ID will depend on your requirements. If you know how many segments you have and how many hosts are on each segment, then you know how many bits you will have to borrow. Make sure that you allow for growth when considering how many host IDs you will need on a particular subnet.

The process to work out how many bits you need to add for a specific requirement is best described with an example. In this example, we will consider a Class B address.

An organization has been assigned a Class B address by the InterNIC. However, the organization has four distinct networks, and you need to route packets between them.

The default subnet mask for a Class B network is 255.255.0.0. In this case, the first two octets are reserved for the network ID, and the last two octets are reserved for host IDs. To achieve the desired result, you will borrow bits from the third octet and add them to the default subnet mask.

To work out how many bits you will need to borrow, the first step is to convert the number of subnets you will need into binary.

```
Number of subnets:    4
Binary value:         100 (3 bits)
```

We now know that we need three bits to create four distinct subnets. As stated earlier, these bits will be taken from the high-order bits of the octet. Therefore, the new subnet octet will be:

```
New subnet octet (binary):     11111111.11111111.11100000
New subnet octet (decimal):    255.255.224
```

So our new subnet mask would be 255.255.224.0. To see how this allows us to have four networks, we need to see how many unique combinations we can make from those new bits. The unique combinations are shown in Table 8.3.

Several methods can be used to determine the number of different subnet masks you can get from a given number of bits. Often, the best method is the one that

Table 8.3 Unique network IDs for subnet 255.255.224.0.

Octet (Binary)	Octet (Decimal)	New Subnet Mask (Decimal)
00100000	32	255.255.32.0
01000000	64	255.255.64.0
01100000	96	255.255.96.0
10000000	128	255.255.128.0
10100000	160	255.255.160.0
11000000	192	255.255.192.0

you find the easiest to use. Here is an alternative method of working out the number of subnets you can gain after you know the number of bits you need.

In the earlier example, our new subnet mask was 11100000. The first thing you must do is convert the rightmost bit of the borrowed bits to its decimal value.

```
Binary placeholders:  128   64   32   16   8   4   2   1
New subnet mask:        1    1    1    0   0   0   0   0
```

As you can see, the rightmost bit we borrowed was 32. This is the increment between the new subnet masks you can use. Remember, you cannot use 0 because that means "local network only." Also, the highest value you can use is the value of all the borrowed bits being set to 1—in this case, 224. So all available subnet masks in this case would be from 32 to 224; they are as follows:

➤ 255.255.32.0

➤ 255.255.64.0

➤ 255.255.96.0

➤ 255.255.128.0

➤ 255.255.160.0

➤ 255.255.192.0

So now you know what your subnet masks will be, but how do you know how many clients are going to be possible on each subnet? Fortunately, there is an easy way to work that out.

Once you have calculated the new subnet mask, you will know how many bits you have left over for the host-ID portion of the address. In the example, we have eight bits from the fourth octet and five remaining bits from the third octet, giving us a binary number of 1111111111111.

Next, you must convert this binary number into decimal and subtract 1 (because you cannot have a host ID of zero). This binary number is 8,191−1 = 8,190. So, in this case, you could have a maximum of 8,190 host IDs per subnet.

Once you learn the basics of the binary and decimal number systems, you can easily convert between the two. One of the best aids in performing this conversion is a scientific calculator. This allows you to enter a number as a decimal and convert it to binary at the touch of a button, and vice versa.

The most common calculator found on desktops is Microsoft Calculator, which also has the added benefit of being free. You can use Microsoft Calculator in your subnetting exercises by switching it to scientific view.

To switch Microsoft Calculator to scientific view, open up the View menu, as shown in Figure 8.3. Select Scientific from the View menu.

The scientific view is shown in Figure 8.4. To convert a decimal number, make sure the Dec option is selected before you enter the number. Enter the number

Figure 8.3   Selecting Scientific view in Microsoft Calculator.

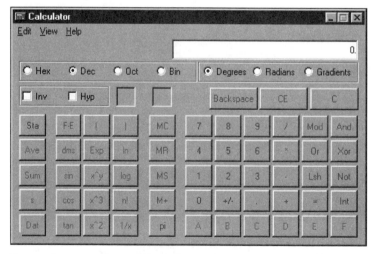

Figure 8.4   Converting from decimal to binary using Microsoft Calculator.

you want to convert. Next, select the Bin option. The calculator will display the decimal number in binary format.

Calculating custom subnet tasks might not be the hardest thing in the world, but it might rank up there with the most boring. To circumvent this, Tables 8.4 through 8.6 detail some of the most common tasks you might be presented with. You might want to keep them handy for future reference.

You have now seen how you can figure out whether two hosts are on the same network. If the destination host is on the same network as the sender host, then the packet is forwarded directly to the destination host. But what if the destination host is not on the same network? Then, the packet would be sent to the default gateway, as explained next.

Table 8.4   Class A subnetting.

Subnets Required	Additional Bit Needed	Maximum Hosts Per Subnet	Subnet Mask
0	0	16,777,214	255.0.0.0
Invalid	1	Invalid	Invalid
2	2	4,194,302	255.192.0.0
6	3	2,097,150	255.224.0.0
14	4	1,048,574	255.240.0.0
30	5	524,286	255.248.0.0
62	6	262,142	255.252.0.0
126	7	131,070	255.254.0.0
254	8	65,534	255.255.0.0

Table 8.5   Class B subnetting.

Subnets Required	Additional Bit Needed	Maximum Hosts Per Subnet	Subnet Mask
0	0	65,534	255.255.0.0
Invalid	1	Invalid	Invalid
2	2	16,382	255.255.192.0
6	3	8,190	255.255.224.0
14	4	4,094	255.255.240.0
30	5	2,046	255.255.248.0
62	6	1,022	255.255.252.0
126	7	510	255.255.254.0
254	8	254	255.255.255.0

8

Table 8.6 Class C subnetting.

Subnets Required	Additional Bit Needed	Maximum Hosts Per Subnet	Subnet Mask
0	0	254	255.255.255.0
Invalid	1	Invalid	Invalid
2	2	62	255.255.255.192
6	3	30	255.255.255.224
14	4	14	255.255.255.240
30	5	6	255.255.255.248
62	6	2	255.255.255.252
126	7	Invalid	255.255.255.254
254	8	Invalid	255.255.255.255

The Default Gateway

TCP/IP is very smart when it comes to knowing what to do with a packet you want to send. As shown earlier in this chapter, ANDing can determine whether the destination host is on the local network or on a remote network. When TCP/IP determines that a destination host is on a remote network, it immediately forwards the packet to the default gateway. This gateway is normally a router, which will use its routing tables to determine whether the destination client is attached to a network it can access. If it is not, then the process starts again with the router passing the packet on to its own gateway.

If a host is on a routed network, the default gateway is an important part of the host's IP configuration. If the host does not have access to a gateway, the host will not have any means to contact hosts outside of its own network. It will, however, function on its own network.

Three Common IP Address Requirements

So far we have talked about IP addresses and how they are broken up into a network ID and a host ID. We have shown how this is done by using a subnet mask. Finally, we have mentioned the default gateway and its role in routing messages.

These three essential elements—IP address, subnet mask, and default gateway—make up the basic building blocks of a TCP/IP configuration. The configuration dialog box on a Windows NT Server computer with these items configured is shown in Figure 8.5.

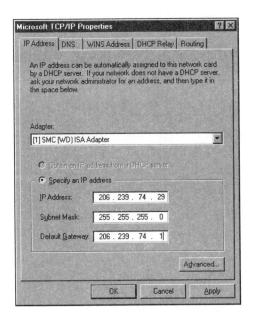

Figure 8.5 The Microsoft TCP/IP Properties dialog box.

SUPERNETTING AND CLASSLESS INTERDOMAIN ROUTING

As the Internet has grown, along with the further acceptance of TCP/IP as the protocol of choice on corporate networks, it has become clear to the Internet authorities that all Class B network addresses will soon be allocated. This is a problem because for large organizations, Class C addresses, with 254 as their maximum number of host IDs, are simply not large enough.

To solve this problem, the Internet authorities came up with a new method of allocating addresses, which would prevent the rapid depletion of Class B addresses. When a request for a Class B address is received at InterNIC, it assigns a range of Class C addresses that matches the applicant's need for network and host IDs. For instance, if the applicant required enough IP addresses for 3,000 hosts, the applicant would be assigned 12 Class C addresses. Although this solution achieves the goal of preventing Class B addresses from being depleted, it also introduces another problem. At each router on the Internet, multiple entries would have to be made for a single organization. In our example, it would mean that a single organization would require 12 distinct entries. This places an extra burden on the routers.

To fix this problem, a technique called *Classless Interdomain Routing (CIDR)* is used. This technique allows for the 12 Class C addresses in our example to be collapsed into a single entry. Conceptually, this can be expressed as follows: The routing-table entry created by CIDR defines the starting network ID (Class C address) followed by the number of addresses that were allocated, thereby defining the entire range that belongs to the organization. A range of CIDR addresses is known as a *CIDR block*.

In reality, a supernetted subnet mask is used to convey this information. Supernetting allows for an extension of the concepts explained in the section on custom subnet masks. In this case, however, bits are borrowed from both the network ID and the host ID.

Here is how the entries would be supernetted in a real-world example. Let's say an organization requires IP addresses for 2,000 clients and therefore requires 8 Class C addresses. The organization is assigned the following range of addresses:

➤ 199.56.43.0

➤ 199.56.44.0

➤ 199.56.45.0

➤ 199.56.46.0

➤ 199.56.47.0

➤ 199.56.48.0

➤ 199.56.49.0

➤ 199.56.50.0

Given this information, we need to calculate what the routing-table entry needs to be. We do this by looking for common bits between the lowest IP address in the range and the highest IP address. This can be done by converting these addresses to binary, as follows:

```
First IP Address:   11000111  00111000  00101011  00000000
Last IP Address:    11000111  00111000  00110010  00000000
Common Bits:        11000111  00111000  001
```

Note that the first 19 bits of the addresses are the same. The remaining five bits of the third octet are different. From this information, we are able to mask the common bits to arrive at the supernetting mask for this range of IP addresses. The supernetting mask is then entered into the routing tables of the Internet's routers as the first IP address with a subnet mask that matches the supernetting mask we just calculated, as shown in Table 8.7.

Support for CIDR has to be built into many routers, but not all routers support this form of subnetting. RIP for IP version 2, OSPF, and BGPv4 are routing protocols that support CIDR.

Table 8.7   The calculated supernetting mask.

Network ID	Subnet Mask (Decimal)	Subnet Mask (Binary)
199.56.43.0	255.255.224	11111111 11111111 11100000 00000000

Saving IP Addresses By Using A Proxy Server

If your network will remain private—that is, it will never become part of the Internet—then it does not matter which IP address range you decide to use. Because you are going to be routing only within your own network, conflicts will not occur.

When you want to connect your network to the Internet, however, you are required to have a unique IP address range. This rush to the Internet has rapidly depleted the supply of IP addresses. To combat this, you could also choose to use a proxy server for your Internet communications. Proxy servers have many useful functions, but a byproduct of their many advantages is that only the proxy server needs to have a unique address on the Internet.

When using a proxy server, a client contacts the proxy server, indicating that it needs something from the Internet. It is the proxy server that actually makes the connection and fetches the information, routing it to the client when the data has been received. In this case, the client itself never actually goes live onto the Internet. Therefore, it does not require a unique address for itself. Proxy servers also have other uses, such as security.

THE PROTOCOLS OF THE TCP/IP SUITE

As stated earlier, TCP/IP is a suite of protocols. Some of these protocols are used to move data from point A to point B. Other protocols are used to resolve addresses or to report errors. Each of the major protocols of the TCP/IP suite will be discussed in this section. (The order is arbitrary and has no significance. Each protocol has its own place within the suite. This is not an exhaustive list, and new protocols are being added all the time.)

Protocols defined by the TCP/IP suite include:

➤ Transmission Control Protocol (TCP)

➤ Internet Protocol (IP)

➤ User Datagram Protocol (UDP)

➤ Internet Control Message Protocol (ICMP)

➤ Internet Group Management Protocol (IGMP)

➤ Address Resolution Protocol (ARP)

➤ Hypertext Transfer Protocol (HTTP)

➤ Post Office Protocol (POP)

➤ Simple Mail Transfer Protocol (SMTP)

➤ Network News Transfer Protocol (NNTP)

➤ Simple Network Management Protocol (SNMP)

➤ File Transfer Protocol (FTP)

Each protocol in the TCP/IP suite performs a unique function. Some protocols are more reliable than others; others have management tasks. Each protocol has its own Request For Comments (RFC) associated with it.

Transmission Control Protocol (TCP)

This protocol is one of the two primary protocols of the TCP/IP suite. TCP offers a connection-oriented, reliable delivery service. This is achieved because TCP demands a connection be established before communication can begin. It also views data as a stream that is broken down into segments and assigned sequence numbers when sent.

Connection Oriented

Being connection oriented is a significant feature of TCP. It works by organizing data into segments. Each segment is sent, and the sender requires an acknowledgement (ACK) for each segment that is received without problems. If an ACK is not received, then the segment is re-sent. If a segment arrives at the destination but has been corrupted, the receiver discards it without sending an ACK, thereby forcing the sender to re-send. If an ACK is received, then the sender continues with the transmission.

This process is commonly known as the TCP three-way handshake, as illustrated in Figure 8.6.

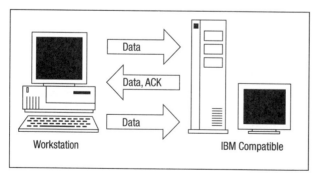

Figure 8.6 The three-way handshake.

Reliable

This characteristic of TCP refers to the sequencing of segments, which facilitates the reassembly of data at the destination host. Each packet that is transmitted is assigned a sequence number. If a receiving host receives data that is out of sequence, then it knows more data is on the way. The host will wait until it has a complete sequence before sending an ACK. After all the packets of a message have been received, they are put back into sequence and processed. The receiving host uses a checksum to figure out whether a segment has been corrupted or not.

TCP has all kinds of safeguards built into it, so you might wonder why anyone would want to use anything else. The answer to this is overhead. TCP has a lot of overhead, and not all services require the guarantees that TCP offers.

TCP is defined in RFC 793.

Internet Protocol (IP)

Unlike TCP, the Internet Protocol is not connection oriented and is not guaranteed to be reliable. However, it does attempt a "best effort" when sending data. This is achieved by adding routing information with the data.

With IP, which is a connectionless protocol, all packets are independent. The receiving station does not send an ACK, and the sender is not informed when a packet has been lost. IP assumes that connections between the sender and the receiver are going to be difficult. To help with this, IP provides routing information from the sender to the receiver. This is the prime function of IP. IP sets rules regarding how routers handle the fragmentation and reassembly of packets.

IP is defined in RFC 791.

User Datagram Protocol (UDP)

Like IP, this protocol is a connectionless, unreliable, "best-effort" datagram service. Nothing is guaranteed.

UDP is used for applications that do not require guarantees of delivery and that do not require an acknowledgment. An example of this type of application is the Simple Network Management Protocol (SNMP). Typically, applications that use UDP send only small amounts of data.

UDP is defined in RFC 768.

Internet Control Message Protocol (ICMP)

ICMP's purpose is to report errors on datagrams and to report specific conditions. Because ICMP simply reports errors, it does nothing to attempt to make IP a reliable protocol. Moreover, because ICMP travels over IP, it is itself not guaranteed.

An example of a use of ICMP would be when a router recognizes that a sending host is sending packets that are either saturating the links between itself and destination host or overwhelming a router. In this case, the router will send an *ICMP Source Quench*. This message requests that the sending host slow down its rate of transmission.

ICMP is defined in RFC 792.

Internet Group Management Protocol (IGMP)

This protocol is used to pass information between routers that support multicasting. It is used to inform the routers which host groups are on which network.

IGMP is defined in RFC 1112.

Address Resolution Protocol (ARP)

For two IP hosts to communicate, there has to be a mechanism where each of the hosts' IP addresses can be resolved to their respective MAC addresses. This resolution is the purpose of ARP.

ARP broadcasts an IP address locally and then gathers the MAC address when it gets a reply. When it gets this information, it stores the information in a cache so it can be retrieved without resorting to a broadcast at a later date. Entries in the ARP cache generally remain there for 10 minutes before being removed. If they are used before this time, the 10-minute limit is reset. When a request for communication is made, ARP always checks its cache first, before making the broadcast.

Reverse lookup is a similar process, but in this case the host is resolving a MAC address to the IP address. (ARP will be discussed in more detail in Chapter 9.)

ARP is defined in RFC 826.

Hypertext Transfer Protocol (HTTP)

This protocol is familiar to most people who use Web browsers. Uniform Resource Locators (URLs) are often prefixed with this protocol name.

HTTP was originally designed as a method to publish and view linked text documents. However, it was later extended to provide support for multimedia capabilities such as sound, graphics, and video. HTTP manages the application-to-application communication. It is not connection based. This means that as each dialog is complete, the connection is broken, and it has to be reestablished before another dialog can take place.

HTTP1.1 is defined in RFC 2068.

Post Office Protocol (POP)

POP is a widely deployed mail-access protocol. Many programs access POP message stores. POP is used to receive mail from a message store. It is not used to send mail; SMTP is used for this purpose. POP uses TCP as its transport protocol and is therefore reliable.

POP is defined in RFC 1939.

Simple Mail Transfer Protocol (SMTP)

This protocol defines methods for the exchange of mail messages between applications. This exchange includes messages going from one client to another client (as in sending mail) and in SMTP-server-to-SMTP-server communication (the passing of a message from one post office to another). Because SMTP uses the TCP protocol for its communication, it is reliable and connection based.

SMTP is defined in RFC 821.

Network News Transfer Protocol (NNTP)

NNTP is used on a network of newsgroup servers on the Internet. These news servers contain newsgroups, which hold information on a variety of subjects. You can think of newsgroups as discussion areas. NNTP is used for the transfer of messages from the newsgroup to the client and from the client back to the newsgroup.

NNTP is defined in RFC 977.

Simple Network Management Protocol (SNMP)

Simple Network Management Protocol (SNMP) provides the ability to communicate status information between a variety of hosts and to then monitor that status. The original intention was that the protocol would be used to monitor bridges and routers, but this protocol has now been extended to include many network resources, including wiring hubs, servers, and mainframe computers.

SNMP is defined in RFC 1157.

File Transfer Protocol (FTP)

FTP allows for bidirectional file transfers between two systems. Because it uses TCP/IP, the underlying operating system is not a concern. FTP servers offer all of the security options you could want, including user lists and passwords. This means that FTP is fast, secure, and error free.

FTP is defined in RFC 959.

Port Numbers (HTTP, FTP, SMTP) and Sockets

Now that we have some of the basics down, let's take a look at how communication between applications really takes place. Before a TCP/IP application can communicate with a server, it needs to create a connection. After the connection is established, the application will then use that connection to send and receive data.

A good example of how this works is the telephone. You pick up the receiver and dial a specific point on the network (someone else's telephone number). When the other person picks up the telephone, the system knows where your voice should go and routes it accordingly. With the advent of features such as call waiting, it is possible to have your telephone continue to listen for further callers, even though it is being used.

In the world of computers, sockets and port numbers are used to achieve the same capability. Your telephone waits to be contacted—a process that is similar to the function of an application waiting on a port number. When the phone rings and you pick it up, the connection is made—a process similar to a socket being opened.

TCP/IP Sockets

A *socket* is a connection to an endpoint. When you start an application that requires a socket, the application makes a connection to a port on a remote computer and opens a socket. This line of communication is then used for data as it is passed between the host and the destination. When the socket is in place, data can be sent reliably. The process has an advantage because communications do not have to be guaranteed and can therefore use protocols with the minimum of overhead, such as UDP. A socket can also be created between applications.

The process for creating a socket connection is simple. The sending application sends its IP address to the host, along with the type of service it wants and the number of the port the application is listening on. (Ports are discussed in more detail in a moment.) When this information is received, a socket is created and communication can begin.

TCP/IP Ports

Every application or process that uses the TCP protocol for transport is assigned a unique identification number called a *TCP/IP port*. The TCP/IP port has many names, including "port address," "TCP port address," and simply "port," among others. However, they all mean the same thing.

These port numbers range from 0 to 65356. When client applications use TCP, they are automatically assigned a port number by the operating system. Applications running on the server, however, are assigned specific port numbers as defined by the IANA.

The IANA took a range of numbers and reserved them for use by server processes and applications. The range set aside and defined was 0 through 1023. The port numbers beyond that are open for use, although some have actually been established as a standard beyond the original 0 to 1023.

Port numbers that fall within the reserved range of 0 through 1023 are known as "well-known port numbers." These port numbers are well documented in RFC 1060. Microsoft Windows NT computers have a text file called SERVICES that details some well-known port numbers and what they have been assigned to. This file can be found at \systemroot\system32\drivers\etc. It can be read and printed from Notepad.

Some of the most common port numbers you will need to know are shown in Table 8.8.

With FTP, the initial communication is processed through port 21. Once established, data is passed over port 20.

In order to understand ports and how they work, it is useful to see this process in action. Once a connection is made through this process, the connection is called a *socket*. In the following example, a client establishes a communication with an FTP server.

If FTP is running on a server, it will constantly monitor port 21 for incoming requests. Because this is a well-known port, it is easy for the client to know where to send data. The following is an example of this process:

1. At the command prompt, a user types "FTP 10.23.34.123".

2. The operating system at the client assigns a TCP/IP port number in the range 1023 to 65356 to the FTP client application.

Table 8.8 Well-known port numbers.

Port Number	Process Name	Description
20	FTP-data	File Transfer Protocol—Data
21	FTP	File Transfer Protocol—Control
23	Telnet	Telnet
25	SMTP	Simple Mail Transfer Protocol
80	HTTP	Hypertext Transfer Protocol
119	NNTP	Network News Transfer Protocol
161	SNMP	Simple Network Management Protocol

3. The packet that is sent will contain the following information:

- ➤ Source IP address   192.23.78.65
- ➤ Source TCP/IP port number   1199
- ➤ Destination IP address   10.23.24.123
- ➤ Destination TCP/IP port number   21

4. The packet is sent across the network to the destination.

5. The destination host receives the packet, and TCP forwards it to the correct port (port 21).

The FTP service receives the information and sends an acknowledgment back to the source host by using the Source IP address and the Source TCP/IP port number in the packet it received.

As you can see, in this process, both the source of the packet and the destination host are always aware of the other computer's IP address and of the application that requested it.

THE DOMAIN NAME SERVICE (DNS)

Along with the benefits of TCP/IP come some problems. For instance, although all hosts on a TCP/IP network (the largest of which is the Internet) have a unique TCP/IP address, it is difficult, if not impossible, to remember what the number is. There are literally millions of hosts currently on the Internet, and the sheer size of the problem demands that a solution be found.

To help with this problem, computers were given friendly names, such as CORIOLIS. This name is known as an *alias*. Aliases are easier for people to remember, but the underlying networks cannot use aliases. What is needed is a scalable method of translating these aliases to their IP addresses. This translation is the purpose of the Domain Name Service (DNS).

The DNS system was created and is operated by InterNIC. It is a hierarchical client/server-based database management system. DNS operates at the Application layer of the TCP/IP architectural model and uses both UDP and TCP as its underlying protocols.

DNS servers contain a database of both the aliases and the corresponding IP addresses. When a client application—called a *resolver*—needs to contact a system, it firsts asks a DNS server—called a *name server*—for the IP address that belongs to the alias. The DNS server returns this information, and the connection can be made. UDP is used for this initial conversation. However, if data becomes corrupted during this dialog, TCP is used, which ensures a reliable communication.

Resolvers

The purpose of a resolver is to pass name requests between a client application and name servers. The name requests are in the form of queries. For example, the resolver might send a query asking for the IP address of **www.coriolis.com**. This information is then returned. The resolver is most often built into each application, but it can also be a library routine on a computer.

Name Servers

Name servers contain the database of translation information. Their purpose is to receive queries from the resolvers and to return the IP data. With the large amount of information on the Internet, it would clearly be difficult, and unwieldy, to have all possible alias-to-IP-address translations on every name server. That is why DNS is a hierarchical system. If a name server cannot resolve a name, the server can be configured to pass a query to another name server that can resolve it. Name servers that are at different levels are considered to be in different domains. Domains define different levels of authority, with the most authoritative being at the top of the tree.

This hierarchical system is known as the *Domain Name Space*. This is an inverted tree that branches out from the top. This is shown is Figure 8.7.

As you can see, at the top of the domain structure is the root-level domain. This contains a null value and can be denoted with a period. Below that are various top-level domains, followed by second-level domains. You will most likely be familiar with most, if not all, of the top-level domain names through your use of browsers on the World Wide Web. These top-level domain entries indicate a type of organization.

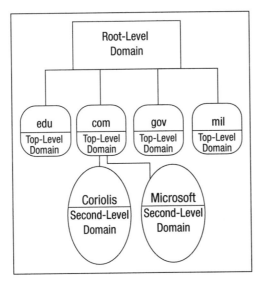

Figure 8.7   Hierarchical Domain Name Space.

Table 8.9 Top-level domains.

Domain Name	Meaning
com	Commercial organization
edu	Educational institution
gov	Government institution
mil	Military group
net	Major network support provider
org	Organizations not covered above
int	International organization
<country code>	Two-letter country code

Top-level domains are defined by an Internet Society Committee and can change over time. The current top-level domains appear in Table 8.9.

Second-level domains identify a specific organization beneath its top-level domain. This organization can include both hosts and other domains. An example of a second-level domain is **coriolis.com**. Hosts can reside at this level, or there can be additional domains here. Additional domains could include **author.coriolis.com**. Hosts at this level might be things like **ftp.coriolis.com**.

The InterNIC is responsible for naming of domains at the second level, but names below the second level are controlled by individual organizations.

Hostnames

When hostnames are added to the beginning of the domains, such as "ftp" in **ftp.coriolis.com**, they are known as the fully qualified domain names (FQDN).

Zones Of Authority

Each domain server is responsible for answering queries in its own name space. This name space is known as its *zone of authority*. The name server stores all information relevant to its zone of authority in its database and will answer all queries that relate to it.

A zone of authority encompasses at least one domain, and it may or may not contain information from subdomains. An illustration of this is shown in Figure 8.8.

In the example in Figure 8.8, the name server in **coriolis.com** has a zone of authority for the domain **coriolis.com**. All the subdomains have their own name servers with their own zones of authority.

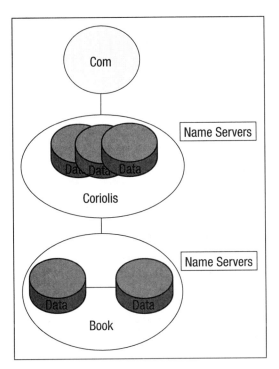

Figure 8.8   Name servers and zones of authority.

There must be at least two name servers in each zone of authority. Each name server is assigned a role. There are two roles: primary name servers and secondary name servers. These servers work together to offer name resolution.

Primary Name Servers
Primary name servers offer zone data from files stored locally on the computer. All changes made to a zone are made on the Primary Name Server.

Secondary Name Servers
Secondary name servers get their zone data from another name server that has authority in that zone. When information is passed from one name server to a secondary name server, this process is called a *zone transfer*.

Secondary name servers are used primarily to provide scalability and to protect against a zone losing its capability to resolves names entirely. The three reasons for this hierarchy are:

➤ **Redundancy** You must have at least one primary name server and one secondary name server. This redundancy ensures that if anything happens to one of the servers, the domain will still be able to offer name resolution.

The two systems should be as independent as possible, which means that there should be a minimal chance that each can be knocked out by a single incident.

➤ **Reduction of load** In a domain with a lot of clients, it is possible for a primary domain server to become overwhelmed. This will slow the hosts that are trying to get names resolved. This problem can be avoided by having at least two name servers in a domain.

➤ **Scalability** Being mindful of where hosts are located in relation to the name server will ensure that name resolution takes place in the fastest way possible. Having multiple name servers means that you can stage them at a location closest to the hosts that need them. For instance, if you have hosts at the other end of a slow link, it makes sense to have a secondary name server near them to offer name resolution.

You should know that a primary name server could also operate as a secondary name server for another domain. This allows a name server to offer resolution for names not only in its own domain, but in other domains also. It also allows for all the benefits listed above for name servers operating in other domains.

Master Name Servers

As stated earlier, you can designate a name server as a secondary name server. It gets its zone information in a zone transfer from another name server in the domain. The supplying name server is also considered to be the *master name server*.

A master name server does not have to be primary name server. Secondary name servers can also supply other secondary name servers with information. When secondary name servers start up, they will automatically contact their master name server and initiate a zone transfer.

The final part of the puzzle involves how the data in a zone transfer is stored. Though it is useful to have zone data transferred from a primary name server to secondary name servers, doing this can also cause problems. For instance, with a name server that is on the other side of a slow link, it might be undesirable to have a zone transfer take place every time the name server is started. In cases such as these, you can use a caching-only server.

Caching-Only Servers

Caching-only servers operate in much the same way as secondary servers. However, the difference is that a zone transfer does not take place when the server is started. No data is stored locally. When started, this type of server will have no data with which to respond to requests. Only as requests are resolved do those results get cached.

Domain name servers do not tell the whole story of how name resolution takes place on a network. There are other mechanisms that can be used locally on the client and on different types of networks. For instance, Microsoft offers alternative methods of registering names on its networks and having them resolved. These methods will be described in detail in Chapter 9.

However, it is worth noting that Microsoft is moving toward using domain name servers as its standard name-resolution method in the forthcoming Windows 2000 product.

CHAPTER SUMMARY

➤ TCP/IP is an industry-standard protocol suite.

➤ There are four layers in the TCP/IP architectural model: Network Interface layer, Internet layer, Transport layer, and Application layer.

➤ There are five classes of IP address, but only three are used for network IDs and host IDs. The three main IP Classes are A, B, and C.

➤ Each class has a default subnet mask. Class A is 255.0.0.0. Class B is 255.255.0.0. Class C is 255.255.255.0.

➤ TCP/IP uses a process called ANDing to figure out if the destination host is on the same network as the sending host.

➤ You can break your assigned IP address range into smaller parts to make it better model your needs; this process is called subnetting.

➤ The three main settings a host needs to be assigned are a unique IP address, a subnet mask, and a default gateway.

➤ TCP is a connection-oriented reliable protocol.

➤ IP is a connectionless, unreliable protocol.

➤ TCP achieves reliability by first performing a "three-way handshake."

➤ There are currently eight top-level domain names: com, edu, gov, mil, net, org, int, and <country code>.

➤ A name server operating in a domain is considered to have a zone of authority in that domain.

➤ Primary name servers have a copy of the name database stored locally.

➤ Secondary name servers pull the name database from a primary name server when they start up. This process is called a *zone transfer*.

➤ Caching-only servers do not store a permanent copy of the name database on them. They store only lists of names and IP addresses that they resolve.

REVIEW QUESTIONS

1. Which governing body coordinates the design, management, and engineering of the Internet?

    a. IAB

    b. IRTB

    c. Microsoft

    d. IANA

2. An IP address is:

    a. A 24-bit number

    b. A 64-bit number

    c. A 32-bit number

    d. An 8-bit number

3. A TCP/IP address represents two pieces of information that help identify a host. What are these two pieces of information called? [Choose the two best answers]

    a. An octet

    b. A network ID

    c. The user's name

    d. A host ID

4. Which part of a TCP address must be unique on each host?

    a. None; TCP/IP addresses can be shared

    b. The network ID

    c. The host ID

    d. All parts

5. How many classes of TCP/IP addresses are in use for network and host IDs today?

    a. 6

    b. 3

    c. 5

    d. 1

6. What is the maximum number of hosts a Class A network can have?

    a. 65,534

    b. 255

    c. 16,777,214

    d. A Class A network is not used for hosts. It is used for multicasting.

7. What is the maximum number of hosts a Class C network can have?

    a. 254

    b. 1,024

    c. 16,777,214

    d. 65,432

8. The first octet of a TCP/IP address identifies its class. What is the range of numbers identifying a Class B address?

    a. 192 to 223

    b. 1 to 126

    c. 128 to 191

    d. 127 to 191

9. In a Class B address, what is the number of octets used for the host-ID portion of the address?

    a. 3

    b. 2

    c. 1

    d. 4

10. What does the binary number 01011010 represent in decimal?

    a. 99

    b. 67

    c. 128

    d. 90

11. What does the decimal number 189 look like in binary?

    a. 01001001

    b. 10011011

    c. 10111111

    d. 10111101

12. Why can't the decimal value of a TCP/IP octet exceed 255?

    a. Internet routers cannot process TCP/IP addresses above this number.

    b. Because it is an agreed-upon standard.

    c. Because each octet is only 8 bits in length.

    d. To provide backward compatibility.

13. What are the three things you should configure in the TCP/IP protocol suite of each workstation? [Choose the three best answers])

    a. The correct date and time

    b. A unique TCP/IP address

    c. The user's name

    d. A default gateway

    e. A subnet mask

14. The binary address 11111111.11111111.11111111.00000000 is the default subnet mask for which class of TCP/IP addresses?

    a. Class D

    b. Class C

    c. Class A

    d. Class B

15. When it sends data to a destination TCP/IP host, TCP/IP performs a check to determine whether the host is on the same or a different network. What is this process called?

    a. Subtraction

    b. Calculating

    c. ANDing

    d. Processing

16. Subnetting allows you to break a single IP address assigned to your organization into different parts. What are some of the reasons you would want to do this? [Choose the two best answers]

    a. IP addresses are too large to remember.

    b. You have a mix of cabling types.

    c. You want to give each department its own network ID.

    d. You want to reduce traffic on a network segment.

17. If the host you are sending a message to is on a different network, where is the message sent?

    a. To a server for distribution.

    b. It is not sent. It is discarded.

    c. To the next computer in line.

    d. To the default gateway.

18. The TCP/IP protocol suite includes which of the following protocols? [Choose the three best answers]

    a. FTP

    b. HTTP

    c. IPX

    d. NetBEUI

    e. IP

19. Which of the TCP/IP protocols is connection based?

    a. TCP

    b. HTTP

    c. IP

    d. ICMP

20. The Internet Control Message Protocol (ICMP) provides non–connection-based protocols with connection-based capabilities. True or false?

    a. True

    b. False

21. Which protocol can be used to read mail, but not to send it?

    a. SMTP

    b. HTTP

    c. POP3

    d. IP

22. TCP applications have conversations over ports, which range from 0 to 65356. Of these, what is the range reserved for and known as "well-known ports"?

    a. 1024 to 6000

    b. 1023 to 65356

    c. 0 to 1024

    d. 0 to 1023

23. What is the well-known port for the initial conversation over File Transfer Protocol (FTP)?

    a. 25

    b. 80

    c. 21

    d. 119

24. Some applications have well-known ports associated with them. When is the well-known port number assigned at the client?

    a. When the client's workstation is turned on.

    b. Only when an application using a protocol is used.

    c. Well-known port numbers are assigned not on the client, but on the server only.

    d. When the service running the application is started.

25. How many layers are there in the TCP/IP architectural model?

    a. 3

    b. 7

    c. 5

    d. 4

26. What layer of the TCP/IP architectural model maps to the Network layer of the OSI model?

    a. Internet layer

    b. Intranet layer

    c. Session layer

    d. Network Interface layer

27. Common top-level domain names include which of the following? [Choose the two best answers]

    a. edu

    b. com

    c. txt

    d. man

HANDS-ON PROJECTS

Project 8.1

If you are new to TCP/IP, the area of subnetting can be one of the most difficult to deal with. This is partly due to the fact that you are new to the process, and partly because you are probably not used to working in binary. The following exercises walk you though a couple of examples of how to use a simple (and free) tool to convert numbers between decimal and binary. We will then use this skill in a subnetting exercise.

First, we will use Microsoft Calculator to convert a number from decimal to binary, and then from binary to decimal. (This exercise assumes that you have access to a Microsoft Windows or Microsoft Windows NT computer.)

1. Click on your Windows Start button and choose Run.

2. Type "calc" and press Enter.

3. By default, the calculator is in standard mode. Click on View and select Scientific.

4. The calculator will change to scientific view. Make sure the Dec radio button is selected.

5. Enter "100" with the keypad on your keyboard.

6. Click on the radio button next to Bin. The calculator display now shows the decimal number 100 as a binary number.

7. Click on C to clear the display.

8. With the radio button next to Bin still selected, type "11011011". (Note that because binary allows the use of only 1 and 0, these are the only numbers available on the keypad.)

9. Click on the radio button next to Dec.

The calculator display now shows the binary number 11011011 as a decimal number.

That was fairly simple. Now we will take this knowledge a little further. In the following steps, we will consider the problems of a midsized company. The company has a Class B IP address (128.98.0.0), but needs six subnets with at least 150 hosts on each.

10. Click C on the calculator to clear the display.

11. Because we need six subnets, this is the initial number we will work with. Make sure the Dec radio button is selected and enter "6" with the keypad on your keyboard.

12. Click on the radio button next to Bin. The calculator now shows the decimal number 6 in binary. As you can see, the decimal number 6 takes 3 bits.

13. Click on C to clear the display.

14. With the radio button next to Bin still selected, type "11100000". (Note that because binary allows the use of only 1 and 0, these are the only numbers available on the keypad.)

15. Click on the radio button next to Dec.

The display now shows you the binary number 11100000, represented as a decimal number, 224. This is the number of the new subnet mask (255.255.224.0).

All we need to do now is to find out the six network IDs that we have created. To do this, we will use the method described in this chapter.

16. On a piece of paper, write out the binary placeholders. These are 128 64 32 16 8 4 2 1.

17. We know from the previous exercise that the subnet mask we created was 224. In binary, this number was displayed as 11100000. Write this number under the placeholder.

18. To calculate the increment between the network IDs, we need to know the decimal number represented by the rightmost digit in our subnet mask. In this case, the number is 32.

19. Now we know that the increment of our network IDs is 32. Don't forget, you cannot use 0, and the value of a network ID cannot be all 1s. Working on that basis, write down numbers incrementing from 32 to 224.

20. You should end up with the following network IDs:

   ➤ 255.255.32.0

   ➤ 255.255.64.0

   ➤ 255.255.96.0

   ➤ 255.255.128.0

   ➤ 255.255.160.0

   ➤ 255.255.192.0

21. These represent the new network IDs.

Project 8.2

Once again, in this exercise we are going to be making extensive use of binary. Hopefully, by the time you have completed these steps, you will begin to feel more comfortable working outside of Base10. In this project, we will examine two IP addresses and use the ANDing technique to determine whether they are on the same subnet. While it is entirely possible to use a tool such as Microsoft Calculator for this exercise, it might be more beneficial to perform this task using traditional pen and paper. However, use whichever method makes you feel most comfortable. The two IP addresses in question are 199.123.71.10 and 199.124.71.11. Both have default subnet masks of 255.255.255.0.

1. First we need to write out the binary placeholders for the 8 bits of each octet. Don't forget, binary is Base2. That means values double as you move to the left. Start with 1 and write eight placeholders across. You should end up with something that looks like the following:

   ```
   128 64 32 16 8 4 2 1 128 64 32 16 8 4 2 1 128 64 32 16 8 4 2 1
   128 64 32 16 8 4 2 1
   ```

2. Now you will have to convert the first IP address to binary. We are going to do this with Microsoft Calculator. If you still have it open from the

previous exercise, then click on C to clear the display. If not, perform the following steps to open it up:

3. Click on your Windows Start button and choose Run.

4. Type "calc" and press Enter.

5. By default, the calculator is in standard mode. Click on View and select Scientific.

6. The calculator will change to scientific view. Make sure the Dec radio button is selected.

Now that we have the Calculator open, we will start to convert the IP address 199.123.71.10 into binary.

7. Enter "199" with the keypad on your keyboard.

8. Click on the radio button next to Bin. The calculator display now shows the decimal number 199 as a binary number (11000111).

9. We will now write this number down. You should place it beneath the left-most octet placeholders.

10. You will now need to do this for the other three numbers in the octet. If some of the numbers are fewer than eight characters, you should pad to eight characters by adding zeros on the left. You should end up with the following set of binary numbers:

```
11000111    01111011    01000111    00001010
```

11. Underneath this number, write the binary values for the subnet mask. It should now look like this:

```
11000111    01111011    01000111    00001010
11111111    11111111    11111111    00000000
```

12. Now, perform the ANDing. ANDing is performed by writing a 1 beneath any two matching 1 values and a 0 beneath for anything else. You should get the results shown below:

```
11000111    01111011    01000111    00000000
```

13. Now, we will perform Steps 1 through 12 of Project 8.2 on the other IP address. First, convert the address to binary and write it down. Then, write the subnet mask beneath that number. The results of the second conversion should look like this:

```
11000111    01111111    01000111    00001011
11111111    11111111    11111111    00000000
```

14. Now, perform the ANDing on the two numbers. You should see the following results:

11000111   01111111   01000111   00000000

15. Finally, compare the two results to see if they are on the same network. At this point you are doing a simple compare.

11000111   01111011   01000111   00000000
11000111   01111111   01000111   00000000

Because the numbers are different, this means the machines are not on the same network.

## CHAPTER NINE

USING TCP/IP

After Reading This Chapter And Completing The Exercises, You Will Be Able To:

➤ Explain the normal configuration options for a workstation

➤ Explain IPCONFIG, WINIPCFG, PING, TRACERT, and other TCP/IP utilities and how to use them to test, validate, and troubleshoot connectivity

➤ Explain the purpose and use of TCP/IP services, including WINS, DHCP, DNS, HOSTS, and LMHOSTS files

---

This chapter describes how to use some of the tools that were mentioned in Chapter 8. Because Transmission Control Protocol/Internet Protocol (TCP/IP) is such an important part of the world's networks, many utilities are available to enable you to see it at work and to help you when things go wrong.

For all you Microsoft Windows users who are used to nice graphical user interface (GUI) tools, you might be surprised to find that most of the utilities that you will use with TCP/IP are, in fact, command-line tools. Although some have been given a graphical overhaul, the vast majority will take you to the command prompt. The command-line tools are worth learning, though, because you'll be able to use your newfound TCP/IP skills on all platforms.

These tools will answer most of the questions that come up in day-to-day work using TCP/IP. For example, what do you do if you have a workstation that does not recognize a server on your network? How does a workstation know who "My Computer" is? What is the best way to get IP addresses out to hundreds or thousands of computers?

These questions and others will be answered in this chapter as we get down to the nitty-gritty of using TCP/IP every day. So let's get started!

Standard TCP/IP Settings

Before you can begin playing with the various TCP/IP utilities, you first need to make sure that the protocol has been installed and is working properly on your system. Of course, the protocol includes utilities to help you do just that. But first, let's talk about the essential elements that are included in a TCP/IP configuration for a workstation or server.

Before we look at the specific screens available on your computer, let's list the values you will need to ensure that your TCP/IP configuration works. Although some of these values are optional—your computer will work just fine without them—a complete installation of TCP/IP requires most of them. These values are:

➤ IP address

➤ Subnet mask

➤ Default gateway

➤ DNS (Domain Name Service)

➤ Internet domain name

➤ Hostname

➤ IP proxy configuration

➤ WINS

➤ DHCP

We will discuss each of these items in detail. Some of them were covered in Chapter 8, but others will be new to you. In fact, not all of these parameters are actually used to access resources. Some are used to assign IP addresses automatically to you when you log on to your network. Others will help you resolve computer names on your local area network.

IP Address

The IP address is the unique identifier that allows you to be located on your network or the Internet. Each host must be assigned an IP address, and no two machines on the same network—either your local area network or the Internet—can share an IP address. An IP address has two parts: the network ID and the host ID. These addresses can be assigned manually or automatically when you are logging on to a network.

Subnet Mask

TCP/IP uses a subnet mask and a process called ANDing to determine which part of an assigned IP address is the network ID and which is the host ID. Without a correct subnet mask, your TCP/IP stack will not be able to find other computers on its network.

Default Gateway

Your computer uses the default gateway parameter when it has determined that the system to which you want to send information is on a different network. Instead of directly contacting the remote system, the packet is sent to the default gateway so it can find a route to the destination.

Domain Name Service (DNS)

The Domain Name Service (DNS) is the IP address of the computer that will resolve domain names for you. One of the most common examples of using DNS occurs when you use the Internet with a Web browser such as Netscape Navigator. The DNS name of a host helps you remember common locations of interest, and also gives a server's IP address a friendly name. For instance, it is easier to remember **www.comptia.org** than it is to remember 207.158.205.174. Also, if the server's IP address changes, DNS makes sure you can still find it by using the friendly name.

Internet Domain Name

The Internet domain name works with DNS, providing a method for assigning your computer a friendly name that DNS can then use. The Internet domain name includes three elements: the computer name (unique); the second-level domain to which your computer belongs (for example, **coriolis**); and the top-level domain (for example, **com**).

Hostname

The hostname is the name given to the first element of the Internet domain name. The hostname must be unique on your network. Although you can change the hostname, you should leave it as it is unless you can be certain that the new name is unique.

IP Proxy Configuration

Standard TCP/IP dialog boxes—like those found on your Microsoft Windows computer—usually do not include IP proxy configuration. An IP proxy contacts hosts on the Internet on behalf of hosts on your own network. With an IP proxy, you do not have to make sure that your internal IP addresses (on your local corporate network) are unique on the Internet. This is because only the computer with the IP proxy, not each individual host, will have direct access to the Internet.

Dynamic Host Configuration Protocol (DHCP)

The Dynamic Host Configuration Protocol (DHCP) automatically assigns IP addresses to clients when they log on to a network. The protocol also can assign most of the other common TCP/IP parameters. DHCP eases TCP/IP administration on medium to large networks and offers an easy method of updating TCP/IP configurations, thus minimizing the need to visit each machine when you need to make a change.

Windows Internet Name Service (WINS)

Despite the name, Windows Internet Name Service (WINS) servers are not used on the Internet. Instead, WINS Servers resolve computer names on local area networks, just as with DNS. The difference between the two systems, however, is that WINS does not resolve Internet domain names to IP addresses. Instead, WINS resolves NetBIOS names to IP addresses. NetBIOS, a protocol that Sytek Corporation designed for IBM, is commonly used on Microsoft Windows networks.

You will need to assign some or all of these parameters to your computer to ensure that your system's network functions are fully operational. We will discuss each parameter in more detail as we go through this chapter. More information on some of the parameters also appears in Chapter 8.

TCP/IP Services

As you go from network to network, you are likely to encounter several protocols. These protocols, such as TCP/IP and Internetwork Packet Exchange (IPX), are the lifeblood of your networked machine. Without them, you will not be able to access resources on the network or the Internet.

More than one protocol can be installed on your computer. For instance, you can have TCP/IP installed for accessing the Internet, and IPX installed for accessing local Novell servers and network resources. If you find that you can log on, share files, and print, but cannot access the Internet, it might be because IPX has been installed correctly, but your TCP/IP configuration has failed. Some of the tools mentioned later in this chapter—such as IPCONFIG— will help you determine if this is the case.

Given these parameters' importance, several methods of implementing TCP/IP have been developed. Which method you use will depend on your machines' locations, their uses, and the number under your management. The most common methods currently used include:

➤ Manually assigned IP addresses

➤ Automatically assigned IP addresses

➤ No IP address assignment at the workstation; use a proxy server instead

This chapter will look at all three methods, from the simplest to understand (yet the hardest to manage) to the most convenient for large enterprises.

Manually Assigning An IP Address

Now that you know the different types of information needed for a fully working TCP/IP stack on your computer, let's look at how these values are assigned. The easiest method, although the one most likely to cause you problems, is to manually assign your IP addresses and parameters.

Manually assigning an IP address involves typing information directly into the TCP/IP stack's configuration boxes. Some advantages to assigning IP addresses manually include the following:

➤ You have complete control over your configuration.

➤ You do not need network connectivity to do it.

For people using their home computers to dial in to the Internet, this method might be the best solution. Once you have entered the information, you can basically forget about it.

However, manually assigning TCP/IP address has disadvantages. In fact, these disadvantages are so great that most corporations use one of the other methods of assigning TCP/IP addresses. The disadvantages to manual assignment include the following:

➤ A typing error can prevent the TCP/IP stack from initializing.

➤ You have to make sure that the IP address is unique on your network; otherwise, you will have IP address conflicts.

➤ The dialog boxes can be complex for novice users to understand.

Still, there are some valid reasons for assigning IP addresses manually. Figure 9.1 shows a typical TCP/IP configuration screen from a Windows 95/98 workstation.

As you can see, this dialog box has seven tabs. You will have to visit most, if not all, of these tabs to completely configure a Microsoft Windows 95/98 workstation. Before you start, make sure you have all the necessary information on hand. Also, if your workstation is on a corporate network, be careful not to change any values unless you are sure the new values will work.

Manually assigning TCP/IP parameters makes management of IP addresses a little more difficult, but in small offices of 50 users or fewer, you can create a paper record of who has been assigned which address. Home users who load the TCP/IP stack do not have to be concerned about IP address conflicts because they are not attached to a network or the Internet.

9

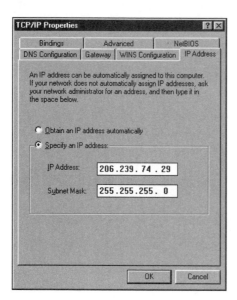

Figure 9.1   A typical TCP/IP configuration dialog box.

Automatically Assigned IP Addresses

Let's imagine that you have 500 hosts on your internal network. One department in your company is moving from your building to another building across the street. Moreover, the company plans to add 100 new employees with the move. Because you have two Class C addresses right now, you quickly realize that you will need additional IP addresses. Not only that, but you also want to change the default gateway address because the computer currently performing the task is getting bogged down with other tasks.

You soon realize that if you previously assigned IP addresses manually, you are going to have a lot of work to do now to accommodate the changes. First, you must visit all of the desktops that are moving and change their TCP/IP configurations. Then, you must manually enter new TCP/IP information into the 100 new machines. To top that, you must visit every other machine using the current default gateway and change that IP address. That's a lot of work!

Fortunately, computers are great for automated tasks, and the problem of changing TCP/IP configurations and adding machines was thought through in great detail. The answer was assigning TCP/IP addressees automatically. This is what happens: When a user starts his or her workstation, the operating system broadcasts a request for an IP address. Another host (in Microsoft terms, this is a DHCP Server) on the network has a range of IP addresses it can give out. When the host receives a request for an IP address, it checks to see if it has one free. If it does, the host assigns an IP address to the workstation, which now can continue to load. If not, the host can tell the workstation that it cannot have an IP address (and therefore is denied access to TCP/IP resources), or it can tell the workstation to use a default IP address (that is, the one it used the day before).

The central host keeps a database of IP addresses assigned to the hosts, so you can easily find out who has an IP address. Because you have to enter only the beginning IP address of the used range, along with the ending address, you have little chance of entering an incorrect IP address. Thus, you can be assured that all assigned IP addresses are accurate. What's more, you also can configure the central host to assign default gateway addresses—all without lifting a finger. If you want to change the default gateway address on all hosts, simply change the gateway IP address in the central host. When the clients log in the next day, they will automatically pick up the new information. Sounds great, doesn't it?

Dynamic Host Configuration Protocol (DHCP)

That is why we have something called the Dynamic Host Configuration Protocol, an implementation of a system to do all of these automated tasks.

You can see what the resultant TCP/IP configuration dialog box looks like in Figure 9.2. The box is simpler than what we saw in Figure 9.1. Because most of its information comes from the DHCP server, you do not have worry about making typing errors or mistakenly assigning an IP address twice.

In DHCP terminology, IP addresses are "leased" to clients. You can configure many parameters in DHCP, such as how long a client can keep an IP address, or how often the client should request to have its lease extended. The details of these tasks are beyond the scope of this book. However, keep in mind that large organizations commonly use DHCP to assign IP addresses because the system greatly reduces administration and eliminates human error. And because DHCP does not have a minimum number of users, you'll also find it in organizations with 50 users or fewer—it just makes sense.

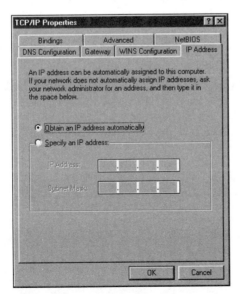

Figure 9.2 TCP/IP configuration dialog box set up to use DHCP.

Name Resolution Services

Even when TCP/IP is fully initiated, lots of things go on behind the scenes to make it work. Some of these activities were discussed in Chapter 8. One of the most important issues involves resolving friendly names to IP addresses. Chapter 8 discussed DNS extensively, so it will not be covered in detail here. However, it is unlikely that DNS is the only method of name resolution taking place on your network. Other methods are covered in this section.

As is often the case, you have a choice to make among various methods, as listed in Table 9.1.

As with DHCP, some of the options shown in Table 9.1 are more attractive than other options. We will discuss each of these options in turn, see how they fit together, and discuss why you might choose one over another.

Before we do that, however, let's briefly discuss how a Microsoft Windows NT computer achieves name resolution. (This scenario assumes a standard configuration in which all of the options in Table 9.1 have been implemented. Also, different resource requests might involve a slightly different set of steps.)

1. When a resource is requested, the first question a Microsoft Windows NT computer asks is, "Am I trying to access myself?" It checks its local name against the requested name. If they are different, it continues.

2. The computer now checks the local HOSTS file. This file must reside on the local computer. If an entry is in the HOSTS file, then the name is resolved to an IP address. If not, the process continues.

3. The client computer next attempts to contact its assigned DNS to resolve the name. Due to network traffic, the DNS might not reply to the first request. If it doesn't, the client will try up to seven times before moving on to the next method.

Table 9.1   Name resolution methods.

Method	Description
NetBIOS Name Server (NBNS)	A central server that resolves NetBIOS names to IP addresses.
Domain Name Service (DNS)	A central server that translates hostnames/ domain names to IP addresses.
Local broadcast	A broadcast on the local network for the IP address of the destination host.
LMHOSTS file	A text file that maps NetBIOS hostnames to IP addresses.
HOSTS file	Similar to LMHOSTS, except that this file is most commonly used for TCP/IP hostname/ domain name to IP address resolution.

4. Next, the client checks its local cache, which holds the addresses it most recently accessed. Because IP addresses can change, however, checking the local cache is not considered an authoritative resolution method. Therefore, it occurs later in the process than you might have imagined.

5. The client next contacts the NetBIOS Name Server (NBNS). The most common NBNS you will find on a Microsoft network is WINS. WINS is often used with DHCP, so references to them often appear together.

6. If all else fails, the client broadcasts on the local network. Broadcasting occurs three times before the client finally gives up and displays an error message. Because the application that is making the request handles errors, the actual error or message the user receives can vary.

As we discuss each name-resolution method in detail, keep the above list in mind. It will help you to picture how the items are used in the real world. Don't worry if you don't know some of the list's terms; we're about to cover all the important stuff right now.

Windows Internet Name Service

TCP/IP has quickly become a standard protocol for desktops around the world. Along with its meteoric rise, we have seen Microsoft Windows become a de facto desktop standard. Unfortunately, adoption of these two technologies did not quite go hand in hand.

Most people are aware that their Windows 95/98 computers have been given friendly names. You assign a friendly name when your operating system is installed, so your computer might be called "Mybookmachine." You use this name often when sharing a hard drive or, in Microsoft speak, when you "connect to a share." In this case, you might enter a command such as "net use * \\Mybookmachine\SharedCDrive". After this is done, your computer will have a new drive letter, which is connected to space on a remote Windows 95/98 client. You will most often use drives to share files.

The question becomes: How did your Windows 95/98 computer know where "Mybookmachine" was? Chapter 8 discussed DNS servers and how they resolve domain names to IP addresses. Can this method be used in this case also? No, it cannot, because the friendly computer name that has been assigned to your Windows 95/98 computer is, in fact, rooted to a network interface called NetBIOS (Networked Basic Input/Output System).

The Sytek Corporation developed NetBIOS in 1983 on behalf of IBM. NetBIOS is an application programming interface (API) for user applications that enable them to submit network I/O and control directives to the underlying network protocol. NetBIOS can travel across any protocol that supports the NetBIOS interface, including TCP/IP. One of the most common early protocols that supported NetBIOS was NetBEUI.

So what would be the best way to allow friendly computer names to find each other in a Microsoft network? The answer is a NetBIOS Name Server. Microsoft's implementation of this is called WINS. WINS works in much the same way as DNS does. The difference is that NetBIOS does not use the same hierarchy that domain names use.

WINS Servers can reduce network traffic because your hosts no longer need to broadcast in order to resolve names. WINS also has the advantage of creating a database of hosts on your network so you can see what is going on.

 If you access a WINS database, you might see the same computer name registered multiple times. This occurs because each service on a Windows NT box registers itself separately. A NetBIOS name is 16 bits long; 15 bits are used to assign the unique name, and the 16th bit is used to identify a specific service. When you're looking at these apparent duplicates, note that the last number is always different.

WINS is a useful way of centrally administering NetBIOS name resolution. You can cut down on network traffic and generate reports on which computers are registered.

Domain Name Service (DNS)

Domain Name Service offers translation between hostnames and IP addresses in much the same way as WINS does. The differences are that DNS has a hierarchy of names, and these names have to be registered with the InterNIC.

It is possible to configure a Microsoft Windows NT computer to use DNS for Windows network name resolution (meaning, to resolve NetBIOS names to IP addresses). However, because the NetBIOS names are organized differently, you will most often see WINS in place for this type of name resolution.

For more information on DNS, see Chapter 8.

Local Broadcast

This option is the least efficient of all those mentioned. In large enterprises, a local broadcast could cause problems because of the amount of network bandwidth that would be eaten up by hosts screaming out, "Hey, 'Bob's computer,' where are you?"

However, on small, simple networks (without routers) where there is little traffic, a local broadcast might be the easiest method of resolving names. What happens is that a host tries to contact another computer on the network. Because it needs to resolve the friendly name to an IP address, the host broadcasts a packet onto the network, saying, "If you are 'Bob's computer,' then let me know your IP address." All the hosts on the network read the message, and if they are not "Bob's computer," they ignore it. When the correct host hears the message, it will send a packet back to the calling host, saying, "Yes, I'm 'Bob's computer,' and this is my IP address."

There is little management of such a method. Because all hosts on the network have to examine the packet to make sure it is not for them, the local broadcast is fairly inefficient.

The LMHOSTS File

As you should now be aware, the original TCP/IP networks had no use for NetBIOS and its associated naming scheme because they fully implemented domain names with DNS Servers. However, Microsoft implemented NetBIOS and supplied its own method of resolving these names to their respective IP addresses.

The LMHOSTS file performs almost the same function as the HOSTS file does. However, instead of resolving domain names to IP addresses, the LMHOSTS file resolves NetBIOS names to IP addresses. The "LM" that has been appended to the name stands for "LAN Manager," which was a predecessor for Microsoft Windows NT.

The LMHOSTS file is a text file, which can be edited in Notepad or your preferred text editor. The file contains a list of names and their associated IP addresses. It also allows you to perform a couple of tricks by giving these names "tags." These tricks include preloading names and IP addresses into the local cache for a faster response and grouping entries.

An LMHOSTS file can use five tags, as outlined in Table 9.2.

Table 9.2   LMHOSTS file tags.

Tag Name	Description
#INCLUDE	Allows you to specify a path and name for another LMHOSTS file, which will then also be parsed. This file can be on the local host or on a remote host.
#BEGIN ALTERNATE	Allows you to have multiple #INCLUDE tags parsed. Each LMHOSTS file will be parsed until name resolution is achieved. This method is called a "block inclusion."
#END ALTERNATE	Marks the end of a block inclusion.
#PRE	Forces the entry to be loaded into the NetBIOS name cache on the local host even if the destination host information has not been requested.
#DOM	Specifies domain names. Names preceded with this tag are loaded into the NetBIOS cache in an Internet Group. This tag is useful on Windows NT domain controllers because the browser and Netlogon services direct NetBIOS over TCP/IP messages to all hosts that are part of the Internet Group.

These tags allow you to customize your LMHOSTS file. Along with the tags, you might also see a couple of ways to improve the performance. For instance, because LMHOSTS files are parsed one line at a time, it's a good idea to make sure that all lines with the #PRE tag are kept at the bottom of the file so they don't have to parsed every single time. Conversely, the most commonly used entries should be written at the top of the file.

On a Microsoft Windows 95/98 computer, you will find a sample LMHOSTS file in the <systemroot>\Windows directory. On a Microsoft Windows NT client, you will find it under <systemroot>\system32\drivers\etc. The file will have the name LMHOSTS.SAM. The extension indicates that this file is a sample. Be careful when editing the file in Notepad or—more importantly— in your word-processing application. Notepad has the tendency to save files with the TXT extension, which will invalidate your LMHOSTS file. Applications such as Microsoft Word have propri- etary formats, which are not text files, so these also will invalidate the file. To save a file in Notepad without the TXT extension, simply put the file name in quotes when saving.

It's a good idea to have an LMHOSTS file stored on the network for everyone to share. To do this, make sure that you use the #INCLUDE tag in your LMHOSTS file. Also, make sure that your LMHOSTS file has an entry—before the #INCLUDE statement—that will enable the host-name-to-IP-address resolution of the network host that stores the LMHOSTS file to be included.

Here is a typical LMHOSTS.SAM file that will be loaded with the Microsoft TCP/IP stack; as you can see, it includes guidance on how the file should be created and information on each of the tags that can be applied to entries:

```
# Copyright (c) 1998 Microsoft Corp.
#
# This is a sample LMHOSTS file used by the Microsoft Wins Client
# (NetBIOS over TCP/IP) stack for Windows98
#
# This file contains the mappings of IP addresses to NT computernames
# (NetBIOS) names.  Each entry should be kept on an individual line.
# The IP address should be placed in the first column followed by the
# corresponding computername. The address and the computername
# should be separated by at least one space or tab. The "#" character
# is generally used to denote the start of a comment (see the exceptions
# below).
```

```
#
# This file is compatible with Microsoft LAN Manager 2.x TCP/IP lmhosts
# files and offers the following extensions:
#
#       #PRE
#       #DOM:<domain>
#       #INCLUDE <filename>
#       #BEGIN_ALTERNATE
#       #END_ALTERNATE
#       \0xnn (non-printing character support)
#
# Following any entry in the file with the characters "#PRE" will cause
# the entry to be preloaded into the name cache. By default, entries are
# not preloaded, but are parsed only after dynamic name resolution
# fails.
#
# Following an entry with the "#DOM:<domain>" tag will associate the
# entry with the domain specified by <domain>. This affects how the
# browser and logon services behave in TCP/IP environments. To preload
# the host name associated with #DOM entry, it is necessary to also add
# a #PRE to the line. The <domain> is always preloaded although it will
# not be shown when the name cache is viewed.
#
# Specifying "#INCLUDE <filename>" will force the RFC NetBIOS (NBT)
# software to seek the specified <filename> and parse it as if it were
# local. <filename> is generally a UNC-based name, allowing a
# centralized lmhosts file to be maintained on a server.
# It is ALWAYS necessary to provide a mapping for the IP address of the
# server prior to the #INCLUDE. This mapping must use the #PRE direc-
# tive. In addition the share "public" in the example below must be in
# the LanManServer list of "NullSessionShares" in order for client
# machines tobe able to read the lmhosts file successfully. This key is
# under \machine\system\currentcontrolset\services\lanmanserver\parameters\
# nullsessionshares in the registry. Simply add "public" to the list
# found there.
#
# The #BEGIN_ and #END_ALTERNATE keywords allow multiple #INCLUDE
# statements to be grouped together. Any single successful include
# will cause the group to succeed.
#
# Finally, non-printing characters can be embedded in mappings by
# first surrounding the NetBIOS name in quotations, then using the
# \0xnn notation to specify a hex value for a non-printing character.
```

9

```
#
# The following example illustrates all of these extensions:
#
# 102.54.94.97    rhino      #PRE #DOM:networking #net group's DC
# 102.54.94.102   "appname   \0x14"              #special app server
# 102.54.94.123   popular    #PRE                #source server
# 102.54.94.117   localsrv   #PRE                #needed for the include
#
# #BEGIN_ALTERNATE
# #INCLUDE \\localsrv\public\lmhosts
# #INCLUDE \\rhino\public\lmhosts
# #END_ALTERNATE
#
# In the above example, the "appname" server contains a special
# character in its name, the "popular" and "localsrv" server names are
# preloaded, and the "rhino" server name is specified so it can be used
# to later #INCLUDE a centrally maintained lmhosts file if the
# "localsrv" system is unavailable.
#
# Note that the whole file is parsed including comments on each lookup,
# so keeping the number of comments to a minimum will improve perfor-
# mance. Therefore it is not advisable to simply add lmhosts file
# entries onto the end of this file.
```

As you can see in Figure 9.3, the sample includes information on the tags and how they can be used. It also includes an example mapping of NetBIOS names to IP addresses.

A few circumstances make the LMHOSTS file (and the HOSTS file) inefficient:

➤ Because the LMHOSTS file is generally not centrally managed, it must exist on the local client. Therefore, each client will need to be updated individually.

➤ These files are parsed line by line, so if a double entry is made, then only the first entry that matches the NetBIOS name is used. Human error is a definite possibility!

➤ These files are used late in the resolution process.

Having said that, the LMHOSTS file can provide a good method of mapping IP addresses to NetBIOS names and can be used for troubleshooting.

The HOSTS File

The HOSTS file shares a lot of the attributes of the LMHOSTS file. One major difference is that this file is used to resolve domain names to IP addresses, not NetBIOS names to IP addresses.

Another major difference is that the HOSTS file does not have the tags that LMHOSTS uses. HOSTS files are commonly used on Unix machines for name resolution. Originally, Microsoft's documentation discussed this file as though it were included for compatibility with Unix hosts. However, with the advent of Microsoft Windows 2000, we will see Microsoft moving away from NetBIOS to a pure DNS name-resolution method. Therefore, the HOSTS file will become more important over time.

Figure 9.3 shows the sample HOSTS file that is installed with Microsoft TCP/IP. This file can be edited with Notepad or your favorite word processor. Keep in mind that this file must be saved without a file extension. Notepad and most word processing programs save files with an extension automatically. If you use a word processor, make sure you save the file in ASCII format.

As you can see, this sample includes information on how the HOSTS file can be used. It shares the concerns mentioned in the LMHOSTS section. Although it is a good method for troubleshooting, it can be cumbersome to maintain on each host, so other methods, such as DNS, are very much preferred.

TCP/IP SUITE: UTILITIES

After you have assigned the necessary TCP/IP parameters to a computer, you should be ready to go—but you might not be. Sometimes you'll think you have done everything right, but perhaps you still can't log on or can't get to the Internet.

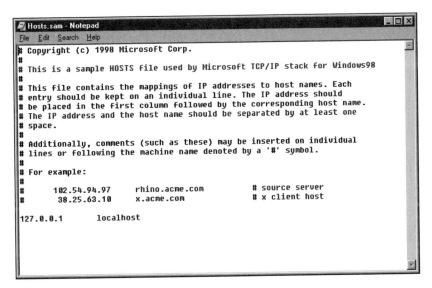

Figure 9.3 A sample HOSTS file.

Fortunately, TCP/IP is not simply a set of protocols that enable communication. It also provides a suite of utilities that can be used to troubleshoot problems. Many of these utilities are available on all platforms (Unix, Microsoft Windows, and OS/2, among others), and some are unique to a platform (such as the Microsoft family of operating systems).

Knowing all of the major utilities and how to use them will aid you in troubleshooting the inevitable problem. Their use is the difference between being a TCP/IP user and being a power user. The utilities we will cover in the following pages are:

➤ IPCONFIG

➤ WINIPCFG

➤ PING

➤ TRACERT

➤ ARP

➤ NBTSTAT

➤ NETSTAT

➤ FTP

➤ Telnet

Although there is some crossover in functionality between some of these utilities, each utility has its own niche in the TCP/IP suite. In addition to discussing what each utility does, we will look at some examples of where you might use them.

Viewing TCP/IP Configurations

Now that we have definitions for most of the common parameters, let's look at some of them in action. When viewing these parameters, be careful not to change them. If you change them, you might lose connectivity to your network or to the Internet.

The IPCONFIG Command-Line Utility

One of the simplest methods of viewing your TCP/IP configuration is to use the IPCONFIG command-line utility. Figure 9.4 shows a standard IPCONFIG screen.

In Figure 9.4, you can see that this computer has an assigned IP address and subnet mask, but no default gateway. That means that this computer will be able to talk to computers on its local network, but not to hosts on the Internet. You will also notice that the Ethernet adapter is listed twice. The first listing has an assigned IP address, but the second one does not. This happened because the

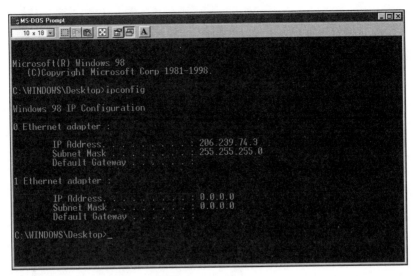

Figure 9.4   A standard IPCONFIG screen.

workstation in question has a Dial-Up Adapter (Microsoft parlance for a modem) installed. Because the Dial-Up Adapter is not in use right now, it shows that no IP address has been assigned to it.

This screen does not tell the whole story about the TCP/IP configuration on this workstation, however. To get a better view of the entire TCP/IP configuration, you will need to use the IPCONFIG utility with one of its switches. This utility has many switches, which we will look at in a moment. Figure 9.5 shows the output for an **IPCONFIG** command when the **/ALL** switch is used.

If you try this on your own workstation, you might notice that the information scrolls off the screen. To prevent this, use the **|more** parameter, as shown in Figure 9.5.

This switch gives you a lot more information about the workstation, including the hostname, the Media Access Control (MAC) address, and the IP addresses of both a DHCP Server and a WINS Server. In most cases, this is the most useful view of the TCP/IP configuration.

Other switches are also available with the IPCONFIG command-line utility. The other options are shown in Figure 9.6. You can often use the **/?** parameter with command-line utilities to get help on using them.

Some of the command-line options shown in Figure 9.6 are applicable only to hosts on a Microsoft network that use DHCP. They are worth mentioning here because they can offer you powerful tools when troubleshooting TCP/IP. Table 9.3 explains what these options mean.

Figure 9.5 An IPCONFIG screen with the **/ALL** switch.

Figure 9.6 Listing the various IPCONFIG switches with the **/?** switch.

By using these commands, you can quickly update client configurations. You might need to do this when you have changed the information stored at the DHCP Server and want the new information (such as the default gateway) to be read without having to reboot the host.

 Different versions of IPCONFIG offer different parameters, so it is worth using the **/?** switch to check when you're using it on operating systems that you're not familiar with. You can also use the **/HELP** switch.

Table 9.3 IPCONFIG command-line switches.

Switch Name	Description
/renew_all	Causes all of the TCP/IP information supplied by the DHCP server to be released. The host will then reapply for updated information.
/release_all	Causes all TCP/IP information to be released, but new information will not be requested by the client.
/renew N	Causes all of the TCP/IP information supplied by the DHCP server to be released on a particular adapter. This switch is useful for hosts with more than one network adapter. After the information is released, the adapter will request new information.
/release N	Causes all of the TCP/IP information supplied by the DHCP server to be released on a particular adapter. This switch is useful for hosts with more than one network adapter. After the information is released, the adapter will not request new information.

If you prefer to work with a graphical user interface, you can use WINIPCFG—Microsoft's GUI utility that duplicates the functionality of IPCONFIG. This utility, shown in Figure 9.7, does not offer significant options beyond what the command-line program offers, but you might find it easier to use.

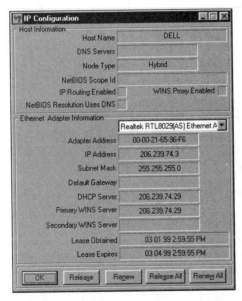

Figure 9.7 Displaying your TCP/IP configuration with WINIPCFG.

Troubleshooting Connectivity

You have loaded TCP/IP correctly. Does that mean that you have access to your network or the Internet? Nope. If it were that simple, we wouldn't need all of those troubleshooters running around solving our problems.

A common problem is that users either cannot log on or can log on but can't print or access network shares. Users might also be able to access computers local to them, but not those on remote networks. What can you do in circumstances like these?

Packet InterNET Groper (PING)

The answer is to use the Packet InterNET Groper, or PING, utility. The PING utility was designed to test connectivity to other systems. It uses Internet Control Message Protocol (ICMP) packets to determine whether or not another host is available.

PING is another command-line utility. Its output is shown in Figure 9.8. This figure shows a successful PING. A successful PING is one that connected to the remote host and received a reply.

When a PING is successful, a packet—called an *ICMP echo request*—is sent to the remote host, which replies with an ICMP echo reply. In our example, the packet that was sent was 32 bytes, and the round trip took less that 10ms each time—a pretty good setup!

Keep a close eye on the **time=** parameter. If the PING takes a long time, it could mean that you have a router problem and that the packet is taking a long time to arrive at the destination. It could also indicate congestion on your network.

Figure 9.8   A successful PING.

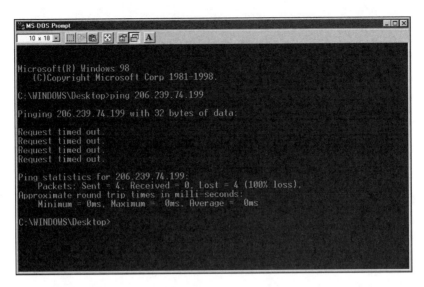

Figure 9.9   An unsuccessful PING.

So what happens when things are not going as well as this? Figure 9.9 illustrates a PING that was unsuccessful. In this case, unsuccessful means that a packet was sent to the IP address that was being PINGed, but the remote host did not reply.

The "Request Timed Out" message is the indicator that something is wrong. For some reason, you could not contact the IP address you were PINGing. Although this message does not tell you why the remote host isn't available, you have at least confirmed that there is a problem.

 You do not have to use a computer's IP address when using the PING utility. If you are using a DNS Server, you can also use the Internet domain name of a remote host. For example, you can use the syntax "ping www.comptia.org". The name will get resolved to its IP address, and then the PING will occur as normal. If you have a WINS Server or a correctly configured LMHOSTS file, this method also works for Microsoft Windows hostnames.

PING is one of the most commonly used TCP/IP utilities. It is easy to use and confirms one of the basic questions of networking: Can I see the remote host? By running PING on the remote host, you can find out if the host can see your computer.

Of course, like most of the command-line utilities, PING has its share of switches that enhance it or supply additional information. Because PING is an older tool, though, it isn't particularly user friendly, and it doesn't have the same syntax as other utilities. Figure 9.10 shows the command line for viewing PING's switches and options.

```
MS-DOS Prompt                                                    _ □ ×
 10 x 18 ▾  ☐ 🖺🖺 ▨ 🖺🖺 A

C:\WINDOWS\Desktop>ping

Usage: ping [-t] [-a] [-n count] [-l size] [-f] [-i TTL] [-v TOS]
            [-r count] [-s count] [[-j host-list] | [-k host-list]]
            [-w timeout] destination-list

Options:
    -t              Ping the specifed host until stopped.
                    To see statistics and continue - type Control-Break;
                    To stop - type Control-C.
    -a              Resolve addresses to hostnames.
    -n count        Number of echo requests to send.
    -l size         Send buffer size.
    -f              Set Don't Fragment flag in packet.
    -i TTL          Time To Live.
    -v TOS          Type Of Service.
    -r count        Record route for count hops.
    -s count        Timestamp for count hops.
    -j host-list    Loose source route along host-list.
    -k host-list    Strict source route along host-list.
    -w timeout      Timeout in milliseconds to wait for each reply.

C:\WINDOWS\Desktop>
```

Figure 9.10   Getting a list of switches for the PING utility.

Note that you don't need to use the **/?** or **/help** switches to get a list of PING options. Simply entering "ping" without an IP address is sufficient.

What if you can't PING any other IP addresses? How can you be sure that TCP/IP has initialized properly on your computer? Use the special IP address 127.0.0.1. This IP address has been reserved and means "localhost" or, in simple terms, "PING myself!" Type "ping 127.0.0.1", and the output should look the same as any other successful PING. If it is not successful, then TCP/IP has not been initialized on your computer. Also, if you can't PING a remote computer, try to PING the default gateway to make sure it is available.

Trace Route (TRACERT)

Now you know how to contact another host to see if it is there. Although this is good information, it is always useful to know more. This is where TRACERT comes into play.

Your local area network (LAN) is a complex set of cables, routers, hubs, gateways, and hosts. The Internet is on a scale many times greater. So although it is good to know that a packet can arrive at a host, wouldn't it be neat to be able to see the route it took to get there?

TRACERT draws you a map of the journey your packet is taking when it is on its way to the remote host. TRACERT reports the name and IP address of every router it traverses on its trip, along with a response time. This response time will tell you where bottlenecks are occurring on your local network or on the Internet.

You will often hear the term "hops" when people talk about packets moving from one host to another. A "hop" is considered to be one step of the journey. For instance, if a datagram travels through 10 routers on its way to a destination, it is considered to have had "10 hops." There is a finite number of hops (30) that utilities will monitor by default. This number can be changed by using the **-h** switch.

TRACERT is a command-line utility. A typical example of screen output is shown in Figure 9.11.

Notice that one of the hops shown in Figure 9.11 has an asterisk (*) beside it. That means that the particular hop timed out. If this were to happen consistently, you would know that you have a problem—perhaps congestion—with the router.

Address Resolution Protocol (ARP)

With all this talk about mapping IP addresses to hostnames, you have to wonder if that is all there is to it. Because IP addresses can change, and hostnames can be changed, how can we be sure that the destination host is correct? Obviously, hostnames and IP addresses do not offer unique identifiers. So what does?

The answer to this is the Media Access Control (MAC) address of the network card in the host. MAC addresses are unique. They are assigned at the factory where the network card was manufactured. The required level of uniqueness is

```
C:\WINNT\System32\cmd.exe                                              _□X
Microsoft(R) Windows NT(TM)
(C) Copyright 1985-1996 Microsoft Corp.

C:\>tracert www.comptia.org

Tracing route to www.comptia.org [207.158.205.174]
over a maximum of 30 hops:

  1    70 ms    70 ms    70 ms  isdn6.wt.net [205.230.159.98]
  2    70 ms    70 ms    70 ms  gw.hou.wt.net [205.230.159.1]
  3   201 ms   170 ms   210 ms  Fddi3-0-0.GW1.HOU1.ALTER.NET [137.39.32.193]
  4   170 ms   180 ms   180 ms  113.ATM3-0.XR2.HOU4.ALTER.NET [146.188.240.150]

  5   180 ms   200 ms   201 ms  292.ATM2-0.TR2.HOU4.ALTER.NET [146.188.240.186]

  6   210 ms   201 ms   210 ms  112.ATM7-0.TR2.ATL1.ALTER.NET [146.188.136.45]
  7   220 ms   210 ms   201 ms  298.ATM7-0.XR2.ATL1.ALTER.NET [146.188.232.109]

  8   221 ms   220 ms   200 ms  194.ATM11-0-0.GW1.MIA1.ALTER.NET [146.188.232.13
3]
  9     *      261 ms   230 ms  rapidsite-t3-gw.customer.ALTER.NET [137.39.141.5
0]
 10   200 ms   210 ms   251 ms  www.comptia.org [207.158.205.174]

Trace complete.

C:\>_
```

Figure 9.11 Typical output of the TRACERT utility.

provided by an IP-address-to-MAC-address translation. This translation is the purpose of the Address Resolution Protocol (ARP).

The translations that ARP performs are stored locally on the client. This storage place is called the *ARP cache*. The entries in the ARP cache are time stamped to prevent the cache from becoming too large. The default timestamp for an ARP entry is 10 minutes. The effect that accessing data in the cache has on this timestamp varies with the TCP/IP stack you have loaded. For some stacks, accessing an entry will restamp it for another 10 minutes, but with others, it has no effect.

When an IP datagram has to be sent from one host to another, the flow of resolution will look something like this:

1. The local host has the hostname of the destination. The local host resolves the destination's hostname to the IP address.

2. The local host then resolves the IP address to the MAC address.

3. This information is appended to the IP datagram and the packet is sent.

When all of these things have taken place, you can be assured that the data you're sending will arrive at the correct place.

 In computers with multiple network cards, each card will have its own ARP cache.

How does your MAC address get into the ARP cache? When the TCP/IP stack is initiated (when your computer is turned on), it broadcasts your MAC address on the network. This address is then stored in the ARP cache of every computer that "hears" the broadcast.

There are two kinds of entries in the ARP cache: static entries and dynamic entries. You can add permanent entries by using an ARP command-line switch. To find out what options are available, type "arp" at the command line. An example of this command is shown in Figure 9.12.

You can add a static entry (one that does not expire) by using the **-s** switch, as illustrated in Figure 9.12. The ARP cache is a key tool in making sure that the datagrams your client is sending arrive at the correct destinations.

One of the most common uses of ARP is troubleshooting. ARP enables you to display what the current cache holds. This might be important when the local host can no longer contact a destination. It's possible that the destination host entry in the ARP cache is incorrect. To resolve this issue, you would clear the entry in the cache.

Using the **ARP −a** switch displays the ARP cache. Figure 9.13 shows an example of what you are likely to see when you're looking at the ARP cache.

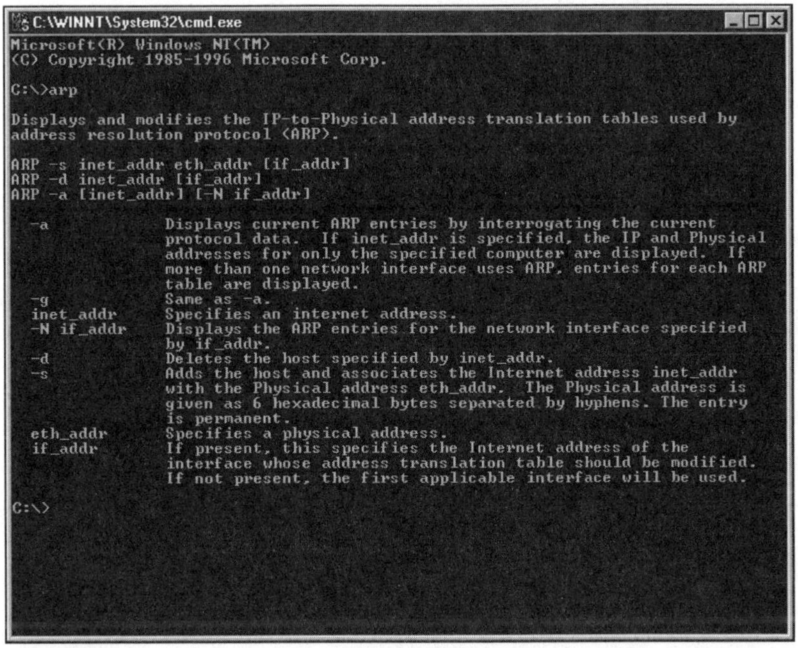

Figure 9.12   Command-line switches for ARP.

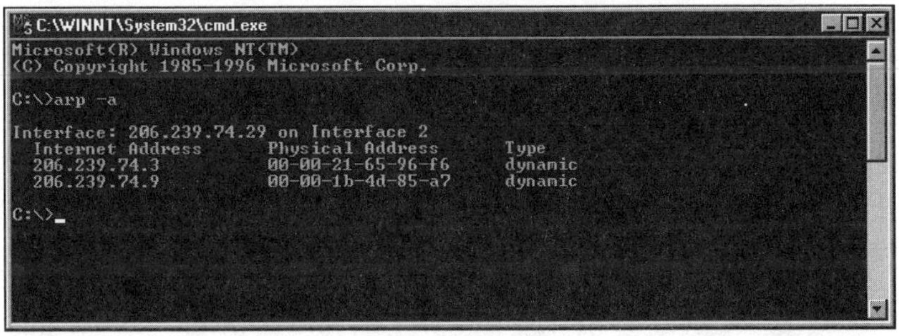

Figure 9.13   Displaying the ARP cache.

If an entry is not in the ARP cache, then ARP will broadcast for the data on the local network. If this is not successful, then ARP will append the MAC address of the default gateway to the datagram.

NBTSTAT

Two companion command-line utilities are available to help you when you're working with NetBIOS over TCP/IP to get the state of your TCP/IP connections. The first of these utilities is NBTSTAT.

The NBTSTAT command-line utility displays protocol statistics and current TCP/IP connections using NBT—or NetBIOS over TCP/IP. You can use this command to find out which services on your computer are registered on the network. You can also use NBTSTAT to find out how many of your client's name requests were resolved by an NBNS Server (or, most commonly, a WINS server) and which were resolved by a broadcast on your network.

NetBIOS uses a local cache of resolved names. When a name is resolved, it is stored in the cache. When your LMHOSTS file has entries with the #PRE tag, these entries are preloaded into the NetBIOS cache. Holding entries in the volatile memory speeds up the process of retrieving them.

Figure 9.14 shows the switches available with the NBTSTAT command-line utility on a Microsoft Windows 98 client.

As you can see, the NBTSTAT command switches offer you some management capabilities for the NetBIOS cache. Keep in mind that this cache operates in unison with an NBNS Server.

NETSTAT

NETSTAT displays protocol statistics and current TCP/IP network connections. You can think of NETSTAT as a companion for NBTSTAT on Microsoft networks. As with NBTSTAT, you can use command-line switches to manage the local cache.

You might use NETSTAT to find out the state of your TCP connections. For instance, entering "netstat" at the command line gives you a list of all connections from your host. From this list, you can determine which connections have been established.

Figure 9.15 shows the switches that are available with the NETSTAT command.

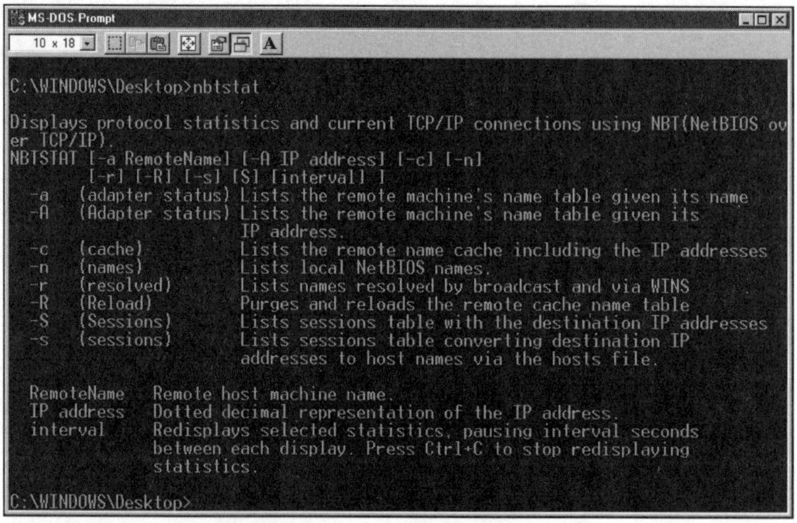

Figure 9.14 Command-line switches for NBTSTAT.

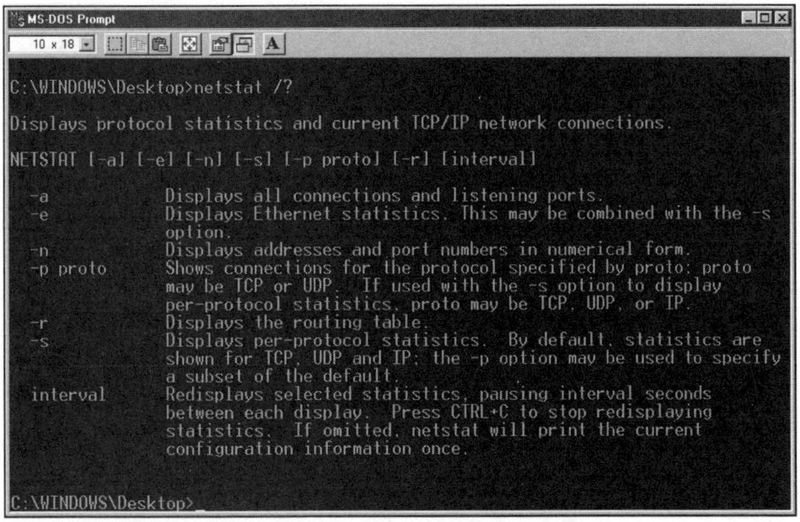

```
C:\WINDOWS\Desktop>netstat /?

Displays protocol statistics and current TCP/IP network connections.

NETSTAT [-a] [-e] [-n] [-s] [-p proto] [-r] [interval]

   -a          Displays all connections and listening ports.
   -e          Displays Ethernet statistics. This may be combined with the -s
               option.
   -n          Displays addresses and port numbers in numerical form.
   -p proto    Shows connections for the protocol specified by proto; proto
               may be TCP or UDP.  If used with the -s option to display
               per-protocol statistics, proto may be TCP, UDP, or IP.
   -r          Displays the routing table.
   -s          Displays per-protocol statistics.  By default, statistics are
               shown for TCP, UDP and IP; the -p option may be used to specify
               a subset of the default.
   interval    Redisplays selected statistics, pausing interval seconds
               between each display.  Press CTRL+C to stop redisplaying
               statistics.  If omitted, netstat will print the current
               configuration information once.

C:\WINDOWS\Desktop>_
```

Figure 9.15   Command-line switches for NETSTAT.

To have the cache display every *n* seconds, enter "netstat *n*", where *n* is any number of seconds, at the command line. This switch can be useful when you want to see how the cache changes over time.

TCP/IP Applications

Many applications run over TCP/IP. It would be impossible to list all of them here, but you should be aware of at least two of them: File Transfer Protocol (FTP) and Telnet. These are the two most common TCP/IP application protocols that you will see supported on just about every platform. In fact, they are so common that it is easy to forget that they are simply application protocols and are not part of the core suite.

File transfers are most commonly done through an FTP application; however, file transfers with Web browsers are becoming more popular. Telnet offers the capability to emulate operating systems.

File Transfer Protocol (FTP)

FTP is often used in its command-line form. However, many FTP utilities with GUIs are now available. Some of these are available as shareware and can be downloaded from the World Wide Web.

FTP has two parts: a server component, which is often known as File Transfer Protocol Server; and a client application. The role of the FTP Server is much like that of a Web server. The client FTP connects to this server and can perform file operations.

We are concerned only with the client in this book, and we are not highlighting any of the GUI versions of the client. This is because the command-line utility is installed by default during the installation of TCP/IP and therefore is the most common implementation. Don't overlook the GUI versions, though. They can simplify your use of this application.

FTP allows you to perform file management and transfer tasks on your network or the Internet. The rights for performing the various tasks are assigned in the server portion of FTP, so if you try to delete a file and cannot, you probably have insufficient rights and will have to contact the server host.

To get a list of all available commands in FTP, you first have to start the application by opening a command window and typing "ftp". After you have done this, the command prompt changes to "FTP". At this command prompt, enter "help" and press Enter. You will now see the available commands, as shown in Figure 9.16.

Many of the commands displayed in Figure 9.16 have obvious uses. To help you get a head start on using FTP, we've listed some commands in Table 9.4.

Table 9.4 is not an exhaustive list of FTP commands, but it does list the most common ones. If you learn these commands, you will know enough to perform 90 percent of the tasks that you normally will find yourself doing with FTP.

Another important point to remember with FTP is that you have to log on to the FTP Server. To do this, you need a username and a password. How can all the FTP Servers on the Internet possibly keep this information up to date? They don't. In the example shown in Figure 9.16, that session was opened with

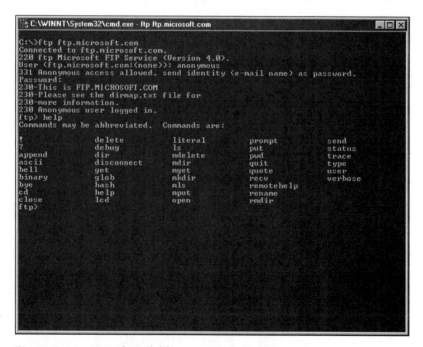

Figure 9.16 List of available commands in FTP.

Table 9.4   File Transfer Protocol commands.

Command Name	Description
OPEN	Opens a connection to an FTP Server. There are two common ways to open a connection to an FTP Server: either type "ftp *<ftpservername>*"; or type "ftp", press Enter, and then use the OPEN *<ftpservername>* method.
PUT	Copies a file to the FTP Server—for example, "PUT chapter9.doc".
GET	Allows you download a file from the server—for example, "GET mydoc.txt".
MGET	Similar to **GET** except that MGET allows you to use wildcards.
MPUT	Similar to **PUT** except that MPUT allows you to upload multiple files by using wildcards.
CD	Same as the DOS command. Stands for "Change Directory."
BYE	Closes the connection to the FTP Server and returns you to the command prompt.
LS	Lists the files in the current directory (same as the DOS command **DIR**).
ASCII	Specifies that the following file transfers will be ASCII files.
BINARY	Specifies that the following file transfers will be binary files.

the account "anonymous"—the password, which was optional, is usually the email address of the person trying to access the server. If you do not have specific access to a server, try "anonymous"; it usually works. Of course, because the access being granted is generic, you are likely to find that you cannot use all the available commands, but you can probably at least download files.

You will most often use FTP to download patches and fixes to the software on your system. Most of the major vendors have FTP sites, which you can access for updates.

FTP is defined in RFC 959.

Telnet

The Telnet utility is provided as a means of performing terminal emulation over TCP/IP. This means that systems running dissimilar operating systems can be accessed from your client as long as both are using TCP/IP as the underlying protocol. These systems include Microsoft, Unix, and mainframe systems. Before the Internet, most of these types of connections were run without local infrastructures in organizations or were run across the public telephone network—hence the term "Telephone Networking," or Telnet.

For Telnet to work, the system you are trying to connect to must be running as a Telnet Server (also known as a Telnet daemon). There are many Telnet Server products on the market. For the client to connect, you will need to have a username and a password on the Telnet Server.

Terminal emulation opens a window into the remote system. As you enter commands in the Telnet window, the commands are processed on the remote system. Telnet applications tend to create heavy network traffic because every character you type into the terminal application is sent as a packet between your host and the server.

When using Telnet, you should be aware that several types of terminals are available. Before you will have complete success, you have to know which terminal the server is expecting to support. The four most common terminals supported are vt100, ANSI, DEC VT-100, and VT-100. Note also that Telnet is a character-based system. This means that menus are generated by using alphanumeric characters, so do not expect a fancy GUI to the remote system.

Telnet is often used as an alternative to FTP and for using legacy applications and databases.

Telnet is defined in RFC 854.

Proxy Servers—An Alternative For Internet Connectivity

The widespread use of TCP/IP raises several issues:

➤ How can you protect against exhausting a finite supply of IP addresses?

➤ How can you protect your organization from those wanting to break in through the Internet?

➤ How can you control what your users do on the Internet?

As the Internet has grown, it has become an essential tool for businesses, and security has become an important issue. Organizations need to make sure that the communication between themselves and the Internet is controlled somehow. The control of communications needs to work both ways. To protect your organization, you need to know how your organization's employees are using the Internet. You also need to prevent data on your network from being accessed by those on the outside. These are the purposes for which proxy servers were designed.

Proxy servers and firewalls are very similar. Originally, they performed different tasks, but as time goes on, their jobs are being combined. Generally, a firewall is used to prevent data from going in and out of a network by blocking TCP ports. For instance, by blocking port 80 going out of your organization, you could prevent your employees from browsing the Internet. Increasingly, we are seeing proxy servers that also perform this function.

Essentially, proxy servers work like this: You have a number of hosts on your internal network. There are literally millions of hosts on the Internet. In between these two sets of hosts is a computer (or several computers) acting as a proxy. Communication from your organization to the Internet, and from the Internet to your organization, travels through the proxy server. This route is illustrated in Figure 9.17.

All the clients on the internal network pass their requests for Internet data to the proxy server. All requests coming in from the Internet are directed to the proxy server, which then passes them to the internal clients.

A proxy server offers benefits both for IP management and end users. Let's look at each separately.

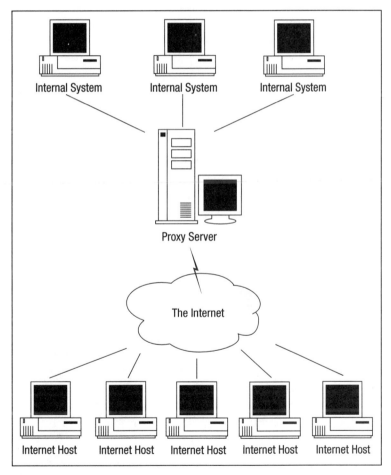

Figure 9.17 A typical example of a proxy server in use.

Benefits For IP Management

A typical proxy server will offer services to both aid the internal client and help you manage your network connectivity. From a management perspective, a proxy server offers the following advantages:

➤ You can limit the Internet resources that your internal clients access, including specific Web sites and FTP Servers, as well as ports.

➤ You can control when access is granted to Internet resources.

➤ You can generate reports of traffic that is being passed to the Internet.

➤ You can manage traffic coming into the local network from the Internet.

➤ You can grant access to Internet resources to clients that are not using TCP/IP.

➤ You can have nonunique Internet IP addresses on your internal network.

Let's look at a couple of these points in detail so it is clear why proxy servers are becoming more popular.

Why would you want to limit the Internet resources that your internal hosts can access? Well, for most organizations, this limitation helps protect them against liabilities. The Internet is a large mass of data, and just about anyone with any opinions can have access to it. Enterprises have to be mindful of every one of their users. Is the material on the Internet likely to offend someone? Are the organization's resources, such as hard–disk space and time, being used for productive matters? The option to control Internet access helps organizations filter out those Web sites or FTP Servers that are not deemed appropriate.

Why is it important to have nonunique IP addresses on the internal network? For the Internet to work, each host must have a unique IP address. Although the current addressing schemes allow for billions of clients, the number of new hosts appearing on the Internet every day means that this supply will soon be exhausted.

Wouldn't it be nice if you could use any old IP address scheme that you wanted to within your organization, so all you had to worry about was getting a unique IP address for the computer that's connected directly to the Internet? That's what proxy servers allow you to do! Typically, a proxy server has two network cards: one connected to the internal network, and one connected to the Internet. Hosts on the internal network pass their requests for Internet resources to the network card that is connected to the internal network. The proxy server routes these requests to the network card that is attached to the Internet. This card is the only interface that is required to have an address that is unique on the Internet.

Let's say that you want to have as much security as possible. You want to make sure that no hosts on the Internet can directly access hosts on your internal network. You could isolate the internal machines by limiting the protocols they use. If the hosts were not running TCP/IP, then they couldn't run FTP Servers or their own Web sites. The trouble is, they wouldn't be able to use the Internet for legitimate business. To solve this problem, you can have both IPX and TCP/IP running on the proxy server, while using only IPX on the clients. The proxy server will accept requests for Internet resources by using IPX from the internal clients and will make requests for the resources externally by using TCP/IP. When the external resources send packets back to the requesting host, the proxy server will receive the IP datagrams and reply to the internal host by using IPX. This scenario is just one example of making a network more secure.

Benefits For The End User

The following are some advantages that a proxy server offers its internal hosts:

➤ Bandwidth to the Internet is limited, and proxy servers can optimize the speed of browsing the Web.

➤ Bandwidth is conserved by making sure that others are not using the Internet connection for nonessential work.

➤ Proxy servers can run FTP Servers, so hosts on the Internet cannot gain access to them.

➤ Proxy servers can host internal intranet sites and prevent unauthorized access.

Of these reasons, one of the best is the extra performance you are likely to see when browsing the Web. Performance improves because many proxy servers can cache the pages of the Web sites they access. So, let's say that one host accesses the pages at Coriolis's Web site. Three minutes later, another host on the network tries to access the same Web site. Instead of this host having to wait for the proxy server to connect to the Internet and retrieve the page, the proxy server delivers the page directly from its cache. This is obviously much faster.

The use of proxy servers has grown. With their ability to both protect data on an organization's internal network and increase performance for those going out to the Internet to get data, they are a great asset. Although firewalls offer the same—or, in some cases, more—security, they do not offer the same performance benefits that a proxy server does.

CHAPTER SUMMARY

In this chapter, we discussed some of the essential things you will need to know about workstation configuration, both for your real-world work with TCP/IP and in order to pass the Network+ examination.

The essential items that a TCP/IP configuration should contain include a unique IP address, a subnet mask, and a default gateway. Other items include WINS Servers and DNS Servers for name resolution, DHCP for IP address assignment, and the hostname of your workstation.

This chapter discussed the three methods of handling IP addresses when TCP/IP is implemented. These are:

➤ Manually assigning IP addresses to all workstations. This method involves a lot of administration and becomes unmanageable when the number of workstations grows.

➤ Using DHCP (Dynamic Host Configuration Protocol) to automatically assign IP addresses to workstations. In this method, DHCP stores a pool of IP addresses and assigns them to workstations as users log on. These assignments are called *leases*. When a lease expires, the workstation can request a lease extension or can request a new IP configuration.

➤ Using a proxy server to handle communication.

Several methods of resolving names are available:

➤ NetBIOS names are resolved to IP addresses by two primary methods: WINS (Windows Internet Name Service) and the LMHOSTS file.

➤ Domain names are resolved to IP addresses by using DNS and the HOSTS file.

➤ IP addresses are resolved to MAC addresses by using the ARP protocol.

Various TCP/IP utilities are available to help you with troubleshooting.

➤ The IPCONFIG and WINIPCFG utilities allow you to see the TCP/IP configuration of a host. IPCONFIG is a command-line utility, and WINIPCFG is a GUI that gives you the same information. WINIPCFG is available only in Windows 95/98 systems. Although the IPCONFIG utility will work with these operating systems, the Microsoft standard tool is WINIPCFG.

➤ The PING utility allows you to send echo requests to a destination host. If the host does not reply, either it is not available, or the TCP/IP stack on your own system is not initialized correctly. Or there might be a network problem between your host and the destination host. In any case, a failure when PINGing indicates a problem.

➤ The TRACERT utility draws a map between two hosts. It could almost be thought of as super-PING. Rather than simply replying, "Yep, I heard you," it draws a map of every router it travels through on its way to the destination host. This map is useful in letting you know when a router is causing a problem.

➤ ARP is both a protocol and a utility that translates IP addresses to MAC addresses.

➤ The NBTSTAT and NETSTAT utilities allow you to get protocol statistics on your network. NBTSTAT is used to get statistics and information on NetBIOS over TCP/IP (also known as NBT) and therefore works in Microsoft networking environments. NETSTAT works similarly in TCP/IP.

Two major TCP/IP applications are FTP and Telnet. FTP is a file management protocol and a server service. One of the most common uses is to download and upload files. You can also create directories and delete files. Telnet is a terminal emulation program. You can use Telnet to allow your host to become a dumb terminal off another host, such as a mainframe. Common uses are to access legacy applications and to transfer files.

Proxy servers are used to perform two important functions. They enhance the users' experience on the World Wide Web by caching Web pages as they are requested. Proxy servers can also act as a firewall by blocking certain ports. This prevents people outside an organization from using the utilities discussed here to get proprietary data.

REVIEW QUESTIONS

1. Which of the following standard TCP/IP settings must be assigned before you can contact hosts on other networks?

   a. PING

   b. Default path

   c. Default gateway

   d. Domain Name Service (DNS)

2. You are having trouble communicating on your network and are not sure if your computer is configured correctly. To check the TCP/IP configuration, what command would you use?

   a. **IPCONFIG**

   b. **PING <default gateway>**

   c. **WINIPCFG**

   d. **TRACERT**

3. Communication on your local area network (LAN) appears to work correctly, but when you try to contact a vendor's Web site, your Web browser hangs. You want to know if the problem is within your own building or on the Internet itself. What command would you use to determine the problem's location?

   a. **PING**

   b. **FTP**

   c. **WINIPCFG**

   d. **TRACERT**

4. You must spend a lot of time troubleshooting TCP/IP configurations on your Windows NT- and Windows 98-based network because the last administrator didn't document the configurations. To ease and automate troubleshooting, what would you do?

   a. Visit each desktop and document each host's TCP/IP configuration.

   b. Send email telling people not to change their TCP/IP configurations because doing so can cause problems on the network.

   c. PING each workstation to make a list of unassigned IP addresses and then use only these unassigned addresses for new workstations.

   d. Implement DHCP and visit each workstation to set its TCP/IP stack to "Obtain an IP address automatically."

5. You have just installed a new server. Because it is not in production yet, you don't want to assign a WINS Server IP address to it. However, you do want to configure your workstation so you can use the PING utility to find out when the new server is available. Which file would you edit so you could PING this server with its assigned NetBIOS name?

   a. Enter the information into the DNS Server.

   b. Edit the HOSTS file.

   c. You cannot PING the server without using a WINS Server.

   d. Edit the LMHOSTS file.

6. You have just created a new Web server. The intranet site is being tested, and you want to enable 10 people in the finance department to access it with their Web browsers and then provide feedback. No one else, however, should be able to access the site. How could you accomplish this?

   a. Add the Web server information in the DNS Server.

   b. Add the Web site information into the WINS Server.

   c. Edit the LMHOSTS file on the 10 hosts in the finance department.

   d. Edit the HOSTS file on the 10 hosts in the finance department.

7. Why would it *not* be a good idea to have no name-resolution methods on your network?

   a. If you don't have a name-resolution method on your network, then hosts will not be able to see each other.

   b. If you don't have a name-resolution method on your network, each host will broadcast when it needs to contact another host, causing network congestion.

   c. Having no name-resolution methods on the network won't matter. Hosts will still find each other.

   d. Without a name-resolution method on the network, TCP/IP will not initialize properly.

8. If you want to load an LMHOSTS file entry into the NetBIOS name cache every time your host starts, what tag would you use in the LMHOSTS file?

   a. #INSERT

   b. #INCLUDE

   c. #DOM

   d. #PRE

9. Which TCP/IP utility would you use to find out NetBIOS over TCP/IP protocol statistics?

   a. NBTSTAT

   b. PING –N

   c. NETSTAT

   d. TRACERT

10. When you try to go to a Web site to download a much-needed patch for a new application, the site will not come up. Which TCP/IP utility would be most useful for solving this problem?

   a. Microsoft Internet Explorer

   b. Telnet

   c. FTP

   d. TRACERT

9

11. Someone gained access to your network from the Internet and planted a virus. After spending an entire day eradicating it from your network, you want to prevent such a disaster from happening again. What is the best way to prevent another virus, knowing that several employees have FTP Servers on their desktops?

    a. Email employees, reminding them always to shut down their FTP sites.

    b. Make sure that everyone turns their computers off at night.

    c. Make sure that everyone tells you about any viruses on their machines so you can fix the problem right away.

    d. Install a proxy server.

12. After a server reboots, you keep using the PING utility to see if it is available yet. It is not. You get tired of typing the PING command. What command-line switch would you use to PING the server infinitely?

    a. **−A**

    b. **−t**

    c. **−N**

    d. **−a**

13. Your users complain that the office's Internet connection is slow during lunch. You know that the sluggishness stems from employees browsing the Internet while eating lunch. Because lunch times are staggered, however, their browsing affects others' work. When your boss asks you to solve the problem, you install a proxy server. How does a proxy server solve the problem?

    a. By limiting the number of sites users can access

    b. By caching Web pages

    c. By increasing the bandwidth between your office and the Internet

    d. By limiting the protocols that can use the Internet

14. You go to a user's desktop to troubleshoot his problems accessing the Internet with his Windows 98 host. You check his machine and discover that the user can access all the hosts on your own network, map drives, and print documents. But you cannot browse the World Wide Web with the user's browser, although everyone else can access the Web without trouble. Which TCP/IP parameter is likely to be wrong or missing?

    a. DNS

    b. WINS

    c. Subnet mask

    d. IP address

15. You have a 1,000-user network and use IPX as your only protocol. All users have Microsoft Windows 95. Now you must ensure that everyone can access the Internet. You contact an ISP who has already installed a T1 line and a router. What is the easiest method of giving users access to the Internet?

    a. Install a DNS Server on your network.

    b. Install a WINS Server.

    c. Install TCP/IP on every system.

    d. Install a proxy server.

16. You are sitting at a Microsoft Windows NT Server and want to know the machine's IP configuration. Which utility would you use to find this information?

    a. PING

    b. IPCONFIG

    c. WINIPCFG

    d. PING –N

17. You have a Microsoft network with all clients using Windows 95. You want to organize your TCP/IP configurations to ensure that they can be centrally managed. What application would you choose to do this?

    a. DNS

    b. WINS

    c. IPCONFIG

    d. DHCP

18. You recently installed a new server. Because it is not in production yet, you add it to your LMHOSTS file for testing purposes. You will not be using the server much, so you add the entry to the bottom of the file. However, you still cannot PING the machine by using its NetBIOS name. What is the most likely reason for this?

    a. You have the NetBIOS name wrong.

    b. There are two entries in the LMHOSTS file with the same IP address and different NetBIOS names.

    c. The LMHOSTS file is not used for NetBIOS name resolution. You need to make an entry in the HOSTS file instead.

    d. You cannot PING NetBIOS names.

19. You are on a host and want to get its TCP/IP configuration information. You type "ipconfig" and press Enter, but the information it gives is incomplete. Which switch would you use to get better information?

   a. **/MORE**

   b. **/EVERYTHING**

   c. **/?**

   d. **/ALL**

20. You are trying to access the FTP site of a vendor so you can download a patch. You can gain access to the site, but it is asking you for a username. You weren't told that you would need one. What is the most likely username you could use?

   a. Your network username

   b. Your Social Security number

   c. You will have to get a username from the vendor

   d. Anonymous

HANDS-ON PROJECTS

The hands-on projects in this chapter will walk you through testing some of the subjects we have discussed in this chapter. Neither of these hands-on exercises will be possible if you do not have TCP/IP loaded at your workstation. The exercises were written for Microsoft Windows 9x. If you are using Microsoft Windows NT or a version of Unix, the steps may be a little different. If you do not have TCP/IP loaded on your system, you will have to install TCP/IP. Steps 1 through 3 in Project 9.1 will determine if TCP/IP is installed and working correctly.

Project 9.1

In this exercise, you will check the TCP/IP configuration of your Windows 9x workstation.

To check the TCP/IP configuration:

1. Go to a command prompt. To do this, do either of the following:

   ➤ Go to Start | Programs | MS-DOS Prompt.

   ➤ Go to Start | Run, type "command", and press Enter.

2. At the command prompt, type "ping 127.0.0.1" and press Enter.

If you receive a reply, then TCP/IP is installed and configured correctly on the system, and you can continue. If you do not receive a reply, then TCP/IP is either not installed or not initialized correctly. You will not be able to continue with the exercise without correcting the problem.

3. Type "exit" and press Enter. The DOS Command window will close.

4. Open the TCP/IP configuration window. There are two ways to do this:

  ➤ Go to Start | Settings | Control Panel. Then, double-click on the Network applet.

  ➤ Right-click on the Network Neighborhood icon on your desktop and choose Properties.

5. There are three tabs in the Network dialog box. Click on the Identification tab. You will now see the NetBIOS name of the computer you are on, plus the domain or workgroup name and a description.

6. Click on the Configuration tab. This tab provides information about the network card you have installed and the protocol you have loaded. You should see an icon that looks like a network interface card (NIC). Click on the icon and then click on Properties.

If you perform Step 6 and get the Dial-Up Adapter Properties dialog box, then you have selected the Dial-Up Adapter from the Network dialog box. The Dial-Up Adapter icon is the same as the NIC in your computer. Click on Cancel and select the correct adapter; then select Properties.

7. In the dialog box for your network adapter, click on the Bindings tab. If you have more than one protocol loaded on your system, there will be multiple entries in this tab. If you cannot see all of the entries, scroll down and look for the one named TCP/IP. This confirms that TCP/IP has been bound to your NIC.

8. Click on Cancel. You should be returned to the Network dialog box, and you should be in the Configuration tab. Look for the entry that corresponds to what you saw in Step 7. If you have more than one protocol loaded, you might need to scroll down the list until you find the correct binding. When you find it, click on it and then click on Properties to open the TCP/IP Properties dialog box.

9. Which option is selected? If Obtain An IP Address Automatically is selected, then your network probably is using DHCP. If Specify An IP Address is selected, then you have been assigned a manual address. You should have an entry in the IP Address box and in the Subnet Mask box.

10. Click on the Gateway tab. Look at the IP address of the installed gateway. Write this down.

If you do not have any installed gateways, your organization might be using a proxy server for connections to the Internet. If you have a standalone workstation, then it is likely that you are having a default gateway assigned when you are dialing in to your Internet Service Provider (ISP).

11. Click on the DNS Configuration tab. Look at the DNS Search Order. Write this down.

9

If you do not have any entries in the DNS Search Order, it may be that DNS entries are automatically assigned to you, either through DHCP or by your ISP when you dial in to the Internet.

12. Click on the WINS Configuration tab. Write down the IP address specified in WINS Server Search Order.

If you do not have any entries in this tab, the values are most likely assigned by a DHCP server.

13. Click on Cancel. You will return to the Network dialog box. Click on Cancel.

14. Click on Start | Run, type "winipcfg", and press Enter. This should start the WINIPCFG utility. Click on the MORE INFO button.

15. If you were unable to write down the IP addresses in Steps 9 through 12 because your system is being assigned this information from a DHCP server, you will now see it displayed. Write down the IP addresses for the DNS Servers, the default gateway, and the primary WINS server for the following exercises.

16. Click on OK.

17. Go to a command prompt.

18. At the command prompt, type "ping *<default gateway>*". The default gateway parameter should be replaced with the IP address you wrote down in Step 10 or 15.

If an IP address was displayed in WINIPCFG or your TCP/IP setup, and you fail to get a reply in Step 18, then you may have a problem on your network. You will not be able to send information to computers that are not on your subnet.

19. At the command prompt, type "ping *<DNS Server>*". The DNS Server parameter should be replaced with the IP address you wrote down in Step 11 or 15.

If an IP address was displayed in WINIPCFG or your TCP/IP setup and you fail to get a reply in Step 19, then you may have a problem on your network. You will not be able to resolve hostnames to IP addresses for your network.

20. At the command prompt, type "ping *<primary WINS server>*". The Primary WINS Server parameter should be replaced with the IP address you wrote down in Step 12 or 15.

If an IP address was displayed in WINIPCFG or your TCP/IP setup and you fail to get a reply in Step 20, then you may have a problem on your network. You will not be able to resolve NetBIOS host names to IP addresses for your network.

Project 9.2

In this exercise, you will practice using some of the TCP/IP utilities discussed in this chapter. It is extremely beneficial if these exercises are run on a network that has Internet connectivity. If this is not the case, then you will not be able to perform some of the tasks in this exercise. If you are on a standalone PC and have a dial-up connection to an ISP, then it is strongly suggested that you connect to your ISP before performing these tasks.

First, we will look on your system to see if you have a HOSTS and/or LMHOSTS file. The location of these files depends on the operating system you are using. If you are using a Microsoft 95/98 or Microsoft Windows NT 4 product, then there are two methods you can use to view the file.

Once we have looked at the HOSTS and LMHOSTS files on your system, we will use PING to contact a server on the Internet. After that is complete, we will view your computer's IP configuration and use this information to find out details of NetBIOS name resolution your computer has performed.

1. If you are using Windows 95/98, click on Start|Programs|Windows Explorer. You will need to open the *<systemroot>* folder, which is usually on the C: drive. If you have a nonstandard installation, then locate the *<systemroot>* directory by looking for the WINDOWS directory on your hard disk.

2. When you have located the WINDOWS folder on your hard disk, open the folder by clicking on the folder in the left pane. This will list the files in the right pane. In the right pane, locate and double-click on the HOSTS.SAM file.

3. If you have never created a file association for the SAM extension on your system, you will see the Open With dialog box. This lists applications on your system. Scroll down the list until you locate Notepad. Click on Notepad and then on OK. The HOSTS.SAM file will open in Notepad.

4. If you have a file called "HOSTS" (missing a file extension) in your *<systemroot>* folder, this means that you have a HOSTS file configured on your system. If you want to look at the working file, rather than at the sample, double-click on the HOSTS file and follow the instructions in Step 2. Do *not* alter this file; otherwise, you might lose connectivity to network resources.

5. Alternatively, you can start Notepad first and then use it to open the file. You can do this by selecting Start|Run and then typing "notepad" and pressing Enter. While in Notepad, click on File|Open. The Open dialog box will default to the *<systemroot>* folder because this is the last folder that was accessed. Type "lmhosts.sam" and press Enter. The last file you were looking at will close and LMHOSTS.SAM will open.

9

6. If you changed the file you had open (even pressing the spacebar by accident), you will be asked if you want to save the changes when you attempt to open the LMHOSTS.SAM file. If this happens, do *not* save changes because this could cause you to lose access to network resources.

7. Click on File | Exit to close Notepad.

8. You will now take a closer look at the PING command-line utility. We are going to check to see if you have access to the World Wide Web. Click on Start | Run and type "command". A Command window will open.

9. In the Command window, type "ping www.coriolis.com" and press Enter.

10. If you receive the message, "Destination Host unreachable," this could signify one of several things. It could mean that you do not have access to the Internet, that the Web site is not currently available, or that your organization uses a proxy server for access to the Internet. When a proxy server is used, the protocol used by the PING utility (ICMP) is often blocked.

11. In the Command window, type "ping www.comptia.org" and press Enter.

Step 11 tests your connection to the Internet even further. Although it is possible that a single site is not currently available, it would be bad luck to find that two popular sites have gone down simultaneously.

12. In this test, we will PING a machine that we know works—your own! We will PING it using some of the available switches. Click on Start | Run and type "winipcfg". The WINIPCFG utility will run. Write down the IP address of your machine.

13. At the Command window, type "ping <IP address> -n 9", where <IP address> is the IP address you have just written down.

You have performed a PING, but instead of seeing the usual four replies, you receive nine. That occurred because the –n switch allows you to specify how many echo requests are generated by the command.

14. At the Command window, type "ping <IP address> -t>", where <IP address> is the IP address you wrote down in step 12. In this case, you will send an infinite number of echo requests.

15. Press Ctrl+C to stop the infinite echo requests.

You might wonder what such a function is good for. You would use infinite echo requests when a remote server has been restarted. For part of the reboot process, the server will not be available on the network because the operating system has yet to initialize. If you need to know that it has restarted successfully, simply PING, using the syntax in Step 14. As soon as the TCP/IP stack has initialized on the server, you will begin to receive replies from the remote host.

16. We will now view all of the command-line parameters that are available in the PING utility you have installed. At the command line, type "ping" and press Enter. The list of parameters will be displayed.

This is worth doing because different operating systems will offer variations on the PING utility. A quick look at the parameters will tell you what you have.

17. We will now use a utility to find which NetBIOS names are being stored in your computer's NetBIOS name cache. At the command line, type "nbtstat –A <IP address>", where <IP address> is the IP address you wrote down in Step 12.

You will likely see several interesting pieces of information, including your computer's NetBIOS name and domain name. You might be wondering why there are so many entries. This is because different services on your system register themselves using a slightly different name (the 16th bit is unique among the services, but they all share a 15-bit portion). The hexadecimal code to the right of the computer name is the unique portion of the name.

So what is a useful situation for such a tool? You would use this switch in NBTSTAT to track down duplicate IP addresses on your network. Duplicate IP addresses are a no-go on a network. All IP addresses must be unique. Sometimes a person will type in a manual IP address while DHCP is giving out addresses to everyone else. This will lead to DHCP giving out a duplicate IP address because it had no way of knowing that one was already taken. One or both of the users will begin to receive error messages telling them that they have a duplicate IP address. To track down the rogue machine name, try the following. Check the machine that just received the error to make sure it is configured correctly. If it is, shut down the system. Go to another system, open a Command window, and type "ping <IP address>". The IP address should be the IP address that was generating the error message. Next, at the command line, type "nbtstat –A <IP address>" and press Enter. This will display the machine name of the host that has the duplicate address.

18. To find out what switches are available to you when using the NBTSTAT utility, go to the command line, type "nbtstat", and press Enter. All available switches will be displayed.

9

## CHAPTER TEN

REMOTE CONNECTIVITY

After Reading This Chapter And Completing The Exercises, You Will Be Able To:

➤ Understand modem protocols SLIP and PPP

➤ Configure modem parameters

➤ Define remote node vs. remote control

➤ Configure and establish a dial-up networking connection.

➤ Understand the purpose and function off PPTP and Virtual Private Networks (VPNs)

➤ Discuss newer remote connectivity methods and their advantages and disadvantages compared to POTS

No longer reserved for business users needing to work from the road, remote connectivity has become commonplace with the enormous growth and popularity of the Internet. In fact, many of the connectivity methods—such as SLIP/PPP and virtual private networks—were developed for the Internet. In this chapter, we will look at SLIP and PPP, the most common methods of accessing a remote network such as the Internet, and we'll compare them to the older host dial-up method (shell access) and direct connections.

The most common means of accessing a remote network is with a modem, so we will discuss modem configuration parameters and setting up a modem under Windows 9x and NT 4. After we have our modem configured, we can configure and establish a connection through dial-up networking.

With the wide availability of the Internet and the desire to keep remote dial-up costs down, many companies have implemented virtual private networks that use the Internet as a communications facilitator. We'll explain what that means and how to do it. Last, we'll compare traditional POTS (Plain Old Telephone System) with newer digital services, such as ISDN and DSL/ASDL, and discuss what the future holds for remote connectivity.

MODEM PROTOCOLS SLIP AND PPP

In the dark ages of the 1980s, before the World Wide Web, the Internet was a text-based world. If you had access to the Internet from home, it was by dialing in to (almost always) a Unix machine at a local university where you had a shell account. In this method, your computer functioned as a dumb terminal on the remote network you were dialing in to, and you dialed in with terminal emulation software such as Procomm Plus. The server you connected to did all of the processing work, and your computer only sent and received screen updates. For an example of how that worked, look at the common FTP utility. With a dial-up to a shell account, you logged in to an account on the remote server. When you used FTP (File Transfer Protocol) to transfer a file from another remote computer on the network or on the Internet, the file was not transferred to the PC you were using; rather, it was transferred to the host server you were dialed in to. From there, you would have to use a transfer protocol such as Kermit, xmodem, or zmodem to bring the file from the host server to your computer. In effect, you had an indirect connection to the network.

SLIP (and later PPP) was born out of frustration regarding the limitations of shell account access. SLIP is short for Serial Line Internet Protocol. SLIP encapsulates the TCP/IP (Transmission Control Protocol/Internet Protocol) protocol for use over asynchronous lines (such as standard telephone lines). Most commonly, it's used as a way to connect a system to a TCP/IP network using a modem. With an implementation of SLIP, your system can act as a full-scale Internet network host. This allows you to run network applications directly on your home computer. The only difference in principle between a SLIP connection and Ethernet is that a serial line is normally a lot slower than Ethernet.

SLIP provides the ability to transport TCP/IP traffic over serial lines, such as dial-up telephone lines, between two computers. Both computers run TCP/IP-based network software. This allows a home user to get direct Internet access from his or her own PC with just a simple modem and a telephone line. With SLIP, you can run your favorite GUI (graphical user interface)-based Web browser or FTP client right from your own PC. In our FTP example above, with shell access, the files are downloaded to the host server you are dialed in to. With SLIP, the file is downloaded directly to your computer because you have a direct connection to the Internet.

 SLIP is a form of direct Internet connection in the sense that:

> ➤ Your computer has a communications link to the Internet, even if it is via a service provider.

> ➤ Your computer has the networking software that can speak TCP/IP with other computers on the Internet.

➤ Your computer has an identifying address (IP address) at which it can be contacted by other computers on the Internet.

PPP, which stands for Point-To-Point Protocol, is very similar to SLIP. To most users, the two are functionally equivalent. SLIP was never approved as an Internet standard, but PPP has been approved. With SLIP, you usually have to enter your configuration parameters manually. If IP addresses are not dynamically assigned (this depends on your service provider), you will need to set them up. You might also need to configure such details as MTU (maximum transmission unit), MRU (maximum receive unit), use of VJ (Van Jacobson) compression header, and so on. All these details can get confusing pretty fast.

PPP addresses this problem by negotiating configuration parameters at the start of the connection. This can greatly simplify the configuration of a PPP connection. PPP's most significant advantage is its automatic login and configuration negotiation features. With these features, the PPP software needs to know only your login user ID and password, and the telephone number of the dial-up server. The software can then dial in to the remote network and figure out everything else on its own.

PPP has some additional benefits. Unlike SLIP (which can transport only TCP/IP traffic), PPP is a multiprotocol transport mechanism. This means that PPP not only transports TCP/IP traffic, but can also transport IPX (Internetwork Packet Exchange), NetBEUI, and AppleTalk traffic, to name just a few. Also, PPP lets you transport all of these protocols at the same time—on the same connection. Although it is not relevant to the Internet, which relies solely on TCP/IP traffic, PPP is a boon for corporate users who need to dial in to networks running other LAN (local area network) protocols, such as IPX/SPX (Internetwork Packet Exchange/Sequenced Packet Exchange) and NetBEUI (NetBIOS Extended User Interface). PPP works by encapsulating the network packets into IP packets for transmission over the Internet's TCP/IP network. PPP is currently the most popular method of dialing in to a remote network over a modem, with a marginal performance gain over SLIP.

The other type of connection you could have is a direct connection. This is not really a remote connectivity method because it involves having your computer directly attached to the network. This is the fastest type of connection, but also the most expensive. Figure 10.1 illustrates the different types of connections.

PPP is the software side of the dial-up equation, with the hardware side typically involving the use of a modem on the user's side. With that in mind, we'll look at modems and at what you need to configure to use a modem for remote dial-up.

10

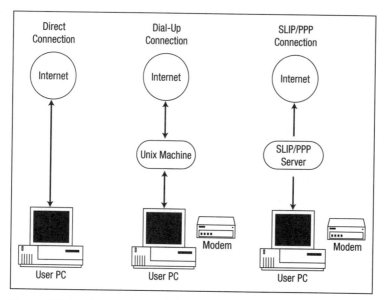

Figure 10.1   Comparison of the shell access, SLIP/PPP, and direct types of connections.

MODEM CONFIGURATION PARAMETERS

There are two types of modems: internal and external. In setting up an external modem, you must do little with the actual modem other than plug it in and turn it on. All of the settings come from the serial port that the modem is plugged into. Configuring an internal modem, however, has often been an exercise in frustration. Internal modems have virtual serial ports (also known as COM ports) that must be configured by the user before the modem can be used. To make matters worse, most computers have two serial ports hardwired to the motherboard; both ports use resources that must be accounted for when configuring an internal modem. Resources that must be configured for modems include the IRQ (interrupt request) and I/O address. The combination of the two determine the COM port the modem is using. Table 10.1 shows the de facto standard COM-port assignments.

Table 10.1   Standard modem COM-port settings.

COM Port	IRQ	I/O Address
COM1	4	03F8h
COM2	3	02F8h
COM3	4	03E8h
COM4	3	02E8h

Notice that COM ports 1 and 3 share an IRQ, and COM ports 2 and 4 share an IRQ. If your computer has two ISA (Industry Standards Architecture) devices that share an IRQ, you'll often run into problems if you attempt to use them at the same time. For example, your serial mouse might stop working when you dial in to the Internet, but start working again when you disconnect from the dial-up session. The newer PCI (Peripheral Component Interconnect) bus handles IRQ sharing much more effectively than the ISA bus does and is not as susceptible to those types of problems, but this issue is something to keep in mind when you're dealing with older systems.

Until recently, most internal modems had jumpers for configuring the COM-port settings. Some modems also offered a Plug and Play option, which was configured by not jumping any of the configuration jumpers (COM, IRQ, I/O address). The vast majority of internal modems being sold today, however, are Plug and Play only. That means if you are not running a Plug and Play operating system, such as Windows 95 or Windows 98, you will need an external modem. Windows NT has very rudimentary support for Plug and Play devices, starting with NT 4 Service Pack 3, but PC-based Unix operating systems, such as Solaris and Linux, do not support Plug and Play and cannot use these newer jumperless modems.

10

With a Plug and Play modem and a Plug and Play operating system, installation is generally a matter of physically installing the card and booting up the computer. If all goes well, Windows will detect the new hardware device and prompt you for the driver disk. As Windows installs the driver, it configures the modem automatically, using available resources. Usually this works fine, but sometimes Windows will assign nonstandard resources to the modem. These nonstandard resources, such as IRQ15, have to be changed manually if you have communications software that demands a standard COM-port setting. In Windows 9x (95 or 98), this is done through the Device Manager, which can be accessed through the Control Panel System applet.

For an internal modem that is not Plug and Play, you will have to set the resources manually. To do this, you must know which resources are currently in use. In Windows 9x, you can view the resources in use in Device Manager. In Windows 3.x, you can exit Windows to DOS and run the MSD.exe utility. In Windows NT, you can use the Windows NT Diagnostics administrative utility to view the resources in use.

After you know which resources are in use, you can configure the modem to use them. Chances are, your computer has two built-in serial ports that are not being used. If COM1 and COM2 are being used, which is typical, you can set the modem to COM3 or COM4 through jumpers. Plug and Play-only modems (modems without jumpers) come with a software setup utility to configure the settings. If you are not using one or both of the built-in serial ports, you can disable them in the CMOS setup to free up those resources.

Most people use only one of their COM ports, and use it only if they have a serial mouse rather than a PS/2-port mouse. Getting into CMOS setup (sometimes mistakenly referred to as the BIOS) involves hitting some key sequence such as F10 (for Compaq computers) or <Del> (for Gateway computers, among others).

After the modem is configured and physically installed in the computer, you can boot up. In Windows 9x and NT, open the Modems applet in Control Panel. If this is the first modem being installed on this computer, the Add Modem Wizard will automatically launch and ask whether you want Windows to detect your modem or whether you want to specify it manually. If you have configured the modem correctly and there are no hardware conflicts, Windows will detect the modem successfully. Windows 9x and NT 4 have a large database of modem information, so if the operating system can detect the modem but cannot figure out its specific brand and model, the modem will be assigned the "Standard Modem" generic driver. At that point, you can change the driver to the correct one by supplying the driver disk that came with the modem.

In addition to configuring the COM-port settings, you must also set the maximum port speed. This is done in the modem's Properties dialog box. Table 10.2 shows modem speeds and recommended maximum port speeds.

We say "recommended" maximum port speed because there is no hard-and-fast rule. There is nothing to prevent you from setting your maximum port speed to 115200 with a 14400 bps modem. There are reasons not to do that, though. The modem will not use that much port bandwidth, even if you set it that high, and setting the port speed too high can cause communication errors because the port is handling data faster than the modem can process it.

Remote Node Vs. Remote Control

One area of potential confusion when discussing remote connectivity is the distinction between a remote node and remote control. It is important to understand the difference between the two methods and the consequences of using each method.

Table 10.2 Modem speeds and their recommended maximum port speeds.

Modem Speed (bps)	Maximum Port Speed (bps)
14400	19200
19200	38400
28800	57600
33600	57600
56000	115200

Remote Node

When it comes to remote connectivity, most people are familiar with the remote node method because it is the most commonly used. When you dial in to a remote network via SLIP or PPP, your PC is functioning as a remote node on that network. As was mentioned earlier in the book, a node is just a device—such as a PC or a printer—attached to the network. When you dial in, you are not directly attached to the network through Ethernet or token ring or whatever other architecture the network might employ; you are remotely connected. Dialing in to the Internet from home is a perfect example of the remote node concept.

Remote Control

Remote control, on the other hand, is the method that allows you to physically control a remote computer through software such as PCAnywhere or Microsoft Systems Management Server. When you remote-control a computer, it is as if you were sitting at the remote computer. Your mouse and keyboard execute commands on that remote system, and the display on your PC reflects what is on the remote PC's monitor.

Remote control over phone lines is much faster than remote node because remote control is only sending keyboard and mouse events and screen updates over the phone lines. All of the application and system processing is taking place on the PC being remote-controlled. Applications such as PCAnywhere make it possible for users to work remotely as if they were in the office. This is often not completely possible with remote node because of the phone-line limitation. If you need to work in an application that transmits large amounts of data between the server and the workstation (such as a database application), the performance will often be unacceptably slow in a remote-node setting. Remote-controlling a PC that is on the same LAN as the server lets the application perform as it would if you were physically sitting at the computer being controlled, with some performance loss due to the lag time of processing screen updates over the phone lines.

PCAnywhere is the most common end-user remote-control software, but there is also software, like Microsoft's Systems Management Server (SMS), that is designed for administrators. SMS contains remote-control features that allow an administrator to gain control of and troubleshoot a machine remotely. This can help reduce maintenance costs, because fewer support technicians are needed to go out to users' desks to work on software problems. (Maintenance is covered in more detail in Chapter 15.)

10

DIAL-UP NETWORKING

Up to this point, we have discussed the components of a dial-up connection, which includes SLIP/PPP software, modems and their configuration, and the principles of remote node versus remote control. All of these topics come together with a dial-up networking connection.

Dial-up networking is a remote-node type of connection. The PC that is dialing in to the remote network functions as if it were a node on that network. Each command and request that is issued from the PC is transmitted over the phone lines; other than the performance issue, use of the network is the same as if you were on a PC in the office. Remote node is many times slower, though. Consider the best modem connection one could establish at 53.3Kbps versus a standard 10BaseT Ethernet connection. 10MB would be the same as a 10,000Kbps connection. A Fast Ethernet LAN (100BaseTX) would be the equivalent of a 100,000Kbps connection.

Configuring a dial-up networking connection differs depending on whether you are in Windows 9x or Windows NT 4, though the principles are largely the same. To best understand them, we will address the topics separately.

Windows 9x Dial-Up Networking

Dial-Up Networking is an optional component that can be installed either during the initial Windows setup or afterwards through the Add/Remove Programs applet in Control Panel. Dial-Up Networking is not to be confused with HyperTerminal, which is the communications software that allows you to establish host/shell access to a remote system. After Dial-Up Networking is installed, it can be accessed through the Accessories group in the Start Menu or as a folder in My Computer. After Dial-Up Networking is open, you create a new connection by double-clicking on the New Connection icon. If no modem has been configured on the system, the Add Modem Wizard will automatically launch when you attempt to create a new connection. Otherwise, you will be taken into a wizard that steps you through the creation of the connection, as shown in Figure 10.2.

When the Make New Connection Wizard finishes, you will have a connectoid that contains the information you just entered. You may be able to double-click on it and successfully connect to a remote network, but chances are, the connection will not perform optimally. In most cases, additional configuration is needed.

Connection Properties Vs. Network Properties

To provide PPP services that allow your computer to function as a remote node to a network, Windows uses a dial-up adapter, which is a virtual network device. By *virtual*, we mean that the dial-up adapter is not a physical network card; rather, it's a software layer that uses your modem as if it were a network interface card. If you view the Network properties, as shown in Figure 10.3,

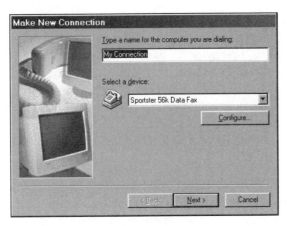

Figure 10.2 The Make New Connection Wizard helps you to set up a dial-up networking connection.

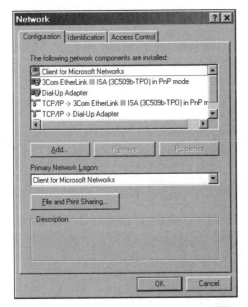

Figure 10.3 The Network applet of the Control Panel allows you to configure the protocols to be used with the dial-up adapter.

you will see that the dial-up adapter is listed and bound to the installed network protocols.

Through the Network applet of the Control Panel, you can add or remove network protocols to be used with the dial-up adapter in addition to the NIC (network interface card). By going into the protocols that are bound to the dial-up adapter, such as TCP/IP | Dial-Up Adapter, you can configure the specific settings—such as IP address, DNS (Domain Name Service) servers, and gateways—required for the remote network you are dialing in to. This is not the recommended method of changing those properties, however, because the settings here are global. That is, they affect every dial-up networking connection created. That is not a problem if you have only one connection set up, but what if you need separate connections with different TCP/IP settings for dialing in to a corporate LAN and for dialing into an ISP (Internet Service Provider)? Editing the properties from the Network applet of the Control Panel won't work. You will need to edit the properties of the connections separately.

Editing the connections is as simple as going into Dial-Up Networking, right-clicking on the connection, and selecting Properties. You are presented with the properties of the connection, and you can edit the network properties of the connection through the Server Types tab, as shown in Figure 10.4.

The settings configured in this dialog box apply only to the specific connection whose properties you are viewing. This restriction allows you to customize the connection for optimal performance. For example, if you are dialing in to an ISP, you would uncheck NetBEUI and IPX/SPX as allowed network protocols because only TCP/IP is used on the Internet. You could then go into TCP/IP properties and configure IP addresses and DNS servers if they needed to be manually specified; otherwise, they could be set at the default option, which is to obtain the information automatically when dialing in. As was previously mentioned, PPP will encapsulate protocols other than TCP/IP, something that SLIP doesn't do. If the remote network you are dialing in to runs multiple protocols or runs a protocol other than TCP/IP, here is where you would configure them.

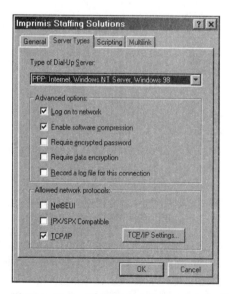

Figure 10.4   The Server Types tab in the Connection Properties dialog box is where you can configure connection-specific network properties.

After you create the dial-up connection, you can launch it by double-clicking on the icon for it. Enter your username and password for the remote network and click on Connect. You should be able to establish a successful connection and start using network-based applications over that link.

Windows NT 4 Remote Access Service

Whereas Windows 9x calls its PPP service "Dial-Up Networking," in Windows NT it is part of the Remote Access Service (RAS). RAS is not installed by default during NT Setup, though it can be selected during the installation of networking services. To install RAS after the initial setup of NT, you would add it as a service on the Services tab of the Network applet of the Control Panel.

If RAS does not detect a "RAS capable device" (e.g., a modem), NT will launch the Add Modem Wizard, which is similar to the one in Windows 9x. You have the option of manually specifying the modem or having the operating system attempt to detect and configure it for you. It is recommended to let NT detect your modem. Even if NT does not know the brand and model, if the modem is installed correctly with no conflicts, NT will detect it and offer the standard generic modem driver. You can change to the correct driver, and NT will have already determined the correct COM port for the modem.

After the modem is installed, you will be presented with the window shown in Figure 10.5.

Clicking on the Configure button in the Remote Access Setup window will open a dialog box that allows you to configure RAS for dial out only, receive calls only, or dial out and receive calls. Unlike Windows 95, NT 4 can function as a dial-up server as well as a client. You can download a dial-up server option, though, for Windows 95, and one comes with Windows 98 as an optional component installable through Add/Remove Programs or during Windows Setup.

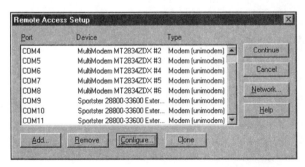

Figure 10.5 Setting up RAS in Windows NT 4.

Clicking on the Network button opens a window that is similar in scope to the Connection Properties' Server Types tab in Windows 9x. The Network Configuration window is shown in Figure 10.6. In this window, you can define the network protocols RAS can use for dial-up and for receiving incoming calls, and configure their properties. After you have completed the configuration of RAS, Windows NT will prompt for a system reboot.

Installing RAS will also install the Dial-Up Networking client application in the Accessories group and place a Dial-Up Networking icon in My Computer. Unlike the Windows 9x Dial-Up Networking client, the Windows NT version uses a phone book rather than having you create and maintain separate connection icons. When you open Dial-Up Networking for the first time in NT, you will need to create a new phone-book entry. The windows are different from those in Windows 9x, but the information you need to supply about your username, phone number of the server you want to call, and protocols is the same.

Unlike with Windows 9x, which allows you to edit the network properties globally for dial-up networking, NT forces you to edit each connection separately through the phone book. There is no way to globally set the properties, such as IP address or default gateway, across all phone-book entries. Although NT does use a WAN (wide area network) wrapper interface around the modem so PPP can work, NT does not create a virtual network device that has editable properties in the Network applet of the Control Panel, as Windows 9x does with the dial-up adapter.

Another difference is that, once connected to the remote network, the NT Dial-Up Networking Monitor provides more details than Windows 9x does about the state of your connection, as shown in Figure 10.7.

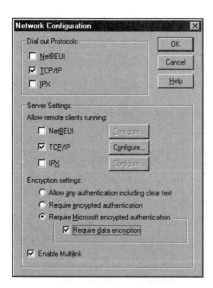

Figure 10.6 The Network Configuration dialog box.

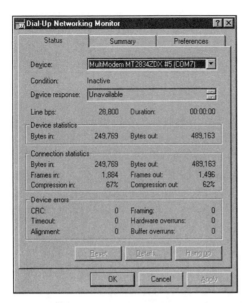

Figure 10.7   The Windows NT Dial-Up Networking Monitor shows connection statistics.

10

The biggest advantage of Windows NT RAS over Windows 9x Dial-Up Networking is that once RAS is installed, a user can log in to a remote network over a dial-up connection. Windows 9x requires that you boot up and log in to Windows before launching a dial-up connection and logging in to a network. Although this is not a problem for Internet connections, Windows 9x often has a difficult time dialing in to corporate LANs running NT RAS services. Because Windows 9x already considers itself logged in, sometimes it has trouble finding a domain controller and running login scripts on a remote NT network. When the Logon Using Dial-Up Networking option in the NT logon screen is used, the operating system dials in and logs the user directly into the remote network without logging in to Windows first. This provides a more reliable connection. Because RAS runs as a service under NT, it loads and runs whether or not a user is logged into the computer. Windows 9x does not support the concept of services, so an application can run only if the user is logged in.

PPTP AND VIRTUAL PRIVATE NETWORKS (VPNS)

A virtual private network (VPN) is a network that uses a public network, such as the Internet, as a backbone to connect two or more private networks. A VPN is a dynamic network, unlike the expensive permanent leased connections maintained in traditional WANs. A link is established on a VPN only when a connection is needed; at the end of that session, the link is destroyed, and the bandwidth is returned to the public network.

VPN Structure

The most common form of a VPN today is shown in Figure 10.8. In this example, VPN uses the Internet as a means to connect remote sites or to

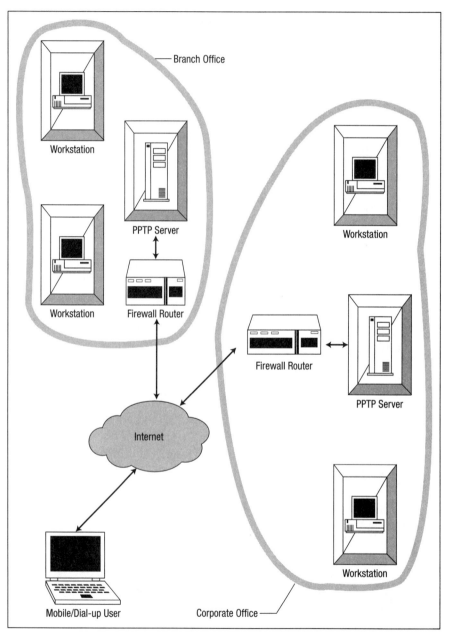

Figure 10.8 A VPN uses a public network, such as the Internet, to connect two or more remote networks.

connect remote users to corporate offices. If you have users who travel, they can use a national ISP so that they can almost always get on the Internet with a local call from wherever they are, and then go across the Internet to gain access to the corporate office. This is much more cost effective than dialing long distance back to the corporate office. Another cost saver is that the corporate office does not have to maintain a large modem pool on a RAS server for employees to dial in.

Companies set up connections to the local POPs (points-of-presence) of their ISP and use that connection to provide connectivity over the Internet to the remote office. The ISP's switching and routing equipment manages the flow of data on each side, as does the infrastructure of the Internet in the middle. Because of the public nature of the Internet, companies that use VPN strategies also employ encryption methods to prevent the data from being intercepted and read by a system other than the intended destination.

If a VPN does not use a permanent virtual circuit (PVC), such as a traditional leased line, how does it establish connectivity? Through tunneling. Tunnels are what put the "virtual private" in VPN. Much like the PPP protocol, which encapsulates other network protocols for transmission between remote connections, PPTP (Point-To-Point Tunneling Protocol) encapsulates private network data in IP packets that hide the underlying routing and switching infrastructure of the Internet from both senders and receivers. At the same time, these encapsulated packets can be protected against snooping by outsiders using encryption techniques. (Encryption is covered in Chapter 11.)

10

The types of end points on a tunnel are either a LAN device—such as a router or firewall—or an end-user workstation. These end points make VPN connections of either LAN-to-LAN or LAN-to-network-client. With a LAN-to-LAN connection, a security device such as a firewall is used as a gateway between the private LAN and the public Internet. (Firewalls are covered more extensively in Chapter 11.) On a client workstation, PPTP software establishes the VPN link to the corporate office. The user initiates the connection and then, after completing the desired task, terminates the connection. The PPTP software protects the data that the user sends to and receives from the corporate LAN.

VPN Protocols

Four protocols are available for creating VPNs over the Internet:

➤ Point-To-Point Tunneling Protocol (PPTP)

➤ Layer 2 Forwarding (L2F)

➤ Layer 2 Tunneling Protocol (L2TP)

➤ IP Security Protocol (IPSec)

Multiple VPN protocols are available because a VPN has multiple uses, and certain protocols provide different benefits, depending on the situation in which they are used. Confusing enough? In some companies, a VPN is a substitute for remote access servers, allowing off-site users (such as a sales staff) and branch offices to dial in to the protected corporate network via a local ISP. In other companies, a VPN may consist of corporate LAN traffic traveling in secure tunnels over the Internet. The protocols that have been developed for VPNs reflect the fact that there is not a "one size fits all" VPN solution. PPTP, L2F, and L2TP are predominantly aimed at dial-up VPNs, and IPSec's main focus has been LAN-to-LAN connections.

PPTP

One of the first protocols deployed for VPNs was PPTP. One of the biggest reasons for its popularity is that PPTP has been widely supported for dial-in VPNs by Microsoft, which included support for it in Routing and Remote Access Service (RRAS) for Windows NT Server 4. RRAS is a downloadable replacement for the standard Windows NT Server RAS software. Microsoft also offered a PPTP client in a service pack for Windows 95 and included a PPTP client in Windows 98. With its dominant market share, Microsoft has ensured the continued use of PPTP for the next few years, although PPTP has never been accepted as a formal standard.

As we discussed earlier in this chapter, the most commonly used protocol for remote access to the Internet is Point-To-Point Protocol (PPP). Point-To-Point Tunneling Protocol (PPTP) builds on the functionality of PPP to provide remote access that can be tunneled through the Internet to a destination site. Like PPP, PPTP can handle packets other than IP, such as IPX and NetBEUI. This ability to work in non-TCP/IP and multiple protocol environments gives PPTP great flexibility.

Because PPTP is used in conjunction with PPP, the standard PPP authentication methods PAP (Password Authentication Protocol) and CHAP (Challenge Handshake Authentication Protocol) are used. With Microsoft backing the PPTP protocol for VPN use, there is a strong tie between PPTP and Windows NT. An enhanced version of CHAP, called MS-CHAP, was developed by Microsoft and is capable of utilizing information within NT domains for security. Also, even though PPTP can encrypt data though PPP, Microsoft has incorporated a stronger encryption method called MPPE (Microsoft Point-To-Point Encryption) for use with PPTP.

L2F

L2F is very similar to PPTP in that it is designed to work with PPP. However, L2F builds on the functionality of PPTP by adding support for other authentication standards—such as TACACS+ and RADIUS—that provide authentication from the beginning of the transmission. L2F differs from PPTP, though, in that it does not rely on IP, giving it the ability to work with other types of networks, such as Frame Relay and ATM (Asynchronous Transfer Mode). L2F also allows multiple connections through a single tunnel, which PPTP cannot do. Like PPTP, L2F supports non-IP protocols like IPX and NetBEUI.

L2TP

L2TP is also predominantly a dial-up VPN protocol, though it is being designed as a successor to PPTP and L2F. L2TP is being created from the beginning to be an Internet Engineering Task Force (IETF) approved standard. While using PPP to provide dial-up access, L2TP defines its own tunneling protocol and works with the advanced security methods of IPSec (discussed next). Building on the philosophy of L2F, L2TP is not tied to TCP/IP and can support multiple types of network packets, including X.25, Frame Relay, and ATM. L2TP is poised to become the standard protocol in the future for dial-up VPN use.

10

IPSec

In a TCP/IP-only environment, IPSec is considered to be the best protocol for VPN use. IPSec has been built from the ground up to be based on existing standards approved by the IETF. Support for strong security standards— involving authentication, encryption, and key management—positions IPSec as the key VPN player for the future.

IPSec allows the sender of a packet, which can be a client workstation or a LAN gateway, to either authenticate or encrypt each IP packet, or to do both. The separation packet authentication and encryption have led to two different modes of using IPSec: transport mode and tunnel mode. In transport mode, only the transport-layer segment of an IP packet is authenticated or encrypted. With tunnel mode, the authenticating or encrypting is applied to the entire IP packet. Although transport-mode IPSec can be useful in many situations, tunnel-mode IPSec is the more secure method because it provides even more protection against attacks and traffic monitoring over the Internet.

IPSec is built around a number of standardized cryptography technologies to provide confidentiality, data integrity, and authentication. For example, IPSec uses:

➤ Diffie-Hellman key exchanges to deliver secret keys between peers on a public network

➤ Public-key cryptography for signing Diffie-Hellman exchanges, which guarantee the identities of the two parties

➤ DES (Data Encryption Standard) and other bulk encryption algorithms for encrypting data

➤ Keyed hash algorithms (HMAC, MD5, SHA) for authenticating packets

➤ Digital certificates for validating public keys

IPSec provides two ways to handle key exchange and management: manual keying and automated key management through Internet key exchange (IKE). Both of these methods are mandatory requirements of IPSec. Manual key exchange can be suitable for a VPN with a small number of sites, whereas VPNs covering a large number of sites or supporting many remote users benefit from automated key management.

VPN Protocol Summary

PPTP, L2F, and L2TP are designed to run at OSI (Open Systems Interconnection) Layer 2 (the Data Link layer). IPSec runs at Layer 3 (the Network layer). By supporting data communications at Layer 2, PPTP, L2F, and L2TP can transmit protocols other than IP over its tunnels, whereas IPSec is IP only. PPTP, although currently the most popular VPN protocol, does have some limitations. Its authentication and encryption schemes are weak when compared to IPSec, which is built around industry-standard cryptographic technologies that provide confidentiality, data integrity, and authentication. For now, PPTP is an easy choice because of its wide deployment and its backing by Microsoft in the Windows operating systems. For the future, L2TP should replace PPTP for dial-up VPNs, and IPSec will be the standard for LAN-to-LAN VPN communications.

REMOTE CONNECTIVITY SERVICES

Choices are greater than ever for consumers when it comes to selecting a telephony service for connecting to a remote network. For the consumer, that remote network is almost always the Internet, though mobile business users also rely on dial-up technologies to access corporate networks. With choice often comes confusion. Some technologies use existing twisted-pair wiring to transmit voice and data, whereas alternative technologies break from traditional telephone service to offer new ways to connect to remote networks. In this last section, we will look at the following remote connectivity services:

➤ PSTN/POTS

➤ ISDN

➤ ADSL

➤ Cable modem

PSTN/POTS

PSTN stands for Public Switched Telephone Network and is the same thing as POTS, which stands for Plain Old Telephone System. PSTN refers to the world's collection of interconnected public telephone networks that are both commercial and government owned. PSTN is the infrastructure that involves all the equipment required for connecting one location to another, including the wiring that runs from homes and offices to the local telephone exchange, the local and long-distance exchanges, and the satellites and submarine cable that link countries and continents.

The PSTN is a digital network, with the exception of the connection between local exchanges and customers, which remains analog. That is why modems exist—to convert a computer's digital data into an analog format for transmission over the POTS analog connection.

PSTN/POTS is the connection service we all love to hate when it comes to connecting to a remote network. Even with the best of modem connections (currently 53.3K in the United States, due to FCC regulations and aging telephone wiring), the connection is too slow to run applications or to use high-bandwidth multimedia technologies such as streaming audio and video. No matter how much Intel hypes its latest processor, suggesting that it will dramatically improve your Internet performance, a 486 with a T1 connection will run circles around the latest Pentium III with a 56K modem. The advantage of PSTN/POTS is that practically everyone has it already for regular telephone service. A modem is cheap, and Internet service is inexpensive as well, making it the choice for most people at the present time.

ISDN

ISDN, or Integrated Services Digital Network, is a form of DSL (Digital Subscriber Line). ISDN is an internationally adopted standard for end-to-end digital communication over PSTN. It makes use of the enormous investment in PSTN, except for adding the last loop between the customer and the local exchange to the digital domain. That is why IDSN is considered end-to-end digital communication. ISDN has two defined interface standards: BRI and PRI.

Basic Rate Interface (BRI)

The term "ISDN" or "ISDN line" is often used synonymously with the Basic Rate Interface (BRI). The Basic Rate Interface defines a digital communications line consisting of three independent channels: two Bearer (or B) channels, each at 64Kbps; and one Data (or D) channel at 16Kbps. For this reason, the ISDN Basic Rate Interface is often referred to as 2B+D. ISDN Internet service comes in 64K and 128K flavors that use one or both B channels for data transmission.

The B channels are used for carrying the digital information (either data or voice). These B channels can be linked together to provide a 128K data channel. The D channel is used to carry signaling and supervisory information to the network.

Each of the two B channels is treated independently, allowing for simultaneous voice and data or data-only connections. With specialized hardware and software, multiple B channel connections can be linked to achieve much higher data-transfer rates. This feature is one of the best advantages over POTS. Call waiting allows you to switch from one voice call to another over a POTS line, but does not work with data communications yet. Simultaneous voice and data transmission requires two separate phone lines in a POTS environment.

To access BRI service, you need to subscribe to an ISDN phone line. The termination point of the connection (such as a home or office) must be within 18,000 feet (about 3.4 miles or 5.5 km) of the telephone company's central office for BRI service. Special equipment to communicate with the phone company switch and with other ISDN devices is also needed. These devices include ISDN Terminal Adapters (sometimes called, incorrectly, "ISDN modems") and ISDN routers.

Primary Rate Interface (PRI)

The Primary Rate Interface (PRI) standard is a higher-level network interface defined at the rate of 1.544Mbps. This particular rate was selected for compatibility with the T1 digital lines commonly used today. The Primary Rate Interface is composed of 23 B channels, each at 64Kbps, and 1 D channel, at 64Kbps, for signaling. These B channels can interconnect with the Basic Rate Interface or when carrying voice services to any POTS line.

ADSL

ADSL, which stands for Asymmetric Digital Subscriber Line, is a service that transmits digital voice and data over existing POTS lines. This technology provides high-speed data access over a single pair of ordinary telephone wires, utilizing the unused portion of the frequency spectrum in POTS. The service is termed "asymmetric" because the downstream speeds from the central office to the customer are not necessarily equal to the upstream speeds from the customer to the central office. ADSL works well for Internet connectivity, where the vast majority of data flows from the Internet to the user rather than the other way around.

ADSL uses the frequency spectrum between 0kHz and 4kHz for POTS and 4kHz to 2.2MHz for data over twisted-pair copper telephone lines, which allows the simultaneous operation of voice calls (using the POTS range) and data transmission. The POTS channel is split off from the digital modem by filters, guaranteeing uninterrupted voice service even if ADSL fails. This line then provides asymmetric transmission of data, up to 9Mbps downstream to the customer (though typically service offerings peak at 1.544Mbps connections, T1 speed) and up to 800Kbps upstream, depending upon line length and line and loop conditions. In other words, ADSL technology can achieve connections that are at or just below the speed of a fully dedicated connection to the Internet while running over regular telephone wires. ADSL is like having a dedicated connection, though, in that it is "always on" once the modem is installed and configured. ADSL has all of the benefits of ISDN and is significantly faster and cheaper because it does not require replacing any telephony equipment at the customer location. Like ISDN, ADSL is available only to customers who are within 18,000 feet of the telephone company's central office.

Cable Modem

Cable modem is not a telephone service but is rather an attempt by cable television providers to cash in on the Internet craze. The nature of cable television, where data travels in only one direction (from service provider to the home), has meant difficulties and delays in establishing cable-modem Internet service in many areas. In areas where two-way data transmission is possible, cable modem has grown in popularity as an alternative to traditional dial-up modem Internet service.

Whereas ADSL provides a dedicated service over a single telephone line, cable modems offer a dedicated service over a shared medium. Although cable modems have greater downstream bandwidth (up to 30Mbps), that bandwidth is shared among all users on a line, and performance therefore varies with traffic. Cable-modem upstream traffic is often slower than ADSL because of contention among users for upstream bandwidth slots. Cable modem is very much like a LAN; more users on it results in the network becoming more taxed, so performance drops.

Security is an important concern for cable modems, which rely on existing coaxial cable to transmit data. The medium is not physically secure. Lines outside of the home can be tapped and data intercepted, making cable modems a dubious choice for transmitting sensitive data such as credit card information.

CHAPTER SUMMARY

Methods of accessing a remote network include shell access and SLIP/PPP.

➤ Shell access allows a computer to function as a dumb terminal on a remote network. The host server does the data processing, and only screen updates are transmitted back to the client.

➤ SLIP/PPP came about out of frustration with the limitations of shell access. SLIP/PPP is a direct connection method in that the client computer communicates directly with the remote network. Data is sent to and from the client workstation rather than to a host server.

➤ SLIP is older than PPP and supports only TCP/IP. PPP also supports other LAN protocols, such as IPX/SPX and NetBEUI.

➤ Modems are the most popular means for connecting to a remote network and are configured to use COM ports on a PC.

When you dial in to a remote network via SLIP or PPP, your PC is functioning as a remote node on that network.

➤ When a client workstation is connected to a remote network and is functioning as if it were part of the LAN, it is said to be a remote node.

➤ When a client workstation is connected to a remote network and controls the mouse and keyboard of a computer on that network, it is using remote control.

Dial-up networking is a remote-node type of connection, which you need software to use.

➤ Windows 9x PPP software is called Dial-Up Networking. It creates a virtual network device called the *dial-up adapter* to bind to the TCP/IP protocol.

➤ Windows NT PPP is part of RAS (Remote Access Service), which offers both PPP server and client functionality out of the box.

A virtual private network (VPN) is a network that uses a public network, such as the Internet, as a backbone to connect two or more private networks.

➤ PPTP is currently the most common VPN protocol because it was one of the first and because it has been widely deployed and supported through Microsoft's Windows operating systems.

➤ IPSec is the newest VPN protocol. It's best for TCP/IP communications between two or more LANs due to wide support for industry cryptography standards.

➤ L2TP is an emerging VPN standard that should ultimately displace PPTP for use in dial-up VPN scenarios.

Several technologies are available for connecting to a remote network. Some technologies use existing twisted-pair wiring to transmit voice and data, whereas alternative technologies break from traditional telephone service to offer new ways to connect to remote networks.

➤ PSTN/POTS is the standard phone service infrastructure in use all over the world.

➤ ISDN provides end-to-end digital communications over POTS with the addition of specialized hardware. ISDN allows simultaneous voice and data transmission, a significant advantage over standard POTS, which requires the use of two telephone lines for similar functionality. ISDN BRI, the most common ISDN interface, supports 128Kbps connections with both B channels linked.

➤ ADSL is an end-to-end digital communications service that uses existing POTS lines with no additional hardware required (other than the modem). ADSL service offers up to T1 speeds (1.544Mbps) downstream, significantly faster than ISDN. ADSL is asynchronous because downstream speeds are not equal to upstream speeds.

➤ Cable modem is an alternative high-speed Internet-access method that relies on the existing cable television infrastructure rather than on the telephony system. Cable modem is similar to a LAN in that bandwidth is shared among all users on a particular segment. Individual bandwidth drops as more users utilize the network. Security concerns make cable modem a dubious choice, however, for secure transactions over the Internet.

10

REVIEW QUESTIONS

1. PPTP stands for:
    a. Point-To-Point Transport Protocol
    b. Point-To-Point Tunneling Protocol
    c. Padded Packet Transport Protocol
    d. Point-To-Point Tunneling Procedure

2. Which protocol would be best used in a LAN-to-LAN connected VPN in a TCP/IP environment?
    a. PPTP
    b. L2F
    c. L2TP
    d. IPSec

3. COM2 is usually associated with which IRQ and I/O address configuration?

   a. IRQ3, I/O 02F8

   b. IRQ3, I/O 03F8

   c. IRQ4, I/O 02E8

   d. IRQ4, I/O 03F8

4. ISDN offers all of these benefits over POTS except:

   a. ISDN provides simultaneous voice and data transmission.

   b. ISDN provides end-to-end digital communications.

   c. ISDN is cheaper.

   d. ISDN is faster.

5. The most common dial-up VPN protocol at present is:

   a. PPTP

   b. L2F

   c. L2TP

   d. IPSec

6. Dialing in to a system and having your PC function as if it were the remote PC is called:

   a. Remote node

   b. Remote control

   c. Remote management

   d. Remote configuration

7. Windows 9x Dial-Up Networking is:

   a. A remote-node networking method

   b. A remote-control networking method

   c. A downloadable add-on component for Windows 9x

   d. A shell-access networking method

8. Why is ADSL said to be asymmetric?

   a. Because data can be transmitted upstream and downstream simultaneously

   b. Because available bandwidth fluctuates with the number of users on the network

   c. Because upstream data rates are usually faster than downstream rates

   d. Because upstream and downstream transmission rates are usually unequal

9. All of the following are weaknesses of cable modem technology except:

   a. Bandwidth is reduced as more customers utilize the network.

   b. Coaxial lines used for data transmission are inherently insecure.

   c. Infrastructure problems mean that it is not available in all areas.

   d. It is slow when compared to ISDN.

10. This dial-up VPN protocol will most likely emerge as the protocol of choice due to its rich support for industry standards.

    a. PPTP

    b. L2F

    c. L2TP

    d. IPSec

11. ISDN "2B+D" service yields how much bandwidth?

    a. 56Kbps

    b. 64Kbps

    c. 128Kbps

    d. 1.544Mbps

10

12. How close must a customer be to the local exchange for ADSL to be an option?

    a. 10,000 feet

    b. 18,000 feet

    c. 30,000 feet

    d. 36,000 feet

13. Which of the following is not true about ADSL?

    a. It uses existing POTS lines to provide end-to-end digital communications.

    b. It is less expensive than ISDN.

    c. It requires specialized network hardware like ISDN.

    d. Upstream and downstream data-transmission rates are usually unequal.

14. Which of the following is not a component of an Internet dial-up RAS configuration in Windows NT?

    a. TCP/IP protocol

    b. Dial-up adapter

    c. Phone-book entry

    d. Modem

15. What is SLIP used for?

a. Dialing in to a remote network and establishing a TCP/IP-only remote-node connection

b. Dialing in to a remote network and establishing a remote-node connection with any major LAN protocol, such as TCP/IP, IPX/SPX, NetBEUI, or AppleTalk

c. Dialing in to a remote network and establishing a shell access connection

d. A replacement for the older, slower PPP protocol

HANDS-ON PROJECTS

The following hands-on projects are designed to tie together many of the concepts of this chapter: dial-up connectivity over a modem, using PPP software, and using PPTP and VPNs. In the first lab, a Windows NT server is being set up as a PPTP server that will allow us to establish a couple of VPNs. The second lab will work with the client side—in this case, a Windows 95 workstation being configured to dial up an ISP through PPP and then connect to a remote LAN through PPTP.

Project 10.1

A PPTP server has a couple of basic hardware requirements. First, it needs to meet all of the requirements to run Windows NT Server successfully. Second, it needs to have a minimum of two network adapters installed—one connected to the Internet, and one connected to the private LAN.

Configuring a computer running Windows NT Server as a PPTP server involves the following procedures.

To install PPTP on a Windows NT Server:

1. Open the Network applet of the Control Panel and click on the Protocols tab. Click on the Add button to open the Select Network Protocol dialog box. You will see a window similar to that shown in Figure 10.9.

2. Select Point To Point Tunneling Protocol and click on OK.

3. Type the drive and directory location of your Windows NT Server installation files in the Windows NT Setup dialog box, and then click on Continue. The PPTP files are copied from the installation directory, and the PPTP Configuration dialog box appears, as shown in Figure 10.10.

4. Click on the Number Of Virtual Private Networks drop-down list, and select the number of simultaneous VPNs that you want the server to support. You can select a number between 1 and 256, the maximum

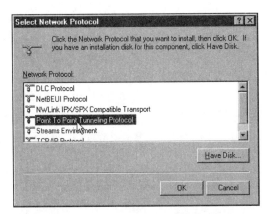

Figure 10.9   The Select Network Protocol dialog box allows you to add protocols.

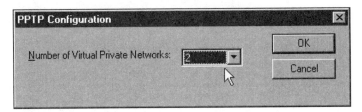

Figure 10.10   Configuring the number of VPN devices in PPTP Setup.

10

number of VPNs supported. Multiple VPNs are usually installed on a
PPTP server to enable multiple clients to connect simultaneously to the
PPTP server.

5. Continue installation of PPTP by clicking on Add to add the VPN devices
installed with PPTP to RAS.

To add the VPN devices as RAS ports and devices:

After installing PPTP, you must add the VPN devices to RAS. VPN devices are
virtual in that they do not physically exist. However, they are installed and
configured in RAS just like a modem. Clicking on Add in Step 5 above opens a
window similar to that shown in Figure 10.11.

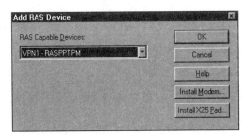

Figure 10.11   VPN devices are added through the Add RAS Device dialog box.

1. Select a VPN device and click on OK. Repeat Step 5 above and Steps 1 and 2 of this procedure until all the VPNs are added to the Remote Access Setup dialog box.

2. Select a VPN port and click on Configure. Verify that the Receive Calls Only option in the Port Usage dialog box is selected and then click on OK to return to the Remote Access Setup dialog box.

3. Repeat the last step for each VPN device that is displayed in the Remote Access Setup dialog box. (By default, VPN devices on a computer running Windows NT Server are automatically configured with the Receive Calls Only option, but you should verify this configuration.)

4. Click on Network to open the Network Configuration dialog box. Verify that only TCP/IP is checked in the Server Settings box. Click on OK to return to the Remote Access Setup dialog box.

5. Click on Continue and then close the Network applet of the Control Panel and restart the computer.

To configure authentication options:

If remote or mobile users connect to the LAN by using the PPTP server and the Internet, PPTP filtering should be enabled on the server adapter that is connected to the Internet. Enabling PPTP filtering provides a form of security for your private network by configuring an adapter on the computer to block all packets except PPTP packets. In a multihomed computer (a computer with multiple network cards installed)—such as a PPTP server with one adapter connected to the LAN and another adapter connected to the Internet—PPTP filtering should be enabled on the adapter over the Internet connection.

1. After you have logged back in to the system, launch the Network applet of the Control Panel again and go to the Protocols tab. Go into TCP/IP properties and click on the Advanced button. You will see a window similar to the one shown in Figure 10.12.

2. Check the box for Enable PPTP Filtering and click on OK. Click on OK again and reboot the computer. Log back in to the system.

To configure LAN routing:

To enable the PPTP server to forward a packet from a PPTP client to the correct destination computer, you must configure RAS to access your private network. Once RAS is configured to access the private network, a PPTP server requires the following configuration:

➤ The TCP/IP protocol must be configured to enable IP forwarding.

➤ The default route on the private network (intranet) must be suppressed by adding a Registry entry.

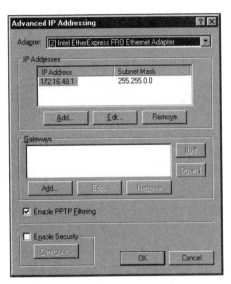

Figure 10.12   Enabling PPTP Filtering in Advanced IP Addressing.

10

➤ You must prevent RAS from changing the source IP addresses of incoming packets.

➤ Static routes to the private network must be established.

Specific steps are described below.

To enable IP forwarding:

You must enable IP forwarding on the PPTP server. To enable IP forwarding:

1. After you have logged back in to the system, launch the Network applet of the Control Panel again and go to the Protocols tab. Go into TCP/IP properties and click on the Routing button.

2. Click on Enable IP Forwarding.

3. Click on OK twice and then close the Network applet of the Control Panel.

To add the DontAddDefaultGateway Registry entry:

By default, Windows NT Server and Windows NT Workstation both place a default route (0.0.0.0) on each network adapter in a computer. This setting causes the server to send packets of unknown IP addresses to the network adapter configured with the default route. This is the normal and desired action of a router.

However, you must change this default setting if a server is connected to a private LAN and the Internet. You must disable the automatic addition of a default route on the network adapter for the private network. You do this on the PPTP server by editing the Registry. Run Regedit or Regedt32 and navigate to the following key:

```
HKEY_LOCAL_MACHINE\System\CurrentControlSet\Services\network
adapter\Parameters\Tcpip\DontAddDefaultGateway
```

Select Edit | New and then click on DWORD Value. Give the entry a name of **DontAddDefaultGateway** with a value of REG_DWORD 0x1.

This entry prevents the default route from being added to the PPTP server's network adapter. Use a Registry editor to add this entry and then shut down and restart the computer.

After the **DontAddDefaultGateway** entry is created, you must add static routes for the network adapter. These static routes must configure the PPTP server to route incoming data from the Internet to the correct server on the private network. This procedure is explained below.

To prevent RAS from changing source IP addresses:

By default, RAS changes the source IP address of packets it routes, from the IP address of the client sending the packets to its own source IP address.

You must disable this functionality for LAN-to-LAN routing to function. You do this on the PPTP server through editing the Registry. Run either Regedit or Regedt32 and navigate to the following key:

```
HKEY_LOCAL_MACHINE\System\CurrentControlSet\Services\RasArp\Parameters
```

Add the Registry entry **DisableOtherSrcPackets** with a value of REG_DWORD 0. This is done by selecting Edit | New and clicking on DWORD Value. The Registry will create a "New Value#1". Change the name to the above value and edit the value by double-clicking on the name of your entry (**DisableOtherSrcPackets**).

This entry prevents the RAS server from changing the source address of packets it forwards.

To add static routes for the private network:

You add static routes to your private network on the PPTP server by using the **ROUTE** command at the command prompt.

The **ROUTE** command causes all subnets and computers on the private network to be known to the PPTP server. Without the necessary **ROUTE** commands, the PPTP server would broadcast for every address required by PPTP clients.

To add the static routes to the PPTP server, run **ROUTE** with the **-p** option at the command prompt, as shown in the following example:

```
C:\>route -p 209.6.87.21
```

The **ROUTE** command must identify all the computers or networks that you want PPTP clients to reach.

At this point, you have successfully set up a PPTP server, the more complicated portion of the VPN setup. In the second project, we will take it a little easier and set up a Windows 95 PPTP client to access your server.

Project 10.2

For this lab, we will assume that you already have a modem installed and configured correctly on your lab PC. If you have any trouble getting that portion working, you can refer to Chapter 15 of the *A+ Exam Prep* by Jean Andrews.

The first step is to ensure that Dial-Up Networking is installed on your Windows 98 PC. Double-click on the My Computer icon on your desktop. If you have a Dial-Up Networking folder within the My Computer window, then it has been installed. If the folder does not exist, you will need to install it by going into Control Panel's Add/Remove Programs applet and adding it to the communications section.

You will need to configure and be able to establish a connection to an ISP through Dial-Up Networking. Most readers will already have an Internet connection set up; if you do not, now is a perfect time to get online. Chapter 16 of the *A+ Exam Prep* has detailed instructions on setting up Dial-Up Networking to connect to the Internet.

PPTP is most commonly used for enabling secure and encrypted communications to private LANs using a dial-up connection to the Internet. In this scenario, you must configure both connections: one connection to the Internet through an ISP and one tunnel connection through the Internet to the PPTP server on the target network. We will assume that you already have a standard PPP connection to an ISP through Dial-Up Networking, and we'll concern ourselves only with the PPTP portion of the configuration.

To install and configure PPTP on Windows 95:

Virtual Private Networking is provided as a standalone upgrade to Windows 95, titled "Dial-Up Networking 1.2 Upgrade." For this exercise, you will need to download and install MSDUN12.exe from **www.microsoft.com**. Windows 98 has this update built into it so there is no need to download it first. After the

10

Dial-Up Networking 1.2 Upgrade is installed and your computer has been restarted, proceed as follows:

1. Open the Dial-Up Networking folder through Start | Programs | Accessories or by double-clicking on My Computer and then double-clicking on Dial-Up Networking.

2. Double-click on Make New Connection. The Make New Connection Wizard starts, as shown in Figure 10.13.

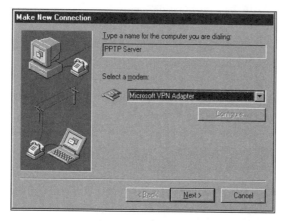

Figure 10.13 Making a new connection for the PPTP server.

3. Type a connection name, such as the name of your PPTP server, in the Type A Name For The Computer You Are Dialing box.

4. Select Microsoft VPN Adapter in the Select A Modem box, and then click on Next. The dialog box shown in Figure 10.14 appears.

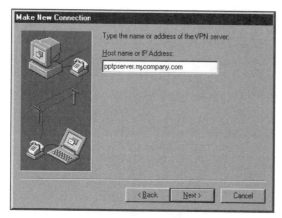

Figure 10.14 Entering the address for the PPTP server.

5. Enter either the DNS name or the IP address of the PPTP server; then click on Next and on Finish.

6. Verify the configuration of your PPTP connection by right-clicking on your new connection in Dial-Up Networking and selecting Properties.

7. Click on the Server Types tab, shown in Figure 10.15, and configure the protocol settings to match what is in use on your PPTP server and the private LAN you are connecting to.

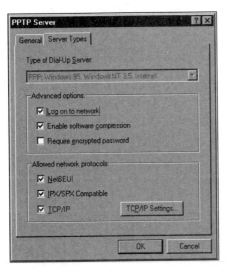

Figure 10.15   Configuring the properties for the connection to the PPTP server.

8. When you have finished configuring the PPTP connection, it is a two-step process to establish the VPN connection. First, you establish your normal PPP connection to your ISP by double-clicking on the icon for the ISP and dialing into its system. When you're successfully connected to the ISP, double-click on the connection for the PPTP server and supply your username and password information. Then, click on Connect and watch it connect across the Internet to your PPTP server.

After you connect successfully to the PPTP server on the remote network, the ISP routes all traffic sent from your workstation over the Internet to the PPTP server. The PPTP server then routes the traffic to the correct computer on the remote network. Consequently, you will see only computers and servers on the remote network. You will no longer see the Internet unless the remote network itself provides access to the Internet.

NETWORK SECURITY

After Reading This Chapter And Completing The Exercises, You Will Be Able To:

➤ Understand network security threats

➤ Physically secure network components

➤ Establish standard password practices and procedures

➤ Select the appropriate network security model (share level versus user level)

➤ Establish an audit trail to track resource usage

➤ Use encryption to protect network data

➤ Understand firewalls and their usage

What network–related subject is the most talked about but probably the least understood? Security. Why do we say it is the least understood? Because, although many people talk about the need for security, few people understand what, exactly, is involved in having a secure network. Network security is more than just passwords, although passwords do play an important role. In this chapter, we will look at the elements that make up network security and establish some guidelines that will enable you to keep your network as secure as possible.

NETWORK SECURITY THREATS

For each type of security threat to your network, certain responses should be made before the threat is realized. Having procedures and measures in place to combat the threats might not completely eliminate the possibility of a security breach, but establishing procedures can help. You can drastically reduce not only the likelihood of a successful breach, but also the damage done from one. Network security threats fall into the following categories:

➤ Theft

➤ Industrial espionage

➤ Hackers and crackers

➤ Disgruntled employees

➤ User error

➤ Viruses

We'll look at each of the types of threats in turn and then discuss how to be proactive in minimizing the risk of a successful breach of your network.

Theft

Consider the hardware components that make up your network—servers, routers, switches, hubs, workstations, printers, and so on. How physically secure is your network environment? Would it be fairly easy for someone to walk out with a vital piece of your network? Does your environment have contractors or temporary employees that have access to servers or other expensive hardware? If a server did disappear, would it be easy to figure out who took it and when?

The first line of defense in securing a network is physically locking up critical network components. Servers and expensive network hardware like switches and routers should be kept in locked, ventilated rooms, and only authorized personnel should have access to those rooms. Network workstations that are easily removed, such as laptops, should have locking mechanisms that physically bolt them to the desk wherever possible. Computer equipment is easy to resell, which makes it an enticing target for thieves.

Having equipment stolen can result in losses far greater than the cost of replacing the hardware. For example, the data stored on a file server is usually much more valuable than the server itself. Even if the data is restorable from a backup, the fact remains that confidential corporate data has been removed from your company and might be used for industrial espionage (see the next section).

Protecting against theft is fairly simple, but requires diligence. If the office has multiple entrances and exits, make sure they are monitored. No one should be able to come or go unnoticed. If the office has a lobby or reception area, institute a company policy that people who are not employees must be escorted at all times if they are in the office area. Be diligent about keeping server-room doors closed and locked, and restrict access to those rooms to only those people who require it as part of their jobs. The goal is to minimize the likelihood that unauthorized access to your facility could result in theft of equipment.

Industrial Espionage

Sure, it sounds like cloak-and-dagger stuff, but most companies would love to get their hands on confidential information from a competitor. Confidential information includes customer lists, employee lists and salaries, financial data of all types, databases of product problem histories, manufacturing data, and so on. Stop for a moment and consider the business field your company is in, and think of who your competitors are. Can you think of ways to exploit insider knowledge of their businesses that would give your company an advantage in the marketplace? Your competitors probably can.

Sometimes industrial espionage can come in the form of theft: Get someone inside a competitor's company and have him physically remove data from the location. This data can, of course, come in a number of forms, from regular paper files to data downloaded onto disks or removable storage drives. The ways that data can be stolen are limited only by the imagination. Physically stealing a server is a brute-force way to go about getting access to insider information, so it's extremely likely that more subtle approaches would be taken. Industrial espionage attempts usually come from the outside rather than from inside the company. The approaches to espionage are very similar to hacking and cracking; therefore, the threats and responses to those threats are similar.

Hackers And Crackers

The term *hacker* used to have a positive meaning, referring to someone who tried to "hack at" or take things apart to figure out how something worked or how to improve something. Inventive and ingenious people did hacking, and some of the industry's best innovations started out as hacks that were attempting to improve on an existing product or technology. A *cracker*, on the other hand, was a malicious individual who used technology as a way to cause disruption or loss for others. Crackers were the ones who tried to break into computer systems or use computers to steal phone services or generate credit card numbers. Mostly through media ignorance, the terms *hacker* and *cracker* have been melded into one, and now hacking has a negative connotation. With that in mind, we will use *hacker* and *cracker* interchangeably, even though traditionalists will argue that they are not the same.

Hacking into a network or server can evoke visions of a teenager or a bored college student or some social outcast sitting in a dimly lit bedroom surrounded by empty pizza boxes and soda cans, dialing randomly, looking for a computer to answer. When a computer answers, hackers then try different username and password combinations until they get a match. After that, they wreak havoc on the system they are connected to, uploading viruses, downloading sensitive data, deleting files, and generally interfering with the normal operation of the system. Hacking is more than these Hollywood scenarios, however, both in methods used to breach network security and in actions taken after the breach is made.

Breaches Through Modem Pools

Dialing in through a remote-access server or a modem pool is still among the most common methods that hackers use to gain access to a private network. A common trick among hackers is to use a utility called a *war dialer*, which dials a range of phone numbers, one after another, logging the modems that answer. Hackers might put in a range of phone numbers, such as 555-1111 to 555-9999, and let the computer work overnight dialing the phone numbers in succession. With their log files of phone numbers that were answered by modems, hackers then go to work picking out systems that look "interesting" and trying to get in.

Hackers using this method will not know any specific user-account names of employees at the company they are trying to get into, so they will try to hack the standard administrative accounts, depending on the operating system of the server they are dialing in to. This approach holds a twofold advantage for hackers: first, they will not waste time trying to guess a valid account name; second, if they are successful, they will have full access to all resources on the network. Table 11.1 summarizes the network operating systems with their common administrative accounts.

Sometimes hackers pick out specific targets and try to find out modem numbers for the companies they are trying to get into. These targets are usually either high-profile companies or companies that the hackers have had some sort of relationship with in the past. If a hacker has had a relationship with a company, the hacker will often know at least some valid usernames and possibly some passwords as well. This is a dangerous situation because the hackers will often appear to be legitimate users on the network, so their activity might go

Table 11.1 Network operating systems and their administrative accounts.

Network Operating System	Administrative Account Name
NetWare 3.x	Supervisor
NetWare 4.x	Admin
NetWare 5.x	Admin
Windows NT 3.5x	Administrator
Windows NT 4.0	Administrator
Unix	Root

unnoticed for some time if they are careful about not drawing attention to themselves.

Breaches From The Internet

The Internet has become a source of security woes, with corporations increasingly establishing an online presence. Many companies that are online have dedicated full-time connections to the Internet because the cost of service has dropped dramatically over the past few years. With that connection comes the need to make sure that it is secure on a 24×7 basis.

Unlike with a modem pool, where hackers have to supply a valid username or password to access your network, a dedicated Internet connection allows hackers to attempt to capture network packets from your network to compromise security. Hackers use elaborate techniques to gather and manipulate network data and are apt to cause more damage (deleting files, uploading viruses, stealing sensitive data, and so on), if only because the increased connection speed between them and your network makes it more convenient for them. Depending on what the hackers want to do, they might upload viruses to your network, delete files from servers they are able to access, or download confidential corporate data. A relatively recent utility called BackOrifice even lets hackers remote-control a computer that the utility is installed on without the user's knowledge, creating an ongoing security problem for your network.

Hackers can also be ex-employees or contractors who know enough about your network to gain access and who have a motive for stealing data or causing damage.

It is interesting to note that many of the industry's top security analysts are former hackers, who have reformed and are now using their hacking skills to help companies find and close security holes. Some companies consider hiring a former "known" hacker as a security analyst too much of a risk, but many have benefited from having someone on staff who understands the hacking mindset and has hacking skills.

Disgruntled Employees

Potentially even more dangerous than hackers and crackers are threats from inside the company. Employees already have access to the network and aren't generally suspected of engaging in any malicious acts against the company. In probably more companies than employers would like to admit, passwords are not very secure. Users post them on sticky notes next to their monitors, leave them written on a piece of paper in a desk drawer, or use easily guessed passwords. That makes it possible for employees who want to cause problems to use a different username to hide their actions. If employees want to cause trouble on the network, preventing their efforts from succeeding is difficult because it requires a sound internal security policy. Inside threats are often overlooked as a potential destructive breach.

In addition to security breaches related to the malicious intent of some employees, many users are naturally curious when it comes to the network. It is probably human nature to want to get involved with someone else's private business, so users often browse the network just to see what they can access. Although this type of activity seems innocent enough, it can still lead to a security leak.

User Error

Although user error is not strictly a network security threat, it does play an important role in network security. Users with too little training and too much access can inadvertently corrupt or destroy network data. Whether a user intended to delete last year's tax information from your database or did it accidentally is not relevant; the data is just as gone. Chapter 15 discusses backup strategies that would at least allow you to recover the data, but there could still be downtime. This is true particularly if the data that was deleted or corrupted is not noticed for some time, until it is needed. You might find yourself having to recover data from off-site backups (discussed in Chapter 15), and you might find the business losing time and money while the tape is retrieved and the data is restored.

Viruses

Viruses are covered in more detail in Chapter 15, but we will touch on them briefly here as they relate to network security. Viruses are but one mechanism used by malevolent employees or hackers to damage the network. The effects of viruses can be anything from slowing down or crashing the network through increasing activity to an unmanageable level (denial-of-service attacks), to deleting data, to emailing confidential information—such as a contacts list—to an outside source.

Viruses are usually not introduced intentionally, however. More often than not, viruses are transmitted unknowingly by users who bring in software from an outside source (such as their home) or download software from the Internet. It is important to take precautions because, as was seen in the recent Melissa virus outbreak, a virus can spread rapidly and cause widespread damage before it is contained.

So What Do You Do?

By now, you may be asking yourself, "How can I possibly protect my network against all of these threats?" Fortunately, you are provided with some countermeasures from the accumulated wisdom of thousands of administrators who have learned (often the hard way) how to deal with network security threats. Keep in mind that even the most stringent security should not be considered foolproof. Consider this quote from Emmanuel Goldstein, editor-in-chief of *2600:The Hacker Quarterly* (the preeminent magazine on hacking), in an interview with CNN: "Hacking isn't really about success—it's more the process of discovery. Even if real security is implemented, there will always be new systems, new developments, new vulnerabilities. Hackers are always going to be necessary to the process and we're not easily bored."

 One of the keys to maintaining good network security is to frequently review existing strategies for weaknesses. Hackers develop new techniques almost as quickly as vendors figure out ways to plug security holes. In many cases, hackers discover holes before vendors even know they exist, as has been seen continually by both Microsoft and Netscape with the ongoing security bugs in their respective Web browsers. Discovering attacks early becomes as important as, if not more important than, preventing them outright. Checking with your vendors for updated patches and fixes should be part of your regular routine. Vendor patches and fixes are discussed in more detail in Chapter 15.

In the rest of this chapter, we'll discuss the countermeasures that are available to combat the network security threats you'll face. These countermeasures can be grouped into the following categories:

➤ Physical security

➤ Passwords

➤ Network security models

➤ Audit trails

➤ Encryption

➤ Firewalls

PHYSICAL SECURITY

Physically securing your network is the most basic step in preventing security breaches. In addition to the threat of equipment theft, discussed earlier, an absence of physical security can result in other problems as well.

Cable Plant

An oft-overlooked area of network security is the cable plant. It's just a bunch of cables lying around, right? How is that a potential threat? Twisted-pair or coaxial cable uses copper wire to transmit signals as electrical impulses, and this type of cable can be easily tapped to capture packets and therefore data going over the network. The opportunity for a breach increases when there is cable running between two or more buildings. The best choice in this case would be to use fiber-optic cable in any exposed areas where it would be easy for unauthorized individuals to get to, because fiber-optic cable transmits light signals and cannot be tapped. If copper-wire cabling must be used, it should be run through a conduit or buried to limit access to it.

Inside the building, cable runs should be inside the walls or ceilings for security. Limit the use of long cable runs that trail along floors behind cubicles or are otherwise out in the open, particularly in areas where fewer people are around or where a lot of people come and go throughout the day.

Modems

Modems present a physical security risk when the network uses remote-access servers to handle incoming calls and to allow network access. The simplest security measure to take is to keep the phone numbers private. Do not post the phone list in public view; the dial-up modem numbers should not be accessible except to the employees who need to use them.

Along the same lines as keeping the phone numbers private is giving dial-up permission to only those users who need it specifically to do their jobs. Fortunately, if your servers are running Windows NT Server, users must explicitly be given dial-in permission; by default, they are not given access. Dial-in permission is given through the User Properties dialog in User Manager for Domains, which is accessed by double-clicking on the user account whose properties you want to view. Clicking on the dial-in button opens the dialog box shown in Figure 11.1.

By granting dial-in access to only the users who need to work remotely, you are reducing the number of accounts that could be used to break into your network.

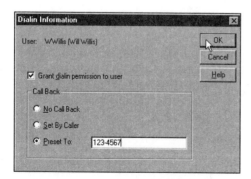

Figure 11.1 Granting dial-in permission for a user account in Windows NT.

You might also want to consider changing the default authentication of NT Server's Remote Access Service (RAS), which is to let users dial in to the network from anywhere. That is the *least* secure configuration. NT also supports restricting users to dialing in from a preset location, an option that is a step up in security.

The most secure method, however, is to implement call-back authentication. When call-back authentication is implemented, users supply the network administrator with the phone number of the location they are dialing in from. When a user dials in to the network, the RAS server answers and detects the user's identity through the PPP information passed between the two systems. The RAS server then disconnects the call and calls the user back at either a phone number specified in its database (most secure) or a phone number specified by the caller at the time of the call (less secure). The method of calling a user back at a number maintained in the server database ensures that, at a minimum, a successful connection attempt would have to come from the user's location, making it difficult for a potential hacker to gain access with that username and password. This method doesn't work for companies that have traveling remote users, such as sales staff, but it works very well for managers and others who need to dial in and work from home. Having a call-back phone number set by the user does work well for traveling employees, and it provides more security than no call-back because the phone number the server called back is logged. Figure 11.1 also shows how to configure RAS for call-back authentication.

11

Servers And Tapes

The most high-profile device on your network is the server, where the company's data is stored and where critical applications are run. When it comes to the server, physical security is just as important as any other security measure. No matter what kind of policies you have in place to prevent users from hacking in from inside or outside of the company, all of it is for naught if someone can come in and physically remove your server or gain access to the server console and make changes. Servers should be kept under lock and key, with only authorized personnel having access to the server rooms.

In addition to physically locking up the servers, if tape backups are performed and the tapes are stored away from the servers, then steps need to be taken to make sure that the tapes are locked up in a secure location and that only the appropriate people have access to them. Tapes can easily be transported off site and restored to a different computer, letting someone have access to all of your corporate data without you ever knowing about it.

If someone has access to the server room, and the tape drive is there as well (which is likely), this person could make a quick backup of your server onto tape and walk out with all of your company's information. Part of physical security is not only keeping the server in a locked room, but also *not* keeping the server console logged in. That way, someone who sits down at the console needs to supply the administrative password in order to perform any functions on the server—an extra measure of security.

Workstations And Other Network Components

Protecting workstations can be difficult because there are usually many of them, and they are spread across multiple rooms, floors, and even buildings. Devices exist to physically bolt PCs and laptops to users' desks, preventing their physical removal without a key. Although this method is often cost-prohibitive to implement on all workstations, it is very effective for small, portable items, like laptops, that have a way of disappearing. A more cost-effective means to protect equipment physically is to have all entrances and exits monitored either through closed-circuit video or by a receptionist. Require that any visitors or guests be signed in and be escorted at all times when they're beyond the lobby or reception area.

Other network components—such as routers, switches, patch panels, and hubs—should be kept in locked wiring closets, and, as with server rooms, only the appropriate personnel should have access. Someone who gains access to a hub or a switch can easily patch a laptop into the network and start capturing data. This is much easier than having to physically tap the copper wire of a twisted-pair or coaxial cable. If a router or switch has a console, make sure that it gets logged out between uses, even if it is in a locked room. That way, even if people managed to gain access to the wiring closet, they would have to know the appropriate passwords to change the configurations (though they could still get on the network and cause other problems).

With the network physically secured, it is time to turn our attention to software-driven threats.

PASSWORDS

Almost everyone is familiar with passwords—those pesky things you have to remember in order to gain access to a resource of some type, such as an ATM machine, a voice-mail system, or a computer network. It seems that we are forced to remember more and more passwords, each one unique. Therefore, people want passwords that are easy to remember, or people want to use the same password in multiple places. The password is a key element to network security, however, so extra care needs to be taken to ensure that users' passwords are "good" passwords.

So what's a good password? A good password:

➤ Has a minimum length

➤ Is composed of a combination of letters and numbers

➤ Is not easily guessed

➤ Is kept private

Minimum Password Length

Although they are not as common as they once were, password-cracking utilities that rely on "brute-force" methods to discover passwords are still in use. *Brute-force method* means that the utility attempts to discover the password by trying every possible combination of letters and numbers until it gets the one that works. The shorter the password, the shorter the time necessary for a brute-force password cracker to arrive at the correct password. Opinion varies as to what the minimum length should be, but generally, fewer than four characters is not very secure, and more than eight characters becomes difficult for the average user to remember. A six-character minimum length is a nice compromise to strive for.

Letters And Numbers

In addition to having a minimum length, passwords should be both alpha and numeric. That simply means that they should contain both letters and numbers, plus, ideally, an extended character, such as !, @, #, $, %, ^, &, *, (,), ?, ", +, -, =, or _. Some password-cracking utilities combine brute-force methods with a large database of words, like a dictionary. Passwords that do not spell common English words are harder to crack and therefore more secure.

Don't Guess That Password

A friend of mine worked at a large health insurance company, and some co-workers doing desktop support bet that they could go to any user's desk or office and within five tries successfully guess the user's password. More often than not, they were right. Bad passwords include the names of family members or pets, birthdays, or anything else that someone who knows you might be able to guess. Other common bad passwords are the word "password" and a password that's the same as the user account name.

What's a good password? A good password employs the techniques previously listed. If a minimum length and alphanumeric strategies are used, chances are better that a password will not be easily guessed. Just because a password is long and has special characters or numbers in it, however, doesn't mean that it will be hard to remember. For Windows NT domain accounts, you have up to 14 characters to play with. The cool thing is that you can use spaces as well as any

11

of the characters listed above, so you can be creative. I like to come up with short, easily remembered phrases as my passwords, such as "I'm @ my job." This is a 12-character password, with an apostrophe, two spaces, and an "at" symbol, yet it's easy to remember. Although passwords traditionally have been thought of as a single word, they can be almost anything within the character limit. Often I find myself wanting passwords that are too long rather than too short! Encourage your users to be inventive with their passwords. It's easy to create a password that is not easily guessed but is easy to remember.

Passwords Are Private

One of the more frustrating things as an administrator is to stop by a user's desk to look at a problem and find the user's password on a sticky note attached to the monitor. What is the point of even having passwords if they are out in the open for anyone to see? Earlier, we mentioned a game in which some technicians bet that they could guess a password within five attempts. Often the reason for success was that the password was written on a note attached to the monitor, or taped underneath the keyboard, or placed on a piece of paper in a desk drawer, on a paper under the phone, or somewhere else in the near vicinity. Usually, we didn't even have to attempt to guess the password. Users should be strongly encouraged to keep passwords private. In fact, this should be part of a comprehensive policy on information systems usage. In many companies where data is highly confidential, the disclosure of a password is grounds for dismissal. That may be going overboard for most companies, but nonetheless, there should be strict rules about keeping passwords private.

Network Password Policies

The first step in a successful password policy is what we have already discussed: making sure that passwords are kept private. No matter what policy you implement, if passwords are public knowledge, the entire strategy is undermined.

As an administrator, you can take steps to minimize the risk of a security breach through passwords. These steps involve configuring account settings, which is done through the Account Policy dialog box, shown in Figure 11.2.

This screen is reached through User Manager For Domains by clicking on the Policies menu and selecting Account. The settings here apply globally, which means that they apply to all of the user accounts in this domain. Here the administrator can define the following characteristics of user accounts: minimum password length, password expiration, and account lockout.

Minimum Password Length

You can force a minimum password length rather than trusting users to create passwords of the appropriate length. As we discussed, longer passwords are more difficult to crack.

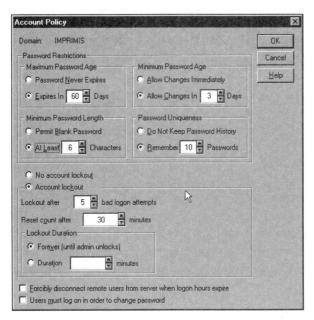

Figure 11.2 Configuring account settings to strengthen network security.

Password Expiration

For a password policy to be effective, regular password changes should be required. Rather than trust users to change their passwords periodically, you can force the passwords to expire on a regular basis. Some discretion needs to be applied here. Requiring changes too often will become an inconvenience for users and will make it more likely that users will write down their passwords or choose bad passwords in order to remember them. Requiring changes too infrequently, however, does not provide the level of protection necessary and defeats the purpose of expiring them.

The length of time a password is allowed to be in use before a required change varies depending on the environment. In highly secure environments, password changes might be forced on a weekly or biweekly basis. In a "normal" business environment, 30 to 60 days is usually about right.

Account Lockout

In conjunction with setting passwords so that they expire periodically, you should configure the server so that a user account is locked out after a certain number of bad attempts. A locked account can be reenabled only by an administrator. You don't want to set the lockout count so low that users might type their passwords incorrectly a couple of times and find their accounts locked out. At the same time, you don't want to allow a potential hacker to enter a lot of bad passwords while attempting to break in. Setting the lockout count value to 4 or 5 should be sufficient.

Another configuration option with account lockout is to set the duration of a lockout (how long a locked-out account stays locked). The duration can be set for a certain length of time, such as 30 or 60 minutes, but the most secure setting is for the account to stay locked until the administrator unlocks it manually. Not only do users have to ask you to unlock their accounts (and you have the opportunity to ask them what happened), but it is less likely that an ongoing attempt to hack into that account from somewhere else will go unnoticed.

Disabling Accounts

You should immediately disable user accounts for employees who are fired or who quit. Also, it can be a good idea to disable accounts for users who are on extended leaves, such as maternity leave. That minimizes the chance of those accounts being used for inappropriate network access. Disabling an account does not delete it or do anything that requires setting it up again later. In NT Server, open the User Properties dialog from User Manager For Domains and check the box for Account Disabled. This option is shown in Figure 11.3.

Renaming Administrative Accounts

Earlier, in Table 11.1, we mentioned that the Windows NT administrative account is, by default, called "Administrator," whereas in NetWare 3.x, it is called "Supervisor," and in Unix, it is called "Root." In Windows NT and NetWare, these accounts can be renamed for added security. Hackers are going to try to gain as much access to a network as possible, and hacking an administrative account gives them the access they want. Renaming the administrative accounts from their defaults provides an extra level of security because hackers then have to guess not only the password, but also the new account name.

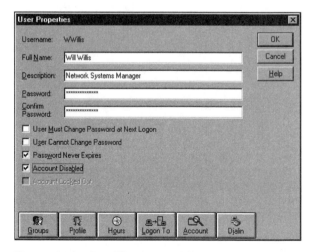

Figure 11.3   Disabling an inactive account prevents its use for gaining network access.

NETWORK SECURITY MODELS

Network security models help control access to resources for user accounts that are logged in to the network. The Windows networking environment has two basic models: share-level security and user-level security. The administrator configures the security model from the workstation when setting up network connectivity. This is done through the Access Control tab of the Network Control Panel, as shown in Figure 11.4.

Share-Level Security

Share-level security is the more basic of the two security models and the less secure. Share-level security provides only password protection to a network resource. If people know the password, they can access the resource. Figure 11.5 shows the configuration of a shared directory with share-level security. This screen is reached by right-clicking on the desired folder in My Computer or Windows Explorer and selecting Sharing.

The only extra measure of protection is being able to assign two passwords: one for read-only access to a resource and one for full access, which is read, write, delete, and change. You can give the read-only password to people who need only that level of access and give the full-access password to others. Again, this level provides only rudimentary security because if a user who knows the full-access password tells someone who is supposed to have only read-only access or no access at all, that person now has full access to that resource. For stricter control over who can access a shared resource, you need user-level security.

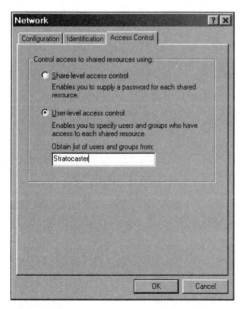

Figure 11.4 Configuring share-level versus user-level security.

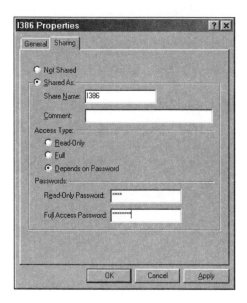

Figure 11.5 Configuring share-level security on a shared directory.

User-Level Security

The downside to Windows 9x is that by default the share-level security model is employed. User-level security requires membership in a Windows NT domain that holds the accounts that will be granted access. Windows NT workstations automatically employ user-level security if they have been added as members of a domain. When configuring a Windows 9x system to log in to an NT domain, you should also go to the Access Control tab and enable user-level security, supplying the name of the domain in the box, as shown in Figure 11.4.

Unlike share-level security, which relies on passwords to protect access to a resource, user-level security grants access to specific users or groups of users in a domain. Figure 11.6 shows the configuration of a shared directory through user-level security. Notice how it differs from the share-level configuration in Figure 11.5.

User-level security provides a higher level of security than does share-level security because when users try to access a shared resource, the account they are logged in with is compared against a database of accounts that have been granted permission. The account is checked for read-only and full-access permissions because it can have either, and the most restrictive permissions apply. That means that if user Bob belongs to multiple groups that have access to a particular resource, and one group has full access but another group has read-only access, Bob will have read-only access. This configuration can be difficult for an administrator to manage, but ultimately provides a higher level of control over who can access which network resources.

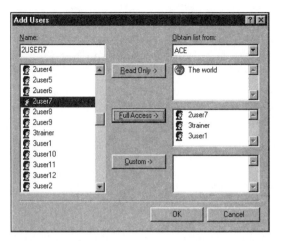

Figure 11.6 Configuring user-level security on a shared directory.

AUDIT TRAILS

Even with physical security in place, great password policies, and user-level security, how can you tell if someone is trying to circumvent your security and gain inappropriate access to network resources? By creating an audit trail.

Creating an audit trail means configuring the system so that specific events occurring on the network are logged into a database called the *event log*. In Windows NT, the event log is viewed with the Event Viewer utility, which is found in Windows NT's Administrative Tools (Common) menu.

By default, security events are not logged in Windows NT, so if you want to track these events, first you must configure the types of events you want to log. As with configuring account policies, configuring auditing is done through the User Manager For Domains utility. Figure 11.7 shows the Audit window, which is entered by clicking on the Policies menu and then on Audit.

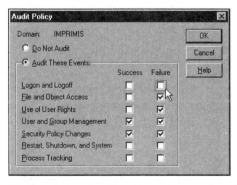

Figure 11.7 Configuring events to log through the Audit menu.

11

You can configure both successes and failures for each of the events selected. Initially, it may seem like a great idea to just select everything—after all, that yields the maximum amount of reporting—but some care needs to be taken in choosing events. Whenever an event occurs that is being tracked, an event is logged into the event log. You can easily get too much information, especially on a large network, making it more difficult to pick out potential trouble spots. Sorting through screens of successful print jobs and successful logons and logoffs can be a hassle. Process tracking, especially, will generate a lot of events. By clicking on the Log menu in the Event Viewer, you can select to view the System, Application, and Security logs (one at a time). The Security log is where our audit information will appear.

The boxes that are checked off in Figure 11.7 represent a good level of auditing for most environments. Possibly, you can add logon failures, but if you have a large network and a lot of users with marginal keyboard skills, you can find yourself wading through screens of bad password attempts being logged as users type their own passwords incorrectly. We find that generally if you have Account Lockout enabled to prevent repeated attempts to crack a password, it is not usually necessary to also enable logging of failed attempts. In environments that require a high level of security, failed password attempts can be logged to determine trends (to find out if the same user account is being flagged for one or two bad attempts a day).

Employee Morale

Audit trails are very useful in tracking attempts by internal network users (employees) to gain access to resources for which they're not authorized. Audit trails protect against curious user who just want to see what they can get into and against malicious users who want to cause problems or extract some revenge for a perceived wrong. The best way to handle malicious users is not related specifically to IT at all: You need to ensure that they do not become malicious in the first place.

Although employee morale is a Human Resources issue, it is also an important issue for IT personnel to keep in mind. Happy employees are far less likely to commit acts of vengeance on your network than are disgruntled employees. Companies that place an emphasis on doing business ethically and on treating their employees well are usually rewarded with employees who won't intentionally disrupt the network and who are apt to be forthcoming when they notice a problem. This can be categorized more as psychological protection of the network than real security, but employees with low morale value their jobs and the company less and are more willing to attempt to damage the company's ability to do business.

ENCRYPTION

Up to now, the security measures we have covered are primarily ways to prevent unauthorized access to network resources. How do you prevent someone from eavesdropping on your network data communications, though, if they do manage to gain access and start capturing or intercepting packets destined for other workstations or servers? The answer is encryption, which involves these three levels of security:

➤ Encryption of network packets

➤ Integrity assurance

➤ Authentication

Encryption Of Network Packets

The goal of encryption is privacy—being assured that information you send can't be intercepted and read except by the intended recipient. The most common approach to encryption is to send data using software such as Pretty Good Privacy (PGP), which scrambles (encrypts) the data before transmission, and to rely on the recipient to have software that unscrambles (decrypts) the message on the other end.

Note that if the encryption software uses the same algorithm for communicating with multiple people, each of them can impersonate the others when communicating with you. Because multiple people can have the same algorithm, there's no way for the software to know that a message really originated from the source it claims to be from. The encryption software could use a different encryption algorithm for each recipient, but managing more than a few such algorithms would make it difficult to keep up with them. Algorithms are like languages. For a rough comparison, imagine that in order to keep conversations with friends private, you had to learn a separate, distinct language to speak with each of them. Most of us would quickly tire of learning new languages, and there would still be duplicates in use, minimizing the effectiveness of separate languages as a way to keep others from understanding your conversations.

Instead of using different encryption algorithms for each recipient, software vendors use algorithms that require that users provide "key" values. Even if someone who knows the encryption algorithm intercepts a message, they can't decrypt it without the encryption key, and because the key is usually a large number, the chances of discovering it are minimal. This means that a software vendor can ship one algorithm (or a few of them), and users can control security by giving keys to only certain people. Think of the key as an unlisted telephone number, which you give out only to people you want to have it.

11

Where a key differs, though, is that it is much longer than a telephone number (and you aren't going to be bothered by pesky telemarketers who are randomly plugging in numbers to call).

The two basic types of key encryption technology are secret-key and public-key.

Secret-Key Cryptography

Secret-key cryptography employs a method that uses the same key to encrypt and to decrypt a message. Using a secret-key algorithm—such as that within DES (the government-sponsored Data Encryption Standard)—requires each party to exchange secret encryption keys. This is usually not a problem in small networks, but as a network grows, the secure exchange of secret keys becomes increasingly expensive and unwieldy. Consequently, this solution is impractical for even moderate-sized networks.

DES has an additional drawback: It requires sharing a secret key. Each person must trust the other to guard the pair's secret key and to reveal it to no one. Because users must have a different key for every person they communicate with, they must trust each and every person with one of their secret keys. This means that secure communication can take place only between people with some kind of relationship, be it personal or professional. The advantage of secret-key cryptography, however, is its speed. Because there is only one key, there aren't a lot of mathematical calculations required to verify the source and destination of the data.

Two popular secret-key algorithms are Data Encryption Standard (DES) and International Data Encryption Algorithm (IDEA).

Public-Key Cryptography

Public-key cryptography actually uses two keys. The first is a public key (where the name comes from) that is distributed to the people you communicate with. This key can be sent across a network unencrypted without any consequences. The second key is a private key that is just that—private. It must not be sent across a network; if your private key is compromised, then your encryption is worthless. The public and private keys are mathematically related and work together to encrypt and decrypt data. Key-encryption techniques generally use multiplication, exponentiation, and division on very large numbers (250 or more decimal digits), making them more difficult to crack without extensive processing power and time.

With public-key cryptography, the public key is used to encrypt the data, and the private key is then used to decrypt the data. So the process works this way: The sender encrypts data with the public key and sends it over a network, and the receiver of the data decrypts it with the private key. Therefore, the sender can be sure that only the intended recipient of the data can decrypt it. If you are the only one who knows your private key, anyone who successfully uses your public key to decrypt a message knows that you (not an impostor) encrypted it. Other people use your public key to encrypt messages to you, but without your private key, they can't decrypt messages to you that they intercept.

Some public-key methods also provide the capability to use the secret key to "sign" a message that anyone who has the associated public key can verify. If a certificate is successfully decrypted with the public key, it must have come from the owner of the corresponding private key. This capability is known as *integrity assurance.*

The popular cryptography program PGP (Pretty Good Privacy) uses public-key encryption technology.

Integrity Assurance

The goal of integrity assurance is to assure recipients that a message has not been intercepted and altered in transit. It is the equivalent of sealing an envelope or shrink-wrapping a product package. The process, often called "signing" or "sealing," is based on "hash" algorithms. Here's where we get technical.

Hashing

A *hash algorithm* takes message data as input and produces as output a "digest" value (typically a very large number) based on the message contents. A simple example: Add all the bytes of the message together, and then use the rightmost three digits as the digest, so each message is mapped to a number between 0 and 999. The algorithm produces digest values reliably: The same algorithm running on two computers produces the same digest from the same message.

Hashing is "one-way" encryption: You can encrypt a message, but you can't decrypt the resulting digest. The reason is that there are countless messages whose bytes add up to any given three-digit number (to use our previous example). That means that if you could decrypt a digest, you would be back in the situation of not knowing for sure that the data arrived unmodified or even arrived from the source address listed in the data. So even if you know the algorithm and the digest value, you can't use them to reconstruct the original message.

Hash algorithms are useful for integrity assurance, especially if they produce a wide range of possible digest values. The software on the sending end hashes the message and then sends both the unencrypted message and the digest. The software on the receiving end rehashes the message and compares the resulting digest with the one that accompanied the message. If the two digests match, the message was not altered in transit. The sending software encrypts the digest to keep anyone who intercepts and alters the message from also altering the digest. This method lets software protect a message without the overhead involved in encrypting and decrypting it.

Email And Key Encryption

Messaging (email) software that uses public-key encryption has the useful side effect of also ensuring authenticity. The software uses your private key to encrypt the message digest. When recipients successfully decrypt the digest with your public key, they know that you (not an impostor) sent the message.

There are two major ways to apply integrity assurance:

➤ **Message signing** This means applying a "digital signature" to a message. Message signing can be useful in e-commerce applications, where a message is signed with your private key to validate a credit-card purchase, for example. Another use might be in a "paperless office," where managers can digitally sign purchase orders or expense reports without having to print them and manually sign on them. Digitally signing messages with a private key ensures that the CFO—and not some guy that works out on the docks—signed that purchase order.

➤ **Code signing** Application software delivered over the network can contain the vendor's digital signature, assuring you that your copy hasn't been altered (say, infected with a virus) in transit. This technology has become increasingly popular on the World Wide Web for use in browsers.

Authentication

The goal of authentication is to verify the identity of the person you're communicating with. The most intuitive strategy is one we've already discussed: using a password known only to you and the people (or computers) you trust. For example, when you log on to a Windows NT network, you provide your user ID and your password. The server looks up your user ID in its security database to find your password and then compares it to the password you typed at the client computer. If the two passwords match, the server gives you access to its resources.

Certificates

Another approach to validation and authentication uses public-key technology. Instead of a password, the user provides a certificate. A *certificate* is a document that is issued by a certificate authority (CA) and that contains a user ID and a public key. Your IT department might be a CA for your network, an online service could be a CA for its users, and so on. The CA puts its digital signature onto the certificate document so that the recipient of it knows that it hasn't been forged or altered.

Certificates close a potential security hole. An example: Suppose that your encryption software lets you manually enter a person's user ID and public-key value. Someone you don't trust forges a message from someone you do trust and includes the trusted person's ID paired with the untrusted person's public key. You then enter the invalid information (right key from wrong person) into your encryption software's database. At that point, the untrusted person can impersonate the trusted one. If, instead, the encryption software obtains public-key values only from certificates, then the impostor can't impersonate someone else without forging a certificate.

Ultimately, cryptography techniques protect the integrity of network data should a security breach occur. To prevent outsiders from breaching your network from a connected network such as the Internet, you need to use firewalls.

FIREWALLS

A *firewall* is a hardware or software device (or a combination of the two) that is used to control access between a trusted network (such as your corporate local area network [LAN]) and an untrusted network (such as the Internet). Firewalls can be employed between any two network segments, but most commonly they are used between private networks and the public network known as the Internet.

Firewalls are called firewalls as a metaphor for what they do. A firewall is a building construction term that refers to materials placed within walls to prevent fires from spreading from one room to another. In an automobile, a firewall is built between the engine and the passenger compartments to stop engine fires from burning through into the passenger compartment. Similarly, a network firewall is designed to prevent traffic from entering your private network from sources you don't want.

The four basic types of network firewalls are:

➤ Packet filters

➤ Circuit-level gateways

➤ Application-layer firewalls

➤ Dynamic packet filters (stateful inspection)

Packet-Filter Firewalls

A packet-filter firewall is a first-generation firewall technology that analyzes network traffic at the Transport layer of the OSI (Open Systems Interconnection) model. By first-generation, we mean that it is the original firewall technology. Each IP network packet is examined to see if it matches a rule defining what data is allowed to pass through the network. Such rules, which identify whether communication is allowed, are created by the administrator and maintained by the firewall software in the TCP/IP (Transmission Control Protocol/Internet Protocol) kernel. These rules are based on information contained within the Internet and Transport-layer packet headers and on the direction in which the packet is headed (internal to external network or vice versa).

Packet-filter firewalls are hardware based, built into routers, and typically enable the administrator to control the transfer of data based on the following controls:

➤ The physical network interface that the packet arrives on

➤ The source IP address

➤ The destination IP address

➤ The type of Transport layer, such as TCP or UDP (User Datagram Protocol)

➤ The Transport layer's source port

➤ The Transport layer's destination port

Packet filters generally do not understand the Application-layer protocols used in the communication packets. Instead, they work by applying a set of rules that is maintained in the TCP/IP kernel. These rules contain an associated action that will be applied to any packets matching the criteria mentioned above.

Denied Or Permitted

When a rule is applied to a packet, the resulting action takes on one of two values: "deny" or "permit" the network packet. The firewall maintains two lists: a deny list and a permit list. For a network packet to be routed to its proper destination, it must first pass a check of both lists—that is, it must not be expressly denied, and it must be expressly permitted. (Some packet-filter firewalls that are incorporated into routers implement a different policy. In these types of packet filters, the packet must be expressly denied; otherwise, it is permitted.)

Packet filters typically implement command sets that allow the checking of the source and destination port numbers on the TCP and UDP Transport-layer protocols. This check determines whether a permit or deny rule exists for the specific port and protocol combination contained in the packet data. Because the ICMP (Internet Control Message Protocol) protocol layer does not utilize port numbers for its communications protocol, it is difficult for packet filters to apply any security policy to this form of network traffic. In order to apply an effective security policy to ICMP, the packet filter must maintain state tables to ensure that an ICMP reply message was recently requested from an internal host. This ability to track the communications state is one of the primary differences between simple packet filters and dynamic packet filters (discussed later in this chapter).

Least-Secure Firewall

Because packet filters are implemented in the Transport layer, they generally do not understand how to process state information in the high-level protocols, such as FTP (File Transfer Protocol). The more sophisticated packet filters can detect IP, TCP, UDP, and ICMP. Using a packet filter that includes the TCP/UDP port-filtering capability, you can permit certain types of connections to be made to specific computers, while prohibiting other types of connections to those computers and similar connections to other computers.

The complete network-packet inspection adheres to the following general rules:

➤ If no matching rule is found, then drop the network packet.

➤ If a matching rule is found that permits the communication, then allow the network packet to pass.

➤ If a matching rule is found that denies the communication, then drop the network packet.

Because this type of firewall does not inspect the network packet's Application-layer data and does not track the state of connections, the packet-filter firewall is the least secure of the firewall technologies. It allows access through the firewall with a minimal amount of scrutiny. In other words, if the checks succeed, the network packet is routed through the firewall as defined by the rules in the firewall's routing table. However, because it does less processing than the other technologies do, it is the fastest firewall technology available and is often implemented in hardware solutions, such as IP routers.

Packet-filter firewalls often readdress network packets so that outgoing traffic appears to have originated from a different host rather than from an internal host. The process of readdressing network packets is called *network address translation (NAT)*. Network address translation hides the addressing schemes of the private network from untrusted networks.

Circuit-Level Firewalls

A circuit-level firewall is a second-generation firewall technology that validates TCP and UDP sessions before opening a connection, or circuit, through the firewall. The firewall examines session setup for legitimate TCP or UDP handshaking and does not forward packets until the handshaking is complete. When the session is established, the firewall maintains a table of valid connections and lets data pass through when session information matches an entry in the table. When the session is over, the table entry is removed, and the circuit is closed until another process begins.

When a connection is set up, the circuit-level firewall typically stores the following information about the connection:

➤ A unique session identifier for the connection, which is used for tracking purposes

➤ The state of the connection: handshake, established, or closing

➤ The sequencing information

➤ The source IP address

➤ The destination IP address

➤ The physical network interface through which the packet arrives

➤ The physical network interface through which the packet goes out

Using this information, the circuit-level firewall checks the header information contained within each network packet to determine whether the transmitting computer has permission to send data to the receiving computer and whether the receiving computer has permission to receive that data.

Circuit-level firewalls have only limited understanding of the protocols used in the network packets. They can detect only one Transport-layer protocol: TCP. Like packet filters, circuit-level firewalls work by applying a rule set that is maintained in the TCP/IP kernel.

Connection State

Circuit-level firewalls allow access through the firewall with a minimal amount of scrutiny by building a limited form of a connection state. This means that only those network packets that are associated with an existing connection are allowed through the firewall. When a connection-establishment packet is received, the circuit-level firewall checks its rules to determine whether that connection should be allowed. If the connection is allowed, all network packets associated with that connection are routed through the firewall, as defined in the firewall server's routing table, with no further security checks. This method is very fast and provides a limited amount of state checking.

Circuit-level firewalls can also perform additional checks to ensure that a network packet has not been *spoofed* (forged or faked) and that the data contained within the Transport protocol header complies with the definition for that protocol, allowing the firewall to detect limited forms of modified packet data. As with packet-filter firewalls, circuit-level firewalls can often perform network-address translation on packets to hide the addressing scheme of the internal network.

Application-Layer Firewalls

An Application-layer firewall is a third-generation firewall technology that evaluates network packets for valid data at the Application layer before allowing a connection. This firewall examines the data in all network packets at the Application layer and maintains complete connection state and sequencing information. In addition, an Application-layer firewall can validate other security items that appear only within the Application-layer data, such as user passwords and service requests.

Proxies

Most Application-layer firewalls include specialized proxy services. *Proxy services* are special-purpose programs that manage traffic through a firewall for a specific service, such as HTTP (Hypertext Transfer Protocol) or FTP. Proxy services are specific to the protocol that they are designed to forward, and they provide increased access control with careful detailed checks for valid data. Proxy services can also generate audit records about the traffic that they transfer, enabling an administrator to see if employees are accessing inappropriate services or sites on the Internet.

Each application proxy requires two components that are typically implemented as a single executable: a proxy server and a proxy client.

The Proxy Server

All connection requests on a trusted network are funneled through the proxy server. That means that all communication between internal users and the Internet passes through the proxy server, rather than having users communicate directly with other servers on the Internet. An internal client sends a request to the proxy server for connecting to an external service, such as FTP or HTTP. The proxy server then evaluates the request and decides to permit or deny the request. The decision is based on a set of rules that apply to the individual network service. Proxy servers understand the protocol of the service that they are evaluating; therefore, they allow only those packets through that comply with the protocol definitions.

11

The Proxy Client

A proxy client is part of a user application, such as a Web browser, that talks to the requested server on the external network on behalf of the internal client. When a client requests a service, such as viewing a Web page on the Internet, the proxy server evaluates that request against the policy rules defined for that proxy and determines whether to approve it. If it approves the request, the proxy server forwards that request to the proxy client. The proxy client then contacts the external server on behalf of the client (thus the term *proxy*). The proxy client proceeds to relay requests from the proxy server to the external server and to relay responses from the external server to the proxy server. Likewise, the proxy server relays requests and responses between the proxy client and the internal client.

Proxy services never allow direct connections, and they force all network packets to be examined and filtered for suitability. Instead of communicating directly with the real service, a user communicates to the proxy server (the user's default gateway is set to point to the proxy server on the firewall). The same is true from the perspective of the real service communicating with a user. The proxies handle all communications between the user and a real service on the external network.

A proxy service is designed to operate transparently between a user on the internal network and the real service on the external network. From the user's perspective, the user is dealing directly with the real service on the Internet. From the real service's perspective, it is dealing directly with a user on the proxy server (instead of the user's real computer).

Performance

Proxy services are implemented at the Application layer of the OSI model. Because of that, each packet must pass through the low-level protocols before being passed up the protocol stack to the Application layer for a thorough inspection of the packet headers and packet data by the proxies. Then, the packet must travel back down to the kernel, and then back down the stack for distribution. Because each packet in a session is subject to this process, proxy services are notoriously slow. Slower performance is the tradeoff for the higher level of security provided by the Application-layer firewall. Like circuit level firewalls, Application-layer firewalls can perform additional checks to ensure that a network packet has not been spoofed, and they often perform network-address translation.

Dynamic Packet Filters

A dynamic packet-filter firewall is a fourth-generation firewall technology that allows modification of security rules on the fly, or *dynamically* (which is where the name comes from). It can monitor an in-progress FTP session, for example, to detect when a file is about to be transferred. On noting the port number negotiated with the server, the dynamic firewall generates a new temporary rule permitting an inbound connection on that port number from that specific source IP address. The firewall then monitors the file transfer and removes the temporary rule when the transfer finishes or times out.

A dynamic packet-filtering facility can also monitor for threatening activities. For example, a dynamic packet filter could watch for a systematic probe for addresses on your LAN and create a filtering rule to block further probes from the offending source address. A dynamic filter also can take actions other than simple blocking. A standard feature is the ability to issue log messages when certain events, such as a suspected attack, occur. Some firewalls can even page someone, providing a realtime problem alert.

Dynamic packet-filter firewalls have the same advantages and disadvantages associated with first-generation packet-filter firewalls, with one notable exception: the advantage of not allowing unsolicited UDP packets onto your internal network. This feature is useful for allowing Application-layer protocols, such as the Domain Name System (DNS), to operate across your security perimeter. An internal DNS server must originate requests to other DNS servers running on the Internet to retrieve address information for unknown hosts. DNS servers may make these requests using a TCP connection or a UDP virtual connection.

A dynamic packet–filter firewall can also be used to provide support for a limited subset of the ICMP protocol. ICMP is often used to test network connectivity by *pinging*—sending a pair of network packets between two cooperating hosts. Because the firewall server can allow a response to cross the firewall at the request of an internal host, the internal host can deduce that a host exists on an untrusted network.

Performance Vs. Security

When considering various firewall technologies, in addition to cost factors, most people want to know the trade-offs between performance and security. These trade-offs depend on how far up the protocol stack a network packet must travel, as well as what level of security checks are being performed on each packet. Packet-filter firewalls generally provide the highest performance, followed by circuit-level firewalls, dynamic packet-filter firewalls, and Application-layer firewalls. The level of security checks generally follows the reverse order because as network packets pass through more protocol layers, they are inspected in more detail. As a result, Application-layer firewalls are considered the most secure type of firewall, being more secure than dynamic packet-filter firewalls, which are considered more secure than circuit-level firewalls, and last, packet-filter firewalls. Selecting a firewall for a company involves balancing the amount of security required against costs and performance issues. A simple packet-filter firewall may cost only $1,000, whereas a state-of-the-art firewall could cost $50,000 or more.

11

CHAPTER SUMMARY

Network security threats come from both internal network users and external hackers who attempt to breach security through modems or public networks. Threats come from intentional acts—including theft and industrial espionage— and from accidental sources, such as user error and viruses brought into the network inadvertently.

➤ Physical security is the first line of defense in a successful network security policy. Servers and critical network components should be kept in locked rooms that only authorized personnel have access to. The cable plant also has to be protected.

➤ Modem telephone numbers should be kept private to reduce the risk of their being hacked. Only users who need to dial in to the network to do their jobs should have dial-in access permissions enabled on their user accounts.

➤ Network connections to public networks like the Internet should be protected by firewalls to prevent hacking.

➤ Maintaining a high level of employee morale will go a long way toward reducing the threat of disgruntled employees attacking the network.

➤ Password policies should strictly enforce the concept of privacy, and no one should be able to guess a user's password. Passwords should have a minimum length, be alphanumeric, and be changed every 30 to 60 days.

➤ User accounts that are known not to be in use or that will not be used for an extended length of time should be disabled.

There are two network security models: user-level security and share-level security.

➤ User-level security is more secure than share-level security but requires membership in a Windows NT domain for its list of users that can be assigned access.

Audit trails can be created so that specific events occurring on the network are logged in to a database called the *event log*.

➤ Auditing policies should be enabled and configured to track security events on the network.

➤ The event log can be analyzed for suspicious activity or trends.

The goal of encryption is privacy, which is accomplished through integrity assurance and authentication.

➤ Secret-key encryption uses the same key for both encrypting and decrypting a message and requires that private keys be given out.

➤ Public-key encryption uses a private key (known only to the owner of the key), which is used to encrypt a message. A second, public, key is distributed by the key owner and is used to decrypt messages.

➤ Certificates offer a higher level of authentication than passwords and are based on public-key encryption.

Firewalls shield internal, private networks from traffic on public networks like the Internet. Firewall technologies that have evolved over four "generations" include packet filters, circuit-level firewalls, Application-layer firewalls, and dynamic packet filters.

➤ Application-level firewalls provide the slowest performance, but also provide the highest level of security.

➤ A packet-filter firewall, which is typically built into a hardware router, is the cheapest and least secure firewall technology.

REVIEW QUESTIONS

1. What must be done to share a directory with user-level security?
   a. A password must be created for users to enter when they want access to the directory.
   b. A list of users from an NT workstation who can access the directory must be configured.
   c. A list of users from the NT domain who can access the directory must be configured.
   d. The user sharing the directory must manually create a list of users who can access the directory.

2. What is the administrative account in Windows NT called by default?
   a. Administrator
   b. Supervisor
   c. Root
   d. Admin

3. The fastest firewall technology in terms of performance is:
   a. Packet filter
   b. Circuit level
   c. Application level
   d. Dynamic packet filter

4. The most secure firewall technology is:
   a. Packet filter
   b. Circuit level
   c. Application-layer
   d. Dynamic packet filter

5. The encryption process of taking message data as input and producing as output a "digest" value based on the message contents is called:
   a. Key encryption
   b. Scrambling
   c. Hashing
   d. Randomizing

11

6. How many keys does secret-key encryption use?

    a. One

    b. Two

    c. Three

    d. A number defined by the user

7. To whom would you distribute your private key in a public-key encryption system?

    a. Only people you trust

    b. No one

    c. Anyone who would need to decrypt a message you sent

    d. The CA (certificate authority)

8. What authentication method offers the highest level of security?

    a. Alphanumeric passwords at least eight characters long

    b. Certificates

    c. DES encryption

    d. Encrypted passwords

9. Approximately how often should passwords be changed in an average networked environment?

    a. Every week

    b. Once a year

    c. Every six months

    d. Once a month

10. Which firewall technology can monitor for threatening activity?

    a. Packet filter

    b. Circuit level

    c. Application-layer

    d. Dynamic packet filter

11. When auditing is enabled, where are tracked security events stored?

    a. Event log

    b. Event Viewer

    c. Audit log

    d. Alert Manager

12. Which type of firewall technology are proxy servers associated with?
    a. Packet filter
    b. Circuit level
    c. Application-layer
    d. Dynamic packet filter

13. Which NOS (network operating system) doesn't allow you to rename the administrative account?
    a. Windows NT
    b. Novell NetWare
    c. Unix
    d. None of the above

14. The default security model used in Windows 9x is:
    a. User level
    b. Share level
    c. Workgroup
    d. Domain

15. Servers should be kept:
    a. In a locked room
    b. In the CEO's office
    c. In the break room
    d. Easily accessible by anyone who needs to sit down at the console and look up information

11

HANDS-ON PROJECTS

In the following hands-on projects, you will be presented with some situations that require establishing appropriate security policies for companies. The projects will put into practice many of the concepts discussed in this chapter, including passwords, RAS security, auditing, account security, and security models. To do these projects, you'll need access to at least one NT server that is a domain controller, that has at least one modem, and that is set up as a RAS server. You will also need a Windows 98 machine that is part of the NT domain.

These projects require making changes to security and Remote Access settings. It is highly recommended that you use a test system and not a production server to do these labs. Following the steps in reverse will allow you to undo any changes you make during the labs.

Project 11.1

You are a consultant who has been contracted to address the security concerns of a small company that has recently suffered several hacking incidents. The company (1 domain, 2 NT servers, and about 100 Windows 98 workstations) is not connected to any other networks, such as the Internet. The company does, however, have several modems attached to a RAS server for some sales staff members who work exclusively from home and almost always during business hours. The company is not 24×7; it operates weekdays from 8 A.M. to 6 P.M. and Saturdays from 8 A.M. to noon. The company has two part-time IS guys: Ace (who is also in marketing) and Peter (who is also the credit manager). They do the IS work in addition to their regular job functions.

Your mission is to shore up the security for the network by implementing new policies and procedures and increasing accountability. You will use your NT Server lab machine as if it were the server you were reconfiguring for this company.

RAS

Because there are no network connections to untrusted networks, you decide to focus your attention first on the RAS server, which provides the only means for an outsider to breach network security from a remote location. Because of limited network administration skills and time constraints, you find that Ace and Peter have granted all users dial-in permission to the network. As we learned, by default, NT grants no one dial-in access; it must be explicitly given. NT does have an option, though, to "grant all." You can reach this option through the Remote Access Admin utility, found under Administrative Tools (Common), by selecting Permissions in the Options menu. In the Remote Access Permissions dialog box that appears, click on the Grant All button and then click on Yes (see Figure 11.8).

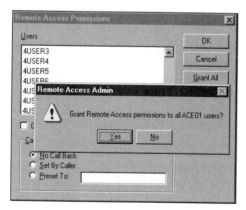

Figure 11.8 Granting dial-in access to every user is a potential security problem.

To change dial-in permissions:

1. The first step you want to take is to ensure that only users who need to work from a remote location have access. So you have meetings with the department managers and create a list of employees who need dial-in access. The list you come up with is as follows:

   ➤ 2USER7

   ➤ 2USER8

   ➤ 3Trainer

   ➤ 3USER1

   In our list, the number preceding USER refers to the floor on which the employee works, and the trailing number is the cubicle number the employee sits in. Using this naming convention (naming conventions are discussed in depth in Chapter 15) saves the administrators from having to rename user accounts whenever an employee leaves the company.

   Notice that Figure 11.9 is similar to Figure 11.8, except that Figure 11.9 shows you how to revoke permissions for all users. You can reach this option through the Remote Access Admin utility, found under Administrative Tools (Common), by selecting Permissions in the Options menu. In the Remote Access Permissions dialog box that appears, click on the Revoke All button and then click on Yes (see Figure 11.9). Perform this action on your server.

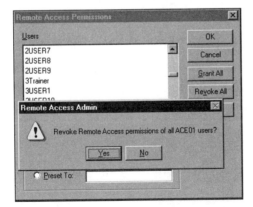

Figure 11.9   Revoking dial-in access for everyone in order to set up permissions appropriately.

2. Now that you have revoked everyone's permission to dial in, you will grant dial-in permission to only the users on the list. For each of these users, open the User Properties window (by double-clicking on the username), and grant access.

3. By default, NT does not require a call back for RAS, which means that a user can dial in to the network from any location. Change the default configuration for each user to require call-back authentication. Do this through the User Manager For Domains utility by double-clicking on the user account and clicking on the Dialin button at the bottom right. When possible, such as with users who work only from one location, set the call-back number so that user account can dial in from only a specified location. This step, in which the phone number of the specified location is entered, is shown in Figure 11.10. Replace the number in the example to reflect the phone number from where your workstation is calling.

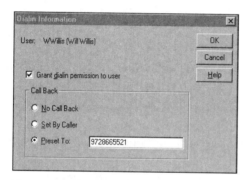

Figure 11.10 Setting the RAS call-back number for increased security.

4. For users, such as traveling salespeople, who are mobile and who dial in from multiple locations, configure the call-back authentication to be set by the caller. While allowing the user to specify any number, this option increases the accountability of the user account and therefore increases the security. In our sample user list, 3Trainer is a roving instructor who travels frequently to other sites in the company. She would need to be able to dial into the network from any number of locations.

Passwords

While looking at the existing security settings, you also notice that the IS guys have left the default account settings, as shown in Figure 11.11.

You interview Ace and Peter and find out that most users have probably never changed their passwords because they're not required to. Furthermore, the average user's account password is probably known by at least two or three people in the same department.

With passwords being neither secure nor changed at all, you will need to implement a new password policy.

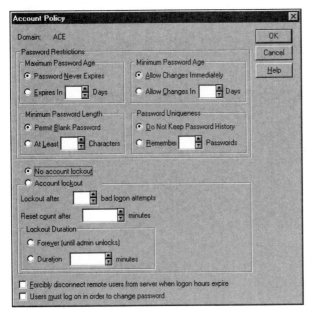

Figure 11.11   Default Windows NT account settings.

To increase password security:

1. Open User Manager For Domains. On the Policies menu, click on Account. This company does not have extensive security requirements, but a reasonable level of security should be set. Configure the account settings as shown in Figure 11.12. The information you need to enter is as follows:

   ➤ Password expires in 45 days.

   ➤ Password must be at least six characters.

   ➤ The system should remember 10 passwords. This option prevents users from simply choosing the same password again or rotating between two or three passwords upon expiration.

   ➤ Password changes can be made after three days. This setting prevents users from undermining the password history just configured. Allowing immediate changes would allow users to change their passwords 10 times in a row to get back to their original passwords. Some users hate change enough to go through this routine!

   ➤ Check the box at the bottom for Users Must Log On In Order To Change Password.

   ➤ Account lockout should be turned on, and users should be locked out after five bad password attempts.

   ➤ The lockout duration should last until the administrator manually unlocks the account through User Manager For Domains. This is a more secure setting than letting the account unlock itself after a predetermined length of time has passed.

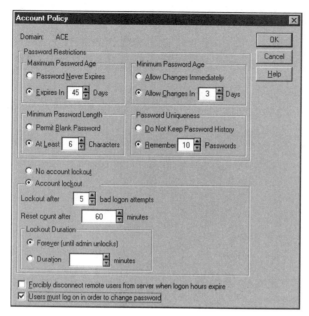

Figure 11.12 You can greatly tighten security by configuring the account policies.

Compare the settings in Figure 11.12 with Figure 11.11, and notice how much stronger you have made account security through these simple steps.

Login Hours

Because the company does not operate on a 24×7 basis, you can tighten security even further through login hour restrictions.

To restrict login hours:

1. Open User Manager For Domains and double-click on any user account to view the User Properties. Next, click on the Hours button, which opens a dialog box similar to that shown in Figure 11.13.

2. Set up each user's login hours to reflect the times when his or her account would typically be in use. Some users (such as administrators) always need to be able to use their accounts, at any hour of any day, but most users don't. Configuring users' login hours to coincide with their work schedules decreases the likelihood that their accounts will be used to hack into the network. Notice in Figure 11.13 that the login hours that are set up give some flexibility for coming in early or working overtime. The company's business hours are 8 A.M. to 6 P.M. during the week, and users are allowed access from 7 A.M. to 8 P.M. Similarly, the company's business hours are 8 to noon on Saturdays, and users are allowed access from 8 A.M. to 2 P.M. By restricting the login hours to more or less match business hours, you

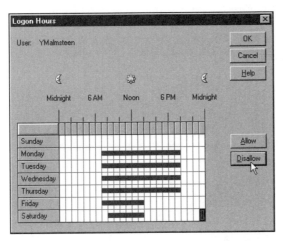

Figure 11.13   Configuring the allowed login hours for a user.

prevent accounts from being used to hack in after hours, when no one should be using the accounts, anyway.

3. Refer back to Figure 11.12, the Account Policy configuration we used in the last section, and look at one of the checkboxes at the bottom, Forcibly Disconnect Remote Users From Server When Logon Hours Expire. If this option is set, the login hours are strictly enforced. If users are working late to finish a project, and their login hours expire, they will be disconnected automatically. In most environments, it is okay to not check this box. If the box is left unchecked, users will be able to continue working if they are already logged in to the network, but they will not able to establish a new connection if the time is outside of their allowed login hours.

Project 11.2

You need to complete Project 11.1 before beginning this project.

Now that you have reconfigured the account policies and increased security on the only source of external attack (the modems), it is time to focus your attention on the possibility of internal attacks.

Configuring the account policies will go a long way toward increasing internal security, as will teaching users to create effective passwords. You've explained to Ace and Peter what they need to do to help ensure that users don't share their passwords with others, and you've taught them how to set up future users in a way that will maintain the same level of security.

Security Model

The next step is to change the default security model from share level to user level on each workstation.

To change the security model used:

1. From a Windows 98 system, open the Network applet of the Control Panel and select the Access Control tab.

2. Select the use User-Level Security option and type the name of the NT domain where the system should get its user list.

3. Complete Steps 1 and 2 on each workstation. If this were a real-life scenario, you would then educate Ace and Peter about the new security model so that they can educate users and discourage them from simply giving "the world" full access when they share a resource.

Auditing

After completing the workstation configurations, you are still faced with a lack of accountability on the network. If potential hackers were employees who already had valid network access, what would stop them from attempting to hack into resources? How would you know if someone were trying to access resources that they aren't authorized for? By auditing.

To create an audit trail:

1. By default, NT does not enable auditing. To enable auditing, open User Manager For Domains. In the Policies menu, click on Audit. You will find that Do Not Audit is selected. Choose Audit These Events and configure the settings so that they're similar to those shown in Figure 11.14.

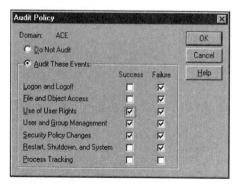

Figure 11.14 Enabling the auditing of network security events.

These settings will provide a large amount of security information without being overwhelming and difficult to sort through. Given the company's recent hacking attacks, Use Of User Rights is enabled for both Success and Failure. After a few weeks, you can remove the check from the Success box to save log space.

2. With these settings, Ace and Peter will be able to view the security log with the Event Viewer and see what kinds of security events are taking place on the network. With the audit settings chosen, click on OK.

3. To see how the Event Viewer works, we will generate a security event that we can view from the server. Open User Manager For Domains (if it is not still open) and double-click on a user account to open a User Properties window. Change the password, confirm it, and click on OK. Close User Manager For Domains.

4. In the Administrative Tools (Common) group, click on Event Viewer. In the Log menu, select Security. Events are listed from newest to oldest. The first event listed should have a gold key to the far left, indicating a successful audit. If you double-click on the event, you will get details similar to those shown in Figure 11.15.

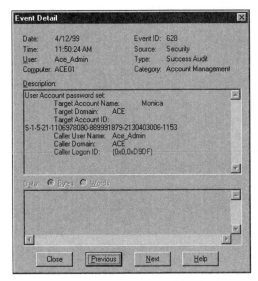

Figure 11.15   Event Viewer detail of a security event.

At this point, you have strengthened the network security policies significantly. Now you are left with documenting your work (discussed in Chapter 14) and with giving Ace and Peter the information necessary to maintain the level of security you have implemented. After all, they will be the ones responsible for the security after you have moved on to your next consulting project.

Maintaining a secure network requires a lot of effort, not just in setting it up but in the day-to-day administration. Event logs have to be read and tracked, and suspicious events have to be documented and acted upon. If you are lucky, security will always be part of preventive maintenance. If your network does get hacked in spite of your efforts, though, you will be glad to have put yourself in a position where you have security logs and a shorter list of possible intrusion points than if you had taken no steps to maintain a secure network.

PART II

NETWORKING
PRACTICES

## CHAPTER TWELVE

NETWORK INSTALLATION

12

After Reading This Chapter And Completing The Exercises, You Will Be Able To:

➤ Describe the planning phases of the process of implementing a network

➤ Set up administrative accounts, user accounts, and groups

➤ Increase network security with password-protection policies

➤ Determine protocol implementation

➤ Understand installation compatibility issues

➤ Explain the impact of various environmental factors on computer networks

---

Installing a network is probably the most exciting part of networking. This is not due to the level of difficulty involved; rather, it is due to the rarity of needing to install a new network server into a network. The most important part of installing a network is what happens before the equipment is ever taken out of the box—the planning phase.

OVERVIEW OF NETWORK INSTALLATION

Installation of a network can be confusing and overwhelming because a network has many elements that must be considered. These include:

➤ The number, capacity, speed, and location of the servers

➤ The topology and wiring to use

➤ The protocols to implement

➤ The configuration of the user directory, if hierarchical

➤ The naming standards for all network elements

➤ The security measures to apply to user and group accounts for file and printer access

➤ The other services required on the network

➤ The client software and its configuration

Deciding some of these issues may lead to further decisions to make on other tangential issues. For example, if a Web service is required on the network, the next decision to make is which Web server software to install. Or, if you're implementing TCP/IP (Transmission Control Protocol/Internet Protocol), the next decision to make may be whether to use static or dynamic addressing.

A network installation can be easier to manage if it is split into smaller sets of tasks and decisions. Although different methods of managing a network implementation are organized in different ways, they all consist of the tasks found in these five basic steps.

The five phases of implementing a network are:

1. **Organization** This first step consists of gathering resources and learning about the new system. In most enterprises, the organization phase includes a review of the costs involved with the project and the procurement of any products. Teams of people are designated to plan, develop, and implement the network and to train users. In small network implementations, this group can be a set of very few people. In larger network implementations, this group can include people in multiple locations.

2. **Standards planning** The second step is dedicated to creating and developing standards, or verifying the standards that are already created. Standards ensure that the final network implementation is cohesive.

3. **Implementation planning** This step focuses on the actual tasks that will be performed and the schedule for performing them. Each team member is assigned a set of tasks with dates by which to complete them. Each part of the network is designed, from the infrastructure to server design and client configuration. The users, groups, and rights assignments are developed. Printer locations are also determined.

4. **Testing** This step sets up a lab. The lab is used for testing various configurations of the network software to determine what will be optimal for the production network. The first administrative users, groups, and rights assignments are created and tested to ensure that applications and files are secured. Login scripts are created and tested. Workstation configuration and automatic installation files are tested.

5. **Deployment** Deployment is the actual rubber-meets-the-road installation of production network equipment. The two phases of deployment are pilot and final roll-out. The *pilot deployment* is the first installation on the production network. The *final roll-out* is the installation of the remaining systems. The pilot deployment is separated in the schedule to allow some time for addressing any errors or issues that were not discovered during the testing phase.

The Planning Phases

Planning a network installation takes an incredible amount of time and effort. The decisions that must be made range from the physical location of each computer to the conceptual design and naming conventions of the directory for user and computer accounts. Even when a network has been completely designed, it must be reevaluated regularly in order to optimize the network as it grows and changes over time.

When one network system is being added to an existing internetwork, you don't create new standards; instead, you must verify and document the standards already in use. The administrative accounts and their passwords need to be gathered so that they can be used to create additional accounts and to access the directory service to install network servers. The implementation team should document all the account names and passwords used to install systems, even if those accounts are already known.

The remaining step in the planning stage is to design the details of the network implementation. Hardware and software must be specified, with a description of the goal configurations. The tasks defined to test and implement the systems must be identified. Then, each task must be given a due date with an estimated task duration to create the project schedule.

Infrastructure Planning

When you're designing an enterprise network, the infrastructure—hubs, routers, switches, and so on—includes many components that must be carefully designed. These components will carry the network traffic for each workstation, printer, and server. Some network implementations are simply additions to existing internetworks, some are new internetworks, and some are replacements of existing internetworks. Basic design factors apply to all versions.

12

A network design can be divided into a hierarchical structure with three main levels:

➤ **Backbone** The backbone provides data transport between different physical sites. The backbone is also a high-capacity infrastructure system that provides optimal transport at each site. The backbone should be designed to move data as quickly as possible and to use as few protocols as possible. To provide the fastest access, the backbone should not be connected to outside systems and should not be filtering traffic.

➤ **Shared systems** This level provides connectivity to servers and other shared systems. Segments of the shared systems are routed directly into the backbone for optimal systems access. This level provides access to the backbone and is best used to handle security to the backbone. This is the level where traffic is filtered.

➤ **Users** This level is composed of the users' workstations. The users level is connected in workgroup systems so that the users' level data is routed directly to the shared-systems segments containing their most often used shared systems.

The hierarchical infrastructure design is depicted in Figure 12.1. This design is flexible enough to apply to any size internetwork, and the network structure lends itself to a standardized, easy to implement, and easy to manage security scheme.

Directory Services Planning

Directory services are the repositories for all user, group, and administrative accounts. The plan for directory services encompasses the naming standards for accounts and network resources, as well as the hierarchy of the tree that contains them.

Using A Naming Convention

Using a standard convention for naming the user accounts and network resources makes the network easy to document. Follow these guidelines when creating a naming convention:

➤ User accounts should be a total of eight characters or fewer. This number provides a backward compatibility with older systems that require eight characters or fewer. Keeping within the strictest confines for naming conventions means that the same names can be used in all systems, providing ease of access for users.

➤ The names of shared systems, especially servers and printers, should include an indication of their locations. This will help users find the shared systems.

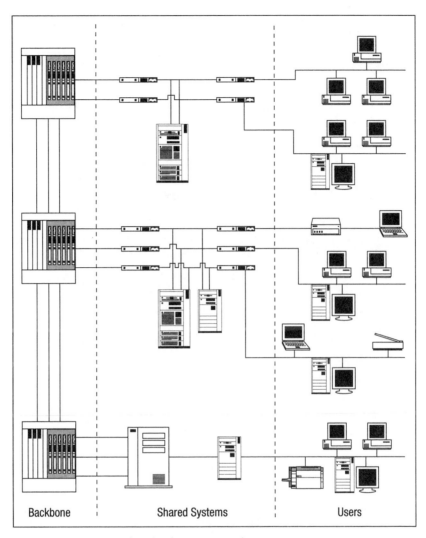

Figure 12.1 Hierarchical infrastructure design.

➤ In an enterprise with a large number of installations, moves, additions, and changes, workstations should not include users' names. Using names would create confusion when a workstation changes hands, and would cause duplication when a user obtains both a laptop and a workstation.

➤ All systems—including routers, bridges, printers, and any other shared resources—should have a naming convention.

➤ Ambiguous naming conventions, such as comic strip character names, should not be used because they tend to confuse users.

➤ Be aware of the naming requirements of the systems that a naming convention will be based on. Many systems exclude special characters, such as the asterisk (*). Domain Name Service (DNS), for example, excludes the use of periods (.) and underscores (_). If a server name will be used as the domain name in DNS, then it should not contain an underscore character.

➤ When you're creating names for organizational units, try to keep them short so that if they are added to a user's account name, they are easy to type.

Examples of naming standards are listed in Table 12.1. This table uses examples for a user account of John T. Robinson, a Hewlett-Packard LaserJet 6P, a workstation, a server in the Phoenix office, and a router in Los Angeles. Incremental numbers are used for multiples of the same type of account in the same area of the directory. So if there are two users with the same account name of JohnR, they become JohnR01 and JohnR02.

Table 12.1   Examples of naming conventions.

Resource Type	Convention Rules	Example For John T. Robinson
User account	First 7 letters of first name + first letter of last name	JohnR
User account	First letter of first name + first 5 letters of last name + incremental numbers	Jrobin01
User account	Three initials (using an "x" if there is no middle name) + incremental numbers	JTR01
Printer	Printer type + hyphen + jack number + hyphen + incremental numbers	HP6P-3141-01
Printer	City + underscore + building + underscore + floor + underscore + printer type	PHX_HQ_3_HP6P
Workstation	PC model + hyphen + jack number	PC330-3141
Workstation	City + hyphen + building + hyphen + PC model	PHX-HQ-PC330
Server	City + hyphen + type of services + hyphen + incremental numbers	PHX-WEB-01
Server	Type of services + underscore + business unit owner + incremental numbers	DATA_ACCTG01
Router	City + hyphen + hierarchy level + incremental numbers	LA-shared01
Router	Hierarchy level (abbreviated) + underscore + nearest airport code + incremental numbers	BK_LAX01

Organizing The Directory Service

You should follow certain basic rules when you're planning and organizing the directory service. These rules are based on the use of a directory service that adheres to the X.500 standard. *X.500* is a standard developed by the ITU-T (International Telecommunications Union—Telecommunication Standardization Sector) to standardize directory architectures. X.500 uses a hierarchy in which each object in the directory uses its location in the hierarchy along with its common name to establish a unique name. An example of an X.500 name is CN=mcraft.OU=Service.O=MicroAge.C=USA. Some directory services are flat and do not support a true hierarchy. In these cases, the rules stated here will probably not apply for upper levels, but the rules for lower levels may be helpful.

Before starting the design, take into account any special requirements that the directory service has. These requirements will drive the design of the directory service and override the other organizational aspects of a hierarchy. For example, each Windows 2000 domain must have a corresponding DNS domain. Domains represent a tree, and are conglomerated into a forest of trees. Each tree contains organizational units in a hierarchical formation. An organizational unit contains the user accounts, groups, and network resource objects.

The very top of the directory service tree should be a single object or a limited number of organization objects. The organization represents the enterprise that is implementing the network system. The top of the directory service remains fairly static, whereas changes are made at the lower levels of the directory service tree.

12

For most of the directory services, the organizational units at the top of the service should mirror the sites separated by wide-area-network links. The reason for this rule is that the directory service is usually distributed across multiple servers. When a piece of the directory containing user accounts is located on a server that is physically close to those users, the users perceive a much faster access to network resources. When an organizational unit spans a wide-area-network link to contain more than one site, the performance for users at both sites becomes degraded.

After the upper part of the hierarchy has been designed, within each site's organizational unit, the lower part of the hierarchy should mirror the company's business units. Using a company organizational chart can help you create this part of the tree. Lower-level organizational units should represent divisions and, below the divisions, workgroups.

You should design the security aspects of the directory service before you add accounts and resources. Security aspects include deciding how the access to files, printers, and other network resources should work. Additionally, if the directory service supports scripts for logging in to the network, the login scripts should be designed at this stage.

The next function is to populate the directory service tree with user accounts, groups, and network resource objects. The flexibility of a directory service is such that an account or a resource can be placed almost anywhere within the hierarchy.

Because the organizational chart is used to design the lower portion of the hierarchy, it follows that the user accounts will be placed in the organizational units representing their workgroups and divisions.

Network resources should be placed in the same organizational units as the users who use them. For example, if a printer is used by the Security group, then the printer should be placed in the Security organization. However, if a printer is used by the Security group and the Fraud group, and they are both in the Operations division, then the printer could be placed in any one of the three organizational units: Fraud, Security, or Operations. As networks grow, the placement of resources can become difficult.

The final design aspect is to provide any logical resources to the hierarchy. Some directory services support the use of aliases or other shortcuts that make network access easier for users. Figure 12.2 depicts a design for a directory service.

Setting Up Administrative And Test Accounts

Administrative accounts and test accounts must be set up before you go forward with a network configuration or installation. Because of the shared nature of directory services, if a directory service is already in place, an administrator account and password are required to install the new systems as part of the directory service.

In order to test the security design, login scripts, and general network access, you need test accounts. A *test account* is simply a user account that is configured in various ways and then tested to ensure that real accounts with the same configuration will be able to access the network resources that they need to. Test accounts are also used to ensure that similarly configured accounts will not be able to access secured resources.

Administrator Accounts

All network operating systems are installed initially with a user account that has full administrative rights to the server or to the network directory service that has been installed with the server. The first server will have this "all-seeing, all-knowing" account installed. However, if changes in the directory service remove or disable this account, a subsequent server installation will not restore it. Table 12.2 lists the default administrative account names for common network operating systems.

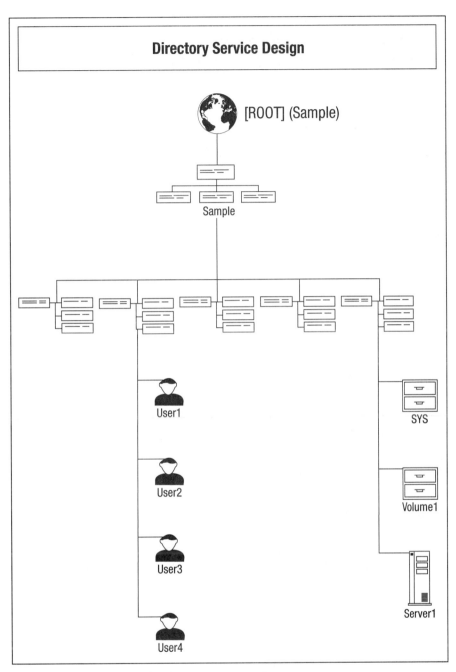

Figure 12.2   Example of a directory service design.

 Be careful to never delete a default Administrative account. Doing so could cause problems later. It is best to disable the account rather than to delete it.

Table 12.2   Administrator account names in various network operating systems.

Network Operating System	Default Administrator Account Name
NetWare 3.x	Supervisor
NetWare 4.x	Admin
NetWare 5.x	Admin
Windows NT 3.5x	Administrator
Windows NT 4.0	Administrator
Unix	Root

Administrative accounts do not have to be the default accounts. Instead, new accounts can be created with full administrative rights to the rest of the directory service, the server, the files, the printers, and other network resources.

Most network operating systems allow multiple levels of administrative access. Some network operating systems provide sample accounts for each administrative access level. Others simply enable the network designer to create the administrative accounts that are required with whatever rights are deemed necessary.

Here's an illustration of an administrator account hierarchy: The Acme company has an internetwork with three sites. Glenda is the MIS Manager. She has an account with full administrative access to every network resource on the Acme internetwork. George is the administrator of the West Branch office. George has full administrative access to the West Branch office network resources, but cannot access East Branch or HQ network resources. George's staff consists of a backup operator, Jolie; the database administrator, Sarah; and the installation administrator, Frank; plus several support people. Jolie, the backup operator, can operate the tape backup systems. She has full access to each server, limited access to the data, and no access to user accounts. Sarah, the database administrator, has full access to the database server database, but no access to other data aside from public data. Frank, the installation administrator, is responsible for installing new systems, moving systems, adding users, and changing accounts. Frank has full access to create user accounts, but can access only public data. The support people have standard user access to the internetwork. This hierarchical system is displayed in Figure 12.3.

To set up a new administrative account, you must use an existing administrative account. The new administrative account is then created as though it were a standard user account. After you create the account, you grant rights to it so that it can have a greater level of access to the internetwork. Depending on the administrative level required for the account, the rights that are granted to the account can vary greatly. Some network operating systems provide groups already created for various administrative levels so that it is easier to grant rights to the accounts.

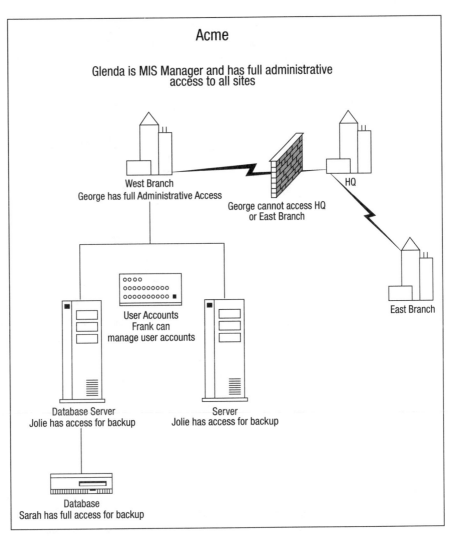

Figure 12.3 A hierarchy of administrative accounts.

Test-User Accounts

If you don't test the network with test accounts, there can be a multitude of problems on the network. For example:

➤ The network can be vulnerable to hackers.

➤ Systems that are available to administrative accounts are not available to user accounts.

➤ Login scripts cause errors.

➤ Rights offer the ability to read files from a directory, but not to change them or add new ones when full access is required to that directory.

A test account is simply a user account in the directory service. Creating a test account is no different from creating a standard network user account. The same procedures apply.

The general process of creating a user account is to begin by logging in to the network operating system as an administrator. The second step is to open the directory service application that manages user accounts. The third step is to follow that application's command sequence to create a new user account. This process can vary from an extreme of adding a line of text to a file on a Unix system to using the GUI (graphical user interface) applications of a Windows NT server. The user account applications are listed in Table 12.3.

Profiles

A *profile* is a template for a user account. Depending on the type of network operating system being used, a profile can be one of several things:

➤ A script that is used to create user accounts with the same basic properties as the template.

➤ A user account that is copied through the user-account management application's copy feature. After being copied, the properties of the account are changed to match the user's specific properties.

➤ A template or profile object that is used to create new user accounts.

Regardless of the type of profile provided, a profile can be an enormous time saver. After creating test accounts and determining the properties for various user types, you can create profiles with the correct properties. The use of profiles prevents errors later on, especially when a large group of user accounts must be created at once.

Groups And User Accounts

Groups are a great time saver when they are implemented correctly. That caveat means that they require a fair amount of planning prior to implementation.

Table 12.3 User account applications.

Network Operating System	User Account Application	Type Of Application
Unix	/etc/passwd	A flat file in which each record represents a user account
NetWare 3.x	Syscon	DOS menu-based application
NetWare 4.x	NetWare Administrator	Windows GUI application
NetWare 5.x	NetWare Administrator	Windows GUI application
Windows NT Server	User Manager For Domains	Windows GUI application

When you create groups, you need to create the user accounts and the group lists, and you need to assign rights to groups.

User Accounts

User accounts are the actual accounts that users will use when they log in to the network. User accounts can be created individually or be based on a profile template to prevent errors. Users will not know what their user accounts are until you give the accounts to them. A good practice for network installations is to provide a short document for users, telling them their account names, their initial passwords, how to change their passwords, and which network resources they can access.

Directory services complicate the names of the user accounts somewhat. A hierarchical directory service based on X.500 will use the entire list of organizational units, from where the user account is placed, up to the root of the hierarchical tree. For example, a user account named JohnR in the SEC organizational unit, which is in the OPS organizational unit, which is in the Acme company, has a name of JohnR.SEC.OPS.ACME. Furthermore, the X.500 standard specifies that the type of object can also be used in the name. A user account type is a common name, or CN. The organizational units are OUs. An organization is an O. The fully qualified name would then be CN=JohnR.OU=SEC.OU=OPS.O=ACME.

Group Objects

12

A group is a collection of user accounts under a single label. An administrator can grant rights to a group one time, and then every member of the group will automatically receive the same rights. A user who is added to the group gains the properties of the group, such as the rights granted to it and the login scripts created for it. A user who is removed from the group loses the properties of the group.

A user account can be made a member of multiple groups at the same time. This arrangement provides a flexible and uncomplicated way to ensure that all users are treated equally for access to an assortment of systems.

In order for you to plan groups, the systems must already be on the network for testing. You should know where users sit and what resources their workgroup will use. Groups can be created for each separate resource, for a group of resources used together, or for a workgroup that accesses the same systems. When you're finished with group design, you should designate the network rights for each job function in the company.

Making Sense Of Groups In Microsoft Windows NT

Most network operating systems contain a single type of group. However, Microsoft Windows NT uses two types of groups: local groups and global groups. This is a confusing concept because Microsoft recommends that rights be granted to local groups, and that global groups be composed of members of local groups, with users being members of global groups.

The confusion is due to the fact that Windows NT is a peer-to-peer network operating system, but acts as a client/server network operating system. Each NT Server contains a server-only (or local) security service, and is a member of a domain-wide (or global) security service that is shared by all servers. The server-only local groups are used to grant access rights to the server's provided resources. Belonging to a global group is the only way that a group of users can be granted access to multiple servers. However, instead of granting access rights to a global group, and granting access rights to a local group for the same resources, the global group can be made a member of the local group and save half the work.

The users who are made members of the global groups are actually global user accounts. They belong to the domain and can be used on multiple servers. A local user account is one that can log on to a standalone NT server that is not acting as a member of a domain. The local user account is rarely used, compared to global user accounts.

Here's an example of a group design in a simple network: The Widget Company has two business units: Production and Sales. There are three servers. Server1 is a Web server that the Sales department manages. Server2 is a file server shared by both departments. Server3 is a highly secure Production server that is restricted from all but a small group of people within the larger Production group. The groups that Widget Company might use are:

➤ **Sales** Granted rights to Server1 and to Server2

➤ **Prod** Granted rights to Server2

➤ **SecProd** Granted rights to Server3

When a new user joins the company, the administrator must find out what the user's position is. Then, the administrator must know which groups grant the rights that the user will need to perform that job function. This is why the groups should be well documented and updated. The administrator can create the user account and add it to the correct groups to automatically grant the user the correct rights to perform the job.

When an existing user account is moved from one position to another, the administrator simply removes the account from the old groups and adds the account to the new groups. Sometimes the user account will not be removed from some of the groups because they are used for both the old and the new job functions.

Rights

File rights are used to grant access to a file or a directory. A different type of right is granted to enable a user or group to perform user-account administration. The administrative design is less of an issue when you're creating user accounts because most network operating systems provide enough basic access for users. Administrative rights are granted by creating administrative-level groups and then adding user accounts to those groups.

Because files and directories are added to the server in a custom structure, the file and directory rights must be designed to match the custom structure.

An Access Control List (ACL) is the name given to the list of total rights granted to a particular user through the group memberships, implied access, and direct explicit access. *Implied access* is the set of rights inherited from an upper-level directory. For example, if a user is granted rights to the SALES directory, then it is implied that the user also has access to SALES\DIR and to all the SALES subdirectories. An inherited or implied access can sometimes be removed from a user account's ACL through a filter or a *no access* right. Each network operating system has a different way of handling inherited access.

Each network operating system has a different set of file rights that can be granted to users. Each version of a network operating system may have an expanded list of rights, too. You must check the documentation of the network operating system to find out what those rights are. Some examples of basic rights are:

➤ **Read-only** The user can open the file and look at the contents, or can execute the file if it is an application. The user cannot change the file or delete it.

➤ **Read-write** The user can open the file, change the file, or execute the file. The user cannot delete the file in some network operating systems, but can in others. The user can create new files in the directory if the right is granted to a directory.

➤ **Delete or erase** The user can delete the file, or delete files in the directory, or delete the directory.

➤ **No access** The user does not have any access to the file or directory. Some network operating systems do not have this right and use a filter instead.

Rights to files are granted through the user-account management application for most network operating systems. Additionally, some network operating

12

systems have command-line applications that can be used to grant rights to files and directories.

Password Protection

Password protection can be set up on one of two levels:

➤ Universally applied

➤ Per user account

A universally applied password-protection scheme is one that enforces password protection rules for each and every account. Usually, these schemes do not affect the accounts that have already been set up. Instead, they affect only accounts set up after the rules have been created.

Password-protection rules may also be enforced on a per-user-account basis for some network operating systems. In this situation, the password-protection scheme is customized for each user. A user-account profile can be used to ensure that each type of user receives the custom password-protection scheme. Table 12.4 shows some of the password-protection rules that can be set up for a network operating system.

A network operating system may or may not require extended password-protection features. For example, as we discussed in Chapter 11, a password that uses a combination of letters and numbers is more secure than one that uses only letters. A password that requires a combination of letters, numbers, and symbols is even more secure. These features might not be supported by the network operating system, but can be written as a network security policy.

A secure network should require a password. It should also force periodic password changes and require that the password is unique or is not the same

Table 12.4 Password-protection options.

Password Option	Function
Require password	The user is required to use a password.
Allow password changes	The user is allowed to change the password.
Periodic password changes	The user is required to change the password on a periodic basis.
Minimum password length	The minimum number of characters must be used for the password.
Unique passwords	The password must be unique, or cannot be reused for a certain number of password changes.
Incorrect passwords	The user has a limit on the number of bad passwords he or she can enter before the network will disable the user account.

one used for several password changes. A minimum password length of six characters should be enforced.

In order to ensure that a hacker is not trying to guess a user's password, the network administrator should enforce intruder detection or lockout features. Most network operating systems include some form of intruder detection. There is a drawback to using a lockout feature, however. When users forget their passwords or inadvertently turn on CAPS LOCK when they log in, they end up locked out of the network. (For an extensive discussion of network security, see Chapter 11.)

Network implementation requires more than a security design. There are more technical aspects, including designing the network servers to access the infrastructure and configuring network servers with the correct protocols.

Protocol Implementation

Protocol implementation can be difficult, because many vendors prefer the implementation of a proprietary protocol. There are all sorts of protocol stacks, including the following:

➤ TCP/IP

➤ IPX (Internetwork Packet Exchange) from Novell NetWare

➤ NetBEUI (NetBIOS Extended User Interface)

➤ DECNet from Digital Equipment Corporation (DEC)

➤ SNA (Systems Network Architecture) from IBM

➤ AppleTalk from Apple Computers

Even when lesser-known stacks are proprietary, their vendors have created methods of using them in heterogeneous internetworks. Determining which protocol to select and use is not a simple decision when so many are available.

The first decision to make is whether to use more than one protocol. It is best to use only a single protocol, but sometimes an internetwork already uses multiple protocols, so when you add a new system, you're forced to use more than one protocol to connect the new system with the other systems. However, when installing a new system, or when redesigning an internetwork, the implementation team should determine the minimum protocols required and remove all extraneous ones.

It used to be that a network operating system governed which protocol could be used. For example, NetWare had to use IPX for full accessibility, and IBM mainframes had to use SNA. But the Internet explosion has expedited a movement toward using a single protocol. Vendors have added the ability to use their network operating systems on the Internet in response to their customers' demand for Internet capabilities. Because the Internet uses the TCP/IP protocol stack, many vendors have incorporated TCP/IP into their network operating systems so that they work as Internet hosts. Therefore, if you're planning a protocol for a network, TCP/IP is a good choice for a single-protocol implementation.

A protocol design should also consider the following:

➤ **Applications** What protocols do the network applications work best with, or require? Will an intranet be implemented?

➤ **Internet connections** Will the network connect to the Internet?

➤ **Other network connections** Will the network be exchanging data with another enterprise's network? What form will this data take? What protocols does the other network use?

➤ **Hosts** Are mainframe or minicomputer hosts being used? Have they been updated to use TCP/IP? If not, is a gateway used to access the host so that a routed protocol can be used? If there's no gateway, is an encapsulation method possible for the nonroutable protocol?

➤ **Growth plans** What are future plans for the internetwork?

➤ **Routers and switches** What protocols do the routers and switches support? Is replacement of the routers or switches possible?

➤ **Clients** What clients are used on the workstations to access the network? Will replacement of any existing client software be part of the implementation?

Regardless of which protocol is selected and implemented on the internetwork, the final protocol implementation must be able to support the network operating systems and the infrastructure that is in place or planned.

IP Addressing Configuration

TCP/IP has several options that need to be configured on the internetwork. These options are:

➤ DHCP or static addressing

➤ The subnet mask scheme

➤ A domain naming convention

➤ A DNS or HOSTS file

➤ A WINS or LMHOSTS file

DHCP (Dynamic Host Configuration Protocol) provides dynamic IP addressing to workstations on the network. DHCP reduces the need for administration of addresses. Static IP addresses are those that are assigned to each network device individually. The use of static addresses can cause duplicates and errors. Servers, however, should always be assigned static IP addresses because a dynamic address may cause problems when a workstation tries to access the server.

Subnet masks should be defined before you implement the network infrastructure equipment. The subnet masks determine which part of an IP address is the network segment's address. Infrastructure equipment provides the boundaries for the network segments and requires those segments' addresses.

The domain name is required for the internetwork. If there is a host naming convention, it will be required to determine the hostnames of any new network servers or workstations.

The use of DNS (Domain Name Service) and WINS (Windows Internet Name Service) will be required for handling name resolution on new network servers or workstations. If DNS is not used, the alternative solution is to use a HOSTS file to resolve IP addresses to hostnames. If WINS is not used, the other solution is to use an LMHOSTS file to resolve IP addresses to NetBIOS names.

IP addressing information should be gathered before you install a network. At a minimum, the network installers must know the IP addresses and subnet masks for critical systems such as:

➤ DNS hosts

➤ WINS hosts

➤ Mainframe hosts

➤ Proxy servers

➤ Network servers

Standard Operating Procedures

During the preparation for the network implementation, the installers will discover some processes and procedures that work best for the enterprise and for the technology on site. These procedures should be documented and tested for use as standard operating procedures.

For example, one of the most common procedures is the management of user accounts (creating, changing, and deleting them). During the network implementation, the installers may create a special administrative account that can create, change, or delete user accounts. The first thing to document is that this particular administrative account should be used. The installers may also decide to require a waiting period after a user-account deletion is requested in case the account can be renamed for the user's replacement. A network operating system may include the capability to disable an account, and the procedures to disable the account would then become documented standards.

OVERVIEW OF THE NETWORK OPERATING SYSTEM INSTALLATION

Each network operating system, regardless of the version, follows a general installation process. Installation procedures will differ somewhat, depending not only on that particular version of the network operating system but also on the configuration required. The configuration of the network operating system should have been determined during the planning phase.

Older operating systems use a manual process of preparing a hard drive for installation and transferring the operating system to that hard drive. Newer operating systems have automated installation programs to guide the installer through the installation.

Each network operating system has a unique installation procedure. Regardless of which network operating system is used, the same basic information about the server and the network will apply to the installation. The general process, regardless of the network operating system, is as follows:

1. Gather information about the server hardware. Hardware information includes the types of adapters used, the types of hard drives, the interrupts set for the adapters, and any other relevant information. Additionally, it is a good practice to document the serial number and any revision numbers for each hardware component. Most of this information can be observed in the BIOS program on the server.

2. Get the latest BIOS update for the server hardware.

3. Install any adapters and internal components into the server hardware.

4. Configure the BIOS.

5. Update the BIOS.

6. Put the network operating system CD-ROM in the drive and begin the installation. Make sure that you follow the configuration that was decided on before the installation.

7. Install any network applications according to their instructions.

8. Set up a new file directory structure for data.

9. Copy any data to the server.

10. Add printers and configure printing.

11. Create user accounts, using the naming convention previously determined.

12. Create group accounts.

13. Add users to the appropriate groups.

14. Grant users and groups the appropriate security rights.

15. Update workstations with new client access software.

16. Perform quality assurance testing to make sure that the server and workstations, accounts and security, applications and data are all working the way that they were intended.

COMPATIBILITY ISSUES

Installation of a network operating system can be a nerve-wracking experience when things do not go smoothly. A problem might be due to a hardware incompatibility, software usage, incorrect information, or wrong versions of drivers.

Cabling

When the server will not connect, check the cable jacks. If you're using a modem to connect, the modem cable may be plugged into a digital jack. If you're using a network interface card, the network cable may be plugged into an analog jack.

Unshielded twisted-pair wiring is used for both analog and digital wiring. The difference in the wiring is nearly undetectable. Not only that, but many jacks are made to support the two types of connectors: RJ-11, which is used for analog lines; and RJ-45, which is used for digital lines.

When a modem cable is plugged into a digital jack, the modem will not dial or connect. The modem software will typically return an error that says there is no dial tone. If a network cable is plugged into an analog line, the network simply does not connect, but there is no error message. The confusion of plugging the wrong cable into a jack is due to the use of standardized cabling that can support either an RJ-11 or an RJ-45 connector.

An RJ-11 connector is smaller than an RJ-45. An RJ-11 connector can have either four or six conductors—most often, four, which are used for two pairs of wires. The red/green pair of wires is used for voice and data, and the black/white pair is used for low-voltage signals.

An RJ-45 connector is wider than an RJ-11, but mostly because it must support eight conductors for four pairs of wires. The way that the conductors are wired depends on the protocol specification and the type of cabling. For example, a standard Category 5 cable uses a different set of pin-outs than does a "straight-through" Category 5 cable. The straight-through cable is used for connecting two network nodes without using a hub, switch, or repeater, whereas the standard Category 5 cable must be used with a hub, switch, or repeater.

Cable Segments

When connecting to the network, if a cable exceeds the maximum length identified for the Physical-layer cable specification, the signal will attenuate. *Attenuation* means that the signal voltage becomes reduced, and it becomes difficult to determine whether a signal represents a 1 bit or a 0 bit. The maximum length of cable is equivalent to the total length of the cable from the port of the hub to the patch panel to the network panel to the drop cable to the network interface card.

For example, a 10BaseT cable is 100 meters long between the patch panel and the cable jack. Because the drop cable between the jack and the workstation is 3 meters long, and the patch cable between the patch panel and the hub is 1.5 meters long, the total length is 104.5 meters. The signal beyond 100 meters is degraded and unreliable, which means that either there will be network errors or the node will not be able to connect to the network. Exceeding the 100-meter threshold does not mean that connectivity does not occur; however, it does mean that you may have intermittent problems. This scenario assumes that the hub is an active hub. A passive hub does not repeat signals, so the total cable length of all cables connected to the passive hub cannot exceed the maximum cable length for the protocol specification. Table 12.5 lists the cable length thresholds for some standard cable types.

ENVIRONMENT AND THE NETWORK

One of the factors that a network designer has to consider is the type of environment the network is being placed in. All sorts of environmental factors can destroy data, and even hardware components, on a network. Destruction of significant data and hardware components is considered a disaster for most production enterprise networks. Disaster recovery is a concern for any enterprise, but prevention of disasters is even more beneficial.

Table 12.5 Cabling standards.

Protocol Specification	Cable Type	Cable Length
10Base5	Coax	500 meters
10Base2	Coax	185 meters
10BaseT	Category 5	100 meters
10BaseFP	Fiber	1,000 meters
10BaseFB	Fiber	2,000 meters
10BaseFL	Fiber	1,000 meters
100BaseTX	Category 5	100 meters
100BaseT4	Category 3, Category 4, Category 5	100 meters

Prevention of a disastrous loss of data and equipment means that the network installer should identify potential hazards before installation and then make appropriate decisions based on those hazards.

The installer should look for any electric or magnetic equipment that could cause electromagnetic interference with cabling or hardware. Electromagnetic interference causes voltage irregularities so that the data traveling through cables and hardware becomes unstable. This means that the installer should not place cabling near fluorescent lighting, TVs, radios, or speakers, because they are known to create electromagnetic interference (EMI).

Power surges are another problem for a network. A power surge can permanently damage network equipment or can simply wreak havoc on it for a short while. Networks in areas that are frequented by thunderstorms, hurricanes, tornadoes, and monsoons are all at risk for a power surge. A surge suppresser or an uninterruptible power supply (UPS) can prevent power surges from damaging network equipment.

Heat creep is a common name given to the effect of humidity and heat on hardware components. In most cases, the problem is not a constant heat, but is more of a thermal shock. Each time the hardware heats up, components expand. As they cool, the parts contract. After this cycle occurs several times, the components can contract to the point that their nodes no longer connect and the components stop working.

Heat is an enemy of computer components. That is why computers are equipped with fans and heat sinks to keep them cool. A processor will fail completely if it gets too hot.

12

Airflow is the number-one necessity for a cooling solution. Keep network servers cool by providing sufficient airflow in the network server room. It is common practice to hide a server in a small, locked room or closet. These closets tend to be airless and to trap heat. A server is far more likely to fail in a small closet than it is in a large room, unless the closet is equipped with appropriate airflow. Racks should be equipped with fans to ensure that airflow can cool the equipment.

CHAPTER SUMMARY

Installing a network involves a significant amount of planning. The network implementation follows a general process of five steps:

1. Organize the resources.
2. Plan the standards.
3. Plan the implementation.

4. Test the design.

5. Deploy the network.

The two planning phases are planning the network standards and planning the implementation. The network standards might already be in place when the network operating system is installed. If that is the case, the standards should be reviewed and validated. Implementation planning is the process of deciding the tasks needed for the installation and the completion dates for each of them.

When you're planning the network infrastructure equipment, use a hierarchical structure. The hierarchy includes the backbone, the shared systems, and the users' workgroups. The network designer should start with the backbone, then design each shared-systems area, and finally design the users' systems area.

The directory service is the organization of the accounts and resources directory. Many directory services are based on the X.500 standard, which uses a hierarchical organization, with subordinate organizational units and with resources placed throughout the tree.

A network installation can be more easily documented and maintained when a naming convention is used. A naming convention provides the rules for naming user accounts and network resources, such as servers and printers.

Depending on the type of network operating system, there may be multiple levels of administrative access. When you're installing a network, the administrator's account name and password are required. After the network is installed, new administrative accounts with different levels of administrative access can be created. Test accounts should also be created for use in testing network access for user accounts.

Groups are a method of simplifying security on a network. An administrator can place user accounts in a group and then grant rights to the group. The user accounts that are members of the group automatically receive the group's rights.

Password protection is another level of security that can prevent unauthorized access to network resources. A password-protection policy can require a minimum number of characters in the password and can lock out an account if the network operating system supports lockout detection.

Protocol selection and implementation depend on the interoperability needs of the network. The protocol, or protocols, used should support the network systems, hosts, and applications installed. The most universally implemented protocol is TCP/IP. If you're implementing TCP/IP, you need to gather the network address scheme, subnet masks, and IP addresses of essential systems so that they can be used when you configure TCP/IP.

The testing and deployment portion of a network implementation will have the best information about the procedures and processes that work on the new network. These procedures can be documented for standard operations.

Network operating system installations vary widely in their individual step-by-step procedures, but overall, the same method of installation can be used. An installer should prepare the hardware and BIOS for the server, and then install the network operating system. After that, network applications can be installed, a file structure can be created, and the directory of user accounts can be created. The workstations and printers can be deployed, as well as the final security elements, such as groups and rights. The final step is to perform a quality-assurance check to ensure that the final structure meets the expectations. If there are problems connecting to the network, the cables should be checked to ensure that they are plugged into the correct jacks.

An ongoing concern is the prevention of data loss. The administrator should review the placement of equipment, ensuring that it is kept away from environmental elements that may cause harm, such as electromagnetic equipment, heat, and humidity.

REVIEW QUESTIONS

1. What should be decided during the planning phase? [Select all that apply]
   a. Directory service design
   b. Naming convention
   c. IP addressing
   d. Password-protection policy

2. What section of the infrastructure plan includes the users' workstations?
   a. Backbone
   b. Internet
   c. Shared systems area
   d. Users' systems area

3. What is not included in the directory services planning?
   a. Internet connectivity
   b. User account placement
   c. Hierarchical structure of the tree
   d. Groups

12

4. Felix found a document that states "All network server names shall begin with the three-letter abbreviation of the city in which the servers are located and end with an incremental number." What type of document did Felix find?

   a. Infrastructure backbone design

   b. Standard operating procedures

   c. Naming conventions

   d. Password-protection policy

5. Brianna wants her network administrators to be able to create, delete, and manage user accounts, but not to access the users' data. What should Brianna implement in her network planning?

   a. Naming convention

   b. Administrative levels

   c. Password-protection policy

   d. Installation procedures for the network operating system

6. During a network installation, George wants to determine whether the security access design he created will work. What should George use?

   a. Groups

   b. Administrative levels

   c. Test accounts

   d. Installation procedures for the network operating system

7. George's test accounts worked correctly. What should he implement to ensure that the user accounts work the same way as the test accounts?

   a. Naming convention

   b. Administrative levels

   c. Installation procedures for the network operating system

   d. Profiles

8. Chris has a network with 250 users. In this network, 100 of the users need access to Server1, 200 users need access to Server2, and 185 users need access to Server3. What can Chris implement to simplify the process of granting access to servers?

   a. Groups

   b. Password-protection policy

   c. User accounts

   d. IP addressing standards

9. Dan creates a password-protection policy for his network. Justine reviews the policy and asks that one of the items be changed because it doesn't offer enough security. If the following are all rules of Dan's original password-protection policy, which one should be changed to tighten security?

   a. Passwords must be changed every 45 days.

   b. A password must have at least 7 characters.

   c. One of the characters of the password must be a number.

   d. No user account is required to have a password.

10. Which protocol can be implemented on a network that consists of 4 OS/2 Warp workstations, 2 Windows 2000 Servers, 2 Macintosh workstations, 6 Windows 98 workstations, 1 DOS workstation, 182 Windows NT workstations, and 14 NetWare 5.x servers?

    a. SNA

    b. TCP/IP

    c. AppleTalk

    d. IPX

11. What type of addressing information should be gathered before you install a network server with TCP/IP? [Choose the two best answers]

    a. The internal server IPX address

    b. The subnet mask

    c. The IP address

    d. The AppleTalk zone

12

12. When you're installing a network operating system, which step should occur before you run the installation program?

    a. Configuring the file structure

    b. Preparing the hardware and BIOS

    c. Creating the user accounts

    d. Installing the network applications

13. Janet documented a quick and accurate way to install a workstation client-access program. What can this documentation be used for after the installation is complete?

    a. Directory-service design document

    b. Naming-convention document

    c. Standard operating procedures

    d. Addressing configuration document

14. What can happen if you plug a modem cable into a network jack?

   a. The modem will connect directly with the network.

   b. The modem will cause the network to fail.

   c. The modem will break and need replacement.

   d. The modem software will display an error message stating that there is no dial tone.

15. Brenda has had problems with a workstation that frequently drops connection to the network. She pulls out the office cabling diagram and finds that the cable is placed close to a fluorescent light, passes through four wooden studs, and is clamped to a beam using a lightweight plastic tie. What could be the cause of the problems?

   a. The fluorescent light is causing EMI.

   b. The wooden studs are interrupting the signal.

   c. The beam is causing heat creep.

   d. The plastic tie is causing electromagnetic interference.

HANDS-ON PROJECTS

The following hands-on projects review the procedures used to create user accounts on a Windows NT 4 Server and to install Novell NetWare. Project 12.1 details how to create a Windows NT Domain Administrator account and how to apply various security access rights to an account. Project 12.2 shows how to install Novell NetWare 5.

Project 12.1

The default administrator account for a Windows NT Domain is named Administrator. This account, or another account that is a member of the Domain Admins group, must be used to create administrator and user accounts for the domain.

To create a user account:

1. Log on to a Windows NT primary domain controller, or to a backup domain controller, as the domain administrator account.

2. Click on Start | Programs.

3. Select Administrative Tools.

4. Click on User Manager For Domains. The User Manager For Domains tool creates the user and group accounts for the NT domain. (Do not confuse this tool with User Manager. The User Manager tool creates user and group accounts for the local computer, whether it is a member server or a workstation.)

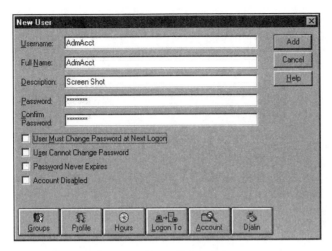

Figure 12.4   The New User dialog box.

5. Click on File | New User. The New User dialog box will appear (see Figure 12.4).

6. The Username box is the name of the user account. This first account will be an administrator account, so type a name that is appropriate for it in the Username box. The name "Administrator" is already taken, so a name like "AdmAcct" could be used instead.

7. Type a password in the Password box, and then type it a second time in the Confirm Password box. This account is now a standard user account.

8. Click on the Groups button.

9. Select the Domain Admins global group, and click on the Add button. The user account is now a member of the Domain administrators. The Domain Admins group is, by default, made a member of the Administrators group on each domain controller and member computer. Therefore, the Domain Admins group can control every computer in the domain. Note that there are other groups that the user can be made a member of. The groups provide the administrative levels for the domain. Backup operators are granted the rights required to perform backups on the NT computers. Print operators are granted the rights required to manage printing within the domain.

10. If the hours that the user is allowed to log on to the network should be limited, click on Hours and remove the hours that the user should not be online. This feature is useful for backing up files. Backups have difficulty with files that are open. When users are forced off the system, the backup can back up frequently used files, which are more likely to be needed if there is a loss of data.

12

11. Extended individual rights can be added by clicking on the Policies menu and then selecting User Rights.

12. The User Rights Policy dialog box will appear (see Figure 12.5). Check the box for Show Advanced User Rights. This option shows all rights that can be granted to an account for systems and user management, but does not include actual file rights.

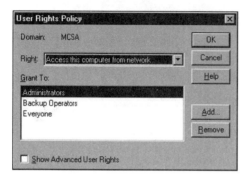

Figure 12.5   The User Rights Policy dialog box.

13. Select the right to act as part of the operating system. This right enables a user account to be used by applications that need to interact with the operating system itself but have access only through a user account. This right is used by Microsoft Exchange Server service accounts and some other network application administrative accounts.

14. In order to assign file rights, you can use Windows Explorer. Right-click on files and select Sharing to grant or remove access to any file or directory.

Project 12.2

This project gets into the guts of a network operating system installation. Novell NetWare 5 is an enterprise-capable network operating system. It does require design before a production installation. This installation, however, is predesigned to create a test server that can be used to try other networking features on.

To install Novell NetWare 5:

1. Before you begin to install the network operating system, you must prepare the hardware. If there are any required components that are not installed in the server, then connect the network interface card to the network.

2. Get the latest BIOS updates for the server, and install them according to the instructions. This step can prevent errors. When you're updating the BIOS, write down the values of the ports, slot numbers, interrupts, and DMA for the hard drive, the CD-ROM drive, and the network interface card. These values will be needed later.

3. Create the DOS partition on the hard drive. The DOS partition must be version 3.3 or later. Boot the server with a DOS system disk. This disk must have the FDISK and FORMAT commands on it, as well as config.sys and autoexec.bat files that can launch the CD-ROM drive from DOS.

4. Type "fdisk" and follow the menu to create a 500MB active partition on the hard drive. Make sure that there is at least 500MB of free space for the server installation.

5. Type "format c: /s" and press Enter. This command assumes that C: is the letter of the hard drive. Copy the config.sys and autoexec.bat files to the C: drive.

6. Reboot the server from the new C: partition.

7. Insert the NetWare 5 CD into the CD-ROM drive.

8. Change to the CD-ROM drive by typing the letter of the CD-ROM drive, such as D:, and pressing Enter.

9. Type "install" and press Enter.

10. Select the country, keyboard, and code page that are appropriate for your region. The default settings are appropriate for most U.S. installations. Go on to the next screen.

11. The installation will detect most hardware storage devices. If the hard drive is not detected, you must supply the hardware manufacturer's device driver for NetWare. Verify that any values for the hard drive on the screen match the ones that were set in the BIOS. Go on to the next screen.

12. The network interface card is loaded and configured in the next screen. The NetWare 5 installation program will detect the card, or you can supply the driver. Verify that the values in this screen match the ones that were set in the BIOS.

13. Next, the installation program will set up the NetWare partition. This is the hard-drive partition that will contain the NetWare file system. Create one partition that is at least 500MB.

14. Next, configure volumes on the server. NetWare 5 requires a SYS volume for the system files. It is recommended that production servers have two or more volumes: the SYS volume; and other volumes for data and applications. For this installation, use the defaults, and create a single SYS volume for the entire space of the NetWare partition (500MB).

15. The next screen is the first graphical screen of the installation, and it asks for the server properties. Provide the server name. Remember that this name must be unique and between 2 and 47 characters long. Click on Next.

12

16. Select the IP protocol for the next screen. Provide an IP address and subnet mask, and provide the IP address of the default router for that segment, if there is one. Click on Next.

17. Select your time zone from the list, and check whether or not to allow daylight savings time. Click on Next.

18. The next screen allows you to select an existing NDS tree to install into, or to create a new NDS tree. For this exercise, we will create a new NDS tree. Select that option and click on Next.

19. Type the new NDS tree name, the organization, and the Admin password in the New Tree dialog box; then, click on Next.

20. The server checks to make sure that the NDS tree name is unique, sets the time, and starts NDS. After that, the NDS summary screen is displayed. Accept the screen and go to the next one.

21. The License screen appears. If a server license is not supplied, the server will install a runtime version allowing two users. Go on to the next screen.

22. You will be prompted for optional applications next. Select all that you want to have installed by checking their options. Then, click on Next.

23. The final summary is displayed. The server has just been installed.

## CHAPTER THIRTEEN

NETWORK COMPONENTS

After Reading This Chapter And Completing The Exercises, You Will Be Able To:

➤ Understand print servers, their types, and their functions

➤ Explain the differences between the three main printer types

➤ Determine the best modem for your network and configure it properly

➤ Explain SCSI technology and its related terms

➤ Understand some of the uses of routers and bridges

➤ Identify UART and its purpose

➤ Explain the different types of power problems that a network might encounter

➤ Determine the best method of power management for your network

➤ Identify the types of tape devices and their technologies

➤ Identify the types of SCSI connectors and their differences

Many hardware components can improve the functions and efficiency of a network. The benefits of these components are often overlooked due to a lack of understanding of their purposes and functions. Many networks allow users to "get by" while not really providing the type of service they are capable of. Your ability to understand and implement the correct devices to transform this type of network to one that can provide fast, efficient service to its users will take you from the area of network administration to network analysis and design. Your value to your employer and your income will both be greatly increased.

In this chapter, we will cover a variety of network hardware components and peripherals that are important to the functionality, structure, and security of your network:

➤ Printers

➤ Print servers

➤ Modems

➤ Tape devices

➤ SCSI devices

➤ Routers, brouters, and bridges

➤ Power control devices

➤ Connectors and adapters

Network administrators should know about all of these devices. Knowing how
and when to use these devices will allow you to transform a network that
merely performs into a solid, well-protected network that serves the needs of its
current users and provides for future growth.

PRINTERS

Various printers on the market today are available for network use. These have
evolved from simple text-based printers, which were attached to personal
computers serving mainly as word processors and report writers, to the high-
speed graphic printer/copier/fax machines that we use today. Printers today can
be grouped as follows:

➤ Dot-matrix printers

➤ Ink jet printers

➤ Laser printers

Dot-Matrix Printers

Dot-matrix printers were some of the first high-speed printers developed for
the data processing market. Patterned after the simple typewriter, these printers
use a print head to strike the inked ribbon onto paper. Printer technology has
since advanced with laser and ink jet printers, but the dot-matrix printer has a
number of features that have yet to be duplicated by the laser technologies. In
addition to being inexpensive, dot-matrix printers benefit from the way they
print. Because of the impact involved in printing, dot-matrix printers can
handle forms that require multiple copies (as with carbon paper), something
that laser and ink jet printers can't accomplish.

Dot-matrix printers usually come in 9- or 24-pin models. A higher number of
pins produces a sharper, clearer letter image. The pins are arranged vertically
and numbered from top to bottom. As the print head moves across the paper,
the pins fire in the numeric order needed to form the desired character. Figure
13.1 shows the dots needed to form the common characters X and Y. The pins
strike an inked ribbon, forcing a dot onto the paper. Nine-pin dot-matrix
printers have became even more clear because of technology that allows two
passes over the same spot. It wasn't, however, until 24-pin print heads became
available that true letter-quality printing with dot-matrix printers became
possible.

Although these seem like simple devices, dot-matrix printers require an advanced
set of technologies. The paper must be accurately moved and stopped at a high,

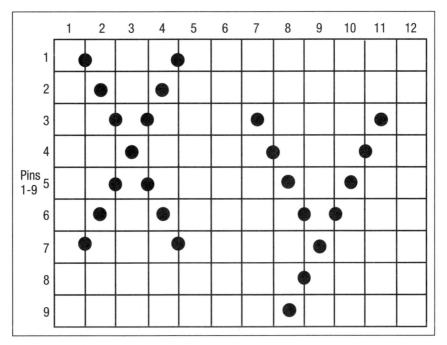

Figure 13.1   Dot-matrix printer impact.

constant speed. The mainboard keeps track of the position of the print head and the paper. Concurrently, the mainboard controls the flow of data from the computer and decodes the data, separating the printable characters from the control characters embedded in the datastream. The printable character codes are then fed into the character generator ROM (CG_ROM), where the pattern of the matrix is formed and forwarded to the printer. A CPU on the main logic board controls all this. The speed of the printer is rated in characters per second (CPS).

Ink Jet Printers

Dot-matrix and ink jet printers are similar. They use the same methods to move the paper and the print heads. The only big difference is the method used to put the ink on the paper. Whereas the dot-matrix printer strikes an inked ribbon, the ink jet printer squirts liquid ink onto the paper.

Ink jet printers use one of two methods to eject the ink from the print head: thermal and piezoelectric. The thermal method heats the ink and creates a bubble that splashes onto the page (hence the term "bubble jet printer"). The thermal method can result in foggy characters. (Figure 13.2 compares a bubble jet dot with an ink jet dot.) The thermal method can also cause the print head to become clogged and require more frequent replacement. In contrast, the print head in a piezoelectric system reacts to voltage that flexes out a spot much cleaner and neater than the thermal counterpart.

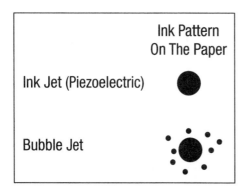

Figure 13.2   Ink jet dot versus bubble jet dot.

Laser Printers

Laser printers use a technology known as electrophotography. Here's how it works: An image is placed on an electrically charged surface. An opposite charge is used to transfer that image from the charged surface to a piece of paper. The image is then bonded to the paper to make it permanent. This is the same method that copy machines have used for a long time. The only difference is that printers use a different method to acquire the image they transfer. Copy machines use a series of lenses and mirrors to bounce light off a document. Laser printers use a low-powered laser beam. They acquire their image by using photoconductive materials that are either conductors in the light or insulators in the dark. The laser beam shines upon a rotating drum and negates the electrocharge in locations where the image is being copied. When the drum then passes over the toner, it either attracts or repels the toner, depending on the charge in a particular location on the drum. The drum then passes onto the paper, which has a positive charge and attracts the negatively charged toner from the drum. An image composed of loose toner is now on the paper. The paper then passes between two rollers that heat and permanently fix the image onto the paper. Next, the drum is recharged, and the process repeats.

PRINT SERVERS

In addition to allowing users to share files and applications, networks allow users to share printers and other peripherals. Workgroups were designed so that many users could share printers, and switch boxes allowed more than one printer to be connected to a single computer. For networks to give all users access to all printers, however, a print server is needed. A print server is a device that allows each printer to function as an independent node on the network, accessible by all computers and capable of acting independently of any particular workstation. Print servers provide the memory and network attachment needed to eliminate the printer's dependence on an attached workstation.

As technology has evolved, print servers have become capable of providing:

➤ Multiprotocol printing

➤ Simultaneous support for multiple operating systems

➤ Automatic language switching between PCL and PostScript

➤ Multiple media connectors

➤ Simultaneous printing on multiple ports

➤ Remote access dial-in support for managing printing services

➤ Protocol-independent operation

The print server is now another software-managed, multiport device, housed in the network-wiring closet, along with the hubs, switches, and routers.

The control of printers is always an important part of an administrator's function. Knowing how and when to use print servers can make that job a lot easier.

MODEMS

A modem—short for "modulator/demodulator"—is a communications device that enables a computer to transmit information over a standard telephone line. Because computers are digital and standard telephone lines are analog, the modem is needed to convert digital signals to analog signals, and vice versa. When transmitting data, modems modulate the computer's digital signals into analog signals that can be carried over the telephone network. When receiving data, a modem demodulates analog signals into digital signals that the computer processor can understand.

13

The definition of the process is simple, but the method used to accomplish this is not as simple. The modulation process begins with a constant signal called a *carrier*, which carries the load of the digital information by mixing in an electrical signal that controls the transfer process. It is a signal of constant amplitude and frequency. Over this carrier, the signal passes across the wire of a dial-up or a leased-line connection, to the demodulator, where the carrier is then stripped away and the encoded information is returned to its original form.

As with many computer devices, modems come with their own set of terminology. Some terms have been used so freely and often incorrectly that they have lost their real meanings. This is particularly true with regard to the newer 56Kbps technologies that have entered the market. We'll explain some of these terms next so you'll be able to choose the best modem for your needs.

Baud Rate

Named after a French telegraphy expert named J.M. Baudot, *baud* is used to define speed or rate of transfer. Technically speaking, the baud rate is the unit of measurement used to describe the number of state changes taking place in the carrier wave in one second. Although it is good to use for comparing the data transfer speed of one device to another's, strictly speaking, one baud is not the same as a one-bit-per-second transfer speed. The actual transfer speed can be more or less, depending on the method of modulation used.

56K Technology

The race to provide 56Kbps technology ended with two finishers, the x.2 technology and the K56flex technology. U.S. Robotics developed its modems using the x.2 technology in 1997 and began an aggressive marketing campaign to make it the standard. At the same time, rivals Rockwell and Lucent introduced their contender, the K56flex modem. Both versions succeeded in providing what many had believed was not possible: They can transfer at speeds up to 53Kbps for receiving data, the maximum allowed by FCC regulations, and at speeds up to 31.2Kbps for sending data. These technologies were well received by the market. They had only one drawback—they couldn't communicate with each other.

V.90 56K Standard

In February 1998, the International Telecommunications Union (ITU), a committee of the United Nations, determined and ratified a standard that could be used worldwide for 56K modem technology. This standard, known as the V.90 56K standard, has replaced both of its predecessors in the new-modems market. Many of the previously sold modems using the proprietary technologies are still in use today. They may be working well while communicating with their exact counterparts, but they are not compatible with the V.90 technology unless the firmware has been flashed to meet the V.90 standards.

Handshaking

Handshaking is the initial communication between two modems. In this initial contact, the two modems transfer information and agree upon which method they will use to govern the rules or protocol they will communicate with. Let's look a little closer at the process that two modems use to communicate over standard telephone lines.

First, the calling modem dials out and the receiving modem answers. It immediately sends out a modem tone notifying the caller that it is a modem so the calling modem does not hang up. The answering modem then sends out a tone or pitch that sounds to the human ear like a lot of static. This signal is the carrier tones we referred to earlier. If the calling modem does not recognize the carrier tone and respond, the answering modem tries another tone until the two modems establish one they can agree upon. When the calling modem recognizes and responds to the answering modem carrier, they enter the equalization stage, in which they establish the communication speed and data-compression method. Next, they establish Request To Send (RTS) and Clear To Send (CTS) pins, which will be used throughout the session to control the transmissions. Then, the noise stops and data transmission begins.

COM Ports

Modems are serial devices and therefore use COM ports to communicate between the device and the main board. Most network administrators have developed a good understanding of COM ports early in their careers. The proper installation of a modem requires the standard information, such as IRQ (interrupt request), I/O address, and COM port number.

Hayes Compatible

One of the early leaders in modem technology was the Hayes Company. It set the standard early on for the technology and for the command set that the modems were driven by. Although Hayes has since been replaced as industry leader by such companies as 3Com (U.S. Robotics) and Rockwell, its legacy still remains in the widely used command set that begins with the two-character sequence, AT, called *attention characters*. The phrase *Hayes compatible*, once a standard in the industry when referring to modems, has vanished from the computing world, along with the 14.4K modems they made famous.

Data Compression

Some modems can provide data compression before data transfer. This feature can vastly increase the amount of usable data received using the same baud rate. This technology and error-correction technology can be very useful in transferring large amounts of data over standard POTS (Plain Old Telephone System) lines. This technology does not increase the rate of transfer over the serial interface; it only increases the amount of usable data that is received. The current 56K technologies do not address or implement data compression.

UART

The Universal Asynchronous Receiver/Transmitter—commonly referred to as the UART—is the chip responsible for communications carried over a serial port. The most advanced version is the Intel 16650, a 16-bit chip with a 32-byte buffer capable of transfer speeds up to 230Kbps, sufficient for any modem-over-COM-port connection in use today. The UART chip is located either on the motherboard or on the interface card of the serial device—in this case, the modem. The UART chip is responsible for the following:

➤ Converting parallel input from a program/application to serial form for transmission

➤ Adding the start, stop, and parity bits to the byte

➤ Maintaining the status of the serial port by monitoring the appropriate control pins

➤ Controlling the timing for the transmissions

➤ Converting the serial transmission to parallel form and then passing the output on to the program/application

The technical information on the working of the UART chip is too broad a topic for this book. What you need to know is that UART chips can often reside both on the motherboard and on the modem's interface card and that the two UART chips can conflict and create potentially baffling problems. Due to this conflict, it's often necessary to disable the onboard COM port when you're attempting to install an internal modem.

RS-232

The cables that attach the modem to the serial port are based on the RS-232 standard. The RS-232 standard defines the particular functions assigned to the wires in a serial cable. These wires connect to devices using the standard DB-9 and DB-25 connectors. The UART controls the flow of signals to and from the serial ports, using the information it receives from the devices attached to this RS-232 cable. (We will cover the pin-outs of the DB-9, DB-25, and RS-232 connectors later in this chapter.)

TAPE DRIVES

The need for file-storage space has grown tremendously over the past decade, and it's likely to continue to grow at an even faster rate. This growth has challenged the computer industry to find methods both to store information in offline locations for later retrieval and to duplicate data for nightly system backups. The tape backup and storage technology has continued to evolve to meet these needs. Whenever hard-disk storage space became available, programs quickly appeared with the capability to produce data to fill them. The tape storage industry not only had to find methods to store these large volumes of data, but also to provide methods for a speedy read-and-write process.

Although the earlier IDE technology still provides an affordable solution for the average user, the DDS technologies provide the functionality needed for the fast pace of modern business. Let's take a look at these two tape-storage technologies.

IDE Drives

The Integrated Disk Electronics (IDE) drive is the most common type of disk drive in use in personal computers today. The controller of an IDE drive is integrated into the device for maximum speed and performance. This technology is also used in tape-storage devices. IDE devices are less expensive than their SCSI counterparts, but provide slower data transfer. This slow rate is acceptable with storage space of a gigabyte or less. However, when you need to back up five or more gigabytes on a regular basis, as is the case in most businesses today, an IDE tape-backup device can be to be too slow. It is still effective and reliable for tape backup and storage, and its low cost is a reason for many companies to accept the lower performance levels. The IDE tape-backup device can be integrated into the onboard IDE controller and can be connected to the same cable as the disk drives. There is no need for a special adapter, for configuration of device IDs, or for termination settings. (There is plenty of more detailed information available on IDE controllers and devices, and most of you should be familiar with the installation and use of them.)

Travan Drives

Travan technology—a form of IDE technology—has evolved to meet the need for more storage space and faster performance. Available in TR-1, TR-3, and TR-4 formats, Travan technology is still an efficient, low-cost data-backup method for smaller PCs and for laptops. Travan tape drives are available in a wide range of interfaces, such as floppy, parallel, ATAPI, or SCSI. The technology provides adequate error protection for this midlevel performance option. The current limitation on storage capacity is around 8GB. A backup strategy for this size storage should include overnight scheduling. This is not a high-speed solution, but the cost compared to other methods does make it an attractive alternative for small to medium size businesses.

DAT Drives

13

Digital Audio Tape (DAT) storage systems for tape backup and storage have become the standard for companies that require a high-speed, reliable tape-storage system. DAT is the same technology that has been used in video tape recorders and video cartridge recorders (VCRs) since the 1950s.

Helical Scan recording is the method behind DAT recording. The Helical Scan method allows extremely high-density recording to be accomplished in a relatively slow-moving tape. In order to accomplish this, both the tape and the recording head must move simultaneously. The read and write heads are located on a rapidly rotating cylinder, which is tilted at an angle in relation to the vertical axis of the tape. The tape enters in an angular manner that allows data to be written diagonally on the tape rather than just straight along the tape's length. The result is that a tape of only one inch can record nearly eight times longer than the width of the tape.

Figure 13.3 is a diagram of how the tape moves through the recording device in an angular pattern, starting with recording at the bottom of the tape as it enters the device and recording further onto the top of the tape as it exits.

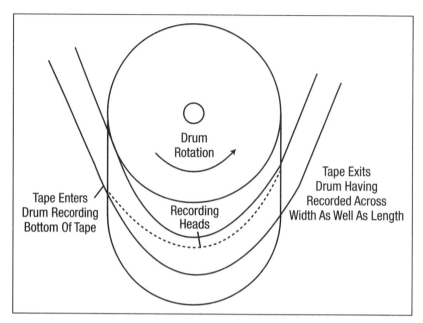

Figure 13.3 The Helical Scan recording method, used in DAT drives.

DAT drives come in two forms: Digital Data Storage (DDS) and Digital Linear Tape (DLT).

Digital Data Storage (DDS)

Digital Data Storage uses the Helical Scan method and combines with Read-After-Write and error-correction technology to create an efficient data-storage technology. Originally designed in 1989, this technology, now referred to as DDS-1, provided 1.3GB capacity on a 60m tape cartridge. In 1992, data compression was introduced and combined with a 90m tape to provide a capacity of up to 4GB. DDS-2 was introduced in 1993 and increased capacity to 8GB using a 120m tape. The increased storage capability was accomplished by increasing the density of the recording by one-half and increasing the length of the tape by one-third.

Error correction is another feature that was implemented with DDS-2. The data group is now a fixed length, divided into 22 data frames and 1 ECC (Error Correction Code) frame for error detection and correction. Read-After-Write was also implemented with DDS-2. This is another, immediate form of error detection, which checks for errors by reading all data immediately after it is written. If a data frame is identified as bad, it is rewritten further down the tape. If consecutive sectors of bad media are encountered, the data can be rewritten multiple times until it is written correctly.

DDS-3 is the current state-of-the-art of recording technology. It uses the same length of tape as DDS-2 to provide twice the storage capability. This is accomplished through the implementation of a 14-step algorithm called Partial Response Maximum Likelihood (PRML). PRML can read whole strings of bits at once, instead of just the two bits at a time the tape head spans. This provides for faster interpretation of data scanned, which is like being able to read a book by reading whole sentences at a time instead of reading each word that makes up each sentence. This increase in the speed of data transfer allows the tape to record twice as much while using the same tape speed.

Other advanced features have been implemented with DDS-3, including advanced Error Correction Codes, Data Randomizing, and a Media Recognition system. The storage of data has become too important to the survival of business today to be trusted with the inefficient backup solutions of the past. The technology of DDS is continuing to evolve, with the standards for DDS-4 technology soon to be introduced.

Digital Linear Tape (DLT)

Digital Linear Tape (DLT) is one of the highest-performance storage solutions available today. (Digital Equipment Corporation developed it for use on its VAX minicomputer systems, but the technology is now owned by Quantum.) DLT is designed specifically for users with storage needs of 40GB or greater. DLT offers storage capacities as high as 70GB on a single data cartridge and can achieve data transfers of up to 10Mbps by using a four-channel read/write feature. Two channels are writing, effectively doubling the transfer rate and recording density. DLT provides the Read-After-Write protection feature and has redundant error-correction-code bit placement to ensure almost error-proof performance. This is an expensive high-end solution for those with major storage needs.

13

It is important that you understand the different backup technologies and strategies that are available. If the past is any indication of the rate of growth of data storage in business, then we can be assured that the amount of data we will be expected to store and back up in the future will continue to grow immensely. Your position in any Information Technology department will most likely involve the storage or transfer of that data. Refinement of your knowledge of the most efficient methods to accomplish this will continue to be a major job requirement.

SMALL COMPUTER SYSTEM INTERFACE (SCSI)

Since its establishment in 1986 as an ANSI standard, Small Computer System Interface (SCSI, pronounced "scuzzy") has become one of the most common specifications in use today. SCSI was created to meet the demand for a faster, more flexible, command-controlled interface for hard-disk drives and peripherals, such as CD-ROMs and scanners. These peripherals connect to a common SCSI bus, which serves as an electrical pathway through a SCSI controller or adapter to the motherboard.

SCSI is not so much one published standard as it is a large group of standards and ideas that have been published, implemented, and refined. Different standards groups, such as the SCSI Trade Association (STA), have been established, but SCSI still remains more of a compilation of many proprietary technologies and standards. Next, we'll explain the main types of SCSI standards and related terms.

SCSI-1

The first set of ANSI standards was known as SCSI-1 because plans for SCSI-2 were already underway. These initial specifications called for up to seven devices called *targets* to be connected to a computer called an *initiator*. Data was passed in both asynchronous and synchronous modes through this intelligent high-level peripheral interface. This was just the start of what continues to evolve as the method most used for high-speed data transfer between devices.

SCSI-2

SCSI-2, which was published as an ANSI standard in 1994, is an upgrade to the SCSI-1 standard. The changes included a mandated message-and-command structure to improve compatibility with the many new devices on the market. SCSI-2 also provided a faster data-transfer rate. SCSI-2 provided a synchronous data-transfer rate of 2.5 to 10Mbps for an 8-bit data bus and 5 to 20Mbps for a 16-bit data bus.

SCSI-3

There is no clear point when SCSI-2 ended and SCSI-3 started. SCSI-3, which is the term related to the SCSI standard most widely used today, simply split the 400-plus pages of documents used to describe SCSI-2 into a series of smaller documents using a more layered approach. This split allows a substitution of parts of the SCSI structure as newer technology replaces parts of the original standards. This does not imply that any of the SCSI terms represent any particular performance or transfer rate; rather, they represent a set of documents that define how the product performs. It is, of course, assumed that replacing the original standards with a better technology should provide a corresponding increase in performance.

Fast SCSI

The timings defined in SCSI-2 for a 10 MegaTransfer/second transfer rate were referred to as *Fast SCSI*. The MegaTransfer rate is a unit of measure referring to the rate of signals on the interface, independent of the width of the bus. To determine the total transfer rate of the bus, you multiply this MegaTransfer rate by the number of bytes wide that the bus is. For example, a narrow bus of one byte would have a 10Mbps transfer rate, and a wide bus of two bytes would transfer at 20Mbps using the same MegaTransfer rate.

Fast-20 SCSI

Fast-20 SCSI, also known as *Ultra SCSI*, was defined in SCSI-3 as a MegaTransfer rate of 20Mbps. This results in a 20Mbps transfer rate on a narrow bus and a 40Mbps transfer rate on a wide bus.

Fast-40 SCSI

Fast-40 SCSI, also known as *Ultra-2 SCSI*, is the latest ANSI-published standard. It uses a negotiated clock rate for synchronous transfers. Like the other Fast SCSI MegaTransfer rates, Fast-40 SCSI can reach transfers of up to 80Mbps over a wide two-byte SCSI bus. Another major improvement to the Ultra SCSI-2 standard was the increase in the maximum allowable cable length. The previous maximum of 3 meters, a very limited distance, was quadrupled to a 12-meter maximum.

Narrow SCSI

Narrow SCSI refers to the one-byte-wide data bus on a 50-pin parallel interface as defined in the ANSI standard SCSI-1. This narrow bus consists of 8 data lines, with parity, and a series of matching control and ground lines.

Wide SCSI

Wide SCSI refers to the two-byte-wide data bus on a 68-pin parallel interface as defined in the ANSI standard SCSI-3. Utilization of Wide SCSI has the effect of doubling the Fast SCSI MegaTransfer rate over the Narrow SCSI interface.

13

Fast-Wide SCSI

Here is the combination of Fast SCSI over a two-byte (Wide SCSI) parallel path. Fast-20 SCSI transfers at 40Mbps, and Fast-40 SCSI transfers at 80Mbps. Fast-20 SCSI over a wide (two-byte) path is known as Ultra-Wide SCSI. Fast-40 SCSI over the wide path is known as Ultra-2 Wide SCSI.

Compare these transfer rates to the 16.7Mbps rate of EIDE (Enhanced IDE), and it's easy to understand why large computing environments that demand quick hard-disk access will consistently choose SCSI devices as storage units and servers. Even Ultra DMA's 33Mbps transfer rate cannot compare with the 80Mbps rate of Ultra-2 Wide SCSI. This performance benefit is not limited to hard-disk storage, either. Zip drives using a SCSI connection can perform up to six times faster than devices using a parallel connection. SCSI scanners have also dominated the market because the difference in the speed of data transfer over parallel connections is very noticeable.

Ultra-3 SCSI

In July 1998, the STA defined a possible set of new features being developed by the ANSI subcommittee. The STA defined data transfers of 160Mbps with improvements that included a CRC (Cyclical Redundancy Check), and named the standard Ultra160/m SCSI or Ultra SCSI-3.

Table 13.1 summarizes the characteristics of the various SCSI specifications.

The SCSI Bus

The secret to SCSI's high speed and performance lies in the architecture of its bus. SCSI is a multithreaded I/O interface. That is, it can process multiple I/O requests at the same time, using the technology incorporated in the SCSI host adapter. This technology allows the bus to remain free while the disk or other device processes the I/O request. When the device has information to send, it connects to the bus, transfers the data, and then breaks free while processing another request.

This ability to bypass the waiting period for data search and retrieval is what allows the bus to handle as many as 15 devices concurrently. Imagine the time difference between delivering 15 letters and waiting each time for a reply before going to the next, or delivering 15 letters and then coming back when the replies were ready for you to pick up. This is the difference between the DMA and the SCSI data-transfer modes. Ultra DMA is a single-threaded I/O interface with the ability to process only one request at a time. SCSI is multithreaded and can handle multiple requests concurrently. The future of data processing lies with the technology that can produce the greater speed. The key to this faster data transfer lies in this multithreaded technology. The SCSI bus, utilizing this key technology, will continue to evolve and dominate the high-speed data transfer market.

Table 13.1 Comparison of SCSI standards.

Feature	SCSI 2	Ultra-SCSI	Ultra-2 SCSI
Width of bus (with wide controller)	8-bit (Fast) 16-bit (Fast Wide)	8-bit (Ultra) 16-bit (Ultra Wide)	8-bit 16-bit (Ultra-2 Wide)
Maximum rate of data transfer (with wide controller)	10Mbps 20Mbps	20Mbps 40Mbps	40Mbps 80Mbps
Maximum number of devices supported (with wide controller)	7 15	7 15	7 15

SCSI IDs

One of the keys to understanding the implementation of SCSI devices is understanding the SCSI ID system. The most common SCSI adapters used today are the Adaptec 2940 cards. The information presented here about SCSI IDs and SCSI devices relates to these devices.

Most SCSI adapters hold 1, 7, or 15 SCSI devices. Each of these devices must be assigned a unique number known as the *SCSI ID*. These numbers range from 0 to15 and identify the priority given to the device when two or more devices are competing for the right to send data on the bus. The numbers do not have to be assigned sequentially, nor do any or all numbers need to be in use. The highest priority is given to ID 7. It is preset to be the ID of the Adaptec SCSI card itself and should not be changed. The remaining IDs are given priority in descending order from 6 to 0 and then from 15 to 8.

Most SCSI disks come from the factory preset to SCSI ID-0. It is best to keep this ID for the drive from which your operating system will boot. The remaining drives need to be reset so that no two drives have the same SCSI ID. (If two drives shared a SCSI ID, your system would not function properly.) With most internal devices, such as hard drives, you set their SCSI IDs by using jumpers located on the drives. Figure 13.4 shows where to look for the SCSI ID jumpers. The jumpers on these devices use binary systems to set the IDs. Figure 13.5 shows the jumper setting for the SCSI IDs. Some hot-swappable or hot-pluggable servers have cables that attach to these jumpers, and the devices are assigned IDs by the operating system. It is important to understand that after these devices have been assigned an ID by the operating system, they cannot be changed or moved because the drives will not be recognized by the system, and the operating system will fail to boot.

External devices usually have a switch, located on the back of the device, for setting the ID. Just be sure that the ID does not duplicate one that is already used by one of the hard disks.

When you are adding a new SCSI device to your system, it is important to determine which SCSI IDs are available. To view your SCSI settings, you can reboot your computer and watch the devices and their IDs appear while the

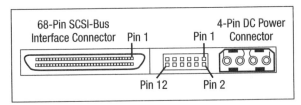

Figure 13.4 SCSI jumper pins on a drive.

Pin Set	6	5	4	3	2	1
SCSI ID Number						
0						
1						X
2					X	
3					X	X
4				X		
5				X		X
6				X	X	
7				X	X	X
8			X			
9			X			X
10			X		X	
11			X		X	X
12			X	X		
13			X	X		X
14			X	X	X	
15			X	X	X	X

X = Jumpered

Figure 13.5 Jumper settings for SCSI IDs.

SCSI BIOS is loading. If you cannot reboot, consult the configuration settings for these IDs that are available in most operating systems.

SCSI Bus Termination

To function properly, both sides of a SCSI bus must be terminated. Termination is managed by a set of electrical resistors called *terminators*. These terminators must be placed at the extreme ends of the SCSI bus. The reason for this is that communication along the SCSI bus is conducted using electrical impulses. When an electrical impulse reaches the end of the SCSI bus, it reaches open air. Open air has extremely high impedance. This open-air impedance causes the signal to bounce back into the SCSI device, enter the SCSI bus, and create echo noise. The presence of this echo noise in the line will cause severe impedance, resulting in errors in the data being transmitted across this bus. Placing terminators at both ends of the SCSI bus creates impedance levels equal to those of the SCSI bus, thereby eliminating the echo signal and allowing the correct transfer of data signals. The adapter at one end of the bus is usually terminated using ID 7. If the last device on the SCSI cable does not have termination capabilities, then you'll need to use a terminator at the end of the SCSI cable.

Two types of SCSI bus termination are available: active termination and passive termination. Let's look at the characteristics of the two and how they differ.

Passive Termination

A passive terminator provides an impedance level close to the level of the SCSI bus cable. It does this by using a terminating resistor pack that is placed at the end of the bus. This resistor pack relies on the interface card to provide it with a consistent level of power that it can convert to a corresponding level of impedance. If the level of power supplied to the system and hence to the adapter remained constant, then the level of impedance produced by the resistor would remain constant also. This would then create noise-free, error-free data transmission. Unfortunately, the power levels throughout the entire network, including the system itself, are in a constant state of fluctuation. This power fluctuation results in a constant state of fluctuation in the level of impedance the terminator provides. This unstable impedance level can cause a number of unnoticed data-transmission errors that slow down the rate of data transmissions throughout the SCSI bus.

Active Termination

To correct some of the limitations imposed by passive termination, a new method of termination was needed. This new method had to provide for a more stable level of impedance even through the constant fluctuation of the power it received. Active termination solves this problem.

Active termination uses a voltage regulator at the end of the SCSI bus to control the impedance levels. Because it regulates the power that it gets from the interface card, active termination is considered to be more stable than passive termination. Voltage regulators can maintain a constant amount of impedance regardless of the fluctuation in the power they receive. This makes for more stability in the SCSI bus, ensuring a more error-free signal flow through the SCSI bus.

13

Passive termination was sufficient for earlier SCSI-1 and SCSI-2 devices. The increase in data-transfer speeds with the improvements later implemented in SCSI-2 called for a more stable SCSI-bus impedance level than passive termination could supply. The technology of the impedance termination needed to be improved to keep up with this improvement in performance.

Some devices allow you to determine the method of termination you wish to use; a jumper located on the adapter card controls this. Figure 13.6 shows the termination setting options on a standard SCSI tape-storage device. In most cases, active termination is a preset standard on the later generation of SCSI adapter devices.

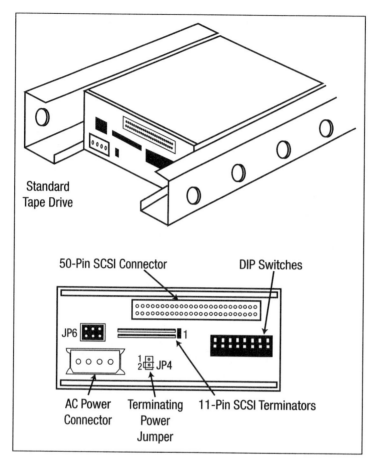

Standard
Tape Drive

50-Pin SCSI Connector   DIP Switches

JP6

AC Power   Terminating   11-Pin SCSI Terminators
Connector   Power
                 Jumper

Figure 13.6   Location of a SCSI terminator on a standard SCSI tape device.

There are a couple more things you need to keep in mind with regard to SCSI termination. One is that the SCSI bus must be terminated at both ends. This also means that the devices on the SCSI bus—in between the end devices—must *not* be terminated. Terminating a device in the middle of the cable will stop the use of the cable at that point. Data can only be transferred among the devices connected to the cable between and including the terminated devices. For example, if you terminate your last hard disk, and the cable continues to your tape device, the system will not recognize the tape device. It is not inside the SCSI data transmission bus, even though it is connected to the cable.

Another thing to remember is that most adapter cards serve as the connection point to your system. These devices are at the end of the SCSI chain and usually come preterminated. Be sure you are aware of all the possible ramifications should you choose to unterminate the SCSI host adapter and specify another device as the end terminator.

Finally, if your SCSI bus is not recognizing the devices connected or is not loading the SCSI BIOS properly, you can probably isolate the problem to two possible causes. Either the SCSI ID is incorrect or is a duplicate, or the ends of the SCSI cables are improperly terminated.

SCSI BIOS

When your computer boots, the SCSI BIOS is installed after your system BIOS installation is completed. The BIOS then loads and lists all devices that are currently located on the SCSI bus, their SCSI IDs, and the type or name of the devices. If one or more of your SCSI devices are not listed here, then you have a problem, and that device(s) will not be available when the operating systems boots (if it does boot).

When it first initializes, the SCSI device's BIOS usually gives you an opportunity to enter, usually by pressing Ctrl+A. It is important that you do not make any changes in the BIOS settings unless you are knowledgeable enough to understand them. The options usually allow you to configure your devices and to detect and diagnose the connections to your attached devices. In the SCSI BIOS, you can also low-level-format disk drives that may not have been low-level-formatted at the factory or that appear to have defects or other types of errors.

If you enter the BIOS, your system will detect and list the SCSI devices and their IDs and then begin the boot process. Do not be alarmed if your SCSI BIOS states, "SCSI BIOS not installed." It simply means that the system is not booting from a device on the SCSI bus. If, however, you are booting from a SCSI device on this adapter and the BIOS does not install, then you have a problem and your system will not boot. If you have multiple adapters, they will load in order. The one that is bootable will say "BIOS installed," and the one that is not bootable will say "BIOS not installed." This is normal.

13

NETWORK COMPONENTS

In Chapters 5 through 7, we covered network connectivity components—such as hubs, bridges, and routers—and discussed how they operate within the OSI (Open Systems Interconnection) layers. In this chapter, we'll discuss these devices in more detail. First, here's a quick refresher.

> ➤ *Hubs* and *repeaters* serve as the central point or intersection of two or more cable connections. *Unintelligent hubs* are those that cannot learn, process, or utilize any of the information that passes through them. *Intelligent hubs* are those that are designed to implement high-end monitoring technologies. Hubs are strictly Physical-layer devices, operating at the bottom layer of the OSI model.

➤ *Routers* are devices that route, or transmit, data between segments on an internetwork. Routers work at the Network layer.

➤ *Bridges* are similar to routers in their connectivity functions; they connect network segments together so that they can function like a single network segment. Bridges operate at the Data Link layer of the OSI model.

➤ A *brouter* acts as a router for routed protocols and acts as a bridge for bridged protocols. It operates at both the Data Link and Network layers of the OSI model.

➤ A *switch* is simply a one-way bridge with multiple ports. It operates at the Data Link layer.

Understanding the technology of these devices is important. It's also important to know when to implement these devices to improve the quality of your network. Let's take another look at the physical aspects of these devices and discuss how we might use them to better control the traffic on our network.

Using Switches

Switches and intelligent hubs work a little differently than their less intelligent counterparts do. In addition to all the things a regular hub can do, switches can remember the addresses attached to their ports.

Segmenting The LAN

Switches use the information found in the packets being sent by the devices connected to the port to determine the MAC (Media Access Control) address of the device on the port. Switches use this information to build tables for each port. When a switch receives a packet, it looks up the destination MAC contained in the packet header and compares it to the table. The switch can avoid sending the packet out to the entire domain; because it knows which port has the destination MAC address, the switch sends the packet to only that port. This arrangement also allows switches to provide full bandwidth on each port. In contrast, hubs send packets to all ports and must share bandwidth with ports where the signal is not intended. The use of a switch instead of a hub will alleviate a bottleneck and provide much faster data flow.

Switches work at the Data Link layer of the OSI model. They operate in the same manner as a bridge, but with multiple ports. This also means that they create multiple segments. These are used to solve problems associated with media. Media problems can be characterized by excessive collisions in Ethernet networks or by long waits during transmissions in token-ring or FDDI (Fiber Distributed Data Interface) environments. Most media problems are caused by having too many devices on a segment. Separating the network into multiple segments by using switches will usually end the problems. Ethernet networks might need to be segmented if the network utilization remains above 40 percent for more than a minute continuously throughout the day. Segmenting token-ring and FDDI networks should be considered if utilization reaches 70 percent.

Modes Of Switching

Switches can work in different ways. The various methods have different purposes and can result in faster or slower transfer times through the switch. The amount of time that a packet takes to move through a switch is called *latency*. Although the latency may be minuscule for a single packet, it can make a big difference as large numbers of packets begin to transverse a large number of switches. Let's take a brief look at the different switching modes:

➤ **Store-and-forward** The store-and-forward method of switching has a higher latency than other switching methods. With this method, the entire contents of the packet are copied into the onboard buffers of the switch, and the CRC (Cyclical Redundancy Check) calculations are performed. The switch then determines whether the packet is free of corruption. If it is, the switch then looks up the destination address in its routing table and forwards the packet to the next node. If the switch determines that the packet has become corrupted, it will drop the packet, causing the sending station to re-send the packet.

➤ **Cut-through** The cut-through method—also known as the realtime method of switching—has a much smaller latency time because the entire packet is not copied into the switch buffers. As soon as the destination address is captured into the switch, the route to the destination node is determined and the packet is quickly dispatched out the corresponding port. A much faster method of switching than store-and-forward, the cut-through method allows the destination workstation to do the CRC computation and to determine the integrity of the packet.

➤ **Fragment-free** The fragment-free method is a small compromise between the other two methods. Usually, the first 64 bytes of the frame are sufficient to determine if the frame is corrupted, because this is often where the corruption starts. This method checks these first 64 bytes; if they are intact, the frame is forwarded. The frame is still subject to the same CRC calculation at the workstation that all frames are, so any corrupt packets not dropped here will be caught and dropped at the destination.

These methods give you the tools necessary to fine-tune your network. When choosing a switch, determine the method of switching that is best for your environment. Most high-end switches allow you to program which method they will use, and it can often be specific to each individual port.

The flexibility of switches and the tremendous increase in performance they provide give this technology a bright future. In the past, the biggest drawback of switches has been their price. Like all network devices, though, they have dropped in price considerably over the past couple of years. The value of switches combined with much lower prices will make these devices a common feature in networks of the future.

Using Bridges In A Network

In a network with no segmentation, only one packet can traverse the network at one time. In a small network, this is not cause for concern. As a network gets larger, though, it might be necessary to segment the network into separate collision domains. Bridges are used to separate a network into logical network segments.

Every bridge maintains a table that lists which segments contain which MAC addresses. Traffic on each side of the bridge crosses to the other side only if the MAC address of the destination computer is determined to be on the other segment. Bridges are not concerned with upper-layer protocols, such as those that deal with IP addresses; rather, they read and route data based strictly on the MAC address of the destination computer.

One of the most significant disadvantages of bridges is that they rely heavily on broadcasts to locate destination addresses. This is a very inefficient method, which can result in broadcast storms. Broadcast storms occur when bridges, not knowing the segment the destination address is located on, begin broadcasting every packet they receive to all segments. This can flood the network with broadcasted packets and can often cripple network performance. In these instances, it is often necessary to use routers.

Using Routers For Traffic Control

Routers work as traffic cops, directing packets down different paths to different segments and to other routers. Here's how the process works: A computer sends out a packet, which is inspected by the router at the first intersection. The router checks the destination address in the packet header, compares it to the routing table, and directs the packet to the next port on the way to the final destination. If necessary, the packet proceeds to the next router, which performs the same inspection. This cycle continues until the packet reaches the segment containing the destination address.

Routers look like hubs, but the ports are normally located in the rear rather than in the front. Routers are very useful in reducing media congestion caused by broadcasts. A *broadcast* is a common method used for name resolution and for providing information on other network services. The number of broadcasts in a collision domain can often create a major slowdown in the transfer of vital information. Broadcasts should not produce more than 20 percent of the traffic on a local area network (LAN). Routers will create separate bandwidths or collision domains and will isolate these broadcasts to the segments where they originated.

Routers send packets based on their destination addresses, just as bridges and switches do. The difference between routers and bridges is that routers work at the third layer—the Network layer—of the OSI model. Routers use the IP (Internet Protocol) or IPX (Internetwork Packet Exchange) address rather than the MAC address. Routers can also be programmed to determine which addresses are allowed to pass through and which are not. This is done through access lists. With access lists, administrators can determine which resources users can access and which resources will be denied, based on entire networks, segments, or protocols (such as FTP).

Using Brouters In A Network

A *brouter* is a device that combines the benefits of both routers and bridges. Its common usage is to route routable protocols at the Network layer and to bridge nonroutable protocols at the Data Link layer. In the past, routers have not often been used because they are needed only in networks using dissimilar protocols concurrently. With the convergence of different networks taking place, brouters are needed more often. They are making a comeback into the networking world and are commonly referred to as "Layer 3 switches."

Using the right network component for the right job is an art to be mastered. Many courses are offered to teach you how these devices can improve your network and how to install them. This is another area of specialty that can consume an entire career and put an administrator in high demand.

ELECTRICAL POWER

13

The reliance on power received from public utilities creates a serious concern in network management. Practically every device in the network relies on electrical power. What's worse is that these devices are easily damaged by fluctuations in electrical power. Data transfers consist of electrical signals that are transmitted across wires and processed through a computer processor powered electrically. Power fluctuations occurring during critical data transfers or processing cycles can cause data loss or corruption of operating systems or databases.

The most obvious change in power is experienced in the form of an outage, or *blackout*. There are, however, more issues regarding the flow of power that can affect your network and the health of its components. Let's look at the common types of power problems:

➤ Brownouts

➤ Blackouts

➤ Spikes

➤ Surges

➤ Electromagnetic interference

Brownouts

The most common form of power disruption is a *brownout*—a short-term decrease in the voltage level. This is usually caused by the startup demands of other electrical devices. The most visual example is often found at home. Do the lights dim momentarily when a large electrical appliance such as a heater or air conditioner starts? This is a brownout caused by the appliance's demand for power. The appliance has drained a lot more power from the common power source than was anticipated. The amount of power sent is quickly increased to meet the demand so all appliances will function properly.

When the supply and demand level out, everything will function normally, but repeated power fluctuations can damage your network hardware and data, and this damage goes mostly unnoticed. The cumulative effect of this constant shortage of power can greatly reduce the life span of any electrical equipment.

Blackouts

A *blackout* is a total loss of power. Its effect is immediate; all functions in process are abruptly halted. All data not written on the hard disk is lost. (This includes all data in transit and in processing, all the bytes being held in RAM, all running applications, and your operating system.) Corruption of operating systems and applications that are open is a common result of blackouts. Even more damaging to your company can be the corruption of a database that was open and transmitting or receiving data. Even though a data transfer in process that is not allowed to proceed will try to re-send the data, this option is not available. In addition, more databases can be totally corrupted by this event, so the damage might not be limited to the data in transit. Your entire database may become corrupt.

When the power returns, you sometimes have to restore an entire operating system. Databases can be harder to restore. Usually, doing so requires a reload from backup, and all data changes that have been made since the backup will be lost. An even worse event is to find that the backup is too old or corrupt. Always pay careful attention to backups; they can save your job.

Spikes

A *spike* is an instantaneous, dramatic increase in the voltage output to a device. A spike can enter from a phone line, a network cable, or a power cable. The most common victims of spikes are hardware components, many of which have sensitive silicon contacts that can be easily destroyed.

Surges

A *surge* is the opposite of a brownout. Its voltage increase is less dramatic than that of a spike, but it can last a lot longer. When a large appliance is switched on, the voltage is increased. When this appliance is shut off, the voltage is decreased, and the power to other devices is increased by the power with nowhere to go. The flow then evens off, and the supply of voltage is dictated by the demand. The short period that the power is increased can also decrease the life of your components.

Electromagnetic Interference

Electromagnetic interference (EMI) is simply the electrical noise caused by one device interfering with another. It is not a major issue with power supply. EMI's most noticeable effects can be felt on data transfers when a cable is too close to machines that generate large electromagnetic fields. EMI can damage packet flow and thereby slow the network.

An IBM study showed that a typical computer is subject to more than 120 power fluctuations a month that are capable of causing problems. To understand the extent of this problem, see Table 13.2, which lists the major causes of data loss (according to information supplied by Contingency Planning Research, Inc.).

By far the largest reported single cause of network data loss is power related. In these cases, in addition to data loss, there is the large loss of productive time used to restore the network to good operating condition after the power has been restored. Although no statistics are available, it would not be surprising to find a corresponding number of lost administrator jobs as a result. If data losses due to power problems occur, there can be no acceptable excuse because there are ample methods available to prevent permanent data loss.

Devices are available for protecting electronic components from power fluctuations. These devices include:

13

➤ Uninterruptible power supplies

➤ Surge protectors

➤ Line conditioners

Table 13.2 The major causes of data loss.

Percentage Of Data Loss	Cause
45%	Power failures or surges
9%	Storm damage
8%	Fires or explosions
8%	Hardware or software errors
7%	Flood or water damage
6%	Earthquakes
17%	All other causes

Uninterruptible Power Supplies

The best protection available against power surges and power outages is the uninterruptible power supply (UPS). A common reference to this is *battery backup*, which is probably a more precise term. The time the UPS gives you before the temporary power interruption becomes permanent is measured in minutes (usually 10 to 20) and can hardly be classified as uninterruptible. The UPS is attached to the power supply, and then each component is plugged into it. A battery inside the UPS can provide sufficient power to all attached devices to allow for an organized shutdown of the server and all attached devices if a power outage occurs.

There is often a misconception that this backup will provide the attached components with sufficient power to continue operation during an outage. This is incorrect. The battery starts to fade immediately; depending on the number of units attached, it will usually be completely depleted in 20 minutes or less. This time is sufficient to close any open programs and databases, avoiding the danger of corrupting these programs with a blackout.

Batteries are rated by the amount of power they can provide after a blackout. Before you purchase a battery backup, it's important that you determine the best match for the devices you intend to connect. Check with the manufacturer's documentation to make sure that the capacity of the battery unit you purchase can handle the load it will be required to carry.

Automatic Shutdown

Most UPSs come with software programs to monitor the power being received and the power being transferred to the attached components. One such program—Powershute Plus from APC—monitors and maintains a consistent flow of power to the components and advises you about problems you may be having with the power you are receiving.

In addition, a serial cable attached from the battery unit to the main component is used to advise the main unit when the battery might be unable to provide power in the near future. Software that is installed in the component will notify the cable to either receive signals or stop receiving a consistent signal, depending on the type of software you are using. When the device has been notified that the power to the battery has been terminated and that the battery will begin to deplete it, then it proceeds with a preprogrammed shutdown cycle. This shutdown cycle can include a series of actions that the administrator has requested, including:

➤ Logging the event

➤ Notifying the administrator

➤ Notifying users

➤ Running a command file

➤ Sending email

➤ Paging users

➤ Shutting down the server

The total loss of power will trigger any or all of the preconfigured actions. These actions can also be triggered by matching them with certain events. For example, you may wish to be notified by email whenever the battery conditions are low. Just set the event for Low Battery Condition and the action for Send Email.

Here is a partial list of the types of events that most power-backup software can respond to:

➤ Low battery condition

➤ Return from low battery

➤ Discharged battery

➤ Power restored

➤ System shutdown

➤ Shutdown canceled

➤ Output overload

➤ Overload condition solved

These events can be configured to notify you when a problem has been detected and to notify you again when the problem has been corrected. These power-backup programs can be very useful when they are properly installed and understood. Read all the information that comes with your UPS. The simple act of plugging it in and connecting a component doesn't provide the benefits you paid for, and when you most need it, you may find it won't be of any help.

Surge Protectors

Surge protectors, also known as surge suppressers, are inexpensive, simple devices. They are often used to turn a single outlet into multiple outlets, rather than to provide protection as they're intended to. They usually have a built-in fuse or switch that can be triggered if a surge or spike occurs. This spike is absorbed by the protector rather than by the attached component. The big danger that comes with these devices is their inability to handle multiple events. After the spike or surge has blown the fuse, the protection no longer exists. The unit, however, continues to function as if nothing has happened, and the user never knows that the expected protection is no longer available. If you use surge protectors, it is best to change them often and to *not* use them with highly sensitive components such as servers or storage units.

13

Line Conditioners

Line conditioners, *power conditioners*, and *voltage regulators* are all different terms for the same device. The line conditioner is a device that is used to stabilize the flow of power to the connected component. Line conditioners have magnetic coils that can retain a certain amount of power to be used after a brownout, and they provide protection from surges and spikes. However, line conditioners are totally ineffective against blackouts and should not be used instead of a UPS for critical components.

CONNECTORS AND ADAPTERS

Many types of connectors and adapters are available on the market today. They send electrical signals between the attached devices in order to provide communication and data transfer between these devices. The items that we'll be covering are the main ones that you'll be encountering on a daily basis. They include the following:

➤ DB-9 and DB-25

➤ Centronics

➤ RJ-45 and RJ-11

➤ BNC

➤ SCSI 50-pin and SCSI 68-pin

➤ Gender changers

➤ RS-232

The more years you spend working with computers, the more types of connectors you will encounter. Just when you think you know them all, another will appear based on a new specification. The best way to classify the basic items currently in use is to categorize them by the manner of connection they use.

The D Connectors

These connectors use pins and sockets to establish connections. They're called D connectors because of their shape. The number that follows "DB" is the number of pins they use for connectivity. A DB-9 has 9 pins, and a DB-25 has 25 pins. These connectors are used mostly for serial-port or parallel-port connections between PCs and peripheral devices, such as modems and printers.

You might sometimes have a cable with a different number of pins than the one you need, yet the device can still use the serial port. Assume that you have a modem with a DB-9 cable, yet the only connection point available is a 25-pin connection. An adapter can be used if it is properly wired to connect the appropriate pins. You can also make custom adapters yourself by using generic unwired connectors. Use the pin charts provided, and be careful; this method does take a certain amount of skill and experience to do it right.

Another D-type connector is the AUI connector. The AUI connector sometimes used with Ethernet connections is a 15-pin, D-type connector.

Centronics Connectors

These connectors use teeth that snap into place. The most common use of Centronics connectors is for printer connections. The cable that runs to the printer has a Centronics connector, which snaps onto the connector attached to the printer so that it won't slip off. The term *Centronics* is usually followed by a number, designating the number of pin contacts available for use. The Centronics-50, for example, is a common 50-pin connector.

RJ-XX Connectors

The most common RJ connectors are the RJ-45, used for Ethernet cable connections, and the RJ-11, the standard telephone cable connector. These connect by catching and locking a plug in place with an overhanging lip that hooks into the internal connector when inserted. The term "RJ" refers strictly to the type of connection because the exact number of wires used in this configuration will vary greatly depending on the type of components being connected. RJ-45, for example, usually uses four pairs of line wires, whereas RJ-11 uses only two. Tables 13.3 and 13.4 show the standard connections used in the four pairs of wire for Ethernet. These pin settings can also be used for token ring.

The other side of this cable needs to be set up using the straight-through setting.

Table 13.3 Pin settings for RJ-45 Ethernet straight-through connection.

Note: Keep the hook underneath and Pin 1 on your left.

Pin Number	Setting
Pin 1	White orange
Pin 2	Orange
Pin 3	White green
Pin 4	Blue
Pin 5	White blue
Pin 6	Green
Pin 7	White brown
Pin 8	Brown

Table 13.4 Pin settings for RJ-45 Ethernet crossover connection.

Pin Number	Setting
Pin 1	White green
Pin 2	Green
Pin 3	White orange
Pin 4	Blue
Pin 5	White blue
Pin 6	Orange
Pin 7	White brown
Pin 8	Brown

BNC Connectors

The BNC connector—known as the British Naval Connector or sometimes as the Barrel and Nut Connector—is used to connect cable with inner and outer cores, such as coaxial cable. We covered this connector while discussing cable in Chapter 4.

SCSI Connectors

The 68-pin and 50-pin high-density connectors are used to connect SCSI-2 and SCSI-3 devices to the SCSI bus. The 50-pin low-density connector is used with SCSI-1 and SCSI-2 devices only. These connectors have adapters available to allow devices with different pin connectors to be attached to the same host adapter. Most tape drives, for example, use the 50-pin connector, and the majority of the SCSI hard drives in production today use the 68-pin connector. To place these on the same cable, you must use a 50-pin-to-68-pin adapter.

RS-232 Connectors

We learned earlier in this chapter that the RS-232 specifies how serial-port communication travels over the nine wires in the serial cable. The most common connector used for this is the DB-9 connector. The pins used for this connection are detailed in Table 13.5. DB-25 cable connectors can also be used if the only serial-port connection available is a DB-25; however, because only nine pins are needed, the DB-9 connector is the logical choice. DB-25 connectors can be used for modems but are most commonly used for printer connectivity. The pin set for a DB-25 connector is shown in Table 13.6.

Gender Changers

It is not uncommon to use a variety of adapter types. Sometimes you may have a cable and a connection socket that are exactly the same. If that's the case, you would need a *gender changer*, which is simply an adapter that allows either a male or female plug to be changed to the other on one or both sides to conform to

Table 13.5 Standard RS-232 serial-port cable pins for a 9-pin connector.

Pin	Function
1	Carrier Detect
2	Receive Data
3	Transmit Data
4	DTR (Data Terminal Ready)
5	Signal Ground
6	Data Set Ready
7	RTS (Request To Send)
8	CTS (Clear To Send)
9	Ring Indicator

Table 13.6 Standard RS-232 serial-port cable pins for a 25-pin connector.

Pin	Function
1	Protective Ground (Printers)
2	Transmit Data
3	Receive Data
4	RTS (Request To Send)
5	CTS (Clear To Send)
6	Data Set Ready
7	Signal Ground
8	Carrier detect
17	Receiver Signal Element Timing (Printers)
19	Secondary RTS (Request To Send) (Printers)
20	DTR (Data Terminal Ready)
22	Ring Indicator (Modems)
24	Transmit Signal Element Timing-DTE Source (Printers)

13

the gender of the devices or cables to which you are attaching. For example, the cable may have the pins sticking out (called "male"), and the device may also have pins sticking out. A gender changer would allow one male end to plug into it and then convert the connection so that another male pin could plug into the other side to complete the connection.

A gender changer might seem like an insignificant item, but when you're planning any type of network changes or installations, be sure to check the types of connections you have. Projects can be delayed hours or even a day or two because small items like these are overlooked. Sometimes it's best to just keep a variety of gender changers and other adapters on hand.

CHAPTER SUMMARY

In this chapter, we looked at various components that provide the services in a network. Printers and print servers work together to provide network printing resources to users. Print servers allow the printers to be directly connected to the network so that they are independent of an attached computer. We discussed three types of printers: dot-matrix printers for impact printing; ink jet and bubble jet printers for low-cost, low-speed color and black-and-white printing; and laser printers for high-speed, high-quality print jobs.

Modems have now become standardized using the V.90 technology. This standard allows 56K-technology modems to communicate with any other modems using the same V.90 standard, regardless of the manufacturer. Whether internal or external, these modems need three parameters configured: the COM port, the IRQ, and the I/O address. Conflicts with these settings and other devices can cause the devices to malfunction. Modems are serial devices that use the UART Intel 16650 chip for the fastest speed transfers. Exterior devices are connected with a serial cable using the RS-232 standard pin set.

Tape drives are either IDE or SCSI devices. SCSI devices, such as DAT drives, provide much faster read/write access using the DDS (Digital Data Storage) technology. DDS-3 uses the Helical Scan method, which allows tapes to be written diagonally, multiplying the amount of storage eightfold. The DDS standard also provides correction protection by verifying the written data before the tape moves off the tape head and rewriting any data that was not correctly written the first time.

SCSI devices are the high-end leaders for fast data transfer. SCSI devices are given numeric IDs, and the devices transfer data across the SCSI bus, which is terminated on both ends. Narrow SCSI has a one-byte channel, and Wide SCSI has a two-byte channel. The terminator can be either a passive or an active terminator. SCSI buses that have been improperly identified or improperly terminated will cause a failure in the transfer. Fast SCSI provides 10Mbps data transfer, and Fast-20 SCSI provides 20Mbps data transfer. This number is multiplied by the number of bytes contained on the bus channel to determine the transfer capability of the device. Shorter SCSI cables provide faster, more secure data transfer.

Hubs, routers, and bridges are used to segment networks for specific purposes. Routers can be used to isolate broadcasts and to direct network traffic. Access lists can be installed to regulate the sender, the receiver, and the protocol passing through them. Switches can be used to segment the network into collision domains to isolate broadcasts and to speed up data transmission on the network.

Electrical problems account for most of the data loss and component damage in a network. Uninterruptible power supplies can be used to regulate voltage, to protect against brownouts and blackouts, and to shut down the network properly if a power outage occurs. Surge protectors are limited to protection against one surge only. Line conditioners are a low-cost alternative but do not provide any battery backup or shutdown protection.

Many types of connectors are used to attach computer peripherals. The D class is named because of its shape. The Centronics connector is known for its clip-on connection, and the RJ series has a lock-in connector. Many of these connectors can be interchanged if the correct pin-outs can be properly connected.

REVIEW QUESTIONS

1. Electrophotography is used in which type of printer?
    a. 9-pin dot matrix
    b. Bubble jet printer
    c. Laser printer
    d. Ink jet printer

2. What type of power management system would you use to provide your server with continuous power?
    a. Surge protector
    b. UPS
    c. Redundant power connectors
    d. Line conditioner

3. What networking component will provide printing services for the entire network?
    a. Print router
    b. Print manager
    c. Print server
    d. Hayes-compatible print sharer

4. Which connector would most likely be on the end of a modem cable?
    a. 50-pin parallel connector
    b. 68-pin parallel connector
    c. DB-9 connector
    d. RJ-45 connector

13

5. Which networking component would you need in order to attach your 50-pin male cable to another 50-pin male connector?

   a. Repeater

   b. Gender changer

   c. Transceiver

   d. DB-25

6. Which networking component can be used to translate between dissimilar network protocols?

   a. Hub

   b. Router

   c. Switch

   d. Gateway

7. Your network analysis has determined that there are too many broadcasts across your network. Which networking component would you use to segment your network to isolate broadcasts?

   a. Router

   b. Bridge

   c. Modem

   d. Hub

8. Which parameters need to be configured when you're installing a modem?

   a. IRQ

   b. I/O address

   c. COM port

   d. All of the above

9. Which networking component maintains a table of MAC addresses?

   a. Hub

   b. Router

   c. Intelligent Hub

   d. Bridge

10. Which network component works with either the Network layer or the Data Link layer of the OSI model?

   a. Hub

   b. Router

   c. Switch

   d. Brouter

11. Which network component can be used to connect multiple devices, providing full bandwidth on each port?

    a. Hub

    b. Managed hub

    c. Switch

    d. Transceiver

12. Which router on your segment would be sent packets destined for a remote network?

    a. Default gateway

    b. Subnet router

    c. Intranet router

    d. External router

13. You intend to create an Ethernet 10BaseT network of three computers. In addition to network cards and network cable, what other item would you need?

    a. Router

    b. MAU

    c. Hub

    d. Bridge

14. What networking component can be installed in place of a hub to alleviate a bottleneck?

    a. Modem

    b. MAU

    c. Switch

    d. Transceiver

15. Narrow SCSI refers to a parallel data bus that is how many bytes wide?

    a. One

    b. Two

    c. Four

    d. Eight

16. Which networking component(s) work at the Data Link layer of the OSI model?

    a. Router

    b. Switch

    c. Hub

    d. Bridge

13

17. Which networking component(s) work at the Network layer of the OSI model?

    a. Router

    b. Switch

    c. Hub

    d. Bridge

18. Which networking component(s) work at the Physical layer of the OSI model?

    a. Router

    b. Switch

    c. Hub

    d. Bridge

19. Fast-20 SCSI can provide what data-transfer rate when used on a Wide SCSI interface?

    a. 20Mbps

    b. 40Mbps

    c. 80Mbps

    d. None of the above

20. Which mode of switching provides the lowest latency?

    a. Cut-through

    b. Store-and-forward

    c. Fast packet

    d. Fragment-free

21. ANSI standards for SCSI-3 define a parallel interface with what type connector?

    a. 50-pin low-density parallel connector

    b. 50-pin high-density connector or 68-pin parallel connector

    c. DB-9 connector

    d. DB-25 connector

22. Which printer would provide the fastest, clearest letter?

    a. 9-pin dot matrix

    b. Bubble jet printer

    c. Laser printer

    d. Ink jet printer

23. Which modem technology has become the standard for 56K technology?

    a. x.2 56K technology

    b. V.90 56K technology

    c. Hayes technology

    d. K56flex technology

24. In an Ethernet network, segmentation should be considered when utilization remains over what percentage on a constant basis?

    a. 20 percent

    b. 40 percent

    c. 70 percent

    d. 95 percent

25. A packet sent to all the computers in the network is known as a:

    a. Multicast

    b. Routed packet

    c. Switched frame

    d. Broadcast

26. What type of connector could be used to connect to an exterior SCSI device?

    a. DB-9

    b. RJ-45

    c. Centronics 68-pin

    d. BNC connector

13

27. What is it called when a modem initiates contact with another modem?

    a. Compatibility

    b. Handshaking

    c. (RTS) Request To Send

    d. Modulation

28. When a tape device using DDS-3 technology writes to a tape, how does it verify the data?

    a. DDS does not provide verification.

    b. It must rewind and then compare for verification.

    c. It is immediately read and verified.

    d. None of the above.

29. Which tape solution would provide the most storage on a single tape?

    a. Travan

    b. DAT

    c. IDE

    d. DLT

30. If your SCSI device has the proper ID, but you cannot get it to function, what would you check for next?

    a. Make sure the patch cable is connected.

    b. Check for proper termination.

    c. Be sure you have proper permission for the device.

    d. Make sure the BIOS is connected properly.

HANDS-ON PROJECTS

Project 13.1

In this project, we will install a SCSI tape drive onto a SCSI bus. To do this, we must first start with a SCSI tape device, a computer with a SCSI controller card, and a SCSI cable.

To install a SCSI tape drive onto a SCSI controller card:

1. First, we need to properly ID the device we wish to install. To do this, we must determine which SCSI IDs are taken and which ones are available. The easiest way to do this is to reboot the computer and determine upon bootup which SCSI devices have already been identified. We assume that you have planned to do installation during a time when the server can afford to be down. In order to set up and test this device, you'll need multiple reboots as well as time to physically install and connect the device.

2. Upon bootup, locate the SCSI adapter to which you intend to connect this device. The screen will read something like this:

```
SCSI  ID  #0  -  Compaq 915884 -  Drive C:  (80h)
SCSI  ID  #1  -  Compaq 915884 -  Drive D:  (81h)
SCSI  ID  #2  -  Maxtor 7290 -   Drive 82h
SCSI  ID  #3  -  Compaq 915884 -  Drive   83h
SCSI  ID  #4  -  NEC   CD-ROM   DRIVE : 844 -

SCSI BIOS INSTALLED
```

3. Now you know which SCSI IDs are taken and which are available. Turn off your computer and disconnect the power plug. Some computers and

servers still retain power to their motherboards even when the computer is not operating.

4. Now you need to use the jumpers and pins to hard code the SCSI ID setting on the device to a SCSI number not identified in the SCSI BIOS. Use a number under 7 (remember, 7 is most likely the ID of the adapter). To properly identify the SCSI device, look for a chart on the device or refer to Figure 13.5.

5. In this example, we'll use SCSI ID number 5. So jumper the first and the third sets of pins, starting from the left of the drive near the power connector. The third jumper has a value of four; the first jumper has a value of one. That's five.

6. If the drive has a terminator, then it can be enabled if this is the last device in the string. Make sure the prior device is then unterminated. If this device will be physically attached on the cable between SCSI devices currently in use (inside the current bus), then make sure the drive is not terminated, because the terminator is already in place at the end of the cable.

7. Connect the power connector and the SCSI cable to the drive. If the pin-outs are different, you may need an adapter or a gender changer. Insert the drive into the case, secure it, connect the power cable, and power on.

8. Upon bootup, your SCSI BIOS should now show the new device in addition to the previous devices. If it does not, or if one of the other devices is no longer present, then you have made an error or there is a malfunction.

```
SCSI  ID #0  -  Compaq 915884 -  Drive C:  (80h)
SCSI  ID #1  -  Compaq 915884 -  Drive D:  (81h)
SCSI  ID #2  -  Maxtor 7290 -    Drive 82h
SCSI  ID #3  -  Compaq 915884 -  Drive    83h
SCSI  ID #4  -  NEC    CD-ROM    DRIVE : 844 -
SCSI  ID #5  -  HP Tape Drive -  6246

SCSI BIOS INSTALLED
```

9. This output should be the same regardless of the operating system. The operating system should now boot up, and you are ready to install the tape drivers.

Project 13.2

In this project, we will install a SCSI tape drive in a Windows NT 4 operating system. To do this, we must first have a SCSI tape device connected to a SCSI controller and properly identified. If you do not have a tape device that is identified upon bootup in the SCSI BIOS as shown in Project 13.1, then

follow the steps in Project 13.1 to install one. Once this is complete, you will be
ready to proceed with Project 13.2.

To install the drivers for the tape device in a Windows NT Server:

1. Click on Start | Settings | Control Panel and double-click on Tape Devices.
   The Tape Devices window will appear with two tabs, Devices and Drivers.

2. Click on the Detect button on the Devices tab (see Figure 13.7) and see if
   Windows NT detects your tape device. If it does, it will begin to load the
   drivers, so just follow the instructions.

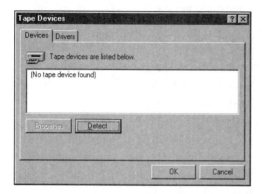

Figure 13.7   Windows NT 4 Tape Devices properties window.

3. If Windows NT fails to locate your tape device, click on the Drivers tab,
   and then click on Add. Figure 13.8 shows the Install Driver window, listing
   the drivers you have to choose from.

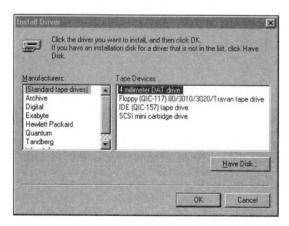

Figure 13.8   Windows NT 4 Install Driver window.

4. Choose the driver that most fits the device you want to install. Most DAT
   drives will work with the standard "4 millimeter DAT drive" driver. We will

choose that one. If yours does not appear, and you have a manufacturer's disk, then click on Have Disk, insert the disk in drive A:, and follow the instructions.

5. After you have successfully restarted your system, your tape drive should be available for use with NTBACKUP. If you have another backup utility program, install it now.

6. If you attempt to start a tape backup and your program states the "tape device cannot be found" or "device is not working", try the backup program in Windows NT. It can be found under Administrative Tools. If you receive these messages in Windows NT backup, your SCSI adapter drivers for Windows NT 4 may not have been properly loaded.

7. To check if your SCSI drivers have been properly loaded, go to Control Panel|SCSI adapters and double-click on the SCSI controller upon which your device is located. Next, double-click on the device to open the properties window. It should say: "This device is working properly". Click on the Drivers tab to be sure the device is started. If you have not located the problem by this time, you need to start from the beginning and double-check all of your settings.

13

## CHAPTER FOURTEEN

ADMINISTERING THE
CHANGE CONTROL SYSTEM

After Reading This Chapter And Completing The Exercises, You Will Be Able To:

➤ Document and maintain records

➤ Maintain records for workstations, servers, and network components

➤ Return a Windows 9x and Windows NT 4 system to its original state and recover from operating system crashes

➤ Understand general administrative practices

Proper documentation is one of the more boring chores you will face as a network administrator, but it is perhaps one of the most important. Although the task can be tedious, documenting your network as you go can save you an immense amount of time and save your company significant dollars because you won't have to hunt for information every time there is a problem. In this chapter, we will talk about what types of things need to be documented, when they should be documented, and how records should be maintained.

Just as important as documenting the network is maintaining the configuration of servers and workstations such that they can be restored or recovered in a minimal amount of time and with no data loss in the event of a crash or other catastrophe. We will discuss these types of issues on the Windows 9x and Windows NT 4 platforms. Backups will be covered extensively in Chapter 15.

Many functions performed by a network administrator are the same tried and true activities that administrators have collectively learned over the years, so we will also discuss good, general administrative practices and habits to develop that can be applied in almost any network environment.

DOCUMENTING AND MAINTAINING RECORDS

Documenting and maintaining records falls under the broad category of *configuration management*, which includes the following elements:

➤ Configuration identification

➤ Equipment status

➤ Change control

➤ Auditing

Configuration management is necessary because it will cost more over the lifetime of a network *not* to do it than it would cost to do it. For example, let's look at the following real-life case.

Joe took over the network administrator position for a company that had approximately 75 to 100 workstations and 7 servers spread across three floors of an office building. In this position, he was a "one-man show," which is common in a network of this size. That means that Joe was everything from desktop support/Help Desk to network administrator to network engineer. The previous two administrators had more or less inherited that position (they had been working in other departments) and, not having any kind of a background in network administration, let a lot of basic tasks like documentation slide. So documentation had not occurred since the company had the network installed a couple of years before Joe's arrival. (Previously, there were some standalone PCs and a network of dumb terminals connected to a VAX server.) Not even the server passwords were documented, though luckily at least somebody knew an administrator password for each domain.

So what is the big deal about not having anything documented? Well, in Joe's case, entering a new environment, where the previous network administrator had left over a month before his arrival, Joe was placed in a situation where initially it would have been impossible to troubleshoot any kind of network problems. Fortunately, no major problems occurred while he was figuring out what everything was. He was with the company for about three months before he knew exactly what each server was running and what was connected in a local area network (LAN) environment that included WINS, DHCP, Exchange Server, SMS, SQL Server, Lotus Notes, and Internet Information Server, plus a dedicated connection to the Internet. No one knew whether applications were running locally on workstations or from the servers or a combination of both, or even what hardware configurations the servers and workstations had. The hardest part to figure out, though, was the cable plant. None of the wiring was labeled; after investigating, Joe found that some workstations on the fourth floor terminated on the second floor, some on the second floor went to the first floor, and so on. There was no rhyme or reason to the configuration. In the first year, Joe often found himself spending hours tracking down cable runs while trying to fix problems.

The last straw for that network came when, due to growth, it was time to go to a wide area network (WAN) environment. The company went to Frame Relay connections between four locations and replaced the remaining 100 to 125 dumb terminals with PCs. The network in that year and a half grew from what was mentioned above to 250 or so workstations and 10 servers. After a careful cost analysis, it was determined that it would be cheaper in the long run to redo the entire network from scratch than to try to fix the mess and add the new PCs and WAN technologies on top of it. A properly documented network would have saved an untold amount of money in hours wasted over the life span of that network. This situation made a believer out of Joe that configuration management is vital. The complete replacement ran well over $300,000 for a network that is not terribly large.

As you can see, this network was a disaster waiting to happen, especially when Joe started. Although some administrators may enjoy the "fly by the seat of your pants" thrill of tempting disaster, most would probably prefer to know what their networks consist of. Also, although this may have seemed like an extreme example, it is definitely a real-world scenario. Configuration management is not the sort of thing that will wow people when you tell them what you have done, but it can allow you to find and fix network problems quickly. And that will make you a hero in your company.

Configuration Identification

Configuration identification is the basic documentation of the network. That includes documenting the equipment, its location, how it is used, and how it is connected. If configuration identification has not been done on your network, now is probably a good time to start working on it. Documenting an existing network is more difficult than documenting a new network as it is being installed, but it can still be done. If you are involved with the implementation of a new network, you should have the network installers include in their bid the cost of documenting their work. After that, make sure they do it and do it right; if the documentation is half complete or not completely accurate, you will find yourself having to go in behind them and finish the job. Documenting an existing network will usually be done internally within a company by the Information Systems (IS) department. It may be difficult to find the time to do the work, especially if you are a one-man show, but the time it takes to do the work will be made up for in the future in time saved. What you will specifically need to document is covered a little later in this chapter.

Equipment Status

Documenting equipment status is the process of keeping track of which components are working and which are broken in a network. This task coincides with maintenance because tracking broken equipment (equipment being serviced by an in-house tech, waiting on parts, or being sent out for repairs) is generally done when there are problems. Equipment status usually does not change very often and can be kept in a software database that can be updated by appropriate people in the IS department. Network maintenance is covered in more detail in Chapter 15.

Change Control

Change control means keeping a detailed record of every change made to the network. The three key goals are:

➤ To ensure that when a system is modified, there is always a good reason for the changes and that the reason is known, documented, and traceable

➤ To ensure that when a part of a system is modified, all the necessary consequential modifications are also made to other parts of the system

➤ To ensure that any required version of a system can be constructed and, if necessary, reconstructed

Changes get made to a network on a frequent basis—users install software applications on their computers, an administrator changes a login script, a faulty network card is replaced in a workstation, or a service pack or update patch is applied to a server. In an environment with many Information Technology (IT) personnel, it can be very difficult to keep track of changes that have been made without a process in place to manage change. Even if you are the only IT person in a company, you can still have difficulty keeping up with the changes you have made.

In an environment where you are the only network administrator, change control is obviously your responsibility. In companies with many IT personnel, there is often a Change Control Committee made up of people with from different parts of the IT department, such as the Help Desk, Network Engineering, and Network Administration. In these environments, if you want to update a network card driver or install a service pack, you have to fill out a *Change Request Form* that is evaluated by the committee. Information required on the form includes the change being requested, the reason for the change, a back-out plan if the change goes awry, the applications or services affected, the downtime expected, and the time the change will be made.

In addition to helping you know when changes have been made and what they are, change control forces you to evaluate your proposed changes and, most important, determine the consequences of the change. Consider the following example, which describes a common network administration situation with two resolutions: one without change control and one with change control.

The Situation

You're the administrator of a server that is running with a 10MB Ethernet card. You know that the network engineering group recently upgraded to

10/100MB hubs, and you want to upgrade your server to take advantage of the additional bandwidth. You already have a name-brand 10/100MB network adapter on hand that you can use to perform the upgrade to Fast Ethernet.

The Resolution (No Change Control)

Because you are perfectly capable of installing a new network card yourself, you send out a global email on Friday afternoon letting your users know that you'll be doing some maintenance on the server Sunday afternoon and that you expect the server to be unavailable to them for a couple of hours. On Sunday, you wander into the office a little after lunch and go through the shutdown sequence to shut down the server gracefully. You power off the server, take the case off, and remove the original 10MB card. You follow the manufacturer's instructions and install the new 10/100MB card, put the case back on, and power up the system. Your NT server boots up without trouble, and you install the new network card driver from the disks supplied by the manufacturer. After another reboot, the system comes up. You don't get any errors, but the card shows itself running at only 10MB. You visit the manufacturer's Web site, find a newer driver, download it, and install it. The network card still runs at only 10MB. You aren't sure what is wrong, but the system seems to work okay, so you decide that you've done enough work for a Sunday afternoon and head for the beach after making a mental note to look at this again some time next week.

The Resolution (Change Control)

Because you are the administrator of the server needing to be upgraded, you open your Web browser to the corporate intranet and go to the page with the Change Request Form, which looks similar to the one shown in Figure 14.1.

You fill out the form and submit it through the intranet, where it is automatically routed to the appropriate location to be reviewed by the committee. Once a week, the Change Control Committee reviews all of the change requests and decides to approve, deny, or require further testing for requested changes.

At the Change Control Committee meeting, your request comes up. The committee head reads it to the group and opens up the topic to the table for discussion. Joe from the Help Desk points out that an approved software rollout taking place on that weekend will require updating an application on SERVER07. Jane from network engineering points out that your department still has CAT3 cabling run, which would need to be replaced with CAT5, at least for the server link, to support 100MB Ethernet. George, the manager of the IT department, notes that the marketing department is finishing a big project next week, so server downtime would be unacceptable. Nick, the NT operating system guru, remembers a specific problem that he ran into while upgrading a different server with that same network card; he needed to upgrade to the latest service pack plus add a few hot fixes.

14

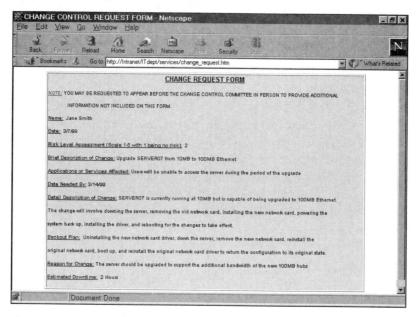

Figure 14.1   A sample Change Request Form.

With all this in mind, the committee decides to delay approval pending further testing of the upgrade and the completion of the necessary other projects, such as the wiring replacement required to complete this upgrade successfully. The committee changes the Risk Level Assessment from 2 to 4 and asks that you submit a new Change Request Form after thoroughly testing the upgrade on a test server.

So now you might be saying to yourself, "Sheesh, what a lot of work!" It might seem like a lot of work, but it really isn't when compared to how much time you could waste trying to sort out undocumented systems. Think about the benefits of change control when you are the sole IT person:

➤ Change control makes you stop to consider the consequences of your actions before you take them. As the lone administrator/technician, with no one around to challenge your authority on a technical level, you are probably used to making changes on the fly and worrying about them later.

➤ Change control provides a detailed record of what you have done. If a problem arises and users or management gets angry, you have the documentation available to show what changes were made and why, and what the potential consequences of those changes were.

In an environment where you are one of many IT professionals, change control offers the following benefits:

➤ Change control provides a means to communicate potential changes to the entire group so that everyone is "on the same page."

➤ Change control eliminates the common excuses, such as "I didn't make any changes" or "I don't know who changed that," because all changes are documented. You will always know who made what change and when to a system.

Auditing

Most likely, no matter how diligent you are in configuration identification and change control, changes and additions will occasionally slip through the cracks and go undocumented. For that reason, a process for periodic audits of the network should be in place. An audit should be performed annually, and, as when configuration management is implemented, the audit should inventory all equipment.

An audit also allows you the opportunity to evaluate your current configuration-management processes to ensure that they are working correctly for you. If you find a large discrepancy between what you have documented and what the audit finds, then you know that you need to refine your change control procedures. The audit is your system of checks and balances that ensures that policies and procedures are being followed.

What will it cost to implement configuration management? That will depend on a couple of factors, notably whether you do the work internally or outsource it, and the size and complexity of the network. Some costs are fixed, also known as *hard costs*. Those include items such as a software database used to collect and store configuration information. Other costs are *soft costs*; they vary with the complexity of the network and with how long it takes to do the documentation. Soft costs include developing procedures to document the configuration and to maintain the documentation, as well as developing procedures for change control.

What will it cost *not* to implement configuration management? Definitely more than if you did implement it. Why? Well, there are not any hard costs associated with not doing configuration management; they are all hidden costs. Estimating the money saved by configuration management is difficult if you are trying to pitch your proposal for it to the corporate executives, but if you look closely enough at your network, you might be able to get an idea of the savings.

The biggest time and money waster involved with not implementing configuration management lies in having to rediscover the configurations of the same components every time you go to troubleshoot a problem or make a change. Thinking back to the case of Joe, many times—during his first year at the company—he would have to grab a network cable and yell to a helper, "Which one does this plug into?" while tugging on the line. The time he could have saved by not repeatedly going through this routine could have been spent working on much more interesting projects, and would have allowed users to

14

get their problems resolved and be productive sooner. That is why Joe finally started documenting as he went—very much a case of "learning the hard way" that configuration management is necessary.

Configuration management also makes capacity planning a lot easier. It is much more difficult to plan upgrades for an undocumented network. When you want to upgrade the workstation operating systems, or when backups are taking too long or users are complaining that the network is running slowly, you will need to know what you have and where it is to effectively handle the situation. On a small network, you might be able to keep up with the majority of your equipment by memory. As your network grows in size and complexity, though, the details start becoming sketchy. As you need to make changes to that network, you need to document them. Otherwise, you will find yourself bogged down with maintenance and unable to spend much time on more productive and exciting projects.

MAINTAINING RECORDS FOR WORKSTATIONS, SERVERS, AND NETWORK COMPONENTS

Now that we know why configuration management is important, we will talk about what, specifically, we should be documenting.

The areas of a network that need to be documented can be organized into the following categories:

➤ Workstations and servers

➤ Network components

Workstations And Servers

When you start documenting your workstations and servers, it is helpful to have a basic annotated system diagram that shows how your network is laid out and how the systems fit in. Figure 14.2 is a sample of that kind of diagram. This kind of diagram is helpful for a quick review of what your network consists of.

The basic system diagram, however, is just that—basic. Many more details need to be recorded. For that task, you will need to create a workstation configuration sheet and a server configuration sheet.

Workstation Configuration Sheet
The following list contains the types of items that you should consider including on your workstation configuration sheet:

➤ Workstation processor

➤ RAM type (SDRAM, EDO, Fast Page, etc.) and quantity

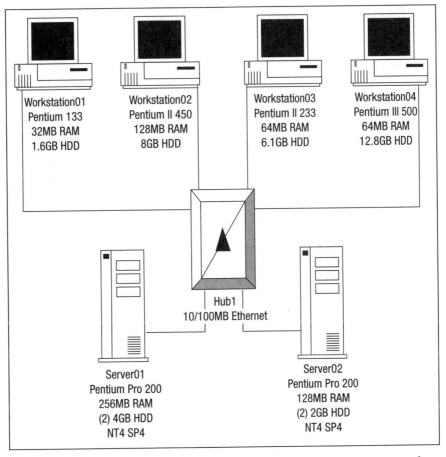

Figure 14.2 A system diagram shows how a workstation or server is configured and how it is connected to the network.

14

> Hard-drive manufacturer, capacity, and settings

> Other disk drives and settings (floppy drives, CD-ROM drives, Zip drives, and so on)

> Disk-drive types (SCSI versus IDE)

> BIOS date and manufacturer

> IRQ, I/O, and DMA settings for all adapter cards

> Operating system and version, as well as any revision/patch levels

> Printouts of system files (autoexec.bat, config.sys, win.ini, system.ini, and any other relevant files)

> Applications installed on the system and whether they are run from the server or locally

> Serial numbers

You can create configuration sheets by using the table feature of your favorite word processor or by using any popular spreadsheet program.

You can manage these configuration sheets in one of two ways. The first is to keep a sheet at each user's workstation, where it will always be available when a technician arrives to perform some troubleshooting or maintenance. The upside to this method is that it is easier to update the sheet while at a user's workstation, making it more likely that the technician will take the time to do it. The downside is that it does not fit in very well with an overall change control plan. Also, the lack of a centralized database of workstations can make it difficult to be proactive in determining when a system needs an upgrade. You are also trusting users not to lose the sheet either in their own stacks of paperwork or by throwing it away. Last, if you want to roll out a new operating-system upgrade or application, you cannot determine at a glance which machines are compatible with the new software and which machines will need upgrades first.

The other method is to maintain a software database of workstations that can be accessed by technicians over the network. This approach is more flexible, allowing you to run reports or queries to obtain information about specific workstations or a group of workstations. If you need to know how many systems have less than 32MB of RAM and which ones they are, you can easily pull that information from the database. Several software packages, including Microsoft Systems Management Server (SMS), will even gather inventory information automatically as users log their workstations in to the network; the software will then store the information in a database. Figures 14.3a and 14.3b show two pages of an example basic workstation configuration database.

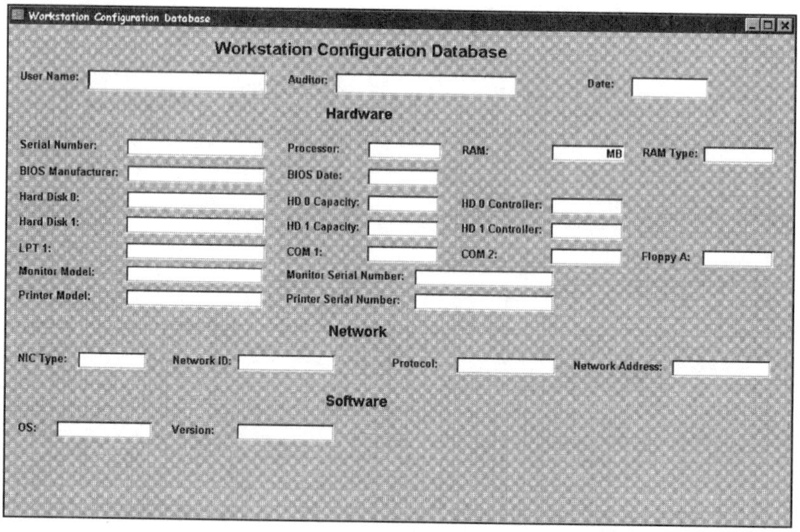

Figure 14.3a   Page 1 of a sample workstation configuration database.

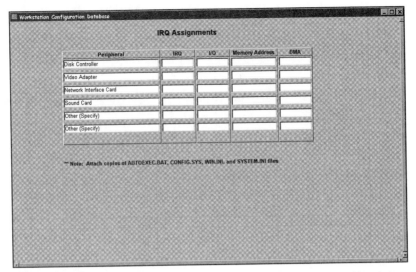

Figure 14.3b Page 2 of a sample workstation configuration database.

Server Configuration Sheet

Even if you do not take the time to document every workstation on your network, you should definitely take the time to document the servers. In practically every case, a single server crashing is going to cause a bigger problem for you than a single workstation crashing. Servers often have more components than workstations, a fact that adds time to the documentation process and makes keeping track of system files much more critical. In many companies, users store no data locally, so if a workstation crashes, the desktop support technician usually does not think twice about formatting the hard drive and reinstalling either from a preconfigured software image or from other installation media. The complex nature of the functions of servers makes that quick fix impossible, especially as you deal with user accounts stored on the server, shared directories with varying levels of permissions, and so on. Many tape-backup programs have disaster-recovery functions to restore a server from tape, but if a catastrophe occurs, you should have enough hard-copy documentation of your server configurations to be able to restore a server to its working configuration manually.

The server configuration sheet will contain a lot of the same hardware information contained in the workstation configuration sheet, such as processor, RAM, and disk drives. In addition to that information, the server configuration sheet should also contain the following:

➤ Operating system and revision/service-pack level

➤ Types and addresses of network adapter cards

➤ Network protocols in use and binding orders

14

➤ Network protocol configurations (e.g., for TCP/IP [Transmission Control Protocol/Internet Protocol]: the IP address, subnet mask, default gateway, WINS [Windows Internet Name Service] configuration, etc.)

➤ Server programs running and their configurations

➤ User accounts (names, group memberships, profile settings, other settings)

➤ Domain name, server name, server role (PDC [primary domain controller], BDC [backup domain controller], standalone), and trust relationships for NT servers

➤ Server name, IPX/SPX (Internetwork Packet Exchange/Sequenced Packet Exchange) configuration, NDS (Novell Directory Services) information, and network number for NetWare networks

With servers, it is helpful to keep the documentation stored both electronically in a database (either collected automatically or entered manually) and in a hard-copy log book. The server log book should be kept near the server and should contain printouts of the important text files, such as login scripts. The log book should also be a change-control helper: The log should document every change made to the server, including the date and time, a detailed explanation of the change that was made, and the reasons for the change. Server errors should also be noted in the log. If your server crashes and your log book is entirely electronic, you do not have any documentation from which to reconstruct your server.

Logging a problem history is especially important. The log book should record all of the problems the server has had and how they were resolved. This history gives you information to analyze in order to determine the factors involved in a server crash. If you do not have a record of any errors or changes that might have caused the crash, it will be difficult to understand why the crash occurred and how to prevent it from happening again after you get the server back online.

The history might also help you to spot a trend in the types of problems that have occurred. This might lead you to the culprit of the crash, if it is not obvious, and keep you from having a repeat performance.

Other helpful items to include in the server log book are a detailed description of standard network procedures and a list of server passwords. This documentation can also be stored electronically, but care should be taken to ensure that only appropriate personnel have access permissions to the directories containing this sensitive information.

The server log book can be as complicated or as simple as you want to make it, though there is eventually a trade-off between completeness and the time it takes to generate the documentation. The more complete the log book is, the more useful it will be.

Network Components

Documenting most network components—such as hubs, switches, routers, and printers—is similar to documenting workstations and servers. You create a configuration sheet, where you document relevant details, such as the following:

➤ Make and model of equipment

➤ Serial number

➤ BIOS/firmware revision

➤ Port speeds

➤ Network MAC (Media Access Control) address and logical address (TCP/IP address and NetBIOS name, such as Corp_Router1)

The above list is by no means exhaustive; it merely shows some of the more common elements and is intended to give you a starting point. Your configuration sheet will probably contain additional information specific to the type of device you are documenting.

Probably the most important network component to document, even more so than servers, is the cable plant. The cable plant consists of all of the wiring, where it starts, and where it terminates. The cable plant is the most important aspect of the network because 70 percent or more of network problems are due to cable faults of one type or another. Initially, documenting the cable plant consists of the following steps:

1. Obtain and annotate floor plans.

2. Obtain or create systems diagrams.

3. Create a numbering system.

4. Perform the inventory and label everything.

Obtain And Annotate Floor Plans

The first step you'll need to take in preparing to document the cable plant is to obtain floor plans from building maintenance (or the person in your company who's responsible for holding them). Make copies, and then start annotating the basic floor plans by drawing a grid on the blueprints to separate areas of the floor into zones. Figure 14.4 shows a sample floor plan, divided into zones.

14

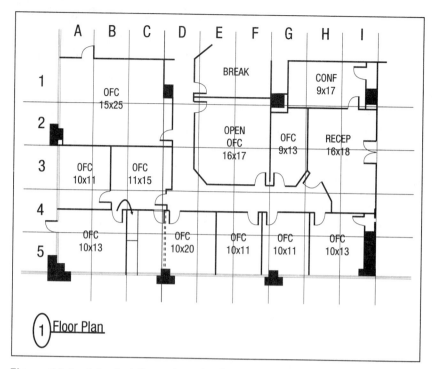

Figure 14.4 A typical floor plan, divided into zones.

The key to annotating your floor plans is to devise a standard naming convention for your cabling scheme that will accommodate any future growth. In our sample, notice how the grids are used to create zones that are no bigger than 10'×10' and are easily identifiable, such as A3, C1, and so on.

Obtain Or Create Systems Diagrams

If you or someone else in the company has already created systems diagrams such as those in Figure 14.2, you are already ahead of the game. If not, you will need to create diagrams that show not only how servers and workstations connect to the network, but also how hubs, routers, switches, patch panels, and other cabling components connect. Your annotated floor plan should show the location of each piece of equipment as it relates to the floor plan, and your systems diagram is where you document the equipment in more detail. Such systems diagrams include labels for the network cable termination points, and for those points you will need a numbering scheme.

Create A Numbering System

When creating a numbering system, keep in mind that you will need to label both the cables and the components that the cables connect to. An easy system to use for labeling the components in a network where everything terminates into patch panels is to use a component's zone, such as B2, followed by a port number. The resulting number looks like B2-07. In that case, you know that this network jack in zone B2 runs back to a patch panel, where it is terminated at port 7. Network jack B2-07 can be patched to a PC or network printer or some other network device, and port 7 on the patch panel is patched into a switch or hub or MAU (Multistation Access Unit) to provide connectivity to other network devices. The cable run between the jack and the patch panel should be labeled with the type of cable (Cat5 UTP [unshielded twisted-pair], RG-58, etc.), the start zone, and the termination zone. (The cable runs should probably be labeled by the installer, because typically these runs will be inside walls, underneath floor panels, or above drop ceilings.) If the patch panel is in zone A6, you could create a numbering scheme such as UTP5/A6-B2/07, which translates to Category 5 unshielded twisted-pair starting at zone A6, running to zone B2, and terminating in port 7 on the patch panel.

Also important to add is the length of the run. Because 10BaseT, in our sample network, has a maximum segment length of 328 feet, you will want to make sure that none of your cable runs exceeds that length. In using the above scheme, you could add the length entry at the end, such as UTP5/A6-B2/07/ 225. You would put a tag on the cable near its termination points. For patch cables that usually run only 6 to 25 feet, you would tag the cable with the name of the port that it plugs into (such as B2-07), near where the cable is connected to the network device. In English, that means that if you were connecting a PC to the network, you would tag the patch cable near where the cable is plugged into the network card. That way, even if the cable is run underneath a desk, you can easily tell which jack it plugs into on the wall.

Perform The Inventory And Label Everything

This step is where you get to do the grunt work. As was mentioned earlier, you should have the cable installers label the cable runs that reside within walls and ceilings and underneath floors. You can do the patch cables yourself, though. You should label both ends of a cable. Use a cable tie to hold your label on, rather than a sticker or anything else that uses gluelike substances to hold itself in place. Over the course of time, the glue will wear off, causing the label to fall off.

Some people like to label each device on the network as well as the cabling runs, but that is a matter of personal preference. In this scenario, each PC or hub or router (or whatever) would have a number assigned to it, following a scheme, and labeling the cable would also include which devices the cable connected. Although this method provides more information, which is always good, it does not really provide any additional help in troubleshooting a problem; you have already carefully labeled your cable runs on your systems diagrams and can clearly see the devices that are connected by the cables.

14

Once you have documented your cable plant, you can add that information to a database or spreadsheet, which can be updated in the future when changes are made. As with other documentation, you will need to be diligent about keeping it updated, or its value will quickly fade.

RETURNING WORKSTATIONS AND SERVERS TO THEIR ORIGINAL STATES

Windows 9x ("9x" refers to either Windows 95 or Windows 98) and Windows NT 4 appear to be similar because on the surface they share the Explorer GUI (graphical user interface). Underneath the hood, however, there are many differences. These differences make it worthwhile to consider separately the processes of recovering and returning Windows 9x and Windows NT systems to their original configurations.

Windows 9x

Windows 95 and Windows 98 are often identical in how they function as operating systems; in fact, Windows 98 is really just an improved Windows 95. Because Windows 98 is the newer operating system and will gradually replace the aging Windows 95, we will focus primarily on Windows 98 in our discussion of recovery and repair. However, we will also point out the areas of difference, because chances are high that at some point you will have to troubleshoot a Windows 95 system.

Before we describe how to restore a Windows 98 system to its original configuration, you need to understand the foundation upon which such a system is built. From there, we can move on to recovering the system and to knowing when and how to reinstall the operating system.

The Registry

In the dark days of Windows 3.x, configuration information was mostly stored in special initialization files that had an .ini extension. The file system.ini had system configuration information, including hardware settings and driver settings. The win.ini file configured the Windows environment with information such as file associations, what programs would load or run as Windows started, and some program-specific settings that were added by individual programs, such as Lotus cc:Mail or Microsoft Office. Other common ini files, such as protocol.ini, contained network-related configuration information. Usually when you installed software in Windows, the program would create its own ini file with configuration information specific to itself. There was also a Registration Database, the Registry, which contained OLE associations.

With the introduction of Windows 95, the concept of the Registry came into its own. The Registry is a database, a central repository, of configuration data. Rather than having configuration information scattered about in multiple files, all information for a Windows 95-compliant application had to be stored in the Registry. That concept carried over into Windows 98 and Windows NT 4 as well. The ini files still exist, but are there only to provide backward compatibility with older 16-bit applications that were designed to use ini files and not the Registry.

The Registry is organized into subdivisions called *keys,* which are organized in a treelike manner. These keys are actually stored in two separate read-only, hidden system files in the root of the Windows installation directory. These files are system.dat, which contains all of the hardware and program data, and user.dat, which contains user-specific data, such as customized menus and color schemes. Editing of these two files is done through the Registry Editor (shown in Figure 14.5), which provides a unified graphical interface to the entire Registry.

As you can see in Figure 14.5, the Windows 98 Registry is organized into six keys. Table 14.1 summarizes the keys and their functions.

As you can imagine, with all of the system configuration settings stored in the Registry, there is a single point of failure for your Windows 98 operating

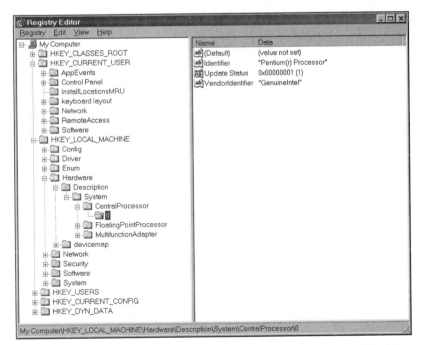

Figure 14.5   The Registry is organized into keys, which are laid out like branches of a tree.

Table 14.1   The six keys of the Windows 98 Registry.

Key	Function
HKEY_CLASSES_ROOT	Contains the file association and OLE data that made up the original Windows 3.x Registration database.
HKEY_CURRENT_USER	This is identical to HKEY_USERS if there is only one user of the computer. If there are multiple users, this key contains the settings and preferences of the user currently logged in.
HKEY_LOCAL_MACHINE	Contains data about the system hardware and the installed software, the type of information stored in the Windows 3.x system.ini file.
HKEY_USERS	User settings and preferences, including color schemes, desktop settings, and mapped network drives. This information in Windows 3.x was found in the win.ini file.
HKEY_CURRENT_CONFIG	Much of the information in this key is identical to that under HKEY_LOCAL_MACHINE. This key also contains printer information.
HKEY_DYN_DATA	Built dynamically at bootup, this key contains Plug and Play information and information about the current state of the system.

system. Lose the Registry, and you've lost Windows. To prevent this from happening, Windows automatically backs up the system.dat and user.dat files to system.da0 and user.da0 upon each *successful* Windows bootup. If your Registry gets corrupted and you cannot boot Windows, you can replace system.dat with system.da0 by booting to a command prompt either from a boot disk or by pressing F8 at the system beep and choosing Command Prompt Only. Both system.da0 and system.dat are in the Windows directory. If, however, you make a configuration change—such as installing a device driver that renders another device inoperable—without preventing Windows from booting, then rolling back to system.da0 will not work because the "bad" configuration will have already been copied to system.da0.

Recovery

There will be times when simply restoring system.da0 will not fix the problems. It might be that the problems have already been copied from system.dat to system.da0. The three recovery options, depending on the current state of your system, are:

➤ Emergency Boot Disk (EBD)

➤ Safe Mode

➤ Reinstalling the operating system

Emergency Boot Disk

You are first given the option to make the Emergency Boot Disk (EBD), also known as the Startup Disk, during the installation of the operating system. If you chose not to make one then, you can easily create one now through the Control Panel's Add/Remove Programs applet's Startup Disk tab, as shown in Figure 14.6.

You will be prompted for a single disk, and, depending on how your system was set up, you might be prompted to insert the Windows 98 CD. Systems that come preconfigured from original equipment manufacturers (OEMs) usually have the installation files stored on the hard drive, so you won't be prompted for the CD whenever you make a change that requires files to be installed.

The Emergency Boot Disk is used primarily when your system will not boot. You might be getting the infamous "Non-system disk or disk error" message when you turn on your computer. The EBD allows you to boot your computer from the floppy drive and, we hope, regain access to your C: drive. The EBD contains a number of useful commands for managing your drives and getting your system booting again. If you were getting the above error message, yet were able to get to the C: drive and see all of your data, you would run the SYS command to restore the three system files io.sys, msdos.sys, and command.com on the boot sector of the hard drive. You can edit boot files such as config.sys and autoexec.bat. Other utilities that can help you recover from worst-case data loss are FDISK and FORMAT.

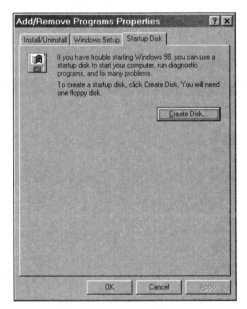

14

Figure 14.6   Creating an Emergency Boot Disk through Add/Remove Programs.

The Windows 98 Emergency Boot Disk does offer one significant advantage over the Windows 95 EBD: support for standard ATAPI CD-ROM drives. You had to customize the Windows 95 EBD in order to boot up and gain access to your CD-ROM drive and reinstall Windows. Windows 98, however, takes care of that for you.

There are still some recommended customizations for the EBD, though. Even though there is sufficient disk space, the EBD does not contain a few of the more useful commands, which can be copied to it from the C:\windows\command directory. These commands are summarized in Table 14.2.

Safe Mode

More commonly, you will run into the situation in which your system boots but then locks up or gives a Fatal Exception message or otherwise does not load Windows. For times like this, Windows provides Safe Mode, which boots a minimal configuration and allows you to correct the problems that are preventing Windows from loading normally. Safe Mode is engaged by pressing F8 right before the Windows splash screen would normally appear. This brings up a boot menu with numbered options, such as Normal Mode (the default), Safe Mode, Step by Step (lets you choose which device drivers to load), and Command Prompt Only, among others. In Windows 95, there was a short delay while "Starting Windows 95..." was displayed, but that delay has been eliminated in Windows 98, so you will have to be quick on the F8 key to get the boot menu.

Safe Mode, as was previously mentioned, loads a minimal configuration—the bare minimum necessary to start Windows. The standard VGA video driver is

Table 14.2   Useful commands to add to the Emergency Boot Disk.

Command	Function
Attrib.exe	If you need to edit a system file, such as msdos.sys, you will need to be able to remove the read-only, hidden, and system attributes in order to make the changes.
Deltree.exe	Deletes a directory and all of its subdirectories. Very helpful if you are trying to delete C:\windows, for example, to reinstall an operating system.
Move.exe	You can't rename a directory from a command prompt without move.exe. When you're working with files, move.exe saves you the trouble of first copying and then deleting the original files.
Xcopy.exe, Xcopy32.exe, Xcopy32.mod	This trio of files allows you to bulk-copy files and directories. The original copy command will work on only one directory at a time, but with xcopy, you can work on a directory and its subdirectories. This is much faster and more flexible.

loaded, and there is no CD-ROM or sound support, or even network support unless you specifically chose "Safe Mode with Network Support." If you have installed a device that conflicts with another and is preventing Windows from loading normally, you can go into Device Manager in Safe Mode and remove the driver that is causing the problems. Safe Mode is often helpful for user-induced errors, such as changing the video display to an unsupported mode that causes the display to be distorted or otherwise unreadable. If you are unable to correct the problems through Safe Mode, or if Windows won't boot even in Safe Mode, then it is time to consider reinstalling Windows.

Reinstalling The Operating System

For one reason or another, you will at some point be faced with the prospect of reinstalling a system that is "hosed" (the technical term for "messed up to the point of needing a reinstall"). The goal, of course, is to get the computer working in the shortest amount of time, so we will take the types of reinstalls in order of time involved from shortest to longest.

Cheat Method

The first type is what I like to call the "cheat method." When you install Windows 95 or 98, it creates a hidden file called system.1st in the root of the C: drive. This file is the original Registry, unblemished by user-installed applications. If you copy system.1st to system.dat and reboot, you will see Windows go through the last stage of setup, where it configures hardware, the Start menu, and the Control Panel, and asks you what time zone you are in. When you reboot, the system usually comes up fairly clean.

The main advantage of the cheat method is that it is quick: You can restore the original configuration of Windows in a few minutes.

There are a couple of disadvantages, though. The first is that it is messy; it doesn't take into account all of the application files or .dll files that might have been added to the C:\windows\system directory. Nor does it consider 16-bit applications that might have written to win.ini and system.ini and created their own ini files. Second, you are faced with having to reinstall all of your 32-bit applications because you have replaced the corrupted Registry with a copy that knows nothing about any installed applications. All of that configuration information is gone. You have saved yourself time reinstalling Windows, but now you have to reinstall applications.

Reinstall Over The Top

Another method of reinstalling is to simply reinstall Windows over itself. Without making any changes, you simply run Windows setup (you can boot from the EBD and access the CD-ROM drive to run Setup) and let it install to the same directory that Windows was originally installed in, usually

C:\windows. Setup runs in its entirety, which can be as much as an hour for
Windows 98 (usually 20 to 40 minutes for Windows 95, depending on
processor speed).

The advantage to reinstalling Windows over itself is that Windows Setup will
glean information from the existing Registry and incorporate it. Application
settings will transfer intact, and you probably won't have to reinstall any of your
applications once setup is complete.

The disadvantages are similar to those of the cheat method. This type of
reinstall does not do any cleanup, so you are still potentially left with old,
unused files in the hard drive taking up space. Reinstalling Windows over itself
is a compromise in that it takes longer than the cheat method, but saves time
later by not requiring applications to be reinstalled. Ultimately, both methods
are of the "quick-and-dirty" variety, designed to get the user working as quickly
as possible.

Clean Reinstall

The clean reinstall takes the "reinstall over the top" method a step further. Here,
you delete the C:\windows directory and its subdirectories before running
Windows Setup. A fresh Windows directory is built, and the Registry is clean,
with no artifacts from a previous setup.

The advantage is that you know that the Windows installation is clean. There is
no potential for rogue dll or ini files cluttering up space or interfering with the
successful operation of Windows by being different versions than what
Windows installed.

The disadvantage of the clean reinstall is twofold. Although you have a clean
installation of Windows, the hard drive still has dead application directories that
will no longer work because the configuration data they had put in the
Registry and the dll files they had copied to C:\windows\system are gone. You
will have to clean up the drive by either reinstalling those applications into
their existing directories to fix them or deleting unwanted application
directories. The other disadvantage is that this is a time-consuming
reinstallation. Depending on the number of applications previously installed
and the speed of the system, it might take you half a day to get the computer
working.

Start From Scratch

When you start from scratch, you go so far as to reformat (and possibly even
repartition) the hard drive. In all other respects, this is similar to a clean reinstall,
but this time you are completely wiping the hard drive clean of all data. If the
user stores his or her data files on the server, this method is a better choice than
the clean reinstall method. Why? Because you are ensuring that the system is

being set up totally cleanly, giving you maximum control over how it is set up. If the user stores data on the hard drive, be sure to have a current backup. Also, make sure that you have all of the necessary driver disks to set back up the video card, the sound card, and so on when you install Windows. Unfortunately, many OEMs do not distribute driver disks, but rather put the installation files in a directory on the hard drive. The OEMs leave it up to the buyer of the computer to make disks. If disks haven't been made and you format the hard drive, you will find yourself spending some not-so-quality time on the vendor's Web site downloading the files you need.

So you know how to reinstall, but when should you do it and which method should you use? That is more or less a personal preference. Some people believe that Windows is inherently unstable and should be reinstalled periodically just to keep it running properly. For others, reinstalling is a last resort. Most people fall somewhere between those two extremes, however. If the user's system is crashing frequently, and you have gone through the standard troubleshooting steps of isolating the cause and attempting to correct it without success, it is time to reinstall. If Windows won't boot even in Safe Mode, you will definitely need to reinstall. Which method you use depends on the severity of the problem and on how much time you can spend on it. If the computer used by the VP of Finance crashes on a Friday morning, and he or she needs to get a project involving payroll done by the end of the day, you are not going to opt for starting from scratch. In that case, you would start as simply as possible with the methods that take the least amount of time. You can always schedule a time to go back later when the pressure of a deadline is off. So, ultimately, the answer is, "It depends." As an IT professional, you will need to analyze each case on its own merits and determine the appropriate course of action. Having a solid knowledge of all of your options will enable you to choose the best plan for a given situation.

Windows NT 4

Even though it shares a common interface with Windows 9x in the Explorer GUI, under the hood, Windows NT 4 is significantly different from Windows 9x. Part of the difference is that NT 4 owes its heritage to NT 3.51, which was designed from the ground up to be everything that the consumer-level Windows 3.x and Windows 9x were not: stable, secure, and not concerned with backward compatibility with legacy applications and devices. These differences mean that different processes are involved in troubleshooting and repairing a Windows NT 4 system. In discussing repairing an NT 4 system or restoring it to its original configuration, we will consider:

➤ The Registry

➤ Emergency Repair Disk (ERD)

➤ "Blue Screen of Death"

14

➤ Reconnecting to the network from a boot disk

➤ Reinstallation methods and when to use them

The Registry

The Registry used in Windows 95 and 98 was born with NT 3.x. The NT Registry contains the same keys as the Windows 9x Registry, with one exception. Because NT does not support Plug and Play and does not detect hardware devices at bootup, it does not have the HKEY_DYN_DATA key that Windows 9x builds dynamically at bootup. Actually, NT does provide very limited plug-and-play support through PnPISA.inf, which can be installed from the installation CD-ROM. The functionality is somewhat sketchy, however, and can be frustrating to those used to Windows 9x Plug and Play, which has a much higher success rate. PnPISA can detect a limited range of Plug and Play devices, such as soundcards and video cards.

Editing the NT Registry is much like editing the Windows 9x Registry, with one notable difference. NT also includes the older regedt32.exe command, which opens the Registry Editor with the keys organized in separate windows, as shown in Figure 14.7.

Notice how the appearance differs from Figure 14.5. Windows NT 4 offers the same regedit.exe command that Windows 9x uses. So which one should you use? It is a matter of personal preference. Our experience is that those who come from an NT 3.51 background typically use regedt32. out of habit, whereas those who started with NT 4 typically use regedit.exe, especially if

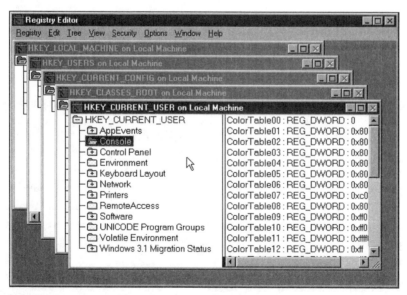

Figure 14.7 Regedt32.exe organizes the Registry keys in separate windows.

they have had experience with Windows 9x. Regedt32 also has the benefit of allowing you to browse the Registry in read-only mode, which is beneficial if you are just looking for a particular piece of information and don't want to accidentally change anything.

Emergency Repair Disk (ERD)

It is ironic that the topic of the Emergency Repair Disk comes up at this point. Even experienced IT professionals sometimes forget about keeping this disk up to date, so they experience headaches later. Consider the experience of Will:

While working on this book (on the previous Windows 9x section) on one of his NT servers at home, Will decided to take a break and install a new sound card he had purchased. No worries—just pop the case and swap out the old ISA 16-bit card with the fancy new PCI card, and boot up. He installed the drivers seemingly without a hitch, but then, when he was prompted to reboot, the system hung. "Hmm... strange," he thought, but after letting it sit for 10 minutes or so to make sure that NT was not going to regain control, Will tapped the Reset button and watched as the system rebooted. It went through the boot sequence and started loading, but right before it would bring up the "Press Ctrl+Alt+Del to log in" dialog, the system would hang. "Okay, no problem," he thought. "I'll just use the Last Known Good configuration to boot the system back up as it was before I loaded the sound card drivers." Doing that resulted in the computer rebooting itself as it switched over from the text-based mode to the GUI mode. After that, he tried the Last Known Good configuration after physically removing the sound card from the computer. It still rebooted itself. By that time, Will figured it would be time to run a repair installation (discussed later in this chapter) ... until he realized that he had not bothered to create an Emergency Repair Disk. To make a long story short, he tried a few other things, including running an *upgrade install* and finally a *parallel install* (both are discussed later in this chapter). The end result found him with a new installation of NT (a dual boot with Windows 98) and the task of having to reinstall all of his applications when he could have done a repair install and been back up and working in a short amount of time. Instead, he had to spend a Friday night rebuilding his system, rather than finishing with his writing early and going out. The only thing he had done properly before shutting down to install the sound card in the first place was backing up his documents to another system on his home network so at least he would not lose his work if something happened.

The previous example, although embarrassing to admit as an experienced IT professional, should show the importance of the ERD. Spending three minutes to create the disk during setup or after the fact would have saved hours of reinstalling the operating system and applications.

In a home environment, having to reinstall NT doesn't cost you anything other than lost time, but in a business environment, the consequences are much greater. Consider the situation a consultant colleague found when he went on a call to a small company.

The company had a single PDC that supported about 50 users who logged in from a mix of Windows For Workgroups 3.11 and Windows 95 workstations. Data files were stored in user directories on the server. The server had a tape-backup drive with limited capacity, so full backups were not done. In fact, the only data that was backed up consisted of a couple of large databases that were shared among many users and some other application data that couldn't be reproduced. The company's network administrator did it only part time; his regular job involved something completely different, and he was the network administrator only because he was a power user who happened to know more about computers than did anyone else in the office. So far, we have a fairly typical scenario.

The day before he was summoned, the server had apparently crashed right after lunch. Rebooting the computer resulted in an error message stating that NT could not start because ntoskrnl.exe was missing or corrupt. That was the state of the server when he arrived.

The "missing or corrupt ntoskrnl.exe" error is a common error that can be repaired by doing a repair install of NT. However, because the system was first set up by an outside consultant two years prior, the network administrator had never updated the ERD, rendering it for all intents and purposes useless. He ended up reinstalling NT Server, and in the process, he lost the Security Accounts Manager (SAM) and the security information that was assigned to files and directories. Without that information on tape, a painful couple of days were spent manually recreating all of the user accounts and security information. In the meantime, the company was more or less shut down, and users were unable to access the shared databases on the server. A small consolation was that shortly after the operating system reinstall, the consultants were able to spend an hour copying user data files onto disks so users could work on them locally on their PCs. The lost productivity probably cost this small company thousands of dollars, not only in paying employee salaries while they were essentially unproductive, but also in lost business because they were not able to work effectively during the unscheduled downtime.

The fallout from not having an updated ERD on hand can be substantial, and it takes only a few minutes to create one. The utility is called rdisk.exe and can be executed by clicking on Start|Run, typing "rdisk /s", and pressing Enter. The /s switch updates the SAM and security data files of the Registry—something that is not done otherwise. After the rdisk utility completes the update, you will be prompted to create a new ERD.

Label the Emergency Repair Disk with the computer name and date of creation and put it in a secured location, because it contains sensitive security information about your system. Be aware that ERDs are specific to the computer they were created on because of the Registry information they contain.

"Blue Screen Of Death"

"Blue Screen of Death" is the affectionate term for the blue-screen STOP errors that occur and halt the system. Anyone who has worked with NT for any significant length of time has probably experienced one, and troubleshooting a blue screen can be difficult at best. When a STOP message (fatal system error) occurs in Windows NT, it enters Debug mode for troubleshooting purposes. This mode appears as a blue screen similar to the one shown in Figure 14.8.

You can configure Windows NT to save STOP-message information to a "dump" file called memory.dmp. This option is enabled by default in Windows NT Server. However, for Windows NT Workstation, you must enable the option manually, and you must do so *before* encountering a fatal error in order for the information to be recorded. To enable this feature, follow these steps:

1. In the System component of Control Panel, choose the Recovery button.

2. Select the Write Debugging Information To checkbox.

3. Choose OK until you are asked to restart the computer.

```
               DSR CTS
*** STOP:   0x0000000A   (0x00000000,  0x0000001a,  0x00000000,  0x00000000)
IRQL_NOT_LESS_OR_EQUAL

p4-0300 irql:1f  SYSVER: 0xf000030e

Dll Base  DateStmp -  Name              Dll Base  DateStmp -  Name
80100000  2e53fe55 -  ntoskrl.exe       80400000  2e53eba6 -  hal.dll
80010000  2e41884b -  Aha154x.sys       80013000  2e4bc29a -  SCSIPORT.SYS
8001b000  2e4e7b6b -  Scsidisk.sys      80220000  2e53f238 -  Ntfs.sys
fe420000  2e406607 -  Floppy.SYS        fe430000  2e406618 -  Scsicdrm.SYS
fe440000  2e406659 -  Es_Rec.SYS        fe450000  2e40660f -  Null.SYS
fe460000  2e4065f4 -  Beep.SYS          fe470000  2e406634 -  Sermouse.SYS
fe480000  2e42a4a4 -  i8042prt.SYS      fe490000  2e40660d -  Mouclass.SYS
fe4a0000  2e40660c -  Kbdclass.SYS      fe4c0000  2e4065e2 -  VIDEOPRT.SYS
fe4b0000  2e53d49d -  ati.SYS           fe4d0000  2e4065e8 -  vga.sys
fe4e0000  2e406655 -  Msfs.SYS          fe4f0000  2e414f30 -  Npfs.SYS
fe510000  2e53f222 -  NDIS.SYS          fe500000  2e40719b -  elnkii.sys
fe550000  2e406697 -  TDI.SYS           fe530000  2e47c740 -  nbf.sys
fe560000  2e5279d9 -  nwlnkipx.sys      fe570000  2e53a89e -  nwlnknb.sys
fe580000  2e494973 -  tcpip.sys         fe5a0000  2e5256b8 -  afd.sys
fe5b0000  2e5279d3 -  netbt.sys         fe5d0000  2e4167f7 -  netbios.sys
fe5e0000  2e406db3 -  mup.sys           fe5f0000  2e4f9f51 -  rdr.sys
fe630000  2e53f24a -  srv.sys           fe660000  2ef16062 -  nwlnkspx.sys

Address     dword dump Build [1057]                                      -  Name
FF541E4c    fe5105df  fe5105df  00000001  ff640128  fe4a8228  000002fe  -  NDIS.SYS
ff541e60    fe501368  fe501368  00000246  00004002  00000000  00000000  -  elnkii.sys
ff541eb4    fe481509  fe481509  ff6688c8  ff668288  00000000  ff668138  -  i8042prt.SYS
ff541ee0    fe481ea8  fe481ea8  fe482078  00000000  ff541f04  8013c58a  -  i8042prt.SYS
ff541ee4    fe482078  fe482078  00000000  ff541f04  8013c58a  ff6688c8  -  i8042prt.sys
ff541ef0    8013c58a  8013c58a  ff6688c8  ff668040  80405900  00000031  -  ntoskrnl.exe
ff541efc    80405900  80405900  00000031  06060606  06060606  06060606  -  hal.dll

Restart and set the recovery options in the system control panel
or the /CRASHDEBUG system start option if this message reappears,
contact your system administrator or technical support group.
CRASHDUMP: Initializing miniport driver
CRASHDUMP: Dumping physical memory to disk:   2000
CRASHDUMP: Physical memory dump complete
```

Figure 14.8 The "Blue Screen of Death."

Troubleshooting the blue screen is a two-step process. The first step is to consult the Microsoft Knowledge Base, found online at **www.microsoft.com** and on Microsoft's TechNet subscription service. You can search for the specific error code, such as 0x0000000A in the above example. You can also search for phrases, such as "Unhandled Kernel exception" Often, you will find articles that describe how to fix the problems you are experiencing, such as by upgrading to the latest service pack or replacing a particular device driver file.

If the Knowledge Base is unable to help and you are not a programmer experienced in reading Assembly language, your second step is usually to call Microsoft. You can send Microsoft the memory.dmp file for analysis and debugging and, hopefully, get a resolution. Otherwise, you might be faced with the prospect of reinstalling the operating system.

Reconnecting To The Network From A Boot Disk

Another useful tool to have in your network administrator arsenal is a network client boot disk. You can create one in Windows NT in the Network Client Administrator applet, shown in Figure 14.9.

Being able to boot from a disk and attach to the network is useful in a number of cases. If you need to reinstall an operating system, and the system does not have a CD-ROM drive, you can connect to a network share to run Setup. Many administrators have resorted to using preconfigured software images that contain the operating system and a company-standard set of applications. With a network boot disk, you can download that image to a freshly formatted hard drive, saving time by not installing the operating system and applications separately.

Having network boot disks that can boot and connect any system in your organization to the network is desirable, but managing those disks becomes difficult as the number of network cards in use increases. The ideal scenario is

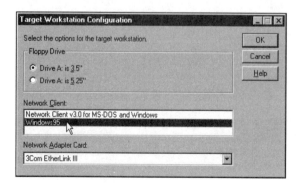

Figure 14.9 The Network Client Administrator is used to create a network boot disk.

to have all computers use a standard network card, allowing you to have a single disk that can be used on any system. If that is not possible, you will want to try to at least minimize the number of different network cards.

Reinstallation Methods

With any operating system, reinstallation is the option that is left after all other options have been explored and failed. With Windows NT 4, there are several types of reinstalls, which are:

➤ Repair install

➤ Upgrade install

➤ Parallel install

➤ New install

Repair Install

The repair install, mentioned earlier, involves the use of the Emergency Repair Disk. When you run NT Setup either from the boot floppies or from a command prompt with the floppyless /b option, a Setup Menu presents you with installation options, as shown in Figure 14.10.

When you perform a repair install, you are prompted to insert the Emergency Repair Disk, and you are given the options shown in Table 14.3.

The repair install lets you recover from many types of errors that prevent NT from booting correctly, without forcing the reinstallation of the operating system and applications.

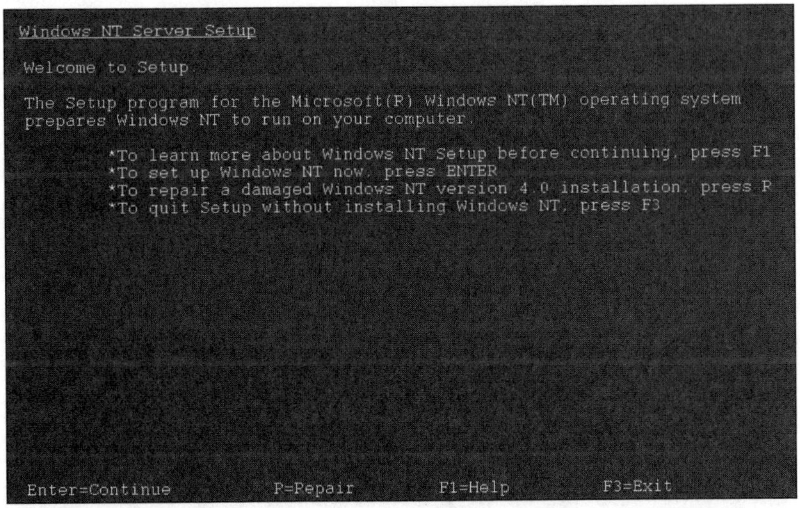

```
Windows NT Server Setup

Welcome to Setup

The Setup program for the Microsoft(R) Windows NT(TM) operating system
prepares Windows NT to run on your computer.

        *To learn more about Windows NT Setup before continuing, press F1
        *To set up Windows NT now, press ENTER
        *To repair a damaged Windows NT version 4.0 installation, press R
        *To quit Setup without installing Windows NT, press F3




  Enter=Continue        P=Repair        F1=Help         F3=Exit
```

Figure 14.10   The Windows NT Setup Menu lets you choose the type of install.

Table 14.3 The Repair menu options and their functions.

Repair Option	Function
Inspect Registry files	Gives you the option to replace Registry files with those stored on the ERD.
Inspect startup environment	Fixes the boot.ini file so that it points to the correct disk and partition to load NT.
Verify Windows NT system files	Identifies files that have been changed since NT was originally installed on the system and gives the option to replace them with the originals.
Inspect boot sector	Fixes the boot sector if (needed) to correctly refer to NTLDR. Useful if someone uses the DOS SYS command to overwrite the boot sector.

If you have selected the option to verify Windows NT system files, Setup will probably report that a lot of files have been changed. Most likely, the system has had one or more service packs applied, which have updated the files. After you run the repair installation, it is advisable to reapply the latest service pack to ensure that there will be no problems related to older files having replaced newer ones.

Upgrade Install

To install Windows NT from the Setup Menu shown in Figure 14.10, you would press Enter. Setup will look for an existing NT installation. If it finds one, you are given the option of upgrading the existing installation or installing a new copy of Windows NT.

An upgrade installation is typically used to upgrade an older version of Windows NT, such as 3.51, to the current version, or to upgrade NT Workstation to NT Server (NT Workstation can be upgraded to a standalone server, but not a PDC or BDC). However, in lieu of an ERD, an upgrade installation can be used to install NT over itself and maintain Registry and application settings. As with installing Windows 98 over itself, it is rather messy in the sense that it does not clean up any clutter on the hard drive that might have been a source of trouble previously. Also, sometimes the upgrade installation cannot fix the problems that caused you to have to reinstall in the first place, and you get through Setup only to find that the system still does not work properly. If that is the case, you can consider a parallel install, described next.

Parallel Install

A parallel install sounds exotic, but it's really not. A parallel install is just installing Windows NT into a new directory in order to get the system booting so you can restore the old directory. Confusing enough? Here is an example.

You have an installation of NT Server installed in C:\winnt that gets corrupted, but you have full and incremental backups (discussed in Chapter 15) available to restore from. Restoring the backup while booted up from the C:\winnt installation will not work because the restore will not be able to replace files that are currently in use. So how do you get around it? By using a parallel install. You install another copy of NT Server on that machine to a different directory—for example, C:\winnt4—and set up your tape drive and backup software. When you restore your full backup, you let the files get restored to their original locations in the C:\winnt directory. Because you are not booted up from that installation, no files are in use from it, and the restore can replace all of the files and the Registry in the C:\winnt directory and its subdirectories. After the restore, you can reboot from your original installation and have the system working again. Once the server is back online, you can safely delete the C:\winnt4 installation and remove references to it from the boot.ini file.

New Install

A new install is simply installing Windows NT into its existing directory without choosing the upgrade option. This type of installation will overwrite any existing files and replace all Registry files and settings. Why would you want to do this? This is a last resort, used when you do not have a good backup to restore from and either you don't have an ERD, or a repair installation didn't work. A new installation would be run only if an upgrade install had been previously attempted and failed. This type of installation is only one step from formatting and reinstalling everything, so it should be used only if none of the previous methods get NT working properly.

Unlike with reinstalling Windows 9x, when the reinstallation method was subject to personal preference, with NT it is generally accepted to follow the order laid out in this chapter. With NT, you should attempt a repair installation before resorting to reinstalling the operating system through upgrade or parallel installations. A parallel installation should be used when you have a way to correct the problems with the existing installation, even if it is through restoration of a backup. An upgrade install works by loading NT over itself, maintaining existing applications and Registry settings. You should attempt an upgrade install before you resort to a new installation, which will take you back to square one and require setting up user accounts, network shares, security information, and applications again. Knowing the options and consequences of the types of installations should illustrate the need to keep backups and ERDs on hand to allow for recovery of a server with a minimal amount of hassle.

GENERAL ADMINISTRATIVE PRACTICES

So far, this chapter has extensively covered the common network-administration chores of documenting and maintaining records and recovering and repairing servers and workstations. This last section is a hodgepodge of general administrative practices that you will be expected to know how to perform as a network administrator. They include:

➤ Updating and removing outdated or unused drivers

➤ Drive mapping and connecting to network shares through Universal Naming Convention (UNC)

➤ Printer port capturing

➤ Verifying functionality of critical hardware and software after a move

➤ Obtaining appropriate permissions

Updating And Removing Outdated Or Unused Drivers

An oft-overlooked administrative chore is updating and removing outdated or unused drivers. Many administrators view this task with the rationale of "If it isn't causing any problems, why mess with it?" Well, there are a few reasons.

As new software and hardware become available, and as existing applications are updated, new device drivers are designed to improve device performance and interaction, and even to fix problems. Usually, these drivers are created and provided by the same company that manufactures the component device, and they are available for download from the company's Web site or FTP site, or are made available on disk or CD for a fee.

Even a brand-new computer system may have been assembled months before it was purchased, so right out of the box it can have "outdated" drivers installed. This happens because the current drivers are not available when the system is built and configured. So, in many cases, even a new computer can be enhanced with updated device drivers to improve system performance and integration.

Outdated drivers contribute to a large number of issues that users experience with any software application. This is why one of your first system troubleshooting or maintenance steps should always be to make sure that your drivers are up to date, are installed properly, and are the newest versions recommended.

Remember that manufacturers don't provide new drivers for the fun of it. Producing drivers costs manufacturers money, not just to manufacture and distribute the new drivers, but for research and development as well. Manufacturers do not usually spend time improving a driver unless there is an issue that causes users problems or unless a newer operating system demands an update for the hardware to work. Therefore, it stands to reason that if newer device drivers exist for your devices, you should get those drivers and install them on your computer.

Unused drivers on a system are usually from devices that have been physically removed from the system, such as a failed network card that was replaced with a different model card. Although these drivers may appear to lie dormant, sometimes they can cause conflicts later on when they have been forgotten. It is a good practice to check your systems periodically for unused drivers and remove them.

Drive Mapping

A *mapped drive* is an alias that makes a network path appear as if it were a local drive. Computers have local drives, which are the floppy, hard, CD-ROM, and any other removable storage drives that are physically installed in the computer. The floppy drive is always drive letter A:, and if there are two floppy drives, the second is drive B:. The first physical hard drive's active partition is C:, and if there are multiple hard drives or multiple partitions on a hard drive, they take on the letters following C:. CD-ROM drives and removable storage drives take drive letters after the hard-drive partitions have been assigned letters. A mapped drive, on the other hand, is not a physical drive in the computer but is rather a "virtual drive." A user's system may have a mapped drive letter W: that does not refer to any drive in the computer, but refers rather to a directory on a file server in another part of the country. By using drive mappings, users can refer to that shared directory as if it were a local drive, rather than having to browse for it or explicitly type in the path to it every time they need to access that directory.

Mapping a drive, like many other tasks, can be done in several different ways in Windows 9x and NT. The easiest way is to browse to the shared directory in Network Neighborhood, right-click on the directory to display the Context menu, and select Map Network Drive. Assign it an unused drive letter, and the task is complete.

14

A more useful method, especially if you work in a cross-platform environment, is mapping drives through Universal Naming Convention (UNC) names. As the name implies, the Universal Naming Convention is an industry standard. It provides a common syntax that should work universally across most systems, including Windows, Unix, and NetWare. The syntax is *servername\sharename*. For example, if I had a directory called "apps" on a server called "finance", the UNC path would be \\finance\apps.

To map a drive from a command prompt in Windows 9x or NT, you would use the **net use** command.

 Several **net** commands owe their heritage to Microsoft's pre-Windows NT LAN Manager. Typing "net /?" at a command prompt will display a summary of the commands.

Command Prompt

```
Microsoft(R) Windows NT(TM)
(C) Copyright 1985-1996 Microsoft Corp.

H:\>net use w: \\wwillis\clients
The command completed successfully.

H:\>
```

Figure 14.11 The **net use** command allows you to connect to a network path
through its UNC name.

To see a properly formed **net use** command to map a drive letter to a UNC
network path, refer to Figure 14.11.

Printer Port Capturing

Capturing a printer port is similar to mapping a drive. Most computers have an
LPT1 printer port, and some have a second port, LPT2. Printer port capturing
lets you establish virtual printer ports—such as LPT3 and LPT4—that connect
to printers that have been shared on the network rather than physically
connected to the computer you are using.

Printer paths are shown in UNC just as network directories are, in the syntax
*printservername**printersharename*. Connecting to a shared printer is done through
the Printers Folder in Windows. From there, you open the File menu and select
Capture Printer Port. This opens the dialog box shown in Figure 14.12.

For the device name, you are given the option of LPT1 through LPT9, and you
want to make sure *not* to select a device that is the same as a physical printer
port on your computer. The path is the UNC name of the shared printer. You
can make the capture permanent by reconnecting the captured port at logon, or
you can capture the port only for this current session.

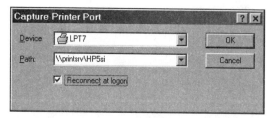

Figure 14.12 Capturing a printer port in Windows 98.

Verifying Functionality After A Move

One of the bigger headaches for a network administrator is a move—for example, one or more departments moving to another side of the floor, to another floor, or even to another building. Servers and workstations are moved, as are routers and hubs and switches, and network cabling is redone. So how do you know that when you throw on the power after the move, everything will work as it has previously?

The answer lies in proper planning and testing. That sounds obvious enough, but in the chaos that surrounds a move, it is entirely too easy to postpone testing until it is too late to be done effectively.

Planning and testing go back to the documenting and change control topics we discussed earlier in this chapter. Well before it is time for the move, floor plans for the new site should be analyzed and the locations of the equipment should be determined. The wiring should be completed as early as possible, and all links should be certified and tested.

The next step is to analyze any consequences of the move. Will workstations and servers be on different subnets than they were previously? Will domains change at all? If so, are the necessary trust relationships in place to guarantee that users will have access to necessary data? With the same type of change control procedures that would be followed before making any other kinds of network or system changes, you would carefully consider as many potential repercussions as possible. Unlike with change control procedures in other circumstances, though, a back-out plan is almost never an option for a move. That raises the stakes for failure to get all critical systems online right after the move. A written checklist of all expectations should be generated. Call a meeting of all managers of affected departments to ensure that relevant information is not missed.

14

If your planning is solid and the change issues have been managed, then verifying functionality after the move should be fairly simple. It is wise to do the move on a Friday after hours or on a Saturday so that you have some time to test the systems before employees come in Monday morning expecting to be able to work. In testing, it is necessary to verify that the workstations can connect to the network and log in to the appropriate servers, that network applications launch and are functional, and that workstations can access other subnets or the Internet, as appropriate. Verifying this will be easy if you have already laid the groundwork in planning.

Permissions

In an environment where you are the sole administrator, obtaining permissions is not particularly relevant. However, when you are one of many IT professionals and have responsibility over only a small area, you will often have to obtain account permissions to add, delete, or modify users. This issue relates to change control in that changes should not be made without cause and without proper documentation.

Obtaining permissions is relevant in another way as well: If you attempt to make a change and you do not have the authorization to do it, any number of things might happen. At best, you will get an error stating that you do not have the proper authorization and the change is denied. At worst, the change may seemingly go through successfully, but will have you chasing down phantoms when you start having strange problems. The resultant waste of time and energy will benefit neither the company nor your frustration level. It is sensible to make sure that you have the appropriate permissions to carry out a task before it is done. As always, document your changes so that you will be able to backtrack and quickly discover the error should there be a problem.

CHAPTER SUMMARY

➤ Although it's not the most glamorous part of network administration, documentation is essential to be able to review previous changes.

➤ Documenting and maintaining records falls under the broad category called *configuration management*, which includes configuration identification, equipment status, change control, and auditing.

➤ An annotated systems diagram is a helpful tool for understanding the layout and pieces of a network.

➤ Workstation configuration sheets should be kept near each workstation for ease of updating as a technician performs work on a system.

➤ A server log book should be maintained, documenting configurations and a history of changes and problems. This log book should be kept in a secured location near the server it documents.

➤ The single most important aspect of the network to document is the cable plant.

➤ The Windows 9x and NT Registry is a database that stores all of a computer's system and applications configuration information. The Registry is organized into keys that are arranged in a treelike fashion, with subkeys and values branching off.

➤ Creating an Emergency Boot Disk in Windows 9x—done through Control Panel—allows you to boot and repair the system from a floppy drive.

➤ There are several methods of reinstalling Windows 9x, depending on the current state of the operating system and its ability to boot: the cheat method of replacing system.dat with system.1st, reinstalling Windows over itself, installing Windows clean, and starting from scratch by formatting the hard drive and reinstalling Windows.

➤ The Windows NT Emergency Repair Disk is updated and created through the rdisk.exe utility.

➤ The "Blue Screen of Death" is a fatal crash that occurs in Windows NT. Troubleshooting is done by analyzing the memory.dmp dump file or by consulting the Microsoft Knowledge Base.

➤ The Windows NT Network Client Administrator allows you to create a boot floppy that will connect your system to the network, allowing you to reinstall from a network share.

➤ Windows NT installations can be repair installs, upgrade installs, or new installs (parallel or into the same directory).

➤ Updating and removing unused device drivers should be done on a periodic basis for optimal system performance.

➤ Mapping a network drive allows the user to use a network share as if it were a local drive.

➤ Capturing a printer port allows a user to print to a remote printer as if it were a locally attached printer.

➤ Verifying functionality of hardware and software after a move involves employing change control methodology and thorough planning before the move.

➤ Proper permissions should be verified before you make network changes that require a higher level of authorization than is standard. Failure to guarantee proper authorization can result in errors and prevent users from gaining access to necessary resources.

14

REVIEW QUESTIONS

1. What file is generated when Windows NT encounters a fatal error and blue screens?

   a. Memory.txt

   b. Dump.mem

   c. Memory.dmp

   d. Crash.dmp

2. The Windows NT Registry contains the same keys as the Windows 9x Registry except:
    a. HKEY_CURRENT_USER
    b. HKEY_DYN_DATA
    c. HKEY_LOCAL_MACHINE
    d. HKEY_CURRENT_CONFIG

3. Configuration management involves all of the following concepts except:
    a. Change control
    b. Auditing
    c. Equipment status
    d. User policies

4. Which of the following examples has correct UNC syntax for a server named "FileSrv1" and a directory named "clients"?
    a. \FileSrv1\clients
    b. \\FileSrv1\clients
    c. \clients\FileSrv1
    d. \\clients\FileSrv1

5. Reinstalling NT into a new directory for the purpose of repairing the original installation is known as which type of installation?
    a. Parallel install
    b. Repair install
    c. Clean install
    d. Upgrade install

6. Which key would you press to display the Windows 9x boot menu?
    a. F10
    b. F1
    c. F8
    d. F4

7. In what situation would you use printer port capturing?
    a. To print to a remote printer as if it were a local printer
    b. To print to a local printer
    c. To make a local printer available to remote users
    d. To prevent remote users from printing to a local printer

8. To map a drive to a remote share through UNC from a Windows command prompt, which command would you use?

   a. **net share**

   b. **net use**

   c. **net connect**

   d. **net link**

9. Which utility is used to create an Emergency Repair Disk?

   a. Control Panel's Add/Remove Programs applet

   b. ERD.exe

   c. Rdisk.exe

   d. An ERD can be created only during the installation of NT

10. Which troubleshooting mode boots Windows 9x with only a minimal configuration?

   a. Diagnostics Mode

   b. Safe Mode

   c. Safe Mode Command Prompt Only

   d. Emergency Boot Mode

11. How often should network auditing be done?

   a. Once per year

   b. One per month

   c. Daily

   d. Whenever a lot of changes have been made

12. The single most important aspect of a network to document is:

   a. Server configurations

   b. Cable plant

   c. Workstation locations

   d. Router and switch configurations

13. Device drivers should be updated:

   a. Only when there are problems with the current driver

   b. Whenever a new version is released

   c. Only if the update offers features you want or need

   d. Only if the manufacturer requires an update for support

14

14. The Windows NT utility used to create a network boot disk is called:

    a. Network Client Administrator

    b. Network Boot Administrator

    c. Remote Boot Administrator

    c. Rdisk

15. What utility would you edit the Windows 98 Registry with?

    a. Regedt32.exe

    b. Regedit.exe

    c. Regclean.exe

    d. both a and b

HANDS-ON PROJECTS

Project 14.1

Knowing how to repair a Windows NT installation is a valuable skill for a network administrator. Fortunately, the procedures are identical for both NT Workstation and NT Server. In this project, we will create the three installation floppy disks and a repair disk. When that is complete, we will intentionally "break" NT and boot up in order to see it fail. Then, we will go through a repair installation, reboot, and verify that NT is working properly. This project requires access to an NT Server or Workstation to be successfully completed. Preferably, this computer will not be used in a production environment.

The first thing that is needed to recover a Windows NT installation is the three boot floppies that start the Setup program. If you purchased the retail NT product, you might already have a set of boot floppies. Most OEMs, however, give you only the installation CD. It is up to you to make the disk. Use the following steps to create the boot floppies.

To create boot disks:

1. Shell out to a command prompt through Start|Programs|Command Prompt.

2. Insert your Windows NT CD-ROM into the CD-ROM drive and change to that drive letter.

3. Change to the i386 directory for x86-based platforms by typing "cd \i386".

4. From a D:\i386 prompt (or substitute your CD-ROM drive letter for D:), type "winnt32 /ox" and press Enter. Figure 14.13 shows how your screen should look.

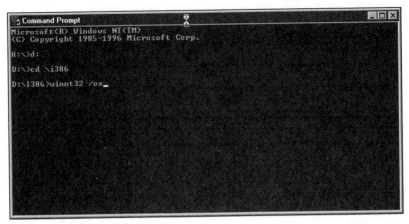

Figure 14.13   Creating the three NT boot floppies from a command prompt.

The /ox switch for winnt32.exe tells Setup to create the three boot floppies, but not to actually run Setup. If you were creating these floppies on a Win9x system, you would use the winnt.exe command, rather than winnt32.exe, because winnt32 is used to upgrade an existing version of NT.

5. You will be prompted to label and insert three disk. This process actually creates the disks in *descending* order, starting with Disk 3. Many new network administrators mistakenly assume that the disks are being created 1 through 3 and later wonder why they can't boot off of Disk 1 when it is really Disk 3.

   The next step is to update and create the Emergency Repair Disk.

6. From a run line (Start|Run), type "rdisk /s" and press Enter.

   The system starts saving the current configuration. The /s switch updates the SAM and Security information, which is not done by default.

7. When the saving of the current configuration is complete, you will be given the option to create the ERD. Click on "Yes" after you have inserted a blank, formatted floppy disk that has been labeled with the server name and date.

To intentionally break NT and then repair it with the ERD to demonstrate the repair process:

1. Open up Windows NT Explorer and make sure Show All Files is selected under View|Options.

2. Navigate to C:\ and delete the boot.ini file. Reboot the computer. When the computer starts to reboot, you will see that it fails because there is no boot.ini file to determine where NT is installed on the system. The boot sector is effectively corrupted at this point.

14

3. Reboot the computer from the first boot floppy, and then insert the second when prompted.

4. When given the Setup menu (as shown earlier, in Figure 14.10), select R for repair.

5. Setup will display the following options:

```
[X]  Inspect Registry files
[X]  Inspect startup environment
[X]  Verify Windows NT system files
[X]  Inspect boot sector
     Continue (perform selected tasks)
```

In our situation (a boot problem), we would want the repair process to inspect the startup environment. Because the ERD is known to be current, you could also optionally have Setup perform the other tasks to see how the process works. Otherwise, take the X's out of the boxes for all except Inspect Startup Environment.

6. After you've made your selections, you'll be prompted for Disk 3 and then to insert the Emergency Repair Disk. Follow the on-screen instructions to perform the repair.

Inspect Startup Environment verifies that the Windows NT files in the system partition are the correct ones. If any of the files that are needed to start Windows NT are missing or corrupt, the repair process replaces them from the Windows NT CD. On x86-based computers, if Windows NT is not listed in the boot.ini file, repair adds a Windows NT option to the file. If there is no boot.ini file, repair creates one. In this case, the repair process will create a new boot.ini pointing to the correct location of our NT installation.

7. When the repair process has completed, you will receive the following message:

```
Setup has completed repairs.
If there is a floppy disk inserted in drive A:, remove it.
Press ENTER to restart your computer.
```

8. Reboot the computer, and notice that the system boots up correctly again. The repair process has successfully re-created our boot.ini file.

This lab example was a simple illustration of the power of the repair process. From the menu options provided by the Setup program, you can see how the Emergency Repair Disk can be used to repair problems with the Registry, with the boot process, or with system files that might be corrupt. If you get in the habit of updating your ERD whenever you make a configuration change, you will always have that option available when you run into system troubles.

Project 14.2

In this lab, you will implement configuration management. To do so, you will need a couple of computers, an NT Server, and an NT workstation or Windows 9x workstation.

Configuration management involves each of the following elements:

➤ Configuration identification

➤ Equipment status

➤ Change control

➤ Auditing

Configuration Identification

For both the server and the workstation, create a configuration sheet similar to that in Figures 14.3a and 14.3b. The worksheets should contain similar types of information, such as:

➤ Workstation processor

➤ RAM type (SDRAM, EDO, Fast Page, and so on) and quantity

➤ Hard-drive manufacturer, capacity, and settings

➤ Other disk drives and settings (floppy drives, CD-ROM drives, Zip drives, etc.)

➤ Disk-drive types (SCSI versus IDE)

➤ BIOS date and manufacturer

➤ IRQ, I/O, and DMA settings for all adapter cards

➤ Operating system and version as well as any revision/patch levels

➤ Printouts of system files (autoexec.bat, config.sys, win.ini, system.ini, and any other relevant files)

➤ Applications installed on the system and whether they are run from the server or locally

➤ Serial numbers

➤ Types and addresses of network adapter cards

➤ Network protocols in use and binding orders

➤ Network protocol configurations (e.g., for TCP/IP: the IP address, subnet mask, default gateway, WINS configuration, etc.)

➤ Server programs running and their configurations

➤ User accounts (names, group memberships, profile settings, other settings)

➤ Domain name, server name, server role (PDC, BDC, standalone), and trust relationships for NT servers

14

Equipment Status

After documenting the configurations of the server and workstation, devise a procedure for tracking equipment status. Some options are:

➤ Writing a database application in a program such as Corel Paradox, Microsoft Access, or Lotus Approach to manage your equipment. This option is most useful in an environment with more than 100 servers and workstations to maintain.

➤ Extend the scope of your workstation configuration sheet to include a problem history and maintenance section. In effect, you create mini-logbooks for each workstation. This works best in smaller environments with fewer than 25 computers to maintain.

➤ Design a spreadsheet to fulfill the same function as a workstation configuration sheet, except in electronic format. You can have a separate file for each piece of equipment, use one file with a separate worksheet for each PC, or build one large table that includes all of the equipment in separate columns or rows. This solution is best suited to environments with up to 100 PCs.

Change Control

You are the network administrator of a network that consists of five NT servers in three domains and 100 Windows 98 workstations on one floor of an office building. Users have been complaining a lot in the last several months about the degrading performance of the 10BaseT network, but your existing CAT3 wiring will not support a higher bandwidth. Management has decided to move the company to another floor that has more space. The move is in three months. You decide that this would be the perfect time to upgrade to 100BaseTX because a new cable plant will be installed and you can have it done in CAT5.

Applying change control methods, determine the risk factor of replacing all server and workstation 10MB network adapters with 10/100MB cards before the move and replacing the 10MB hubs with 100MB hubs at the time of the move. Use the sample Change Request Form shown in Figure 14.1 to document the details of the change, the risk factor, and a back-out plan. Describe what methodology you will use to replace the existing network adapters (for instance, a department at a time or by least critical PC to most critical).

After analyzing the potential consequences and creating an implementation and back-out plan, determine the procedures for testing the new location before the move (assuming that your company is given free reign of the new space for a month before the move). Consider the installation and documentation of the cable plant and installing the new hubs. Also, plan for testing network links before the move by hooking up critical servers and workstations during off hours to ensure that they will function in the new environment without modification.

Auditing

Document a plan to audit your network configuration from the previous example on an annual basis. In an audit, you will not need to completely redo your configuration identification, though you will want to hit on the aspects most likely to change. Your server serial numbers and processor will probably not change, but installed applications and the operating-system revision level (as service packs are applied) are likely to have changed. Decide how you will approach discrepancies between your existing documentation and what you find in your audit. A potential solution is to hold a department meeting if there are multiple IT personnel and discuss ways to improve the change control process to ensure that all changes are being documented.

14

## CHAPTER FIFTEEN

MAINTAINING AND SUPPORTING THE NETWORK

After Reading This Chapter And Completing The Exercises, You Will Be Able To:

➤ Maintain hardware

➤ Understand what a vendor's role is in a network, including methods of obtaining and implementing patches, fixes, upgrades, and maintaining system software

➤ Manage Users and User Accounts

➤ Utilize standard backup procedures and backup media practices

➤ Understand the need for installing anti-virus software on workstations and servers and the need to frequently update virus signatures

After the network has been installed and configured, the day-to-day process of maintaining and supporting it is what is known as *network administration*. Although specific procedures vary depending on which NOS (network operating system) is in use, the principles of network administration are largely the same, regardless of whether you work in a Unix, NT, or NetWare environment. In larger companies, where there is usually more than one network administrator, job duties can become specialized, and you may or may not come in contact with all of the different areas involved in network administration. In smaller companies, where Information Technology (IT) resources are not as abundant, you will often be expected to handle all of the chores, as well as provide some user support.

NETWORK MAINTENANCE

As with a well-called game by a professional referee or umpire, the work of network administrators often goes unnoticed. In fact, more often than not, when a network administrator gets attention, it's usually because there is some sort of problem that needs to be addressed. Effective administration, besides reducing the number of problems that arise, can also allow the administrator to respond to and resolve problems more quickly than if routine maintenance is lacking or not up to date. Chapter 14 covered the general principles involved, which can be followed throughout your organization to help maximize network uptime and minimize user disruption.

What Do You Need To Know?

Before you can effectively maintain your network, you first need to understand what it is you are trying to maintain. That sounds simple enough, but usually will require some investigation on your part. From strictly a hardware perspective, your network will at least include servers, workstations, a cabling plant, and hubs or switches to tie all of that together. More complex networks,

Is My Hardware Still Supported?

It is vitally important to know the vendor support status of each piece of hardware you have. Take, for example, the true story of a network administrator colleague of mine at another company. We'll call him Joe to protect the guilty. Joe took over an administrator position at a company that had quite a bit of old hardware still in use. He went about his day-to-day routine, which included performing server backups. One night he got paged at home because an emergency had come up. It seemed that a user had accidentally deleted a substantial portion of an accounting database. The department needed that information back ASAP, so Joe went to the office to restore the database from a backup tape. When he tried to restore the database, the tape drive stopped responding.

A little troubleshooting determined that the tape drive had a hardware failure. "No problem," he thought. "I'll just restore these tapes from a different drive in another department." Quickly he realized that this tape drive was the only one of its type left in the company. A call to the drive manufacturer revealed that this drive had been discontinued for several years and was no longer even supported. In the end, it took Joe three days to track down a working drive of that type, at another company that was willing to lend it to him (for a fee) long enough to restore the missing data. The company estimated the lost revenue from the downtime at close to half a million dollars. A lesson hard learned about ensuring the availability of replacement parts or units in case of a hardware failure.

including those connected to other networks such as the Internet, will have routers as well. Your organization may also have bridges, dedicated RAS server hardware, repeaters, hardware RAID arrays, and so on. So the first step is to have an accurate inventory of the hardware in your organization. As was discussed in Chapter 14, not only will you want to keep your documentation in electronic format for ease of updating, but you'll also want a hard copy of your critical network information.

Once you have determined exactly what your hardware assets are and where they are located, the next step is to identify existing warranties and maintenance agreements. Knowing this information will save you from many headaches down the road. Equipment that is past its warranty period should be flagged for periodic review. Not only is out-of-warranty equipment more likely to be a little older and more susceptible to problems, but you also have to be careful about the vendor discontinuing support of your hardware. A good local area netword (LAN)-based inventory package—such as Microsoft's Systems Management Server, Tivoli Systems' Tivoli Enterprise, HP OpenView, or Computer Associates' Unicenter—can go a long way toward helping you get a handle on what hardware and software you have on your network.

The Economics Of Hardware Maintenance

Although network hardware at times seems quite expensive, the costs of supporting that hardware and the people that use it over its lifetime far outweigh the initial hardware expense. Figure 15.1 shows a breakdown of the total cost of ownership (TCO) for a network.

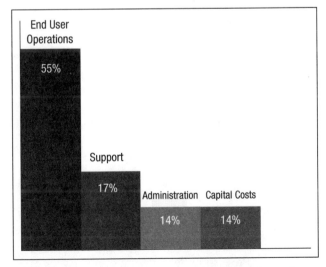

Figure 15.1 Total cost of ownership breakdown for a network.

As with other business units within a corporation, the IT department works within the constraints of a budget. Out of the budget come personnel expenses, such as salaries and bonuses, as well as education and training costs. There are the actual hardware and software expenditures as well. In many companies, the IT department is the cost center that absorbs the computer-related costs for other departments. It is imperative to know the warranty and maintenance status of your equipment because the support costs can really be a budget buster. Say, for instance, that your company buys 10 new servers and 1,500 new PCs this year. The servers have three-year warranties, and the PCs have one-year warranties. You also replace some older switches and routers that have one- and two-year warranties. Your organization also has an additional 3,000 PCs and 15 servers that are either in the last year of their warranties or are not under a manufacturer's warranty. This year the budget is okay, but what happens next year? You have to make decisions regarding support of the equipment as the warranties expire, and you have several options, which are outlined in the following sections.

Departmental Support

This first model is often used in larger corporations. With departmental support, a designated individual within a particular corporate department, such as finance or marketing, is responsible for handling computer-related issues. The advantages to this model are cost and response time. The cost is lower because the computers are just a part of the job for the person charged with their care. Invariably, their "main" job is something else within the department. Because they are in the department, the response time is faster than calling up a Help Desk or a centralized IT department. The biggest disadvantage is obvious: expertise. Because IT work is not the full-time profession for the people in charge of the computers, they usually do not have the background of a professional IT worker, nor do they have the time (or often the inclination) to devote to developing that level of knowledge and skill. Their skill set tends to be limited to what they do on a daily basis, such as user management (changing passwords, setting up user accounts) and rudimentary troubleshooting. Complex problems usually require outside help. This model can offer an excellent first line of defense, however, in a hybrid model that also incorporates a centralized IT department.

The Information Technologies Department

The next option is to support the company internally through a centralized IT department. This department can go by many different names, such as the Information Systems (IS) department, the Management Information Systems (MIS) department, the Data Processing department, the Network Support Center, or simply the Help Desk. This model employs any number of IT professionals (the number depends on the size and complexity of the network) in a centralized department. These people have a background in IT and work full time with computer- and network-related issues. In large corporations, this model is often combined with the departmental model to create a hybrid support model. In those cases, the departmental LAN administrator handles the day-to-day chores of user management and basic troubleshooting, and calls the IT department when a problem exists that he or she cannot solve.

The IT department is usually divided into two or more categories, depending on the size of the network. The first level of support is the Help Desk, where users call in with problems and try to resolve them with a technician over the phone. A call-tracking system is used to log calls, and a support call can be closed by solving the problem, left open for further research, or escalated. When a call is escalated, it goes to a second-level team that does hands-on desktop support. The Help Desk generates a "trouble ticket" or "problem ticket" that is passed on to the Desktop Support group for review and response. This Desktop Support team takes the problem tickets, or cases that have been escalated by the Help Desk, and goes out to the user's environment to solve the problems. Most problems are solved at this point. If not, the case is escalated to the third level, also known as the "senior-level" support team. This team is primarily responsible for high-level support and for supporting the physical network and server infrastructure. If a problem cannot be resolved by the time senior-level support has looked at it, the only place to go from there is outside the company.

Many smaller companies are large enough to have a full-time support person. These companies usually have between 30 and 150 workstations and servers. In this environment, where the network administrator also functions as the desktop support technician and the Help Desk, a third-party vendor is usually called in to assist with major upgrades or system changes, or to provide additional manpower for specific projects like a PC rollout.

Third-Party Support

15

Companies choose third-party support solutions for a number of reasons. Companies with very small networks might not find it necessary to incur the costs of having a full-time support person on staff. These companies will either contract out their support altogether or use a mix of departmental support and third-party support. As with the mix of departmental support and a centralized IT department, this model has the departmental support people handling day-to-day tasks as a sideline part of their jobs and calling for help when they run across a situation they cannot resolve.

Companies also use third-party support when they use highly specialized or proprietary equipment. A temporary agency that uses a proprietary staffing software package will find it more convenient and less costly to pay the vendor for support and maintenance of the program, rather than have someone in-house attempt to become just as knowledgeable about it. The convenience factor is important because you have the people that created the product at your fingertips. The cost is important because if a company does take the time to have an individual in-house trained, what happens when that person leaves? Because the equipment is specialized, it is difficult, if not impossible, to find a replacement without training someone else, which is another cost. Having the knowledge base walk out the door in search of greener pastures has burned more than one company.

Some corporations with very large support operations find that outsourcing is less costly over the long term than handling support in-house. As the size and complexity of the network grows, so does the number of IT professionals required to maintain it, and so does the budget required to pay the salaries. The nature of the business is that it comes in spurts. One week can be extremely slow with very few problems, which results in high-priced IT talent having a lot of downtime. The next week can be extremely busy with more work than can possibly be done by the team on hand.

For an ideal situation, a network requires one full-time support person per 100 to 125 workstations in a nonmanaged environment. *Nonmanaged* means that there is no systems management software in place that allows support personnel to remote control user workstations or otherwise manage workstations remotely. These numbers are ideal numbers; however, real-world economics often force companies to keep less staff than needed. IT professionals often find themselves expected to work more than the "standard" 40-hour workweek to make up for being understaffed.

Our sample network, which has 25 servers and 4,500 PCs, would require between 35 and 45 IT personnel, depending on the logistics of the particular network (number of locations, complexity, etc.). A reasonable breakdown based on a department of 35 people working 40 hours per week would be 7 level-one Help Desk people, 18 level-two desktop-support people, and 10 level-three (senior-level) people. The bulk of the salaries will be at the second and third levels, which will naturally be a lot higher. Third-party vendors often offer substantial discounts when the volume gets as high as in our example, which makes outsourcing the support quite attractive as compared to maintaining that big an IT payroll. The downside is that the response time is almost always significantly slower than having an internal support team. Table 15.1 summarizes the advantages and disadvantages of each model.

Most likely, the support model is already clearly defined in your organization. That provides the basis for handling the example network we started earlier, where our PCs and servers were having their manufacturers' warranties expire.

Table 15.1   A cost-benefit analysis of the support models.

Support Model	Response Time	Cost
Departmental	Very fast, usually within an hour or two	Cheapest; support person has "main" job separate from IT
IT Department	Moderate, usually same day or next day	At low volumes, cheaper than third party; at high volumes, the most expensive model
Third Party	Slow, usually 48 to 72 hour response time	Varies; consultants are expensive at low volumes, often charging more than $100/hr; volume discounts often available to make this model attractive at higher volumes

Busting The Budget Busters

Your budget can get burned in a number of ways when it comes to network maintenance. Here are some strategies for keeping in check the costs associated with hardware:

➤ Know when your warranties expire.

➤ Don't buy cut-rate components.

➤ Minimize the number of vendors.

Know When Your Warranties Expire

It might sound like we're beating a dead horse here, but this cannot be emphasized enough. The quickest way to blow your budget is to have a router or server go down and find out that you aren't covered by a warranty or maintenance agreement. Knowing when your coverage runs out could save you from expensive replacement costs should a key piece of hardware fail.

Don't Buy Cut-Rate Components

The old cliché that "you get what you pay for" definitely applies in the networking world. You may think you got a great deal on those no-name hubs because you saved so much money when you bought them instead of name-brand units, but usually you end up paying more in the end. Why? Inexpensive no-name brands are often built to less exacting standards, and shortcuts are taken to keep costs down. Quality control is not as good, and, although a product may appear to work just fine, down the road you may experience intermittent, "flaky" problems on your network that are difficult to track down. On more than one occasion, I've had to track down intermittent network problems to a no-name hub or a network adapter that was mostly working but was having problems. This is not to say that name-brand components will not have problems, but the percentage of problem units is a lot lower.

15

In addition, a hidden cost that many administrators don't consider is the support. If a no-name network adapter fails and is covered under warranty, how easy is it to get a replacement? Does the company have a Web site with the latest drivers and support information? Is Tech Support open 24/7, or, if your hub breaks on a Saturday morning, do you have to wait until Monday morning to call the manufacturer? Is the support number still active, or has it been disconnected? Will the vendor send you a replacement overnight, or do you have to return the original before you can get a replacement? In general, the name-brand manufacturers have better warranties and support policies.

Minimize The Number Of Vendors

Few things are more confusing than trying to figure out where you got a particular piece of equipment from when your company works with a dozen different vendors. When you have a lot of vendors, it's also easier to get caught up in "vendor tag" when you have a problem, as one vendor blames another and passes your problem on. The fewer vendors your organization works with, the easier your life will be when trying to maintain your network. The only "gotcha" to look out for is to make sure you don't get locked into an exclusive contract with a particular vendor. When competition doesn't exist, prices tend to rise (a look at your electric bill should convince you of that). If you work with a sole vendor, chances are good that you won't be getting the best deal on your purchases. For significant purchases, you should get price quotes from a minimum of three vendors. How you define "significant" is up to your company policy. The larger the corporation, the larger the price tag has to be before a purchase is considered significant. It's a waste of energy to implement a rigid across-the-board policy of getting quotes for everything. A maximum of five quotes is a good ceiling. Beyond that, you won't find many differences.

THE ROLE OF THE VENDOR IN NETWORK ADMINISTRATION

The vendor's role goes beyond merely supporting the hardware. The vendor, in this case, refers to either the manufacturer of the hardware or the developer of the software application or operating system in use. Part of the routine maintenance of a network is updating applications and installing patches. The issues involved are:

➤ Obtaining patches and upgrades

➤ Testing

➤ Rolling out the upgrades to the entire network

In most cases, these issues will be the responsibility of the network administrator. However, in some instances, smaller vendors who deal in specialized hardware or software might assist or even perform these functions themselves if there is a maintenance contract in place.

Obtaining Patches And Upgrades

There are a number of ways to obtain a patch or upgrade from a vendor. In the "old days," vendors maintained Bulletin Board Systems (BBSes), which you dialed in to with a modem to download the latest upgrades. BBSes have been almost completely usurped by the popularity of the World Wide Web, however. With the growing number of people with Internet access, vendors have increasingly opened up Web sites with the latest support information and patches. Some still offer the BBS option, and some also make the files directly available through FTP, but most commonly you'll find that a vendor's Web site is the primary means of obtaining upgrades. All you need is an Internet connection and a Web browser, and you're set. Most vendors still make updates and patches available on disk or CD-ROM, but you have to call Customer Service to request them, and it often takes days or weeks to receive your product.

Testing Upgrades

One of the most dangerous things you can do is download an upgrade or receive an upgrade in the mail and start installing it on production systems. In many cases, a vendor's patch introduces new problems in addition to resolving old ones. A classic example of this situation is when Microsoft initially released Service Pack 2 for its Windows NT 4 operating system. It was a disaster. The service pack caused many systems that had been working perfectly to crash. This fiasco created a big public relations problem for Microsoft. Network administrators were warned by others who had problems not to install the service pack without thorough testing in their environments.

Of course, Microsoft is not the only vendor that has ever had this type of problem with an upgrade or patch. It does illustrate the need for caution, though. Sometimes we get a little too anxious to load the latest and greatest without stopping to look at the bigger picture. Are the servers currently having any problems? Does the update add any functionality that you require? What exactly does it fix or upgrade? Is that relevant to your network? Loading an upgrade just because it is newer is a foolhardy way to maintain a network. After asking yourself the previous questions and determining that applying the upgrade is the best course of action, the first step is to put it through a test run.

In general, you should never install an update on a production system without testing it first. This cannot be emphasized enough. Even in smaller companies with tight IT budgets, it's important to have at least one or two computers available that can be used for testing purposes. These systems should be configured comparably to a production system. For servers, you should install

15

the same NOS with the same service packs and the same software already in use. That way, when you apply the upgrade or patch you have downloaded, you can put the system through its paces and see if you run into any problems as a result of the upgrade. Once you have tested the update to your satisfaction, you're ready to plan the rollout to the production environment.

Rolling Out The Upgrade To The Entire Network

You've identified and downloaded the latest service pack for your server operating system, and you've tested it on a test server configured similarly to your production servers. Now you're ready to update your company's 25 servers. So, do you just go around and install it on every server? No. First, you have to come up with an implementation plan. The first part of your plan is to ensure that you have current backups in case you need to roll back your configuration because of a problem with the update. Most patches and upgrades have uninstall features, but if your server crashes, you might not have the option of trying to uninstall. For Windows NT networks, make sure you have an up-to-date repair disk for each server. The update should be completely transparent to the users, so an obvious part of planning is to determine when a particular server can be updated while having the smallest impact on user productivity.

Also, if you have multiple servers configured in a cluster or working together in other ways, those servers will need to be updated at the same time. When you have the CYA (cover your assets) mechanisms in place and have determined an appropriate schedule for updating the servers, you're ready to start rolling out the update.

After completing the update, you'll want to keep a close eye on the servers for the first week or two. Run performance-monitoring tools and compare the results to your baseline. Document any differences you notice and test major functions of the server to ensure that they still work properly. Document any trends so that if a problem comes up a month later, you can trace it back to the update and not wonder where it came from.

MANAGING USER ACCOUNTS

User management is part of the day-to-day job of the network administrator. Chapter 11 covered the security aspect of user management. Here, we'll discuss the more general administration issues involved. These issues include setting up a naming scheme for user accounts, creating the accounts, assigning users to groups, and maintaining security.

Using A Naming Scheme For User Accounts

When you're managing a network with a lot of users, it's a good idea to have an established, consistent account-naming convention. The network can be confusing to administer if you have some user accounts named by the employee's first name, some by first initial and last name, others by first name and last initial, and so on. When establishing your naming convention, you'll want to consider company growth. For instance, if you work for a company that has only 15 employees, chances are good that everyone will have a different first name. So you might set up all of your user accounts with the users' first names as their account names.

But what happens when the company hires someone that has the same first name as an existing employee? Your naming scheme just broke. So instead, you might give everyone first-name last-initial account names, such as "WillW." That may work for a long time, but as the company grows, you're more likely to run into a problem with two employees with the same first name and with last names starting with the same initial. The best method then becomes first-initial last-name, such as "WWillis." The chances of having two people with the same last name are usually a lot lower than having multiple people with the same first name. It happens, of course; there are many common last names, such as "Smith" or "Jones." You'll find, though, that this naming scheme is the easiest way to support the largest number of users.

Creating User Accounts

Managing user accounts in a Windows NT environment involves the use of the User Manager For Domains administrative utility, shown in Figure 15.2.

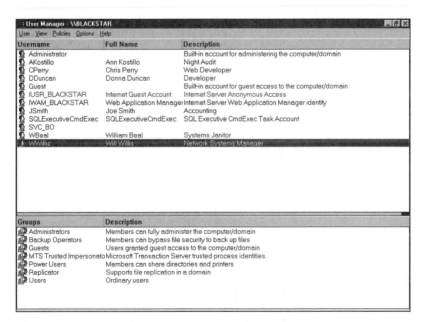

Figure 15.2   User Manager For Domains is the central location for administering user accounts in Windows NT.

Creating a new user account on your network can be done in a couple of ways. The first way is to click on the User menu and then click on New User in User Manager For Domains. Figure 15.3 shows the New User window.

As you can see, creating a user is a matter of filling in the Username field, following the format of your naming convention, and then entering the user's full name and a description. The description is optional, but in a large environment where you might not be on a first-name basis with every employee, it is helpful to use the Description field to enter the department or job title of the employee. Then, if that user account shows up in the Event Viewer security logs or otherwise has problems, you can quickly determine who the employee is and what department he or she is in. This is especially critical in a wide area network (WAN) environment where the user might be in another city or state. The Password field gets filled in according to your corporate policy. As was mentioned in Chapter 11, some administrators will set a generic password, such as "password", when creating a user account and check the box for User Must Change Password At Next Logon. Other administrators will assign an initial password for the user account to prevent someone else from logging with that user account before the intended employee and gaining access to the network.

After you've filled out the New User screen, you will most likely want to assign the user to a group for easier administration. To do so, click on the Groups button at the bottom of the User Properties screen, which you get to by either double clicking on the user whose properties you want to see or highlighting the user and selecting File | Properties. When it comes to administering a large network, it's easier to manage access rights at the group level than at the user level. What that means is that you group your employees logically, creating, for example, a group called Sales for the sales staff. When you want to give those users access to a resource on the network, you simply give access rights to the Sales group, rather than having to add each individual user account to the access list. Figure 15.4 shows how to define which groups a user belongs to.

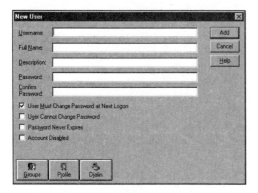

Figure 15.3   Creating a new user account.

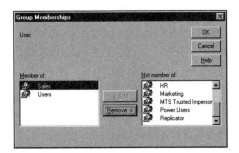

Figure 15.4   Managing group membership.

In addition to group membership, you can also assign a login profile or script to a user and specify which hours the user is allowed to log in to the network. You can allow a user to log in from a specific set of workstations or from any workstation. As was discussed in Chapter 10, you can allow or disallow the user the ability to dial in to the network if you have RAS services installed.

Creating a user account from scratch can be tedious if you have many accounts to set up. If you are setting up multiple user accounts with the same basic settings (same login script and security policies), it's easier and more efficient to work from a template.

To use a template, you select an existing user account and choose Copy from the User menu. This makes a copy of that user account, retaining all of the settings except Username, Full Name, and Password. All group memberships are maintained, and so are any profile settings, login hours, and dial-in permissions. Usually you'll want to set up a "clean" user account to use as a template for this purpose. You can even call that account "template" so that you don't mistake it for an active user account. For security purposes, you should have the Account Disabled box checked, except for when you are using the account to set up other accounts.

Managing user accounts also includes enforcing security, discussed in Chapter 11, and keeping up with active versus inactive user accounts. When an employee leaves the company, you'll want to deactivate that account by checking the Account Disabled box in User Manager For Domains. Employees that are on extended leave (such as maternity, short-term disability) should also have their accounts disabled for the term of their absence. Once you're sure an employee will not be returning to the company, you can delete that account.

If a replacement is hired right away, you can simply rename the account to reflect the new employee and reset the password. This saves you the trouble of deleting the old account, creating a new account, and then assigning properties to that account. User accounts are often tied to other network services, such as email.

15

Renaming a user account and mailbox also lets you maintain any relevant email from the ex-employee that would be beneficial for the new hire or the department to have.

SUPPORTING USERS

Part of the network administrator's job is to support the end users in their use of the network. In addition to managing their accounts, the administrator also has to manage the network resources that enable employees to do their jobs.

Shared Directories And Applications

The administrator is responsible for ensuring that all users have sufficient access rights to do their jobs. That means they need to have permissions to access appropriate network directories, applications, and printers. On a network with a centralized server farm, you'll want to create departmental or individual user directories for data files to be stored. On a network with departmental servers, you'll need shared directories on each server for users to store files. Users should have access to only the resources they need. As was discussed in Chapter 11, periodic security audits should be performed to make sure that users are not able to access locations on the network where they should not be.

Data files created by users should be stored on a server so that they are backed up each night. Most companies back up only servers, not individual user workstations. Ideally, users should be able to sit at any computer and accomplish their work. If they have data on their own PCs, then they can work on only that PC, and this restriction is a problem waiting to happen.

Many networks have server-based applications, where users run applications, such as word processors, off of a network share rather than from a copy installed locally on their hard drive. Each user should be able to access only those applications that are necessary for their work, and some sort of software metering program should be employed to monitor licensing. If a company has 25 licenses for an office suite and 30 employees are accessing it, that is a violation that could result in legal troubles and severe fines. It's the network administrator's job to protect the company in this situation. If you knowingly allow software to be used illegally, you can be held liable along with management should you ever face a surprise external audit.

Communication

An often-overlooked side of network administration is communication. Nothing is more frustrating for users than reporting a problem and then not knowing when it will be resolved. Even if the administrator is unable to address the problem immediately or has to research the problem, he or she should inform the users of their problem's status and let them know that it's being worked on. Poor communication often fosters animosity between the IT department and the rest of the company in many organizations. As a network administrator, usually you will be called by users only when there is a problem, and when there is a problem, people are often upset or impatient. If users are griping, the best policy is to let them blow off steam and to not take it personally. Users might be frustrated by a problem that is interfering with their ability to meet their deadlines. A good network administrator needs people skills in addition to technical skills. If you can assure your end users that their technology problems matter to you and that you're there to fix them, they will be more understanding even if you can't work on their problem immediately. That understanding will go a long way toward building trust, and it will help reduce the stress and anxiety level as you put out one fire after another.

BACKING UP THE FORT

Although it's not the most glamorous aspect of network administration, performing backups is one of the most important duties of an administrator. Take a look at your servers and ask yourself some questions: If this server crashed, could all of the data be recovered? What would be involved in recovering it? What would the cost be? Sure, you could reinstall the server operating system and all of the applications and have the system back online in a fairly short amount of time. But what about the data files created by the users? What about the financial information, such as accounts payable, accounts receivable, and payroll? There are probably hard copies of most of this information, but how long would it take to track all of it down in various filing cabinets and off-site storage facilities and piece it all back together? The hundreds or thousands of hours it would take to rebuild the data and the interrupted or lost business for the company in the interim would have enormous costs. Some companies never recover from a disastrous loss of data and have to close down. Even if the company doesn't close down, having a loss of data could cost you your job. I like to use the motto: "If it's worth saving in the first place, it's worth backing up."

When it comes to performing backups, there are many more considerations than just sticking a tape in a drive and walking away. The issues you will need to be familiar with are:

➤ Backup technology

➤ The different types of backups and their usage

➤ Planning and scheduling the backup of your enterprise

➤ Protecting your backup tapes

15

Backup Technology

Storage technology has grown quite a bit over the past few years, and now there are several options available when it comes to storage. These are:

➤ Storage area networks

➤ Converted mainframes

➤ Removable storage drives

➤ Tapes

Storage Area Networks

Storage area networks (SANs) draw their origin from the mainframe days. However, they have only recently gained prominence in the world of client/server networking. Rather than having a storage device attached to each individual server, you have a collection of storage devices linked together and connected back to the network through a switch and high-speed fibre channel or gigabyte Ethernet connections. Although costs are initially quite expensive (in the tens of thousands of dollars for setup), performance is greatly improved because your servers don't spend as much time processing basic I/O requests for data from user workstations. Improved performance increases efficiency and lowers overall costs. The speed ensures that data is always available, an advantage over traditional storage devices that back up to media such as tape. With those technologies, data that isn't still on the server due to disk-space usage must be restored from tape or similar media before it can be accessed. With storage centrally managed and the storage devices backing each other up for redundancy, reliability is greatly strengthened. Figure 15.5 shows how a basic LAN looks with a storage area network.

Converted Mainframes

Some companies have converted old mainframes to serve as huge, fast storage devices for their networks. This model is similar in concept to a storage area network, but initial costs are lower than they are for implementing a new SAN because most of the supporting hardware is often in place already, and companies get the benefit of being able to further exploit their existing technology.

Removable Storage Drives

Removable storage drives such as those made by SyQuest and Iomega have grown in popularity in recent years as the media costs have come down and data files have gotten bigger. Data files are now often too large to fit on a single floppy disk. The technologies start with floppy-drive replacements, such as the LS-120 Superdisks (which are 120MB floppy drives that can also read standard 1.44MB floppies), the Iomega Zip drives of up to 250MB capacity, and the

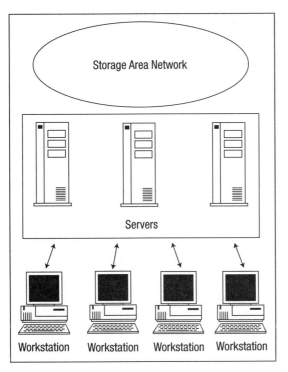

Figure 15.5   A storage area network provides fast centralized storage of data.

SyQuest EZ-Flyers at 230MB capacity. From there, they move on to hard-drive capacities and speed with Iomega's Jaz drive and SyQuest's SyJet, with capacities of 1GB and 1.5GB, respectively. Recordable CD-ROM drives and rewritable CD-ROM drives also fit into this category of removable storage. These technologies are better suited to the world of workstation backups, though, because of their capacities. Backing up a multiple-gigabyte hard drive would require several disks and would make backups even more tedious.

Tapes

For all of the criticism tape drives get for their lack of speed, tapes still offer the most bang for the buck when it comes to price per megabyte, usually costing around $.03 to $.05 per megabyte. That price point and their wide availability make tapes the overwhelming choice for the vast majority of companies. Tape drive speeds have dramatically increased as technology has advanced, and some drives today will back up at a rate of well over 100MB of data per minute. Digital Data Storage (DDS) drives, an outgrowth of the older DAT (Digital Audio Tape) technology, are the most popular type of tape drives on the market. They use tapes in either the older 8mm format or the newer 4mm format.

15

Tape drives work the same way that cassette recorders work: Data is read or written sequentially as the tape passes over the heads of the drive. This fact makes restoring data sometimes take a lot longer than you think it should. For instance, if you need to restore a 30K Word document that a user accidentally deleted, the drive has to read the tape until it comes to the file it's looking for. Some software packages actually give the tape drive a drive letter on the system it's attached to. The speed, however, is why tape is sometimes referred to as "secondary storage," whereas drives with faster access times, like hard drives or floppy drives, are considered "primary storage." *Secondary storage* really means that the data is not available in a manner that makes it efficient to work with the data directly off of that particular medium. Secondary storage is sometimes also called *near-line storage*. The data is available without the intervention of an administrator to restore files for the user, but the slow performance makes secondary storage inefficient for the user to store and access frequently used or updated files.

The Different Types Of Backups And Their Uses

For our purposes, we're going to assume that your backup strategy will involve the use of tape drives and tape media, because these are used by the vast majority of companies today.

Once you have your backup hardware in place, you have to decide how, exactly, you're going to do your backups. As was mentioned earlier, there's more to a backup strategy than just feeding tapes and walking away. The first step in planning is to determine precisely what you're going to back up. That will help you decide on the appropriate backup method. The different types of files on a network to be backed up are:

➤ Operating-system files and settings

➤ Applications

➤ Users' data files

Operating-System Files And Settings

Operating-system (OS) files are the files that are essential to the operation of the computer. Without an operating system, the computer can do nothing when you turn it on, so the OS is of vital concern. The Windows Registry maintains system configuration settings that Windows and its applications refer to during its operation. The Registry also maintains security and policy information, as well as the hardware device settings of the system. Chapter 14 discussed protecting this information by creating and maintaining an emergency recovery disk or repair disk.

Applications

Applications are not just the programs users access and run from the server, but also the applications, such as the backup software, that you run on the server. In most cases, applications don't need to be specifically backed up unless doing so is part of an overall scheme of performing full backups. If you're not backing up applications, you should ensure that you have any special configuration settings documented and kept with your original installation media.

Users' Data Files

Arguably the most important of the files to back up, users' data files are the files that cannot be reinstalled from a vendor's disk or CD-ROM. User data is the company's livelihood and is what you are there to protect. If you have a solid network design that enables users to back up their data to a central location, life will be much easier than if you have to attempt to track down data files on users' hard drives and various locations on a server.

 In addition to backing up files on the server to tape, it's wise to train users to save their files to floppy disks whenever possible. Not only does that give users quick access to their files if they delete or accidentally damage the copies on the server, but it also provides an extra layer of protection in case the tape drive fails or otherwise can't read the tape media to restore the files.

After you've determined what you want to back up—either user data only or the entire server—you're ready to start designing your backup strategy based on the different types of backup methods available. Any decent backup software will allow you to perform the following types of backups:

➤ Full backup

➤ Incremental backup

➤ Differential backup

➤ Copy backup

➤ Program-specific backup

Full Backup

The full backup is exactly what it implies: a backup in which every file on your hard drive is saved, including system files, applications, data, and the Registry (Windows) or Bindery (NetWare). If you ever have a server crash, this is the easiest type of backup to restore from because it requires only a single backup set (which is usually a single tape).

15

Getting a good full backup is sometimes difficult because some files will always be in use, and many backup programs require exclusive access to a file to back it up successfully. Files that are open or in use are generally skipped and noted in the backup log file. Many commercial backup programs have *agents*, which are plug-in utilities to the backup software that allow the program to successfully back up open files. Two of the more popular backup programs, ARCServe and Backup Exec, have optional modules to back up open files, as well as open databases from third-party server products such as Microsoft Exchange Server and Lotus Notes. The bundled NT Backup program with the Windows NT software does not back up open files or open databases, though the Exchange Server product does include a replacement NT Backup, which backs up the open Exchange Server databases. The NT Backup backs up the system Registry, though.

 Disk-space usage on a server doubles roughly every two years. Ideally, a full backup should be able to fit on a single tape, so keep growth in mind as you plan your backup strategies. Also, be aware of the usable life of a tape. You should replace your tapes annually to ensure the best-quality backups. As a tape gets older, it becomes more susceptible to stretching and wearing out. As with a cassette tape, the metal oxide that holds the data to the tape begins to flake off, creating dead spots on the tape. This results in more tape errors and an increased risk of being unable to restore data from a tape when it's necessary.

Incremental Backup

Whereas a full backup backs up the entire hard drive, an incremental backup backs up only those files that have changed since the last backup. So how does the backup software determine what files have changed? This is done through the archive bit.

The *archive bit* is a property of a file that is manipulated during the backup process. When a file is backed up, the backup software clears the archive bit for that file. That tells the software that the file has not been changed. When a file is modified later by a user or by the system, the archive bit is set again. That way, the next time a backup is run, the backup software is able to tell which files have been changed since the last backup.

As we briefly mentioned, an incremental backup backs up only those files that have changed since the last backup of any type. It does this by clearing the archive bit for any file it backs up. That way, only the files that have been modified (had their archive bit set) since the last backup will be backed up. If you have a server crash and need to perform a full restore, you'll need to have the last full backup tape *plus* all of the incremental backups that have occurred since that time. For example, let's say you have a backup schedule where you do a full backup on Friday and incremental backups Monday through Thursday. You have a server crash on Wednesday morning. To restore that drive, you will need the previous Friday's full backup, plus Monday's and Tuesday's incremental backups.

Incremental backups are ideal for daily backups because they typically back up far less information than a full backup does and are therefore much quicker to perform. The disadvantage is that there will be more tape shuffling than with any other backup method because your data is spread across more tapes.

Differential Backup

A differential backup is very similar to an incremental backup in that it backs up only data that has changed since previous backups. The difference is that a differential backup backs up only those files that have changed since the last *full* backup (not since the last incremental backup). Whereas an incremental backup clears the archive bit from files it backs up, the differential backup leaves the archive bit set. This way, if you need to restore a server, the only tapes you'll need are your last full backup and your last differential backup.

The advantage of a differential backup is that, like an incremental backup, only files that have been modified are backed up. The disadvantage, as compared to incremental backups, however, is that with each day that passes since the last full backup, the data takes longer to back up. Because the differential backup doesn't clear the archive bit, it will back up all of the files it backed up previously *plus* any new ones that have been modified.

Using our backup-schedule example, a Wednesday differential backup will back up all of the files that were backed up on Monday and Tuesday, as well as the files that were modified on Wednesday.

Copy Backup

A copy backup is a type of full backup. Like a full backup, a copy backup backs up the entire hard drive, but unlike a full backup, the copy backup does not touch the archive bits on files. It leaves them exactly the way they were. So what's the point? A copy backup is useful for doing a one-off full backup of a server without throwing off your backup schedule. For example, say you made a major configuration change on Tuesday night, installing a new piece of hardware and a new application package on the server. You want to do a full backup before you do this as a "just in case" measure. Doing a standard full backup will clear all of your archive bits, which will interfere with the incremental or differential backups that are usually based on the previous Friday's full backup. So instead, you do a copy backup, which gets you what you want—a good full backup of the server—without interfering with your regular backup schedule.

15

Program-Specific Backup

This is a special kind of backup that isn't part of a normal backup scheme. Some programs—most notably, databases such as Microsoft SQL Server—have an internal backup program that backs up to the record or field level and dumps the contents out to another file on the drive to be backed up by your regular backup software. These backups must be configured within the program itself and are specific to the program they come with.

How you set up your backup schedule will depend on a number of factors within your organization. Table 15.2 summarizes the backup types with their advantages and disadvantages.

Planning And Scheduling The Backup Of Your Enterprise

If you have gotten this far, you have seen that there are a lot of considerations to take into account when it comes to planning a backup strategy. Once you've determined what types of backups you're going to do, you'll need to develop a schedule for your backups. The point of having backups is to be able to restore data in the least amount of time with the least amount of hassle. Having a schedule gives you a documented plan; you know exactly when data was backed up and how (by what method).

Not all restores will be full server recoveries. Users often ask for certain files to be restored that have been accidentally deleted or otherwise damaged (such as a user saving unwanted modifications and being unable to revert to the original version). Your schedule allows you to quickly determine which tape to restore from without having to spend a lot of time searching individual tapes for the file you need.

Table 15.2 The different types of backups.

Backup	What's Backed Up	Archive Bit Method	Advantage	Disadvantage
Full	Every file	Cleared on all files	Restore needs only one tape	Time consuming
Incremental	Files changed since last backup	Cleared on files backed up of any type	Fast	Restore requires full plus all previous incremental tapes
Differential	Files changed since last full backup	Unchanged	Faster than full; restore requires full plus last differential tape	Backup time is slower as days pass since last full backup
Copy	Every file	Unchanged	One-off backup doesn't affect backup schedule	Time consuming

A backup schedule should be set up in a way that provides the maximum amount of data protection with the easiest amount of administration. The best of these schedules is what is known as the Grandfather-Father-Son (GFS) method.

Grandfather-Father-Son (GFS)

The GFS backup strategy is a method of maintaining backups on a daily, weekly, and monthly schedule. GFS backup schemes are based on a five-day or seven-day weekly schedule (depending on your organization), beginning any day (typically Friday or Monday). A full backup is performed at least once a week. On all other days, full, partial (incremental or differential), or no backups are performed. The daily incremental or differential backups are known as the Son. The last full backup in the week (the weekly backup) is known as the Father. The last full backup of the month (the monthly backup) is known as the Grandfather. Tables 15.3 and 15.4 show examples of a weekly backup schedule using full and differential backups.

You can reuse daily tapes after four days (for a five-day schedule) or six days (for a seven-day schedule). Weekly tapes can be overwritten after five weeks have passed since they were last recorded on. Monthly media are saved throughout the year and should be taken off site for storage. The primary purpose of the GFS scheme is to suggest a minimum standard and consistent interval at which to rotate and retire the tapes. Table 15.5 shows a sample GFS implementation over the course of two months, using a month with the first day conveniently falling on a Sunday. Although I use differential backups for the daily backups, the schedule would be the same using incremental backups instead.

From the above rotation, you can quickly calculate that the two-month rotation will take a total of 21 tapes. There are four daily tapes (Sons), which are recycled (reused) weekly; five weekly tapes (Fathers), which are recycled after the fifth full weekly backup is complete; and 12 monthly tapes (Grandfathers), which are the last full backups of the month and are taken off site. The need for storing monthly tapes leads us into the next topic.

15

Table 15.3   An example of a weekly backup on a five-day schedule (Diff=Differential).

Sun	Mon	Tue	Wed	Thur	Fri	Sat
None	Diff	Diff	Diff	Diff	Full	None

Table 15.4   An example of a weekly backup on a seven-day schedule (Diff=Differential).

Sun	Mon	Tue	Wed	Thur	Fri	Sat
Diff	Diff	Diff	Diff	Diff	Diff	Full

Table 15.5 An example of a two-month GFS rotation scheme on a five-day schedule (Diff=Differential; Full-W=Weekly backup; Full-M= Monthly backup).

Sun	Mon	Tue	Wed	Thur	Fri	Sat
1	2	3	4	5	6	7
None	Diff	Diff	Diff	Diff	Full-W	None
	Tape1	Tape2	Tape3	Tape4	Tape5	
Sun	**Mon**	**Tue**	**Wed**	**Thur**	**Fri**	**Sat**
8	9	10	11	12	13	14
None	Diff	Diff	Diff	Diff	Full-W	None
	Tape1	Tape2	Tape3	Tape4	Tape6	
Sun	**Mon**	**Tue**	**Wed**	**Thur**	**Fri**	**Sat**
15	16	17	18	19	20	21
None	Diff	Diff	Diff	Diff	Full-W	None
	Tape1	Tape2	Tape3	Tape4	Tape7	
Sun	**Mon**	**Tue**	**Wed**	**Thur**	**Fri**	**Sat**
22	23	24	25	26	27	28
None	Diff	Diff	Diff	Diff	Full-M	None
	Tape1	Tape2	Tape3	Tape4	Tape8	
Sun	**Mon**	**Tue**	**Wed**	**Thur**	**Fri**	**Sat**
29	30	31	1	2	3	4
None	Diff	Diff	Diff	Diff	Full-W	None
	Tape1	Tape2	Tape3	Tape4	Tape9	
Sun	**Mon**	**Tue**	**Wed**	**Thur**	**Fri**	**Sat**
5	6	7	8	9	10	11
None	Diff	Diff	Diff	Diff	Full-W	None
	Tape1	Tape2	Tape3	Tape4	Tape10	
Sun	**Mon**	**Tue**	**Wed**	**Thur**	**Fri**	**Sat**
12	13	14	15	16	17	18
None	Diff	Diff	Diff	Diff	Full-W	None
	Tape1	Tape2	Tape3	Tape4	Tape5	
Sun	**Mon**	**Tue**	**Wed**	**Thur**	**Fri**	**Sat**
19	20	21	22	23	24	25
None	Diff	Diff	Diff	Diff	Full-M	None
	Tape1	Tape2	Tape3	Tape4	Tape11	
Sun	**Mon**	**Tue**	**Wed**	**Thur**		
26	27	28	29	30		
None	Diff	Diff	Diff	Diff		
	Tape1	Tape2	Tape3	Tape4		

Protecting Your Backup Tapes

You've been diligent in your backup practices, performing a perfect GFS tape rotation and keeping your tapes readily available on a shelf in your server room. What's wrong with this picture? Although your data is protected against a server failure, it is not protected against natural disaster. What if a wiring fault causes a fire in your server room? Your precious backup tapes will get melted down, along with the server, and all data will be lost. A wise investment for the server room is a heavy-duty fireproof safe for storing tapes. That way, if you have a fire, your tapes should be able to survive.

But what if you have flooding? Even if you don't live in a floodplain, stranger things have happened than one of the restrooms on the floor above you having a busted pipe that causes water to rain down through the ceiling tiles. Fireproof safes aren't waterproof, and while your server shorts out and crashes, your tapes are going under water. And what if your building is hit by a tornado?

The only way to really ensure that your data is protected is to store copies of it off site. In the GFS tape rotation, the monthly backups, or Grandfathers, are taken off site for storage. If you have a natural disaster that strikes the office building and server room and wipes out your data, you have the ace in the hole, so to speak, and can probably recover enough of the company data to at least be able to carry on with business. In addition to protecting against natural disasters, storing tapes off site also protects against the possibility of losing all corporate data to theft or vandalism. The exact location of off-site backups depends on the individual company. Some companies store off-site backups in safe deposit boxes at banks. Companies that span multiple cities or states sometimes ship backup tapes to another site out of town as a means to protect against a natural disaster, such as a tornado, that might cause widespread destruction in a single city. No matter where they are stored off site, the tapes should be in a secured, locked location where only authorized personnel can access them. Chapter 11 discussed the security ramifications of losing backup tapes filled with corporate data.

15

VIRUSES AND YOU—A PRIMER

Most people know that a virus is not a good thing for your computer to have—for one thing, it just sounds downright nasty. You might even know a little about what computer viruses are and what they do, but if not, here is a quick primer to get you up to speed. This is what you need to know:

➤ What is a virus?

➤ How can you protect computers from viruses?

➤ What are virus signature files?

What Is A Virus?

A virus is a software program, just like any other application on your hard drive. The difference between a virus and a regular application is that a virus is written specifically to affect your system or network adversely without your knowing about it. Viruses do not magically appear; they are specifically written by someone and are transmitted by manipulating files. The two basic functions of a virus are to spread itself from one file or system to another without the user's knowledge and to implement whatever symptom or damage is planned by the author of the virus.

The action the virus performs on your system is whatever the author designed it to do. Some viruses are mere annoyances, popping up messages, changing your icons, or performing similar functions that, although they are annoying, do no real damage. At the other extreme, some viruses will move your hard-drive partitions around or erase all of your files. Most are somewhere in between, such as a virus that removes from your word processor the option to save documents as anything other than templates.

How Can You Protect Computers From Viruses?

Protecting computers from viruses is a two-step process. The first step is to use common sense. Do not use disks of unknown origin in your computer, and be careful about downloading or executing files from unknown sources. The second step is to invest in anti-virus software and learn how to use it.

On a network, viruses can obviously infect both servers and user workstations. In fact, many companies have had virus problems get out of hand and bring down the network because of the ease of transmission from system to system. Therefore, it is imperative to install anti-virus software on both the servers *and* the workstations on the network. Server-based anti-virus software works a little differently in that it offers network-management features—such as remote monitoring, alerting the administrator when a virus is detected, and so on—that are not in workstation versions. Essentially, the virus scanning technology is the same, though. The better programs will automatically scan floppy disks as they are inserted into the computer, files as they are downloaded from the Internet (compressed and noncompressed files), and email attachments. These programs also offer scheduling features that allow you to run them automatically during nonwork hours. The more automatic the program is, the more likely it is that viruses will be detected.

What Are Virus Signature Files?

It is estimated that approximately 200 to 300 new viruses are created every month. For that reason, as you can imagine, anti-virus software quickly becomes outdated. Anti-virus software manufacturers have gotten around that by updating the virus signature files on a regular basis, usually monthly. Virus signatures are the lists of viruses that the scanning engine can detect. So, rather than repeatedly having to install an entirely new product, you merely update your existing anti-virus software. That way, your software stays up to date, and your computers stay as protected as possible. Many programs even offer automatic update features that will use your Internet connection to download updated signature files when they become available.

CHAPTER SUMMARY

- ➤ Network administration is the day-to-day process of maintaining and supporting the networking environment.

- ➤ Knowing when hardware warranties expire is necessary to keep a network budget under control.

- ➤ The cost of hardware alone is a small percentage in the total cost of ownership of a network.

- ➤ Network support can be done on a departmental, centralized, or out-sourced third-party basis, or with a hybrid combining two or more of those models.

- ➤ You should maintain hardware from a small number of vendors, because the more brands of equipment you have, the more difficult it is to figure out where a particular piece of hardware came from.

- ➤ Always test software upgrades and patches on a test server or workstation before applying them on a production unit.

- ➤ Plan your naming scheme for user accounts to allow for growth. First-initial last-name formats, such as "WWillis," lend themselves especially well to larger environments.

- ➤ Effective communication between you and your end users will go a long way toward reducing tensions and frustrations when problems arise.

- ➤ The most common backup technology still remains the tape drive, which has a lower cost per medium than any of the other available technologies.

- ➤ Full, incremental, differential, and copy are the different types of backups that can be performed. Some applications, such as Microsoft SQL Server, have built-in proprietary backups as well.

- ➤ The Grandfather-Father-Son (GFS) backup scheme is the most common backup schedule. The Grandfathers are the monthly backups stored off site, the Fathers are the weekly backups, and the Sons are the daily backups.

15

➤ Monthly tapes should be stored off site to protect against natural disasters, theft, and vandalism.

➤ Viruses are programs written to adversely affect a computer without the user's knowledge.

➤ New viruses are created at a rate of 200 to 300 every month, making it essential to keep anti-virus software up to date.

➤ Virus signature files are the listings of viruses that an anti-virus program knows how to detect.

REVIEW QUESTIONS

1. In the total cost of ownership of network maintenance, in which area is the majority of the IT budget spent?

   a. Administration

   b. Support

   c. End user operations

   d. Capital (hardware) costs

2. Why is getting a good full backup often difficult?

   a. A full backup usually takes up more than one tape.

   b. Open files do not get backed up.

   c. A full backup takes too long.

   d. Full backups are done only once per week.

3. In a GFS tape rotation scheme, which set of tapes is the Father?

   a. Daily

   b. Weekly

   c. Monthly

   d. Yearly

4. In a GFS tape rotation scheme, which set of tapes is the Son?

   a. Daily

   b. Weekly

   c. Monthly

   d. Yearly

5. An incremental backup:
   a. Backs up all files since the last full backup
   b. Backs up all files on the hard drive
   c. Backs up all files since any previous backup
   d. Backs up all files without an archive bit set

6. The Windows NT Server tool for managing user accounts is:
   a. Server Manager
   b. User Manager For NT
   c. Server Manager For Domains
   d. User Manager For Domains

7. The type of backup that backs up only files modified since the last full backup is a:
   a. Differential backup
   b. Incremental backup
   c. Copy backup
   d. Selective backup

8. All of the following are sources for obtaining drivers from a vendor except:
   a. BBS
   b. Web site
   c. Email
   d. Disk

9. When a vendor releases a new patch or upgrade, you should do all of the following except:
   a. Download it and install it immediately to get the latest features.
   b. Wait for others to install it to see if it has problems.
   c. Download it and install it on a test server.
   d. Ask yourself if you really need the patch in the first place.

15

10. Which support model offers the quickest response time to end users?
    a. Centralized IT department
    b. Third-party support
    c. Departmental support
    d. Help Desk

11. Which support model offers the slowest response time to end users?

    a. Centralized IT department

    b. Third-party support

    c. Departmental support

    d. Help Desk

12. Assigning user permissions to shared files and directories should be done at what level?

    a. User level

    b. Group level

    c. Organization level

    d. Domain level

13. The best protection for backup media is to be stored where?

    a. Off site

    b. In a fireproof safe in the server room

    c. In the CEO's locked filing cabinet

    d. On a shelf above the servers in case of flooding

14. What should you use if you need to create multiple user accounts with the same basic properties?

    a. Batch files

    b. Login scripts

    c. Profile editor

    d. Template

15. All of the following are viable backup media except:

    a. Tape

    b. SAN

    c. Removable drive cartridges

    d. Spare server hard drive

HANDS-ON PROJECTS

In these hands-on projects, you will be performing some basic network administration tasks, including creating a new user account, managing permissions through groups, and defining a login script and home directory for a user with User Manager For Domains. You will also be performing a server backup with NT Backup and installing Windows NT Service Pack 4. These projects assume that you have access to a Windows NT server in at least a test-lab environment as well as having access to the Internet. However, even if you do not have access to an NT server, there are sample screenshots to guide you through the exercises.

Project 15.1

In this project, you will create a new user account through User Manager For Domains, assign your new user to the Domain Admins group and set that group as the default group, and assign a login script to your new user and connect the user to a home directory on the server.

To create a new user account through User Manager For Domains:

1. From the Windows desktop, click Start| Programs| Administrative Tools (common)| User Manager For Domains.

2. On the User menu, click New User, as shown in Figure 15.6.

3. When the New User window appears, as in Figure 15.7, enter your information.

4. Check the box for User Must Change Password At Next Logon.

5. When you're finished, click on the Add button to create the user account, and then click on Cancel to exit the New User window.

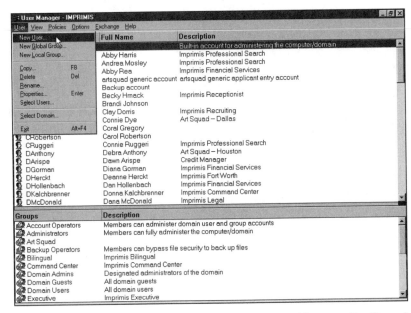

Figure 15.6   Creating a new user account in User Manager For Domains.

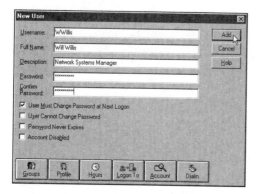

Figure 15.7 The New User properties window.

To assign your new user to the Domain Admins group and set that group as the default group:

1. In User Manager For Domains, double-click on the user account you just created.

2. Click on the Groups button in the lower-left corner. A dialog box appears.

3. In the right-hand panel (Not Member Of), click on Domain Admins and click on Add.

4. Highlight Domain Admins and click on the Set button to set this group as the default group for this user (see Figure 15.8).

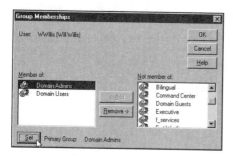

Figure 15.8 The Group Memberships dialog box for assigning user accounts to groups.

5. Click on OK to return to the User Properties dialog box.

To assign a login script to your new user and connect the user to a home directory on the server:

1. From the User Properties dialog box, click on the Profile button. This will open a dialog box similar to the one shown in Figure 15.9.

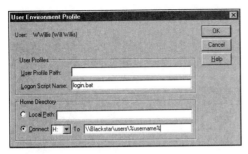

Figure 15.9   The User Environment Profile dialog box.

2. On the Logon Script Name line, type in the name of an existing login script on your network or make up a name. This file needs to be in the NETLOGON shared directory for it to be executed when the user logs on to the network. A *share name* is a descriptive name given to a directory by the person who "shares" a directory, meaning the person makes a directory available for use by other people on the network. The NETLOGON directory is the network share name for the \winnt\system32\repl\ import\scripts directory.

3. Connect the user's home directory to drive letter H:. You should create a directory called "Users" (or something similar, such as "Home") on one of the server hard drives and share it. The %username% option is a system variable that automatically substitutes the user's account name for that field. In our example, drive H: would be mapped to \\Blackstar\users\WWillis because the user account name is WWillis.

Project 15.2

In this project, you will perform a server backup with NT Backup, and then you will update the server to Service Pack 4. Whenever you plan to make a significant change to your server, you should always perform a backup first, to ensure you can get back to your previous configuration if the update does not go as planned.

15

To perform a server backup:

1. From the Windows desktop, click on Start|Programs|AdministrativeTools (common)|Backup. This will open the Backup window seen in Figure 15.10.

2. Double-click on the C: drive to see the list of directories and files on the drive. The list will look similar to Figure 15.11.

3. After you have selected the files to be backed up, click on the Backup button at the top left. This will open the dialog box shown in Figure 15.12.

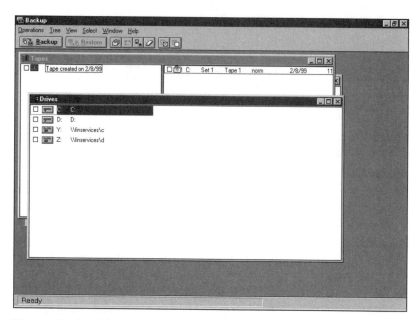

Figure 15.10   Windows NT Backup program.

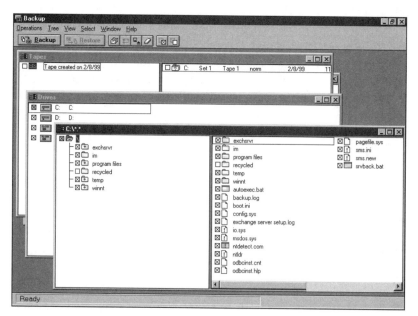

Figure 15.11   The directories and files on a hard drive ready for selection.

4. Enter the appropriate information, such as naming your backup tape, choosing whether to verify and/or back up the system Registry, and so on. After you have completed the fields in this window, click on OK. You will see the window shown in Figure 15.13, which shows the backup status all the way through completion.

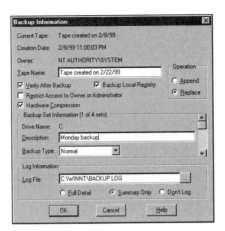

Figure 15.12   The Backup Information dialog box, where you configure backup options.

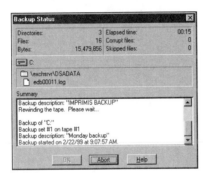

Figure 15.13   The Backup Status dialog box is where you monitor the progress of your backup.

To update your NT server to the latest service pack (now that a complete backup is in place):

1. Connect to the location that contains the Service Pack files. In Figure 15.14, that location is a shared directory on the network.

2. Double-click the ntsp4.exe file to start the setup. Service Pack setup will extract the files needed for setup and present you with the license agreement shown in Figure 15.15. You must check the first checkbox to accept the license agreement before continuing, and you must check or uncheck the second checkbox to specify whether you want Service Pack setup to back up your existing files in case you want to later uninstall.

3. Agree to the license and click on Install.

4. Watch the installation run, as shown in Figure 15.16.

5. Click on Restart to reboot your computer at the end of the setup process.

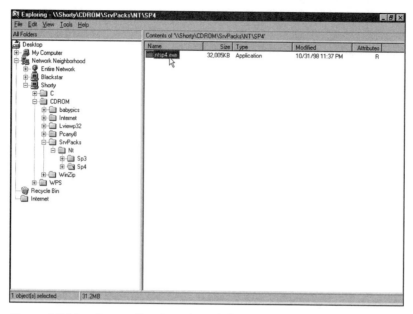

Figure 15.14 Connecting to a shared directory containing the installation files.

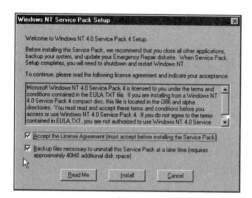

Figure 15.15 Service Pack 4 setup and license agreement.

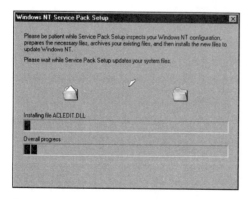

Figure 15.16 Service Pack 4 installation.

## CHAPTER SIXTEEN

TROUBLESHOOTING THE NETWORK

After Reading This Chapter And Completing The Exercises, You Will Be Able To:

➤ Identify and prioritize common network problems

➤ Use a systematic approach to resolving network problems

➤ Analyze the symptoms and characteristics of a problem

➤ Troubleshoot the major operating systems

➤ Identify and resolve network connectivity issues

➤ Troubleshoot name-resolution problems

➤ Locate and utilize vendor troubleshooting resources

Every network administrator struggles on a daily basis with a never-ending stream of hardware, software, and connectivity-related problems. In a well-managed network, most of these fall into the category of minor problems or inconveniences. Little things like file locations and application peculiarities are often simple configuration issues or could be due to lack of user understanding of the product.

On the other extreme, we are often faced with major issues: networks down and unable to respond to user requests, files or databases lost or corrupt, and applications that will not function. These are the issues that cost companies a lot of money in nonproductive hours or lost work. Here is where the experience and knowledge of the administrator can make a big difference.

In this chapter, you will learn how to identify real network problems (as opposed to user errors). You will also learn how to prioritize problems and respond to them in an analytical and systematic manner. The many troubleshooting tools that are available for your use will be explained, and some step-by-step approaches to common connectivity issues will be detailed. We will then show you how to access the tremendous resources of technology information that are available.

IDENTIFYING, ASSESSING, AND RESPONDING TO PROBLEMS

In a large network, it is normal for an administrator to have many problems to attend to simultaneously. The accountant has a monitor that flickers, an engineer has a computer that locks up once in a while, a new inventory application needs to be installed and configured, and then someone says that the entire third floor can no longer access the network. In instances like this, it's easy to tell where the priorities are. Sometimes, however, it's not as easy to determine which problem requires the most immediate attention. Often the decision is based on a "first come, first served" list, or, in some places, it's the "squeaky wheel" method, where the loudest complainer takes priority. Whatever method your company uses, it will require an ability to determine how serious one problem is in comparison to another. You won't be employed long if you spend the afternoon trying to get a sound card working while an entire department is unable to access its files.

To prioritize problems that are not so easy to differentiate, we often need some guidance. Problems need to be categorized to determine in which order they should be handled. Let's look at the different categories of problems you will encounter:

➤ **Serious** These problems require immediate attention. If a number of users cannot work, time and money in the form of productivity are being lost. Serious problems are often caused by a glitch related to a connectivity component, such as a hub, a router, or a switch. Problems might also be related to a specific application and can be caused by an inoperable server or a problem with the application or related database. The priority here is to get the network operational so that the workers can continue being productive.

➤ **Normal** Normal problems are those you encounter on a daily basis. A user can't log on, or someone's workstation keeps giving error messages. These problems need attention, but for the moment, there is little loss of productivity, or at least it is limited to only one or two people. These problems take priority over adding applications or checking on last night's backup, but they should be weighed against more serious issues, based on the number of users affected or potentially affected.

➤ **Minor** Minor problems are usually in the form of a steady stream of complaints. They are often small hardware or software incompatibilities or simply a matter of perception. The program doesn't work the way the user thinks it should work or would like it to work. These problems are often categorized more by the importance of the person expressing the concern than by the nature of the problem itself. If your general manager's workstation locks up, it will be a bigger concern than if it happens to the assistant to the junior accountant's secretary. This may not seem to be the proper way to prioritize a problem, but it's a reality of the business world.

Of course, it is our goal to solve all these problems. If you work in a company that is adequately staffed with technical personnel, then you will have a much better chance of achieving this goal. If you don't, then often your day is dictated by a constant prioritizing of situations as they appear against those that are still outstanding. The most serious of those get the more immediate attention.

However you may choose to prioritize your problems, unless you can quickly determine that different problems are related, you still need to look at them individually. Once you understand the nature of the problem, you can determine if other problems might be related. Let's look at some different types of problems and some systematic methods for troubleshooting.

A SYSTEMATIC APPROACH TO IDENTIFYING NETWORK PROBLEMS

It would be nice if there were a simple way to determine and fix a computer-related problem. Unfortunately, instead of using a simple chart or procedure, you often have to approach the situation like a detective, gathering information and formulating a theory of what happened before determining exactly what the culprit is and how it can be corrected.

Let's discuss some of the things we need to consider when a problem is first brought to our attention and how we might isolate the cause and solve the problem. The steps of troubleshooting a network problem can be generalized as follows:

1. Analyze the symptoms and characteristics of the problem.
2. Determine whether the problem is related to other problems and whether the problem affects more than one user account or workstation.
3. Isolate the source of the problem.
4. Solve the problem, if you can, or consult technical support resources.

I know it's easy to just say, "OK, find the problem, fix the problem," but is it as easy as that? Let's look at how we would use these guidelines to troubleshoot network problems.

Analyzing The Symptoms And Characteristics Of The Problem

This step is probably the most critical part of problem solving. This is the information-gathering phase, in which you determine what may have caused

16

the problem and, therefore, how you might correct it. Here are some questions you need to ask:

➤ Exactly what is not working?

➤ Has it ever worked before?

➤ What has changed since it last worked?

➤ Under what conditions does this problem occur?

➤ Can this error be reproduced or does it happen at random?

➤ What specific hardware, software, and firmware is involved, and have any of these been changed recently?

➤ Is this problem specific to an application or to the operating system?

These types of questions will help you narrow down the issues and the causes of the problem. Most often, problems are caused by some change that has taken place. It is necessary to answer the questions just listed before you try to institute quick-fix changes based on assumptions. It's easy to make a problem worse and to confuse the real nature of an issue by trying to correct a symptom without determining the cause of the problem.

Getting The User's Assistance

When a network problem is brought to your attention, your first step is to rule out user error. A user might have entered the wrong password without realizing it, or might have inadvertently made a problem worse by changing a configuration incorrectly or by trying to solve a problem with insufficient knowledge. Whatever the situation, you'll often need the user's help to isolate the problem and its cause.

Whenever possible, if you have not identified the problem quickly, try to have the user with you when you attempt to re-create and solve the problem. As a general policy, you can ask users to write down any error messages they received, to list all the steps they took just before the problem occurred, and to list any steps they took to try to solve the problem. Be patient and polite, and don't embarrass users who have made mistakes. Not everyone is a computer expert (or wants to be).

Usernames And Passwords

Users sometimes forget their usernames and passwords or type them incorrectly without realizing it. When this happens and the users think that there's a network problem, they might say something like, "Is the network down? I can't log on," or, "My computer isn't working; I can't see the network." The easiest way to determine the cause of this problem is to log on using your administrator name and password. If you can log on and access the network, then the problem is a user-related issue. Make sure that the user is using the correct name and password (including the correct combination of uppercase and lowercase). If doing this does not allow the user to log on, but it worked yesterday, then most likely the user's password has expired. Check your logon server for verification.

To determine if a problem is user related, you can do two things:

➤ At the user's workstation, log on as administrator, or ask another user to log on to his or her workstation, and see if the problem surfaces again.

➤ Have the user log on to another workstation, and see if the same problem occurs.

These two methods will help you determine if the problem is specific to the computer or is a permissions issue related to the user. It is important that you determine this before you change any hardware or software configurations.

Isolating Problems

The first step in determining the exact nature of a problem is to isolate the problem. This means determining the scope of the problem—that is, which users, machines, and applications are having the same or related symptoms. If the problem is occurring on only one machine, then you need to determine the cause. If you used the previous method to eliminate the user as the cause, then you have probably isolated the problem to the computer configuration or hardware or to the application the user is accessing.

The General Approach To Isolating A Problem

At this point, you must further isolate the problem by determining whether any other users that attempt this same event on a different computer are having the same problem. This step will tell you whether you need to focus on the computer or on the task.

To isolate problems, follow these steps:

1. Have a second user, preferably an administrator, perform the same task on an equivalent workstation. This will tell you if the problem is related to the task or to the user or computer.

2. If that is successful (the task can be performed), then have the successful user perform the task on the machine that experienced the failure. This will tell you if the problem is user related or computer related.

If the second user can perform the task properly, then the problem is somehow associated with user rights and permissions. If the second user cannot perform the task on the original machine after having successfully performed it on another machine, then the computer or its connection is the problem, and that is what you'll have to tackle next.

16

The Strip-Down Approach To Isolating A Problem

Sometimes every effort to determine the cause of the problem provides no relief. All resources have been checked, and no conflicts have been noted. The problem might just be a bad hardware item. In these cases, the strip-down method is used to isolate the cause of the problem. Here's how it works:

1. All cards not needed to operate at the basic level are removed from the system. Disconnecting cables will often be sufficient. This includes modems, sound cards, SCSI adapters, tape devices, etc. The computer is brought to its original configuration and rebooted.

2. If the problem still exists, then it has to be related to the motherboard or another remaining device. It may be necessary to replace one of these items.

3. If the problem has gone away, then you may begin by adding each peripheral card, rebooting, and testing for the same problem until it recurs.

4. When you have experienced the problem again, you have isolated it to the last device you just installed. Replacing this device will usually solve the problem.

Viruses

When you have trouble isolating the cause of a problem, a virus might be the culprit. Viruses can be hard to detect. Sometimes a problem does not seem logical. You might be unable to trace the problem to a particular application or hardware item. The problem's occurrence might be totally random or might affect unrelated files or tasks. When there appears to be no logical connection between the problem and any specific hardware and application, suspect a virus.

Viruses can cause a variety of problems ranging from minor to extreme. Make sure you always have an updated virus detection disk available. When all logical troubleshooting methods produce no results, or when the symptoms seem unusual, often a virus scan will solve the problem. If you find a virus, be sure to clean not only that computer but also any other computers that may also be infected. All floppy disks in the area must also be checked or (if possible) discarded. Be sure that the virus is not allowed to continuously infect the network due to a haphazard approach to eradicating it.

TROUBLESHOOTING THE OPERATING SYSTEMS

Most of the time, you will be able to isolate your problem to a single workstation. Workstation troubleshooting can vary greatly depending upon the operating system in use. Most workstations you encounter will be running one of the three main operating systems, discussed here in the order they were released:

➤ Windows 95

➤ Windows NT 4

➤ Windows 98

You might occasionally encounter a Windows 3.x or DOS workstation, but by the end of 1999, these operating systems will be as scarce as 14.4K modems. Let's concentrate on this Windows group because a majority of the desktop workstations use a Microsoft Windows product.

Windows 95

Windows 95 ushered in a new era of network operating systems. It has continued to evolve through the release of Windows 95 B and Windows 95 C versions, as well as numerous service packs. There are a number of versions of Windows 95 in existence, with the earlier ones being less stable than the later ones.

In Chapter 14, we learned how Windows 95 technology replaced many of the autoexec.bat, config.sys, and .ini files that were previously used to maintain information about the applications, the hardware, and the general configuration of the operating system. These files were all replaced by a central set of system files called the *Registry*. The Registry is where all the system information is stored and where all the configuration changes you make are recorded. We covered the details of the Registry keys in Chapter 14. What we need to remember when troubleshooting is that all software-related configurations are kept in the H_KEYS database. Any change we make using the utilities in the Control Panel or through the Device Manager is simply a graphical display of a text change in the H_KEYS database. Let's look at this graphical display and see how it tells us what's in the Registry and how we can make changes.

To open the Device Manager, you open the Control Panel, double-click on the System icon, and click on the Device Manager tab of the System Properties window. The Device Manager lists the categories of hardware installed in the computer. Double-click on any category to view the specific hardware contained in that category. Double-click on a specific hardware item to see the driver installed for that item and the resources (such as the IRQ [interrupt request] and the I/O address) that are associated with it. The Device Manager even shows resource conflicts associated with the item.

16

The Device Manager

The Device Manager lists all the devices in your computer. If you double-click on the icon labeled Computer, you'll open the Computer Properties window. The View Resources tab lists your system's resources, including the IRQ settings. Click on Input/Output (I/O) to view a list of all the memory addresses. When easier methods cannot locate hardware conflicts, you'll often have to write down the IRQs and I/O addresses and their associated hardware devices. Checking them against the jumpered settings or the configuration programs will often uncover misidentified resources. The resources listed in the Windows 95 Device Manager are the resources that Windows 95 *thinks* are being used by the device. If the actual device you have hard-jumpered is different, then this discrepancy is probably the cause of the malfunction.

The tools in the Device Manager often make the diagnosis much simpler. Check the Device Manager list to see if any of the device icons are covered with a yellow circle with an exclamation point in it. Figure 16.1 shows a Device Manager list with a circle on the Gameport Joystick line. This yellow circle identifies a hardware conflict that Windows has detected. Remember that two devices can share a resource as long as they do not attempt to use that resource at the same time. Should they attempt this, both devices will fail, and an error will be noted in the Device Manager in the form of a yellow circle.

The yellow circle can also mean other problems with the device. Resources may be properly allocated, but if you are using an incorrect driver, or if the device is defective and Windows is unable to properly communicate with the device, then this yellow circle will appear.

Resolving Resource Conflicts

Once you have located a yellow circle, open the device's Properties window and click on the Resources tab. This tab lists the parameters that are in conflict. It should look something like Figure 16.2. These settings need to be reconfigured to match the settings you have manually configured on the card. If the resources that are shown match the card but conflict with another device, then you'll need to manually change the settings on the card. If the device settings are Plug and Play and can be set through the Device Manager, then changing to a resource that is not in conflict will often solve the problem.

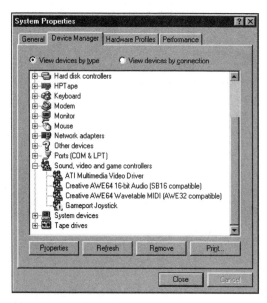

Figure 16.1   Windows 95 Device Manager with error icon.

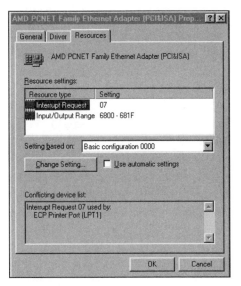

Figure 16.2   Resources tab of a device's Properties window in Windows 95.

Safe Mode

When problems occur upon startup of a Windows 95 operating system, this can often create difficulties for troubleshooting. If the video driver is causing major distortion, or if the system is locking upon startup, then it may be impossible to operate the system long enough to make the necessary configuration changes. Safe Mode for Windows 95 allows you to troubleshoot the system by bypassing the current Real Mode configuration and loading a minimal Protected Mode configuration, disabling Windows 95 device drivers and using a standard VGA display adapter.

To access Safe Mode, press the F8 key when the screen says "Starting Windows 95." You'll see a menu of startup options, including a normal startup, a startup with the minimal number of drivers, or a startup that lets you specify, driver by driver, which ones you want loaded. If you are experiencing lockups and major conflicts that do not allow Windows to start normally, you should load only the minimum number of drivers. Then, open the Device Manager and remove or replace the incorrect or offending drivers. (Remember that in Safe Mode, several drivers will not be loaded, so a number of your components—such as the modem and the sound card—will not operate until you have rebooted in a normal manner.) After making changes, try to restart the computer. Reload or reconfigure the correct drivers and resources, and test them to be sure that the computer is working properly.

If your system is still having major problems after you have used Safe Mode, and if you have used the procedure discussed in "The Strip-Down Approach To Isolating A Problem" section earlier in this chapter, then you most likely have a

16

defective motherboard or a corrupt Registry, or maybe both. Try reloading your operating system. If this does not solve the problem, then new hardware will be required.

Windows NT 4

Due to its use as a server, Windows NT 4 provides even more troubleshooting tools than Windows 95 and 98 do. Troubleshooting tools in Windows NT 4 include the same tools for listing hardware resources, plus tools that allow you to closely monitor the performance of the server and the network. NT 4 even includes an Event Log, which records errors and problems, providing the administrator with some indication of what the problem is, what may have caused it, and where to find further information to assist in its resolution. Let's look at these tools and how we might use them.

The Event Viewer

The Event Viewer is a valuable tool available in both NT Workstation and NT Server. The Event Viewer has three categories: System, Security, and Application. These logs provide you with details regarding possible errors in a configuration. When you are experiencing a problem on a Windows NT 4 computer, the Event Viewer is the first place you should look to isolate the problem. Often, the nature and cause of the problem will be logged for you.

To open the Event Viewer, click on Start | Programs | Administrative Tools | Event Viewer. These are the logs you will find:

➤ **System** The System log contains events logged by Windows NT 4 system components. These events may include driver failures, device conflicts, Read/Write errors, timeouts, and bad block errors.

➤ **Security** The Security log is used mostly to audit events that you have determined to be security related. These events include logons, attempts to log on, attempts to access areas that are denied, and attempts to log on outside of normal hours.

➤ **Application** The Application log lists events that occur within an application in the system. For example, a service might have failed to load so an application is unavailable, or a database might have registered an error. The errors recorded here are specific to the application tasks running on the server.

Let's look at one of these logs and what it tells us. Figure 16.3 shows a typical Windows NT 4 System log. At the left of each date is an icon that indicates the seriousness of the event.

Although only three types of icons are visible in Figure 16.3, five types of icons can appear. The icon types are as follows:

➤ **Information icon** This icon—a blue circle with an "i" in it—indicates a successful operation.

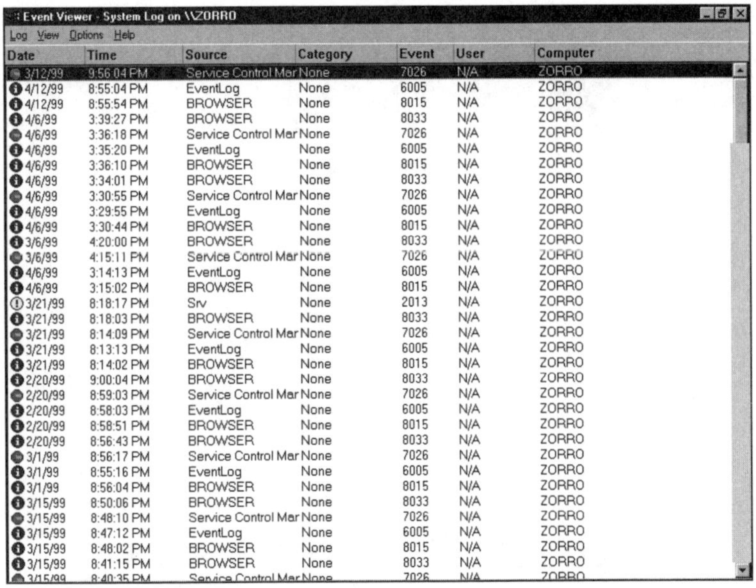

Event Viewer - System Log on \\ZORRO

Log View Options Help

Date	Time	Source	Category	Event	User	Computer
3/12/99	9:56:04 PM	Service Control Mar	None	7026	N/A	ZORRO
4/12/99	8:55:04 PM	EventLog	None	6005	N/A	ZORRO
4/12/99	8:55:54 PM	BROWSER	None	8015	N/A	ZORRO
4/6/99	3:39:27 PM	BROWSER	None	8033	N/A	ZORRO
4/6/99	3:36:18 PM	Service Control Mar	None	7026	N/A	ZORRO
4/6/99	3:35:20 PM	EventLog	None	6005	N/A	ZORRO
4/6/99	3:36:10 PM	BROWSER	None	8015	N/A	ZORRO
4/6/99	3:34:01 PM	BROWSER	None	8033	N/A	ZORRO
4/6/99	3:30:55 PM	Service Control Mar	None	7026	N/A	ZORRO
4/6/99	3:29:55 PM	EventLog	None	6005	N/A	ZORRO
4/6/99	3:30:44 PM	BROWSER	None	8015	N/A	ZORRO
3/6/99	4:20:00 PM	BROWSER	None	8033	N/A	ZORRO
3/6/99	4:15:11 PM	Service Control Mar	None	7026	N/A	ZORRO
4/6/99	3:14:13 PM	EventLog	None	6005	N/A	ZORRO
4/6/99	3:15:02 PM	BROWSER	None	8015	N/A	ZORRO
3/21/99	8:18:17 PM	Srv	None	2013	N/A	ZORRO
3/21/99	8:18:03 PM	BROWSER	None	8033	N/A	ZORRO
3/21/99	8:14:09 PM	Service Control Mar	None	7026	N/A	ZORRO
3/21/99	8:13:13 PM	EventLog	None	6005	N/A	ZORRO
3/21/99	8:14:02 PM	BROWSER	None	8015	N/A	ZORRO
2/20/99	9:00:04 PM	BROWSER	None	8033	N/A	ZORRO
2/20/99	8:59:03 PM	Service Control Mar	None	7026	N/A	ZORRO
2/20/99	8:58:03 PM	EventLog	None	6005	N/A	ZORRO
2/20/99	8:58:51 PM	BROWSER	None	8015	N/A	ZORRO
2/20/99	8:56:43 PM	BROWSER	None	8033	N/A	ZORRO
3/1/99	8:56:17 PM	Service Control Mar	None	7026	N/A	ZORRO
3/1/99	8:55:16 PM	EventLog	None	6005	N/A	ZORRO
3/1/99	8:56:04 PM	BROWSER	None	8015	N/A	ZORRO
3/15/99	8:50:06 PM	BROWSER	None	8033	N/A	ZORRO
3/15/99	8:48:10 PM	Service Control Mar	None	7026	N/A	ZORRO
3/15/99	8:47:12 PM	EventLog	None	6005	N/A	ZORRO
3/15/99	8:48:02 PM	BROWSER	None	8015	N/A	ZORRO
3/15/99	8:41:15 PM	BROWSER	None	8033	N/A	ZORRO
3/15/99	8:40:35 PM	Service Control Mar	None	7026	N/A	ZORRO

Figure 16.3 System log in the Windows NT 4 Event Viewer.

➤ **Warning icon** This icon—a yellow circle with an exclamation point in it—might or might not be cause for concern. This event needs to be checked by an administrator in case a corrective action is required.

➤ **Error icon** This icon—a red stop sign—indicates a potentially serious problem. Try to address and correct all of these items. Your Event Viewer should be free of stop-sign icons. If you are having problems with your system, these icons will often tell you the cause.

➤ **Successful Audit icon** This icon—a gold key—Indicates that an audited security event was successful.

➤ **Failure Audit icon** This icon—a lock—Indicates that an audited security event has failed.

These logs also contain the time of occurrence, the application or component that logged the event, and an event number. All this information is valuable for isolating the cause of the problem. In Hands-On Project 16.1, you will use this information to help define and correct problems.

Windows NT Diagnostics

The Windows NT Diagnostics tool assists in the diagnosis of hardware and driver problems. Although it is a good access point for information regarding the configuration of your system, it falls short of providing any real diagnosis or hardware testing capabilities. Probably the most useful section is the Resources tab, shown in Figure 16.4. The Resources tab can be accessed through Start|Programs|Administrative Tools|Windows NT Diagnostics.

16

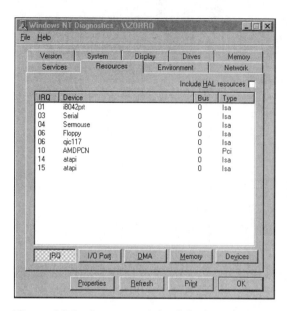

Figure 16.4   Resources tab of the Windows NT Diagnostics window.

Like the Windows 95 Device Manager, the Resources tab of the Windows NT Diagnostics window lists resources that your hardware uses. It doesn't, however, allow you to change the IRQs or I/Os that it lists. This is strictly an information database for you to use when troubleshooting the configuration of your devices. Any changes you need to make must be made through the specific Properties subsection of your Control Panel.

The Task Manager

The Task Manager is a useful tool for checking which tasks are working on your system or for stopping tasks that are not responding. In addition, Task Manager is an excellent place to quickly view the memory and processor usage. Often, if a system appears to be locked up, you can look in the Task Manager to see how it is performing and what may be causing the lockup. You can then quickly stop the offending service and allow the system to continue in a normal manner.

The Task Manager is also a good place to monitor your computer's memory usage. Figure 16.5 shows the Performance tab of the Task Manager. This tab shows the computer's resource usage. If you find that the computer is constantly over its physical memory and using its virtual memory (pagefile.sys), then it's time to add more physical memory to the system.

Pressing Ctrl+Alt+Delete and pressing the Task Manager button in that dialog box opens the Task Manager dialog box. The Task Manager will appear over any application you are running. From there you can choose one of the three tabs: Applications, Processes, or Performance.

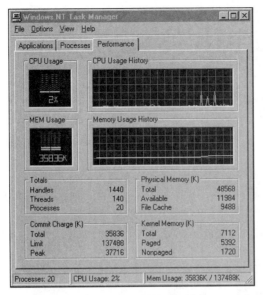

Figure 16.5   Performance tab of the Windows NT Task Manager.

Performance Monitor And Network Monitor

Performance Monitor and Network Monitor are two diagnostic programs that allow you to set baselines and log variances. These are complex programs that, when mastered, can provide a lot of good information about the health of your hardware and application subsystems. Performance Monitor (see Figure 16.6) is concerned with the operation of the computer and its hardware. Network

16

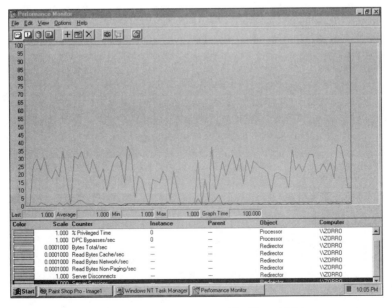

Figure 16.6   Performance Monitor in Windows NT 4.

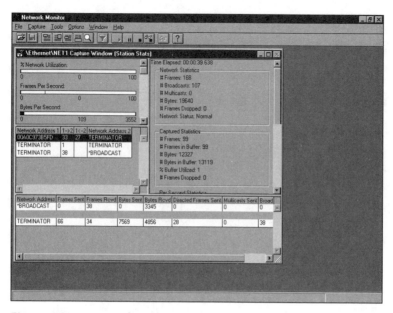

Figure 16.7 Network Monitor in Windows NT 4.

Monitor (see Figure 16.7) can help you diagnose problems between computers and other network devices. We will not go into detail here about how to use these very effective programs, but a lot of good information is available elsewhere.

Dr. Watson

Dr. Watson is a program error debugger that interprets program errors in Windows-based applications. Dr. Watson automatically creates a log file whenever an application fault occurs. This file indicates the program that faulted, the program the fault occurred in, and the memory address where the fault occurred. You can read this information by accessing the log file that is stored in the \\Winnt\system32\Drwtsn32 directory.

Although it's nice that Dr. Watson can provide this type of information, this utility is an after-the-fact monitor—it doesn't give much detailed information, such as error codes, that might be used to prevent a recurrence.

The NT Registry

Windows NT completed the cleanup and consolidation of the autoexec.bat, config.sys, and .ini files that the Windows 95 Registry had started. The Windows NT Registry is much more complex and robust. It acts in the same manner as the Windows 95 Registry, in that it stores all the configuration changes made using the different installation and configuration methods. The NT Registry should not be tampered with by anyone who does not have a strong understanding of the effects any changes might have.

Windows 98

Windows 98 has expanded immensely on the few tools that Windows 95 provided. The Device Manager is much the same and works in much the same manner. It can be used to access the information needed about the devices within the system and the resources that these devices are using.

The Windows 98 Registry

The Windows 98 Registry is patterned more after the Windows NT Registry than after the Windows 95 Registry. One major difference is that the Windows 98 Registry can support Plug and Play, whereas the one in Windows NT cannot. Also, Windows NT supports security features that the Windows 98 Registry does not need.

Dr. Watson For Windows 98

Microsoft included its application debugger, Dr. Watson, in the Windows 98 troubleshooting tool chest. Dr. Watson log files are stored as .wlg files in the \\Windows\Drwatson directory. Dr. Watson functions here the same as it does in Windows NT.

Windows 98 Hardware Conflict Troubleshooter

The Windows 98 help file provides a Hardware Conflict Troubleshooter (see Figure 16.8), which can be used to detect and solve a variety of hardware-related configuration problems. It's easy to use and can be accessed through the Help menu.

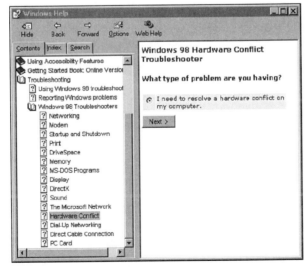

16

Figure 16.8   Windows 98 Hardware Conflict Troubleshooter.

Windows 98 Safe Mode

Windows 98 Safe Mode works in much the same manner as the Windows 95 Safe Mode does. Safe Mode can be used to load Windows without drivers in order to make changes. Actually, Windows 98 has two Safe Modes: Safe Mode with network support and Safe Mode without network support. To access Safe Mode without network support, press F5 when the screen says "Starting Windows 95." To choose Safe Mode with network support, press F6 instead. Both options are also available by pressing F8 and then choosing one of the two.

Other Windows 98 Tools

Windows 98 also offers other hardware and software troubleshooting tools that are too numerous to explain or even list here. Many are error-checking systems that work without user intervention. These tools include:

➤ A system file checker that scans for altered files

➤ A Microsoft System Information program to assist with configuration

➤ An Automatic Skip Driver Agent that detects devices that might prevent Windows from starting

➤ A System Recovery tool that operates in Protected Mode to assist in the recovery of files through Microsoft Backup

➤ A Version Conflict Manager that can handle file version conflicts

➤ Windows and DOS Web-based report tools that can gather system information for reporting to Microsoft engineers

Editing The Registry

Whenever possible, changes to the Registry should be made using the appropriate graphical user interface. Sometimes, however, a solution to a problem may call for a direct change in the Registry of the operating system.

Changing the Registry directly should always be done with care and only when specifically indicated by Microsoft documentation or under the direct instruction of a Microsoft Technical Support Engineer. Should you need to change the Registry, be sure to create a backup copy before you begin. After the Registry has been altered, you may be unable to continue operation. In these instances, a repair installation or a complete new installation may be required. Do not attempt any changes based on "friendly suggestions" or quick "tricks and tips" unless you are fully prepared to reinstall if necessary. There are also many unofficial guides to Registry changes; again, you need to proceed with extreme caution.

To open the Registry Editor, choose Start|Run and enter "regedit" (in Windows NT, you can use "regedit", or you can use "regedt32" for a tiled display). The Registry Editor will display the keys described in Chapter 14. Figure 16.9 shows the Registry interface for Windows 95. Remember that any changes, even minor ones, may render your system inoperable.

TROUBLESHOOTING COMMON NETWORK CONNECTIVITY PROBLEMS

We have looked at a number of methods to determine the nature of problems at the workstation. The problems we've discussed in this chapter thus far can be isolated by identifying who can and who can't perform certain tasks. Sometimes, however, you can't get this far. Sometimes all components of the network appear to be operating properly, yet one workstation or more is unable to log on or cannot recognize the network. You have checked the workstation, and it is functioning properly, as far as you can tell, and other users are able to access the network without any problems. You attempt to log on to the workstation as administrator and still can't get any validation. In an NT network, you would receive a message such as "Domain controller not found." Now you must begin to isolate the problem. This is not a question of user permissions. The problem lies in the specific computer and its configuration or in some other component on the network. Here is where the protocol you are using on your network can provide the tools you need to determine the cause of the problem.

Using The **PING** Command To Test Connectivity

The TCP/IP utility suite is full of commands that can be used to isolate problems. These commands are included in all Windows operating systems and

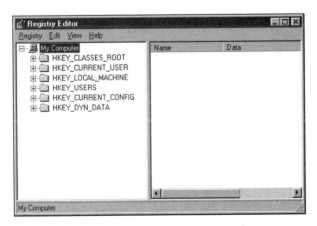

Figure 16.9   Windows 95 Registry interface.

are independent of the rights and permissions you have. Often the major issues involve the inability to log on and therefore to receive the rights and permissions that you need. If you needed these rights to troubleshoot your network, you could be in serious trouble.

One of the most valuable commands in the TCP/IP (Transmission Control Protocol/Internet Protocol) protocol stack is PING. The **PING** command can be used on any operating system using the TCP/IP protocol stack. This includes Windows 95, 98, NT, Unix, and the Macintosh OS. PING sends a packet to a TCP/IP address and records the response time. Figure 16.10 is a reply from a host that has been PINGed. Let's look at how we can use the **PING** command to isolate the cause of a connectivity problem.

Let's assume that you have been called to a Windows 95 workstation where the user is unable to access any resources on the network. You attempt to log on as administrator and are unable to reach the primary domain controller (PDC), the validation server for your network which is located in the same subnet as the workstation. TCP/IP is the default protocol in your network, and you believe it is installed on both your local host and your remote host. Here is a systematic approach you can take to test your connection and isolate the location or cause of the problem:

1. After bootup, go to the MS-DOS Command Prompt.

2. Type "ping *IP address of PDC*" and press Enter. (Be sure to include a space between "ping" and the IP address of the PDC.)

   If you receive a reply, see Step 5. If you do not receive a reply, or if you receive a "timeout" or "destination host unreachable" error, see Step 3.

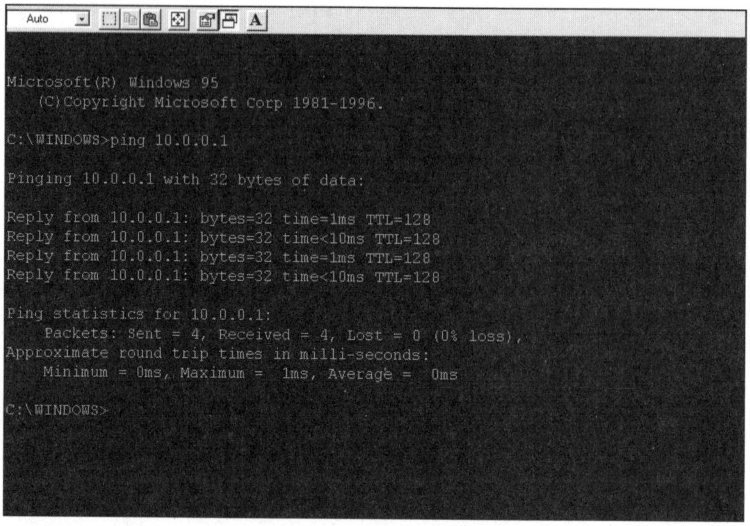

```
Microsoft(R) Windows 95
   (C)Copyright Microsoft Corp 1981-1996.

C:\WINDOWS>ping 10.0.0.1

Pinging 10.0.0.1 with 32 bytes of data:

Reply from 10.0.0.1: bytes=32 time=1ms TTL=128
Reply from 10.0.0.1: bytes=32 time<10ms TTL=128
Reply from 10.0.0.1: bytes=32 time=1ms TTL=128
Reply from 10.0.0.1: bytes=32 time<10ms TTL=128

Ping statistics for 10.0.0.1:
    Packets: Sent = 4, Received = 4, Lost = 0 (0% loss),
Approximate round trip times in milli-seconds:
    Minimum = 0ms, Maximum =  1ms, Average =  0ms

C:\WINDOWS>
```

Figure 16.10   The reply from a **PING** command.

3. Type "ping *IP address of your workstation*" and press Enter.

   If you receive a reply, see Step 8. If you do not receive a reply, see Step 4.

4. Type "ping 127.0.0.1" and press Enter.

   The IP address 127.0.0.1 is an internal loopback address. If you PING this address when your workstation is disconnected from the network, you will receive a reply if your TCP/IP protocol has been installed properly. The reply does not indicate that you have any parameters—such as the IP subnet or the subnet mask—correct.

   If you receive a reply when you PING the 127.0.0.1 address, this indicates that TCP/IP has been correctly installed and is working on your computer. This does not indicate that you have properly bound TCP/IP to the network card you are using or that you have properly configured your TCP/IP address and other parameters. If you are unable to PING your own IP address, you might attempt to disconnect it from the network and try again because there may be a conflict with another workstation. Also, be sure to check for hardware conflicts with IRQs or I/O addresses that may be causing this problem. You might also try resetting and rebinding your TCP/IP parameters or reinstalling TCP/IP. If none of these strategies works, you might need to replace the network interface card. In extreme cases, the Registry might be corrupt, and a complete reinstall of the operating system might be required.

   If you do not receive a reply when you PING the 127.0.0.1 IP address, then TCP/IP is not installed or configured correctly. This could also be the result of a defective network interface card or incorrect drivers. You should verify that the hardware settings on your network interface card (NIC) are correct and are not in conflict with another device. You might also use a hardware loopback to complete a more thorough set of diagnostic tests on your network card. If you are confident that your NIC is configured and working properly, then you should remove and reinstall TCP/IP, being sure to use the correct address and subnet mask for your network.

5. Type "ping *name of PDC*" and press Enter.

   If you receive a reply, see Step 7. If you do not receive a reply, see Step 6.

6. If you can PING the IP address but not the name, then you have a name resolution problem. Refer to the "Troubleshooting Name Resolution Problems" later in this chapter.

7. If you can PING the PDC by name but you cannot log on (this is applicable only if your message is "Domain controller not found"), then your computer can locate and communicate with the primary domain controller. The problem here is that the workstation doesn't recognize the PDC or does not know that you want to log on at startup. The client might not be configured correctly in Network Neighborhood.

16

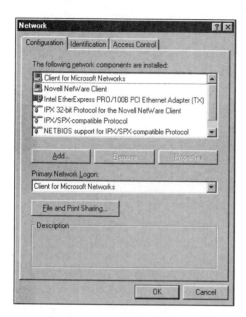

Figure 16.11   Network Properties dialog box.

Figure 16.11 shows the Configuration tab of the Network Properties dialog box and the location of the client software. (To open this window, right-click on the Network Neighborhood icon on your desktop and click on Properties.) Check that the proper client is installed. If you are logging on to a Windows NT Server, then Client for Microsoft Networks should be installed. If you are logging on to a Novell NetWare server, then Client for NetWare should be installed. Also, be sure that the client you wish to use for logon when you first boot up is in the box labeled Primary Network Logon. Next, double-click on the client (in this case, Client for Microsoft Networks) and check the box labeled Log On To Windows NT Domain, as shown in Figure 16.12. A similar dialog box will appear if you're using Novell NetWare.

Another cause of this problem (you can PING the PDC by name but you cannot log on) might be an incorrect locator, such as an LMHOSTS file that may be on the computer and incorrectly pointing to another address for the logon server. This can happen if the computer has been relocated from another network and an LMHOSTS file is resident in the operating system. Check for an LMHOSTS file to determine if you have one incorrectly pointing to a different IP address. If so, then remove the file and reboot because the incorrect information may be cached in memory.

LMHOSTS files are text files used in TCP/IP networks to provide NetBIOS name resolution. We will cover them a little more in the section on name resolution. If you're trying to log on to your server over a router or across a wide area network (WAN), then you may need to install an LMHOSTS file.

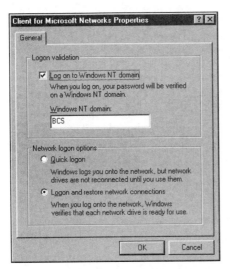

Figure 16.12 Client for Microsoft Networks Properties.

8. If you have a connectivity problem, check the following:

> ➤ Are both the workstation and the server on the same subnet?

> ➤ Are both the workstation and the server using the same subnet mask?

If both are not on the same subnet or not using the same subnet mask, then you will not be able to use the **PING** command to test communications between them. If you have any questions regarding this, refer to Chapters 8 and 9 for more detail.

If you have been able to PING your own workstation (Step 3), and you are sure that the TCP/IP configuration is set correctly, proceed to Step 9.

9. Type "ping *another workstation*" and press Enter.

If you receive a reply, see Step10.

If you do not receive a reply, you have a broken physical connection. In a star topology using UTP (unshielded twisted-pair) cable, trace your cabling, starting from your NIC. Check that it is properly connected to both the computer and the outlet from the wall. Now, go to your patch panel and trace the cable from the patch panel to the hub to be sure that it is properly connected. Some hubs have connectivity indicator lights above or below each port. If you have a trouble light or the light is not on, then make sure the connection is secure, or move the cable to an open port switching, and look for a green light indicating that you have a good connection. If these things do not resolve the problem, then you must start replacing cables.

Replace the patch cables both at the workstation and at the hub, and try again. If you are still unable to connect, then try using another computer at the same location to see if you still have the same problem. If you do, then

16

you will need to use a cable tester to check the wiring in the wall and at the outlets. If the new computer can see the network, then the problem lies within the old system, probably with the NIC. Try replacing it.

Sometimes a router of a hub might be the cause of the connectivity problem. Try bypassing all the network devices by directly connecting the computer to the server, one to one. This can be done using a crossover cable. With a crossover cable, the wiring is different than a straight-through cable (refer to Chapter 13). This is a good troubleshooting method to isolate and determine if the cause is a computer/NIC problem or a network device/cabling problem.

In a bus topology using coaxial cable, one break can bring the entire network down. This is the most common cause of a downed coaxial-bus network. Check to be sure that all cables are securely connected. Also, check to make sure each end is terminated. The method to use here is to segment the network in halves by using the terminators and determine which segment does not function. Continue to halve that segment until you isolate the location of the problem.

10. If you can PING other workstations but not the server, check the following:

➤ Can you PING the server from the other workstation?

➤ Can these workstations PING the server?

Probably not. There is a connectivity problem. Start at the server. Check to see which computers are connected and trace connectivity back from there by checking the cable connections.

The **TRACERT** Command And Bottlenecks

The **TRACERT** command can expand a little on the troubleshooting advantages of PING. Not only does TRACERT give you a reply from the destination workstation, but it also shows you each hop or node that it encounters along the way and how long it took to get to that hop. TRACERT is an excellent tool for locating devices that are bottlenecking your network. Try the **TRACERT** command, and watch how long it takes to move from each node to the next. To use this command, type "tracert *IP address*". If any device takes more time to reply than the others do, this device is probably the location of the bottleneck.

TROUBLESHOOTING NAME RESOLUTION PROBLEMS

Name resolution is the process by which the IP address is "resolved" or linked to its NetBIOS or domain name. When you need to access a resource on the network, your computer mapping will usually refer to it by its NetBIOS or

Share name. For example, if you need to use the printer shared as HP4, attached to the "receptionist" computer, it would be mapped as \\receptionist\HP4. This is meaningless to TCP/IP unless an IP address is associated with it. By using name resolution, an IP address can determine where the "receptionist" computer is located, and the request can be directed to that computer.

On the Internet, we refer to sites by their domain name. The browser searches using the IP address. Somewhere, there needs to be a source of data about which name corresponds to which IP addresses. In actuality, there are many places this information is stored and many ways in which it can be obtained. Chapter 9 detailed some of the methods that the TCP/IP protocol stack uses for name resolution. These include:

➤ HOSTS file

➤ LMHOSTS file

➤ DNS server

➤ DHCP server

➤ WINS database

➤ Broadcasts

Your operating system may use some or all of these, depending on whether they are available or have been installed. Most often they are used so that if one fails to resolve the name, the system immediately tries another until the name is resolved to its IP address. If none of these methods can resolve the name, then most likely the name does not exist, does not have an IP address, or has been entered incorrectly.

Other problems that can occur with name resolution include the incorrect resolution of the name. If there is an incorrect entry in the HOSTS or LMHOSTS file, or in the WINS (Windows Internet Name Service) or DNS (Domain Name Service) server, then your computer may be attempting to locate a resource at an IP address that doesn't have that resource. So how would you go about determining where the name resolution issue is?

16

To solve a name resolution problem, try to PING the name from another computer on the network. If you are able to PING by name from there but not from your workstation, then you have isolated the problem to your workstation. Look for a HOSTS or LMHOSTS file that may be set up incorrectly on your workstation. Here is a sample LMHOSTS file:

```
128.1.1.3    BIG    #PRE  #DOM:BADDOG
```

The file shows that the computer BIG has an IP address of 128.1.1.3 and is the primary domain controller for a domain named BADDOG. The #PRE tells the computer to load this information into cache memory when the computer starts up. Cache memory takes precedence over other name resolution methods, so if this file is in place, it is located first, and a WINS server will never even be checked to resolve this name. If this file is incorrect, the wrong information and mappings will be used when looking for the Domain Controller. You will then receive a "Domain Controller not found" message.

If the problem is consistent throughout the network, then look for one of the network name-resolution databases. If the name you are trying to resolve is a domain such as .com or .net, then look at your DNS server and see what has been entered as a static mapping for that name. If the name you are trying to resolve is an internal computer or server name, then you need to determine if it is related to your WINS or DHCP (Dynamic Host Configuration Protocol) server. They may have become corrupt or may have an incorrect static entry.

OTHER SOURCES OF INFORMATION

Technology changes rapidly, so you might need some outside help to keep up with it. That help can include subscriptions to resources such as the Microsoft TechNet and Novell Connections CDs, as well as technical support by telephone.

Microsoft TechNet And Novell Connections

Microsoft TechNet is a monthly CD available for an annual subscription fee. Information compiled by Microsoft engineers is stored in a database that has search capabilities. You can search for error IDs from the Event Viewer and for other error messages that appear in Microsoft products, and you can find information that can assist you in the resolution.

Novell's CD-ROM, Novell Support Connections (or simply "Connections"), also provides information that can help you solve problems associated with the Novell NetWare network operating system. If you work with either of the Novell or Microsoft network operating systems, these information CDs can save you a lot of time and effort, so they are well worth the investment.

Telephone Technical Support

When you've used all the resources discussed in this chapter and you still can't solve a problem, it might be time to contact the technical support engineers for the vendor of the product. Usually, these contacts are free for the first 30 or 90 days that you own the product, but sometimes there is a charge right from the start. The cost varies tremendously from one vendor to the next. Proprietary software programs usually have annual technical support contracts that average about 15 percent of the cost of the program. Hardware items often have free technical support as long as you are using the product. Some larger companies that produce operating systems often charge by the "issue" and will provide support until the problem is resolved.

When it's time to call, here are some helpful items to remember:

➤ Get the name and a direct phone number for the person you are talking to. If you are given a case number, write it down. Keep good notes of your conversation.

➤ Try to be at the location of the item you are calling about. It's hard to answer questions about the configuration of a server across town. It's helpful to step through procedures as the support technician gives you instructions.

➤ Have information about the product and about any support contracts you may have available. This information includes your client number or contract number and the serial number of the item you are calling about.

➤ If at all possible, try to make sure that the problem is really resolved before you disconnect the call. Often, the representative will have other calls and will try to give you some directions and end the call. Most often, you will end up calling back when the quick advice doesn't work.

➤ Most technical support departments have different levels called *tiers*. If you have been unable to get the problem resolved after a few hours or a few calls, and you think that the technical support representative may have exhausted his or her resources, then you might want to request that the issue be elevated to a higher tier. Sometimes the representative might resist, but often the second level will provide engineers who are much more experienced in that particular product.

➤ Don't feel that asking for help from technical support diminishes your knowledge or expertise. In addition to the tremendous amount of knowledge these support people can provide for your future use, they have available much more product and interaction information than you could possible have. Don't waste hours or days trying to do something that might involve issues you couldn't know. Remember that knowing how to find the answer can be just as important as knowing the answer. The important thing is that you correctly resolve the issue as quickly as possible.

16

CHAPTER SUMMARY

In this chapter, we looked at methods to identify common network problems, which we classified as minor, normal, or serious, depending on the effect they have on the network. You should use a systematic approach to analyze problems and isolate their causes. This approach involves checking certain factors, one at a time, to determine whether a problem affects one workstation or more, and whether a problem is caused by user error, a resource conflict or other problem with the operating system, an application error, or faulty hardware.

Windows 95 and 98 have a Device Manager that can help you identify IRQ and I/O conflicts. Windows 95 and 98 also have a Safe Mode that can be used to troubleshoot problems that can cause startup errors. Windows NT provides several troubleshooting tools:

➤ An Event Viewer to log configuration and application errors

➤ NT Diagnostics to detail IRQs and I/O addresses in use

➤ Task Manager to show processor and memory usage

➤ Performance Monitor and Network Monitor to establish baselines and track long-term performance

The TCP/IP protocol stack provides a number of utilities that can help you troubleshoot connectivity problems on TCP/IP networks:

➤ PING can be used to test physical connectivity and responses between computers.

➤ TRACERT is used to track the path a packet takes between nodes and to record the amount of time the packet takes to pass through network devices. TRACERT can be very useful in determining the location of network bottlenecks.

➤ Name resolution problems can be resolved using TCP/IP utilities. HOSTS and LMHOSTS files can be created to map IP addresses to computer and domain names. DNS and WINS servers have databases that can be accessed for name resolution.

Many hardware and software vendors provide technical information and support through Web sites, CDs, and telephone services. Check to see what type of support is available for any proprietary software you have or intend to purchase.

REVIEW QUESTIONS

1. Which of the following questions are relevant when you're troubleshooting a problem?

   a. Exactly what is not working?

   b. Has it ever worked before?

   c. What has changed since it last worked?

   d. All of the above

2. What is the most common problem associated with the bus topology?

   a. One cable break can down the network.

   b. The protocols do not scale well.

   c. Only one server can be placed using a bus topology.

   d. It is subject to continuous broadcast storms.

3. When all workstation tests show that there are no local problems, but you can't see or even PING any other nodes on the network, what should you look for next?

   a. Check the protocols installed on the server.

   b. Make sure that the DNS and the WINS are properly configured.

   c. Make sure that the patch cable is properly connected.

   d. Check the user's rights and permissions.

4. You cannot access the Web server using the IP name, but you can access it using its IP address. Which utility is most likely configured incorrectly?

   a. RAS

   b. DNS

   c. TechNet

   d. IRQ

5. Due to a bottleneck, it takes longer than expected to PING across your network. What command would you use to determine the location of the bottleneck?

   a. **NBTSTAT**

   b. **IPCONFIG**

   c. **TRACERT**

   d. **SHOW PATH**

6. You arrive at work, and several users are complaining they cannot log in to the file server. Where would you look first?

   a. Run your network adapter diagnostics at one of the workstations.

   b. Run the **NBTSTAT** command at one of the workstations.

   c. Run the **NETSTAT** command at one of the workstations.

   d. Check the server's active user connections to see if anyone has successfully logged in to it.

7. What is a common cause of user-related problems?

   a. Bad network connections

   b. Faulty hardware

   c. User error

   d. Corrupt operating system

16

8. A user cannot log on to the network. He could log on yesterday. You can log on to his workstation without a problem. What is the most likely cause of the problem?

    a. The Registry is corrupt.

    b. The server is unavailable to authenticate the logon.

    c. The user's password has expired.

    d. A hardware component is faulty.

9. What is the startup option that allows you to load with minimum drivers in Windows 95 and 98?

    a. Quickstart

    b. Logon

    c. Registry

    d. Safe Mode

10. You can PING a workstation by its IP address but not by its name. What is the most likely problem?

    a. A hardware problem

    b. No connectivity; probably a cable issue

    c. A name resolution problem

    d. Corruption in the operating system Registry

11. What three logs are located in the Windows NT Event Viewer?

    a. System log

    b. Security log

    c. Dr. Watson log

    d. Applications log

12. What does the yellow circle with an exclamation point in it signify in the Windows Device Manager?

    a. A PCI device

    b. A Plug and Play configuration

    c. A serial device

    d. An error in the configuration

13. To fully test your network adapter with diagnostic testing, what device must you use?

    a. Crossover cable

    b. Hardware loopback

    c. Modem

    d. DB-25 connector

14. What tool in Windows NT can be used to see the current CPU and memory usage?
    a. Network Monitor
    b. Task Manager
    c. Windows NT Diagnostics
    d. The Registry

15. If the problems you are having on a computer occur erratically, what might you check for?
    a. A virus
    b. Proper rights and permissions
    c. Cable connectivity
    d. Network interface card configuration

16. If you can PING an IP address but not the related NetBIOS name, what type of problem are you having?
    a. A cabling problem
    b. A hardware failure
    c. A rights and permissions problem
    d. A name resolution problem

17. What type of cable would you use to bypass the network and directly connect a computer to a server?
    a. A patch cable
    b. A straight-through cable
    c. A crossover cable
    d. A SCSI cable

18. What IP address is used as the universal loopback address?
    a. 10.0.0.0
    b. 127.0.0.1
    c. 255.255.255.255
    d. None of the above

19. Which two files are parsed for name resolution information?
    a. LMHOSTS
    b. SYSTEM
    c. HOSTS
    d. DHCP

16

20. To see the IP configuration on your Windows 95 workstation, what command would you use?

    a. **NETSTAT**

    b. **WINIPCFG**

    c. **TRACERT**

    d. **IPCONFIG**

21. Where will an error message appear when you assign a static IP address that is in use by another workstation?

    a. An error message will appear at the workstation to which you just assigned a new address.

    b. An error message will appear at the workstation that had the address previously.

    c. Neither workstation will receive a message; they will both just stop operating.

    d. Both workstations will receive the error message that the IP address is conflicting.

22. What are the names of the Microsoft and Novell support CD-ROMs?

    a. Tech-Know

    b. TechNet

    c. Connections

    d. NetWare

23. You have determined that you have a connectivity problem. Where would you first look for a disconnected cable?

    a. Server room

    b. Hub connection

    c. Network adapter patch cable

    d. Interwall connection

24. Upon reaching a vendor tech-support contact, what are the first things you need to know?

    a. The representative's name

    b. The representative's direct number

    c. The city in which the representative is located

    d. Both a and b

25. How would you start the Task Manager in Windows NT?

   a. Ctrl+A

   b. Ctrl+Alt+Del

   c. F8

   d. Start | Programs | Task Manager

HANDS-ON PROJECTS

Project 16.1

Over the past few years, network applications have become much more complex, and so have the problems associated with them. Proper troubleshooting techniques require an understanding of the monitoring tools available in the operating system and knowledge of how to use them to solve a problem.

In this project, we are going to take you through a simulated problem. We'll use a systematic troubleshooting technique to identify it. Next, we'll determine the cause of the problem, and then we'll use the vendor-supplied resources to determine the resolution.

Because you will be unable to create the problem for yourself, we will provide the Event Viewer and Event Detail that you would see if you had this problem. If you have a TechNet CD available, please follow along as we search for the answers to the problem.

To troubleshoot a problem:

1. On your Windows NT 4 server, go to Start | Programs | Administrative Tools and click on Event Viewer.

2. Click on Log and click on Application.

3. Assume that when you open the Application log, it appears as it does in Figure 16.13.

4. You have just received a stop error advising you that at 10:50 A.M. the application MS Exchange alerted you to a serious error. The event was logged as Event ID 1005. For more detail, you would double-click on the line item. The Event Detail appears as shown in Figure 16.14.

5. You are notified of details regarding the cause of this error. "The Microsoft Exchange Server computer is not available. Either there are network problems or the Microsoft Exchange Server computer is down for maintenance."

   You know that the server is not down for maintenance, so you must look for more detail. Insert your TechNet CD into your CD-ROM drive. It has an autorun for setup. When the setup is complete, go to Tools | Query. Enter in quotes "Event id 1005", as shown in Figure 16.15, and click on the Run

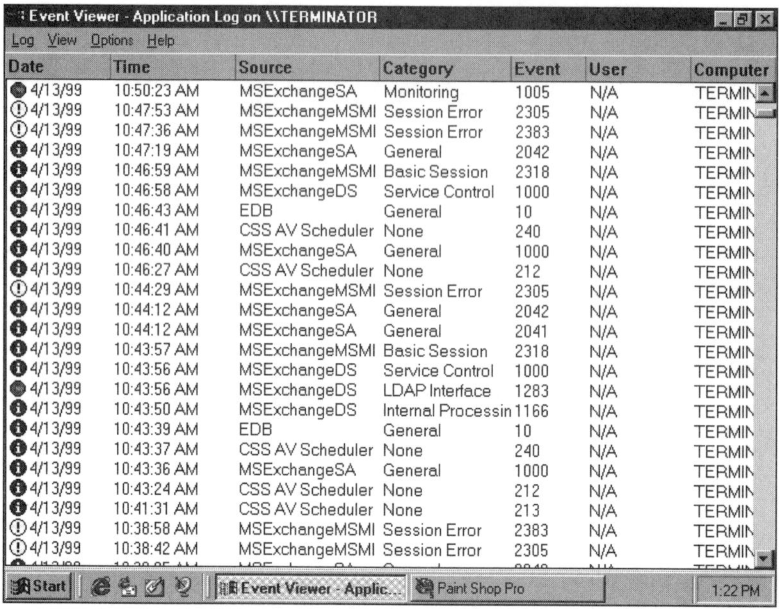

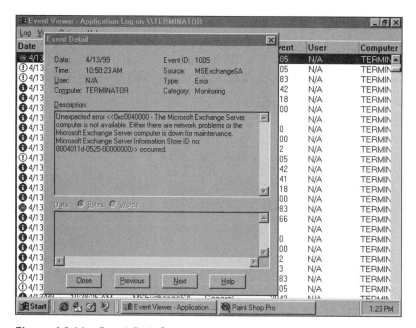

Figure 16.13 Windows NT Application log.

Figure 16.14 Event Detail.

Query button. You will now have a list of results to choose from, as shown in Figure 16.16.

6. Double-click on the results, one at a time, and evaluate each one to determine the one that details your symptoms and/or your error message.

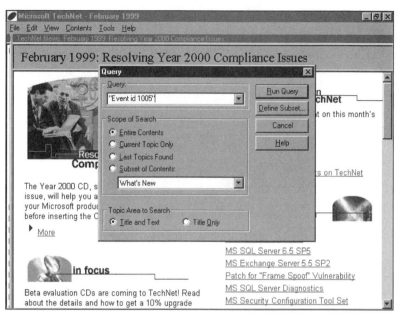

Figure 16.15   Microsoft's TechNet Query dialog box.

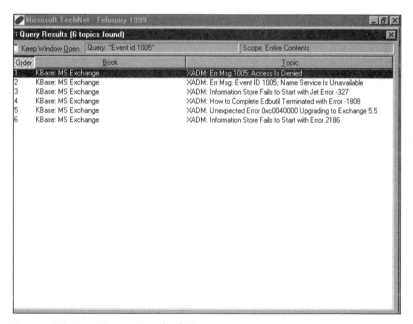

Figure 16.16   Query Results list.

7. Figure 16.17 shows the exact message you received in the Event Detail, so you know you are at the right spot. Figure 16.18 gives you the cause and the solution. If this were a real problem, you would print this screen's information and then take the steps it indicates to resolve the problem.

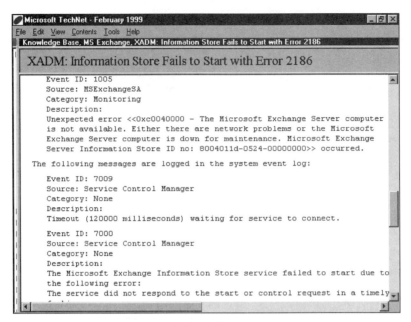

Figure 16.17 TechNet results detail for an error event.

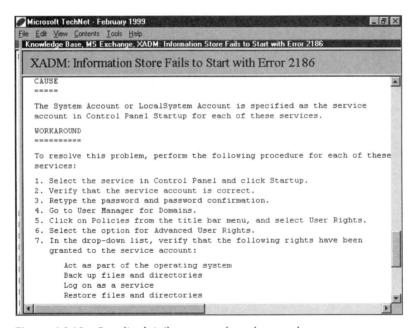

Figure 16.18 Results detail cause and workaround.

Project 16.2

In this project, we will resolve a workstation connectivity problem. A user has called to tell you that he cannot log on to the network. (In this exercise, you can play both roles—administrator and user—for convenience.) You respond and follow the steps outlined here to find out what the problem is and correct it. To perform this exercise properly, you must be on a network that has TCP/IP installed, and you must know the IP address of at least one other workstation and the server on your subnet.

First, let's set up the problem by disconnecting the cable from the back of the computer.

To isolate the connectivity problem:

1. Ask the user to attempt to log on again, and watch to be sure that he has entered the username and password correctly. Read the error message he receives.

   If this is an NT network, the message will read "Domain Controller not found."

   You know that this is not a username/password issue. If you had been given a message to that effect, such as "Incorrect username or password," you would have then tried to log on with your administrator username. In this instance, the message you received has advised you that the domain controller could not be found and therefore was not queried with the username you entered.

2. Go to Start | Programs | Command Prompt (MS-DOS Prompt in Windows 95). Type "ping", then a space, and then the name of your server.

   You will receive one of the following messages: "Destination host unreachable" or "Request timed out." (See Figure 16.19.)

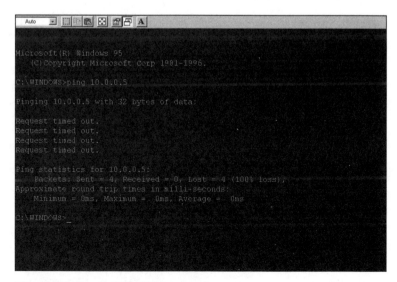

Figure 16.19   Failed PING request.

16

3. Try the **PING** command again, but this time try to PING the IP address of another workstation on the network. You will receive the same message. PING your own IP address or the 127.0.0.1 loopback. You receive a reply, so TCP/IP is properly set up and bound to your adapter card. Go to another workstation and PING this one. No reply? You now know that your computer is not connected to the network.

4. Check the cable connected to your computer. Then, go to the hub, look for a green light, and check your cable connection there. Of course, by now you would have realized that the cable at the back of your workstation had been accidentally disconnected, and you would have reconnected it. What would you have done next if the cables were all connected and the light on the hub was not on?

5. The next thing to check would be the network card. Open the Device Manager and check the network-card icon. If there were a yellow circle over your network-card icon, what would that mean?

6. Let's assume that there's a yellow circle over the network-card icon. Display the Properties tab and then Resources, and see if there are any conflicting IRQ or I/O addresses. Click on Change Settings and browse through the available settings. Notice that some of them will show a conflicting device. If you needed to reset an IRQ, you would pick one that did not have a conflict. Now, click on Cancel all the way out of the dialog boxes so that you don't accidentally save any settings.

7. Let's assume that there were no conflicts and that your Intel Network Adapter Diagnostics program showed the network card to be working fine. What could the problem be?

A number of things could be causing this problem. You might want to replace the patch cable, both locally and at the patch panel, and look for a light. Have there been any changes lately? Maybe a new network card was added recently. You might move the workstation to another location and try there. The connection in the wall may have been severed. You can isolate the problem's location by changing the variables until one variable works but another doesn't. Then, you know where the problem is.

NETWORK+ EXAM OBJECTIVES

Knowledge Of Networking Technology

Basic Knowledge	Chapter
Demonstrate understanding of basic network structure, including the characteristics of star, bus, mesh and ring topologies, their advantages and disadvantages, and the characteristics of segments and backbones.	1
Identify the major network operating systems, the clients that best serve specific network operating systems and their resources, and the directory services of the major network operating systems.	2
Associate IPX, IP and NetBEUI with their functions.	3
Define mirroring, duplexing, striping, volumes, and tape backup.	4
Define the layers of the OSI model and identify the protocols, services, and functions that pertain to each layer.	1
Recognize and describe the characteristics of networking media and connectors, including the advantages and disadvantages of coax, Cat 3, Cat 5, fiber optic, UTP and STP, and the conditions under which they are appropriate, the length and speed of 10Base2, 10Base5, 10BaseT, 100BaseT, 100BaseT4, 100BaseTX, 100BaseVG-AnyLAN, and the visual appearance of RJ-45 and BNC and how they are crimped.	4
Identify the basic attributes, purpose, and function of full- and half-duplexing, WAN and LAN, server, workstation and host, server-based networking and peer-to-peer networking, cable, NIC, router, broadband, baseband, default gateways, and gateway systems.	4

Physical Layer	Chapter
Given an installation, configuration, or troubleshooting scenario, select an appropriate course of action if a client workstation does not connect to the network.	5
Identify hubs, MAUs, switching hubs, repeaters, and transceivers and the differences between them.	5

Data Link Layer	Chapter
Describe bridges, what they are and why they are used.	6
Describe the 802 specification series, including 802.2, 802.3, and 802.5.	6
Describe the function and characteristic of MAC addresses.	6

Network Layer	Chapter
Explain the fact that routing occurs at the network layer.	7
Explain the difference between a router and a brouter.	7
Explain the difference between routable and nonroutable protocols.	7
Explain the concept of default gateways and subnetworks.	7
Explain the reason for employing unique network IDs.	7
Explain the difference between static and dynamic routing.	7

Transport Layer	Chapter
Explain the distinction between connectionless and connection-oriented transport.	7
Explain the purpose of name resolution.	7

TCP/IP Fundamentals	Chapter
Demonstrate the knowledge of the concept of IP default gateways, the purpose and use of DHCP, DNS, WINS, and host files, the identity of the main protocols in the TCP/IP stack, that TCP/IP is supported by every operating system, the function of Internet domain name server hierarchies.	8
Demonstrate knowledge of TCP/IP addressing, including Class A, B, and C addresses and default masks, and the use of a port number for a given service (HTTP, FTP, SMTP).	8
Demonstrate the knowledge of TCP/IP configuration, including an IP proxy definition, normal configuration parameters for a workstation—IP address, DNS, default gateway, IP proxy, WINS, DHCP, hostname, and Internet domain name.	9

TCP/IP Suite: Utilities	Chapter
Explain how and when to use each of the following TCP/IP utilities to test, validate, and troubleshoot IP connectivity: ARP, TELNET, NBTSTAT, TRACERT, NETSTAT, IPCONFIG, or WINIPCFG, FTP, PING.	9

Remote Connectivity	Chapter
Define and explain remote connectivity concepts.	10
Explain the distinction between PPP and SLIP, the purpose and function of PPTP and the conditions under which it is useful, the attributes, advantages, and disadvantages of ISDN and PSTN.	10
Specify the dial-up networking elements, including the requirements for a remote connection and the modem configuration parameters.	10

Security	Chapter
Identify good practices to ensure network security, including the selection of a security model (user and share level), standard password practices and procedures, the need to employ data encryption to protect network data, and the use of a firewall.	11

Knowledge Of Networking Practices

Implementing The Installation Of The Network	Chapter
Demonstrate awareness that administrative and test accounts, passwords, IP addresses, IP configurations, relevant SOPs, etc., must be obtained prior to network implementation.	12
Explain the impact of environmental factors on computer networks. Given a network installation scenario, identify unexpected or atypical conditions that could either cause problems for the network or signify that a problem condition already exists.	12
Recognize visually, or by description, common peripheral ports, external SCSI (especially DB-25 connectors), and common network components, including print servers, peripherals, hubs, routers, brouters.	13
Given an installation scenario, demonstrate awareness of cabling issues, such as the consequences of trying to install an analog modem in a digital jack, the differences in usage of RJ-45 connectors, and that patch cables contribute to the overall length of the cabling segment.	12

Administering The Change Control System	Chapter
Demonstrate awareness of the need to document the current status and configuration of the workstation (i.e., providing a baseline) prior to making any changes.	14
Given a configuration scenario, select a course of action that would allow the return of a system to its original state.	14
Given a scenario involving workstation backups, select the appropriate backup technique from among the following: tape backup, folder replication to a network drive, removable media, multigeneration.	14
Demonstrate awareness of the need to remove outdated or unused drivers, properties, etc., when an upgrade is successfully completed.	14
Identify the possible adverse effects on the network caused by local changes (e.g., version conflicts, overwritten DLLs, etc.).	14
Explain the purpose of drive mapping, and, given a scenario, identify the mapping that will produce the desired results using Universal Naming Convention (UNC) or an equivalent feature. Explain the purpose of printer port capturing and identify properly formed capture commands, given a scenario.	14
Given a scenario where equipment is being moved or changed, decide when and how to verify the functionality of the network and critical applications.	14
Given a scenario where equipment is being moved or changed, decide when and how to verify the functionality of that equipment.	14
Demonstrate awareness of the need to obtain relevant permissions before adding, deleting, or modifying users.	14
Identify the purpose and function of the following networking elements: profiles, rights, procedures/policies, administrative utilities, login accounts, groups, and passwords.	12, 14

Appendix

Maintaining And Supporting The Network	Chapter
Identify the kinds of test documentation that are usually available regarding a vendor's patches, fixes, upgrades, etc.	15
Given a network maintenance scenario, demonstrate awareness of the following issues: standard backup procedures and backup media storage practices, the need for periodic application of software patches and other fixes to the network, the need to install anti-virus software on the server and workstations, and the need to frequently update virus signatures.	15

Identifying, Assessing, And Responding To Problems	Chapter
Given an apparent network problem, determine the nature of the action required (i.e., information transfer versus handholding versus technical service).	16
Given a scenario involving several network problems, prioritize them based on their seriousness.	16

Troubleshooting The Network	Chapter
Identify the following steps as a systematic approach to identifying the extent of a network problem, and, given a problem scenario, select the appropriate next step based on this approach: 1. determine whether the problem exists across the network, 2. determine whether the problem is workstation, workgroup, LAN, or WAN, 3. determine whether the problem is consistent and replicable, and 4. use standard troubleshooting methods.	16
Identify the following steps as a systematic approach for troubleshooting network problems, and, given a problem scenario, select the appropriate next step based on this approach: 1. identify the exact issue, 2. re-create the problem, 3. isolate the cause, 4. formulate a correction, 5. implement the correction, 6. test, 7. document the problem and the solution, and 8. give feedback.	16
Identify the following steps as a systematic approach to determining whether a problem is attributable to the operator or the system, and, given a problem scenario, select the appropriate next step based on this approach: 1. have a second operator perform the same task on an equivalent workstation, 2. have a second operator perform the same task on the original operator's workstation, 3. see whether operators are following standard operating procedure.	16
Given a network troubleshooting scenario, demonstrate awareness of the need to check for physical and logical indicators of trouble, including link lights, power lights, error displays, error logs and displays, performance monitors.	16
Identify common network troubleshooting resources, including knowledge bases on the World Wide Web, telephone technical support, vendor CDs.	16
Given a network problem scenario, including symptoms, determine the most likely cause or causes of the problem based on the available information. Select the most appropriate course of action based on this inference. Issues that may be covered include recognizing abnormal physical conditions, isolating and correcting problems in cases where there is a fault in the physical media (patch cable), checking the status of servers, checking for configuration problems with DNS, WINS, HOST file, checking for viruses, checking the validity of the account name and password, rechecking operator logon procedures, selecting and running appropriate diagnostics.	16

Troubleshooting The Network (continued)	Chapter
Specify the tools that are commonly used to resolve network equipment problems. Identify the purpose and function of common network tools, including crossover cable, hardware loopback, tone generator, tone locator (fox and hound).	**16**
Given a network problem scenario, select appropriate tools to help resolve the problem.	**16**

Appendix

GLOSSARY

10BaseT
The IEEE 802.3 specification for running Ethernet at 10Mbps over shielded or unshielded twisted-pair wiring. The maximum length for a 10BaseT segment is 100 meters (328 feet).

10Base2
The IEEE 802.3 specification for running Ethernet at 10Mbps over thinnet coaxial cable. The maximum length for a 10BaseT segment is 185 meters (607 feet).

10Base5
The IEEE 802.3 specification for running Ethernet at 10Mbps over thicknet coaxial cable. The maximum length for a 10BaseT segment is 500 meters (1,640 feet).

56K technology
The serial transfer of data over analog modems at rates of up to 56Kbps. Although 56K technology started as two competing technologies, the x.2 and the K56flex, eventually the V.90 standard was established. The transfer rate of 56Kbps is theoretical and is not a reality in any of these technologies.

100BaseTX
The IEEE 802.3u specification, also known as Fast Ethernet, for running Ethernet at 100Mbps over shielded or unshielded twisted-pair.

100BaseT4
This technology allows the use of Fast Ethernet technology over existing Category 3 and Category 4 wiring, utilizing all four pairs of wires.

100BaseFX
The IEEE specification for running Fast Ethernet over fiber-optic cable.

100BaseVG (Voice Grade) AnyLAN
The IEEE 802.12 specification that allows data transmissions of 100Mbps over Category 3 (data grade) wiring, utilizing all sets of wires.

1000BaseX
This IEEE 802.3z specification, known as Gigabit Ethernet, defines standards for data transmissions of 1,000Mbps.

Access Control List (ACL)
The name given to the list of total rights granted to a particular user through group memberships.

Access layer
In the Hierarchical Model, the layer where the workstation connects to the network. It is here where hubs reside and where workgroups access the network.

active directory
The user, group, and security information database distributed across a Windows 2000 internetwork.

active termination
Used with SCSI devices to provide a more stable flow of signals across the bus.

address
A set of numbers, usually expressed in binary format, used to identify and locate a resource or device on a network.

Address Resolution Protocol (ARP)
The protocol used to map the IP address to the MAC address.

administrator
Person responsible for the control and security of the user accounts, resources, and data on a network.

Administrator account
In a Windows NT system, default account with rights to access everything and to assign rights to other users on the network.

American National Standards Institute (ANSI)
The organization that publishes standards for communications, programming languages, and networking.

ANDing
The process of comparing the bits of an IP address with the bits in a subnet mask to determine how a packet will be handled.

anti-virus
A type of software that detects and removes virus programs.

anycast address
An address used in ATM for shared multiple-end systems. An anycast address allows a frame to be sent to specific groups of hosts (rather than to all hosts, as with simple broadcasting).

Application layer
The layer of the OSI model that provides support for end users and for application programs using network resources.

Application log
A log, located in Windows NT 4 Event Viewer, that provides information on events that occur within an application.

ARCnet
Token-bus LAN technology used in the 1970s and 1980s.

Asymmetric Digital Subscriber Line (ADSL)
A service that transmits digital voice and data over existing (analog) phone lines.

Asynchronous Transfer Mode (ATM)
International standard used in high-speed transmission media—such as E3, SONET, and T3—for cell relay in which multiple service types (such as voice, video, or data) are conveyed in fixed-length, 53-byte cells.

Asynchronous Transmission Synchronization (ATS)
A process used in serial data transfer in which a start bit and a stop bit are added so the receiving station can know when a particular bit has been transferred. Also known as bit synchronization.

attachment unit interface (AUI)
IEEE 802.3 specification used between an MAU (Multistation Access Unit) and a network interface card.

attachment unit interface (AUI) connector
A 15-pin D-type connector sometimes used with Ethernet connections.

attenuation
The loss of signal that is experienced as data is transmitted across network media.

backbone
A high-capacity infrastructure system that provides optimal transport at each site.

backup domain controller (BDC)
A server that provides a redundant backup of the primary domain controller's user, group, and security information.

bandwidth
The rated throughput capacity of a given network protocol or medium.

base bandwidth
The difference between the lowest and highest frequencies available for network signals. The term is also used to describe the rated throughput capacity of a given network protocol or medium.

Basic Rate Interface (BRI)
An ISDN digital communications line that consists of three independent channels: two Bearer (or B) channels, each at 64Kbps, and one Data (or D) channel at 16Kbps. ISDN Basic Rate Interface is often referred to as 2B+D.

baud rate
Named after a French telegraphy expert named J. M. Baudot, this term is used to define the speed or rate of signal transfer.

binary
A Base2 numbering system used in digital signaling, characterized by 1s and 0s.

Bindery
The user, group, and security information database on a NetWare 3.x server.

binding
The process of associating a protocol and a network interface card (NIC).

bit
An electronic digit used in the binary numbering system.

blackout
A total loss of electrical power.

Blue Screen of Death
The term for the blue-screen STOP errors that occur and halt the system in Windows NT.

bridge
A device that connects and passes packets between two network segments that use the same communications protocol. Bridges operate at the Data Link layer of the OSI Reference Model. A bridge filters, forwards, or floods an incoming frame based on the MAC address of that frame.

bridging address table
A list of MAC addresses kept by bridges and used when packets are received to determine which segment the destination address is on before sending the packet to the next interface or dropping the packet if it is on the same segment as the sending node.

broadband
A communications strategy that uses analog signaling over multiple communications channels.

broadcast
A packet delivery system in which a copy of a packet is given to all hosts attached to the network.

broadcast storm
An undesirable condition in which broadcasts have become so numerous as to bog down the flow of data across the network.

brouter
A device that can be used to combine the benefits of both routers and bridges. Its common usage is to route routable protocols at the Network layer and to bridge nonroutable protocols at the Data Link layer.

Glossary

brownout
A short-term decrease in the voltage level, usually caused by the startup demands of other electrical devices.

bus
A path used by electrical signals to travel between the CPU and the attached hardware.

bus mastering
A bus accessing method in which the network interface card takes control of the bus in order to send data through the bus directly to the system memory, bypassing the CPU.

bus topology
A linear LAN architecture that uses a common cable with multipoint connections for the flow of data in a serial progression to all nodes on that network segment.

byte
A set of bits (usually eight) operating as a unit to signify a character.

cable modem
A modem that provides Internet access over cable television lines.

caching-only server
A server that operates the same way as secondary servers, except that a zone transfer does not take place when the caching-only server is started.

Carrier Sense Multiple Access with Collision Avoidance (CSMA/CA)
A contention media-access method that uses collision avoidance techniques.

Carrier Sense Multiple Access with Collision Detection (CSMA/CD)
A contention media-access method that uses collision detection and retransmission techniques.

Centronics connector
A common connector that uses teeth that snap into place to secure the connector.

change control
A process in which a detailed record of every change made to the network is documented.

channel
A communications path used for data transmission.

Channel Service Unit (CSU)
Network communications device used to connect to the digital equipment lines of the common carrier, usually over a dedicated line or frame relay. Used in conjunction with a DSU (Data Service Unit).

Class A network
A TCP/IP network that uses addresses starting between 1 and 126 and supports up to 126 subnets with 16,777,214 unique hosts each.

Class B network
A TCP/IP network that uses addresses starting between 128 and 191 and supports up to 16,384 subnets with 65,534 unique hosts each.

Class C network
A TCP/IP network that uses addresses starting between 192 and 254 and supports up to 2,097,152 subnets with 223 unique hosts each.

classless interdomain routing (CIDR)
A technique that allows multiple addresses to be consolidated into a single entry.

client
A node that requests a service from another node on a network.

client/server networking
Networking architecture utilizing front-end "client" nodes that request and process data stored by the back-end or "server" node.

coaxial cable
Data cable, commonly referred to as *coax*, made of a solid copper core, which is insulated and surrounded by braided metal and covered with a thick plastic or rubber covering. This is the standard cable used in cable TV and in older bus topology networks.

collision
The result of two frames transmitting simultaneously in an Ethernet network and colliding, thereby destroying both frames.

collision domain
Segment of an Ethernet network between managing nodes where only one packet can be transmitted at any given time. Switches, bridges, and routers can be used to segment a network into separate collision domains.

common carrier
Supplier of communications utilities, such as phone lines, to the general public.

communication
The transfer of information between nodes on a network.

communication port (COM port)
A connection used for serial devices to communicate between the device and the motherboard. A COM port requires standard configuration information, such as IRQ (interrupt request), I/O (input/output) address, and COM port number.

conflicting devices list
Located in the Device Manager of Windows 95, this list details IRQ (interrupt request) or I/O (input/output) conflicts with other devices.

connectionless-oriented communication
Refers to packet transfer in which the delivery is not guaranteed.

connection-oriented communication
Refers to packet transfer in which the delivery is guaranteed.

connectivity
The linking of nodes on a network in order for communication to take place.

Copper Distributed Data Interface (CDDI)
The implementation of the FDDI standard using electrical cable rather than optical cable.

copy backup
A backup of the entire hard drive; similar to a full backup except the copy backup does not touch the archive bits on files.

Core layer
In the Hierarchical Model, it is the backbone of the network, designed for high-speed data transmission.

crosstalk
Electronic interference caused when two wires get too close to each other.

cut-through packet switching
A switching method that does not copy the entire packet into the switch buffers. Instead, the destination address is captured into the switch, the route to the destination node is determined, and the packet is quickly sent out the corresponding port. Cut-through packet switching maintains a low latency.

Cyclical Redundancy Check (CRC)

A method used to check for errors in packets that have been transferred across a network. A computation bit is added to the packet and recalculated at the destination to determine if the entire packet contents have been transferred correctly.

D connectors

Connectors shaped like a "D" that use pins and sockets to establish connections between peripheral devices using serial or parallel ports. The number that follows is the number of pins they use for connectivity. For example, a DB-9 connector has 9 pins, and a DB-25 has 25.

daemon

A service or process running on a Unix server.

Data field

In a frame, the field or section that contains the data.

datagram

Information groupings that are transmitted as a unit at the Network layer.

Data Link layer

This is Layer 2 of the OSI Reference Model. The Data Link layer is above the Physical layer. Data comes off the cable, through the Physical layer, and into the Data Link layer.

Data Service Unit (DSU)

Formats and controls data for transmission over digital lines. Used in conjunction with a CSU (Channel Service Unit).

data terminal equipment (DTE)

Device—used at the user end of a user-network interface—that serves as a data source, a destination, or both. These devices include computers, protocol translators, and multiplexers.

DB-9

This connector has 9 pins and is used for serial-port or parallel-port connection between PCs and peripheral devices.

DB-25

This connector has 25 pins and is used for serial-port or parallel-port connection between PCs and peripheral devices.

dedicated line

Usually used in WANs to provide a constant connection between two points.

default gateway

Normally a router or a multihomed computer to which packets are sent when they are destined for a host that's not on their segment of the network.

Delete or Erase

The right given to users that allows them to delete a file or files in a directory, or to delete the directory.

destination address

The network address where the frame is being sent. In a packet, this address is encapsulated in a field of the packet so all nodes know where the frame is being sent.

Destination Service Access Point (DSAP)

This one-byte field in the frame combines with the SAP (service access point) to inform the receiving host of the identity of the destination host.

Device Manager

A Windows 95 and 98 tool that lists all the devices in your computer and keeps records of the resources and drivers they use.

dialed number identification service

The method for delivery of automatic number identification using out-of-band signaling.

dial-up networking
Refers to the connection of a remote node to a network using Plain Old Telephone System (POTS).

differential backup
A backup of only the data that has changed since the previous backup.

Digital Audio Tape (DAT)
Tape-recording technology that uses the Helical Scan recording method. This technology has been used in video tape recorders and video cartridge recorders (VCRs) since the 1950s.

Digital Data Storage (DDS)
This tape-recording technology uses the Helical Scan method and combines with Read-After-Write and error-correction technology to create an efficient data-storage technology.

Digital Data Storage 3 (DDS-3)
This is the current state-of-the-art of recording technology. It uses longer tape length and faster speed than previous DDS technology.

Digital Linear Tape (DLT)
One of the highest-performance storage solutions available today. This technology is designed specifically for users needing very large database backups.

Digital Subscriber Line (DSL)
A public network technology that delivers high bandwidth over conventional copper wiring at limited distances.

direct memory access (DMA)
The process of transferring data directly into memory at high speeds, bypassing the CPU and incurring no processor overhead.

directory services
The organization of the accounts and resources directory to help network devices locate service providers.

disk duplexing
Fault-tolerance method, defined as RAID 1, that uses disk mirroring and duplicate controllers to duplicate the information stored on a disk.

disk mirroring
Fault-tolerance method, defined as RAID 1, that uses a duplicate disk to duplicate the information stored on a disk.

disk striping
A technique used to bind multiple disks together as a single volume referred to as a *stripe set*.

Distribution layer
In the Hierarchical Model, this layer functions as the separation point between the Core and Access layers of the network. The devices in the Distribution layer implement the policies that define how packets are to be distributed to the groups within the network.

domain
Networking system used worldwide on the Internet and in Windows NT networks to identify a controlled network of nodes that are grouped as an administrative unit.

Domain Name Service (DNS)
The part of the distributed database system responsible for resolving a fully qualified domain name into the four-part IP (Internet Protocol) number used to route communications across the Internet. DNS can also stand for domain name server. See also *Domain Name System (DNS)*.

Domain Name System (DNS)
A hierarchical client/server based database management system. The DNS was created and is operated by the InterNIC to provide alpha-based names for numeric-based IP addresses. See also *Domain Name Service (DNS)*.

dot matrix

A type of printer that uses a number of pins to strike a character impression upon a form. Useful for printing multiple-layer forms.

drive mapping

An alias that makes a network path appear as if it were a local drive.

Dr. Watson

An error debugger that interprets program errors in Windows-based applications and creates a log file whenever an application fault occurs.

dumb terminal

A keyboard/monitor combination that accesses a mainframe computer for data but provides no processing at the local level.

Dynamic Host Configuration Protocol (DHCP)

A protocol that provides dynamic IP addressing to workstations on the network.

dynamic window

Used in flow control as a mechanism that prevents the sender of data from overwhelming the receiver. The amount of data that can be buffered in a dynamic window varies in size—hence its name.

electromagnetic interference (EMI)

The term used for the external interference of electromagnetic signals that causes reduction of data integrity and increased error rates in a transmission medium.

Electronics Industries Association (EIA)

The group that specifies electrical transmission standards.

electrophotography

The photocopy process technology used by laser printers and copy machines.

Emergency Repair Disk (ERD)

A floppy disk that contains security files and resource configurations used for recovery when a Windows NT operating system becomes corrupt.

encapsulation

The technique used by layered protocols in which a layer adds header information to the protocol data unit (PDU) from the layer above.

encryption

The modification of data for security purposes prior to transmission so that it is not comprehensible without the decoding method.

Event Viewer

A troubleshooting tool available in both NT Workstation and NT Server. The Event Viewer provides three logs that record system information: the System log, the Security log, and the Application log.

Extended Industry Standard Architecture (EISA)

The successor to the ISA standard, it provides a 32-bit bus interface used in PCs.

Fast Ethernet

IEEE 802.3 specification for data transfers of up to 100Mbps.

Fast SCSI

The term given for the technology defined in SCSI-2 for a 10Mbps transfer rate.

Fast-20 SCSI

Also known as Ultra SCSI, Fast-20 SCSI was defined in SCSI-3 as a MegaTransfer rate of 20Mbps.

Fast-40 SCSI
Also known as Ultra-2 SCSI, the latest ANSI-published standard. It was defined in SCSI-3 as a MegaTransfer rate of 40Mbps. Another major improvement over Fast-20 is the increase in the maximum allowable cable length to 12 meters.

Fast-Wide SCSI
The combination of Fast SCSI over a two-byte (wide SCSI) parallel path. Fast-Wide SCSI 20 transfers at 40Mbps; Fast-Wide SCSI 40 transfers at 80Mbps.

fault tolerance
This is a theoretical concept defined as a resistance to failure. It is not an absolute and can be defined only in degrees.

fiber channel, fibre channel
This technology defines full gigabit-per-second data transfer over fiber-optic cable.

Fiber Distributed Data Interface (FDDI)
A high-speed data-transfer technology designed to extend the capabilities of existing local area networks using a dual-rotating ring technology similar to token ring.

fiber-optic cable
Also known as fiber optics or optical fiber, this is a physical medium capable of conducting modulated light transmissions. Compared with other transmission media, fiber-optic cable is more expensive, but is not susceptible to electromagnetic interference and is capable of higher data rates.

file rights
The method of granting access to a file or a directory.

File Transfer Protocol (FTP)
The set of standards or protocols that allow you to transfer complete files between different computer hosts.

flow control
A method used to control the amount of data that is transmitted within a given period of time. There are different types of flow control. See also *dynamic window* and *static window*.

fragment-free
A fast packet-switching method that uses the first 64 bytes of the frame to determine if the frame is corrupted. If this first part is intact, then the frame is forwarded.

frame
Grouping of information transmitted as a unit across the network at the Data Link layer.

Frame Check Sequence field
This field performs a Cyclical Redundancy Check (CRC) to ensure that all of the frame's data arrives intact.

Frame Length field
In a data frame, the field that specifies the length of a frame. The maximum length for an 802.3 frame is 1,518 bytes.

Frame Relay
Data-Link-layer switching protocol used across multiple virtual circuits of a common carrier, giving the end user the appearance of a dedicated line.

Frame Type field
In a data frame, the field that names the protocol that is being sent in the frame.

frequency
Expressed in hertz, it's the number of cycles of an alternating current signal over a unit of time.

Glossary

frequency division multiplexing (FDM)

This technology divides the output channel into multiple, smaller bandwidth channels, each using a different frequency range.

full backup

A backup method in which every file on the hard drive is copied.

full-duplex

The transmission of data in two directions simultaneously.

fully qualified domain name (FQDN)

The entire domain name that specifies the name of the computer as well as the domain. Example: mail.aol.com.

gateway

A hardware and software solution that enables communications between two dissimilar networking systems or protocols. Gateways usually operate at the upper layers of the OSI protocol stack, above the Transport layer.

gigabit (Gb)

Term used to specify one billion bits or one thousand megabits.

Gigabit Ethernet

IEEE specification for transfer rates up to one gigabit per second.

Grandfather-Father-Son (GFS)

A backup strategy of maintaining backups on a daily, weekly, and monthly schedule. Backups are made on a five-day or seven-day schedule. A full backup is performed at least once a week. All other days are full, incremental, or differential backups (or no backups at all). The daily incremental or differential backups are known as the Son. The Father is the last full backup in the week (the weekly backup). The Grandfather is the last full backup of the month (the monthly backup).

Group object

A collection of user accounts represented by a single label.

guaranteed flow control

A method of flow control in which the sending and receiving hosts agree upon a rate of data transmission. After they agree on a rate, the communication will take place at the guaranteed rate until the sender is finished. No buffering takes place at the receiver.

half-duplex

A circuit designed for data transmission in both directions, but not simultaneously.

handshaking

The initial communication between two modems, during which they agree upon protocol and transfer rules for the session.

Helical Scan method

An extremely high-density recording method on a relatively slow-moving tape. The tape enters in an angular manner that allows reads and writes diagonally across the tape rather than just straight across it.

High Speed Serial Interface (HSSI)

The network standard for high-speed serial communications over WAN links. It includes frame relay, T1, T3, E1, and ISDN.

HKEY_CLASSES_ROOT

The Windows Registry key that contains the file association and OLE data that made up the original Windows 3.x registration database.

HKEY_CURRENT_CONFIG

The Windows Registry key that contains information about the hardware your computer had at the original bootup.

HKEY_CURRENT_USER
The Windows Registry key that contains the settings and preferences of the users currently logged in.

HKEY_DYN_DATA
The Windows Registry key that contains Plug and Play information and information about the current state of the system.

HKEY_LOCAL_MACHINE
The Windows Registry key that contains data about the system hardware and the installed software (the type of information stored in the Windows 3.x system.ini file).

HKEY_USERS
The Windows Registry key that contains user settings and preferences, including color schemes, desktop settings, and mapped network drives. (This information in Windows 3.x was found in the win.ini file.)

host
Used generically for any system on a network. In the Unix world, used for any device that is assigned an IP address.

host ID
Identifier used to uniquely identify a client or resource on a network.

hostname
The NetBIOS name of the computer or node, given to the first element of the Internet domain name. It must be unique on your network.

HOSTS file
Similar to LMHOSTS except that the HOSTS file is most commonly used for TCP/IP name resolution of domain names.

hub
Also known as a concentrator or multiport repeater, this is a hardware device that connects multiple independent nodes.

HyperTerminal
A communications program that allows you to establish Host/Shell access to a remote system.

Hypertext Transfer Protocol (HTTP)
A protocol used by Web browsers to transfer pages and files from the remote node to your computer.

IEEE
See *Institute of Electrical and Electronics Engineers (IEEE)*.

IEEE 802.1
Standard that defines the OSI model's Physical and Data Link layers. This standard allows two IEEE LAN stations to communicate over a LAN or wide area network (WAN) and is often referred to as the "internetworking standard." It also includes the Spanning Tree Algorithm specifications.

IEEE 802.2
Standard that defines the LLC sub-layer for the entire series of protocols covered by the 802.x standards. This standard specifies the adding of header fields, which tell the receiving host which upper layer sent the information. It also defines specifications for the implementation of the Logical Link Control (LLC) sub-layer of the Data Link layer.

IEEE 802.3
Standard that specifies Physical-layer attributes, such as signaling types, data rates and topologies, and the media-access method used. It also defines specifications for the implementation of the Physical layer and the MAC sub-layer of the Data Link layer, using CSMA/CD. This standard also includes the original specifications for Fast Ethernet.

Glossary

IEEE 802.4

Standard that defines how production machines should communicate and establishes a common protocol for use in connecting these machines together. It also defines specifications for the implementation of the Physical layer and the MAC sub-layer of the Data Link layer using token-ring access over a bus topology.

IEEE 802.5

Standard often used to define token ring. However, it does not specify a particular topology or transmission medium. It provides specifications for the implementation of the Physical layer and the MAC sub-layer of the Data Link layer using a token-passing media-access method over a ring topology.

IEEE 802.6

Standard that defines the distributed queue dual bus (DQDB) technology to transfer high-speed data between nodes. It provides specifications for the implementation of metropolitan area networks (MANs).

IEEE 802.7

Standard that defines the design, installation, and testing of broadband-based communications and related physical media connectivity.

IEEE 802.8

Standard that defines a group of people who advise the other 802-standard committees on various fiber-optic technologies and standards. This advisory group is called the Fiber Optic Technical Advisory Group.

IEEE 802.9

Standard that defines the integration of voice and data transmissions using isochronous Ethernet (IsoEnet.)

IEEE 802.10

Standard that focuses on security issues by defining a standard method for protocols and services to exchange data securely by using encryption mechanisms.

IEEE 802.11

Standard that defines the implementation of wireless technologies, such as infrared and spread-spectrum radio.

IEEE 802.12

Standard that defines 100BaseVG-AnyLAN, which uses a 1,000Mbps signaling rate and a special media-access method allowing 100Mbps data traffic over voice-grade cable.

implied access

Term referring to rights inherited from an upper-level directory.

incremental backup

A backup of only those files that have changed since the last backup.

Industry Standards Architecture (ISA)

The standard of the older, more common 8-bit and 16-bit bus and card architectures.

ink jet

Printer technology that splashes or ejects ink onto the paper.

input/output (I/O)

Any operation in which data is either entered into a computer or taken out of a computer.

Institute of Electrical and Electronics Engineers (IEEE)

Professional organization that develops standards for networking and communications.

Integrated Disk Electronics (IDE)

The most common type of disk drive in use in personal computers today. These devices have the controller integrated into the device.

Integrated Services Digital Network (ISDN)
An internationally adopted standard for end-to-end digital communications over PSTN (Public Switched Telephone Network) that permits telephone networks to carry data, voice, and other source traffic.

intelligent hubs
Hubs that contain some management or monitoring capability.

interface
A device, such as a card or a plug, that connects pieces of hardware with the computer so that information can be moved from place to place (for example, between computers and printers, hard disks, and other devices, or between two or more nodes on a network).

internal IPX address
A unique eight-digit number that is used to identify a server. Generally generated at random when the server is installed.

internal loopback address
Used for testing with TCP/IP, this address—127.0.0.1—allows a test packet to reflect back into the sending adapter to determine if it is functioning properly.

International Standards Organization (ISO)
A voluntary organization founded in 1946, responsible for creating international standards in many areas, including communications and computers.

Internet Assigned Numbers Authority (IANA)
The organization responsible for Internet protocol addresses, domain names, and protocol parameters.

Internet Control Message Protocol (ICMP)
Network-layer Internet protocol, documented in RFC 792, that reports errors and provides other information relevant to IP packet processing.

Internet domain name
Name used on the Internet. Made up of three elements: the computer name, the top-level domain to which your machine belongs, and the root-level domain.

Internet Engineering Task Force (IETF)
A group of research volunteers responsible for specifying the protocols used on the Internet and for specifying the architecture of the Internet.

Internet Group Management Protocol (IGMP)
Protocol responsible for managing and reporting IP multicast group memberships.

Internet layer
In the TCP/IP architectural model, this layer is responsible for the addressing, packaging, and routing functions. Protocols operating at this layer of the model are responsible for encapsulating packets into Internet datagrams. All necessary routing algorithms are run here.

Internet Network Information Center (InterNIC)
The group that provides Internet services, such as domain registration and information, directory, and database services.

Internet Protocol (IP)
Network-layer protocol, documented in RFC 791, that offers a connectionless internetwork service. IP provides features for addressing, packet fragmentation and reassembly, type-of-service specification, and security.

Glossary

Internet Research Task Force (IRTF)
The research arm of the Internet Achitecture Board, this group performs research in areas of Internet protocols, applications, architecture, and technology.

internetwork
A group of networks that are connected by routers or other connectivity devices so that the networks function as one network.

Internetwork Packet Exchange (IPX)
The Network-layer protocol usually used by Novell's NetWare network operating system. IPX provides connectionless communication, supporting packet sizes up to 64K.

Internetwork Packet Exchange/Sequenced Packet Exchange (IPX/SPX)
Default protocol used in NetWare networks, it is a combination of the IPX protocol to provide addressing and SPX to provide guaranteed delivery for IPX. Similar in nature to its counterpart, TCP/IP.

interrupt request (IRQ)
A number assigned to a device in a computer. The number is used to determine the priority and path in communications between a device and the CPU.

IPCONFIG
Windows NT command that provides information about the configuration of the TCP/IP parameters, including the IP address.

IPSec
A protocol designed for virtual private networks (VPNs). Used to provide strong security standards for encryption and authentication.

IPX address
The unique address used to identify a node in the network.

isochronous transmission
A method of asynchronous transmission requiring a node other than the sender or receiver to provide the clock signaling.

jumpered, jumpering
Refers to the physical placement of shorting connectors on a board or card.

K56flex technology
One of the original two 56Kbps data-transfer technologies designed for modems. They were both replaced by the V.90 standard.

Kermit
Commonly used terminal-emulation and file-transfer program.

kilobit (Kb)
Term used for one thousand bits.

kilobyte (K)
Term used for one thousand bytes.

laser printer
A type of printer that uses electrophotography.

latency
The time used to forward a packet in and out of a device. Commonly used in reference to routing and switching.

Layer 2 Forwarding Protocol (L2F)
A dial-up VPN protocol designed to work in conjunction with PPP to support authentication standards, such as TACACS+ and RADIUS, for secure transmissions over the Internet.

Layer 2 Tunneling Protocol (L2TP)
A dial-up VPN protocol, it defines its own tunneling protocol and works with the advanced security methods of IPSec. L2TP allows PPP sessions to be tunneled across an arbitrary medium to a "home gateway" at an ISP or corporation.

learning bridge
A bridge that builds its own bridging address table, rather than requiring you to enter information manually.

line conditioner
Also known as a power conditioner or voltage regulator. This is a non–battery-operated device that is used to stabilize the flow of power to the connected component.

LMHOSTS file
A text file that contains a list of NetBIOS host-name-to-IP-address mappings used in TCP/IP name resolution.

local area network (LAN)
A group of connected computers located in a geographic area, usually a building or campus, that share data and services.

local broadcast
A broadcast on the local network, looking for the IP address of the destination host.

logical addressing scheme
Refers to the addressing method used in providing manually assigned node addressing.

Logical Link Control (LLC) layer
Sub-layer of the Data Link layer of the OSI reference model. Provides an interface for the Network-layer protocols and the Media Access Control (MAC) sub-layer, also part of the Data Link layer.

loop
A continuous circle that a packet takes through a series of nodes in a network until it eventually times out.

loopback plug
A device used for loopback testing.

loopback testing
A troubleshooting method in which the output and input wires are crossed or shorted in a manner that allows all outgoing data to be routed back into the card.

MAC address
See *Media Access Control (MAC) address.* A six-octet number that uniquely identifies a host on a network. It is a unique number, burned into the network interface card, so it cannot be changed.

mainframe
A large computer network in which the central computer handles all the data processing and storage, and only the results requested are sent to the requesting node.

Master Name Server
The supplying name server that has authority in a zone.

Media Access Control (MAC) address
A six-octet number that uniquely identifies a host on a network. It is a unique number, burned into the network interface card, so it cannot be changed.

Media Access Control layer (MAC layer)
In the OSI model, the lower of the two sub-layers of the Data Link layer. Defined by the IEEE as responsible for interaction with the Physical layer.

Media Access Unit (MAU)
IEEE 802.3 specification referring to a transceiver. Not to be confused with a token-ring MAU (Multistation Access Unit), which is sometimes abbreviated MSAU.

megabit (Mb or Mbit)
One million bits. Term used to rate transmission transfer speeds (not to be confused with megabyte).

Glossary

megabyte (MB)
One million bytes. Usually refers to file size.

MegaTransfer rate
Bus signal transmission speed, detailed in SCSI standards and measured in megabits per second (Mbps).

memory address
Usually expressed in binary, this is the label assigned to define the location in memory where the information is stored.

message
A portion of information that is sent from one node to another. Messages are created at the upper layers of the OSI Reference Model.

microsegmentation
The process of using switches to divide a network into smaller segments.

Microsoft Point-To-Point Encryption (MPPE)
Microsoft's proprietary, point-to-point, secure data-encryption method, designed for use with PPTP (Point-To-Point Tunneling Protocol).

microwaves
Very short radio waves used to transmit data over 890MHz (megahertz).

modem
A device used to modulate and demodulate the signals that pass through it. It converts the direct current pulses of the serial digital code from the controller into the analog signal that is compatible with the telephone network.

multicast
A single packet transmission from one sender to a specific group of destination nodes.

multiplatform
Refers to a programming language, technology, or protocol that runs on different types of CPUs or operating systems.

multiplexing
Method of transmitting multiple logical signals across the same channel at the same time.

multiprocessor
Term referring to support for multiple processors in a single machine.

Multistation Access Unit (MAU or MSAU)
A hub used in an IBM token-ring network. It organizes the connected nodes into an internal ring and uses the RI (ring in) and RO (ring out) connector to expand to other MAUs on the network.

multitasking
The running of several programs simultaneously. In actuality, the processor is sharing its time between them, and it only appears as if they are running concurrently.

multithreading
A form of multitasking in which the different tasks that appear to be running concurrently are coming from the same application rather than from different applications.

name servers
These contain the databases of name resolution information used to resolve network names to network addresses.

Narrow SCSI
This technology refers to the one-byte-wide data bus on a 50-pin parallel interface as defined in the ANSI standard SCSI-1. This narrow bus consists of eight data lines with parity and a series of matching control and ground lines.

NBTSTAT

A command-line utility that displays protocol statistics and current TCP/IP connections using NBT (NetBIOS over TCP/IP).

NetBIOS Extended User Interface (NetBEUI)

A nonroutable, Microsoft-proprietary networking protocol designed for use in small networks.

NetBIOS Name Server (NBNS)

A central server that provides name resolution for NetBIOS names to IP addresses.

NETSTAT

A command-line utility that displays protocol statistics and current TCP/IP network connections.

Net Use command

A Windows NT command that allows you to connect to a network path through its UNC name.

NetWare Core Protocol (NCP)

NetWare protocol that provides a method for hosts to make calls to a NetWare server for services and network resources.

NetWare Loadable Module (NLM)

A service or process running on a NetWare server.

network down

A term used when the clients are unable to utilize the services of the network. This can be administrative, scheduled downtime for upgrades or maintenance, or the result of a serious error.

Network Driver Interface Specification (NDIS)

Microsoft proprietary specification or standard for a protocol-independent device driver. These drivers allow the NIC (network interface card) to bind multiple protocols to the same NIC, allowing the card to be used by multiple operating systems. Similar to ODI (Open Data-Link Interface).

network ID

The part of the TCP/IP address that specifies the network portion of the IP address. This is determined by the class of the address, which is determined by the subnet mask used.

Network Information Services (NIS)

The user, group, and security information database utilized in a Unix internetwork.

network interface card (NIC)

Also known as a network adapter, this is the hardware component that serves as the interface, or connecting component, between your network and the node. It has a transceiver, a MAC address, and a physical connector for the network cable.

Network Interface layer

The bottom layer of the TCP/IP architectural model. Responsible for sending and receiving frames.

Network layer

The third layer of the OSI Reference Model, this is where routing based on node addresses (IP or IPX addresses) occurs.

Network Monitor

A program used in Windows NT to monitor and analyze the packet traffic on the network.

Network News Transfer Protocol (NNTP)

An Internet protocol that controls how news articles are to be queried, distributed, and posted.

network operating system (NOS)
Refers to networks where there is one operating system running the servers on the network. Network operating systems include NetWare, Unix, and Windows NT.

No Access
File right used to specify that the user does not have any access to the file or directory. Some NOSs do not have this right and use a filter instead.

noise
Also known as EMI. See *electromagnetic interference (EMI)*.

Novell Directory Services (NDS)
The user, group, and security information database of network resources utilized in a NetWare 4.x and/or NetWare 5.x internetwork.

Open Data-Link Interface (ODI)
These drivers, heavily used in both Novell and AppleTalk networks, allow the NIC (network interface card) to bind multiple protocols to the same NIC, allowing the card to be used by multiple operating systems. Similar to NDIS.

Open Systems Interconnection (OSI) Reference Model
A seven-layer model created by the ISO to standardize and explain the interactions of networking protocols.

Packet InterNET Groper (PING)
A TCP/IP protocol-stack utility that works with Internet Control Message Protocol and uses an echo request and reply to test connectivity to other systems.

Parallel Install
A second installation of Windows NT into a new directory in order to get the system booting so you can retrieve data or restore the old directory.

passive termination
A SCSI bus terminator using a terminating resistor pack that is placed at the end of the bus. This resistor relies on the interface card to provide it with a consistent level of power.

password
A set of characters used with a username to authenticate a user on the network and to provide the user with rights and permissions to files and resources.

patch panel
A device where the wiring used in coaxial or twisted-pair networks converge in a central location and are then connected to the back of this panel.

PCAnywhere
A common remote-control software program that allows users to gain control of a computer remotely.

peer-to-peer networking
A network environment without dedicated servers, where communication occurs between similarly capable network nodes that act as both client and server.

Performance Monitor
A Windows NT diagnostic program that allows you to set baselines and log variances—regarding such things as processor, memory, and disk usage—to monitor the operation of the computer and its hardware.

Peripheral Component Interconnect (PCI)
Newer high-speed bus designed for Pentium systems.

permanent virtual circuit (PVC)
A logical path—established in packet-switching networks—between two locations. Similar to a dedicated line. Known as a *permanent virtual connection* in

ATM terminology. (Not to be confused with Private Virtual Circuit, also known as a PVC.)

permissions
Authorization provided to users, allowing them to access objects on the network. The network administrators generally assign permissions. Slightly different from but often used with *rights.*

physical addressing scheme
Refers to the MAC address on every network card manufactured. Cannot be changed.

Physical layer
Bottom layer (Layer 1) of the OSI Reference Model, where all physical connectivity is defined.

piezoelectric
Method of printing—used in ink jet printers—that shoots ink onto the paper.

Plain Old Telephone System (POTS)
The current analog public telephone system.

Plug and Play
Architecture designed to allow hardware devices to be detected by the operating system and for the driver to be automatically loaded.

points-of-presence (POPs)
Physical location where a long-distance carrier or a cellular provider interfaces with the network of the local exchange carrier or local telephone company.

Point-To-Point Protocol (PPP)
A common dial-up networking protocol that includes provisions for security and protocol negotiation and provides host-to-network and switch-to-switch connections for one or more user sessions. The common modem connection used for Internet dial-up.

Point-To-Point Tunneling Protocol (PPTP)
A protocol that encapsulates private network data in IP packets. These packets are transmitted over synchronous and asynchronous circuits to hide the underlying routing and switching infrastructure of the Internet from both senders and receivers.

polling
The media-access method for transmitting data, in which a controlling device is used to contact each node to determine if it has data to send.

Presentation layer
Layer 6 of the OSI Reference Model. Prepares information to be used by the Application layer.

primary domain controller (PDC)
In a Windows NT network, this is the server that acts as the main repository for the user, group, and security information of the domain.

primary name server
The server that offers zone data from files stored locally on the machine.

Primary Rate Interface (PRI)
A higher-level network interface standard for use with ISDN. Defined at the rate of 1.544Mbps, it consists of a single 64Kbps D channel plus 23 (T1) or 30 (E1) B channels for voice or data.

primary site server
A server that is responsible for all changes made to a zone.

print server
A network device or computer that manages and executes print requests from other nodes on the network.

Private Virtual Circuit (PVC)

Provides a logical connection between locations through a Frame Relay/ATM cloud. Example: A company has three branch offices. Each location physically connects to the Frame Relay provider's network through a series of switches, but it appears to the end users as if the three branch offices are directly connected to each other, as if it were an unbroken circuit. (Not to be confused with Permanent Virtual Circuit, also known as a PVC.)

profile

A template for a user account.

program-specific backup

A backup program specific to an application, usually of a database such as Microsoft SQL Server.

proprietary

A standard or specification that is created by a single manufacturer, vendor, or other private enterprise.

protocol

A set of rules or standards that control data transmission and other interactions between networks, computers, peripheral devices, and operating systems.

Protocol Identification field

In a frame, a five-byte field used to identify to the destination node the protocol that is being used in the data transmission.

protocol stack

Also known as a protocol suite, it's two or more protocols that work together, such as TCP and IP or IPX and SPX.

proxy server

A program that makes a connection and retrieves information on behalf of a client.

Public Switched Telephone Network (PSTN)

A general term referring to all of the telephone networks and services in the world. The same as Plain Old Telephone System (POTS), PSTN refers to the world's collection of interconnected public telephone networks that are both commercial and government owned. PSTN is a digital network, with the exception of the connection between local exchanges and customers, which remains analog.

RAID

See *Redundant Arrays of Inexpensive Disks (RAID)*.

RAID 1

Fault-tolerance method that uses disk mirroring to duplicate the information stored on a disk.

RAID 2

Fault-tolerance method that uses disk striping with error correction.

RAID 3

Fault-tolerance method that uses disk striping with a single disk for parity.

RAID 4

Fault-tolerance method that uses disk striping with a single disk for parity. Striping is done across the disks in blocks.

RAID 5

Fault-tolerance method that uses disk striping with distributed parity. Striping is done across the disks in blocks.

Read-Only

An assigned right that allows the user to open the file and look at the contents, or to execute the file if it is an application. The user cannot change the file or delete it.

Read–Write
An assigned right that allows the user to open the file, to change the file, or to execute the file. The user cannot delete the file in some NOSs, but can in others. The user can create new files in the directory if the right is granted to a directory.

Redundant Arrays of Inexpensive Disks (RAID)
Fault-tolerance methods that use multiple hard disks to duplicate information that can be accessed if one of the disks becomes inoperable.

regedit (regedit or regedt32 in Windows NT)
Command used to open the Registry editor so that you can access the Registry HKEYs and make changes.

Remote Access Service (RAS)
A Windows NT service that controls the access to the network through dial-up connections.

remote control
In networking, this refers to physically controlling a remote computer through software such as PCAnywhere or Microsoft Systems Management Server.

remote node
A node or computer that is connected to the network through a dial-up connection. Dialing in to the Internet from home is a perfect example of the remote node concept.

Repair Install
An option in Windows NT Setup that allows you to repair your current operating system directory by overwriting the corrupt or damaged files.

repeater
A device that regenerates and retransmits the signal on a network. Usually used to strengthen signals going long distances.

Request For Comments (RFC)
Method used to post documents regarding networking or Internet-related standards or ideas. Some have been adopted and accepted by the Internet Architecture Board as standards.

resolver
Utility designed to pass name requests between a client application and name servers.

resource conflict
Term used when multiple devices are using the same IRQ (interrupt request) or I/O (input/output) address at the same time, usually causing the devices to fail and the program to halt.

rights
Authorization provided to users, allowing them to perform certain tasks. The network administrators generally assign rights. Slightly different from but often used with *permissions.*

ring in (RI)
A connector used in an IBM token-ring network on a Multistation Access Unit (MAU) to expand to other MAUs on the network. Counterpart to the RO (ring out), the ring-in connector on the MAU connects to the media to accept the token from the ring.

ring out (RO)
A connector used in an IBM token-ring network on a Multistation Access Unit to expand to other MAUs on the network. Counterpart to the RI (ring in), the ring-out connector on the MAU connects to the media to send the token out to the ring.

Glossary

RJ-11 connector

This connector is used with telephone systems and can have either four or six conductors. A red/green pair of wires is used for voice and data; a black/white pair is used for low-voltage signals.

RJ-45 connector

An Ethernet cable connector, used with twisted-pair cable, that can support eight conductors for four pairs of wires.

RMON

The remote monitoring standard established in 1992 by RFC 1271 for its usage in Ethernet networks. It provides network administrators with comprehensive network fault diagnosis and performance information.

router

A device that works at the Network layer of the OSI Reference Model to control the flow of data between two or more network segments.

Routing Information Protocol (RIP)

Protocol that uses hop count as a routing metric to control the direction and flow of packets between routers on an internetwork.

RS-232

The communications standard that defines the flow of serial communications and the particular functions assigned to the wires in a serial cable.

Safe Mode

Windows 95 and 98 mode, used for troubleshooting, that loads a minimum number of drivers upon startup. Can be accessed only at the time of startup by pressing F8.

SCSI

See *Small Computer System Interface (SCSI)*.

SCSI-1

The first set of ANSI standards for small computer systems, which called for up to seven devices, known as targets, to be connected to a computer known as an initiator.

SCSI-2

The second set of ANSI standards for small computer systems, published in 1994. An upgrade to the SCSI-1 standard, SCSI-2 provides a synchronous data-transfer rate of 2.5 to 10Mbps for an 8-bit data bus and 5 to 20Mbps for a 16-bit (or *wide*) bus.

SCSI-3

The term related to the SCSI standard most widely in use today, SCSI-3 simply split the 400-plus pages of documents used to describe SCSI-2 into a series of smaller documents. SCSI-3 does not define any particular performance or transfer rate, but is rather a set of documents that define the architecture of the updated SCSI specification.

SCSI BIOS (Basic Input/Output System)

Installed after your system BIOS installation is completed, it loads, locates, and provides drivers for all attached SCSI devices.

SCSI bus

The SCSI's high-speed channel between the SCSI devices on the chain and the resources of the motherboard (CPU, memory, etc.). Its architecture contains a multithreaded I/O (input/output) interface that can process multiple I/O requests at the same time.

SCSI bus termination

The use of a set of electrical resistors called terminators at the extreme ends of the SCSI bus to reflect the electrical impulses being transmitted across the bus.

SCSI IDs
Numbers assigned to the SCSI devices, ranging from 0 to 15, to identify the device and its priority when two or more devices are competing for the right to send data on the bus.

secondary name server
A server that gets its zone data from another name server that has authority in that zone.

Security Account Manager (SAM)
The database of user, group, and security information on a Windows NT Server.

security log
A log, located in the Windows NT 4 Event Viewer, that provides information on audit events that the administrator has determined to be security related. These events include logons, attempts to log on, attempts to access areas that are denied, and attempts to log on outside of normal hours.

Sequenced Packet Exchange (SPX)
Protocol used in conjunction with IPX when guaranteed delivery is required. Used mainly in NetWare network environments.

Serial Line Internet Protocol (SLIP)
A method of encapsulation that allows the TCP/IP protocol to be used over asynchronous lines, such as standard telephone lines. Previously used for most Internet access, it has been replaced by PPP because of SLIP's lack of error-checking capabilities.

server
A node that fulfills service requests for clients. Usually referred to by the type of service it performs, such as file server, communications server, or print server.

server-based application
An application that is run off of a network share, rather than from a copy installed on a local computer.

server-based networking
A network operating system that is dedicated to providing services to workstations, referred to as clients. See *client/server networking*.

service access point (SAP)
This field in a frame tells the receiving host which protocol the frame is intended for.

Service Advertising Protocol (SAP)
NetWare protocol used on an IPX network. SAP maintains server information tables, listing each service that has been advertised to it, and provides this information to any nodes attempting to locate a service.

Service Advertising Protocol agent (SAP agent)
Router or other node on an IPX network that maintains a server information table. This table lists each service that has been advertised to it and provides this information to any nodes attempting to locate a service.

session
Term used referring to the dialog that exists between two computers.

Session layer
The fifth layer of the OSI Reference Model, it establishes, manages, and terminates sessions between applications on different nodes.

shared systems
The infrastructure component routed directly into the backbone of an internetwork for optimal systems access. Provides connectivity to servers and other shared systems.

shielded twisted-pair (STP)
Twisted-pair network cable that has shielding to insulate the cable from electromagnetic interference.

Simple Mail Transfer Protocol (SMTP)
An Internet protocol used for the transfer of messages and attachments.

Simple Network Management Protocol (SNMP)
A protocol used almost exclusively in TCP/IP networks to do several things: to provide network devices with a method to monitor and control network devices; to manage configurations, statistics collection, performance, and security; and to report network management information to a management console.

Simple Network Management Protocol trap (SNMP trap)
An SNMP protocol utility that sends out an alarm notifying the administrator that something in network activity differs from the established threshold, as defined by the administrator.

Small Computer System Interface (SCSI)
A technology defined by a set of standards originally published by ANSI for use with devices on a bus known as a SCSI bus.

smart bridge
Also known as a learning bridge, it builds its own bridging address table, rather than requiring you to enter information manually.

socket
A logical interprocess communications mechanism through which a program communicates with another program or with a network.

socket identifier
Also known as a socket number, this is an eight-bit number used to identify the socket. It is used by IPX when it needs to address a packet to a particular process running on a server. The developers and designers of services and protocols usually assign socket identifiers.

source address
The address of the host who sent the frame is contained in the frame so the destination node knows who sent the data.

source route bridges
Used in source route bridging, these bridges send the packet to the destination node through the route specified by the sending node and placed in the packet.

Source Service Access Point (SSAP)
This one-byte field in the frame combines with the SAP to tell the receiving host the identity of the source or sending host.

Spanning Tree Algorithm (STA)
Defined by IEEE 802.1 as part of the Spanning Tree Protocol to eliminate loops in an internetwork with multiple paths.

Spanning Tree Protocol (STP)
Protocol developed to eliminate the loops caused by the multiple paths in an internetwork. Defined by IEEE 802.1.

spike
An instantaneous, dramatic increase in the voltage output to a device. Spikes are responsible for much of the damage done to network hardware components.

static IP addresses
IP addresses that are assigned to each network device individually, often referred to as hard-coded.

static window

A mechanism used in flow control that prevents the sender of data from overwhelming the receiver. The amount of data that can be buffered in a static window is a set size.

station IPX address

A 12-digit number that is used to uniquely identify each device on an IPX network.

storage area network

A subnetwork of storage devices, usually found on high-speed networks and shared by all servers on the network.

store-and-forward

A fast packet-switching method, it produces a higher latency than other switching methods because the entire contents of the packet are copied into the onboard buffers of the switch, and the Cyclical Redundancy Check (CRC) calculations are performed before the packet can be passed on to the destination address.

StreetTalk

A global naming service created by Banyan and included with the Banyan VINES network operating system.

subdomains

Privately controlled segments of the namespace; they exist under other segments of the namespace as divisions of the main domain.

subnet mask

A 32-bit address that is used to mask or "screen" a portion of the IP address to differentiate the part of the address that designates the network and the part that designates the host.

subnetting

The process of dividing your assigned IP address range into smaller clusters of hosts.

Subnetwork Access Protocol (SNAP)

An Internet protocol that specifies a standard method of encapsulating IP datagrams and ARP messages on a network.

supernetting

The aggregating of IP network addresses and advertising them as a single classless network address.

supernetting mask

Mask—similar to the subnet mask—used in supernetting.

Supervisor account

In a NetWare network, default account with rights to access everything and to assign rights to other users on the network.

Support Connections

A monthly CD that provides information and technical support for Novell's NetWare operating systems.

surge

The opposite of a brownout. A surge's voltage increase is less dramatic than that of a spike, but it can last a lot longer.

surge protectors

Also known as surge suppressers, these are inexpensive and simple devices that are placed between the power outlet and the network component to protect the component from spikes and surges.

switch

A Layer 2 networking device that forwards frames based on destination addresses.

Glossary

Switched Multimegabit Data Service (SMDS)

Defined by IEEE 802.6, it is the Physical-layer implementation for data transmission over public lines at speeds between 1.544Mbps (T1) and 44.736Mbps using cell relay and fixed-length cells.

switched virtual circuit

A virtual circuit that is established dynamically on demand to form a dedicated link and is then broken when transmission is complete. Known as a *switched virtual connection* in ATM terminology.

symmetrical multiprocessing (SMP)

The utilization of multiple processors on a single system.

synchronous transmission

Digital signal transmission method using a precise clocking method and a predefined number of bits sent at a constant rate.

System log

A log, located in the Windows NT 4 Event Viewer, that provides information on events logged by Windows NT system components. These events include driver failures, device conflicts, Read/Write errors, timeouts, and bad block errors.

T1

Digital WAN carrier facility that transmits DS-1-formatted data at 1.544Mbps through the telephone switching network, using AMI or B8ZS coding.

Task Manager

A monitoring and troubleshooting tool in Windows NT, used to check the tasks that are running on the system and the amount of resources they are using.

TCP/IP

See *Transmission Control Protocol/Internet Protocol (TCP/IP)*.

TechNet

Published monthly, this CD provides information on troubleshooting and other items related to Microsoft programs and operating systems.

Telecommunications Industry Association (TIA)

An organization that develops standards—with the EIA (Electronics Industries Association)—for telecommunications technologies.

Telnet

Standard terminal-emulation protocol in the TCP/IP protocol stack. It is used to perform terminal emulation over TCP/IP via remote terminal connections, enabling users to log in to remote systems and use resources as if they were connected to a local system.

thicknet coaxial

Thick cable most commonly used as the backbone of a coaxial network. It usually comes about .375 inch in diameter.

thinnet coaxial

Thinner than thicknet but still about .25 inch in diameter, it is commonly used in older bus topologies to connect the nodes to the network.

token

A frame that provides controlling information. In a token-ring network, the node that possesses the token is the one that is allowed to transmit next.

token ring

IBM proprietary token-passing LAN topology defined by IEEE standard 802.5. It operates at either 4 or 16Mbps in a star topology.

token-ring adapters

Traditionally ISA or Microchannel devices with 4 or 16Mbps transfer capability, they are used to connect nodes to a token-ring network.

topology
Defines the shape or layout of a physical network and the flow of data through the network.

transceiver
A coined word that combines *transmitter* and *receiver*.

Transmission Control Protocol (TCP)
Part of the TCP/IP protocol stack, it's a connection-oriented, reliable data-transmission communication service that operates at the Transport layer of the OSI model.

Transmission Control Protocol/ Internet Protocol (TCP/IP)
The suite of protocols combining TCP and IP, developed to support the construction of worldwide internetworks.

Transmission Control Protocol/ Internet Protocol (TCP/IP) sockets
A socket, or connection to an endpoint, used in TCP/IP communication transmissions.

transmit
The process of sending data using light, electronic, or electric signals. In networking, this is usually done in the form of digital signals composed of bits.

transparent bridging
A situation in which the bridges on your network tell each other which ports on the bridge should be opened and closed, which ports should be forwarding packets, and which ports should be blocking them—all without the assistance of any other device.

Transport Driver Interface (TDI)
A kernel-mode network interface that is exposed at the upper edge of all Windows

NT transport protocol stacks. The highest-level protocol driver in every such stack supports the TDI interface for still higher-level kernel-mode network clients.

Transport layer
Layer 4 of the OSI Reference Model, it controls the flow of information.

Travan technology
Available in TR-1, TR-3, and TR-4 formats, it is an efficient, low-cost data-backup method for small PCs and laptops. Travan tape drives are available in a wide range of interfaces, such as floppy, parallel, ATAPI, or SCSI.

Trivial File Transfer Protocol (TFTP)
A simplified version of FTP, allowing files to be transferred over a network from one computer to another.

twinaxial
A type of coaxial cable more commonly found in IBM mainframe environments or used with AppleTalk networks. Contains two insulated carrier wires twisted around each other.

twisted-pair
A type of cable that uses multiple twisted pairs of copper wire.

Ultra SCSI
Also known as Fast-20 SCSI, it is defined in SCSI-3 as a MegaTransfer rate of 20Mbps.

Ultra-2 SCSI
Also known as FAST-40 SCSI, this ANSI published standard uses a negotiated clock rate for synchronous transfers. It can reach transfers of up to 80Mbps over a wide 2-byte SCSI bus. Another major improvement in Ultra SCSI-2 was the increase in the maximum allowable cable length from 3 to 12 meters.

Ultra-3 SCSI
The STA-defined standard defining data transfers of up to 160Mbps.

Ultra-Wide SCSI
The combination of Ultra SCSI data-transfer technologies with a two-bit (or *wide*) bus.

uninterruptible power supply (UPS)
Also referred to as battery backup, it provides protection against power surges and power outages. During blackouts, it gives you time to shut down the network before the temporary power interruption becomes permanent.

Universal Asynchronous Receiver/ Transmitter (UART)
A chip that's responsible for communications carried over a serial port, converting between data bits and serial bits.

Universal Naming Convention (UNC)
An industry naming standard for computers and resources that provides a common syntax that should work in most systems, including Windows, Unix, or NetWare. For example: *servername\sharename*.

Unix
An open standards operating system in wide use, with over 100 variations.

unshielded twisted-pair (UTP)
A type of cable that uses multiple twisted pairs of copper wire in a casing that does not provide much protection from EMI. The most common network cable in Ethernet networks, it is rated in five categories.

Upgrade Install
An option you are given during Windows NT Setup to upgrade the existing installation to a newer version of Windows

NT. Also refers to any installation of a software product that has the effect of upgrading the software to a newer version.

user accounts
The accounts that end users will use when logging in to the network, they contain the rights and permissions assigned to the users.

User Datagram Protocol (UDP)
A communications protocol that provides connectionless, unreliable communications services and operates at the Transport layer of the OSI Reference Model. It requires a transmission protocol such as IP to guide it to the destination host.

username
Name used with a password to identify the person requesting logon permission to the operating system.

V.90 standard
The standard that replaced both the K56flex technology and the x.2 technology as the standard for 56K serial data transfer over phone lines.

virtual LAN (VLAN)
Group of devices located on one or more different LAN segments whose configuration is based on logical instead of physical connections so that they can communicate as if they were attached to the same physical connection.

virtual memory
A paging or swapping process from memory to disk, used to increase the amount of RAM available to the system.

virtual private network (VPN)
A network that uses a public network such as the Internet as a backbone to connect two or more private networks. Provides users with the equivalent of a private network in terms of security.

virus
A software program that is written specifically to affect your system or network adversely. Usually designed to be passed on to other systems that it comes in contact with.

virus signature
A list of viruses that the scanning engine of an anti-virus program can detect.

volume set
Multiple disks or partitions of disks that have been configured to read as one drive.

wide area network (WAN)
Data communications network that serves users across a broad geographical area. Often uses transmission devices such as modems or CSUs/DSUs (Channel Service Units/ Data Service Units) to carry signals over leased lines or over common carrier lines.

Wide SCSI
ANSI standard for SCSI-3 that refers to the two-byte-wide data bus on a 68-pin parallel interface. It has the effect of providing double the Fast SCSI MegaTransfer rate provided by the Narrow SCSI interface.

window flow control
Flow-control method in which the receiving host buffers the data it receives and holds it in the buffer until it can be processed. After it is processed, an acknowledgment is sent to the sender. See also *dynamic window* and *static window*.

Windows Internet Name Service (WINS)
NetBIOS name-to-IP address resolution program available in the Windows NT operating system.

Windows Internet Name Service (WINS) database
Dynamically built database of NetBIOS names and IP addresses used by WINS.

Windows NT Diagnostics
A troubleshooting tool provided in Windows NT that helps you diagnose hardware and driver problems. It provides a graphical database of system devices and resources, similar to the Device Manager found in Windows 95 and 98.

x.2 technology
Developed by U.S. Robotics in 1997, one of the original two 56Kbps data-transfer technologies that were replaced by the V.90 standard.

X.21bis
This Physical-layer communications protocol used in X.25 supports synchronous, full-duplex, point-to-point transmissions with speeds up to 19.2Kbps.

Xmodem
One of the most popular file-transfer protocols. It sends data in blocks along with a checksum and waits for an acknowledgment of receipt by the receiver.

Zmodem
A communications protocol similar to Xmodem. However, Zmodem provides better transfer rates and error checking. It achieves faster transmission by allowing larger blocks of data to be transmitted.

zone
A logical grouping of network devices in an AppleTalk network.

zone transfer
The passing of information from one name server to a secondary name server.

Glossary

INDEX

D

S

X

Y

Z

WHAT'S ON THE CD-ROM

The *Network+ Exam Prep*'s companion CD-ROM contains elements specifically selected to enhance the usefulness of this book, including:

- Two 75-question practice exams—The practice exam questions simulate the interface and format of the actual certification exam.

- Answers to end-of-chapter review questions.

- *PPPShare Pro*—An evaluation version of a proxy server that enables multiple networked computers to share a single Internet connection that can be dial-up TCP/IP, ISDN, ADSL, cable modem, or Ethernet.

- *EventReader(tm) for Windows NT(tm)*—A configurable utility that can read the event log from multiple Windows NT workstations and servers. This tool enables an administrator to collect event information and store it in ODBC-compliant databases for later evaluation and baseline tracking.

- *OstroSoft Internet Tools*—OstroSoft has developed a complete suite of Internet utilities. This suite includes domain scanner, port scanner, ping, traceroute, netstat, Whois client, Finger utility, FTP client, mailbox watcher, and HTML document watcher, among others.

- *Alot MoniCA*—This utility is for those who are curious to know what happens when they are not using their computers. Alot MoniCA lets you know who was using your standalone or networked computers, and when and what they were doing.

- *LMHosts Generator*—Netadmintools developed this snappy utility for Windows networks with more than 10 computers. It generates an LMHOSTS file automatically, plus the batch file to use in distributing it to other computers.

- *SNMP Trap Watcher*—This tool is designed to receive SNMP traps from network equipment, including routers, switches, and workstations. Traps are sent when errors occur on the network.

- Many other useful utilities!

System Requirements

Software
- Windows 95, Windows 98, Windows 2000, or Windows NT

Hardware
- Pentium with 16MB of RAM minimum
- Hard disk with at least 110MB free space
- Network interface card connected to a network
- CD-ROM drive
- Internet access and a browser